G000229333

The Rugby Clubs Of England

By MALCOLM CRANE

ALYCIDON LTD

Published by Alycidon Ltd

© Malcolm Crane 2015

First published in the UK in 2015 by Alycidon Ltd

A CIP catalogue record for this title is available from the British Library.

ISBN: 978-0-9933217-0-2

Typeset and Design by Andrew Searle
Photographs courtesy of the clubs

Printed and bound by CPI Ltd.

Alycidon Ltd,
69 Tarn Road,
Little Thornton,
Blackpool FY5 5AY
Malcolm.Crane@rugbyclubsofengland.com

DEDICATION

This book is dedicated to everyone who ever played the strange game of rugby union, especially to those who have played in the scrum and noticed the blackness at the heart of the scrum – and perhaps in the hearts of their fellow rugby players.

CONTENTS

INTRODUCTION

THANK YOU FOR taking an interest in 'The Rugby Clubs of England'. It is, I think, the largest book ever written about the sport and certainly took the longest period of any rugby book (25 years).

The idea for the book came in September 1989 whilst I was promoting the Provincial Insurance Cup (later known as the RFU Junior Vase). It was my job as one of the founders (the others were John Shields and Chris Rea) to decide which club had done best in each round and to award them £500. This task involved me becoming an expert on the 512 entrants, most of which were unknown to 99.9% of the population.

The entrants may have been unknown but it soon emerged many had great histories and links to some of rugby's greatest characters.

The Provincial Cup disappeared in 1992, but I kept collecting stories of the clubs of English rugby. In 1996, Tony Hallett of the RFU circulated a letter which said there was a strange man in Blackpool who is collecting club histories. Over the following months, clubs forwarded details to me, which now appear in this book. Those contributions were augmented with stories I collected on my travels from Cornwall to Cumbria. I was fortunate my work took me all over England and provided an opportunity to visit clubs or to delve into the local archives.

Over 25 years, I have interviewed thousands of people to get their stories and spent countless hours looking at microfilmed newspapers in innumerable public libraries. So here is the end product.

My apologies if I have made any mistakes and I would be pleased if you could send any corrections to me by email to 'Malcolm.Crane@rugbyclubsofengland.com' marked 'Correction'.

I must express my thanks to the thousands of informants for their time and patience. Can I also thank my team of heroes who laboured long and hard on this book: Hazel Oakes, Andy Searle, Kevin Willman, Sam Birkett and J.V. Ward; not forgetting my wife Pat and daughters Emma, Stephanie and Laura.

Thanks to you all.

Malcolm Crane, July 2015

CHAPTER ONE – BEGINNINGS

*"I may have wasted my life, but at least I didn't spend every Saturday afternoon pursuing
a piece of white leather around a muddy field with a bunch of like-minded lunatics."*
Christopher Tetlow 1974

ODD! RUGBY IS an odd pastime. It is a sport where a collection of friends indulging in moderate levels of violence and organised cheating battle against a bunch of complete strangers whose only crime is wearing a different coloured shirt. All this is in pursuit of a piece of inflated leather that has to be placed behind the goal-line of the opposition. After 80 minutes, the two teams shake hands and then cheer their opponents off the field without the slightest sign of ill-feeling. This strange process is marked by inevitable minor injury to all the participants. The injuries are even accepted as a mark of esteem. Truly odd!

This is a pastime that preoccupies hundreds of thousands of intelligent people, who spend months preparing for 80 minutes of sporting endeavour that offers little opportunity for personal glory. To find the taproot of this strange modern pursuit, one must examine the society that created the game: 19th Century England and the public school system in particular.

The modern image of an English public school is one of an establishment run by avuncular, well-educated teachers who oversee an assembly of upper-class children whose parents are prepared to pay large sums to give their offspring the best possible start in life. This view is a long way from the truth about the 19th Century public schools that were so important in shaping British life. The public schools of that era were madhouses. They were so under-staffed that pupils were left to their own devices, leading to drunkenness, squalor, bullying and cruelty.

It wasn't always so. The oldest public schools trace their origins back to the Middle Ages. They were founded by philanthropists to provide free education and accommodation for poor and orphaned children. Rugby School began as just such a charity in 1597. The original charity schools gradually became centres of excellence and the orphans were returned to the streets and replaced by the sons of the well-to-do.

By modern standards, those in search of a good education in the 19th Century were misguided. A handful of teachers tried vainly to control hundreds of unruly youths. At Eton in 1809, seven masters supervised 515 boys. What control there was, in the Victorian public school, rested in the brutish hands of prefects and their lieutenants, 'the fags'. They ran the schools, which was a recipe for trouble. Winchester School had seven full riots between 1770 and 1828, whilst Rugby had four. The usual cause of the riots was animosity between the students and the local townsfolk. The usual solution was to bring in the local militia to keep the two sides apart. Thomas Arnold, the first great icon of English education and legendary headmaster of Rugby School, was a master at Winchester during the riotous years.

Dr. Arnold arrived at Rugby as headmaster in 1828 with his memory fresh from "most difficult times" (riots) at Winchester. He must have been aware that his predecessor at Rugby had presided over two riots. Arnold arrived to face serious problems on several fronts. The school had financial problems because parents were reluctant to spend money at a school with disciplinary problems and the local farmers resented the students shooting and hunting on their farmland without permission.

In the short term, Arnold solved one problem by keeping the pupils within the school confines and organising sports, such as an in-house version of street football, to keep them preoccupied. It is a misconception that Rugby School had kept a continuous link to the days of street football because it is unlikely, due to a shortage of space, that the old game of 'footballe' was played at Rugby School until 1816.

Dr. Arnold eventually became the most influential reformer of the 19th Century. He was to improve the status of everything connected with education, not least the profession of the schoolmaster. Arnold saw that the root of education's problems lay in the lowly status of schoolmasters, who were poorly paid and the social inferiors of their pupils. He also preached 'Muscular Christianity', the creed that godliness could be achieved through a healthy body.

Christianity and sport became two of the obsessions of Victorian England and Arnold was the great apostle. 'Muscular Christianity' was the driving force behind 19th Century Britain's obsession with sport. It is no exaggeration to say that Dr. Arnold's little local difficulties with the farming community gave birth to much of the world's sport. It suited Victorians to talk of a "healthy body and healthy mind", but Arnold thought more in terms of keeping his charges too tired from playing games to cause trouble.

The image Arnold sought to present was that the schoolmaster was a caring, paternal figure who favoured all God's children. Yet he once actually said, "The first, second and third duty of a schoolmaster is to get rid of unpromising pupils." One contemporary commentator described Dr. Arnold as "a fearful prig and hypocrite, with a genius for self-publicity."

Football was played at many public schools, including Rugby, in the early 1800s and had a variety of different names. It was rooted in the medieval pursuit of 'street footballe', where hundreds of hooligans pursued a pig's bladder, encased in leather, through the streets on 'high days and holidays'. Street football was synonymous with violence and bloodshed; deaths were an occasional occurrence and damage to property was unavoidable.

The game began at first light of the public holiday and continued until one side carried the leather ball across an ancient boundary, such as a bridge or river, hence the expression 'Uppers' or 'Downers', referring to which part of town a player represented. Surprisingly, street football still survives today in places such as Workington in Cumbria and Ashbourne in Derbyshire. Street Football is an anachronism today, but perhaps it is wrong to be over-critical of Arnold for letting his charges play the game. By modern standards, the original game of rugby was a brutal and violent sport but came at a time when cock fighting, dog fighting and bear baiting were only just being outlawed.

Football as played at Rugby School had few rules, except that you did not handle the ball because it was an open invitation to be maimed. Kicking and hacking were the standard ways of discouraging the opposition. Risk of injury was considerable because everyone wore boots with metal toecaps. One small concession to civilisation was that kicking an opponent above the knee was considered unsporting. The risks were reduced by the presence of hundreds of players on the field, which offered ample opportunity to keep out of harm's way. There was, however, pain in abundance because matches could last over five afternoons of a school week. Later the game of football adopted the length of a match as being two 45-minute sessions; 45 minutes being the approximate length of a lesson in some of the old schools. The game of rugby preferred 40-minute sessions.

Rugby School's version of football was closer to a sport called 'camp ball', a game that was played in Lincoln, Colchester and St. Albans until the 19th Century. Camp ball used a pitch of approximately 100 yards in length with small goals at either end. The aim was to carry the ball between the goals. Rugby's version had the aim of moving the ball behind a set of posts that marked the opposition's line. Most of the players were, however, oblivious to the positioning of the posts because they were embroiled in huge scrums, where players ferreted for the ball amid a mass of muddy bodies. Given the chaos, the impartial observer could be forgiven for wondering how this madness gave rise to a sport that swept the world.

The accepted legend is that the game was changed forever in 1823 when William Webb Ellis, a pupil at Rugby School, picked up the football and ran "with fine disregard for the rules". This single act is credited with changing rugby from a school pastime to a national sport.

But was Webb Ellis the great original? True, he played football at Rugby School, but he never made any claim to changing the game, or even took any interest in the game after leaving school. His sporting prowess was on the cricket field, where he represented Oxford University. Webb Ellis later became a vicar and lived a long and comfortable life before dying in 1872 in the South of France. It is fair judgement that there is no historical provenance to support the Webb Ellis legend because no contemporary evidence exists.

William Webb Ellis, pictured as a vicar in later life, who is credited with founding the game of rugby despite minimal evidence.

The evidence for Webb Ellis starting rugby comes from an Old Rugbeian called Martin Bloxom, who had left Rugby School before the alleged incident. He first mentioned Webb Ellis's act in 1876 and never suggested a date for the exploit, or supplied any evidence to support his claim.

The testimony of other Old Rugbeians casts doubt on the Webb Ellis legend. T. Harris, who left Rugby in 1828, described Ellis as inclined to take unfair advantage at football, but "picking up the ball was forbidden" at that time. George Benn, who arrived at Rugby in 1830, said that he knew nothing of Webb Ellis's alleged act. Thomas Hughes, the famous author, said a boy called Jem Mackie was the culprit in 1838 or 1839 and was revered as the great 'runner in'. Hughes arrived at Rugby in 1834 and said Webb Ellis was never mentioned as a footballer in his day. Other sources give Theodore Walrond, who later became a leading player, as the sport's founder. The evidence for Webb Ellis is further undermined by the fact that he had already left Rugby when Dr. Arnold arrived in 1828.

All the eyewitnesses were long dead before anyone decided that Webb Ellis was the great original. In 1895, a committee of Old Rugbeians decided, based largely on Bloxam's evidence, that Webb Ellis was the sport's founder and gradually the legend became fact. Rugby School reveres William Webb Ellis, but the evidence that he founded rugby is unsatisfactory.

Jennifer Macrory, the Rugby School librarian, in her book 'Running with the Ball', argued that Webb Ellis is recalled as the 'great original' not because he was a hero but because he took liberties in many areas of life which made him unpopular and memorable with his contemporaries. Amongst Webb Ellis's crimes was getting his pushy mother to do a Latin essay, which won him a lucrative place at Oxford University. The fact remains that the only evidence for Webb Ellis is the memories of Bloxom; no other contemporary ever defined Webb Ellis as the great innovator.

Webb Ellis, Mackie or Walrond, something happened at Rugby School around 1830 that changed football into a handling game, although the name remained the same. Thomas Hughes was one of the few witnesses who took the time to record his experiences. Hughes is best remembered for his fictional account of Dr. Arnold at Rugby School in his book 'Tom Brown's Schoolboys', which was published sixteen years after the doctor's death. Hughes recalled that, by his time, 'running in' was permitted subject to three conditions: the ball was caught on the bound; the handler was 'on-side' (in front of the last defender) and the handler did not 'knock-on' (made a clean catch).

Hughes's book of 'Tom Brown's Schooldays' helped promote Dr. Arnold and Rugby School to a position where the school became one of the most desirable centres of education in the world. As the establishment became famous, its teachers and pupils were in great demand at other public schools and took prominent positions throughout British educational life. They also took 'Muscular Christianity' and their game of 'Rugby Football' with them to such an extent that the game became popular across Britain and it was soon played by adults on a 'kickabout' basis. This encouraged Rugby School to publish 'The Laws of Football as played at Rugby School' to help followers of the emerging sport. These laws consisted of a set of decisions on disputes arising in play, rather than giving a basic description of the game.

Players could now run with the ball, but only the player holding the ball could be held. Hacking was permitted, but only below the knee. There was, however, no positional play, although some players stood behind the scrum with the aim of collecting the ball if it ever emerged. The 'stand offs', as they were called, then ran towards the opposition's line to place the ball over their opponent's goal line. A successful touchdown gave the scoring team the right to 'try' to kick a goal between the posts. In rugby terms, a 'goal' still remains a touchdown and the successful conversion.

The first rugby club to be formed was by medical students at Guy's Hospital in London in 1846. The game had spread to Trinity College, Dublin by 1854, where its earliest known members came from Cheltenham and Rugby Schools. R.H. Scott, an old Rugbeian, signed a notice advertising the first Trinity match.

The Old Rugbeians were an organised rugby side from 1840, when they played the first of what became annual matches against the School side. Seventeen years later, Rugbeians organised the first ever club match when a group led by Frank Mather and Richard Sykes organised a match played at Liverpool Cricket Club. Sykes had been captain of football at Rugby and he supplied the ball used in the Liverpool match. Fifty players turned up, including enough Rugbeians to call the match 'Rugby versus the World'. The game was far from serious because the non-Rugbeians didn't know the laws and had to be taught the game as they went along.

Richard Sykes, who helped organise the first ever club rugby match.

The football game was already fragmented by 1860, despite Rugby School remaining the primary influence on the game. Pupils of other schools wanted to play the game, but used the version of football they had learnt at their own school rather than the Rugby rules. When non-Rugbeians formed a club they understandably opted to use their own laws rather than those used at Rugby.

The problem grew worse as clubs were being formed all over Britain and rarely did two clubs play the same rules. The local solution was for the two captains to decide what set of laws was to be used before the kick-off. It was common for a match to stop whilst a point of order was discussed. One instance is recorded where the match was halted after 20 minutes to dispute the validity of a try. The matter was settled by starting the game all over again, thus ensuring that "the players had no wind left to query further decisions".

The first 'open' club (i.e. not restricted to former pupils of a school or college) was Blackheath FC, formed in 1862. Their rules include much that is familiar to modern rugby, plus some acknowledgement of the barbarous nature of the early game:

- Running with the ball was only permitted if the ball had been caught off the first bounce; or from a ball kicked by an opponent, or from a knock-on (handling mistake) by an opponent. Then, and only then, could the catcher run with the ball.
- Any player holding the ball could be hacked, but no player could be hacked and held at the same time. Hacking above, or on the knee, was unfair unless the player was holding the ball in his hands.
- It was unlawful to attempt to throttle or to strangle an opponent, which was totally opposed to the principles of the game (and also a capital offence at the time).
- A player could pass to another player on his side, provided the team-mate was not in front of him.
- No one wearing projecting nails, iron plates on the soles, or heels, of their boots were allowed to play.

Things were so disorganised that the shape of the ball was a matter for local arrangement. The Rugby School ball was oval in shape, but other sides preferred a round ball depending on what had been used at the old school.

With so much disorganisation, some clubs began to press for one central organisation to take control of the game. The Football Association was formed in October 1863 by a meeting at the Freemasons' Arms in Covent Garden, attended by 11 clubs, including Blackheath FC. Over the next few weeks, the clubs met six times before the majority voted to abolish hacking and handling. The major public schools and Blackheath FC disliked the new game of 'association', which they felt was too far removed from the Rugby game. They preferred to stick to their own rules and voted, with their hacking boots, to stay independent. Two separate games had been created: Association Football and Rugby Football. The Victorians even gave them nicknames: 'soccer' and 'rugger'.

There were enough rugby clubs in London to cope with the decision to stay independent, but clubs in other parts of the country had difficulty in finding and organising matches. It was common in the 19th Century for a club to play both codes and, week by week, to switch from soccer to rugby depending on what fixtures were available.

The rugby lads preferred their freedom, but eventually they had to accept organisation. In 1871 a meeting to consider organising the game was called by Edwin Ash, the Richmond secretary. The meeting was held at the Old Pall Mall restaurant, Charing Cross, and 20 clubs were represented: Harlequins, Blackheath, Richmond, Wellington College, Guy's Hospital, King's College, St Paul's School, Civil Service, Marlborough Nomads, Queens House, West Kent, Wimbledon Hornets, Gipsies, Clapham Rovers, Flamingo, Law, Lausanne, Addison, Mohicans and Belsize Park. Some of the original clubs have disappeared, but many still survive.

The Pall Mall restaurant stood at No. 1 Cockspur Street, W1 until its disappearance many years ago. The meeting resulted in the founding of the Rugby Football Union. The laws of the game, including a ban on hacking, were soon drafted by a committee of Old Rugbeians and adopted throughout the rest of Britain, where local versions of the RFU were set up, primarily to organise the national team.

The RFU's founders were entirely composed of men from the middle classes, but they were not typical of all the rugby clubs in England. Clubs were being formed in shipyards, factories, even offices, whilst other clubs emerged from churches, public houses and youth organisations.

Another major input into the game was from 'Old Boys clubs', which were formed by ex-pupils of public schools other than Rugby School. The first English old boys rugby clubs, which still exist today, are Old Paulines (1871), Old Blues from Christ's Hospital (1873) and Old Milhillians (1879). The dozens of Old Boys clubs that emerged were nicknamed the 'Old School Tie' as the old boys association provided a social circle after matriculation. The claustrophobic world of the public school was a suitable prelude to the closed world of the Old Boys' clubs. The Victorian young man, who had been raised by a nanny and packed off to public school, probably related more closely to his school friends than to his own family.

The Old Boys' clubs really were a closed world because they were open exclusively to former pupils. You may be an England international but, unless you went to the old school, the doors were firmly closed. 140 years later, that rule still applies to a small number of clubs, but most 'closed clubs' have been forced to abandon their exclusivity to preserve their standard of rugby.

Many rugby sides emerged from cricket clubs, which was already an established sport in the 19th Century. For this reason the rugby season was deemed to run from the end of September until Easter, which allowed cricketers to put their rugby boots away and don their cricket whites without any overlap. Eventually the RFU banned all rugby in England between 1st May and 31st August, a ban that lasted until the 1970s.

The OBs clubs were to be become the backbone English rugby, but they had to acknowledge that Old Rugbeians ran the RFU in the 19th Century. Old Rugbeians drafted the laws, gave the RFU its first five presidents and provided ten members of the first England international team, and the RFU adopted the red rose on a white jersey and white trousers for the first international because the ten Old Rugbeians on parade were familiar with 'all-white' from their school matches and the red rose was the badge of the Rugby School team.

Special kit for football had emerged during the early years of Dr. Arnold's reign at Rugby School. It wasn't for decoration, it was intended to prevent school clothes being ruined by mud. Velvet caps were worn for rugby at the school, though they were rapidly abandoned as impracticable except for ceremonial purposes. The tradition was adopted by international rugby teams, who presented 'a cap' to mark playing for your country.

The sport was clearly 'the Rugby game', but the supremacy of the Rugbeians was soon to be under threat from a new breed of players – and from money.

CHAPTER TWO – A DIVIDED HOUSE

"The professional comes from the factory, from the pit and from the slum."
The Country Life Library of Sport (1903)

IN 1860 SPECTATORS at rugby or football matches were unknown, yet within three decades the arrival of the partisan spectator was to threaten the entire game of rugby. The spectator revolution arose from an Act of Parliament that ordered mills and factories to close before two o'clock on Saturdays. The Factory Act of 1850, known as the Compromise Act, was introduced as many employers were ignoring the working week limits. By closing factories on Saturday afternoon, Parliament inadvertently created the tradition of the British weekend. .

The new working week gave workers the right to spend Saturday afternoon as they wished. The newly-liberated masses sought something to do with their half day and, in the North of England, they began watching rugby and football. Working men began to follow their local side in their thousands and soccer clubs such as Blackburn Rovers, Blackburn Olympic and Notts County became so popular and wealthy that they began to dominate the Football Association.

Until the 1880s, the Football Association was proudly amateur but suddenly found itself dominated by the new professional soccer clubs. A splendidly British compromise was negotiated by Charles Alcock, the FA Secretary, which allowed the 'professionals' to set up their own leagues whilst administration remained with the London-based amateurs. This arrangement remained in place for a century. In view of subsequent events in rugby, Alcock's handling of the amateur/professional issue in soccer was a sporting miracle.

Cricket was eventually forced to follow the FA's example. The game acknowledged the need for high-class 'professional' players who could keep the crowds happy, whilst amateurs made up the bulk of the players. A bizarre fact of Victorian sport was that some amateur cricket players, such as W.G. Grace, received appearance fees of up to £20 a match, plus bonuses for good results, whereas a top-class professional cricketer might earn £3 a week, which had to pay for his equipment and accommodation.

Today professional sportsmen are admired as national figures, but in the late 19th Century they were treated as low-grade manual workers by the amateur sport authorities. They were comparable with gardeners or farm labourers in the eyes of the middle classes. The term 'professional' in the 21st Century equates to a doctor or solicitor; it meant something totally different in Victorian times.

Not long after Alcock's compromise, Rugby faced the same crisis. Rugby clubs like Bradford, Leeds and St. Helens adopted a commercial approach to the game, which wasn't surprising as they attracted thousands of spectators in the 1880s. Following their soccer counterparts, the big clubs began to challenge the RFU's control of the sport. The Old Rugbeians resented this attempted takeover by the provincials. They also looked at how the big professional soccer clubs had altered association football, to suit themselves, and the rugby amateurs decided to fight for rugby to remain an amateur game.

In the North of England, rugby was built around leagues and cups and was about entertaining big crowds by winning silverware. Winning was important because the crowds stayed away if the local club didn't win. To this end, some Yorkshire and Lancashire clubs blatantly abused the laws banning payments to players. Big crowds wanted star names; stars wanted special treatment. Cash through the turnstiles provided the means for 'under the counter' payments, as players were enticed from club to club by 'backhanders'. Players mysteriously moved clubs on a whim and gravitated towards the South Lancashire and South Yorkshire clubs, where the huge populations provided huge crowds. They had a greater urge to win and didn't mind bending the laws, on either side of the touchline.

Traditionally the home side provided the referee, but 'the will to win' meant impartiality being eroded. The growth of the game and worries of officials being bribed or coerced saw the RFU introduce referees in 1885. Soon afterwards, they introduced 'the penalty' kick at the goal to penalise unfair advantage on the field. Referees did not, however ,lightly dispense penalty kicks. There were two penalties, one to each side, in the 1895 England v Scotland match and none in any subsequent renewals until 1925.

The era was a trying time for the RFU, who were shocked when a team of foreigners proved better at the game than the people who had invented it. In 1888 a touring team arrived from New Zealand called 'The Maoris'. Although allegedly new to the game, the visitors were too good for their hosts and demonstrated the fragility of English rugby by winning 49 of 74 matches. The tourists created unprecedented interest. Physically the Maoris, who were actually all British emigrants, brought a new dimension to rugby. In England, the national team had previously been picked from a handful of elite clubs and size had not been important. The RFU had little choice but to abandon the previous policy of picking from the best of a limited pool of Oxbridge students and bolster the English team with big, tough forwards from the North who didn't fear the Maoris or any other side. Suddenly the England team was full of northern players, which gave some credibility to their different outlook on the game, but below the surface, northern rugby was in a mess because the unregulated world of illegal payments was draining the clubs of funds.

Eventually the game split on regional grounds over illegal payments to players. Legend has it that the 1895 RFU's North-South split was purely about compensating players for losing wages – the so called 'Broken Time Dispute'. It was true that a six-day working week still existed in some industries, and loss of wages was a problem for journeymen players, particularly if they were injured. This, however, ignored the fact that many of the top northern players had sinecures. A leading player who joined a big club could expect a 'soft job' with a friendly employer, or he could receive the license to a public house as reward for his efforts on a Saturday afternoon. This was perfectly within the laws because the player's income came from outside the game. There was, however, hypocrisy associated with the issue of 'broken time'. This was revealed by Salford RFC's secretary, who pointed out in 1892 that the players lost 12p in wages for missing an afternoon's work, but clubs were paying £2 – a full week's wage.

There had been attempts to rationalise the 'broken time' issue as far back as 1882, but it was another decade before matters came to a head. In 1891, the RFU's Annual Meeting voted in favour of 'broken time' payments by a small majority, but the majority was insufficient to change the laws. Then an unexpected crisis occurred at a time when the northern game was in a mess financially from the money draining out of it to fund rugby's attempts to keep pace with the growth of association football. An economic depression hit Britain, bringing unemployment to many working men. They couldn't afford to pay to watch sport and takings at the turnstiles were reduced alarmingly at a time when some clubs were heavily in debt. The RFU's amateur wing was unhappy at the uncontrolled indebtedness, which they attributed to paying players. The leader of the pro-amateur reformers was the Rev. Frank Marshall, an obsessive Huddersfield schoolmaster who saw the devil in paying players for playing rugby. Marshall led a private war in Yorkshire against those he saw as making illegal payments.

The issue of paying players resurfaced on the 20th September 1893 when a motion was placed before the RFU to allow "compensation for bona fide loss of time". Marshall and his supporters carried the day by 282 votes to 136. The majority included 120 proxy voters from clubs who failed to attend. The RFU were determined to prevent rugby following the example of Alcock and the FA, who had found themselves facing a strike by professional players who wanted more pay. Also, the London-based RFU looked around the capital and saw many of the soccer clubs in financial trouble trying to fund professionalism. Pressure was turned on the 'broken time' supporters when the RFU introduced a new series of measures to drive out professionalism. But before the measures could be introduced, a 'Northern Union' was formed by clubs who disagreed with the changes. War between the RFU and the rebels was inevitable.

On 29th September 1895, 20 of the top northern clubs met at the George Hotel in Huddersfield to discuss solving their financial problems by reorganising their leagues to generate bigger gates. They decided, almost as an afterthought, to quit the RFU and form a Northern Union, which would allow payments to players, but only if they had a full-time job. The Great Schism (as it was termed) was to bleed English rugby for nearly a century. Ironically, the Northern Union soon found difficulty in controlling its own clubs over illegal payments when in 1905 they tried to enforce the 'full-time employment' rules that insisted that players have jobs outside rugby. The NU highlighted the fact that the pay of the best

Rev. Frank Marshall, a Huddersfield schoolmaster, was a leading opponent of the growth of professionalism in the sport in the North of England

players had risen to £4 a match (twice the average wage) at a time when their game's finances were suffering. The Northern Union, which eventually became the Rugby Football League, has often been accused of a lack of sophistication, but it survived by being much more innovative than the RFU.

Eventually the RFU introduced draconian measures to ban NU players from playing rugby union, although most NU players were amateurs. This blanket ban remained in place for nearly a century and proved a public relations disaster for the RFU. It allowed the Rugby League to perpetuate a myth of working class heroes being persecuted by elitist southern bullies. The truth was that the two codes were played, side by side, by the same people, but the RFU wasn't too bothered because it was a northern problem. It was true that the NU game reappeared in the Midlands and the West Country before World War One, but it soon died out because of a lack of money. In contrast, Rugby League became a leading sport in a heartland of a dozen northern towns from which it never expanded. It enjoyed popularity in Wigan, Widnes and St. Helens, but never caught on in Liverpool, a mere ten miles away.

The Great Schism was a self-inflicted wound that created two codes of rugby at a bad moment in history. The end of the 19th Century saw mass migration of working class men to the USA and to the Empire as 5% of the British population went overseas to build a better life. Then, in 1899, came the outbreak of the Boer War, which required a large portion of the nation's young men to fight in South Africa. The manpower needed to field thousands of rugby clubs up and down the country was suddenly reduced to such an extent that hundreds of clubs disappeared between 1895 and 1905.

Some English clubs got round the problem of player shortages by offering their players jobs in their area, or paying generous expenses. The great exponents of this new recruitment technique were Leicester, Coventry, Blackwell and Plymouth Albion. Tom Crombie, Hon. Sec. of Leicester, became synonymous with bending the game's laws to benefit his club. Coventry were accused of paying players, whereas John Todd, founder of Blackwell RFC, simply hired 50 top-class rugby players to work in soft jobs for his mining company.

Abuse was most widespread in the West of England. Amateur players moved to clubs, such as Plymouth Albion, with a gay abandon that equalled what Bradford and the other northern clubs had got up to in the early 1890s. Ironically, more Welsh rugby players moved to English RFU clubs than ever joined NU clubs. Torquay United and Weston-Super-Mare were notorious for recruiting Welsh players with the offer of an attractive job by the seaside. Weston were known for decades as 'Weston Welsh' for their blatant recruitment of players from across the Severn Estuary.

The RFU never opened a 'second front' in the West or Midlands. Individuals were banned from playing rugby union for various professional-related activities, but the RFU never again ejected a big club from its ranks. The 1895 Schism had hit the RFU hard, which it further compounded by discouraging all cup and league competitions. In 1900 the RFU threw out a suggestion from Bristol RFC that leagues should be reintroduced. Rowland Hill, one of the game's leading figures, said: "We all know the evils that must spring from introducing Leagues." The RFU compensated by encouraging the arrangement of friendly matches, which ignored the fact that spectators were lukewarm towards friendlies. This one decision probably did more to limit the popularity of rugby union in England than any other action.

For nearly 90 years, until the reintroduction of leagues, many successful teams were stymied from progressing to better fixtures because the 'system' did not allow them to improve their standards by playing better teams. A senior club would refuse First XV fixtures to a junior club for fear of losing their own status. They skilfully kept their junior rivals in their place by offering a Second XV fixture. This was hardly compulsive viewing, but guaranteed that the existing order was kept in place.

From a tactical point of view, the absence of a cup and league competition kept English rugby rooted in the Victorian era, where backs did the attacking and forwards did the grinding. Interest in rugby union drained away as a spectator sport because it was dull to watch. The inexorable rise of soccer also made life difficult for rugby clubs. Youngsters played soccer from an early age because a round ball is easier to kick on a cobbled street than an oval ball. The laws of association football were also easy to follow, whereas rugby seemed to pride itself on the complicated nature of its tactics and scoring.

The English public's love of soccer, and their own self-inflicted wounds, pushed English rugby to a low ebb in 1905 when the second New Zealand team arrived in Britain, the country that had given rugby to the world.

Unfortunately, the newcomers had improved from 1888 and were far too good for the founding fathers. The Kiwi forwards had developed a versatility that easily overcame the unadventurous, plodding English. A reporter at Hartlepool saw the touring NZ forwards in a provincial match and dubbed them 'All Backs', referring to their all-round competency. A sub-editor thought it was a typing error and changed the reference to 'All Blacks', thus creating a legend. The incredible achievements of the 1905 All Blacks regenerated interest in rugby as a spectator sport in the decade before World War One. A year later, the South Africans came and generated further interest. The All Blacks and Springboks were better at rugby than the British because it was their first choice as a national game, whereas soccer was king in England.

The RFU had a financial problem that was exacerbated by the visiting touring teams; they had no national stadium and they had to hire stadia from other organisations, which reduced the RFU's share of the gate money. The revival in English rugby was further sparked when England played particularly badly at Crystal Palace in 1905. The pitch was terrible, which led the RFU to question its tradition of playing internationals at any suitable venue. The Palace was one of a dozen grounds hired for matches. If gates declined at one venue, they simply moved to another. The Kennington Oval, Manchester, Blackheath, Richmond, Leeds, Dewsbury, Birkenhead, Bristol, Gloucester, Leicester and Crystal Palace all briefly hosted the national team.

In 1905, a group within the RFU, led by Bill Williams, an ex-Harlequin and Middlesex CCC wicket-keeper, proposed an audacious plan to buy some low-lying farmland on the city outskirts and to transform it into a national stadium. The initial cost of £5,572.12.6d for ten and a quarter acres was a huge drain on RFU resources, with another £30,000 to be spent on drainage and erecting stands. Finances were so tight that the RFU agreed to share the huge stadium with the Harlequins club as a cost-saving measure.

The opening of Twickenham brought mystique to the game. The man in the street began to take an interest in how England performed. The RFU found this new interest to be a mixed blessing, especially as they viewed the press with suspicion. After all, the press were being paid for writing about rugby and the laws of amateurism forbad anyone involved in the game from earning a penny from the sport. The result was that, for most of the 20th Century, little of rugby union's activities were committed to print: rugby books were few and rugby magazines were virtually

The opening of Twickenham marked a golden age for English rugby.

unknown until 1960. This law forbidding writing about rugby for money led to many of the finest players in English rugby being banned for life. Critics pointed out that murderers and felons were only banned from rugby if they wrote about rugby or played rugby league.

Despite the lack of publicity, the outrageous gamble of building Twickenham began a golden era of English rugby, with great names such as Poulton-Palmer, Stoop, Lowe and Pillman. It was an era that ended with the outbreak of the Great War in the weeks before the 1914-15 season was due to kick off. Rugby was hard hit by the Great War because a fifth of England's young men were either killed or wounded. The near-destruction of a generation had a profound effect on British society, particularly the officer class, which drew its recruits directly from the great public schools. Casualties were devastating amongst the public school-educated officers and the traditionally elitist recruitment policy of the army was destroyed. Officers were selected from the lower middle and working classes, who filled the void left by a dead generation. And women came forward to plug the gaps left by men away fighting. When the war ended, women refused to retire back to kitchen or the drawing room and some women played sport, even rugby.

Amongst the curious legacies of the Great War was the marching song which helped troops keep a steady pace. Troops would march 30 miles a day and keep in step by singing songs where the beats equated to marching pace. The marching songs dealt with sex, which has been an obsession of soldiers and rugby players down the ages. Sing-songs had always been a part of British life before the arrival of radio and television. Rugby players entertained themselves by standing around a piano and singing bawdy songs borrowed from the Music Hall. They took the Music Hall songs to war where they were changed the lyrics to more than 'Moon and June'.

Men returned to Civvy Street with a rich collection of marching songs, which they used to enliven long journeys home from matches. After-match booze-ups were an excuse to raise the rafters. No one was embarrassed because women were barred from most rugby clubhouses until the 1950s. A thick forward might not know his way home, but he might know 50 verses of some old ditty. They had to be engraved on his soul because the words could never be written down due to the obscenity laws.

It was 1955 before the songs were actually written down, and only then by ex-pats living in West Africa. When the compilers returned home they brought copies of the song book, which eventually reached a record company, who put together a mysterious group called the 'Jock Strapp Ensemble' to sing the ditties. The first rugby songs record was issued in 1965 with the obscenities 'bleeped' out. It became a best-seller, although respectable record shops refused to stock copies which had to be ordered from specialist dealers. The last legacy of World War One finally emerged nearly half a century after the Armistice.

CHAPTER THREE - CONSOLIDATION

"Rugby is a pastime offering a salutary opposition to that tendency of the age towards effeminacy which was surely undermining the constitution and the heart of the nation."
F. Clifford (circa 1900)

THE END OF World War One brought a spell of peace to Britain. People enjoyed themselves as an antidote to the awful experiences of the previous decade. English rugby also went through a golden era as players like W.W. Wakefield, Dave Davies and Sam Tucker became national heroes.

This golden era even reached the grassroots of the game, where the clubs enjoyed a period of consolidation and growth. In 1900 most rugby clubs played on farm fields or public parks; only a handful owned the land they played on. Nobody knew anything about 'pitch maintenance' beyond persuading the landowner to mow the pitch at the start of the season – and that was done with horse-drawn mowers as motorised tractors were virtually unknown. Marking the touchline was done with white paint, or just neglected, depending on the ardour of the volunteers. The private world of the rugby club underwent great change between the wars. Rugby Clubs, like the RFU and Twickenham, developed a great urge to own their own grounds. Pre-1920 few clubs owned their own grounds. In Kent in 1922 only three clubs had their own ground, yet over the next 50 years, hundreds of clubs, up and down the country, followed the RFU's lead.

Rugby clubs were fortunate because the early 1920s were remarkable for the greatest changes in land ownership in British history. Around this time, 25% of all English land changed hands as big landowners were forced to sell their estates because of the introduction of death duties, income tax and other charges. The concept of land ownership was not traditionally a tenet of British life. The age-old view was that land had no intrinsic value; it was something to be used for farming or housing. Suddenly landowners saw it as a financial burden and looked for a way to dispose of it, preferably to reputable people who would put it to good use. Many rugby clubs were therefore able to buy pitches for comparatively modest sums.

Some landowners simply gave away acres of land as an act of altruism. They were cautious though, and found a recipient in the National Playing Fields Association, who guaranteed the long-term future of open spaces, in contrast to the local rugby club who might disappear when interest waned. Some benefactors did, however, trust the longevity of their local rugby club because it was associated with the 'old school', and what better way to shine than in the eyes of your school friends.

No one should underestimate the wonderful work that the RFU did in helping clubs to buy their grounds or make improvements. They lent clubs money, at generous interest rates, which saved many having to worry about keeping the bank manager happy.

The urge to own your own ground gave clubs control over their own destiny, not least the right to open the clubhouse bar on Saturday afternoons whilst pubs and clubs were forced to close after lunch. The law said you couldn't have a drink on Saturday after 3pm unless you were a member of a private club. This guaranteed a good crowd for rugby clubs, particularly in the bar. This strange law arose from a restriction on opening hours that was introduced during the First World War and lasted for 70 years until the John Major government relaxed many of the strictures on licensed premises.

Rugby Union grew rapidly between the Wars, primarily because it was the favoured sport of the new grammar schools that emerged from a series of educational reforms in the 19th Century. Grammar Schools were 'public schools' for the lower-middle and working classes who could not afford schools fees. The new schools modelled themselves on the public schools, but restricted admission to anyone who could pass an examination at the end of their primary school education – or pay to be admitted without passing the exam. The grammar schools slavishly copied the curriculum of their rich cousins and adopted rugby for that reason, and for the slightly more pragmatic reason that it kept 30 boys occupied rather than only 22 with soccer.

The model was set in 1922 when the Headmasters' Conference, the trade union of the public schools, recommended adoption of rugby because it offered a better opportunity for playing after school than association football.

Graduates of the grammar schools produced new generations of rugby players by adopting the idea of the long established Old Boys clubs such as Old Alleynians, Old Merchants Taylors etc., who had emerged in the early days of the sport. Dozens of new Old Boys sides emerged between the wars and soon were supplying players to the big city clubs, and eventually the England team. The new clubs accepted fixtures against the less-established clubs and, in places like the Wirral in Cheshire, fixture lists were built almost entirely around these new Old Boys clubs

An amazing number of rugby clubs were formed initially to provide the school First XV with an annual run out against the cream of the Old Boys. This annual event led many players to talk about forming their own club. These annual matches were banned in the 1970s as the RFU had to clamp down on youngsters playing against adults for fear of injuries. It was known for 12-year-olds to make up the numbers in junior sides.

Another source of rugby talent was works sides, which had first emerged in the 1880s and who drew their players from coalmines, railways, factories, offices and banks. They had a rich source of new talent from the apprentices who had five years of learning their trade on breadline wages. Few works sides would dare ask for first class fixtures, but they added to the growing pool of rugby players in England. The cream of these players gravitated to the big clubs that had emerged before World War One.

The big city clubs, such as Leicester, Gloucester, Bristol etc., could afford to buy their grounds from the gate money they generated. Bristol played over 40 games a season, including mid-week fixtures, against the top Welsh sides which attracted 20,000 paying supporters. The English gate-taking clubs were all eclipsed, in the number of games they played a season, by Cardiff, who in 1928-29 managed an incredible 76 games!

At the other end of the scale were first-class sides who generated little gate money and were known as the 'non-gate-taking' clubs. They mainly comprised Hospitals and Old Boys sides. One Bristol official remarked in 1934 that they had played Cardiff in front of 30,000 spectators and then, a week later, had to travel to London where only 100 supporters watched them play a "bunch of medical students". The best clubs in England knew successful rugby attracted large crowds, which meant no financial problems, but if the First XV were unsuccessful, the crowd went elsewhere and decline was inevitable. Sides like Leicester, Northampton and Gloucester wanted more competitive fixtures to keep the paying public happy than the 'non-gate taking clubs' could provide.

The RFU had mixed feelings about the idea of 'rugby as entertainment' as it had connotations of professionalism. Only players or ex-players understood the laws, which didn't deter the huge crowds who went to Twickenham. O.L. Owen, the rugby writer, wrote: "Rugby between the wars was a semi-private and largely incomprehensible world and the Home Unions did their best to keep it so."

When King George V suggested players should wear numbers to help spectators recognise who was who, he was advised by an RFU official, who said: "It would reduce the game to a cattle market." The very idea of spectator sport brought back memories to the RFU of the events of 1895.

By the middle of the 20th Century, English rugby was developing in a vacuum. The absence of cup and league rugby had reduced the need for tactical development. The tactics were based on the Victorian emphasis on backs running with the ball after the forwards had ground out some advantage. Until 1970, it was considered tactically sound in English rugby for the tight-head prop forward to collapse the scrum at every opportunity; by contrast, the All Blacks, French and Welsh were developing mobile props who actually ran about.

Across the Channel, the French game had developed because the French Clubs Cup gave a focal point for the Tricolours' game and league rugby had existed there since 1892. As a result, the French changed tactics so the forwards became an attacking weapon. Traditionally the French national team were the whipping boys of the Home International Championship, but having league rugby helped them gain superiority over England by the 1960s.

Similarly, smaller countries like Wales, Scotland and Ireland could beat England regularly at rugby, and nobody expected the Whites to cope with the Springboks or All Blacks because they took the game far more seriously. Regionally, English teams had an appalling record against both sets of tourists. The Springboks had only lost twice in England in 50 years, to the East Midlands in 1931 and to London Counties in 1951, yet Welsh town sides, such as Newport and Llanelli, could claim better records against touring teams than the whole of England.

English regional teams had terrible records against tourists because, it was claimed, they were rarely picked on merit. They were artificially created sides formed from neighbouring counties where each county expected, and received, a proportional share of the team regardless of merit. This was great for local pride and democracy but sporting suicide against organised opposition.

The concept of coaching rugby players, outside school, was something players did privately. Players learnt to play rugby at school, joined the local rugby club and developed as a player dependant on their physique: 'Little 'uns at the back, big 'uns upfront'. Fitness was largely a personal matter; after all, many rugby men played cricket in the summer and pre-season training would interfere with that. The old joke was a club coach was the vehicle that took your club to away matches.

Back in 1920, England had an unofficial coach in W.W. Wakefield and enjoyed a brief period of success under his captaincy. Then, in 1936, came another brief moment of glory when England recorded their first victory over the All Blacks. Behind the scenes, the team's experienced members organised private training and coaching without the RFU's knowledge. Until then, English forwards were traditionally viewed as 'a soft touch' by their international rivals, who knew how to intimidate them. The 1936 England pack were a different proposition and were not going to give second best to anyone. They shocked the tourists by matching them physically and creating the platform for Obolensky's glory. In the best British traditions, England and the All Blacks were billeted in the same hotel and even shared the dining room before and after the match.

England's victory came at a dark moment in English history as the Great Depression ravaged a nation. Young men left their towns in search of a better life than that on offer at home. Gates fell as people struggled to find spare money to watch rugby. At the time, a journalist was walking back from a match at Twickenham when he saw a famous former player from the West Country. It transpired the ex-player had walked the 200 miles to London looking for work. After a fruitless search, the ex-player was heading home on foot when he met the journalist. The reporter gave the ex-player a pound to help him on his way.

Prince Obolensky's last match, Rosslyn Park v Harlequins in 1940.

The Second World War brought an end to the Great Depression, but it claimed the lives of many young players. Rugby was played during the war as a way of keeping fit and following a long services tradition of sport. Demobilisation in 1945 brought a new start for rugby as young men who had learnt the game in the Services joined clubs.

Many of the old barriers were breaking down in the late 1940s. Exclusive Old Boys clubs remained, but they were becoming more open to outsiders. However, boots, socks, shorts and jerseys were in short supply and could only be obtained by government coupons, which meant few teams could possess 15 matching jerseys.

The England team enjoyed a brief renaissance in the 1950s under Eric Evans, a firebrand hooker, but soon English rugby lapsed into mediocrity and worse. The national trials system was bizarre as it began each season before the Varsity match and didn't include Oxbridge players. The inexperienced Varsity players were, however, selected for

Eric Evans, who led a brief renaissance for English rugby in the 1950s.

the final trials in preference to experienced club players. The shambolic state of English rugby was demonstrated by the 1961 England trials, where 43 different players from 15 separate clubs were selected for three trial matches. England repeatedly took the field with unproven and inexperienced players who were discarded at the first sign of failure. In 1960 England made ten changes over the four-match season.

Until the 1950s, bad results for the national rugby team were a private matter, mentioned only in the broadsheets, but the arrival of television into people's living rooms transformed entertainment and sport. The Home International Championship was splendid television, coming in the depths of winter when other sports were frozen off and at a time when the Football Association banned soccer from television. Television galvanised national spirit with the plucky Irish, the taciturn bravery of the Scots, the fervour of the Welsh, the unpredictability of the French and, of course, the 'stiff upper lip' amateur-spirit of the English.

The big losers from televised rugby were the big gate-taking clubs, who found their attendances falling dramatically when rugby was on television. They tried, and failed, to persuade the Home Counties to play internationals on Wednesday afternoons, which would have left them Saturdays to attract spectators. The big clubs found little sympathy amongst other RFU clubs, who took little money on the gate and weren't affected.

Unfortunately, television viewers saw England frequently at the foot of the Home International table, yet they sent touring teams to New Zealand and South Africa who won against all the odds. But, back at home, England were the whipping boys for Wales and France in particular. The backbone of the team were proven Lions in Cotton, Neary, Beaumont, Hiller, Burton and Pullen, but one bad defeat meant the axe, regardless of previous form.

The British Lions highlighted England's international shortcomings. Often the Lions' selectors chose England players who were not considered by Twickenham. They pulled on the red jersey of the Lions and were world-beaters. Mr. Average asked why players such as John Pullen, Mike Burton and Peter Dixon were good enough for the Lions, but ignored by England. The country as a whole benefitted when the 1971 and 1974 Lions won test series in New Zealand and South Africa, as thousands of new players joined rugby clubs inspired by the Lions' heroics, and, ironically, one of the biggest benefactors was England. At club level, English rugby boomed, with record numbers of new clubs and players. Things were changing gradually. The old county cups were re-instated and provided a passport to the new National Knockout Cup. Leagues were even creeping in the back-door as 'Merit Tables'.

Gradually, England embraced the fact that sticking by its best players, through thick and thin, might reap better rewards than constant change. The years of humiliation finally came to an end in 1980 when England won the Grand Slam under captain Bill Beaumont and coach Mike Davis. The team was composed of great players who had suffered the vicissitudes of RFU selection during the barren years. Even the 1980 Grand Slam did not come easily, with full-back Dusty Hare kicking an injury time penalty to beat Wales by 9-6. The breakthrough had been made, and never again were England the whipping boys of world rugby. And, within a few years, league rugby was re-introduced, professionalism officially sanctioned and the Southern Hemisphere countries conjured up the Rugby World Cup.

CHAPTER FOUR – THE PROFESSIONAL ERA

"For when the One Great Scorer comes to mark against your name,
He writes – not that you won or lost – but how you played the game."
Henry Grantland Rice (1880-1954)

THE 1980 GRAND Slam was a watershed for English rugby. The national team did subsequently have barren years, but they were never as 'amateurish' as in previous generations. At club level, rugby had also undergone a profound change. The state schools had declined in size following the baby boom of the 1950s. There was more pressure on teachers to produce results in the classroom and declining interest in promoting out-of-hours sport, including rugby. The role of the schoolmaster was changing; they even took strike action, which had been unthinkable in bygone days.

The Wilson Government of the late 1960s decided grammar schools should be abolished because they were viewed as bastions of elitism. They were replaced by comprehensive schools, where equality was the watchword. School sport suffered because schoolmasters were under more pressure and less inclined to give up their free time, at night and/or on Saturdays, to coach sports such as rugby. As a result, famous rugby-playing grammar schools disappeared from the fixture lists and the supply of new players dwindled.

The void was filled by two areas of English rugby: the independent schools and the clubs. Many independent schools had teachers and boarders who, like Arnold's charges, were available seven days a week. If the years after World War Two had seen a dramatic rise in the profile of rugby players from grammar schools, the 1980s and 1990s saw the English national side dependant again on products of independent schools.

A new force also stepped into the breach: the clubs, who wholeheartedly adopted 'mini-rugby'. Parents dropped off their offspring at the rugby club on a Sunday morning. Soon some clubs had hundreds of youngsters playing every Sunday morning under the watchful eye of ex-players. The crisis, in the disappearance of the grammar school, was solved by the hard work of thousands of volunteers.

The clubs coped surprisingly well with the change from the schools producing players to producing them themselves, but clubs up and down the country were to see more change in the 1970s and 1980s than at any time since rugby was invented.

This change had begun with an obscure amateur RFU official called Eric Smith, who compiled a blueprint in the early 1970s for English rugby to embrace league rugby. The RFU rejected his suggestions, and rejected two more attempts, the Mallaby Report in 1975 and the Burgess Report in 1981, to introduce league rugby. A contemporary assessment said: "The local fixtures that went back into the last century, in which old rivals hammered away at each other twice a season, are vanishing and where they still exist, they don't matter a damn."

The RFU allowed two concessions to progress: merit tables and cups. Merit tables were a bizarre gesture to league rugby without acknowledging its existence. Clubs played a dozen or so matches (not necessarily against the same opposition) and based their position in the table on their percentage of wins. The problem was some clubs played a full complement of table matches; whereas other clubs played half as many. An unofficial Merit Table of 40 London clubs existed. The results were bizarre, with Royal Naval College (Greenwich) as champions on 87% and Old Blues second with 85%. The Merit Tables were basically flawed because everybody's fixture list was different

The National Knockout Cup was more merit-based. Qualification initially came through winning the local county cup, which had suddenly reappeared after 70 years. The Lancashire RFU were shocked to learn the Lancashire Challenge Cup was still stored in a Warrington bank vault. It had been stored there at the turn of the century when the RFU discouraged competitions. Its silver content meant it was a seriously valuable item, regardless of its competitive value.

The National Knockout Cup emerged in 1972 and soon gained great popularity, not least amongst the traditionally strong city clubs, such as Leicester, Bath, Gloucester and Bristol. Bizarrely, it was sponsored by a tobacco company

Wilkinson   Dallaglio   Greenwood   Underwood

Gumersall   Underwood   Obolensky   Wakefield

for 15 years, which didn't send out a particularly healthy message. Eventually the Cup's prominence was overshadowed by the emergence of the Premiership and the Heineken European Cup.

Domestic competitions were, in turn, dwarfed by the Rugby World Cup (RWC), which began in 1987. Within ten years, the RWC had become the pinnacle of rugby ambition. When it was first projected, the World Cup split rugby down the middle – or actually the Equator. The Southern Hemisphere nations wanted the competition; the British nations were opposed. A deadlock existed within the IRB until, in 1984, John Kendall-Carpenter of England voted with the Southern Hemisphere countries, which broke the deadlock and led to the approval of the first Rugby World Cup.

1987 was also the year that league rugby was introduced to England after 92 years. Clubs could opt out of league competitions, but most choose to opt in. Like all change, league rugby had its winners and losers. Amongst the casualties were many great names. No longer could a second-rate club cling to top-class fixtures. Great sides of a bygone era tumbled down the leagues and suddenly found themselves playing minor clubs who they had previously viewed with disdain.

Rugby players also needed to register with a club for the first time since the Great Schism. Inevitably, good players gravitated to successful sides and the new breed of club coaches were in demand, with clubs clamouring for their signature. Previously older players supervised training and it was unthinkable that 'a rugby coach' could earn a living within the sport The top-class players and coaches were soon able to find clever ways around the RFU's laws on amateurism by bending the rules governing payment for playing rugby.

The RFU argued the game relied on thousands of amateur volunteers who would disappear if money came into the game and clung desperately to amateurism. But in 1994, the IRB sent a document to its members saying it was impossible to defend the amateur principle and pressure to stop players earning money from the game was impossible. The RFU acquiesced despite misgivings.

The sudden change to professionalism in rugby union was too sudden. The concept of 'financial viability over lofty ambition' was ignored, with catastrophic results. Clubs with small memberships and limited spectator appeal would spend millions of pounds on paying players without considering how to balance the books. The underlying problem for English rugby in the 1990s was that club rugby, even at the top level, did not generate enough income from gate receipts, or ancillary pursuits, to pay the players' wages. A club required 40 professionals at a basic £1000 a week, plus bonuses, which represented outgoings of £2,000,000 a year, plus administration and ground maintenance. This could never be balanced with only 20 home games attracting gates of 5,000 at £10 per head. This resulted in £1,000,000 losses per season. The RFU subsidised clubs from its income, but eventually it had to reduce annual payments to clubs below the top level, which had a devastating effect on clubs committed to player payments.

Inevitably, some famous clubs, such as Moseley, London Scottish and Richmond, went to the wall. They had prospered in the amateur days but couldn't attract enough support to survive at the top level. Many other famous old clubs gave up the uneven struggle and simply went back to be being amateur, although they had to start again at the bottom of the league structure. Unfashionable clubs, who dreamed of a fixture with the Richmonds of the world, suddenly found they were in the same league.

The miracle about the introduction of professionalism in England was that it coincided with a golden era for English rugby. England, under coach Geoff Cooke and captain Will Carling, won successive Grand Slams and the runners-up place in the 1991 Rugby World Cup. No longer could the big Southern Hemisphere countries belittle England, who also recorded several victories over their old colonial rivals.

Sadly, off the field a battle developed for the soul of the RFU, with the top clubs in open warfare with the sport's grassroots. The English First Division Rugby Ltd formed an independent body, EFDR, who threatened a breakaway rugby organisation. Rugby Union's problems were exacerbated by the removal of England internationals from terrestrial television and the massive success of the Premiership in English soccer. The big clubs cast envious eyes at the RFU and Twickenham, with its capacity of 80,000 for internationals and tens of millions of pounds of television money. The EFDR clubs argued that it was their players, in England's colours, who filled Twickenham but the RFU kept all the benefits. With English rugby at an all-time high on the pitch, the off-field ructions were dragging the game into disrepute. In 2000 the England team went on strike over pay, which caused enormous bad feeling amongst the English public. Eventually, the England squad became part-time RFU employees, with the clubs paying part of the wages.

The top clubs seemed to have hijacked the RFU, but the grassroots clubs blocked further control by electing their candidate, Cliff Brittle, as chairman of the RFU Executive. Brittle was committed to keeping rugby under the control of the entire RFU membership. A civil war, for the soul of the RFU, ensued before peace was made.

The elephant in the room for English rugby was that there was never enough money to support a professional game outside a dozen clubs, funded by millionaires. 99% of English rugby had to remain amateur or semi-professional because there was no money for any other option.

The bitterness was cast aside when England beat Australia to win the 2003 Rugby World Cup. Martin Johnson lifted high the Webb Ellis Cup and English rugby had finally lost its inferiority complex. The blessing was that thousands of youngsters suddenly wanted to be rugby players and rushed to join their local clubs. The England rugby team had, with one victory, guaranteed a new generation of rugby players for the nation's clubs, who were inundated with aspiring young rugby players.

Even old antagonisms were forgotten as the RFU head-hunted top players from rugby league; a total reversal of previous generations, where rugby league clubs recruited rugby union players. Now top rugby league players switched codes; the most successful example being Jason Robinson, a Wigan RLFC legend, who swapped South Lancashire for South London and became a national hero.

The England rugby team were high profile and players enjoyed fame and fortune beyond the wildest dreams of their predecessors. But the Premiership clubs lacked exposure and even the top clubs could only attract the gates of

a modest soccer club. Also, the top rugby clubs suffered because England, and other international countries, needed the cream of Premiership players for nearly three months a year for international matches. And obviously the paying public weren't keen on seeing under-strength club sides in the Premiership when England were playing – a complaint made by the big clubs half a century before.

The complaint was made that England's players suffered from too many competitions. The problem was exacerbated by the unparalleled success of the Heineken Cup, which decided the European club champions. In 2012 England's premier clubs even fell out with the European Cup organisers. The pressure on top-class English players was far greater than players from other nations. It was argued that Irish players with central contracts either played for Ireland or their province in the European Cup, whereas English clubs had international, European and a 20-match Premiership season, which meant they were worn out compared to their Irish counterparts. The English and French clubs threatened to form a rival competition. The dispute, in the short term, came to nothing but was an echo of previous generation, with English rugby seemingly at odds with its neighbours. However, in 2014 a new European club championship was introduced that placated English club fears.

English rugby had, however, another problem. In 1999 The Premiership Rugby Ltd introduced a salary cap in an attempt to stem the losses, estimated at £20m a year. Each club had defined limits on how much they could pay their playing squad, which was intended to control club deficits. The top French clubs recognised they could recruit the best English players by offering bigger salaries than their counterparts across the Channel. The RFU responded by refusing to select French-based players for the national team, which caused some ill-feeling because some commentators felt the policy was undermining England's chances of winning the 2015 Rugby World Cup, which was to be held on home soil for the first time since 1991.

The build-up to the 2015 Rugby World Cup saw unprecedented interest and English rugby flourishing on and off the field. But problems still haunt the sport in this country. They are the problems which arise from constant change. Priorities have changed, with winning the Rugby World Cup becoming the pinnacle of achievement and the autumn internationals against the Southern Hemisphere countries becoming increasingly important. The Home International Championship does still retain its place in the sporting calendar, although it seems some of England's opponents view beating England as more important than winning the Rugby World Cup.

CHAPTER FIVE – CUMBRIA

"Mountains! You mean there are mountains in Cumbria."
Reaction of RFU official 1990

AMBLESIDE

AMBLESIDE IS A small town at the heart of the Lake District. The beauty of the area, which is surrounded by England's highest mountains, made it a popular holiday centre with wealthy Victorian merchants from Manchester who bought holiday homes in the district. The town of Ambleside also has an odd connection with Rugby School because Dr. Thomas Arnold, the school's famous headmaster, lived at Fox How, a house he built near Loughrigg on the north side of the town.

Galava Park, Ambleside

Some of the newcomers to the town in Victorian times were ex-public schoolboys, who brought rugby to Ambleside in 1874. Matches were played at Rydal Fields (more famous for Wordsworth's daffodils) or on Rothay Park as a home pitch for nearly 50 years.

Ambleside's first ever match was against Preston Grasshoppers and was followed by fixtures against Ulverston, Windermere College and Stramongate College of Kendal. By 1876 they had arranged matches against Birch, Carlisle, Newcastle, Southport and Bolton. The club received another boost in September 1884, when they merged with Ambleside Swifts, their local rivals.

In February 1886 the club received a letter from Kendal Hornets inviting Ambleside to send delegates to a meeting at Windermere to discuss forming a county union for Westmorland. Ambleside sent four delegates to the meeting and were rewarded when the club had players selected for the county team.

In December 1897 the entire Ambleside team switched to the Northern Union and made their NU debut at Birkenhead Wanderers. The chaos of the era can be gleaned from the fact that Ambleside somehow managed to play both NU and RU in 1898 before the club opted for the latter, although it was another 22 years before it formally adopted the name of Ambleside RUFC. This coincided with the club finding a permanent pitch at Kelswick Field, with changing facilities in the Union Hotel.

All was not luxury as the club minutes for 26th August 1925 record that the club committee had decided to pay extra money for cars with pneumatic tyres for all away matches. It seems solid tyres were both uncomfortable and unpopular.

On 19th September 1966, the club opened a fine pitch and clubhouse at Galava Park, near the site of an old fort occupied by Roman invaders in the 2nd century. Lord Wakefield of Kendal, the greatest Cumbrian player, officially opened the clubhouse, which was followed by a renewal of the ancient fixture against Preston Grasshoppers.

Ambleside's best ever player emerged in the 1980s in Sam Hodgson, a tough farmer from nearby Patterdale. Sam moved on to the Vale of Lune and Sale, with whom he represented the North of England. He received some adverse publicity during his days at Sale when their committee felt he sometimes put his Lakeland farm ahead of top-class rugby. The pinnacle of Sam's career was to play for the North of England against the 1983 All Blacks.

In the 1990s, Ambleside were boosted by the arrival of John Smith, the ex-Sedgley Park forward, as coach. He took the village team to the Fourth Round of the National Junior Cup in 1994 and later led them to the Cumbria League Championship, to give the club their first trophy in 135 years of existence.

(Thanks to the late, great John Smith)

ASPATRIA

ASPATRIA (POP. 3000) occupies a unique place in English rugby, having produced seven internationals and over 100 county players despite being a village. Aspatria is, it is fair to say, a crossroads on the road from Wigton to Workington, but has somehow become a major centre for rugby.

The old game of street football survived late in north Cumbria, but seems to have died out around the 1840s. Aspatria was, at the time, famous for the illegal sport of cock-fighting and for the local breed of scarlet and black fighting cocks. The colours of black and red were adopted by the local rugby team when they were founded in October 1878 and the fighting cock became the club emblem.

Four Aspatria internationals. From top to bottom: James Davidson, David Graham, Tosh Holliday and Bob Hanvey

The instigator of the Aspatria club was James Troughton, an assistant master at the National School in the town, who became the captain, trainer, coach and tactician.

The first report of a game involving Aspatria dates from 20th October 1878 and states that Aspatria played Wigton College in a match split between 'Association' and 'Rugby Football' rules. Wigton College was the precursor of the famous Wigton club formed four years later.

Aspatria sent representatives to the meeting on 25th October 1882 which established the Cumberland county side and agreed to purchase a Challenge Cup to be competed for annually by the best clubs. The inaugural championship in 1883 saw Aspatria beat Whitehaven in the final. The two sides met the following season, with Aspatria winning again; indeed, Aspatria won 12 of their 13 matches that year. Subsequent Cumberland Cup success eluded the club until 1890-91, when they defeated Broughton at Maryport in front of 4,000 spectators.

The following year's cup final against Whitehaven saw victory for Aspatria in unpleasant circumstances as the losers alleged one of the Aspatria backs had worn spikes on his boots.

The end of the century saw Aspatria hit badly by the Great Schism as many of their best players were poached by NU sides and the club's best fixtures were lost. The Cumberland RFU organised a league to engender interest, and in 1897 Aspatria were the inaugural champions. But Cumberland rugby was haemorrhaging talent to the Northern Union, for the county union was reduced to Aspatria, Cockermouth, Penrith and Carlisle.

The Cumberland county team was entirely composed of players from Aspatria and Carlisle. The county side did well, which brought their players to the attention of the RFU selectors. Brothers James and Joseph Davidson were England regulars. Joe won prominence in the 1898 North v South trial at Bristol and was immediately promoted to the England side. The brothers played together for England against Scotland in 1899. James won five England caps, whereas Joseph was awarded only two. When the Davidson Brothers were discarded by England, another Aspatria forward, David Graham, was called up. Graham later joined New Brighton RFC.

In the early years of the 20th century the club was in trouble and only survived by borrowing players from other clubs. Relief was at hand as the Northern Union was in decline and rugby union was recovering. The years before the Great War saw rugby union on the mend, with Aspatria and local rivals Carlisle competing for the title of Cumberland's premier club.

The 1920s saw Workington replacing Carlisle as Aspatria's only rivals for the title of Cumberland champions. One of the two sides were in eight out of ten Cumberland Cup finals, with Aspatria winning in 1923-24, 1927-28 and 1929-30.

The mid-1920s were a golden era for Aspatria. In 1923-24 they won 21 out of 24 matches. The principal scorer during the season was Tosh Holliday, who accumulated a total of 18 tries and 15 conversions. Holliday was a modestly-built three-quarter, who won seven England caps between 1923 and 1926. He had a miserable final appearance for England as Scotland, led by Ian Smith, bombarded him with high kicks. He had been first choice for England for three seasons and was selected for the 1926 Lions tour of South Africa. After beginning well, Tosh dislocated his collar bone and missed the final part of the tour.

After the disaster against Scotland, Tosh joined Oldham RLFC, along with Aspatria's teenage prodigy Fred 'Basher' Ashworth. Tosh played well at Oldham for several seasons before returning home to Aspatria, where he ran a greengrocer's shop. Fred Ashworth stayed in Oldham and made 436 appearances for the Watersheddings club in 15 seasons.

Aspatria had lost several star names, but a new hero came to the fore in the shape of Bob Hanvey, who played in all four England internationals during the 1926 season. Hanvey had attracted the attention of the selectors with some fine performances for Cumberland & Westmorland in the County Championship. In 1926 Hanvey was described as "magnificent" for his performance in the England trial. Two years later, Bob Scott and Owen Errington of Aspatria defected to the new Carlisle RL club.

The Black-Reds had to completely rebuild the whole club after the Second World War and success was hard to come by. The club did, however, recognise the need for its own clubhouse, ground and a championship team. But improvement only came in 1972 when a group of youngsters, captained by Melvyn Hanley, won the Under 21 County Cup and progressed to form the nucleus of a top-class senior side. After 39 years, the Black-Reds regained the Cumberland Cup, defeating Cockermouth in 1976-77. The 1977-78 final against Netherhall went to three games before Aspatria won 13-3. The following season, the First XV became the only team throughout Great Britain to complete their annual programme with a 100% record (P33 W33 D0 L0 F818 A163).

The 1980s saw six successive Cumbria Cup wins. The 1987 final against Moresby was a personal triumph for David Pears; the talented young centre scored four penalties from six attempts, and added a try in the final five minutes.

Pears, along with team-mate George Doggart, signed for Sale in 1988. Within weeks Pears won his first England 'B' international cap, a game in which Doggart came on as replacement scrum-half. Two years later, Pears moved south to join Harlequins and was included in the 1991 Rugby World Cup squad. He was on the bench in all of the games as a replacement for the stand-off and full-back.

In 1990 the club hosted the North of England v Russia match.

In 1998 the Aspatria-Sale connection saw Stephen Hanley progress to international honours. Stephen, son of Mel Hanley, appeared on the wing for England. He was a big winger, but not big enough to tackle the entire Welsh pack, who bore straight down on him. He made the tackle but paid for his bravery by breaking his arm and missing the next two seasons. Hanley played 191 games for Sale, scoring 104 tries.

Aspatria's fortunes declined with the arrival of the 21st century. Too many Cumbrian youngsters left the area in pursuit of work and education. In 2010-11 they were champions of the North Lancs and Cumbria Division.

(Thanks to Mel Hanley)

BARROW

"Barrow is a town that strikes me as being one of the miracles of our time."
Bishop of Carlisle, 1872

FEW TOWNS HAVE grown as rapidly as the Cumbrian port of Barrow did in the 19th century. The importance of Barrow arose from the discovery of haematite (an iron ore) in the vicinity in 1850. The total population was 65 in 1800, which increased to 47,000 with the opening of the Furness Railway in 1864 and the rapid expansion of shipbuilding in the port. Barrow grew from 300 to 80,000 in the second half of the 19th century alone. Mining gave way to iron and steel production and later shipbuilding. Gradually, Barrow became the world's biggest shipbuilders and Vickers shipyard employed 30,000 men. Decline followed the Great War.

Rugby arrived in Barrow in 1875 with the town club arranging 11 matches. The first game was on the 6th November 1875, away to Ambleside, where sadly they could only muster nine men. The match ended after ten minutes because it was no contest as Ambleside ran riot.

Matters improved over the next decade as Barrow became a middle-ranking side which was able to attract fixtures with good clubs, such as Halifax, Dewsbury and Cambridge University. In 1888 Barrow were honoured with a visit from the Maoris, who won by a goal to nil in front of 6,000 spectators.

The early 1890s saw Barrow successful in the 'Second Class Lancashire Clubs League' with 32 victories in 39 matches in one season. They were promoted to the Lancashire Senior League in 1895, but won only 14 of 32 games. The club did,

however, produce its first international in George Hughes, who played for England against Scotland. Hughes was not a big forward, but was described as: "an effective tackler… and a marvel in the (foot) rushes".

In 1897 Barrow joined the exodus to the Northern League, where they established a good reputation as a 'rugby league town' and succeeded in winning the RL Challenge Cup in the 1950s. Sadly, the industrial decline of Barrow was mirrored in the decline of the rugby league club, who dropped out of the leading ranks.

BAe BARROW (formerly Vickers)

BARROW-IN-FURNESS today has two rugby union clubs: Furness and BAE Barrow (formerly known as Vickers). Vickers was formed on 21st October 1930 by 20 enthusiasts as a section of Vickers-Armstrong Shipyard's sports club. Initially Vickers lived in the shadow of Furness, but in 1948-49 they had a splendid season when they won 20 out of 28 games. In the 1930s, the shipyard had a regular intake of apprentices who were the future of the rugby club.

A new pitch was opened in September 1957, with a clubhouse added in November 1963. The Furness Peninsula was traditionally a part of Lancashire, but county boundaries were re-drawn in 1974 and the club joined the Cumbria RU in 1977.

The club changed its name in 2002 to acknowledge the importance of British Aerospace in the entire area. The club are now known as Hawcoat Park.

BRITISH STEEL

THE BRITISH STEEL industry was amongst the nation's biggest employers in the 20th century, but foreign imports undermined its importance. Steel production is closely associated with South Wales, but it was once a major employer in Cumbria. British Steel RUFC was formed in 1954 by staff from Workington Iron & Steel Company. In 1961, the combined club, known as United Steels, won the Cumberland Junior Shield. They joined the Cumbrian League, but suffered badly from the decline in the steel industry in the 1990s.

In 1998 the club won national headlines when they fielded three players whose average age was 65. The unlikely trio were easily the oldest back-line to ever play UK league rugby. Despite good facilities, British Steel RUFC finally closed in 2000.

CARLISLE

THE CITY OF Carlisle has always had importance as the gateway to Western Scotland; the Scottish border is only a dozen miles away. Carlisle can lay claims to having hosted the world's first international club matches as on 28th March 1874, Carlisle played the Langholm club from over the border. This fixture is occasionally renewed and is probably the oldest international club fixture in rugby.

Rugby was the foremost sport in Cumberland before the Great Schism, but the schism had a devastating effect on local rugby. There were 50 clubs in the county before the split; afterwards Carlisle was the only large club left, although several junior clubs struggled on – notably Old Creightonians, Eden Rangers, Cowans, Sheldon Hornets and the Nondescripts.

Eden and Carlisle RFC had reunited in 1894 with agreed terms that the club be called Carlisle FC, but that the colours should be those of Eden Wanderers: white jerseys, red stockings and navy blue knickers. These have remained Carlisle's colours.

The troubled times afflicting English rugby during the Great Schism proved a blessing for Carlisle, who began to appear under the international selectors' scrutiny. Walter Butcher (1878-1957) was the first genuine Carlisle international. He began with the club before moving to Bristol and Streatham, and eventually accrued seven England caps.

William Nanson (1880-1915) was a top-class forward after the turn of the century, but stayed with Carlisle. He too won seven England caps and was part of a Carlisle side that won the 1908 Cumberland Cup, beating Aspatria in the final. Later that year he switched to the NU and joined Oldham, but stayed for only two seasons. He was killed in action in 1915 whilst serving in Mesopotamia.

In 1923 Bernard 'Tommy' Tucker was an England reserve. Army Captain B.H. Tucker, the Cumberland captain, played for Cumberland & Westmorland despite having been posted to India with his regiment. He played for Cumberland and then caught the train to the South of France, where he caught a ship to Malta and joined his regiment.

In December 1925 the RFU held an England trial at the club. A report of the match said, "Carlisle is a nice looking ground but on state occasions the rugby folk have to obtain the use of the better appointed association club." This was a reference to the Carlisle United football ground next door to the rugby ground.

Such plaudits could not be directed at the Cumberland v New Zealand match played in Carlisle the previous year. That match was one of the roughest games ever played. The tourists claimed that the Cumbrians kicked and thumped anything that moved. They claimed Hart, their try-scoring winger, was flattened by a Cumberland forward after the final whistle and only the police stopped a free-for-all involving both sides and the crowd.

Carlisle can take the credit for introducing seven-a-side rugby to England and won their first competition, beating Hawick 7-6 in the final. Sevens had, of course, been created just across the Scotland border at the turn of the century.

Carlisle had a strong team at this time. James Morgan (1890-1961) played for the club after winning an England cap in 1920 when he was with Hawick, and Dr Alexander Gillies, a Scotland international flanker, played for Carlisle after winning 12 caps as a Watsonian in Edinburgh.

Carlisle benefited from the large number of servicemen stationed in the area during World War Two and managed to keep playing for most of the emergency.

After World War Two, Neil Cameron won three Scotland caps whilst with Carlisle, and a number of other players appeared for the club who went on to win international caps – notably Humphrey Luya (the Waterloo and England lock), Alec Valentine of Hawick and Scotland and Ron McCarter, a local lad who played for London Irish and Ireland.

The most recent Carlisle international was perhaps the best of all: Chris Wardlow, a stocky centre who made his club debut at the age of 16. He moved south and played for England six times despite a string of injuries that ended his career prematurely. Wardlow played in the 1971 RFU Centenary match and was selected for the 1971 Lions, but missed out due to injury.

Several attempts were made to establish rugby league in Carlisle. The earliest attempt didn't last long before moving to Maryport and then disbanding. In 1980 a rugby league club called Carlisle Borderers RLFC

Chris Wardlow

opened next door at Brunton Park. Borderers muddled through for 15 seasons before merging with Barrow RLFC.

Carlisle RUFC has now settled into middle-ranking status in the North West leagues. Much of their glory days were built on attracting the best talent from the whole of Cumberland, but the emergence of Aspatria, Wigton and Newcastle Gosforth meant players could look beyond Brunton Park for a rugby career.

(Thanks to Norman Laycock)

CREIGHTON

CREIGHTON RUFC WAS formed in 1927 by former pupils of the long gone Creighton School. They were formerly known as Old Creightonians RUFC and drew their players from Creighton Grammar School in the border city. Opened in 1918, the school took its name from a prominent local family, one of whom, Dr Mandell Creighton, was a Bishop of London. The Bishop founded Kilburn Grammar School in 1898 and also formed an 'Old Creightonians' rugby club in London, which died out decades ago. Fixtures between the Old Boys' clubs were played until the London club closed.

Old Creightonians of Carlisle were a highly successful rugby club between the wars. W.E. Telford, R.S. Lancaster and J. Payton all represented Cumberland & Westmorland in the 1930s; and Jack Sewell played for the county and had an England trial. 1950 was OC's finest hour when they reached the Cumbria Cup final, but lost to Workington. They were runners-up again in 1959 to Egremont.

The most famous Creightonian is Herbert Victor 'Chalkie' White, who is credited with 'teaching the rugby coaches to coach'. Chalky White moved to Truro, where he taught at the school and played scrum-half for Camborne for four years. He played scrum-half for Creighton, Cumberland, Penzance, Camborne and Leicester. Chalkie progressed from player to coach in the 1970s and, as club coach, helped re-establish Leicester amongst England's elite. White enjoyed enormous success at Welford Road, but was consistently overlooked for the job of England coach.

Creightonians dropped the Old Boys title in 1972 as the link to the school fell away. The club have settled in the middle reaches of the Cumbria Leagues and moved to a new sporting complex at Sycamore Lane, Parkland on the south side of the city in 2006.

EGREMONT

West Cumbria is a rare combination of the wild and the functional, and Ennerdale is a spectacular mountain valley that terminates in the mining town of Egremont (population 15,000). Iron ore is still mined today, but the industry is a shadow of the days when five large mines employed thousands of men.

Rugby in Egremont dates from the 21st November 1878, when the local side beat St. Bees Village by three tries and five minor points to nil. Some reports suggest a side called 'Egremont Athletic' also operated in the town for several seasons.

Egremont became a hotbed of rugby in the late 1880s, when the local paper recorded that they had acquired players from arch-rivals Whitehaven Town. The club was becoming a force and enjoyed a double triumph in 1890 when the First XV won the Cumberland Cup and the Second team were Cumberland Shield winners. Egremont's County Cup win came at the expense of a long-forgotten side called Flimby.

Egremont reached the county final again in 1894, when they lost to Maryport. They won the cup again in 1922 and 1932, when they were one of the finest sides in the North West.

A contemporary writer wrote of the 1921-22 cup victory: "Egremont's football was tough and rugged. It was of a type that has fortunately disappeared everywhere else!" It was alleged that Egremont had a team of 14 forwards and a full-back who thrived on a mud heap of a pitch. The forwards steamrollered all the opposition into the ground and the full-back was available in case any survived the juggernaut.

In the 1930s, Egremont bought a new ground at Bleach Green, where they remain to this day.

Rugby in Egremont survived during World War Two thanks to a local miners side. One of the club's finest players was Harry Cook, who joined his home-town club in the mid-1940s and can recall playing against the wartime miners side. Harry was a talented enough youngster to play for the Northern Counties XV against the Wallabies in the late 1940s. He recalled that several of the Wallabies never went home, preferring instead to switch to rugby league and stay in the north, which was surprising because the UK had food rationing after the war.

Some months after the match, an unexpected parcel arrived at Harry's home. The parcel contained food sent from Australia by the Wallabies, who felt that the northern team looked under-nourished! Harry returned to Egremont from university to be part of the club's golden era, when they reached the Cumbria Cup final on seven occasions between 1956 and 1970, including a hat-trick of wins. They were unofficial North West champions in the 1950s, based on their results in friendlies all over the region. Harry Cook regards beating arch-rivals Furness as the highlight of his rugby career.

Harry had an unusual brush with the RFU when he was a star with Egremont. Several of the team were top-class wrestlers who competed in the highly-competitive Cumbrian wrestling circuit (where a competitor could collect a tenner for a big win). The RFU tried to have the Cumbrian wrestlers declared as professionals and banned for life. They eventually failed to impose a ban.

Egremont have declined from those heady days, as has the town's mining industry, forcing an exodus of young people in search of work

The best player to emerge in recent years is John Butler, a huge lock who won an England cap when with Gosforth. Butler was a top-class goalkeeper with Carlisle United FC and county high jump champion before opting for rugby. Other good players to emerge from Egremont include Vince Fox (Tynedale) and Peter Murphy (Newcastle Falcons). Martin Hodgson began with Egremont before becoming a great RL player.

Today the club play in the North Lancs & Cumbria Leagues.

(Thanks to Harry Cook)

Egremont in 2011.

FURNESS

THE PRINCIPAL TOWN of the Furness Peninsula is Barrow. The original Barrow RFC joined the Northern Union on 20th April 1897 and were an important outpost of rugby league for much of the 20th century. In 1902 Furness RUFC was formed to fill the void, but followed the tradition of adopting an alternative name to save confusion with the NU club. The inaugural meeting was held at the Criterion Restaurant, Barrow under Mr. E. Wadham (President), Mr. Mawson (Chairman), F. Taylor (Hon. Secretary) and W. Bagot

(Hon. Treasurer). F.W. Stileman was elected club captain. Initially, the newcomers joined forces with the local hockey club. The club's first ground was on Abbey Road with changing accommodation at the Furness Abbey Hotel.

The opening game was played against Skipton on the 4th October 1902, which Furness lost by 37 points to five. The following week they travelled to Lancaster, but lost 12 points to six. The first home match was played against Whitehaven on the 25th October 1902. Furness's first win came on the 22nd November 1902 by three points to nil against Birkenhead Park 'A' team. The scarcity of good rugby union clubs in the area can be gleaned from the fact that in only their first season Furness had two county players in the Rev. C.R. Burnett (Cumberland) and F.W. Stileman (Lancashire). The Furness peninsula was a part of Lancashire until 1974, but many of its players were Cumbrians.

The 1903-4 season began with a new ground at Monks Croft and victory in their first five games, beginning with Preston Grasshoppers by 32-0. In early 1904, the ex-Yorkshire and Durham half-back Bernard Oughtred arrived. Oughtred (1888-1949) had won six England caps whilst with Hartlepool Rovers in the early 1900s. A product of King Edward's School, Birmingham, the tough little scrum-half was a rover on and off the field, playing for at least four different clubs. His half-back combination with F.W. Stileman was considered the strongest in the north and catapulted Furness into the front rank of northern clubs. By 1908, Hartlepool Rovers, Birkenhead Park, Headingley and Waterloo were among the opposition.

Subsequently, the club had short spells of playing at Railway Meadows, Dalton and Thorncliffe Road, Barrow before the present location of the Strawberry Grounds was acquired – for the then frightening sum of £1,480 – in 1921. A clubhouse was added in 1935 and an adjacent field was acquired in 1957.

Back in 1921, Harry Wilkins and Alfred Aslett represented Lancashire in all five games. The following season the club jersey was changed to blue and white stripes with a white collar and the badge was the mitre crest, denoting Furness Abbey. Aslett subsequently moved to London, winning six England caps whilst with Richmond.

The 1920s were a period of success, culminating in the England selection of Reg Foulds, a No. 8 who arrived from Waterloo. Reg was the first player to be actually capped for England during his spell with Furness. He won three caps and appeared 44 times for Lancashire.

W.W. Wakefield, the great Grand Slam captain, is also recorded as having played for Furness, but details are sketchy.

1929 saw the arrival of J.C. Pank from Marlborough, who was Furness captain for five years, a Lancashire regular and Barbarian. Pank and J. Bowker were first choice for Lancashire for some years, and Pat Horne was an England trialist. However, a decline in Furness's playing fortunes was apparent from the mid-1930s. The impact of the outbreak of war in 1939 saw some unusual fixture lists for the clubs that kept going, with Furness playing Kendal every month during the winter of 1939-40.

Furness v Kendal 1939.

Things improved after World War Two, with a crop of new talent led by Reg Bazley and Bill Ferguson, who were both England trialists. Ferguson played in the trial at Workington, but suffered an early injury and was never selected again. Bazley, however, a flying wing, won ten caps in the 1950s and appeared 55 times for Lancashire. He moved on to Liverpool University and Waterloo, with whom he is most associated. Ron Slater began at the Strawberry Ground before playing for four counties: Cheshire, Lancashire, NLD and Hampshire.

In 1951-52 Alan Milligan, the Cumberland scrum-half, joined Furness. It was a mixed season with a wonderful win against all-powerful Liverpool.

1955-56 was the best season in the history of the club, with only three defeats in the 31 games and 715 points scored and

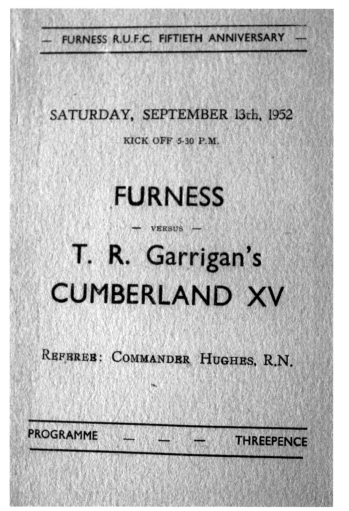

FURNESS R.U.F.C. FIFTIETH ANNIVERSARY

SATURDAY, SEPTEMBER 13th, 1952

KICK OFF 5-30 P.M.

FURNESS

— VERSUS —

T. R. Garrigan's

CUMBERLAND XV

REFEREE: COMMANDER HUGHES, R.N.

PROGRAMME — — — THREEPENCE

Furness in 2008

only 152 conceded. The record lasted until 1971, when A. Bowker contributed a record 49 tries in a playing record of P40, W35, D1, L4, for 935 points scored against 208 conceded.

1970 saw Furness's first victory in the Westmorland Cup. Four years later, government reform saw Westmorland disappear and the Furness area moved into Cumbria, which marked the end of the Lancashire affiliation after 73 years.

The ensuing years of the century saw Furness find their level as a good junior club, but the area's economics took a dive. The drain of young people from the area has hit the town and local rugby hard.

OLD BARROVIANS

IN 1950 FURNESS allowed training facilities to a new team, the Casuals XV, who were later to become the Old Barrovians They died out after only a couple of seasons.

KENDAL

"That dreary Moor"
William Wordsworth

RUGBY WAS FIRST played in the 'Auld Grey Town' of Kendal in 1871, and enthusiasm for the game was so great that within a decade there were eight teams in the town. Matches, all local derbies, were rough and spiteful and attracted up to 600 spectators. The most prominent of the octet was Kendal Town (known as the Cardinals because they wore red jerseys).

The first games of rugby in the Westmorland town were played at the cricket field. In 1872, the local drill field was utilised when not required for the local militia. The drill field, known as the Soldiers' Field, was on the north bank of the River Kent and occupied the site known as Parr Street.

Land flat enough for sport was hard to find in Kendal, which lies in a valley between the Lakeland Fells. Kendal Hornets moved out of the town centre to attract the cream of opposition in the North West, including Preston Grasshoppers, in November 1872.

The Hornets and the Cardinals prospered until the early 1890s, and visiting teams included Halifax, Wigan, Aspatria, Tyldesley, West Hartlepool, New Brighton, St. Helens and Bradford. The rugby talent of Kendal didn't go unnoticed by

some of the visitors and the town's sportsmen became easy pickings for the big clubs from Lancashire and Yorkshire, who 'bent' the laws of amateurism.

The greatest Kendalian of the era was John 'Buff' Berry, who grew up in Fellside, a little hamlet just outside the ton. He left school at eight and in his teens played for some of the town's rugby teams, including Monument Rovers, Castle Mills and eventually Kendal Hornets. It was there he formed a formidable half-back partnership with Billy Cross. A small, wiry individual, Berry recalled that he played football in his boots with strips of leather on the sole. After matches,

'Buff' Berry

he carried his soiled jersey home in an old newspaper and thought nothing of walking miles to and from away matches. He first attracted attention outside Kendal when the Hornets played Broughton Rangers in 1884 before a crowd of 1000. He, Billy Cross and skipper Billy Walker formed a formidable trio for the Hornets. Their reputations were sealed in 1885 when Kendal Hornets joined Kendal Town, Ambleside and Windermere in fielding a Westmorland county team. Berry and Cross made a huge impact with the county and were soon enticed

Billy Cross

to Tyldesley in south Lancashire, who were then one of the best sides in Britain. 'Buff' was even capped by England, but never returned to Kendal. However, he was persuaded to reappear for Westmorland in 1892.

There wasn't much to tempt a top-class player back to Kendal, for the Hornets switched to NU in 1898. They struggled on for six years before folding, along with most of their local rivals.

Alf Charley began with Kendal Town before moving to Halifax. He emigrated to New Zealand and played for the All Blacks against the British Isles.

The present Kendal RUFC emerged in August 1905. The club "reintroduced the good old game in its true amateur spirit!" Their first ground was at Mintsfeet, but in 1906 they moved to Maude's Meadow, which was their home ground for 20 years. Their first match was against Vale of Lune, and although they lost 8-3, they were soon able to attract well-known clubs like Sale, Furness and Heaton Moor on to their fixture list.

The new club made rapid headway and supported the Cumberland & Westmorland side that were making national headlines. This led to Stan Alexander becoming an English trialist.

Kendal lost many of its sons in World War One and a huge memorial was erected in the town centre. Those rugby players who returned from the war were augmented by schoolboys from Sedbergh. One product of the school was W.W.

Lord Wakefield

Wakefield, who was perhaps the finest rugby player of the era. W.W.'s family had local links as they owned much of the land surrounding Windermere. Wakefield got himself fit by running 15 miles at a time across the mountains. He also appeared for Windermere RUFC before he left Sedbergh and headed to London, which denied his services to his home-town club. He proceeded to lead a remarkable life, encompassing becoming a RAF pilot, rugby coach, travelling salesman and MP, and he also led England to a Grand Slam. Although Wakefield never returned to live permanently in Kendal, he kept a close affiliation with his original club.

Kendal may have lost the services of a great England captain, but the years between the two great wars was a golden age for the club, culminating in a three-year period when they were undefeated at home. During this time they won the Manchester 'Sevens' and were even featured in The Tatler magazine as one of England's best sides.

Sammy Martindale

Sammy Martindale was the kingpin. He was selected 51 times for Cumberland, and in 1929 played for England against France in Paris. This led to him touring Australia and New Zealand with the British Lions. A fine full-back, he was badly hurt at the start of the tour but recovered.

Alex Johnson was an England trialist, who, in the 1931-32 season, scored a record 54 tries as Kendal amassed 1,190 points – a huge total in the days when a try was only worth three points. During the 1934 season, Kendal played at mighty Otley with only 12 men – the other three could not get through the floods – but still won 9-0.

In 1932 L.H. Collinson, an Old Millhillian, taught at Sedbergh and played for Kendal.

The club had its ups and downs, but in 1926 decided Maude's Meadow was unsuitable for matches and a move was imperative. A field was purchased at Mint Bridge on the north side of the town. The whole population rallied round to raise the money, including organising a two-day bazaar in the town hall. It took another decade for the move away from Maude's Meadow to materialise when a new clubhouse was opened. The 1937 building was replaced in 1953.

The Second World War years saw the club fielding another of the greatest players in the sporting history: Bob Stuart. The giant Kiwi was based in the area whilst serving with the New Zealand army. He was later to play for the All Blacks, and, indeed, was captain for a time.

The 1950s saw Kendal fielding a young, but talented, team. They were able to claim parity with mighty Sale, who were very

Kendal in action in 1910.

fashionable with the international selectors. By contrast, Kendal had no internationals, but many county players. Two of the best Kendal players, Pym Sharpe and Bobby Hogg, were selected for England trials in 1958. Sharpe later switched to Rugby League. In 1959 Hogg was again an England trialist, but had to drop out with an injury.

The next two decades saw Kendal as a good, but unspectacular, side with an excellent fixture list. The second half of the 20th century was notable for generations of the same families playing for the club: the Nicholsons, the Healeys, the Staverts and the Sharpes.

The outstanding Kendal player of the 1980s and 1990s was David Bell, who, fortunately for the club, stayed loyal for two decades. Year in and year out Bell scored points by the bagful from the fly-half position. They also had an outstanding forward in Peter Kremer, a huge No. 8 who played for the club for a decade before becoming a successful coach. Sadly Kremer died very young.

With the introduction of leagues, Kendal found themselves around level 4 or 5 (North), where they had the pleasure of regularly meeting old friends, such as Preston Grasshoppers, Aspatria, Harrogate and Otley. With modest resources, they could hold their own in such company, but saw wealthier clubs pass them on the stairway to stardom.

They did, however, manage to attract some outstanding talent, including Casey Mee from New Zealand and Jimmy Thompson from Wigton, but the club junior section produced the bulk of the side.

Kendal briefly climbed into National Two (North) before slipping down into North One. The club are reported to be looking to their own home-produced players to take them forward. In 2014, Mark Wilson moved to Newcastle Falcons from and has established a big reputation in the North East.

(Thanks to John Hutton)

KESWICK

THE DELIGHTFUL TOWN of Keswick (pop. 4,800) lies at the heart of the Lake District. Rugby is still popular in Keswick and it has a distinguished history.

The first recorded match was a trial match played in October 1879 and the first recorded inter-club match was against Cockermouth on Thursday 29th November 1879, resulting in a loss by one try to nil. The club's next match was a victory against Workington on the 7th February 1880.

The town is also recorded as being home to four sides in 1881, with Keswick fielding two sides and Skiddaw Rangers and Fitz Rangers having one side apiece. Only Keswick were to survive, but they switched to soccer in 1885-86.

Resurrection came from Keswick School, which has long links to the Keswick club. The school began playing rugby in 1898, which led masters and pupils to reform the club in September 1901 with a match against Carlisle. Keswick were to play on the school fields for many years.

The new club could boast an international in David Graham, who had been capped by England whilst playing for Aspatria. They were held in very high regard as they could boast fixtures against top sides, such as Langholm and Manchester.

Keswick progressed and were Cumberland Cup winners in 1936, 1947, 1948, 1949, 1951, 1952, 1953 and 1955. For almost a decade, they vied with Workington for the premier spot in Cumberland. In 1946 they suffered a severe loss when their best player, Frank Longman, joined Wigan RLFC, for whom he made 213 appearances.

Keswick vacated the school fields in 1958 when the club acquired its own ground and clubhouse near Crossings Bridge.

John Scoon played at outside centre for the NW Counties team which lost 16-9 to the 1951 Springboks.

The club remained a force in Cumbria into the 1980s and could field three or four sides, but they declined towards the end of the 20th century. They survive through promoting junior rugby and their continuing links to Keswick School. In 2005 the club's ground suffered terrible flooding, yet only two years later their Under 17 team reached the national finals of RFU Under 17 Bowl, competing against clubs with vastly greater resources.

(Thanks to Alan Gray)

KIRKBY LONSDALE

KIRKBY LONSDALE IS an affluent little town (pop. 1,771) in the western Pennines about 20 miles from Lancaster and its rugby club was formed in 1877. They played their first match and the following match against Heversham Grammar School. The historic old school on both those occasions.

The club joined the Westmorland RU, but waited a decade before joining the RFU. In 1888 Kirkby provided G. Webster and E. Richardson to the Westmorland team who played the Maoris at Kendal.

Rugby boomed in the area in the final years of the 19th century, and Kirkby were able to fill their fixture list without moving outside of a 30-mile radius.

They ceased playing in the early years of the 20th century but reformed in 1920.

In 1926, the club had a remarkable achievement when one of their players, W.H. Walling, was selected for an England trial in Birmingham.

Kirkby was isolated by the hills that surrounded Underley Park until the M6 motorway opened in the 1960s and the south Lakeland became more accessible. At the time, Kirkby were down to a dozen regular players and it was only the merger with Holme Wanderers – their local rivals – which ensured their survival. Holme were a club built on the local farming community and had a fearsome reputation, based more on brawn than good rugby.

On Friday 31st August 1987, Kirkby and Cockermouth made history when the first official rugby union league match since 1895 was played by the two clubs at Cockermouth. By a quirk of fixture planning, the Cockermouth fixture was arranged the weekend before the start of the rest of the rugby season.

The next decade was a golden era for rugby in Kirkby Lonsdale as they climbed to North West Two and had fixtures against Vale of Lune and Kendal. Since then the club have suffered the 'swings and roundabouts' of rugby fortune. Underley Park itself is one of the best facilities in northern rugby and was home to the North of England selectors in the days before professional rugby ended regional competition.

In 2010, Kirkby were promoted to North 1 West and in 2014 Callum Sheldon from the club was selected for Scotland U18s.

(Thanks to Dave McGonnigal)

MILLOM

MILLOM IS A small seaside town on the northern edge of Morecambe Bay and lies a dozen miles west from Barrow. Isolated by geography, Millom was well 'off the beaten track' until the arrival of the railway in the 1860s, which opened the town to the world.

Millom RFC was formed in 1873 and joined the Cumberland County Union in 1885, winning the Cumberland Challenge Cup in three successive seasons in the late 1880s. All was not, however, sweetness and light as in 1889 Barrow played at Millom and a Barrow player was reprimanded by his committee for 'foul language'. Barrow and Millom enjoyed a long and far from harmonious rivalry that stretched into the NU era.

Stan Northmore

In this period they also produced two England internationals: Stan Northmore, who was capped at fly-half against Ireland in 1897, and Edward Knowles, who won two England caps at forward around the same time. Both players subsequently moved to NU teams. Northmore and Knowles came to England's notice following Cumberland's 1897 County Championship run. That Cumberland side included eight Millom players: J. Buckett, J. Young, R. Moore and W. Cunningham, S. Northmore, T. James, E. Knowles and S. Hoggarth. Cumberland reached the final, but lost 3-9 to Kent at Carlisle.

By this stage, the club were in dire straits after staying loyal to the RFU. Most of the neighbouring clubs had decided to join the NU, including arch-rivals Barrow, and attractive opposition was reluctant to travel to this distant corner of Cumbria. Millom joined the NU in 1897, and were also triple champions of the rebel NU North-Western League in the following years. The NU were glad to welcome the club as they had provided 12 of Cumberland & Westmorland's NU side in 1898, with Northmore at fly-half.

After initially prospering, Millom struggled to field a team in the semi-professional ranks and in 1906 the club returned to the amateur fold. The decision split the town and two separate clubs emerged: a NU team and a RU side. The two teams and their rivalry have survived for a century. Both clubs claim the honour of being the true descendant of the great side.

William Eagers was one of the best NU players of the 1900s. He made his debut for Millom Rangers as a 12-year-old and switched to the town club at 16. In 1900 Eagers moved to Bradford Northern.

Millom RUFC remained a considerable force in Cumbrian rugby throughout the 1920s and were one of only four sides to defeat mighty Furness in 1927-28. During this era, the club produced a top-class player in W.R. Bond, who played for the Possibles in the 1934 England trial without making the final selection.

In 1940, Millom fielded possibly the finest player in its history. Willie Horne, the legendary Barrow RLFC stand-off, was persuaded to play for the club, but he only stayed for a season before returning to rugby league. Willie is credited with inventing the 'round the corner' style of goal-kicking.

Les Bettinson, who played rugby union and league for the two Millom clubs, moved to Salford RLFC, where he made 319 appearances. He was also a reserve for the Cumberland RU team. After a distinguished RL career, he managed the Great Britain RL touring team to Australia in 1985.

Millom in 2011

In more recent times, they produced Jason Slater, who played for Kendal in the National leagues. Millom have developed their facilities and today have a superb clubhouse near the sea front.

(Thanks to Edward Whitfield)

NETHERHALL

NETHERALL RUFC WAS formed in 1950 as Ellenfoot Rugby Club, and played on any farmer's field they could find. In 1960 they were given the use of playing fields at Netherhall School and renamed themselves Netherhall Old Boys, although they never restricted themselves to previous pupils of the school.

The club moved its headquarters in the mid-1960s to the centre of Maryport. Fifteen years later, the club gained its own ground and clubhouse and 'Old Boys' was dropped from the name.

In 1990, they produced two top-class players in Stuart Connell and Mark Cueto. Connell played centre for Fylde and was later coach of the Woodlands club. Cueto played for Netherhall before joining Altrincham Kersal and then Sale Sharks. He became an England regular from 2004 onwards, and was one of the Premiership's top try-scorers.

PENRITH

THERE ARE RECORDS of rugby being played in Penrith in the early 1870s, when a side called 'Penrith Wasps RFC' operated in the town. This side didn't exist for long, but three new clubs emerged in the following decade. Penrith RFC were formed in 1882 with a meeting at Great Dockray under chairman, Rev. W.G.C. Hodgson. The first captain was R. Glasson of a local brewing family. A pitch was obtained at Foundry Field. Records show Penrith played Keswick in 1884 in a match that had to be curtailed as Penrith had to catch the last train home.

The club soon found a local rival in Inglewood Rangers (who were also known as Carleton Rangers). The two sides merged in 1889 as Penrith United, and were able to field a Thursday (half-day) side for players who weren't able to play on Saturdays. United's best players were Jeff Bewsher and Webby Murray, who both played for Cumberland, W.H. Parkin, who played for Oxford University, and Billy Winskill, a tall, rangy forward. Winskill played for Penrith United and Penrith Juniors before moving to Percy Park. He moved to Broughton Rangers NU around 1900 and became a top-class NU player.

Before the Great Schism, they could attract 1,000 spectators, but defections to the Northern Union destroyed Penrith United as they had only three local RU sides to play against. In 1900 United switched to the NU, but their playing resources were so threadbare that their XV lost to Seaton, who could only field ten men. Penrith won only three of 20 games in the NU. A financial crisis loomed and, in September 1902, Penrith United closed its doors.

Penrith reformed after World War One, but it was not until 1954 that Sir Wavell Wakefield opened the club's first pavilion at the Foundry Field. The club's growth led to the formation of a the Development Committee under Joe Jameson and Jim Nicholson, and they purchased 28 acres of land at Winter's Park (a concrete area used as a tank park during World War Two). Winter's Park became three playing pitches and a state-of-the-art clubhouse.

In 1987 Penrith were placed in North West 2, where they started badly with a 9-6 defeat at Heaton Moor. The early years saw them struggling against relegation, and they ere eventually relegated in 1992. They then stayed for two seasons in the peculiarly titled North West East North before regaining a spot in North West 2 by winning nine of their 12 matches in 1994-95 under skipper Joe Dent. That season, the county Performance Development Centre was opened by Rob Andrew MBE.

The club's most famous son is Stuart Lancaster, the England rugby coach, who learnt his rugby at Penrith and St. Bees before moving to Leeds Tykes.

Penrith are probably unique in having played in the North West and North East leagues. The RFU decided at one point that the club should play in North 2 East as only the Pennines separated them from the Durham and Newcastle clubs. Another link to the North East is flanker Mark Wilson, who began with Penrith juniors before moving to Kendal and Newcastle Falcons

The 21st Century began with Penrith struggling as their best players moved to other clubs. They climbed to National 3 North before falling back to North One.

SEATON

A RUGBY SIDE existed in the small town of Seaton near Workington in Victorian times. Its greatest claim to fame is that it produced Tom Fletcher, the first Cumbrian to be capped by England, before he joined Oldham NU in 1898. He played for Oldham until 1906, making 100 appearances. Fletcher was outstanding in the 1899 NU Challenge Cup Final, when Oldham beat Hunslet 19-9. He subsequently returned home to Seaton, who had by then joined the NU.

Tom Fletcher

Lads from the tiny mining town of Seaton were easy pickings for the wealthy NU clubs, and on one occasion three Cumbria players all joined Oldham RLFC in a single swoop.

Billy Little, a half-back from Seaton, joined Halifax in 1901 and played in the first NU international. He was one of the best rugby players in the years before World War One.

Joe Owens was born in and played for Seaton, but joined Oldham NU in 1899 along with Joe Ferguson.

The Seaton club disappeared before the Great War.

SILLOTH

'The Torquay of the North'
Bishop of Carlisle, 1860

SILLOTH-ON-SOLWAY is a tiny port on the Solway coast with spectacular views of the Scottish hills. Its main historical claim to fame was that an unpopular English prince drowned whilst trying to land there in the Middle Ages. Silloth didn't see many more visitors, dead or alive, until the Carlisle & Silloth Bay Railway arrived in 1859. The railway transformed the town into a popular Victorian holiday resort. The railway company also developed Silloth as an outlet for the North Cumberland coalfield.

The earliest reference to rugby in Silloth comes in 1878, when a post-match supper was held in the Queens Hotel. The rugby club was later recorded as having played at Annan across the Scottish border.

Silloth were a serious force in Cumberland rugby in the early part of the century, and were able to arrange fixtures with sides such as Kendal.

A great Silloth player was Jim Brough (1903-1987), who was perhaps the best English full-back of the 1920s. Brough did not take up rugby until he was 17-years-old, yet four years later he was capped by England against the All Blacks. He was a brilliant broken-field runner and an accomplished goal-kicker. Off the field, he came from humble origins and earned a living as a fisherman. He rapidly became the target of rugby league scouts and, after his England debut, he was asked to travel to Carlisle for a meeting with representatives of Swinton RLFC. In the station cafeteria a rugby league official put £350 in cash on the table in front of Jim – a fortune for a working man at the time. Brough declined the offer, saying, "At the time I had a shilling in my pocket, but I said 'No' as I was determined to get my second cap against Wales."

Jim caused consternation when he arrived at Twickenham; he presented a third-class rail ticket from Silloth to London to the RFU Secretary, who expected all players to travel first-class. Brough explained he had expected the RFU to send him a travel pass, but when it never arrived, he just bought the cheapest ticket in case they didn't offer to pay. Jim added that the Cumberland Rugby Union insisted their players travelled third-class.

Unfortunately for rugby union, Brough was a brilliant all-round sportsman. Liverpool Football Club offered him £10 a week to play soccer, whilst Leeds RLFC put £1000 on the table to switch to the 13-a-side code. Not surprisingly Brough took the money in 1925 and became one of rugby league's all-time greats, making 442 appearances for Leeds and touring Australia in 1928 and 1936. Despite Jim's great fame, his career in rugby league was overshadowed by his great contemporary, Jim Sullivan of Wigan. Sullivan and Brough were two of the

Jim Brough with Edward, Prince of Wales, later Edward VIII in 1926

greatest full-backs in rugby league history, and Welsh-born Sullivan always got the nod over his Cumbrian rival in the GB team. Brough's career stretched until World War Two, when he returned home to Silloth. He then switched his attentions to golf and became one of the best amateur golfers in Cumbria, where he took the regional title on several occasions. He was never considered by the England golf selectors because he had played sport as a professional.

At Silloth Rugby Union Club, Jim thought nothing of sweeping the dressing rooms and coaching the youngsters. As an old man, friends asked the RFU to rescind the lifelong ban imposed when he switched to rugby league half a century earlier. The RFU refused point blank, and even blocked an attempt to award him a life membership of his local club. Brough died in 1987, revered in Cumberland but forgotten elsewhere.

Silloth has also produced a number of other top-class players. D. Messenger played for the North in 1930, whilst Ivan Lomas, Ian Cannon and Mike Blake all played for Cumbria.

In 1983 the club built a new pitch on the old railway yard. Silloth's finest hour in recent years came when they reached round five of the National Junior Knockout Cup in 1992-93, a huge achievement for a small club who sometimes struggle to field two teams. Most recently, the best known Silloth rugby player has been John Pearson, who went on to become a top-class referee.

WHITEHAVEN

"Whitehaven possesses the finest harbour between Glasgow and Liverpool."
The Times 1882

AT THE MOUTH of Solway Firth, Whitehaven was the principal port of the region throughout the 19th century. The town's boom at that time was due to the determination of the earls of Lonsdale (the Lowthers) to maximize mining interests in Cumberland.

Rugby Football was introduced into Cumberland in the 1870s. In 1874 a club was started at Whitehaven, so it seems rather unkind of a writer in the Whitehaven News (18th October 1877) to say: "True to its tradition of being behind and in everything, Whitehaven is about the last town in the kingdom to open its gates to football, but 'mieux vaut tard que jamais' (better late than never)."

On the following Saturday they met 15 of the 'fine fleur' of the players of West Cumberland, Whitehaven winning by a goal and three tries to two. Other matches were arranged with Penrith and Ambleside, and second XV fixtures with St. Bees village and the college at St Bees.

The Whitehaven News later admitted (22nd November 1877) that, "The game of football, as played by the Rugby Union Society, is making such wonderful and rapid strides into popularity in the western division of the county. The excellent example set by the Whitehaven Football Club (some amends for their previous criticism) this season has now been followed by several other places in this district, and we understand that besides the clubs at St. Bees and Millom, two new organisations have recently been started at Workington and Cockermouth. Whitehaven beat Workington by 2 goals and 2 tries to a try disputed. There was a County match with Northumberland on Nov. 24, 1877, the former consisting of Carlisle men; Northumberland won by 8 goals and a try to nothing."

Whitehaven RUFC, a member of the Cumberland and Westmorland Rugby Union, was founded in 1877. Unfortunately, the minute books of the club prior to 1911 are not to be found, hence it has not been possible to refer to some of the happenings and the personalities of the period up to that date.

We have a record, however, of a spirited match played on Saturday, 3rd March 1877 between Whitehaven and the Students of St. Bees Theological College. The club won by the margin of three goals, one disputed goal, eight tries and sundry extra to nil. Then, in the following week, there was a match between The Professions and the Non Professional Gentlemen of the town.

In this county, the Cup Competition has been played since 1883, and the Shield Competition since 1888. Although in general it can be said that the Whitehaven club has not been competition-minded, it has nevertheless achieved success in these two fields. In the Challenge Cup there have been four wins (1884, 1914, 1963 and 1969) and nine defeats (1883, 1885, 1892 and 1929 against Aspatria, 1922 against Egremont, 1961 against Carlisle and 1971, 1971 and 1973 against Wigton) in the final.

The 1884 Cup Final against Carlisle was a dramatic affair, sprawling over two indecisive matches at Aspatria, but when the date of the third replay was fixed, the Carlisle club unexpectedly withdrew and left Whitehaven the winners. The club had to wait 30 years before they next won the cup; the final was again spread over the three matches, with Workington as opponents.

The Cumberland Shield was won by the club in 1912, when they defeated Cockermouth 10-3 at Aspatria on 20th January. They won the County Cup twice in the 1960s. In 1963 they beat Carlisle at Workington and six years later beat Wigton at Keswick 9-3 at the first attempt.

Co-operation with Whitehaven Grammar School was maintained over the years. Since its formation, over 60 players at the club have played for the Cumberland & Westmorland County team. In the 1877-1914 period, 34 players had 196 appearances.

In 1953-54 the club adopted an official motto: 'Vitai Lampada' (The Torch of Life) from Sir Henry Newbolt's poem. The club colours are maroon and white hoops.

Since leagues arrived, Whitehaven have played in the Cumbrian and North Lancs/Cumbria leagues.

WIGTON

WIGTON IS THE largest town between Carlisle and Workington and it is where Wigton RFC began as a soccer club in the early 1880s. A rugby section was formed on the 4th October 1882 as Highmoor Rangers. The Rangers were thought to have played fixtures against school sides before their first recorded match against a Scottish side called Burgh. Their first English club fixture was against the long-forgotten Brompton of Carlisle.

The new club suffered an internal schism in 1884 when a number of members broke away and formed Wigton Excelsior, but Highmoor and Excelsior reunited at the end of the season and agreed to change the name to Wigton RFC. It was to no avail as the united club soon disappeared due to shortage of numbers.

The emergence of the Cumberland Challenge Shield in 1887 was the catalyst for Wigton RFC to be reformed, but Wigton's results were modest and the club folded again in 1889.

1906 saw the club's second re-emergence with a match against Aspatria Agricultural College. The club had some decent players, including the local vicar, the Rev. Harold Ewbank, who played for Cumberland & Westmorland on 38 occasions despite being short-sighted and wearing a monocle during matches. During close combat, the monocle hung by his neck and was only lifted to his eye when he broke away from the scrum and needed to see where he was going. This was an unlikely form of leadership, but amazingly Ewbank led the new club to the 1908 and 1911 Cumberland Shield finals. Ewbank was captain of Cumberland from 1907 until 1920.

Wigton were not seeing 'eye to eye' with the RFU, who suspended the club for fielding Northern Union players. Tussles with the authorities were the norm in the years before

World War One, but Wigton still reached the 1912-13 County Cup final, losing to their neighbours Blennerhasset (who have long since disappeared).

Blennerhasset re-occurred in the Wigton story in 1923, when a fixture between the two clubs sparked trouble. A Wigton player was reported for thumping the referee, whilst several of his teammates limited themselves to pelting the official with mud. Mud certainly stuck as Wigton were barred from playing at home for a period, which led to the club folding yet again.

In 1924, a new side emerged in the town called Wigton Hornets. They even used the old club's second team jerseys. During their eight-year existence, the Hornets won the County Shield and were captained by Tosh Holliday, the England and Lions international from Aspatria. The survival of the Hornets was threatened in the early 1930s when an Old Boys side, Old Nelsonians RUFC, emerged from Nelson Secondary School. Old Nelsonians played from 1932 to 1936.

Another Wigton RUFC emerged after World War Two, playing modest fixtures against other clubs' second teams. They proved more reliable than their predecessors and, eventually, became a force in Cumbrian rugby by winning the 1965 Cumberland & Westmorland Cup. The early 1970s saw Wigton lose only ten of 116 matches played in three seasons, and success brought county honours to a string of Wigton players, notably Keith Warwick, Alan Fell and Ray Graham.

The club became regular County Cup winners, which brought automatic entry to the new National Knockout Cup. In 1979 Wigton hit the jackpot when they drew Sale. Sale fielded four internationals and ten North players, but still lost 24-7. The next round brought a fixture against Moseley, who were the Midlands' premier side. Moseley beat the Cumbrians 7-3.

Curiously, the most 'famous' rugby player to represent Wigton barely made the First XV. Melvyn Bragg left his home-town for London in the 1960s, but wrote a number of novels about Lakeland life. He also wrote affectionately of Wigton rugby. Bragg later became a hugely successful TV and radio presenter and producer.

WORKINGTON

THE OLD GAME of street football is still played in Workington every Easter between teams from the upper and lower parts of the town, referred to as 'Uppies' and 'Downies'.

The town's rugby club played its first match in December 1877, against Whitehaven, who had been formed the previous year. Although Workington lost, the press reported that their footballers performed 'very creditably'. The club played at the Valentine Ground, home of Workington Cricket Club, and like many early clubs was formed by cricketers looking for a winter pastime.

Workington RFC played at the cricket club until 1893, when they bought their own ground at Lonsdale Park at a cost of £200. The end of the 19th century was, however, a time of increasing prosperity and population growth in Workington as industrial expansion saw the population rise from 5,000 to 25,000 in just 15 years. The rugby club also grew and won their

Rugby Football Union
International Trial
England v. Possibles
AT
ELLIS SPORTS GROUND,
WORKINGTON, On
SATURDAY, DECEMBER 5th, 1936,
KICK OFF 2-30 P.M.
Referee - Mr. A. S. BEAN, Durham.
Official Programme, 2d.
—Selections by—
Workington Town Band.
Scotts (Workington) Limited, Printers

first major competition, the Cumberland Shield, in 1896. Around this time, the club acquired its nickname, the Zebras, after their jerseys of vertical black and white stripes, which later changed to horizontal hoops. Legend has it that a group of soldiers returning from the Boer War described the team as running around looking "like a herd of Zebras". The unflattering name stuck.

The Shield win coincided with the formation of the Northern Union, and Workington RFC joined the rebels along with the majority of Cumbrian clubs. Initially, the NU club went from strength to strength, winning their league and cup competitions in successive years, but professionalism was unsustainable and threequarters of the NU members went bankrupt or switched to soccer. Workington stayed loyal to the NU until 1909, when the lack of opposition (and gate money) forced the club into voluntary liquidation. The final straw was a dispute with the NU and, despite victory in the NU Cumberland Cup, League and Shield that year, the rugby league club went bust.

Workington Rugby Union Club re-emerged and incorporated an existing organisation, Workington Trades RUFC, which had been formed in 1907. They moved back into the cricket ground and re-joined the Cumberland Rugby Union. The reunion proved difficult as they were soon in trouble.

In 1909 Workington were one of the four Cumbria clubs found guilty of using the services of players who had played Northern Union. Along with Wigton, Cockermouth and Blennerhasset, they were suspended from playing from December 1909 to April 1910.

The Zebras soon recovered, and in 1914 they reached the Cumberland Cup final, where they faced arch rivals Whitehaven. The final was a scoreless draw, as was the replay. A third match was never arranged because of the outbreak of World War One.

The years following the war saw Workington RUFC become one of the UK's best sides when they only lost seven of 150 matches in six years. They won the Cumberland Cup on six occasions in the 1920s and provided six players to the Cumberland & Westmorland side, who were the English county champions.

The best known Workington players of the era were brothers T.M. and R.G. Lawson, who both played for England, and Billy 'Bumley' Little, who was generally regarded as the best northern scrum-half of his era, despite his unusual nickname. R.G. Lawson won 62 Cumbrian caps between 1919 and 1930, Bumley Little won 48 and T.H. Lawson won 41. Tom Lawson (1901-51) played at St. Bees and Workington. Little was a brilliant scrum-half and drop-goal specialist, but he had a reputation for brawling with opponents. He was brought up in dire poverty and worked as a miner before grasping the precious chance to earn a living as a rugby league player. He switched to rugby league in 1932 with Barrow, where he became a local legend.

The success of Workington RUFC brought acclaim to the town. The local steel company were so impressed they provided the Zebras with one of the game's finest stadiums, the Ellis Sports Ground, which cost £10,000 and had a huge grandstand and terraces to hold 21,000 spectators. The stadium was named as a permanent memorial to Mr J.V. Ellis, who was, at the time, general manager of the Workington Iron and Steel Works.

The Ellis Works Ground has hosted many county matches, as well as England trials in 1936 and 1952. Other matches at the ground have involved the Springboks, the Wallabies, Fiji and, most notably, the All Blacks. The 1972 All Blacks team will never forget their trip to Workington, where they lost to an English provincial side, the North West Counties, for the first time.

The Zebras produced three top-class players in the 1960s. Ron McCarten played for Workington, Carlisle and London Irish. He also won three Ireland caps in 1961. Alan Cowman and Peter Dixon both began with Workington before playing for England. Dixon was a member of the legendary 1971 Lions tour.

Workington's fortunes declined in the late 1960s and 1970s, and when leagues were re-introduced into English rugby union in 1985, the club found itself in the lower reaches. However, they have since won promotion on several occasions. In 2000, the club reached North West 2.

UPPER EDEN

UPPER EDEN RUFC operates from the delightful town of Kirkby Stephen, which lies between the Lake District and the Pennines. The side was formed in March 1975 by several ex-Penrith players. Initially the Pennine Hotel was the club headquarters, whilst the local Grammar School loaned a pitch.

The first captain was Sam Fisher, with Clive Williamson as coach, and they won their first match against Penrith Vagabonds.

The club finally found a home in 1982, when five acres were bought for £10,200. Levelling the ground would have cost £7,000, so the club did the work themselves. A clubhouse was added the following year, although a bar wasn't installed until 1985.

Upper Eden were Cumberland Cup inners in 1984, beating several bigger clubs. The club were also Cumbrian League champions 2001-02.

Upper Eden in 2007.

CHAPTER SIX - LANCASHIRE & CHESHIRE

"Lancashire players are the worst behaved of all English sportsmen.
They tend to drink a lot and misbehave."
RFU official selector circa 1900

LANCASHIRE

THE LANCASHIRE COUNTY RFU was formed at the Albion Hotel, Manchester on 22nd December 1881 by representatives from Manchester, Liverpool, Broughton, Birch, Broughton Rangers, Cheetham, Cheetham Hill, Oldham, Preston, Rochdale Hornets, Rossendale, Swinton, Salford, Manchester Rangers, Free Wanderers and Walton.

Previously Manchester FC had been the overriding force that dominated all county selection; indeed, the administration of county matches in Lancashire was solely in the hands of the Manchester club, with a little help from Liverpool RFC. The two clubs had been the entirety of Lancashire rugby in the early days, but the newer clubs wanted equality of representation. The newcomers sent a deputation to meet the Manchester committee in 1881 in the hope of encouraging the formation of a representative committee. Manchester were slow to accept change, but eventually the Lancashire County RFU was formed with the proviso that all home matches were to be played at Manchester.

By 1890 the LRFU could boast clubs from Aspull, Askam, Barrow-in-Furness, Blackley, Blackley Rangers, Boothstown, Broughton, Broughton Rangers, Bury, Crompton, Failsworth, Free Wanderers, Leigh, Liverpool, Liverpool Old Boys, Lancaster, Manchester, Manchester Rangers, Morecambe, Mossley, Owens College, Oldham, Pendleton, Radcliffe, Rochdale Hornets, Rochdale St. Clements, Salford, Stalybridge, St. Helens, St. Helens Recreation, South-East Lancashire Union, Southport, Swinton, Tottington, Tuebrook, Tyldesley, Ilkeston, Walkden, Warrington and Werneth.

In 1893, Lancashire and neighbours Yorkshire were producing the finest players and were the backbone of the England team. The game of rugby in Lancashire transcended class barriers.

The LRU Challenge Cup was inaugurated in 1894 and only lasted four seasons as the game rumbled into discontent and revolution. The traditional giants of Manchester and Liverpool had not been involved in the turmoil; they never entered the various competitions and preferred to play traditional 'friendly' matches against established clubs on a national and regional basis. But the new clubs wanted leagues and the income they could provide to pay their way.

The problem of professionalism threatened to destroy the game. Clubs loyal to the RFU were forced to join the Northern Union because there were insufficient opponents to fill the calendar. The county was hit hard. From gates of £1500 in the early 1890s, income from spectators dropped to £45 in 1899. The offer of a Lancashire fixture against the 1905 All Blacks was refused on the grounds of poor finances. Results were also a worry because the cream of the county's players had joined the NU.

Things were bleak, but two things portended well for the LRU: the re-emergence of town clubs in the wake of the decline of the NU, and the formation of many new sides composed of Old Boys from the new grammar schools that emerged between the wars.

In 1891 Lancashire won the first County Championship and five of their side played in that year's internationals – three for England and two, having joined Oldham from Swansea, for Wales! England's famous 1892 side, the only one from any country to win the Triple Crown without conceding a point, contained players from Wigan, Leigh, Swinton and Salford. Subsequently, all four clubs defected to the new Northern Union, and Lancashire's fortunes slumped so badly that it was 44 years before the Red Rose took their second county championship.

That 1935 Championship team had England star three-quarters Heaton, Leyland and Meikle and forwards in Toft and Fry, together with the legendary Welsh captain Watcyn Thomas. Centre Jack Heaton, one of the most remarkable figures in the history of county rugby, was Lancashire captain when they won their next four championships in 1938, 1947, 1948 and 1949. Lancashire's seventh championship came in 1955, when Eric Evans made his name as such an inspiring skipper that he was earmarked as the next England captain and led his country to the Grand Slam.

Lancashire rugby became enormously popular in the decades following World War Two, with great support amongst the rugby fraternity throughout the county. Unlike many other areas, clubs actively

Eric Evans is chaired off the field after leading England to a Grand Slam.

supported the county and would rearrange matches for the morning of a county match so that players could watch go and watch. Yet, surprisingly, it was 1969 before Lancashire won another championship, under Dick Greenwood, another outstanding England captain.

The 1970s were a golden era for county rugby in general and Lancashire in particular, with British Lions such as Tony Neary, Fran Cotton, Bill Beaumont and Steve Smith. The two northern victories over the All Blacks owed much to Lancashire personnel.

The highlight of the county season was the annual Roses match against Yorkshire, which could attract gates of 5,000 and a dozen international players would take the field.

In 1972 the county even asked for the Lancashire Challenge Cup to be taken from a Warrington bank vault, where it had sat for 75 years. It became a popular competition again and was dominated by Orrell, Waterloo, Fylde and Liverpool St Helens until the advent of league rugby in 1987. From then onwards, clubs preferred their players to concentrate on league commitments, which has led to a decline in county rugby within Lancashire. A handful of counties, led by Lancashire, have kept the flag flying for the County Championship and Lancashire have won the title on seven occasions since 2000.

After restructuring in 2007, the top tier of the championship has been known as the Bill Beaumont Cup, in honour of the Fylde, Lancashire, England and Lions captain.

CHESHIRE

THE FIRST REFERENCE to a Cheshire rugby 'club' occurs in 1875, when the minutes of the Sale club recorded an invitation from J.W.H. Thorp, a local squire from Macclesfield, A.E. Ward of Sale and H.M. Blythe, of Birkenhead Park, arranging a match between Cheshire and Liverpool at Edge Hill. At the time there were few Cheshire clubs, so the county had to depend on men qualified by birth or residence who were playing in Lancashire. The original Cheshire team was composed of players from Birkenhead Park, Birkenhead School, Rock Ferry, Parkgate, Sale and New Brighton. Cheshire beat Liverpool and had the temerity to challenge Lancashire. That game, at 15-a-side, took place at Sale on 24th February 1877, with Lancashire winning by one goal and two tries to a sole Cheshire try. In subsequent seasons Yorkshire (1877), Northumberland (1883), Durham (1887) and Westmorland (1887) were played on a friendly basis until 1888, when the County Championship was officially organised by the RFU.

In 1876, the county introduced the Cheshire Cup, which was stopped in April 1888, presumably because bad behaviour had reared its head. In the short life of the competition, the cup was won three times by Birkenhead Park and once by New Brighton. Other clubs affiliated to the union and taking part in the competition at that time were Alderley, Macclesfield, Bowdon, Dukinfield, Egremont, Hyde, Marple, Northenden and Sale. The county drew its playing strength from a handful of middle-class clubs, but ignored the playing credentials of successful clubs such as Runcorn and Stockport, who had 'working-class' members. These working-class clubs eventually joined the Northern Union.

The loss of the NU clubs allowed Birkenhead Park, New Brighton and Sale to attain 'first-class' status. But, despite the rise of the three clubs, Cheshire county rugby was unsuccessful. The county produced top-class individuals but failed to produce winning teams.

The best Cheshire player between the wars was H.M. Locke, who played 12 times for England between 1923 and 1927. He also had the honour of playing for the combined England and Wales side against Scotland and Ireland in the Centenary match played at Rugby School in 1923.

Cheshire was highly progressive in promoting schools rugby in 1949 and organised coaching courses from 1950. The Cheshire Cup competition was reintroduced in 1969 and Cheshire were county champions in 1998.

ALDWINIANS

ALDWINIANS RFC PLAY in Droylsden. Originally called Old Aldwinians, the club was founded in 1936 as Audenshaw Grammar School Old Boys. The school was founded in 1932 under Headmaster John Lord, who formed the OA Association. The rugby section was allowed to play on the school playing fields at Stamford Road, Audenshaw.

In their first three seasons they lost only seven games and raised £3,000 for the purchase of a ground on Stanhope Avenue. During the war years the club amalgamated with Oldham to keep the game going in the district. Independent existence was resumed in 1945 and a new pavilion was erected as a war memorial.

Old Aldwinians who have gained honours in the game include F.G. Griffiths (Sale and Lancashire), J.K.D. Whaling (Liverpool) and the legendary Eric Evans (1921-1991). Evans later played for Sale from 1945 to 1962, but he began his rugby with OAs in the late 1930s as a 15-year-old. Eric was born in Droylsden and attended Audenshaw GS and Loughborough Colleges. He qualified as a PE master and was an early advocate of total fitness, working with the famous 'Busby Babes' at Manchester United to learn how to improve his fitness skills. Eric belonged to the last generation of international forwards who were expected to play anywhere from prop to flanker. He made his England debut at prop, but was ignored for seasons as his 'professional' attitude bothered the selectors. He was reinstated for the 1954-55 Championship, when England won the Triple Crown. He was again dropped to the 'rags' for the following season's trials, but led the second team to a shock win over the First XV in the final trial. He was immediately made England captain and held the job for 13 consecutive matches to equal the record of W.W. Wakefield and Nim Hall.

He is best remembered as one of England's most successful and charismatic captains. His team talks were many decades removed from the 'let's play the game chums' approach of the era; indeed, he was reputed to often stand on the tables in the dressing room and beseech his men to die for the cause (and to take a few of the opposition with them). Evans eventually won 30 England caps, but had lost his place in the Lancashire team for a part of his time as national first choice. In 1957 he led England to their first Grand Slam and successive championships in the next two seasons. He retired from international rugby in 1959 but played for Sale until 1962. He made 105 appearances for Lancashire whilst retaining his links to Old Aldwinians. He died in 1991 and is commemorated with the Eric Evans Room at Twickenham. After his death, his ashes were spread on the pitch at Twickenham.

After Eric had died, it emerged he had a secret from his youth. When he was young and single he was romantically involved with Julie Andrews, the great film and music star. They met on a flight to Paris when the England team was travelling to an international. Julie was bound for a weekend in the French capital and Eric persuaded Julie to come to the match and they were friendly for a while afterwards. Eric even took his girlfriend home to meet mum.

Evans was unique in Aldwinians history, but they have produced other top-class players in Mike Kenrick and Mike Jackson, who were key members of the senior Lancashire sides that beat Cornwall and Yorkshire respectively in the County Championship Finals of 1992 and 1993. Aldwinians first team won the inaugural Lancashire Plate in 1983, and were Lancashire Trophy finalists in 1996. Not to be outdone, Aldwinians Colts won the Lancashire Cup in 1989 and the Lancashire Plate in 1990. In recent league action, Aldwinians were champions of NWII in 1997-98 and NWI in 1998-99. Perhaps the greatest team honour that Aldwinians have won is the Intermediate Cup, beating Dudley Kingswinford 22-10 at Twickenham in April 1999.

Aldwinians made history in the final as they are the only club outside the National Leagues to win the Intermediate Cup. Remarkably, in that final two future internationals were on display: Shaun Perry of DK and Dean Schofield of Aldwinians. The 6ft 6in Schofield scored two tries in the final. He attracted the attention of both Leicester Tigers and Sale Sharks. He opted for the latter, where he won two England caps. Later he joined the exodus to France and played for Toulon.

Aldwinians had a momentous year in 2002 when the England Sevens squad used Aldwinians ground to prepare for the Commonwealth Games. Also that year the club unveiled a blue plaque to commemorate Eric Evans who died in 1991,

(Thanks to Roy Hallam, Andrew and Steve Rigby).

ALTRINCHAM

AN ALTRINCHAM CLUB existed in the 1880s. They initially stayed loyal to the RFU during the dispute, but, in 1897, the lack of opposition forced them to join the NU. The club suffered badly from its best players being recruited by bigger clubs and eventually the original Altrincham club went bust in 1902.

ALTRINCHAM KERSAL

ALTRINCHAM KERSAL ARE based in the prosperous south-west Manchester suburb of Altrincham, but the club's original home was once 20 miles north at Kersal. Today Kersal is a rundown parcel of land between Salford and Prestwich, but half a century ago the name Kersal specifically related to a prosperous suburb of the city alongside the River Irwell opposite the old Manchester racecourse that became defunct in 1965.

Kersal RUFC was a product of the Great Schism, but not on the Northern Union side. Some of the founders were solid RFU supporters whose clubs had gone over to the NU. A meeting was called on 15th March 1897 in the Deansgate Hotel with a view to forming Kersal RFC. Two of the founders, Dr. A.E. Barclay and F. Miller, were Old Leysians. Another founder, A.S. 'Robin' Robinson, was a playing member of Broughton FC, who had joined the NU. Robinson was also Honorary Secretary of the Broughton School Old Boys' RFC, who went out of existence in 1897. Broughton FC had joined the Northern Union in 1895 and was to survive, in different guises, playing rugby league for a further half a century.

A local bleach manufacturer, Horace Bleakley, donated a pitch on Myrtle Grove (which is now the first hole of the Prestwich Golf Club). The club's first fixture on 6th April 1897 was a 6-6 draw against Broughton Park. This was followed by a game against Manchester 'A' four days later at Manchester's Whalley Range. Things must have been bad that season as E. Arthur Miller, the first secretary, wrote, "We usually lost our games to the tune of anything between fifteen and sixty points against us."

Miller was perhaps being pessimistic as, in their second season, Dr. Barclay was selected for Lancashire and Kersal had the honour of being Manchester's first opponents in Fallowfield. The first international from Kersal was Frank Handworth, a half-back, who continued the tradition of Old Leysians at Kersal. Handworth began there before moving to Manchester, with whom he won four England caps in 1904, and he toured South Africa with the 1910 Lions.

Frank Kershaw, an Oxford Blue, joined Kersal in 1902, bringing with him several other good players. In 1904-5 Kersal only lost two games and had an all-county three-quarter line, including D. Pape of Durham County and C.S. Williams of Cheshire. As the playing strength improved, so did the fixture list. One of their players, Geoff Gowland, won seven Scotland caps.

The club had many different homes, mainly on the north side of the city. After Prestwich, Kersal moved to Old Trafford, Broughton Park, Heaton Park, Oaklands Road, and Kersal before a move to Flixton in 1926, where they stayed for 20 years.

In 1921-22 the club toured France for the first time, visiting the shattered cities of Lille, Nancy and Verdun. The side included Carleton Catcheside, who became one of England's greatest backs. The following autumn Leon Chapuy, a French international, came over to play for Kersal whilst international Geoffrey Conway took over as club coach.

Geoffrey Conway is forgotten today but he ranks amongst the greatest English forwards. He won eighteen England caps during the great era of the early 1920s. Described as 'lightly built', Conway served in World War One and later attended Cambridge University, where he read classics. Whilst at university, he was selected for the North v South trial and was outstanding on the day. His tackling and dribbling projected him into the England team against France as a forward, and his versatility saw him selected at three-quarter against Ireland. A university lecturer by profession, Conway was a rover on and off the field. He was a member of Blackheath in 1920, Rugby FC in 1922 and Hartlepool Rovers the following year. That was followed by periods at Manchester, Kersal, and Fettesian-Lorettonian, before he re-joined Blackheath in 1927. He was amongst the elite who

Geoffrey Conway

played in the 1923 Centenary Match, but his international career ended in the violent encounter between England and New Zealand in 1925. He suffered a knee injury in the match and never appeared for England again, although he carried on playing club rugby until 1932. But Conway's story doesn't end there. He served in the army again during World War Two and was promoted to Lieutenant Colonel. He was also an archaeologist in Greece from 1961 to 1969 before he retired to live in France.

Kersal declined after World War Two, principally because they had lost their home ground. They moved to Flixton before moving to Oldfield Avenue, Timperley. In 1968 they moved to Stelfox Avenue, Altrincham, but kept membership of Lancashire RU. Indeed, it took the club several decades to put down roots in their new home.

In 1987 the club won the Lancashire Plate, and two years later they won the Lancashire Trophy. In 1992 they reached the semi-final round of the knock-out Provincial Insurance Cup.

Altrincham Kersal rose five levels in eight seasons in the 1990s, and gradually emerged as the major club behind Sale Sharks and Manchester FC in the rugby-mad area of south Manchester. Crucial to the improvement was Chris Smith, the Rugby Manager, and long-time captain Will Harrison, who was persuaded to stay on as captain for four years.

Eventually AK switched allegiance to Cheshire, and in 1997 won both North West 2 and the Cheshire Plate. In 2011 they were N1W Champions, which propelled them to National 3 North. At the same time the club's women's team reached National North 1.

The best player to wear Altrincham colours was Mark Cueto. He began his rugby as a student contracted to Sale Sharks, but played for Kersal on Saturdays until he became a Premiership regular. Cueto rapidly progressed into the England side and the 2005 Lions.

Looking to the future, Altrincham have forged a successful link with Sale and have one of the best junior sections in the region (with 325 members).

ANSELMIANS
(formerly Old Anselmians)

OLD ANSELMIANS ARE the old boys of St Anselm's College, an Irish Christian Brothers grammar school, on the Wirral. Formed in 1947, the first home ground was secured at "Solly Rec" in Birkenhead. In the mid-1950s the club relocated to its present home of Malone Field (named after a Christian Brother teacher at the School) in Eastham village

In the 1960s, the Old Boys connection began to fail. The first step, in loosening the nexus, was to open the club "to young gentlemen of Catholic Belief". The club abandoned the restriction because most of the available players "were atheists and far from being gentlemen". Old Anselmians survived and became was a well-established and thriving club running three sides. In the 1980-81 season the club became the first junior club to reach the Cheshire Cup semi-finals, losing narrowly to Birkenhead Park.

In the 1980s St Anselms produced three top class youngsters: Austin Healey, Christian Saverimutto and Simon Mason. Austin Healey, latterly of Strictly Come Dancing, would go on to win 51 England caps at scrum-half, full-back and wing and tour with the British and Irish Lions in 1997 and 2001. Simon Mason and Christian Saverimutto both won three caps for Ireland. Mason steered Anselmians to the last eight of the Junior Vase and their televised match with Kidderminster Carolians was watched by 1500 spectators. His burgeoning reputation led him to be capped by Ireland in 1997 and he was outstanding for Ulster in their 1999 European Cup campaign

In 2002, Ben Johnston was capped twice by England after graduating to Saracens. The Newcastle Falcons scrum-half Chris Pilgrim is the most recent graduate of 'The Saints'.

Visiting teams remember one corner at Malone Field with mixed feelings. The pitch is unusual because it has no dead ball area in one corner because a hedge restricts the available space. Many a would-be try-scorer has suddenly become aware he has little or no room to touch down.

ASHTON-UNDER-LYNE

ASHTON-UNDER-LYNE IS A suburb of Oldham on the east side of Manchester and Ashton RFC was formed in 1878 at the Commercial Hotel on Old Street in the town. Association football was, at that time, almost unknown in Manchester, so Ashton had plenty of opposition in the area from sides such as Stalybridge, Audenshaw, Dukinfield Rangers, Romiley, Tame Valley, Gorton, Oldham, Mossley, Failsworth, Stalybridge, Mottram Hall, Dukinfield and Mossley Rovers.

The club, which drew many of its members from the local army barracks, played its first games on the Old Drill Field near Raynor Lane, but in 1883 moved to a new ground on Manchester Road. During their first season, Ashton reached the final of the local Charity Cup Competition, where they lost to Mossley. Ashton had defeated Newton Heath in the semi-finals by 14 points to eight. The losers, Newton Heath, subsequently switched to association football and changed their name to Manchester United FC!

Soccer was to sweep away rugby in the district and the few surviving rugby clubs found great difficulty in arranging matches. An announcement at the time stated, "When arranging fixtures, clubs are desired to be careful to put the name of their town or village after the names of club, and also to state whether 'Rugby or Association.'"

Ashton's fortunes took a further downturn with the emergence of a local rival, Ashton West End FC, in 1885. The rivalry and disastrous results (P17 W0 D1 L16) eventually saw the demise of the first Ashton-under-Lyne RFC.

The next Ashton rugby club appeared in February 1911, when a NU club appeared in the town and made a great impact by winning the NU Cup and the Oldham Challenge Cup. They were also runners up in the Manchester NU Championship. The success was short lived, however, and they disbanded the following year.

Ashton under Lyne in action in 2011

The next rugby club to appear in the town was 'Old Ashtonians RFC', formed by Frank Jones, an ex-Cumberland forward who taught at Ashton Grammar School. In their first season (1924-25), they played three games against Rochdale, Old Californians and Heaton Moor. They operated from the school playing fields until 1925, when they found a ground on Worthington Street, Waterloo. The club survived until World War Two and resurfaced at Daisy Nook in 1946. The players had changed in farm buildings before the war, but they were no longer available and new changing-rooms had to be built. An Army Nissan hut was purchased and erected for the purpose. Eventually, the club changed their name to Ashton-Under-Lyne RUFC and operated in the North Lancashire leagues.

Ashton have been North Lancs 2 champions three times since 2001 and won their play-offs in the North Lancs 1 League in 2015. AUL have the longest-serving club captain in the area: John Walmsley, who has been skipper for eight years and has played in all their promotions since 2001.

An interesting memory of Ashton rugby comes from an Aldwinian player in the 1990s. He suffered a bad injury at Ashton and clearly remembers being treated by a friendly doctor who was amongst the spectators at St Albans Avenue. He was grateful at the time but several years later was shocked to learn the rugby-loving doctor was called Dr. Harold Shipman and he had murdered over 200 of his patients.

ASPULL

"A treeless tract of land overlooking Wigan."
Peter Hesketh-Fleetwood

ASPULL IS A SUBURB on the east side of the rugby-mad town of Wigan. An Aspull Rugby Club existed in the 19th century. They must have been a good side, for they reached the 1889 West Lancashire Cup Final, where they lost to Wigan. Leigh's first match at their Mather Lane ground was against Aspull on 7th September 1889. Two years later, Tom Atherton, a Leigh-based player, tried rugby with Wigan RFC but didn't make the grade, so he moved to Aspull and attracted the attention of Lancashire. He was picked up by Wigan NUFC in 1895.

The original Aspull club disappeared soon afterwards. The name of Aspull RUFC reappeared in 1975, when Wigan Unionists RUFC changed their name. Wigan Unionists had originally been a cricket club based in Poolstock, but in 1947 they decided to start up a rugby team to keep them occupied during the winter months. They played their home games at Little Lane, Goose Green in Orrell, where life was primitive. It took the club a decade to acquire a wooden hut, which arrived complete with four showers. In 1972 the club moved to Woodshaw Park and renamed themselves.

The clubhouse was burnt down in the "Great Fire" of November 1993. It was the worst possible time for the club as it was the day of an important league fixture. The players had to use changing facilities at the civic centre until their own were re-instated in January 1994.

In the four years after the fire, Aspull were promoted three times and reached the final of the Lancashire Trophy. Although they lost to a very strong Manchester, their appearance in the final speaks volumes for the commitment of both the players and ex-player/coach Paul Keegan. They were also honoured with the title of Junior Team of the Year in 1995-96.

The 1997-98 season saw a double celebration for the club: the new clubhouse was officially opened and it was the 50th anniversary of the founding of Wigan Unionists.

Probably the club's finest moment came on Sunday 3rd May 1998 at Liverpool St. Helens. In the final of the Thwaites Brewery Lancashire Trophy, skipper Mick Yates led his band of players to glory with a resounding 23-0 victory over Leigh, one of the club's closest and bitterest rivals.

The best-known player produced by the club is Peter Anglesea, who moved to Sale Sharks. He was selected for an England XV and toured Japan on an England A tour in 2003.

In 2008 Aspull dropped out of South Lancs/Cheshire 1 and reappeared in North Lancs 2.

Aspull in action in 2002.

BIRKENHEAD PARK

"Birkenhead – the one eyed city."
Leo Carroll

BIRKENHEAD PARK RFC are one of the surviving links to the golden days of the town of Birkenhead. The Park, from which the club takes its name, opened in 1847 as the world's first publicly funded park and the template for Central Park in New York.

Birkenhead lies on the south of the River Mersey, a mere wet and windy 800 yards from mighty Liverpool. Birkenhead emerged from virtually nothing when, in 1821, William Laird opened a shipyard. The population rose rapidly from 2,000 to 35,000 by the middle of the 19th century as shipbuilding and shipping became a major industry.

The rugby club was formed in 1871 by H.M. Blyth and W.H. Wallace from the merger of two clubs, Claughton and Birkenhead Wanderers. Blyth and Birkenhead Park played a large part in the founding of the Cheshire Rugby Union five years later. and have a remarkable history, with 42 internationals and over 330 county players.

The club's results were unspectacular until 1877, when Park benefited from the demise of the original Rockferry club. Gradually Park became pre-eminent in the area and won the original Cheshire Cup competition on three occasions.

Park had its first internationals in 1880-81, when Charles Phillips and John Ravenscroft played in England's win over Ireland at Whalley Range, Manchester. Both Park men were old Rugbeians and Oxford alumni. Ravenscroft was from one of the Wirral's greatest sporting families; Elsie Ravenscroft was the ladies World Golf champion. John Peel, the disc jockey, is a distant relative.

On its foundation the club played at the Lower Park, later moving to the St. Anne's ground before settling at the Upper Park in 1886. A dark shadow was cast over Park in that year when one of their players, James Murphy, died in a match against Litherland after receiving an elbow to the throat.

In the 1887-88 season, England were ostracised by the other Home Countries, but Ireland still played Wales at Birkenhead. Ireland were reluctant to make the journey to South Wales, and eventually a compromise was reached with Ireland and Wales travelling to neutral Birkenhead. Wales proved victorious.

England played an international at the Upper Park in 1894. Besides the novelty of playing in the North West, England also experimented with Hancock's four three-quarters for the first time. Wales had a bad day, which began when they discovered the pitch was rock hard from frost. The game kicked off and the ball went directly to Bradshaw, the tough York forward, who went straight through the Welsh defence like an express train.

Other Park internationals included Frankie Hulme, who won four caps between 1903 and 1905. Hulme and 'Toggie' Kendall of New Brighton developed a great half-back partnership for England in the days when specialised half-back positions were virtually unheard of. Hulme went on the British Lions tour of Australia and New Zealand in 1904 when the Lions won all 13 games, including three tests.

Percy 'Toggie' Kendall (1878-1915) was educated at Tonbridge and Cambridge. He failed to win a rugby blue, but was first choice at scrum-half for the Barbarians. He was selected for England v Scotland in 1901, and although his early appearances went badly, he went on to captain England. He returned to Birkenhead Park and Cheshire.

James 'Bim' Baxter was one of the greatest characters in Park's history. He played three times for England, was England's manager to Argentina in 1927, and also the Lions manager in 1930. He became club president from 1903 until 1940, and was also RFU President. He was even an international referee – of sorts. Never a modest soul, Bim caused an international incident when he refereed the 1913 France v Scotland match. In getting the appointment he exaggerated his command of the French language, which resulted in him baffling the French team and crowd with his attempts at their language. Baxter thought the crowd were shouting praise, whereas they were actually screaming for his blood. He completed the match and was smuggled away from the irate French. In 1908 he won an Olympic gold medal in the 12-metre sailing class.

The years between the wars were Park's golden era. In 1921-22 Park won 24 of 31 games. They could boast a superb fixture list and a string of top international players. Their strength came from being able to draw good young players from the district's junior clubs, the ample employment prospects in the area, and from a number of superb rugby-playing schools that produced great talent.

Birkenhead School produced Harry Locke, who was perhaps Park's finest player. He was one of the greatest three-quarters of the period. He played 12 times for England between 1923 and 1927 and had the honour of playing for the England and Wales side against Scotland and Ireland in the Centenary Match played at Rugby School in 1923. Harry Locke left Park in 1925 to take a job in London, and played for Blackheath.

A contemporary of Locke's was J.R. Paterson, the great Birkenhead Park forward who was to go on to win 21 Scottish caps and 37 Cheshire caps (including three out of position as scrum-half) before retiring from first-class football in 1929.

Wilfred Lowry was another international from Park, although he had perhaps the oddest entry to England honours. He arrived with the rest of the England party, got changed and then took part in the team photograph. At this point, the selectors decided the ground was heavy and goal-kicking was crucial. Harold Day of Leicester was with the party and a superb goalkicker. So Lowry was dropped minutes before kick-off. It proved a good match to miss as Wales won easily. Lowry was recalled and actually played!

Park were perhaps the best rugby club in the North West throughout the inter-war years and popular visitors, particularly to the big London clubs.

Other internationals from Park during this era were A.W. Walker (Scotland), Leslie Haslett (England), Douglas Law (England), Guy Wilson (England and also Tyldesley) and Tom Knowles (England). Knowles, who could play anywhere in the backs, was one of a number of Park players who also toured with the Lions. He toured twice, in 1930 to Australasia and to Argentina in 1936. R.B. Maxwell was selected for the 1924 Lions but never made the England team.

Park can certainly claim to have been the last major club to retain anonymous jerseys and held out for no numbering or letters until the mid-1930s.

Success continued after the Second World War, with Bob Weighill winning four England caps (1947–48). Weighill, who began with Old Wirralians, had a distinguished service career and was a senior figure in RFU administration. In 1984 he was appointed IRB Secretary.

A great Park player in this period was prop John Robins (1926-2007). He was born in Cardiff and

John Robins

served in the Royal Navy during World War Two before playing for Wales from 1945 to 1953. A man of many clubs, he was most closely associated with Birkenhead Park, but also played for Bradford, Sale, Leicester, Coventry, London Welsh, Cardiff, Penarth and Devonport Services. Robins also found time to join the six-month long 1950 Lions tour to New Zealand and Australia, where he made 16 appearances. He later returned 'down under' as assistant manager of the 1966 Lions.

J. P. Quinn was selected for England in the mid-1950s before switching to rugby league with Leeds in 1958.

One Park player who made rugby history was Derek Robinson, who was credited with scoring the last try worth three points in the sport's history. At the start of the 1971-72 season, the IRB increased the value of a try to four points. Due to an administrative mix-up, the Sri Lankan Rugby Union were unaware of the change when an England XV took the field against Sri Lanka in Colombo on the 8th October 1971. England won 34-6 with Robinson scoring the last try and entering history.

Sadly, the world around Park and Cheshire was changing. Sale, their ancient East Cheshire rivals, were pre-eminent. The best North West talent gravitated to Sale or the new boys at Orrell. In 1975 Park merged with the Old Birkonians, but they could not stem the decline. Far from the merger helping both clubs, it proved futile when planning problems blocked the sale of Birkonians assets. It took 25 years before the assets could be realised for considerably more than they had been worth in 1975. Affluent again, Park began the slow climb back up the ladder to national prominence.

Ironically, Park played a part in revitalising another sport as Robert Sangster was a regular for the 'A' team in the 1960s. Sangster gave up rugby to concentrate on racehorse breeding. Over the next decade, his methods paved the way for it to become a multi-billion pound sport. His pioneering approach to international horse breeding transformed 'the Sport of Kings' to the 'Sport of Sheiks' as billions of pounds poured in following his initiatives.

If international players weren't so frequent, the Park became a popular venue for touring teams: Tonga (1974), New Zealand (1978), Romania (1984) and West Indies (2000).

Since the inception of leagues, Park have done well. They won South Lancs & Cheshire One in 2001 and North West Two the following year. They have made solid progress and reached National 3 North in 2010.

(Thanks to Pete Greville)

BLACKBURN

"The dribbling code only is cared for in East Lancashire"
Newspaper article 1899

RUGBY IN EAST Lancashire has always laboured under the shadow of Blackburn Rovers, one of the greatest names in soccer history. Rovers were formed in the 1880s, but rugby had been played in the town for a decade before their arrival.

The first known rugby involving Blackburn was on the 3rd November 1877, when Preston Rovers met them at Penwortham on the west side of Preston. Blackburn lost heavily. The second match saw Blackburn face Clitheroe at Pleck Gate. Most of Blackburn's early matches involved sides from Preston, which is ten miles to the west.

A letter to the Blackburn Standard in March 1879 reported: "At Manchester and Preston, it is all rugby and no association but in Blackburn there is no rugby but numerous Association ones." Harry T. Thomas, secretary of Blackburn Rugby Club, reported a Blackburn Rugby Club had just completed its second season.

Despite modest results, Blackburn were adventurous. They played one match under floodlights which attracted 6,000 spectators. By 1880 Blackburn could boast 100 players, two teams and 21 fixtures, but within a couple of years the club was no more. No explanation is available except the rise of association football in the area. Every street had a soccer team and the town's two professional teams attracted huge gates. Rovers have continued to be a legend of the football league, but Blackburn Olympic disappeared at the end of the 19th century.

Blackburn rugby had a legend of its own: Albert Neilsen Hornby. The son of a Blackburn mill owner, Hornby became a cricketing legend whilst still at Harrow School. He was also an accomplished boxer and rugby player. He made his England debut at rugby at the advanced age of 31, but eventually captained his country. Unfortunately Hornby defected to Preston Grasshoppers as his rugby career developed.

The original Blackburn RFC went out of business in the early 1880s and several replacements came and went until the present club was established in 1921.

The modern Blackburn RUFC began by operating from the Bay Horse (Cog and Billicock) public house and played on the Yellow Hills, which is the upland on the west of the town between Pleasington and Preston New Road. The first match for the new club was against Rossall School of Fleetwood on the 16th February 1921 on the Yellow Hills.

Legendary all-round sportsman Albert Nielsen Hornby.

The club struggled for several years, although H.C. Worswick was capped by Lancashire and D.C. Cumming, a former international, played occasionally. The 'Yellow Hills' ground had a reputation for being the 'bleakest spot' for miles. One club member remarked, "When the east wind blew, the South Col of Everest had nothing on the Yellow Hills."

Between the wars, Blackburn's best fixture was an annual match against high-riding Kendal. It was usually a difficult afternoon for the Royal Blues, and it was 1969 before Blackburn finally overcame the Westmorland side.

In 1932 the members were foresighted enough to purchase the land on which the club now sits (Ramsgreave). The original purchase price was £800. A wooden hut was added as a clubhouse, which survived with its interior decoration of a bison's head. The clubhouse was opened with a fixture against New Brighton.

In 1951 Blackburn were honoured with an exhibition match between a W.W. Wakefield XV and the Scottish Co-Optimists, a Scots trial side, which ended with Wakefield's team winning 13-9. The match led to an annual fixture between Blackburn and the Co-Optimists, which continued until the 1980s. Down the years many of Scotland's finest players appeared for the Co-Optimists at Ramsgreave.

The late Ted Cooper was one of the best players of the 1970s. He is certainly unique in rugby history, as he captained

Blackburn at two centenary celebrations. Due to a mix up, the Royal Blues celebrated their centenary in 1971. When the mistake became know, the club re-celebrated, with Ted again as club captain.

Probably the best player to represent Blackburn was Dick Greenwood, the Waterloo, Lancashire and England flanker. Dick taught at nearby Stonyhurst College and was persuaded to become player coach at Ramsgreave. Blackburn had some of its best results under his guidance and he subsequently moved to Preston Grasshoppers before becoming England coach.

Since the late 1960s the pitches have been drained (the main pitch used to be a quagmire) at substantial cost, further land was added and an extension was built with the help of lottery money. With the aid of a recent Rugby Union loan, the club was able to redesign and refurbish the clubhouse.

Since the arrival of league rugby, Blackburn have been a middle-ranking side with a tradition of social rugby. Their fortunes rose in 2000 with the influx of several ex-Preston players, led by Richard and Phil Crayston, which brought several seasons of success. The best Blackburn player of recent times is probably Andy Morris, a talented flanker who later played for Sale and Manchester.

In 2004, the Royal Blues won the Lancashire Trophy

(Thanks to Ken Woolley, Dave Morris, Ronnie Pickup and Rhodes Greenwood)

BLACKPOOL

"The average Joe's boy doesn't know the meaning of fear – in fact there are lots of words they don't know the meaning of."
- **George Bagot**

THE FIRST BLACKPOOL rugby club were formed in the 1897-98 season, and competed for several years in the Second Division of the NU Lancashire League. Blackpool's ground was at Raikes Hall Gardens on the east side of the town centre. Their first match was played on the 19th March 1898 against Thornton Rangers, a local side whose players worked at the Alkali Works.

Blackpool relied on players from outside the area, and they finished at the bottom of the league by losing all 16 matches. They played their final league game at home to Radcliffe in April 1899.

The best player for the original Blackpool RFC was half-back Harry Hayes, who played for both Blackpool and Fleetwood. He later joined York, where he earned a brilliant reputation in NU circles. Hayes had begun with Tyldesley as youthful partner to the great Buff Berry.

Between the wars a number of the grammar schools in the town played rugby – notably Blackpool GS, Arnold School and St. Joseph's College. Most young rugby players graduated to Fylde and Thornton Cleveleys, but soccer was king, with Blackpool Football Club fielding half a dozen internationals and attracting 30,000 spectators every week.

Blackpool GSOBs were the only rugby union club in the town between the wars, until they merged with Fylde around 1934. Anyone wanting to play the 15-man game was, however, well served with Fylde, Thornton Cleveleys and Fleetwood OBs operating within the district.

Blackpool Borough RLFC was established in 1951 and was accepted into the League in 1954, catering for league fans. They 'borrowed' rugby union players when necessary, although the practice was banned by the RFU. Borough struggled on for 30 years before leaving the town for various other locations. Borough can boast having fielded Billy Boston and Brian Bevan in the twilight of their careers.

The present Blackpool RUFC arose from a schism at Thornton Cleveleys RUFC, which attracted players from Blackpool grammar schools, including St. Joseph's College. 'Joe's Jailhouse', as the college was known, was a grim, red-brick building which was run by the Irish Christian Brothers. In 1954 the Christian Brothers brought several of the All Blacks to the school – the visitors had been educated at Christian Brothers schools in New Zealand.

The social development of the area had seen a curious religious split: the bulk of the population were Church of England whilst the opening of the huge ICI plant at Burn Naze had brought many Irish Catholic workers to the district. In 1959 there was a schism at Thornton Cleveleys when some of the Catholic element (who had attended St. Josephs College) left to form Old Josephians. Some Catholic players gave up the game altogether rather than take sides. Thornton never recovered from the split, whilst the new Blackpool club struggled for a decade before establishing itself.

The founders of Old Josephians included Jack McCann and Ted Schools, who were schoolteachers and first teamers from Thornton. They were joined by Ted Crosland and a handful of ex-pupils.

The small club made headlines in the 1960s by fielding the four Fenney brothers in the First XV. Curiously, all the brothers were hookers!

At first Old Joes played on a school pitch at Normoss before moving to Blackpool Road, Bispham, where they shared the clubhouse with Blackpool Rangers soccer club. The two

Blackpool in 2008.

organisations led an uncertain existence because the soccer club objected to the rugby lads getting into the hot showers ten minutes ahead of the footballers.

The club changed its name to Blackpool Josephians in 1973 before dropping the suffix in 1975 as they sought to become an open club. Doughty cup fighters, Blackpool have improved due to the hard work and dedication of a small band of stalwarts.

They marked their place in Lancashire rugby when they defeated a strong Fylde A side on New Year's Day in 1977. The Ansdell side were so shocked they refused to play the game at New Year, saying the Blackpool side took the match 'too seriously'.

Blackpool were a successful side in the 1990s when they were North Lancs & Cumbria champions as well as North Lancs champions. Famous players who began at Blackpool include Mickey Weir (the Lancashire & Fylde scrum half), Richard Robertson (Leicester & Coventry) and Paul Williams (Leeds & Wales Under-21s). Williams had the oddest club debut of any player; his father, a Welsh hotelier, had a Fijian representative side as his guests in 1993. They spotted the potential of the youngster as the 'White Fijian' against a North of England team. Two years later, the 6ft 4ins youngster was playing for Leeds and Wales U-21s.

(Thanks to George Bagot, Cliff Wainscott, Joe Feeney, Ian Sharples, Tony & Barbara Appleby, John Sumner, Adrian Bradley, etc.)

BOLTON

FEW TOWNS IN Britain have as limited a rugby history as Bolton (population 240,000). Equally, few towns are as committed to soccer as Bolton. Bolton Wanderers is a football team with a great history dating back to the 1880s.

The first Bolton RFC was formed in 1872, seven years before Bolton Wanderers, and was first listed in the "Football Annual" of 1874. The listing reads: "Bolton formed 1872, has 100 members, ground at Burnden. Burnden is one mile south of Bolton railway station." The club died out before the end of the 19th century.

The second Bolton RFC was formed on 2nd May 1904 at the Talbot Restaurant in the town centre. The meeting talked about 'the original Bolton club' and even decided to adopt the original colours of white jerseys and shorts with blue stockings. The 1904 version had distinguished connections. Jessop Hulton MP, Shepherd Cross MP, George Hayward MP and Lord Stanley had already volunteered their support to Mr. A.T. Holden, who took the chair and the president's office. The meeting generated enough interest to find 20 players and plans for an inaugural season. The big problem came with finding a ground. Herbert Taylor, the first Honorary Secretary, began a long trudge around the town to find a suitable venue. He reported back to the club that a field at Chorley New Road was 'too small' and followed that with a succession of near misses. He eventually found a ground on Wigan Road, 300 yards from the nearest tram stop and convenient for the Rumworth Hotel, which agreed to provide dressing facilities.

The first season began with a match against Vale of Lune, followed by 'a smoker' – a form of social gathering where the teams smoked and drank to the capacity of their hearts and lungs. The defeat by Vale of Lune was followed by matches against Parkfield of Salford, Vale of Lune, Owens College, Heaton Moor, Bowdon, Kersal 'A', Trafford Rovers, Broughton Park and Preston Grasshoppers.

The club were sufficiently vibrant to field a second team on Edgar Fields. On the downside, the visitors from Cheadle Hulme were so unimpressed that they wrote asking for "better accommodation should we ever return". Season one ended with the treasurer reporting that the club had 26d in the bank. The second season was ruined by the worst winter in decades which restricted rugby in the region.

The club struggled along for five seasons and even started charging for admission, which brought in £56 in one season. There was, however, no disguising the fact that results weren't great and the first affiliation of the townspeople was to the soccer team.

The end came on the 6th May 1910, when the secretary reported the figures for 1909-10 were P15 W5 L10 D0 F86 A216. He then announced the disbandment of the club due to the increasing difficulty in finding fifteen players to even field a first team.

The best-known rugby player from Bolton was John Sutcliffe (1869-1947), although he never played for the town club. He played for Bradford, with whom he won an England rugby cap. Despite being a rugby player, Sutcliffe attracted the attention of Bolton Wanderers, who persuaded him to try soccer. He proved a fine goalkeeper and turned professional with the Wanderers. He was one of a handful of dual sporting internationals as he won five England soccer caps between 1893 and 1895.

Despite having good fixtures, Bolton RFC in Edwardian times were 'an unreliable side' as they were constantly leaving the Lancashire Rugby Union and re-joining shortly afterwards. Despite their demise, the oval game did continue in the town through the presence of Tyldesley RUFC on the west side of Bolton.

Bolton resurfaced in 1928 as Wilmslow's record shows they played a Bolton side and slaughtered them. One curious incident dates from 1933, when a stranger arrived at Bolton RUFC by bicycle and asked for a game. He played in the pack and was brilliant. After the match, he was asked, "Can you play next week?" His reply: "Sorry, but I'm Scots reserve against Ireland in Dublin"

After the Second World War, an old boys team called the Old Haywardians operated in the town and changed their name to Bolton Wyresdale by the time they joined the Lancashire RU. The club reduced the name to Bolton RUFC in the 1970s, when they played on a council mud heap at Little Lever on the south side of the town. In 1989, the club moved to Leverhulme Park in Horwich. Bolton have worked hard to establish themselves in the town and have a thriving junior section.

In 2000 Bolton were North Lancs Champions

Bolton in action in 2004.

WALKDEN

There were at least three rugby teams in Bolton in the late 19th century: Bolton, Tyldesley and Walkden. The south Bolton suburb of Walkden had a rugby club between 1878 and 1900. They played, and lost, to the Maoris in 1889 in front of 3,500 spectators. In 1890, they joined the RFU's West Lancashire League, and initially stayed local to the rugby union before joining the NU in 1895-96. They disbanded four seasons later. A NU side existed in the neighbouring suburb of Lostock in the 1890s.

BOWDON

BOWDON IS A leafy town in north Cheshire. The exact founding date of the town's club is not known, but we know Bowdon RFC played Sale around 1867, which was five years from the official founding date of the club.

Another report, dated 13th October 1877, reported, "The newly formed Bowdon and Lymm FC played Widnes." The match was noticeable for the fact that Bowdon and Lymm had accidentally fielded an extra man. The error was rectified at half time.

The first Bowdon player to win representative honours was H.C. Rowley, who played for Cheshire against Lancashire at Sale. Rowley later played for England. Rowley, Matheson and Walter Rycroft played for Cheshire in that first season. In the 1880s, F. Wainwright and J.D. Deakin were English trialists.

Eventually, Bowdon and Lymm went their separate ways. Bowdon originally played at Stamford Road before moving to Clay Lane, Timperley, which became their long term home.

The finest player who ever played for Bowdon was Hal Sever, who subsequently joined Sale and won 10 England and 40 Cheshire caps. His most famous appearance for England was in the game against Ireland on 13th February 1937, when

in the last minutes of the game, with Ireland leading 8-6, he intercepted on his own 25 line and beat the Irish defence. He ran 60 yards and brought a try and victory for England. Sever retired from the game in 1945.

During World War Two, Bowdon found they had some top-class rugby players available from the Services, notably All Black Les Hill and Bob Weighill of England. Bowdon were one of the best junior clubs in Manchester, and winger Bill Clephan was one of the top try-scorers in the area.

In 1967 the clubhouse was destroyed by a fire.

Currently Bowdon play in the South Lancs & Cheshire leagues.

BROUGHTON PARK

TODAY BROUGHTON PARK RFC are a middle-ranking side, but were once one of England's premier clubs. They were formed, as their name suggests, in Broughton, a suburb on the north side of Manchester city centre in 1882, but the earliest known reference to Broughton Park comes in October 1877, when Bury Second team beat Park Seconds. After basing themselves at a number of grounds in north Manchester, they eventually settled in the south Manchester suburb of Chorlton.

The Great Schism deprived rugby union of many of the great names of Manchester rugby (Salford, Swinton, Stockport), which allowed Broughton Park to become a magnet for top-class union players. In 1900, Park could field ten county players and, seven years later, Sydney Start (1879-1969) played for Park before winning England honours whilst with the Royal Navy. In 1923 Park fielded three international trialists and nine county players.

The 1930s saw Park produce two more internationals: George Vallance and Bert Toft. Vallance began his career with Broughton Park before playing over 200 matches for Leicester between 1930 and 1939. He was only picked for England once, but never took the field due to influenza. He was never picked again. He served as a Major in World War Two and lived to the age of 99. H. B. 'Bert' Toft was Park's skipper before moving to Waterloo, with whom he won ten England and 64 Lancashire caps. Bert was unlucky that his time as England's captain was brought to an end by World War Two. A schoolmaster by profession, Bert was employed by the RFU in the 1950s to teach PE teachers how to coach rugby to schoolboys.

Park's golden years began in 1950, when they began a two year period when they were undefeated at home. The best Park player of the post-war years was Barry Jackson, who was capped by England and was captain of Lancashire.

During the 1960s, Peter Barratt, Alan Shuker and Ron Greenall all had England trials, and Haydn Walters, a stand-off from Swansea, was a reserve for Wales. The most influential Park player to emerge at the time was John Burgess. He began his career as a fly half before moving into the forwards. He retired as a player in 1965 and became one of the first generation of club coaches. Burgess drew his inspiration from the 1967 All Blacks, which led to success as Lancashire coach.

Three Broughton Park greats: John Burgess, Tony Neary and Tony Bond.

He also had success with the North West Counties, who beat the 1972 All Blacks – only the sixth British team to beat the New Zealanders and only the second English side. Burgess had mixed fortunes with the England team. Some of the England players resented Burgess's lack of international credentials and were uncooperative. He stepped down as coach and became a highly respected RFU official, where he did much good work in modernising the English game.

Park had a tradition of tough, talented forwards. These included Barry Jackson, who won two England caps, and Mike Leadbetter, who won an England cap and made 33 Lancashire appearances before switching to rugby league with Rochdale Hornets. In the 1970s, Geoff Wappett played for Park before becoming one of the game's leading coaches with Bradford GS and Rotherham.

The best player to wear Park's black and white hoops was Tony 'Nero' Neary, who captained England and won 43 international caps and one Lions cap between 1971 and 1980. A product of De Le Salle, Neary was one of the best back row players in the world during a dismal period when England were dogged by poor organisation. Brave and durable, Neary won the respect of opposition throughout the world. The highlights of his career were playing for the unbeaten 1974 Lions in South Africa and finishing his international career in the 1980 England Grand Slam side.

Park played a major part in the 1978 20-9 defeat of the All Blacks by the North at Otley. Four Park or ex-Park players were in the North XV: Tony Bond, Tony Neary, Jim Syddall and Kevin O'Brien.

Tony Bond was another member of the 1980 Grand Slam side. A big, agile centre, Bond established his reputation in that victorious North team at Otley, but his England career ended with a broken leg against Ireland in 1980.

Jim Syddall began at Park as a 17-year-old before moving to Waterloo and being capped by England. Jim is remembered for carrying his size 14 boots in a paper bag.

Kevin O'Brien won two Irish caps at full-back in the early 1980s after first emerging as an outstanding goalkicker for Park and Lancashire. O'Brien was one of the curious breed of international players who stuck with his club and was a regular with the junior teams alongside his sons.

The club suffered in the 1990s with the social changes that transformed Manchester. Chorlton became surrounded by new housing and prosperous young people headed for the leafy suburbs of Cheshire. Despite good facilities, Park had to compete with Sale RFC and the decline in schools rugby in the city. Park could no longer attract the best players and tumbled down the leagues, which eventually forced the sale of their Chelsford Grove ground for housing. They found a new home and future at Hough End Sports Centre, barely 300 yards from their traditional home.

BROUGHTON

THE NORTH MANCHESTER suburb of Broughton also produced three other sides: Broughton FC, Broughton Rangers and Broughton School Old Boys RFC (who went out of existence, precipitating the formation of Altrincham Kersal in November 1897). Although these sides are long forgotten, they were major powers at the time. F. Moss (three caps) and C. Sawyer (two caps) were selected for England from Broughton RFC. Charles Sawyer was a fine three-quarter in the earliest days of rugby. He played for England against Scotland and Ireland in 1881.

In 1878 Broughton Cricket Club fell out with Broughton Wasps, who dropped the suffix which created two Broughton clubs. The original Broughton club eventually became Broughton Rangers to avoid confusion. Broughton RFC disbanded in 1897 due to lack of opposition caused by the defections to the NU.

Broughton Park (founded in 1882) took over their ground at The Cliff, which was later purchased as a training ground by Manchester United.

The present Broughton RUFC were originally called 'Old Salfordians' and were formed in 1912 from the old boys of Salford Grammar School and the Royal Technical College, Salford. The club had roots amongst the members of Broughton Cricket Club, which dates back to 1823. Broughton were regularly running five rugby teams in the 1930s and today remain a decent junior side playing in the North Lancs league.

The club's greatest son was John Burgess, who eventually moved to Broughton Park. As a player, he lost only three of his 36 Lancashire games, and twice led Lancashire to county championship victories. In 1972 he organised the North West Counties team who beat the All Blacks. He had an unhappy spell as England coach in the 1970s, when it was said he had trouble dealing with some internationals because he hadn't played for his country. Later he drafted a blueprint for the reorganisation of English rugby.

(Thanks to Alan Leaver)

BROUGHTON RANGERS/ BELLE VUE RANGERS

BROUGHTON RANGERS WERE founded in 1877 by England international Robert Seddon. He won three England caps and was the vice-captain of the 1888 British tour to Australia, where he died in a boating accident.

Rangers had two subsequent England internationals in Alf Teggin (six caps) and John Payne (seven caps). Payne has a place in rugby history as the first half-back to be recorded as having passed directly to a wing three-quarter, which caused the scrum to be outflanked and created a try-scoring opportunity. This incident occurred in the 1881 North v South match and represented an almost iconoclastic moment in the sport's development. Previously the crowded nature of matches meant half-backs were glued to the heels of their pack and had no room for outmanoeuvring the opposition.

The club precipitated the Great Schism by signing David and Evan James from Swansea for £250 each in 1892. One brother was immediately installed as a publican whilst the other got plumbing jobs. This was described as a 'National disaster' by the Welsh Rugby Union. The WRU were incensed and banned the brothers for professionalism. Seven years later the James brothers returned to the amateur ranks and played for Wales. Shortly afterwards they rejoined Broughton Rangers as professionals.

Rangers first played on Peel Park and were known as "Mrs Boardman's Boys" as they changed at the Bridge Inn on Lower Broughton Road, which belonged to Isabella Boardman. They switched to the NU and eventually moved to the Grosvenor Hotel, on Clarence Street, until 1913 where they leased a new ground at The Cliff, Lower Broughton Road, near the River Irwell and Manchester racecourse.

Between the wars, Broughton Rangers were well known for recruiting players amongst the miners of South Wales and for the meanness of their directors' dealings with the players.

Rangers vacated The Cliff in 1933 for the Belle Vue Zoological Gardens and later changed their name to Belle Vue Rangers. They eventually quit the rugby league in 1955.

BURY

BURY IS AN industrial town to the north of Manchester. At the end of the 19th century the place was famous as the birthplace of politician Sir Robert Peel and for being top of the North's unofficial table for drinking. In 1895, one in eight of the town's population had been arrested for drunkenness. The town's rugby club proved a leader in more acceptable pursuits and in 1875 they were one of the first Northern clubs to join the RFU.

One of the earliest mentions of Bury RFC is dated 17th March 1877, when they beat local rivals Farnworth 12 points to nine, despite playing three men short. Bury's fixture list at the time included a host of local (and some long-forgotten) names such as Birch, Bolton, St. Clements, Rochdale, Prestwich, Rossendale, Bacup Excelsior, Bury Unitarians, Blackrod, Tottington, Horwich and Whitefield. Visitors from further afield included Wigan, Southport (then Southport Olympic), Tyldesley and Skipton. A report from the Southport Visitor states that 400 people watched a second team match between Southport and Bury.

In 1884 Bury were playing on a local cricket field and using the Royal Hotel on Silver Street as headquarters. Three years later, they moved to the Trafalgar Hotel and then to the Fernhill Hotel on Hornby Street. In 1891 Bury moved to a new ground at Chamber Hall, where they used the Derby Hotel for changing. Still, the club weren't particularly nomadic as they never strayed more than a mile from the town centre.

The club finally found a permanent home on Radcliffe Road thanks to Sam Roberts, who was one of the greatest figures in the club's history and was associated with Bury for over 40 years. He played for Swinton, Bury and Lancashire, winning two England caps in 1887 and 1888, both against Wales. At the time Bury were in turmoil, and had temporarily withdrawn from the RFU amid controversy over illegal payments to players. Sam Roberts saved the day by donating the Radcliffe Road ground as a home base that they still use today.

Sam Roberts

In 1888, Bury's best player, Doc Worthington, left the club for Leigh, but the club was boosted by the presence of Tom Kent. He won six England caps in the early 1890s and toured Australasia with the 1888 British team. Kent was, however, a member of Salford RFC at the time of his England honours.

The early years of the 20th Century took their toll on Bury as, geographically, the town and club were at the heart of the breakaway by the Northern Union. This denuded the club's playing strength and fixture lists. By 1912 Bury were restricted to playing mainly against the second teams of local rivals.

The club was revived in November 1919 on a field at Limefield because Radcliffe Road had been commandeered for the war. Eventually, the club regained the Radcliffe Road pitch, which became Bury Sports Club.

Bury were a major force in Manchester rugby until the 1950s, when competition from other local clubs became intense. The rise of Sedgley Park (only three miles south) in particular made life difficult. Matters had improved for Bury's centenary in 1975, which saw the first team amongst the best in Lancashire.

Bury declined in the early 1980s and enjoyed an unusual relationship with the Sports Club. Although they were the senior partner, the rugby team were forced to play and drink in an ancient wooden hut adjacent to the new clubhouse. Bury entered the leagues amongst the better junior sides in Lancashire rugby, and have held their position despite growing competition.

In 2000 Bury celebrated their 125th Anniversary by playing the Anti-Assassins, who were celebrating their 50th Anniversary.

RADCLIFFE RFC was formed in 1875 as Radcliffe Close Wesleyan FC, named after the local Methodist Sunday School. They first played at Cross Lane before moving to Withins and Peel Park. They were members of the NU from 1896 to 1907.

TOTTINGTON RFC was a tiny village that played in the lowest rung of North West rugby, but it nonetheless produced an England international in Tom Coop. A full-back, Coop also appeared for Leigh, with whom he won an England cap in 1892, and Broughton. He also made 20 appearances for Lancashire. Coop is credited with masterminding Leigh's shock win over the touring 1889 Maoris. Tom Coop remained with Leigh when they joined the NU in 1895.

CALDY

CALDY RFC ARE probably the rugby club with smallest catchment area to supply a National League side. Caldy is an affluent suburb on the western side of the Wirral, with spectacular views across to Wales. The rugby club began life as Old Caldeians in 1923, a club that drew their players exclusively from Caldy School.

They started playing on a cow pasture near Caldy crossroads and changed in the farm buildings at Croxton Farm. Bathing facilities were a tin bath with cold water. Salvation came in the shape of Sir Alfred Paton, himself an old Caldeian, who bequeathed 20 acres of land bordering Thurstaston Common to the National Trust. The bequest included a proviso stating that the area was to be available to the rugby club to use as a playing area in perpetuity.

In 1928 the clubhouse opened, although it was four years before electricity was supplied and another seven years before baths were installed. Better facilities were needed as the club was fielding six sides by the outbreak of World War Two.

In 1930 OCs fielded D. D. Evans, a Welsh international scrum-half who played for Cheshire. OCs kept going through World War Two, and in 1943 started an innovative 'seven-a-side' competition for a shield donated by R. R. Okell. The first winners were a side from Rootes Cars Ltd. The 'Caldy Sevens' gradually became a highlight of the North West season, with all the leading clubs competing. The competition became so large that it grew into two days, with 60 teams competing and foreign clubs travelling to Caldy, including Fiji and Western Samoa. At its peak the Caldy Sevens could attract over 5,000 spectators. A schools seven-a-side competition was added in 1947 and ran successfully until 1975.

When the schools sevens were inaugurated, Caldeians were having problems. During the war, the local farmer had been given grazing rights to the pitches at Paton Field. It was not until 1953 that the club were able to resolve the matter and get the farmer off the pitches.

The club never outgrew its roots and always regarded itself as a community club with a successful cricket section. The club changed its name to Caldy in the 1970s when it opened its doors to all-comers.

Caldy have enjoyed middle-ranking status, which meant that its best players inevitably moved to bigger clubs such as New Brighton and Birkenhead Park. This worked to Caldy's advantage in 1970, when the club noticed a loophole in the county regulations that allowed club members to play in the Cheshire Cup despite playing for another side. Caldy won the 1970 County Cup using seven New Brighton RFC players who were still affiliated to them. They beat Lymm 13-9 in the final despite having only 13 players on the field due to injuries.

In 1988 they even fielded two Paraguayan internationals: Reuban Rematoza and Hugo Baez. But they have retained their status by mostly using local talent and have maintained a position amongst Wirral's best.

One of their best players of modern times is Marcus Coast, who appeared for Waterloo in the National Leagues before returning home and coaching Caldy to the 2005 North West

Two title. In 2007 Caldy won the North One title to enter the National Leagues for the first time, rising to National Three.

Caldy have been a modern success story for holding National League status and were 2003 Wirral club of the Year. The club still runs the Caldy Sevens – one of the longest running sevens tournaments in the UK

(Thanks to Roger Flashman and Alan Jeffcoat)

Caldy in 2005.

CARNFORTH

The small north Lancashire town of Carnforth is famous for railways and the 1940s film 'Brief Encounter', which immortalised the town and its railway station. Carnforth RUFC are nicknamed 'the Railwaymen' because they operate from the Railway Social Club.

Carnforth play in the North Lancashire leagues and were founded in the mid-1970s. An earlier Carnforth RFC existed a century earlier and the records of Preston Grasshoppers show a match against Carnforth in the 1870s. The original club disappeared at the start of the 20th century, but the town had produced a number of good players. The best was Bob Campbell, who was an England trialist in 1899. Subsequently, the best players migrated to Vale of Lune RUFC, which is only four miles south of the town.

Another fine Carnforth player was Shane Rich, who played a world record 500 consecutive matches for the Railwaymen between 1989 and 2006. The 500th match came on 29th January 2006, when Carnforth met Blackpool in a league match. A club record crowd of 400 turned out to hail Shane's achievement – and, one suspects, to appear on BBC

Shane Rich

and Sky TV, who covered the match. Shane's achievement was all the more remarkable because he didn't miss a game for four years until injury stopped a previous run of 89 consecutive appearances.

(Thanks to Alan Hardy)

CHESTER

The old game of street football was popular in Chester in the Middle Ages. The game is claimed to have originated with the locals kicking around the head of a dead Viking. Indeed in 1569 two local men, Hugh Case and William Shurlock, were fined two shillings for playing the game. The reason for their fine might have been because they used the cemetery of St Werburgh's Church as a field, and it didn't help that they kicked off during the vicar's sermon!

Research shows that there was a rugby club in Chester in the 1880s, and apparently there was a game between Chester and New Brighton in 1879-80. But this club later disbanded. The current club was formed in 1925 by several military men, which led to the club having links to local regiments. The military link provided the most famous player to grace Chester's colours in Richard Sharp, the outstanding 1960s England and Lions fly-half. Sharp played for the club whilst he was stationed in the army barracks at Eaton Hall.

Chester struggled in the post-war years because there were no rugby-playing schools in the area. Chester RFC had no permanent home until 1961 and operated at a variety of grounds in its early years, including Sealand Road, Blacon Point, the ancient Roudee, Bumpers Lane and Boughton Hall. In 1962 Chester bought 14 acres at Vicars Cross, which have been developed into a superb sporting complex. Finding a permanent home enabled Chester to field a strong side in the 1960s, when they succeeded in getting fixtures against Cardiff. An excellent clubhouse was added in 1994.

Rugby blossomed in the 1960s and 1970s, with a fixture list including some of the then top clubs in the north and many of their players were awarded county honours The 1980s was a quiet period for the club, with playing strength less than before and the fixture list suffering as a result.

The introduction of league rugby, however, revitalised rugby and started a new era. In 1998 Chester were promoted from North West One to North Two, and in 2000 another promotion to North One followed with a (unsuccessful) Cheshire Cup final.

The 2007-8 season was arguably the most successful in the club's history. Not only were Chester promoted as League champions from North West Two (having been relegated from North One the previous season), but they also won the EDF Intermediate Cup at Twickenham with a 21-18 win over local rivals Birkenhead Park.

2010-2011 saw Chester enjoying a fantastic season, finishing in their highest ever position in a highly competitive National Three North. They finished second, granting them the chance to be promoted to National Two. However, they just came up short, losing 16-14 away at Sheffield Tigers. Eventually they made National Two in 2012-13.

Chester in action in 2008.

Chester, like all clubs of their rank, have tended to lose their best players to the Premiership. Amongst the best recent products of the club were props Andrew and Paul Smith, twins who played for Chester RFC before moving to Sale in 1989 and becoming Division One regulars.

That trip up the M56 motorway to Sale was made by Ben Foden in 2004. Ben, son of Chester coach Rob Foden, was capped by England U21s at scrum-half whilst with Sale Sharks. He then played for the England Sevens team before moving to Northampton Saints, where his talent made him an England regular.

(Thanks to Peter Rhodes)

CLITHEROE

CLITHEROE IS AN ancient town in East Lancashire. Records exist of matches between the original Blackburn RFC and Clitheroe in the late 1870s. The first match was played on 16th February 1878, at Ribble Hill, Clitheroe. Although the weather was unfavourable, a large number of spectators were present. At that time the clubs were well matched, although the Clitheroe players were more familiar with soccer. After a keen contest, the home team proved the winners by one disputed try and one touchdown to nil.

Nearby Burnley had a rugby side until they switched to soccer. Their best known player was C.E. Sutcliffe, who once as a soccer referee disallowed seven goals scored by arch rivals Blackburn Rovers.

Rugby in Clitheroe disappeared until 1977, when the present Clitheroe RUFC was formed. The club play in the North Lancs Leagues and have an excellent ground at Littlemoor Park.

CONGLETON

THE CHESHIRE TOWN of Congleton can claim links to the earliest days of club rugby. A side called Congleton Rovers was formed in 1860, and played both codes before adopting the Association rules as Congleton Albion in the 1880s.

The current club, Congleton RUFC, were formed on the 7th December 1931 by a handful of locals who agreed to pay subscriptions of 6d (2p) per week from the outset. On the 30th January 1932, the first practise match took place at Barber's Farm despite no line markings or posts and the fact that most of the players had no knowledge of the laws, being ex-soccer players.

The new club's first game was played against Macclesfield GS on the 5th March 1932. It resulted in a 30-5 defeat, with the first points in the club's history being a try scored by forward Frank Burgess, with Dennis Pirie landing the conversion. Matches were subsequently played that season against Winnington Park, Dominies (who died out in 1939), Wilmslow, Sale and Leek.

Hankinson's Field was acquired in late 1933. It belonged to a local butcher, who kept horses and cows on the pitch during the week and allowed the rugby club to use it on a Saturday for the princely sum of 7s 6d (37p). It was a far from salubrious venue and a club official called Dr. Lowe would, on a match day, march down the High Street and command any small boys he found to follow him. The party would march to Hankinson's Field and pick up all the manure on the playing area. Dr Lowe's concern for the players' infection risk only extended to the horses output; the cow manure was considered to be acceptable.

In 2011 Congleton went into the Guinness Book of Records when they played the world's first 24-hour rugby match for charity. Today Congleton are a thriving club in the South Lancashire & Cheshire Leagues.

CREWE & NANTWICH

THE CHESHIRE TOWN of Crewe is associated with railways and the railway made Crewe the centre of the rugby world. The great and good of world rugby (well, European rugby) headed to Crewe because it was the meeting place of the International Rugby Board in the days before world travel became the norm. The representatives of the home nations decided Crewe, with its excellent railway links, was the centre of Britain.

A side called Crewe Britannia RFC operated in the early 1870s and produced an international in Sir Stephen Finney (1852-1924), who played half-back for England in 1872 (and for whom he scored a try). After one international, he was recorded as looking like "he had been in a prize fight". Finney, who was educated at Clifton College, later pursued his career in India working for the East Bengal Railway Company. There he played for the Calcutta club, who donated the famous cup used for the annual England v Scotland match. Crewe Britannia lasted only three years. The club operated from Crewe Railway Works and included in their ranks the grandson of Richard Trevithic, who developed the steam engine.

Another Crewe rugby club that existed at the same time was called 'Brookhouse RFC', who were based at the mill of Albert Hornby, the famous Preston Grasshoppers and England captain. Hornby, who lived at Poole Hall, Nantwich, raised the side from the mill workers and they played regularly throughout the 1880s.

In 1872 Hornby organised a side called Brookhouse in Nantwich. He later switched to soccer with Blackburn Rovers in the winter and cricket in the summer. He was capable of good performances at cricket but prone to dreadful spells at both sports. He proved a fearless full-back, but retired in 1882 with knee trouble, although he continued to referee matches. He returned to cricket and captained England against Australia. On returning to Nantwich he led the life of a country squire.

The first Crewe RFC was founded in 1877 and flourished until a loss of key players led to its demise in 1887. The present rugby club originated as Nantwich RUFC in February 1923 and operated from Colleys Lane, Willaston. Three years later they moved to Victoria Avenue, Crewe, which precipitated the name change to Crewe & Nantwich RUFC.

Despite operating from the local orphanage, the new club quickly produced another international in Jack Wright, who played for Crewe from 1927 to 1930 when he was top points scorer. Wright was a talented all-rounder who had trials for Stoke City FC before moving to London and joining the Metropolitan Police. He was capped for England against Wales in 1934. He later moved to Newport and played against the New Zealanders. At the outbreak of World War Two he joined the army but became a prisoner of war.

After World War Two, the club moved to Church Farm, Haslington, before moving to Barony Park, Nantwich in 1958. The immediate post-war years were highly successful, but by the early 1960s the club was struggling and almost went out of business. Over the next 20 years, they recovered and began to produce some top-class players, most notably Neil Hitchin (Orrell and England B), Paul Hackett (Waterloo and the North) and John Farr (Coventry and the Midlands).

In 1995 the club moved into a superb multi-sport complex called the Vagrants. The following season the club reached the National Junior Cup Final at Twickenham. The Cheshire side led for most of the match before losing in extra time.

DUKINFIELD

'Open land of ducks'

DUKINFIELD WAS ORIGINALLY a village on the south east side of Manchester until the arrival of the coal and textiles industries revolutionised the area. A club called Hurst Rovers RFC existed in the town in the 1870s, but had disappeared by the time Dukinfield RFC was formed in 1880. Dukinfield may have existed before 1880 because a side from the town competed in the Cheshire Cup from 1876 onwards.

There were nine coal mines in Dukinfield at that time and numerous cotton mills. Dukinfield Colliery was reputably the deepest colliery in Britain at 2,000 feet. The colliery belonged to the Blocksage family, who became closely involved with the local rugby club. A. C. Blocksage played for the Cheshire side in the 1880s whilst representing Dukinfield. At the time they could boast fixtures against top clubs such as Oldham and Wakefield Trinity.

The town of Dukinfield was hit hard by an economic depression at the end of the 19th century, which along with the impact of the Great Schism wiped out most of the area's rugby clubs, although Dukinfield RFC managed to stay afloat. They survived the bad times and eventually enjoyed a purple patch in the 1920s under a Dr. K. Hendrie, a Scots international captain and a member of the 1924 Lions to South Africa.

In the 1930s, they lost their original pitch at Lakes Road and moved to the site of the old Blocksage Colliery. Soon afterwards, the new pitch was requisitioned by the government for storing cotton because of its close proximity to Manchester Docks. The whole area was heavily bombed during World War Two and ships did not linger in the docks. As soon as the boats arrived, their cargoes were unloaded onto lorries, which dumped the cotton on the Dukinfield pitches. The Blocksage ground soon became a cotton tip and totally unsuitable for rugby. The long-term positive result was that, after the war, the rugby pitches were re-laid on top of the cotton waste, which provided superb drainage.

The town was again affected by recession in the 1950s, which also hit the rugby club. The collieries were gone and the mills were in decline, but new industries emerged and Dukinfield RFC recovered to enjoy a brief golden era in 1966, when they ranked amongst the best in Manchester. Their best player of the era was winger Harry Council, who played for Cheshire before defecting to Salford RLFC. Council became the highest scorer in Salford's history.

The club suffered a major setback when vandals burnt down the clubhouse. The club survived, thanks to using council changing rooms and the efforts of a few stalwart members. In 1969 Allan Hilton arranged for the purchase of the Stalybridge grocery and butchers' shop in Dewsnap Land, adjacent to Blocksages, for £5,000. The building was converted into a very serviceable clubhouse with changing facilities for two teams, a comfortable upstairs lounge with bar, a downstairs bar, a kitchen and a dance area.

Dukinfield entered the brave new world of league rugby as a good, middle-ranking club with excellent facilities in an area with a dozen rural clubs within a 20-mile radius.

In 1996 rugby league international Mike Ford joined the club as a fitness coach and the team immediately progressed. Unknown in rugby union circles, Ford led Dukinfield to promotion and the 1997 Griffin Plaque (the Manchester and District Junior Championship), beating Aldwinians in the final. Progress in the league was also secured by winning North West Lancs Two, which took them into the much more difficult South Lancs/Cheshire Three. Nevertheless, they won promotion in consecutive years, missing out on entry to North West Three due to the reorganisation of divisions.

Mike Ford remained at Dukinfield until 2003, when he was recruited as Ireland's defence coach. He later moved to Saracens and Bath and became English defence coach until 2011. Ford also recruited Graham Steadman, the Great Britain rugby league full-back, which made the club a real force.

(Thanks to Allan Hilton)

ECCLES

Famous for its cakes.

Harry Scott

IN THE LATE 19th century there were a dozen rugby clubs in West Manchester. The suburbs of Eccles, Peel Green, Patricroft, Monton, Winton, Barton, Swinton, Pendlebury and Urmston all had clubs. All soon disappeared, leaving Eccles as the only survivor. The first record of Eccles occurs in 1881, when they played another local side, Glodwick Seconds. Glodwick soon disappeared, whilst Eccles joined the Lancashire RU in 1886 and the RFU the following year. Eccles briefly went out of existence but were reformed in 1889. Around this time, a number of Eccles players were selected for Lancashire, notably R.L. Bolton, H. Bowker, R. Cameron, J.E. Kidd, R. Smalley and T.S. Stevens. J.E. Kidd made his Lancashire debut at 18 before moving to Broughton Park, where he was selected for an England trial.

Eccles had a first-class fixture list in those days, with regular opponents including Broughton Park, Manchester, Sale, Heaton Moor, Kersal, Bowdon Rangers, Harrogate, Furness, Vale of Lune, Nottingham, Waterloo, Kendal, Birkenhead Park, New Brighton and Preston Grasshoppers. In March 1903, Eccles drew with Manchester FC, who were regarded as the best team in the North West. Two years later they beat Preston Grasshoppers and Harrogate. They were also popular tourists under the name of the "Northern Wanderers" and had a regular end of season fixture against mighty Bedford. They usually ran them to a close match, but the fixture was discontinued when Eccles received two heavy defeats from Bedford in the years before World War One.

In September 1906, Eccles' ranks were swelled by J. Clerc, the Racing Club de France three-quarter, who had played for France against New Zealand, and R. Worsneys-Smith, the Durham University full-back.

Eccles played on a number of different pitches in the early days. In 1897 they used Chorlton Fold in Monton, with their headquarters at the Blue Bell Hotel, and two years later moved to Barton and the Bridgewater Hotel in Patricroft.

World War One marked the end of Eccles as a top-class side. In October 1919, they resumed rugby with a fixture against the new Fylde club and had a first-class fixture list, but little else. Their playing numbers were thin and based around an enthusiastic young team with no experience. Decline was inevitable and they struggled for many years. On the plus side, they found a stable base from 1925-1948 on farmland just over Barton Bridge by the Manchester Ship Canal. A hut was erected along with a hot water boiler and bath, which eventually developed into a clubhouse. Unfortunately, fixtures were again to be interrupted due to war in 1939. Fixtures were resumed in the 1946-47 season, and in 1948 they moved to their present location in Gorton St, Peel Green, Eccles.

The greatest name to represent Eccles was full-back Harry Scott, who won an England cap in 1955 against France. He also played for United Services Portsmouth, US Chatham and Manchester.

In 1984 the members built a new clubhouse, in 1991 a junior section was formed, and in 1993 new changing rooms were built with help from the Foundation for Sports and the Arts and also from Sportsmatch.

Due to the success of the junior section and the emergence of a women's team, the club was awarded a Lottery grant in 2002 for mixed-use changing facilities, increased training lighting and other various ancillary improvements. In 2003 the club extended and refurbished the clubhouse in order to accommodate the swelling ranks. An all-weather pitch was installed in 2004 funded by the RFU and the government in appreciation of the club's commitment to community rugby.

The club's endeavours over the last 15 years, with regards to facilities and juniors, have resulted in representation for England Schools at U16s level in 2003-2004 and 2005-2006, and also England U18s 2007-2008.

In 2009-2010 the First XV gained promotion to the North Lancs/Cumbria league (level 7), as well as winning the Lancashire Plate for the first time in the club's history. Their Gorton Street ground has been redeveloped, with thriving senior, junior and women's teams

FLEETWOOD

"Fleetwood occupies a bleak and isolated position on the North Lancashire coast. The place is not without charm of a grey and gloomy kind. It is a place sympathetic to the artist or philosopher. There is however little for those seeking every leisure minute spent in pursuit of novel experience."

Sir Thomas Beecham (1944), an Old Rossalian

THE AREA NOW known as Fleetwood had another less salubrious name in the 18th century when it was referred to as the 'rabbit warren'. It had barely a building until the local landowner spent his entire fortune on building 'the new Brighton'. It was Lancashire's first planned town.

The town of Fleetwood had its heyday in the mid-19th century as a port serving western Scotland and Ireland. The port subsequently declined with the opening of the railway over Shap Summit, which opened Scotland to railway travellers. Fleetwood was badly affected, however fishing, chemicals and holidays later brought prosperity back to the town.

The first recorded reference to rugby in the area comes in 1887 with an exhibition match between St. Helens and Kendal Hornets at the Fleetwood Copse Ground. That year two local teams, the Cockle Hall Rangers and the Bourne Hall Turnip Loupers, played a friendly match.

In the mid-1890s, half-back Harry Hayes played for both Blackpool and Fleetwood before joining York, where he earned a brilliant reputation. Hayes had begun with Tyldesley as youthful partner to the great Buff Berry.

A NU match took place between Thornton and Fleetwood sides on the 6th May 1897. Later, a Fleetwood Rangers NU team emerged, but recorded only one league match in their first season. In their second season, the club managed home and away league wins over Blackpool, but the two Fylde clubs propped up the league.

The 1900-01 season saw debt-ridden Fleetwood become Thornton Rangers, who disbanded soon afterwards.

Fleetwood's fortunes as a town benefited from three related events. The first 'Beam Trawlers' appeared in Fleetwood, which made deep-sea fishing more efficient; then World War One came to the North Sea, and metal-bottom trawlers had to escape to the Irish Sea and Fleetwood to avoid German mines; then, in the 1920s, fishing made Fleetwood a boomtown as the world discovered 'fish 'n' chips' as a cheap and tasty meal for working people.

Rugby reappeared in 1924, when Fleetwood RUFC were formed by Stan Hamer, Mark Baxter, Alex Keay, Dr. Ian Preston, Philip Lamb and Ronald and Reg Gilchrist. The latter was a student at Cambridge University. His brother Ronald was a superb winger at Mill Hill School. The first practice game was played on the rifle range adjacent to the famous Rossall School. Unfortunately, it didn't augur well as they lost their first match 70-0 to Fylde Seconds.

The game in Fleetwood slowly prospered and attracted good sides, such as Tyldesley, Kendal and Halifax. This was despite playing on a succession of different pitches, including a pitch at Broadwaters where someone had tried to improve the soil by applying fish waste. When the pitch was churned up on a wet day, the smell was awful and a definite turn-off to the ladies on a Saturday night. Fleetwood's search for a pitch even took them to Preesall 20 miles away.

The need for a ground led to disaster as the club gambled on attracting spectators to the Queen's ground – formerly the home of the Fleetwood soccer club. The annual rental for the Queen's ground was approximately £200 (a fortune for those days), and after two years the rugby club went into liquidation. That year, several players formed a breakaway club at Thornton Cleveleys, which is two miles south.

The game returned to Fleetwood in 1930 when Fleetwood GSOBs played on farmland (which is now the ninth green at Fleetwood Golf Club). In 1932 the Old Boys moved to a ground at Broadwaters and rented changing facilities from the local cricket club. The rugby club later acquired a Nissan hut for £160 which had three domestic baths without hot water.

The club went open in 1946 and changed the name to Fleetwood RUFC (Fleetwood Grammar School itself closed in the 1970s).

Fleetwood RUFC eventually left the cricket club and moved to nearby Melbourne Avenue, where a second-hand RAF building was erected in 1963 by the members. Results in the late 1960s were disappointing, and in 1969 there was a call to wind up the club due to lack of players and problems with funding. A new, young committee was born, which galvanised interest. They fielded a young side who won 21 of its games in 1971.

Christmas Day 1972 brought disaster when the clubhouse caught fire, but within a couple of months the problems had been overcome. Results continued to improve and they were soon rated one of the top junior clubs in the north of England. 1974-75 produced a record season for Fleetwood, winning 32 of 40 matches, scoring 917 points and only 287 conceded. Outstanding in this era was John Dewhurst, who has served the club as player and official since the 1960s.

Fleetwood has produced several internationals for England over the years, notably Peter Winterbottom, John Olver and Bob Hesford. Peter Winterbottom attended nearby Rossall School and played occasional matches for the town club. The blond flanker was, however, nearly dropped after his first game for Lancashire Colts for "failing to make an impact at the breakdown". A selector commented that the much-vaunted loose forward was nowhere to be seen during the match. A more observant bystander pointed out to the selectors that Winterbottom was to be found at the bottom of every ruck, having destroyed the opposition's defence. Winterbottom went on to repeat similar mayhem at every level up to the British Lions. John Olver, the England hooker, also emerged from Rossall. Olver was unlucky to be understudy to Brian Moore throughout his long England career.

Bob Hesford, the Bristol No. 8, came from a Fleetwood sporting family. He moved to Bristol and was an England regular in the 1980s. His brother Steve was a regular for Fleetwood before switching codes and becoming one of the top goal-kickers in the rugby league history.

Fleetwood's finest hour came in 1992 when they were National Junior Champions, having overcome Harpenden in the Provincial Cup Final. The club have risen rapidly since the advent of leagues due to a first class junior set-up. They recruited David Stephenson, the ex-RL international, as coach and reached North West One in 2004. Fleetwood currently rank as one of the best junior sides in the North West.

(Thanks to John Dewhurst, Charles Hughes and Andy Thompson)

OLD ROSSALLIANS

The first known reference to football at Rossall School dates from 1863, when the school played the local School of Musketry under the Harrow rules. This was unusual because Rossall normally played using the Rugby code. The School of Musketry may have been associated with the London Scottish Regiment, who were billeted in the town at this period. Rossall School had a good reputation as an association football school in Victorian times, but it turned to rugby in 1905. An Old Rossallians team established a fixture list between the wars but now only operate as an occasional side.

FYLDE

"Vice has not erected her standard in Lytham. Gamblers, profligates and swindlers find employment elsewhere."

A description of Lytham, 1813

FYLDE IS A distinct parcel of Lancashire bounded on three sides by water. The River Ribble to the south, the River Wyre to the North and the Irish Sea to the West. The whole area was so isolated it has little history. That changed, however, in the 18th century with the first holidaymakers who 'took the waters'. In 1870 Elijah Hargreaves, a Manchester businessman, visited the area. He found sand hills, empty fields and sea, but sensed that there was scope for an up-market holiday resort. He bought the area on a 999 year lease and built the town of St Anne's, which took its name from the parish church. Eventually, many people retired to the coast to escape the smog of the cities and the hamlets of Lytham and St Anne's became thriving holiday resorts. The twin towns even produced a top-class rugby side.

Fylde Rugby Club has been a great bastion of the amateur ideal for most of its history, which is odd as an ex-rugby league player helped to form the club. George Marsden, whose family had a long connection with the Morley club in Leeds, had won three England RU caps in 1901 before joining Bradford RL, and eventually moving to the Blackpool area. Marsden is reported to have played a part in the formation of Fylde in 1919, although he isn't credited in the club's history. Marsden was able to return to the amateur ranks due to the fact that the blanket ban on professionals only became operative in 1901 and players who had switched to the NU between 1895 and 1901 were allowed to resume their place as an amateur in the RFU ranks.

The club attributes its formation to a handful of commuters who became friendly on the Blackpool to Manchester train. The commuters decided to play sport at the weekend but couldn't decide whether to play soccer or rugby, so they tossed a coin and opted for the oval ball. The new club also adopted the colours of maroon and gold of Huddersfield Old Boys RUFC for reasons unknown, but it is known the new club wrote to Huddersfield for permission to use the colours. They found 22 players and arranged a match with a Manchester XV, which was cancelled (ironically) due to a rail strike. The following week they entertained Manchester YMCA at Ansdell School, winning 26-0. A good season ensued with 16 wins in 26 matches.

The club moved to 'the Woodlands' in May 1920. Admission cost 5d (2p) and the first yearly gate receipts amounted to just over £57. In 1922 Harold Brooks was elected president, and through his efforts Fylde progressed. He also generously provided the present stand. As far back as 1924, the club was represented in the Lancashire team by many colourful names, such as 'Ham' Neville, who was capped 33 times, and 'Pop' Ogden, who was regarded as the greatest kicker of the era. Pop was the originator of the 'round the corner' style of kicking now used by more or less all kickers worldwide. Pop Ogden played 29 times for Lancashire. Reports suggest he wasn't a great three-quarters, which meant he was repeatedly dropped by Lancashire but restored when they wanted a goal-kicker.

The autumn of 1929 saw Fylde shock the established order with a string of wins against top names, such as Huddersfield, Ilkley and a 42-3 win over high-flying Bradford. That season, B.D. Butler, the Fylde winger, played in three England trials.

In 1934 the club became embroiled in a dispute over poaching with Blackpool Grammar School Old Boys (BGSOBs). Arthur Bell, the BGSOB secretary, wrote to Fylde to complain, but was surprised when their neighbours suggested a merger. The Old Boys had been under a cloud after an opponent playing for Orrell was killed when he was kicked in the back by an Old Boys player. A post mortem found no one was to blame, but the incident cast a shadow over their club. The merger went ahead and greatly strengthened Fylde. In a compromise the club badge included the waves from Blackpool Corporation's crest.

Arthur Bell was to become a local legend. Head of Fylde Water Board and 'Honorary Secretary' of Fylde, Arthur was a formidable character. He arrived at Fylde to find no clubhouse and only a small grandstand. The dressing rooms were two huts on wheels containing two large zinc baths. An outside boiler provided the heat for the water. Bell played rugby for Fylde from 1934 to 1953. He never gained a county cap, but once took the field against Cheshire in a Lancashire jersey. Just before the kick-off, he was called from the field to say Eric Evans, the England captain, had arrived and that Bell was no longer needed. A great goal-kicker, Bell had one huge disadvantage: being short-sighted in the days before contact lenses. During one match, he called over a young player and said, "Watch this kick will you." When the youngster asked why, Bell replied, "Cos, I can't see anything without my glasses and I need to know if it went through the posts."

Fylde established an excellent fixture list in the 1930s, but they felt like unwelcome new boys alongside other longer established northern clubs. In 1949 the programme editor at the Woodlands felt he had to express an opinion: "Our lack of representatives in the County side is that our fixture list does not give our promising players sufficient sustained experience against players of County and International class. It takes a generation to become senior and once established, another generation will pass before a Club lapses to a primary position. Now that we have passed the clogs stage, we are finding great difficulty in shouldering our way into the good graces of the top clubs, so we must be content for a while to have occasional tilts at windmills."

During the war, Fylde had been able to keep playing using locally-based servicemen. They even picked up several great players who were serving in the forces locally, notably Ken Fyffe and Harry Fry of Scotland. A number of Fylde members were killed during the war, which led to the Ansdell ground being named 'the Woodlands Memorial Ground'.

The first great player to emerge from Fylde was Malcolm Phillips, who won 25 England and Lions caps in the post-war years. Phillips, an elusive centre, was the son of a rugby league player from Oldham. The family moved to Blackpool, where Phillips attended Arnold School, one of Britain's foremost rugby schools. He joined the army before gaining a Cambridge Blue in 1956, and was later RFU President.

Other Fylde players came close to what Phillips achieved. J.T. Hodgson (1955) and Bryn Jones (1964) were England trialists.

Malcolm Phillips

Jones was reputed to have the longest pass in northern rugby. The club supplied Lancashire with a steady stream of county players and received a number of top-class players from elsewhere, notably Stan Purdy and Bob Rowell, internationals from the Midlands. Other top-class Fylde players of the era included winger Tony Richards and prop Mike Hindle, who played for the North West Counties team who defeated the 1972 All Blacks. Hooker Bill Baxter set a club record of 451 First XV appearances, and he also represented the North and Lancashire.

Tony Richards, a long-serving Fylde captain, was unfortunate to only tour with England, but he was undoubtedly one of the best wingers in English rugby. He earned an international reputation after outplaying Bryan Williams, the brilliant New Zealander, in the 1971 England Centenary match. Williams was considered unstoppable, but was shocked when Richards was so quick that he tackled the big Kiwi out of the match.

Bill Beaumont was the greatest player produced by Fylde. Bill captained the 1980 Lions and led England to a Grand Slam. He joined Fylde as a Fourth XV full-back, but, being 6ft 3ins tall and 16st, was moved to the pack, where he never stopped improving. Bill eventually won 34 England caps, including 21 as captain, and also captained the Lions. Sadly his career was terminated at its height by a serious head injury. After retirement, he became a national hero and a popular television personality.

Bill Beaumont

Despite Bill's enormous fame, Fylde remained a side just behind the best. However they did field a number of internationals that are better associated with other clubs. The youthful Roger Uttley played for Fylde's junior sides before moving to Gosforth, and Barrie Jon Mather turned to rugby league after Fylde tried to convert him to a lock-forward, despite his being a flying winger.

Other more recent internationals associated with Fylde include England wingers Tony Swift and Simon Smith, who were capped in the 1980s after leaving the club, and established international locks Steve Bainbridge and Wade Dooley, who won further caps whilst with Fylde.

Steve Gough was a Fylde regular for 15 years who set a UK record of 404 points in 1996-97.

The Woodlands lies only 30 miles from the heartland of rugby league and the 13-man game frequently signed talent from Fylde, notably Mark Preston, David Stephenson and Dave Tanner, who were all distinguished rugby league backs. The connection went the other way when in 2008 Jason Robinson, the legend of both codes, agreed to join Fylde.

With the arrival of professionalism, Fylde 'yo-yoed' between National Two and Three before becoming an established National One side under coach Mark Nelson.

Off the field, re-development of facilities of all kinds at the Woodlands began in January 2005. The spanking new clubhouse, housing some 400 people, was opened in October 2005 and has been a huge success. This was followed by the construction of a floodlit 3G (rubber crumb) all-weather pitch and the installation of floodlights on the main pitch. A totally refurbished gym was also completed in 2009.

In 2011, Fylde reached National One with 26 wins in 30 matches to give them their first ever league title. Recently, the club's youth section produced two England internationals in Kieran Brookes and Richard Wigglesworth.

(Thanks to Alan Townsend)

HEATON MOOR

SINCE THE ADVENT of club rugby, Stockport has had several rugby clubs, notably Stockport RUFC and Heaton Moor. The original Stockport club flourished in the 1880s and they were initially part of the NU split, but they soon went bankrupt. In 1878, there was also a short-lived club in Stockport called Heaton Mersey Ramblers.

A replacement RFU club was formed in 1899 as Heaton Moor RUFC, who adopted that name to disassociate themselves from the NU rebels. Heaton Moor takes its name from the moorland surrounding Stockport. The area was changed in 1852 by the opening of Heaton Chapel train station, when builders soon recognised the potential of the area as a centre for commuters to Manchester.

Heaton Moor RUFC was formed by a group of ex-public schoolboys following a meeting in 1899. The first ground was a rented field on Peel Moat Road with rather primitive changing accommodation at the Chapel House Hotel, Wellington Road North. They played their first match on 23rd September 1899, away to Manchester Athletic at Fallowfield and lost by a goal and two tries to nil. Most of their early fixtures were against the 'A' teams of bigger clubs, plus matches against sides like the Lancashire Fusiliers.

Peel Moat Road was followed by a move to a boggy field near the Chapel House Hotel. In 1906 the club moved to Parsonage Road, where they stayed until World War One. During this time, Moor earned fixtures against top sides such as Waterloo, Birkenhead Park, Sale, Broughton Park, New Brighton, Kendal and Nottingham.

Several Heaton members played for Lancashire, notably J. Brown, R.B. Burns, J.W. Bainbridge and W. B. Croxford (who was a leading rugby writer). The club bought a ground on Green Lane, Stockport, which was formally opened on 14th October 1922. They were earning a big reputation at the time with big wins over Sale, Broughton Park and Liverpool. The standing of Heaton

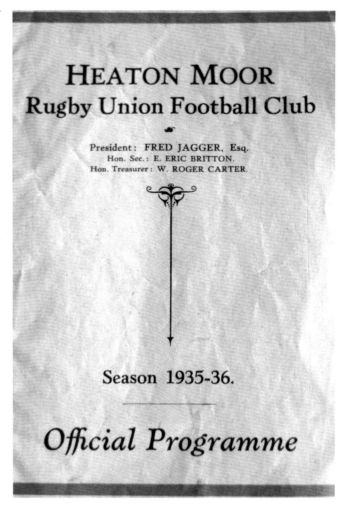

Moor can be gleaned from the records of Old Leysians, then a leading side, who recorded, "Our 1929 Lancashire tour included top class fixtures against Waterloo, Birkenhead Park and Heaton Moor." And the minutes of Chesterfield RUFC record, "We were becoming a respected name and regular opponents included Morley and Heaton Moor."

In 1923 Stuart Tadman joined Heaton Moor, but moved to Sale and played for Lancashire.

The disruption caused by World War Two cost Heaton Moor their senior status because, when peace came, they were unable to find the quality of players who had previously been available. Most of the available players were raw youngsters, although Duncan McLean, a 1946 Scotland international, represented Moor for a time.

Heaton Moor won the 1955 Bowdon Sevens, but the intense competition for good players from other local clubs proved a problem. There was also competition from rugby league, and in the 1970s the club captain, John Knighton, joined Salford RLFC. Despite the competition, Moor reached the semi-final of the Lancashire Cup and ex-colt Simon Roberts played for Cambridge University in the 1983 Varsity Match.

Heaton Moor were struggling when league rugby arrived, and have had to settle for rugby in the Lancashire leagues in recent years. The club's 50th and 75th year anniversaries were marked with a match against Old Leysians, the once great Victorian side that included a Heaton Moor fixture on their end-of-season tour.

HELSBY

HELSBY RUFC WAS formed in 1962 by a group of factory workers at the BICC (British Insulated Calendar Cables) plant in Helsby, a small town on the north Cheshire border. They operated from the BICC Sports and Social Club, which later changed its name to Helsby S & SC. The club's finest hour came in 1989 when they reached the final of the Cheshire Plate. They were defeated by Ashton-on-Mersey, who were two divisions up the league structure.

(Thanks to Chris Johnson)

LEIGH

THE ORIGINAL LEIGH RFC were formed in August 1878. A leading Lancashire side, they were best known at the time for problems with amateurism. Leigh were suspected of illegal payments, and eventually a disgruntled member leaked details of the club's misdemeanours to the RFU, which led to the club being suspended for ten weeks in 1884. Fingers were pointed once more in 1885 when Leigh signed Tom Coop and Doc Worthington. Tom Coop had played for England against Scotland in 1892.

In 1894 Leigh were again suspended by the RFU for professionalism. They had got into the mess by signing the legendary Buff Berry, the much-travelled England half-back, who was at the end of his playing career. Berry was one of the best-paid amateurs of his era and his move to Leigh was just another 'nice little earner' for the declining star.

Leigh joined the NU in 1895 and proved solid supporters of the Northern Union, even winning the RL Challenge Cup in 1921. They changed their name to Leigh Centurions RLFC in the 1990s and continue to be members of the RFL Championship.

Rugby union disappeared in the town for half a century after the Great Schism. Its re-introduction came from the Leigh Technical College, where students formed a rugby club in 1948. Under the guidance of K.R. Isherwood and Eddie Lindley, the students decided to play union rather than league. The Technical College was the initial headquarters, followed by stints at the Sportsman hotel, the Oak Tree and the Village Inn. In 1950 the players got bathed in pit baths and played on Lilford Park. The new club eventually acquired a pitch at Round End Farm and converted its old barn into a clubhouse. In 1957 the club changed their name to Leigh RUFC.

The present ground at Hand Lane was opened on 13th September 1961, when Leigh played a representative side from the Anchor, Ashton-on-Mersey, Burnage, De La Salle and Widnes clubs. Leigh lost 8-3.

During the 1970s, Leigh produced two top-class players in the Tabern brothers, who played in the front row for Fylde and Lancashire. The brothers were sons of local rugby legend Walt Tabern. Leigh had a flourishing junior set up. Rugby League had benefitted with some great names progressing into the 13-man game, notably Mick Hogan (297 games for Leigh RLFC) and Steve Donlan (240 appearances for Leigh RLFC). Today Leigh are one of the best RU teams in Lancashire.

Leigh in 2004.

LEIGH SHAMROCKS

An Irish club existed in the town from 1889 to 1914. The Shamrocks won the 1893 South East Lancashire and Border Towns Junior Cup. They remained a part of the RU during the Schism, and had forward T. Tickle picked for Lancashire. In March 1897 the club joined the NU, but soon disappeared.

LITTLEBOROUGH
(formerly Old Rochdalians)

IF YOU ARE stuck on the M62 motorway near Rochdale and have a look to the north, you will see Hollingworth Lake and the pitches of Littleborough RUFC, who play on a ground adjacent to the water.

A club existed in Littleborough in the 19th century and were the 1897 Lancashire Cup winners before disbanding in 1900. The present club was founded in 1930 as Old Rochdalians and was restricted to the old boys of Rochdale High School. Their first playing fields were at Firgrove, but in 1971 they moved to Hollingworth Saxon burial ground.

Two XVs were first run in 1932, and at the end of 1949 – with a playing membership of 90 – the number of sides had risen to four.

The club produced an international in David Rosser, a three-quarter who won five caps for England and was captain of Wasps from 1966-68. Littleborough also produced Alex and Pat Sanderson, who both played for England. The lads began with Littleborough before moving to Preston Grasshoppers and later to the Premiership.

Other notable players who emerged from the club were Gordon Leach (Sale

David Rosser

and NLD) and Graham Starkey, who captained Rochdale Hornets RLFC. Peter Sutton may not have played for any great clubs, but he built the foundations of the present club by starting Littleborough's mini section in the 1970s. In the 1980s, the club produced Craig Burrill, a brilliant goalkicker who later moved to Orrell and Leigh RLFC

Littleborough has a curious link to the sunny South Seas thanks to rugby league. Rochdale Hornets imported a number of Fijian rugby players in the 1950s and gradually a Fijian community emerged in the town. Many of their offspring preferred rugby union to its rival, and in 2003 a third of the team were Fijians.

Since the advent of league rugby, Littleborough have been middle-ranking. Their finest hour came in 2011 when they had a great unbeaten run, culminating in becoming North Lancs One champions. That year they also reached Twickenham in the final of the RFU Senior Vase, where they took on Teddington. Although beaten 42-8, it was a great achievement for the club. The squad was: Chris Park, Nathan King, Tom Galvin, Chris Duffy, David Kearns, Andy Bairstow, Steve North, Ben Irving, Mark Elvidge, Brook Reader, Graeme Shepherd, Mark Forden, Stuart Bairstow, Michael Fletcher, Mark Murgatroyd, Paul Fino, John Doherty, Adam Wayne, Sam Dickinson, Alistair Towers, Ben Park and Stuart Irving.

Boro's achievements owe much to former coach Rob Rawlinson (ex-Leeds Tykes) and director of rugby Steve Park. Littleborough have teams from the under-eights of the Minis section right up to the first XV, including three senior teams and a ladies side.

(Thanks to Steve Collins & David Geldart)

LIVERPOOL ST HELENS

"We have gone through troubled times in recent years… it was a heady froth at the beginning of professionalism."

Ray French

RUGBY HAS BEEN second best to soccer in the city of Liverpool for over a century, yet Liverpool played an important part in the history of rugby, and there have been dozens of clubs who have played in the city. Waterloo are still a force, but Liverpool St Helens RFC have sadly slipped out of the limelight, which is doubly sad as they organised the first ever club rugby match.

On Saturday, 19th December 1857, several Old Rugbeians, led by Frank Mather and Richard Sykes, organised a game in Liverpool. Sykes later recalled, "When I was a boy at Rugby School, I received a letter from Frank Mather of Bootle Hall inviting me to play in a match, Rugby versus the World, which would take place at Liverpool. I was requested to bring a football from Rugby. As the notice was short, and there being no stock of best footballs, I secured one that had been used in the Bigside [the best school team] matches and was still in good repair. On reaching the rendezvous, which was the ground of the Liverpool Cricket Club adjoining the gas works at Edge Hill, I was agreeably surprised at the preparations which had been made.

"There were nearly 50 players present and some spectators. The players for the most part were members from the chief families of Liverpool and represented the leading public schools of England. The game was a very pleasant one, played in the best spirit, but it was not a match so to speak… Mather afterwards wrote to me that the verdict was favourable and my impression is that the Liverpool Football Club was then and there formed."

Sykes subsequently joined Manchester FC, who played Liverpool on a regular basis from 1862. Later he emigrated to America, where he established huge interests in railways and farming – he even has a town in North Dakota named after him. It is also claimed that he introduced rugby football to colleges and universities in the West.

The new club had an improbable claim to fame as it produced the first American footballer in James Taylor Soutter, who was the chargé d'affaires in Rome and Paris for the Confederate States during the American Civil War. After its outbreak, Souter was unable to return to the South, but found old friends in Liverpool's cotton trade and played for the rugby club during his exile.

Liverpool as always well represented at international level. In the first international match in 1871, England selected eight Liverpool players: J.A. Lyon, F. Tobin, Hon. S. Parker, C.W.H. Clarke, C.L. Verelst, C.J.C. Touzel, H.H. Springman, and H.D. Bateson, whilst J.R. Hay Gordon represented Scotland. The club also provided the first Northern player to captain England in Edward Kewley (1852-1940), who made seven appearances for England from 1874 to 1878.

Liverpool eventually left the cricket club and moved to Aigburth. By this time, they were one of the north's premier sides, but they never attracted great support. A club record states that the gate money for season 1886-87 was only £104, and even that had dwindled to £34 by 1893. Liverpool Rugby had been overtaken by the emergence of the two great soccer clubs, Everton and Liverpool, with whom the rugby club had a mixed relationship. In April 1892, the rugby club objected to a new soccer club using the name Liverpool FC, but the complaint failed because the Football Association (not surprisingly) supported the soccer club. However, the following year Everton donated the use of Goodison Park for a charity match to raise money for the rugby club. A combined Bradford-Runcorn XV beat Liverpool by two goals to nil.

Liverpool's finest hour was immediately prior to World War One, when the club had the captains of England, Scotland and Ireland in their team: Ronnie Poulton-Palmer, F.H. Turner and Dicky Lloyd respectively. Turner was the first Scot to score 13 points in an international, a record that stood until 1972. Sadly, Poulton-Palmer and Turner were both killed in the Great War. Lloyd and Turner were both brilliant goal-kickers.

Dr. Noel Chavasse was a member of the 1913 Liverpool side. The son of the Bishop of Liverpool, Chavasse is one of only three men to win two Victoria Crosses. Chavasse spent World War One rescuing wounded men from no-man's-land and he won his first VC at the Battle of the Somme for rescuing 20 men. A year later, he once again spent his days in no-man's-land, and despite a series of injuries, he was awarded a second VC. Sadly, he was killed by a shell burst.

Between the wars Liverpool remained one of England's top rugby clubs, but rugby as a sport lost ground to soccer. Even the city council were biased in favour of soccer and the council built nearly 200 soccer pitches for amateur players in the inter-war year. At the same time, they provided only a handful of new rugby pitches because they thought rugby was a middle-class game which could afford to buy its own facilities.

There was even a geographic divide, which marginalised rugby in the city. The north and south of the city (Waterloo, Wavertree, etc.) were home to a dozen rugby clubs, whilst the centre and the suburbs were soccer-mad. Liverpool RFC operated in the city centre, which was devastated by bombing in World War Two and by subsequent urban redevelopment which took the heart out of the city.

Mike Slemen

The social fabric of Aigburth declined and Liverpool's ground was plagued by vandalism. In the early 1980s, Liverpool decided to merge with St Helens RUFC and to move to Moss Lane on the city's outskirts. On 3rd May 1986 the last match was played at Liverpool's old ground. It was also Mike Slemen's farewell to club rugby, and he marked the occasion with a hat-trick of tries in a 48-0 victory. Slemen was a tall, fast winger, who was a complete footballer and capable of playing anywhere across the back-line. He first made his name for England with a superb defensive display against France in Paris, and retained his place throughout the Beaumont years. He played for the 1980 Lions and later became a leading coach.

The merged Liverpool St Helens RFC club went into action, on Sunday, 31st August 1986 with a match against Aberavon.

Liverpool's days as the home of internationals came to its end in 1986 when they produced its final international in Dr Kevin Simms, a talented centre who embodied the old tradition of full-time medical and amateur rugby players. Simms was unlucky to have competed with the youthful Will Carling for the England inside-centre berth and he won less caps than he deserved.

LSH began the era of league rugby at the highest level. They, like many clubs, had no grasp of the logistics of top-class league rugby and registered only 30 players for the first season. Injuries soon reduced their squad to barely enough to field one team and eight months of competitive rugby proved a nightmare. The club had to juggle resources in order to field a side worthy of facing the best clubs in England. Relegation was inevitable, and sadly the club tumbled down the leagues over the following seasons. Despite their problems, they were always amongst the most hospitable sides in the game.

In 2008 LSH were the first club in the world to reach the 150-year landmark. Four years later saw the renewal of the oldest open rugby union fixture in the world when Manchester visited LSH.

(Thanks to the late Alan Walker, Ray French and John Williams)

DEFUNCT LIVERPOOL SIDES

The city of Liverpool has been home to dozens of clubs since the 1860s. A long-forgotten team, Dingle RFC, were the first English club to travel to Ireland when they played Trinity College in Dublin in 1873.

The most distinguished side in the city to disappear were Liverpool Old Boys, who were formed in 1887 and produced two England internationals in Robert Wood (three caps 1901-03) and Roger Wilson (three caps in 1891). Liverpool OBs played at Greenhill Road, Allerton. They were thriving in the 1930s, but closed during World War Two. When peace came, the members were unable to re-establish the club, so instead merged with Liverpool RFC.

Rugby union has always struggled to survive in Liverpool due to the pre-eminence of soccer and rugby league has also had a chequered history in the city. Runcorn RFC joined the NU in 1895 and tried to be the leaders in south-west Lancashire. They struggled for a decade before switching to soccer. In their wake came Liverpool City (later Liverpool Stanley), who joined the Northern Union in December 1905. They survived for more than 60 years with minimal interest from the soccer-mad city. In the 1970s they moved to Runcorn as Runcorn Highfield but soon disappeared.

LYMM

"To play rugby football was to enter a higher plane where one straining, struggling half-hour was worth a year of common life."
Michael Dobbs after Thomas Hughes

LYMM IS A smart little town in north Cheshire. The rugby club was founded in 1959 in the Spread Eagle Hotel on the village's main street. Sufficient interest was soon generated to field a team who played seven fixtures in their first season. A pitch and hut were found at Beechwood on the south side of the village and a full fixture list was arranged for 1961-62, including Metrovick 'B', Crewe and Nantwich, Heinz, Vulcan 'A', St Helens Recs 'B', Leek, Padgate Training College, Manchester University Freshers and Old Salfordians 'A'.

The playing side continued to improve, but the clubhouse was primitive; beer was served from a nine-gallon keg, which was placed on a table in the middle of the room. Eventually the club bought 'Beechwood', a very handsome villa in the Italian style, which became its headquarters.

The second season saw the start of a colts team, mostly drawn from Lymm Grammar School, who had introduced the sport into the curriculum that season.

Lymm rose rapidly in the 1960s and produced Tony Wright, who was one of Britain's finest centres of the era. He scored 58 tries for the club in 1973-74, which led him to join Sale, who were the top North West side at the time. Within a month, he was in the Lancashire team. In December 1978, he played for the North of England in the historic match against the All Blacks at Otley. The North's 21-9 victory ranks amongst the greatest ever British provincial results.

The new year brought an England trial for Wright, and a place in the England 'B' team against Ireland at Twickenham. His

Lymm in action in 2008.

season culminated in the County Championship Final victory over Gloucestershire at Vale of Lune. He subsequently played for the North against Australia at Gosforth, when they drew 6-6. Tony was a regular member of the Lancashire side for five seasons. In the summer of 1982 Tony was asked to tour Canada and America with the England team, but his employers refused him leave of absence. It is obvious that had Wright made the transition to senior rugby earlier, he would have won a full England cap. His legendary side-step made him an extremely difficult opponent. He left Sale and Lancashire in 1983 and returned to Lymm. Cheshire noted his eligibility for his home county and persuaded him to change counties. He finished his career at Lymm with a record of 359 tries in 13 seasons.

Despite Lymm's meteoric rise, they could not complete with the 'big boys' and the road to Sale was busy at this time, with Andy Phillips, Hywel Benjamin, Colin Rowe, Colin Meachin, Howard Fitton, Anthony Egan, Simon Plumb, Robin Meachin and Huw Thomas all leaving for Heywood Road.

Lymm RFC has appeared in six Cheshire Cup finals, including their victory in 1989 over Mid-Cheshire Colleges.

The best player to emerge from Lymm was David Strettle who began with the club before playing for England at Sevens and at full international level.

MACCLESFIELD

"People come to Macclesfield as a stepping stone in their march through life. 30 years later they are somewhat surprised they have set up camp in the town."
Macc and the Art of Long Distance Walking
- Graham Wilson (1998)

MACCLESFIELD HAD A sartorial part to play in the development of the English gentleman because this hilly town in east Cheshire was an unlikely world centre for silk weaving. In days gone by, no English gentleman was well-dressed without his silk waistcoat, which were mainly produced in Macclesfield. Unlike the wool and cotton industries, the silk industry in Macclesfield grew in the early 20th century and the town could boast 80 silk mills. Even when the silk industry declined, Macclesfield flourished as a commuter town for nearby Manchester.

A Macclesfield rugby club existed in 1875, and they sent delegates to the meeting that founded the Cheshire county association. The current club was formed on 23rd November 1926 by five local enthusiasts. The first game was on the 1st January 1927, when they were trounced 63-0 by Davenport. At this point it was decided, on the advice of the Rev. W.S. Coad, to postpone more fixtures until the squad had reached a competent standard.

On the 5th February 1927, the club played their second fixture against Marple, which resulted in a draw. A month later, Macclesfield travelled to Dukinfield and got hammered 51-5. They had to wait until April to register their first victory – an 8-0 win over Stoke-on-Trent 'A'. It was clear from early results that Macclesfield needed support. It came when Scots international Dr. A.C. Gillies came to live in the town and stepped in as coach. He also persuaded E. Mucklow, another Scots international, to play for the club. Under Gillies' coaching, Macclesfield improved and the following season the first XV had 11 wins in 24 matches. A second team could also now be fielded. They went from strength to strength and were unbeaten from October 1935 to February 1937.

The club had its first county player in 1967, when Peter Holland was selected by Cheshire. But Macclesfield weren't going to get big-headed as local rivals Leigh dropped fixtures

Priory Park, Macclesfield.

with them, saying, "they weren't good enough". The club was, however, good enough to field an international in 1993 when Simon Hodgkinson, the England full back, shocked rugby by leaving high-riding Nottingham for Macc. He quickly moved onto Moseley, leading to suggestions that it was a ruse to get round RFU registration rules.

Macclesfield were traditionally one of Cheshire's best sides and by 2010 they were playing in the National Leagues and have reached National One on two occasions.

MANCHESTER

MANCHESTER FC APPEARED from the earliest roots of the game because the club's founders included Richard Sykes, who organised the first open match at Liverpool in 1857. The formal founding date of Manchester FC is generally taken as 1860, when the club played a trial game at Pendleton. Subsequently, fixtures were organised against sides from Liverpool, Preston, Rochdale and Sheffield. Sykes and his Manchester team also travelled to Scotland to play friendlies against the Academicals sides from Edinburgh and Glasgow.

By 1869 Manchester could organise a match against a District XX. This was followed by a match against Leeds select, which was advertised as 'Lancashire against Yorkshire'. The notion of a Red Rose county team caught on and county matches became a regular feature of rugby.

Manchester had played originally on Alexandra Park for two seasons before moving to Whalley Range. The players changed at the Queens Hotel in the city centre and drove to the ground in a coach and four. International rugby came to the club itself in 1880 when the first of four international matches was played at Whalley Range. Manchester hosted Scotland (1880 and 1882) and Ireland (1881 and 1883).

Manchester vacated Whalley Range in 1901 in favour of Fallowfield, where they remained for seven years. In 1908 they moved to Kersal near the old racecourse. They stayed for 62 years before moving to Grove Park, Cheadle Hulme.

Manchester were Lancashire rugby for the first dozen years, and this caused controversy. Initially its members composed the county side, but the Manchester committee soon recognised that they did not have exclusivity of talent. The suspicion was harboured by other Lancastrian clubs that Manchester lured the best players to their ranks by offering a ticket to the county team.

Manchester and the other clubs remained at loggerheads until 1881, when a formal agreement was reached to establish 'Lancashire County FC'. Manchester did not relinquish the reins as they were automatically granted a place on the county committee and the right to host the matches. Manchester were one of the north's top sides but lost many of their best fixtures following the creation of the Northern Union.

From the earliest days of the sport, Manchester were a force nationally. They supplied four players – J.C. Turner, A.S. Gibson, W. Maclaren and R.R. Osbourne – to the England team who played in the first international against Scotland in 1871. They also supplied three forwards to the England side who met Ireland in their inaugural match in 1875. Indeed, 25 players who won 65 caps in the first 14 years of international rugby hailed from Manchester.

In 1892 James Marsh of Manchester was the only player to appear for two countries in the Home International Championship. In 1889 he played for Scotland and won two caps before joining Manchester and winning an English cap.

One Manchester international who left a mark on the sport was R. Todd (1847-1927), who is credited with kicking the ball so high that the RFU felt they needed to introduce high goal posts to resolve disputes about kicks. Previously posts were only one foot higher than the cross bar.

In 1949 Arthur Komrover stepped down after 15 years as a great player for Manchester.

1983-84 was a terrible season for Manchester, with only three wins in 32 games. They lost most of their best players to Sale and Orrell, and John O'Driscoll moved to London Irish.

The decline of Manchester FC was perhaps the saddest story of the new professionalism. In 2000, Manchester were playing in the championship, yet just a dozen years later, they had sunk to the middle ranks of Lancashire rugby. Their lowest moment came with one relegation when the RFU funding was cut overnight from £250,000 per year to £30,000. Such a loss inevitably led to an exodus of players.

In 2008, which briefly saw them back in National One, Manchester had a female head coach. Elaine Vassie originally arrived at Grove Park as conditioning coach assisting Paul Reid, only to find just four players present for training. When Paul Reid had to step down, Elaine took over but couldn't stop the rot.

Sadly, once great Manchester have gone into a tailspin and slipped down to North 1 West.

MANCHESTER UNIVERSITY

MANCHESTER UNIVERSITY RC was formed in 1882 under the title of Owens College. The university itself was formed at a later date by the merger of Owens and two other colleges. Owens College had a formidable reputation, and were able to arrange mid-week matches against some of the top northern sides until the Schism of 1895.

Since its formation, the university has fielded several English internationals, including A. Alcock, E. Fookes, H.B. Toft and C.B. Holmes, plus D.G. Schulze-Muller of Scotland.

NEW BRIGHTON

*"Playing at New Brighton is great;
they even run the baths for you."*

Anon

NEW BRIGHTON WAS a small village on the Wirral coast until the late 19th century when it was transformed by a grandiose plan to make it the north's answer to the other (and more famous) Brighton. It became a popular holiday resort, with attractions such as a replica of the Eiffel Tower, fairgrounds, ornamental gardens and a yacht club.

New Brighton FC was formed by members of the local sailing club looking for a winter sport. A trio of youngsters – Edward Holt, Percy Shaw and Walter Petrie – happened upon John Herron and Harry Hiles playing with a rugby ball. They raised two sides for a challenge match between 'Claremont' and 'Egremont'. Egremont proved the more durable club and eventually changed their name to New Brighton after absorbing Claremont. One of the earliest members was Harry Ryalls from the Egremont club, who was to represent England. Ryalls scored a try for England when they beat Wales at Swansea in 1885, despite not having been selected for the trial match. He kept his place against Ireland.

The Wirral was a hotbed of rugby even in those days. Besides the New Brighton club, there were nearly half a dozen small clubs in the area, including Wallasey Old Boys, New Brighton Olympic, Wallasey Ferries and the Magazine Club.

The first known fixture of New Brighton FC was a heavy defeat away to West Derby on 25th February 1876. They were champions in 1880-81 when they beat Birkenhead Park in the final of the Cheshire Cup at Rock Ferry by a try to nil.

New Brighton entertained the county side at their Seaview Road ground in 1882, when Cheshire beat Lancashire for the first time. Five New Brighton men played for Cheshire, including Harry Ryalls and Harry Bell. The latter was originally a member of Liverpool, where he won English honours.

Seaview Road was one of a number of home grounds in the first years. The club began at Rake Lane, but had brief stops at Seabank Road and Sea View Road, Liskeard. In 1898 they moved to the Cricket Ground in Rake Lane, where the club remained until the present ground at Leasowe was ready for use.

A boost for the club was the elevation to grammar school status of Wallasey School, which was to provide them with a steady stream of talent. The school produced Fred Jones, who was the outstanding figure at New Brighton in the 1890s. Jones was fast and a determined tackler, which helped him win an England cap in the 1893 Leeds international against Scotland.

Another New Brighton player of note was a Mr Keir, who in 1897 forced a change in the laws of the game. Keir had to leave the field in a match against Waterloo after suffering concussion. He was sitting on the touchline when he saw a Waterloo player, ball in hand, making towards an unprotected try line. Keir got to his feet, rushed onto the field and tackled the Waterloo player. Waterloo were incensed and complained to the RFU, who instituted on a new law forbidding an injured player from returning to the field until the referee gave permission.

At the end of the 19th century the club had ambitions of becoming a

Fred Jones

gate-taking club and bought two turnstiles from the Woodside River Ferry for £5. Unfortunately, the formation of the Northern Union and the outbreak of the Boer War spiked their plans. Without local fixtures, they tried to expand their horizons and sought fixtures with Swansea, Coventry and Gloucester. The move was unsuccessful as they won only three out of 20 games in 1901-02, and only two out of 24 in 1903-04. Things were grim on and off the field, culminating in the club treasurer paying the club's debts out of his own pocket. Membership fell to 19 playing members. Cheshire were desperate to retain one of its premier sides; the Sale Club offered private financial help and James Baxter of Birkenhead Park organised a "benefit game" for them.

The club survived and became a major force between the wars, when the town reached the height of its days as a tourist resort. The rugby club enjoyed heady days, none better than when 4,500 spectators paid 6d a head to watch a 'friendly' against Birkenhead Park in 1922. Interest was so great that New Brighton could field six sides, who couldn't all be accommodated at the old Rake Lane ground. This led to a situation where the club's junior matches were played all over the Wirral. This was bad for morale, so in 1930 the club began negotiations to buy land at Reeds Lane, Leasowe. They eventually purchased it for £3,178. The Reeds Lane ground was officially opened in September 1933 with a match against Waterloo. Standards improved and, by the end of the decade, New Brighton were playing superb running rugby with Welsh internationals David Evans and Ronald Boon in the three-quarters.

The ample space at Reeds Lane provided an unusual way of raising funds when the New Brighton Horse Show became an annual event that generated much-needed cash until 1960.

During the 1950s and 1960s the club ranked amongst the best club sides in the north. Their best-known player of the era was Dr. Vic Tindall, who played in two England trials whilst with New Brighton and later won four England caps.

1969 saw the oddest fixture in the club's history when they played the Springboks. The tourists were beset by anti-apartheid demonstrations and looked for a friendly fixture away from the protesters. New Brighton were due to play the North of Ireland RFC in a Saturday fixture when they were offered a 'behind-closed-doors' fixture against the South Africans. Rather than upset their Ulster visitors, a combined New Brighton-North of Ireland XV played the Springboks. Unsurprisingly, the tourists won.

New Brighton were still producing internationals in the early 1970s, notably Stewart Maxwell of England. He is best remembered for scoring two tries for the North West Counties against the 1972 All Blacks at Workington, which was the first victory by an English regional team over the New Zealanders.

However, the world was changing for the club. The Merseyside area was in economic decline, the town of New Brighton could no longer attract large numbers of tourists and the club were entering a spectacular freefall.

One club member recalls: "We always expected the best rugby players on the Wirral to join New Brighton. It was their premier local club. But we didn't realise that young men were buying cars and could travel further. Sale, Waterloo and Orrell could offer more than we could. They were only an hour's drive away. Added to which, the growth in university education meant more youngsters went away to college and never came back to Merseyside because the job opportunities had gone. New Brighton was not the magnet it had been."

Sale were now the top club in Cheshire and totally dominated the Cheshire Cup, being unbeaten for 13 successive seasons. The only team to give Sale a fright was New Brighton, who in 1978-79, narrowly failed to wrestle the cup from Heywood Road.

The club was still producing good players such as Mark Williams, who won 27 caps for the USA after emigrating. But the introduction of leagues in 1987 left the club in dire straits, and the club's elders decided that something drastic had to be done. They sought a top-class coach and recruited Lol Connor from Waterloo. Connor reversed the decline and good times returned as a resurgent club climbed back into the National Leagues.

One of the most remarkable characters of this era was Colin Bentley, the publicity manager. A huge mountain of a man, Colin was famous for his generosity, not least to referees. He upset the county authorities during one hugely important promotion decider against Preston Grasshoppers. New Brighton led by a point in injury time when Colin used the PA system to advise the referee that he had played too much injury time. To his chagrin, Preston immediately scored.

Today Reeds Lane (renamed Hartsfield after a stalwart member) is a vibrant centre of rugby and very much the heart of Wirral rugby.

(Thanks to Colin Bentley)

NEWTON-LE WILLOWS

THE TOWN OF Newton-Le-Willows is on the south side of Wigan, and the rugby team have been playing at the Crow Lane Sports Club for well over 60 years. They have provided county players for both Lancashire and Cheshire, as well as England players Paul Kenrick, Dave Roy and, most notably, the formidable Fran Cotton.

Fran Cotton was the son of a rugby league player whose brothers had played the 13-man game at the highest level. Fran first gained attention at Newton-le-Willows before winning a place at Loughborough Colleges when the university was becoming established as a leading physical education establishment. He joined Coventry and later Sale, and won England honours throughout the 1970s (when, sadly, the national side were at a low ebb). The Lions selected Cotton for the 1974 and 1977 tours, where he earned a reputation as the world's best prop-forward. He was also an integral part of the 1980 England Grand Slam-winning side.

After retirement, he used his sporting knowledge to help

Fran Cotton

create a brand of rugby and leisure shirts and revealed himself to be a very good and successful businessman. Despite his enormous contribution to rugby, he was banned for life in 1982 after writing his autobiography. The ban lasted until 1989 when he was reinstated by the RFU. He later managed the 1998 Lions and was Chairman of the RFU.

Newton made national television in the late 1960s, when the screenwriter writer called Colin Welland, who had played for Newton, wrote a TV series about his old rugby club under the title of 'Banglestein's Boys'. The odd title was a reference to a character in a rude rugby song. The series included a character who ate beer glasses as a post-match trick and bore an uncanny resemblance to a real club member, who did, indeed, eat glasses. Welland later won an Oscar for his screenplay for the great sporting film 'Chariots of Fire'.

Today Newton are a modest side who keep going despite intense local competition from soccer, league and union clubs.

OLD BEDIANS

ST BEDE'S COLLEGE, Manchester, was a Roman Catholic school formed in 1876. The origin of Old Bedians RUFC is owed to Des Pastore, a legend of the city's rugby, who had played for Sale and Cheshire. He attended the Old Boys Association A.G.M. in December 1954, when the school captain announced they would like to form an OB's club after two highly successful seasons for the First XV. Des offered his services and found himself involved. Des Pastore went on to become a legend. He played regularly until he was 90 years of age for EGOR (The Evergreen of Rugby] – a world record. His achievements earned him the MBE

The new club had no pitch, no money, no clubhouse and few players. A farmer's field was found on Hardy Lane, Chorlton, but facilities were primitive; a barbed-wire fence provided coat hooks and cars were used for changing. A derelict pavilion was spotted over the fence at Chorlton Lawn Tennis Club, who came to an agreement with the rugby players: the rugby club would maintain it during the winter and let the tennis club have it back in summer. OBs then persuaded St. Werburghs Church on Wilbraham Road to sell the disused land in front of the pavilion. Two parents who had boys at the school, Connel and Finnegan, offered to level the land, which the members seeded. A full fixture list was agreed for the following season, which included the 'A' teams of Sale, Wilmslow, Fylde, Manchester, Broughton Park and Bradford. Under captain Dennis Ryan, an ex-Manchester player, Bedians won 18 games and were finalists in the Shell Sevens.

During the following 10 years, under the enthusiastic captaincy of Vincent Moor, Ron Evans, Mike Lydon, Patrick Chamberlain and Ashley Hall, Old Bedians became the most successful junior club in the Manchester area, with 28, 30 and 32 wins in individual seasons. Success on the field brought problems because four teams were too many for one pitch. A small committee was formed to find a new venue before treasurer Ged Kendrick spotted that Granada TV were selling their sports club at Underbank Farm in Didsbury. It seemed ideal and offered scope for another club to share the facilities.

Old Bedians Football club were invited to join in the new venture and a joint fund-raising effort was made to purchase the ground.

In 1966-67 Bedians moved to Millgate Lane, Didsbury, with two rugby pitches and two soccer pitches. In the September of that year, the club hosted the preliminary rounds of the Glengarth Sevens so successfully that it was decided to start their own sevens competition. This was to run successfully for the next 20 years and, over the years, the club have promoted mini rugby and Colts XVs with varying success.

Keith Marsden was chairman from 1990 to 1993, and it was during this time (April 1991) when car thieves torched a stolen car behind the clubhouse. The flames spread and engulfed the building, destroying it. The members pulled together and a management committee was formed to work on 'Project New Building'. This committee, under the guidance of Keith and Vin Rossall (president 1992-93), together with the help of a very co-operative builder, used the insurance money to build a new two-storey brick and concrete clubhouse with facilities that are envy of clubs of all codes in the Manchester area.

Due to strong Irish connections of the membership, discussions began which led to the Oisin Gaelic Football Club joining the centre and assisting with the viability of the new clubhouse. Oisins became members when a revised constitution was approved.

The First XV now compete in the North Lancashire league. In 2004 they celebrated their 50th Anniversary at Millgate Lane.

OLD BIRKONIANS

ONE GREAT OLD Merseyside club does not attract a single member to pre-season training and hasn't done for years: that club is Old Birkonians RFC (the Old Boys of Birkenhead School). Mind you, the club stopped playing regularly in 1980 and reforms for just one match a year.

Rugby was first played at Birkenhead School from at least 1874, when the school magazine recorded a goal kick of 60 yards by a boy called Kelk. This was a remarkable achievement, even with wind assistance. The next reference is a match between the First Team and a team of Old Boys. The match was replayed on a casual basis in the following years. One unflattering report from the era described the school pitch as being the "worst in England", but said a replacement was "too short and narrow".

Birkenhead Grammar School concentrated on rugby, but produced another piece of sporting history. Dr Walter Bensemann, who taught at the school, initiated the England v Germany soccer matches. Bensemann, the chubby, short-sighted son of a wealthy Berlin banker, founded the first soccer clubs in Germany at Montreux and Karlsricke Kickers, where he played centre-forward with a total lack of ability. In 1899 Bensemann persuaded the Football Association to play a series of matches between England and Germany by paying the £200 costs himself. The results were 13-2, 10-2 and 7-0 to England. Bensemann was an outstanding teacher of languages and well regarded at Birkenhead School, but he was also a mysterious figure who entertained lavishly and gave expensive dinner parties for all the most influential people in Liverpool. The mystery about Bensemann increased when he suddenly disappeared in 1914, on the eve of the First World War, which sparked rumours that he was a German spy.

Traditionally BGS boys graduated to Birkenhead Park, but Old Birkonians RFC emerged from a schism at that club. The founders included Rev. C.A. MacVicar, the school chaplain, who played for Kent and Cheshire. The first match was against the school in September 1922. OBs won 23 of 27 games in the first season. Their success was remarkable and in 1931-32 they won 24 of 28 matches.

OBs were a closed club who played on the school playing fields. In 1928 they bought an adjacent field and erected a pavilion at a cost of £4000. They soon had fixtures against Sale and Manchester. In the 1960s they had four senior teams, and provided five blues in one post-war varsity match. The club could boast one British Lion (Bill Howard 1938), 12 rugby internationals and 110 county players. Howard was one of an elite band who were selected for the Lions but was never capped by his country. It was said Howard was never capped for England because OBs were too unfashionable.

OBs emerged from World War Two with a fixture list composed almost completely of top-class sides. OBs finally produced an England international in Laurie Rimmer and John Walton had an England trial.

Few clubs can have suffered as dramatic a change of fortunes as Old Birkonians. In the early 1960s, they were the premier Old Boys club in the north of England. OBs were the second strongest Merseyside club in 1961-62 when of their local rivals they only lost to Waterloo and won 24 of 30 fixtures. That year they had S.A. Martin (Cambridge) and P.M.W. Stafford (Oxford) in the Varsity match and four players in the Cheshire team. Yet interest was dwindling, and five years later they opened membership to all-comers. Even so, within a decade they were defunct. Some members rejoined Birkenhead Park, but their tradition remains for just one afternoon a year.

A curious footnote to the OBs' demise was that bureaucracy blocked the sale of the club's ground for 25 years and it was 2003 before the pitches were sold.

Their legend lives on each Boxing Day, when a New Brighton XV takes on an Old Birkonians XV. Many of the players travel great distances for their only fixture of the year.

OLD SALIANS

Old Salians were officially formed in 1944 by members of the Old Boys' Association of Sale Grammar School. However, the club must have existed seven years earlier because a newspaper article written by Sir Robert Mark, the Metropolitan Police Commissioner, includes references to training with Sale and to helping form an old boys team in 1937.

The best players from Salians traditionally migrated to neighbours Sale, who were the top club in Cheshire. In 1968-69 Sale beat Old Salians to win the first renewal of the Cheshire Cup since 1881. Salians were a formidable junior club in Manchester rugby until the 1990s and could boast excellent facilities at Conway Road, Sale Moor. The club suffered badly when the Grammar School declined as a rugby school, which coincided with the arrival of leagues. Salians dropped out of the leagues in 1997, but returned five years later.

OLDHAM

"Oldham owes its present magnitude to the factory system of which it is a remarkable outcome"

John Hudson

RUGBY HAD BEEN an important part of Oldham life since 1876, when the original Oldham club was formed at the Prince Albert Hotel on Lee Street. Their first game was on the 21st October 1876, against Stalybridge on a field in Glodwick. Subsequently, the club moved to Clarks Field, Knuckett, and eventually to the Watersheddings in September 1889. The Watersheddings and Oldham rugby became synonymous over the next 110 years.

William McCutcheon, a Welsh back, was the first international from Oldham FC. He was one of many players to 'go north' from South Wales under suspicious circumstances in the 1880s. McCutcheon committed himself to Lancashire after joining Oldham. With McCutcheon, Oldham were Lancashire champions and the county were English champions. McCutcheon was rewarded with a Welsh cap in 1891.

Oldham were amongst the top Northern clubs in the years before the Schism, and were one of the nine clubs who established the Lancashire Championship in 1892. They won the championship in 1894. Oldham's success was overshadowed by accusations of bribing players to leave their original club and to join their ranks. One of the best acquisitions was Harry Varley, a small half-back from Liversedge, who moved to Oldham in 1893 and was capped by Lancashire and England. A. Ashworth began at the Mossley Club then later moved to Oldham and in 1892 was capped for England.

Oldham joined the Northern Union in 1895 and were NU Champions on four occasions between 1901 and 1911 (when they could attract crowds of 20,000). Oldham RLFC were part of the Rugby League until 1998, when they were casualties of the new Super League. Ironically, when the Watersheddings was sold along with its artefacts, the original 1889 turnstiles were bought by the RFU for the museum at Twickenham.

A rugby union club was formed in 1905 by members of the Brighton House College. The club struggled to find a permanent home and played all their matches away for a period.

In 1911, Oldham RUFC were playing at Middleton junction, and after World War One they moved south to the town centre. In 1921 they bought a pitch at Keb Lane, Bordsley for £1,150, which was to be their home for the next century. Unfortunately, the new ground was a mile from the railway station and the uphill walk was unpopular with visiting teams in the days before motor transport. The move led to Oldham going from strength to strength: in 1929-30 they lost only five of 32 matches. Three seasons later they lost only to Tyldesley and Wigan, who were two of the best sides in the region.

Initially, Oldham RUFC had a struggle to survive because many of its players worked in the Lancashire cotton industry, which declined in the 1920s. But their reputation grew, and the 1932-33

season saw only three defeats in 30 matches. This encouraged the county selectors to award a Lancashire cap to A. Heptonstall, the first Oldham player to win a county cap since the Schism.

Oldham became one of the best clubs in the North West but struggled to contain the attractions of rugby league for their best players, who were prime candidates for the paid ranks. Any top-class player at Keb Lane was likely to switch to rugby league. The union club declined badly in the 1990s, and despite excellent facilities were playing their competitive rugby in the lowest leagues. Ironically, it was the arrival of Ian MacCorkindale, a famous rugby league player and coach, that sparked a revival for the East Manchester club, culminating in two victories in the Lancashire Trophy.

CROMPTON AND WERNETH

The shadow of the Oldham town team has always eclipsed the other local teams, but in the 19th century, the best-known junior clubs were Crompton RFC and Werneth RFC. Crompton joined the Lancashire RFU in November 1887 and were second in the Third Division in 1894-95. The NU exodus saw Crompton promoted to the depleted NU Division One, but they disappeared in February 1898. Werneth joined the Lancashire RFU in 1882, but enjoyed little success before defecting to the NU in 1896. They found success equally difficult to find in the NU, and ceased to exist in 1906.

ORRELL

*"Losing to Orrell was bad enough, but to have it happen
in a lay-by on the M6 is too much to bear."*
Nigel Starmer-Smith

ORRELL RUFC ROSE to prominence during the 1980s
and, for a few years, the west Wigan side disputed the title of
England's top club with Leicester, Bath and the London giants.
Yet they were a junior club for many years.

It is thought the first matches were played in 1926, but the
original foundation date is generally accepted as 1927. The club's
inaugural meeting was held in the stables of John Simpkin's
home 'Sunny Side', Chapel Street, Pemberton, Wigan. The
Simpkins were mine owners in Pemberton and John Simpkin,
Jack Gaskell and Charlie Holt organised a rugby match
amongst friends. The first official matches were against Wigan
Old Collegians and Wigan OBs III team and were played at
the Donkey Field, Billinge. The Old Collegians match was
abandoned due to unruly behaviour amongst the players and
the crowd. Captain that day was Bill Liptrot, who had a life-
long association with Orrell RUFC.

1927-28 saw 18 games, mostly away. The few home games
played were either on the Lamber-Head Green, on a field off
Orrell Road, or at the Donkey Field. The teams changed in
the outside washhouse at Charlie Holt's house in Moss Road.
Later the club moved to Alma Hill, Upholland and Winstanley
Road, Orrell.

In 1928 a permanent home was established behind the Abbey
Lakes Hotel, where a small hut served as the changing rooms;
washing came via a bucket or a dip in the lake. Orrell closed its
doors during World War Two. In 1945 they resumed playing
and celebrated Alan Ackers being picked by Lancashire.

In 1949 the club finally found a permanent home at Edge
Hall Road on the Western side of Wigan. Two years later, they
won the prestigious Caldy Sevens. A new clubhouse was opened
in 1955 with Orrell playing a Lancashire XV.

Orrell rose rapidly, and in 1964 recorded a victory over Fylde
– then one of the Lancashire elite. Eric Lyon was outstanding
for Orrell that day, and was picked as reserve for England v
Wales.

In 1972 Orrell produced their first international in prop
Frank Anderson, who played for England against the All Blacks.
Legend has it that Anderson was
fourth choice, but all the more
highly-rated props went down
with injury or illness. The club
also had four players in the
Lancashire team who won the
County Championship. One of
the quartet, Des Seabrook, later
became the club's long-serving
coach. Des was associated with
Orrell for 30 years as a player,
coach and administrator, yet
perhaps his finest hour was
coaching the North to victory
over the 1979 All Blacks.

Des Seabrook

Orrell became regular winners of the Lancashire Cup in the
1970s, but were still unfashionable. In 1980 they established
their credentials by winning the Northern Merit Table.

The club took great pride in being amongst the best run clubs
in the UK. They had a streamlined administrative system, which
used the skills of volunteers. Gradually, the best North players
looked at Edge Hill Road as a place to be seen when looking
for representative honours.

In 1967 Chris Hesketh joined Orrell from West Park St
Helens. He moved to Salford RLFC, where he made 452
appearances, winning every honour the 13-man game can offer.
Another Salford acquisition from Orrell was Colin Clarke, who
made 431 appearances for the rugby league club.

One of the keys to Orrell's success was sheer good fortune;
their ground at Edge Hall Road was close to the new M6
motorway, which made it easy for visiting teams to find them.

Gradually Orrell became one of
the best grounds in British rugby,
but many top sides shunned the
new upstart club. Their cause was
boosted in 1980 when winger
John Carleton established himself
as one of Europe's top three-
quarters. He won 26 England
caps and was capped on the 1980
Lions tour of South Africa.

Orrell established themselves as
one of the North's top sides when
leagues were formed in 1987. Five
years later, they tied for first position
in Division One with Bath, but

John Carleton

their rivals were champions on points difference. It proved a high
point for Orrell, whose fine team had been together for nearly a
decade. They later recruited an England scrum-half, Dewi Morris,
who won 29 caps during the Grand Slam era of the early 1990s.

The arrival of professionalism at the same time made life
difficult for Orrell because bigger clubs could pay bigger wages.
Orrell's modest gates meant their best players were easy pickings
for rugby league clubs and the big RU clubs in the south. What
was once Orrell's strength became their weakness. Being well run
was an asset that was of no value in the professional age unless
you stayed amateur, which Orrell didn't. In 2001 Orrell seemed
to have found a saviour when Dave Whelan, Wigan's foremost
businessman, bought the club as part of his sporting empire
that included Wigan football club and Wigan Warriors RLFC.
He even changed the rugby union club's name to Wigan Orrell
RUFC. Whelan bought the club, its pitch and the clubhouse.

On the field, Orrell lost two of its finest servants in the Cusani
Brothers, Dave and Charles, who were two of the foremost lock
forwards of the era. Dave Cusani won an England cap.

In 2004 an audacious bid was made to buy Orrell lock, stock
and barrel. The bidders, a group of South Africans, wanted to
move Orrell RUFC to London and to rename it the 'London
Tribe'. The colourful idea was to have a top class Springbok side
in English rugby. The bid was rejected.

Despite the changes, Orrell – with an inexperienced squad
– were relegated from National One. Two more successive
relegations followed as terrible results became the norm.

On 21st April 2007, they vacated Edge Hall Road for a local school pitch. They found themselves without a clubhouse and had to use the nearby Station Hotel as a headquarters.

Today they play in South Lancs & Cheshire leagues, having returned to being an amateur club.

PRENTON

'Prenton is a damp winding verdurous place.'
Nathanial Hawthorne

IN 1992, PRENTON RUFC was formed from two of the Wirral's clubs, Old Rockferrians and Old Instonians. Old Rockferrians were formed in the 1920s by the old boys of Rockferry Grammar School, who had produced an international in George Owen, who played in the centre for England after moving to Birkenhead Park. A Rockferry RFC existed in 1876 and provided two players, J.B. Parry and E.C. Kendal, to the first Cheshire side who played Liverpool at Edge Hill that year. Old Instonians were the former pupils of Birkenhead Institute, who played their rugby at West Kirby. The Institute had begun on Wetstone Lane before moving to Bidston. Both grammar schools became comprehensive in the 1970s and the decline of schools rugby impacted on the respective old boys clubs.

Eventually the two clubs decided to come together on OR's ground at Prenton. A change of name took place to seal the union. Today, Prenton are a prosperous club in the South Lancashire & Cheshire leagues.

(Thanks to John Percival)

PRESTON GRASSHOPPERS

"You know things are bad at Hoppers when we count the postage stamps at a committee meeting."
John Hetherington

PRESTON GRASSHOPPERS RFC were formed on 28th September 1869 at the Bull Hotel in the town centre. The club took its quaint name from a side at Cheltenham College. Several of the original Preston players attended the College, where there is a traditional annual game between 'Grasshoppers' and 'Fireflies'.

Preston had its own code of rules. Indeed, the early minute book records that the club declined an early fixture unless the game was played according to 'Grasshoppers Rules'.

There is a report from February 1870 of Hoppers playing Manchester at Winckley Meadows near Penwortham Bridge. It states, "the Prestonians did not get the worst share of the bruises, bleeding noses, discoloured eyes, bruised shins and other marks of assault". A subsequent match against Liverpool was stopped after a player had his teeth knocked out.

From the start, Hoppers were one of the leading clubs in the North of England, with a high quality fixture list from the earliest days: Manchester, Liverpool, Birkenhead Park and Sale were regular opponents.

The Hunt and Hornby brothers.

By 1877 Hoppers provided five members of the Lancashire XV: J. Hulton (Half-back), R. Hunt (Three-quarters-back), F. Storey (Forward), W. Hunt (Forward) and A.N. Hornby (Captain and Back). Additionally, the club could boast four internationals, namely Hornby and the three brothers: J.T., R.H. and W.H. Hunt.

Albert Hornby (1847-1925) and his brother C.L. Hornby – who also played for Hoppers – were Old Harrovians. They were members of the pioneering Butterflies cricket club in 1865 along with school friends Arthur Guillemond and Charles Alcock, who became influential figures in the FA and RFU respectively. Hornby was famous at Harrow for his "sublime indifference to education". He was a staunch opponent of hacking after an incident which left him unconscious from the footwork of the opposition. He played for Hoppers for ten seasons from 1870 and was a three-quarter for England between 1877 and 1882, winning nine caps. Hornby was the first man to captain England at cricket and rugby and later had a long association with Manchester FC. He was also President of the Lancashire RFU from 1884 to 1914.

The Hunt Brothers, William, Robert and James, all won England caps in the early days. William won four caps, including one for the 1877 England v Ireland match, which was the first international match involving teams of fifteen players.

Hoppers ran into troubled times in the 1890s due to their loyalty to the RFU. They suffered because many of their regular – and most attractive – opponents had joined the NU. A compensation was that Lancashire saw Hoppers as the backbone of the county side because nobody else was available and a number of members received England trials. Brothers Stanley and Lewis Smith both played for Cumberland; later Stanley Smith, a Hopper, went with the Australian Waratahs to Argentina. Arthur Blakiston turned out for Hoppers before gaining 17 England caps whilst with Northampton.

After World War One, Hoppers played on the banks of the River Ribble, opposite Avenham Park, and the teams changed at the Bull and Royal Hotel. The club were fortunate to draw some good players from apprentices at the Dick Kerr Works in

The Hoppers in action in 1931.

the nearby Strand Road Factory (later part of English Electric and BAE).

In 1925 the Club took a ten-year lease on a disused cycle track ground at Farringdon Park, which adjoined the Preston Cemetery. Without a club bar, the landlord of The Cemetery public house turned a blind eye to licensing regulations, which proved very helpful but confusing; when the doors of the hotel opened for the general public at 6pm they encountered Hoppers leaving. In 1929 the club granted sub-tenancy to a Speedway team, which went into liquidation after about three years.

The early 1930s saw two significant events: Dr Joe Stewart from Belfast was picked for Ireland whilst playing for Hoppers – the first Hopper for 50 years to be capped. Then in 1932 the club left Farringdon Park after buying farm land at Lea on the west side of the town. Unfortunately, the pitches were still used for cattle-grazing and there were continual problems with cattle droppings and the rough state of the turf. These problems caused a fall in the club's status.

Hoppers kept going during World War Two due to the large number of servicemen billeted in the area. The situation continued after the war, which provided the club with the services of Don Rutherford, the Lions and England full-back, who was stationed with the RAF.

As a club, Hoppers were held back because their ground at Lea was prone to vandalism as suburbia moved closer to Lea. Fortunately, in 1973 the club swapped Lea for the farmland of Lightfoot Green on the north side of town. Lightfoot Green had been a former pig farm.

All was not perfect for several reasons: despite wonderful facilities, financial problems dogged the club and the junior pitches retained the residue of their previous incumbents. The previous use of the pitches was sometimes apparent during matches; one player recalls a scrum collapsing in the mud and suddenly becoming aware of the aroma of "aftershave, perspiration and pig shit".

During this era, some junior matches had to be played on pitches that didn't yet have goalposts. This required the referee to keep diagrams of the penalties and conversions that he awarded during the match. After their match, the two teams were taken on the First XV pitch after the premier side had finished their match, where both sides then had to recreate the kicks

The first team itself suffered because they had to rely on local talent, who were always vulnerable to 'offers' (of an amateur nature, of course) from other local clubs. Consequently, fine players such as Brian Ashton and Keith Aitchison drifted off to bigger clubs in search of success.

In 1988 Steve Kerry switched to Salford RLFC from Hoppers, where he was the leading point scorer in English RU. He made 105 appearances for Salford.

Wade Dooley

Hoppers' most famous son is Wade Dooley, a giant lock-forward who began playing rugby league as a boy in Warrington. When he joined the local police, he tried union with Hoppers, where he was coached by Dick Greenwood, an England selector. At the time, England had a plethora of good, but unexceptional, lock-forwards. Greenwood gambled his reputation that Dooley was better than any other candidate. The 'big fella' admits that on his debut the pace was breathtaking, but he justified Greenwood's opinion and became an integral part of the 1990s Grand Slam side and first choice for the 1988 Lions side to Australia.

Another England player of the era was Paul Grayson, who began his career at Preston. Grayson was an accomplished soccer player in his youth and played for Accrington Stanley before trying his luck as a fly-half with Hoppers. He did well enough to move to Waterloo and Northampton, and won England and Lions caps. He joined Northampton in 1993 and went on to score 2,784 points in 259 games. He won a Heineken Cup winners' medal in 2000, and also scored 400 points in 32 appearances for England – a total exceeded only by Jonny Wilkinson. Grayson later became Saints coach.

Other England players who began at Hoppers were Will Greenwood, Pat Sanderson and Steve Borthwick. Steve joined Hoppers from Hutton GS. Steve's ambition was to play for Preston North End, but he was selected for England Schools at rugby, much to his own surprise. As a 6ft 6 ins junior at Hoppers, he went to see the club manager, Ken Moore, and said: "Ken, Bath have offered me a lot of money to join them. What should I do?" Ken said simply: "Bite their hand off". Steve left Hoppers and eventually won 57 England caps and captained his country on 21 occasions. He also holds the record for having played more games than any other Premiership player.

Hoppers in 2015 are one of the friendliest clubs in rugby. Their ambitions are tempered by financial realism, and they are content to play at Level Four with a team recruited from the ranks of its hugely successful junior rugby set up.

(Thanks to Les Anson, George Thompson,
Ken Moore, John Hetherington et al)

OLD HUTTONIANS

AN OLD HUTTONIANS side was formed in 1927 by the Old Boys of Hutton Grammar School, which lies three miles southwest of Preston. Old Huttonians merged with Preston Grasshoppers in 1932.

ROCHDALE

THE TEXTILE INDUSTRY made Rochdale a boomtown in the 19th century, when it gave birth to the Co-operative Movement. All social classes in Rochdale played rugby – although they did so at different clubs. The earliest recorded rugby involves two sides called Rochdale Juniors and Rakebank, who merged in 1867 as Rochdale United.

R.R. Osborne

The town's most famous club is Rochdale Hornets, who were formed in April 1871 and went on to become a major force in the professional ranks. A year earlier, an upper-class club called 'Rochdale RFC' had emerged. Their most famous son was R.R. Osborne (1848-1926), who played full-back for England against Scotland in the first ever international match in 1871. Osborne was huge in stature, which didn't stop him being flattened by a Scottish forward in the match. Little is known of 'RR', but we know more about his brother, John Osborne. He was the King's jockey and later a legendary trainer of racehorses.

The first Rochdale RFC disappeared in the 1880s and the mantle of the most successful side in town passed to the Hornets. They produced a number of international players, including a British Isles player in John Nolan, who toured Australia and New Zealand in 1888. Hornets were one of the original Northern Union rebels in 1895 and proved one of the most durable rebel clubs, surviving into the 21st century.

A new Rochdale RUFC emerged in 1905, but lasted only seven years. The present club was formed in 1921 by a small band of enthusiasts who met in Smiths Cafe, Townhead. The chairman of this inaugural meeting was Joseph Rigg. The first games were played at Firgrove, but the permanent foundations of the club were laid at Balderstone on ground which was later occupied by Rochdale Grammar School (latterly Balderstone Community School). G.B. Johnston and H.D. Clayton shared the captaincy for nine years. Rochdale were an attractive side to watch, which guaranteed good crowds in a rugby-mad town.

Unfortunately, Rochdale Corporation took over the Balderstone pitches in the early 1930s and the club had

to move to the 'Moss ground' at Norden. The years at Norden were highly successful with regards to results on the pitch.

In the 1950s the club moved to Bamford nearer the town centre. By 1965 the club had several first-class fixtures and Eddie Deasey had been selected to play for Lancashire. Development at their Bamford home continued with the building of a new bathhouse and bar. Still under the presidency of Joseph Rigg, the club grew in strength.

The 1980s saw the development of another golden team, of which the formidable wing forwards R. Fitton and R. Hartley will not be forgotten. As captains and as players they helped to push Rochdale (literally) through the decade. If the players of the 1980s achieved new heights, the officials were never far behind. Following a serious fire, a committee of commitment oversaw the construction of the Osborne Suite development.

In the 1990s Chairman Tom Downham-Clark led the club through a revival in both financial and rugby terms. The result was two league wins and a new belief in the club. The wins on the field had a healthy effect on the social life at the club.

In the new millennium, Chairman Mike Holden took things to new heights. Mike's vision and drive led the club through the construction of a fine new clubhouse and the reconstruction and drainage of all the rugby pitches (which has dispelled the widespread view that Rochdale's pitches are mudbaths).

Under the guidance of Head Coach Mick Gould, the First XV achieved three league wins (plus three Lancashire Trophy triumphs). This gave Rochdale its highest ever league ranking (at level 5) in National Division 3 North. In addition to the four existing playing pitches, in 2009-10 a fully reconstructed and drained training area with floodlights was created from unused club land ('the Hollow') with the aid of an RFU grant. This was to accommodate the greatly increased demand for training facilities by all age groups.

One player who came right through the Mini & Juniors and Colts teams is first team fly-half Steven Collins, who in 2010 played for the Lancashire County XV in their four County Championship games, culminating in a victory over Gloucestershire at Twickenham. Steven led the back-line superbly, scoring 57 points in the four games, and was selected by the county as joint Lancashire Player of the Season. Steven

Rochdale in action in 2008.

was subsequently approached by Fylde, and agreed to sign for their successful team. He still maintains a regular attendance at the Rochdale club.

January 2010 also saw the club gain the RFU's 'Whole Club Seal of Approval', one of the first clubs in the North of England to achieve this prestigious award. Season 2010-11 saw a rare blip when the first team were relegated from National Division 3 North to North 1 West

The 21st century sees Rochdale RUFC as one of the best sides in Lancashire with excellent facilities.

WHITWORTH

Whitworth is the eastern suburb of Rochdale. As a village, Whitworth was famous for the Taylors, a family of doctors who discovered the value of resetting bones in the 18th century – something to which many a rugby player owes a debt. The first Whitworth rugby club, known as the 'Brownbacks', won the Rochdale Charity Cup in 1890. The original club joined the Northern Union in 1897, but went bankrupt in 1901. A second Whitworth rugby club was formed in 1996 and operated on an occasional basis.

RUNCORN

THE INDUSTRIAL TOWN of Runcorn, on the banks of the River Mersey, has known several rugby teams over the centuries. The original club was nicknamed 'The Linnetts' because of their yellow and green jerseys. But the name has a dark origin for, in Victorian times, most of the workers were employed in the town's copper factories and suffered from copper poisoning. The copper filings and its residue that the workers handled every day caused poisoning that gave the workers a 'greeney-yellow' facial colouring.

The first town club was formed in 1876 as Runcorn YMCA and operated from Greenway Road. The 'YMCA' suffix was dropped in 1878, and the following year they moved to Canal Street. The most famous players associated with the original Runcorn club were Sam Houghton (1870-1920) and Harry Speakman. Houghton won two England caps in 1892 and 1896. Speakman was a three-quarter on the first British Lions tour to Australia and New Zealand. He impressed the Australians enough to be offered a well-paid job and he (not surprisingly) never returned.

Harry Speakman and Sam Houghton

Runcorn were a top-class side around this time. They defeated mighty Cardiff in 1886-87 when the Welshmen ventured north. Records of Cardiff matches noted that "Runcorn were the best side that they had met". But all was not plain sailing for the Linnetts; on one occasion they travelled to Sale by a canal barge that ran aground and they missed the prestigious fixture.

Runcorn's decline was brought about by their decision to join the original 22 rebels who formed the Northern Union. They stuck with the Northern Union until the Great War, when their Canal Street ground was bought by the local soccer enthusiasts, who insisted the ground only be used for association football. The Linnetts switched to soccer and have been a major force in the northern semi-professional game ever since.

A Runcorn RUFC operated in the 1930s, but did not reform after World War Two. Whitehouse Park RUFC operated in the town from the 1960s and changed their name to Runcorn RUFC in 1997 in recognition of their hometown roots.

SALE
(Sale Sharks and Sale Amateurs)

"Turn right at the launderette."
Advice to anyone trying to find the original club

THE CITY OF Manchester stretches for miles, and the affluent suburb of Sale has long since been absorbed into the city's expansion. But until 1849, when the railway arrived, Sale was just a small village. The railway made Sale suitable for commuters looking to escape the Mancunian smog.

Rugby football was played as a winter pastime at Sale Cricket Club from 1861 to 1865. Alfred Ollivant was the driving force as he persuaded a few cricketing colleagues to form Sale FC on October 14th 1865 at the local Drill Room. Sale have minute books from 1865 and consider themselves as the oldest club with an unbroken history. Three years later, they adopted the famous blue and white striped jersey, which they have maintained with minor alterations until the professional era.

In the 1871-72 season, Sale won 11 of 14 matches despite not having a regular pitch. They had, however, a regular changing facility at the newly built Brooklands Hotel. A rival club, Northenden, operated in the next village, which created a shortage of experienced players. Sale struggled until the two clubs joined forces in January 1882.

Sale were badly affected by the Great Schism and many of its most lucrative fixtures disappeared overnight. On the eve of the 1896-97 season, Sale Club lost their ground near Brooklands Station, but, fortunately, they were able to lease a field adjoining Ashton-on-Mersey Cricket Club and changed at the Bull's Head in Cross Street, Sale.

In 1905 the club obtained the lease on a field nearer the village centre, at the end of Heywood Road. In 1920 the Heywood Road ground was bought and Sale FC formed with funds raised by the issue of shares. It has always been an oddity that one of Britain's premier rugby clubs was reached by "turning right at the launderette".

The period between the 1890s and World War One saw the club dominated by the five Hartley brothers: Charles, Alfred, Ernest, Louis and Edward. Two of the brothers captained Sale and also played cricket for Lancashire and rugby for the North of England. Charles Hartley was honorary secretary of both the club and Cheshire for 21 years. Alfred's four years of captaincy included 1911-12, when for the only time in its history the club was undefeated. The club record for that season reads: P26 W24 D2 L0 F490 A108.

The mid-1920s saw a new, young Sale team. Pat Davies (1903-1979) played for England in 1927 and appeared 48 times for Cheshire. It was the following decade before Sale finally achieved a top-class fixture list, when they also won the Middlesex Sevens at Twickenham, beating Blackheath in the final. Sale's team of Fyfe, Wooller, Davey, Noden, Mycock, Shaw and Reynolds included some of the best players in the club's history. Ken Fyfe joined Sale from Cambridge, having already collected nine caps for Scotland.

Wilfred Wooller was an attacking genius with incredible pace. He was spotted playing cricket, soccer and rugby at Rydal College as a schoolboy and was persuaded to join Sale before going up to Cambridge. His sporting prowess is astonishing; he won 18 Welsh rugby caps – including for one in Wales' historic victory over the All Blacks – represented Wales at squash, played soccer for Cardiff City, and was captain of Glamorgan CCC for 14 years. Wooller also spent three years in a Japanese prisoner-of-war camp during World War Two.

The Welsh connection also provided Sale with two other all-time greats: Claude Davey and Harold Sedgewick Sever. Davey joined Sale from Swansea in 1930 at the age of 20 with one Welsh cap. He played for Sale for six years, winning 22 more caps. His partner was a local lad, 'Hal' Sever, who joined Sale in 1929. He scored an amazing 57 tries for the club in a single season and also won 10 caps for England, scoring five tries.

During the 1930s, Sale's three-quarters were their main scoring instrument, but in the immediate post-war years, the balance of strength shifted to the forwards. This change led to an inevitable switch in the strategy of attack to one in which the forwards held the key. Jim Birtles joined Sale in 1935, captained the club during the Second World War and was match secretary for 36 years. A stand at Heywood Road was named after him. It was said, disparagingly, that the Birtles Stand held "40 spectators in comfort".

Joe Mycock was one of England's finest forwards, but World War Two overshadowed his achievements, which included captaining his country. Mycock played 43 times for Lancashire and 21 times for England, but 16 of his England appearances were in wartime internationals.

Great Sale players of the 1950s at Heywood Road included Bill Paterson and Peter Stagg, who both played for Scotland and the Lions. Jim Roberts was an outstanding winger for Sale and England.

The club, however, had an England great in Eric Evans, who led his country to the Grand Slam in 1957. Many legends abound about Eric and his fiery leadership. One official recalls entering the Lancashire dressing room to find Eric stood on the treatment table beseeching hellfire and damnation on the opposition. Another legend is that Eric, before an England v Wales international, deliberately knocked on the door of the Welsh dressing room during their warm-up and asked if anyone had any spare tape. Eric was one of the many local players who played for Manchester junior clubs before being invited to Heywood Road for trials.

Other players weren't as lucky as Eric, particularly in dealing with the club's committee, who could be notoriously fussy in the 1960s. One player recalls making his First XV debut for Sale and doing well. He left the field feeling proud until an elderly committee man collared him. The elderly man said: "You did well, young fellow, but you won't be playing again for the Firsts. You're just not good enough." The player never got over the double-edged compliment, or the crass way it was delivered.

Eric Evans

Dick Trickey had a problem with selectors at a higher level; he was perhaps the best uncapped lock of the era. A product of Giggleswick School, he was a Sale and Lancashire regular for a decade, and played for the North West Counties in their victories over the 1970s Wallabies and 1972 All Blacks. Dick was associated with Sale for 40 years as a player and administrator.

Richard Trickey

The late 1960s saw Sale below their traditional best, which caused a fall in gate receipts and membership. In 1969-70 F.G. (Freddie) Griffiths was appointed first team coach, and with Alan Morritt as captain they oversaw a significant improvement in the First XV results. That season Sale played 40, Won 32, Lost 8, For 644, Against 291, and they won the Sunday Telegraph Northern Pennant and the Cheshire Cup.

After Eric Evans had led England to a Grand Slam in 1957, the country had to wait until 1980 for a repeat. Sale men Fran Cotton, Steve Smith and Tony Bond – along with former Heywood Road favourite John Horton – were pivotal to the 1980 Grand Slam. Fran Cotton played on three Lions' tours and was manager of the Lions in 1997, when they won the series in South Africa. He also captained the North West in 1972, when the region became the first in England to beat the All Blacks. Sale were represented that day by Cotton, scrum-half Steve Smith, hooker John Lansbury and Dick Trickey. Six years later, Cotton and Smith became virtually unique in English rugby history to have twice overcome the All Blacks when they

Sale in action in 1988.

played for the North XV who defeated the New Zealanders at Otley. The 1979 North team included hooker Andy Simpson and centres Tony Wright and Tony Bond from Sale.

The 1980s saw Sale overtake Broughton Park as Manchester's premier side, but an ambitious and previously unheralded rival emerged from only 20 miles away: Orrell. In 20 years, Orrell rose from junior ranking status to the new Premiership. Their dynamic approach to amateur rugby and recruitment of top players pushed Sale off their pinnacle.

The retirement of Smith, Cotton and company lead to a downturn in the club's fortunes. They were in National Two when Paul Turner, the veteran Welsh Fly-half, was coaxed to Heywood Road as player/coach. Turner won only four Welsh caps due to the brilliance of Jonathon Davies, but was a unique player who could win any match with deadly accuracy as a goal-kicker and a gift for improvisation. Turner became famous for a trick move where, in full flight, he deliberately used his knee to control the ball. It took pure improvisation, but was a play he had perfected over hours of practice. Turner galvanised an ordinary side into a promotion side. He brought the best out of underrated players like Dave Baldwin, Jim Mallinder and Mike Kendrick. Sale were back amongst Britain's big clubs, but, without warning, Turner was sacked as coach.

John Mitchell, the All Black flanker, replaced Turner and continued the upturn in Sale's fortunes. He helped develop David Rees, Jim Mallinder, Phil Greening, Steve Hanley and Barrie John Mather into England internationals, but Sale's modest gates meant they couldn't cope financially with the richer southern clubs. Mitchell achieved miracles on limited resources. He took Sale to the 1998 Pilkington Cup final (losing 9-3 to Leicester) and provided five players to England, but was sacked as coach in March 1999. Mitchell joined England as the forwards coach before taking the post of New Zealand coach in 2001.

The drain on finances of trying to compete in the First Division led to a consortium taking over the running of the professional team, but relegation loomed until the businessman Brain Kennedy stepped in. When Kennedy bought Sale, they were relegation favourites. He is reported to have made his arrival known to the players by reading them all the newspaper cuttings predicting their relegation. The club was rebranded as Sale Sharks.

Five years later, half the team were internationals. High profile players were recruited, including Scotland captain Bryan Redpath and a convert from rugby league, Jason Robinson. Robinson quickly established himself in the England rugby union team and was rewarded with a Lions' tour at the end of his first season after switching codes. Apollo Perelini, who played for Samoa in a World Cup, also made the switch from rugby league, serving the Sharks well until retiring from the game. And other internationals who have joined the ranks at Heywood Road include England's Kevin Yates; Scots Iain Fullarton, Jason White and Barry Stewart; Springbok Braam van Straaten; and Aussie Graeme Bond.

Jason Robinson and Mark Cueto, two of Sale's more recent Lions.

The turnaround in the fortunes of the Sharks was initially achieved by the coaching duo Jim Mallinder and Steve Diamond, former players who created a strong family ethic in the squad. They also added talented players like Andrew Sheridan and Matt Cairns to the Sharks' squad, who both toured with England along with a bevy of their new clubmates.

Part of the rebranding involved the Sharks moving to Edgeley Park, home of Stockport County. The move worked as the new club again reached the final of the 2004 National Knockout Cup, but were runners-up to Newcastle Falcons.

The Sale Amateur club stayed at Heywood Road, whilst Sale Sharks professional club made the best ever start to the season under Director of Rugby Philippe Saint-Andre and forwards coach Kingsley Jones. When charismatic flanker Sebastien Chabal joined from Bourgoin, France, he wasn't able to speak English. He later became that rarest of birds: a French international playing abroad. Andrew Sheridan, at tight-head prop, proved another man mountain. Mark Cueto set a club record of 14 tries in 11 consecutive matches for Sale. A good soccer player, he tried rugby for Altrincham Kersal and was spotted by Sale Sharks. He played for the 2004 Lions after making his England debut against Canada in 2004.

2005-06 saw Sale Sharks as Premiership champions, and in the following seasons they were always close to honours, but were pipped at the post by southern clubs.

2012-13 was an unusual season. The Sharks moved to the brand new Salford City Stadium at Barton, and they recruited two colourful characters in Danny Cipriani and Andy Powell. Danny Cipriani arrived with a reputation for making headlines. Andy Powell was best known for one incident; after a Wales match, he borrowed a golf cart and drove down the M4 motorway to buy a chocolate bar.

On the field, the Sharks struggled, but a revival followed, and the club reached the European Champions Cup in 2014.

SALE AMATEURS

SALE FC, ALSO known as 'Sale Amateurs', emerged in 2002. When Sale Amateurs were formed, Sue Gardiner, Sale's President, rang up the RFU and said they wanted to join the RFU. "What's the club, where's your ground and what are your colours?" came the request from an RFU official, blissfully unaware that the club had been formed 140 years earlier.

Sale were one of the north's top sides from the 1930s until they embraced professionalism in the 1990s. Their Heywood Road was deemed too small for the brave new world of the Premiership and brand 'Sale Sharks' was invented in Stockport, some eight miles east.

The Heywood Road ground remained in the ownership of the old amateur club when the Sharks moved on and Sale FC filled the breach. Heywood Road doesn't attract thousands of spectators anymore, but visiting teams are flabbergasted to find they run out onto one of rugby's finest stadiums. 2011 saw Sale FC celebrate their 150th anniversary.

In 2012 Sale reached North One West after a 36-match winning run.

Sale on the attack in 2015.

SALFORD

_"Salford is a working class club that does not contain
any gentlemen."_
J. Daniels, 1896

IN THE OLD 20-a-side days of 1873, Salford RFC was
formed by pupils of Cavendish Street Chapel, a Sunday school
off Manchester Road. The link to the church was severed two
years later when the club was renamed 'Cavendish FC'. Four
years later they became 'Salford RFC'. The club had a variety
of pitches, mainly on the north side of the city. The south side
already had a team named 'Crescent RFC', who merged with
Salford in the early 1880s.

The merger gave Salford a great acquisition in Harry Eagles,
who was to be Salford's first international for England. Oddly,
the England match was cancelled, but Eagles was 'capped'
nonetheless. He was never recalled to the team. Three years
later Tom Kent, formerly of Bury, won six England caps whilst
playing for Salford. Kent and Eagles were two of four Salford
players invited to tour Australia and New Zealand with the first
'British Isles' rugby team of 1888. The other Salford players were
Sam Williams and Jack Anderton. Their selection is unusual
because many of the party were middle-class characters and
Salford were viewed as a working-class side.

Swinton RFC were Salford's arch-rivals, and their first visit
to Salford attracted over 13,000 spectators. This attendance
was greater than the one that watched Salford lose to the 1889
Maoris. In 1892-93, Salford were the first Lancashire club
champions. Unfortunately, they were hauled before the county
authorities for offering J.W. Wherwell of Radcliffe the sum of
£2 a week to join them. Salford were found guilty and were
suspended for the rest of the season

Salford initially declined to join the NU breakaway, but,
finding they'd lost all their best fixtures, agreed to join in 1896.
The 'Reds' have remained members of the rugby league ever
since.

SEDGLEY PARK

SEDGLEY PARK RUFC take their name from an area of
north Manchester. Oddly, the rugby club has never played in
the village that bears its name. They were founded in 1932
following Kersal's move from Prestwich to Stretford.

Sedgley Park began playing in a farmer's field at Prince's Park
in Whitefield, which had a disused cowshed that was used as
the changing accommodation. By 1935 Sedgley were fielding
three teams each Saturday and they built a clubhouse costing
£300.

The early 1950s saw the members extend the clubhouse and
undertake a major drainage operation on the pitch. It was all
for nothing, as in August 1953 – a week before the start of the
season – the club was informed that their rented ground had
been sold to build a school. The club had not been warned of the
sale due to 'an oversight'. Matters were dire, and soon Sedgley
did not have enough players to field two sides. However, the
entire club met each Saturday at the Temperance Bar where

they had been formed and divided the total number of players
between the two sides. This meant the first and second teams
both played short for the entire season. The first team won two
games in 1953-54; the second team failed to win one match.
But the gamble paid off, and in the following season the club
were back to two full sides plus reserves.

In 1966 the club fielded a regular Colts XV for the first
time – the first step in what was to become an explosion of
youth rugby in the 1980s. A bold decision was made to build a
large clubhouse. Soon Park had the best facilities in local rugby,
but the view from the luxurious upstairs bar was uninspiring:
two acres of mud, glorious mud. Opponents called the ground
'Sludgley Park'. Gradually, hard work by the members improved
the situation.

Sedgley had an unusual problem during a match in 1980,
when a visiting player dived for the try line and felt a burning
sensation on his arms. An ambulance was called and the player
taken to hospital. The doctor diagnosed that the try lines had
been erroneously marked out using a dangerous chemical that
was hazardous to humans. The club acted quickly to prevent the
mistake being made again.

Sedgley were rising through the ranks and became the best
club in north Manchester. In 1993 Sedgley acquired the services
of two former Orrell stalwarts – Ken Fletcher as coach and
the giant Bob Kimmins as captain. Success was immediate and
spectacular as the club gained promotion in three successive
seasons. The club were determined the improvement wasn't
going to be temporary, and under the leadership of chairman
David Smith, Sedgley embarked upon a massive programme
of expansion and improvement. A large field was purchased
nearby, big enough for three more pitches, whilst the main
pitch was upgraded to meet their continuing ambition.

Sedgley were
promoted to National
Two in 2001, under
coach Tim Fourie, with
a team that included
internationals Christian
Raducani (Romania)
and Colin Stephens
(Wales). Three years
later, they were
bidding for promotion
to National One. In
2006, the club changed
their name to Sedgley
Tigers. Currently they
are one of the top sides
in National Two.

Sedgley Park in action in 2004.

(Thanks to Dave & John Smith)

SEFTON

SEFTON RUFC WAS founded as the Aliens RFC in 1907 by a number of Liverpool schoolmasters, and for the first two years membership was restricted to the teaching profession. The Aliens found life difficult because they had no home pitch and they had to play all their early matches on opponents' grounds. However their first season figures were encouraging (P18 W7 D1 L10). Total expenditure for the season was £3.96p and the assets were listed as one ball and two jerseys.

Eventually the Aliens found a pitch at Clubmoor Cricket Club, but later had to move to Townsend Lane. The club improved rapidly, and by 1913 had fixtures with many senior clubs, notably Birkenhead Park.

After Wold War One the club changed its name to Sefton, but still struggled to find a home. Eventually, in 1929, the present ground was bought, mainly through the efforts of the club's trustees, F.J. Applebee, W.B. Croxford (a well-known player and sports journalist) and H.A. Munro. The euphoria of possessing a settled home didn't last because the club's pitches were commandeered during World War Two by an anti-aircraft battery. The base units of two enormous anti-aircraft guns were buried down to 40ft for stability in the middle of the pitches.

Sefton recovered the ground in 1955 and have continued to operate in the area whilst drawing juniors from Cardinal Heenan and West Derby Schools. In the 1984-85 season, Sefton won the Liverpool Cup 23-9 in a hard-fought match against Merseyside Police at Aigburth.

The club are one of the middle-ranking clubs in the South Lancashire and Cheshire leagues.

SOUTHPORT

"Southport is a dreary sandbank at the lower end of a bay, seventeen fathoms deep, which is now chocked up with sand."
Anon (1792)

THE WEST LANCASHIRE town of Southport is more famous for golf than rugby, but the holiday resort has a long history of the oval ball. There are records of a Southport RFC playing Manchester in 1870, but the first Southport RFC was founded on 29th November 1872, which makes the club the eighth oldest in the world. That year Southport played Birkenhead Park at the Lower Park and the score was 0-0. Three years later, Wigan played Southport. Another rugby side called Southport Olympic occur in the record books in Victorian times.

The first notable player to join Southport was Herbert 'Pinkie' Booth of Bedford. He left the Midlands side to play for Leigh, a club who were noted for paying amateurs at the time. He subsequently left Leigh and joined Southport.

Southport's next notable son was Leonard Haigh (1880-1916), who played for England on seven occasions in 1910-11. Haigh is recorded as having played for a side called 'Sandringham House RFC' in Southport. Haigh subsequently joined Manchester, where he won his England caps. He died in World War One.

Southport had a top quality fixture list between the wars. They bought a large ground near Hillside railway station in 1928, and with their excellent facilities they were able to host the Lancashire v Cumberland game in 1937. Southport were so proud of the occasion they persuaded the Mayor of Southport to welcome the teams when they arrived at Hillside station.

The Southport club closed down during World War Two and many of the club's best players travelled the 20 miles to Wigan.

Leonard Haigh

After the war, Southport produced a string of top-class players. J. Nichol was an outstanding goal-kicker, R. Scott was a versatile three-quarter for Lancashire, and Peter Eastwood began at Southport before having a distinguished playing career with Richmond, Hampshire & the Combined Services.

Gordon Rimmer and Sam Perry were both products of King George V School in the town and played for Southport before moving to Waterloo. Rimmer, a scrum-half, won 12 England

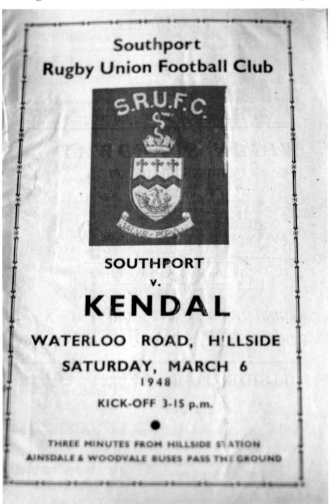

Gordon Rimmer

caps between 1949 and 1954 and played for the 1950 Lions. Sam Perry, a lock, won seven England caps between 1947 and 1948.

Harry Foster was one of the best Lancashire players of the mid-1950s. He began at Southport, but moved to Waterloo and was a member of Lancashire's county title-winning squad.

Southport tried to reverse the habit of good players departing in the early 1980s, when an adventurous recruitment policy saw them rise to rank amongst the best sides in the north west. The catalyst was recruiting prop Frank Anderson from Orrell as player/coach. A bear of a man, Anderson had been the first Orrell player to play for England when he propped against the 1972 All Blacks. He was never recalled to the England colours, but gave Southport several successful seasons.

Southport have settled for middle-ranking since the arrival of leagues. Their best player of recent times is Iain Greenhalgh, a talented fly-half who represented Lancashire. A progressive, community club, Southport's annual Junior Rugby festival attracts thousands of youngsters

ST EDWARDS OLD BOYS

St Edwards School, Liverpool was founded in the 19th century as 'The Catholic Institute'. The school was taken over by the Christian Brothers in 1909 and renamed in 1920. The Christian Brothers were famous for their toughness, in and out of the classroom, and produced many rugby players who embodied that ethos.

St Edwards OBs were formed in 1950. Within four years, the fledgling club had reached the final of the Caldy Sevens – a major competition for Northern clubs – and were Caldy champions in 1958 and 1990, as well as Wallasey Sevens champions in 1989 and 1990.

'Old Teds' played at Yew Tree Drive, Liverpool for the first 30 years, which was followed by a move to the college playing fields at Sandfield Park. The advent of leagues has seen the club amongst the most successful of Old Boys sides in the North of England, although they now have 'gone open' and welcome all-comers. They were unbeaten champions of NW West 2 in 1985-86 and NW West 1 four years later.

Two of their players, Ted Rudd and Mike Slemen, have played on the wing for England. Ted Rudd won six caps in the mid-1960s after winning a Blue with Oxford. Rudd was the cousin of another England man, Tom Brophy. Mike Slemen won 31 caps during a great era of English rugby whilst with Liverpool St Helens. Other top class players who began with St Edwards

OBs include Dave Lupton (Liverpool St Helens) and Justin Cunningham (South East Asia).

(Thanks to Richard Ellis)

ST. HELENS

"St Helens lacks the cosmopolitan charm and sophistication of Liverpool."
Watcyn Thomas

THE LANCASHIRE TOWN of St Helens is famous for two things: glassmaking and rugby. St Helens RLFC are giants of the 13-man sport, but several other rugby sides have played in the locality.

PILKINGTON RECS

St. Helens Recreation RFC was founded on 19th November 1873 by William Herman, a chemist who worked at Pilkington Crown Glass Works. Their first game was against Liverpool Royal Infirmary on 31st January 1874, at the Recreation Cricket Ground, Boundary Road. Recs competed in the West Lancashire League and Border Towns Cup. In their inaugural season (1885-86), they reached the semi-finals of the Border Town Cup, losing to Aspull. Two years later 10,000 spectators saw Recs lose to Wigan in the same competition. They subsequently produced Jimmy Pyke, who won England international honours against Wales in 1892, and William Pilkington (1877-1935) of the famous family and who won an England cap.

In 1895 Recs remained stoutly loyal to rugby union, despite the town team switching to the Northern Union. The club supplied Lancashire with half a dozen county players during the season. The Great Schism cost Recs most of their fixtures, which damaged their finances, and in April 1896 they joined the NU. The NU could only initially offer friendly games, which exacerbated the club's problems. The end of Recs came in 1898 when it was decided to disband the rugby team.

ST. HELENS RUFC

St Helens OBs was formed in 1919 by Mr. E.A.A. Varnish, headmaster of the Cowley School. The first club president was William Pilkington, the St Helens Recs international. Until 1926 home games were played at Cowley School, and even after a move to St. Helens Cricket Club the players still changed at the school. The club set about buying a ground, and in 1930 land at Moss Lane was purchased for £1,000. In 1932, "Old Boys" was dropped from the club name.

The club's first international was Watcyn Thomas, who moved to Lancashire from Llanelli. Thomas was regarded as one of the best Welsh forwards of the inter-war years, but the Welsh selectors

Watcyn Thomas

ostracised him for leaving Llanelli. His 'crime' was that he went North in 1929 to teach at Cowley School, St. Helens and to play for Waterloo. Legend has it that he had upset the selectors by speaking his mind and ignoring their advice. He was recalled as Welsh captain in 1933 and led the principality to their first victory at Twickenham for 25 years.

In 1936 Thomas joined King Edward's School, Birmingham. His principal legacy in Birmingham was developing the England School RU. He wrote a colourful autobiography called Rugby-Playing Man (1977).

After World War Two, J.W. "Jumbo" Scott, who was capped 18 times for Scotland, was St Helens captain. He led the club during its "golden era" when the Sunday Times reported, "in the second class, St. Helens are supreme and rising gradually to first-class status". In 1960 Ray French became the club's first Barbarian, and in 1961 he became the first and only player to be selected for England from St. Helens. He won four caps for England before switching to rugby league. He later combined teaching at Cowley School with his role as a BBC rugby league commentator.

The 1970s witnessed a decline in St. Helens' fortunes. They began the decade under the captaincy of Geoff Pimblett at the top of the Sunday Telegraph Pennant table. But Pimblett moved to rugby league and the team failed to win any of the remaining pennant games that season. The next important departure was that of fly-half John Horton to Sale during the 1971-72 season. Horton eventually became the first choice for the England No. 10 jersey. He was followed in the subsequent season by Dave Gullick, who went to Orrell and was a reserve on the 1971 Lions Tour.

The major beneficiary of the decline were neighbours Waterloo, who recruited players from their rivals. In 1977 Waterloo included six former St. Helens players in their John Player Cup final squad. The surviving St. Helens team was weak and members put a great deal of time and energy into re-building the side.

In 1981 Nigel Heslop won a place in the England Colts side, where he was joined the following season by twins John and Dave Ingram. All three took part in St Helens' victory over Orrell in the 1981 Lancashire Cup final. Ironically, Heslop moved to Orrell and won England honours.

Fred Howard joined St. Helens RUFC as a schoolboy in 1966, but developed knee trouble and tried refereeing instead. He reached the International Referees Panel.

Eventually St Helens acknowledged the changing world of rugby and merged with Liverpool RFC on 31st August 1986.

STOCKPORT

"An artisan side"
Anon 1895

THREE SEPARATE CLUBS have had the name of Stockport RFC. The original Stockport Rugby Club was founded in 1874, and initially shared a ground on Bramhall Lane with Stockport Crusaders before the former moved to Adswood Lane and Cale Green. In 1891 they moved

Stockport in action in 2012.

again, this time to Edgeley Park. The first Stockport were a competent side in the 1880s before joining the Northern Union rebels. Stockport did not attend the George Hotel meeting that formed the NU, but sent a telegram showing interest and were accepted. The switch to the NU was initially successful, with 10,000 spectators for their first ever match. Stockport hosted several NU county matches over the next five years. However, by 1902 the original club were deep in debt and rock bottom of the NU Second Division. They tried to ground-share with the local soccer club, Stockport County, but eventually were liquidated.

The second Stockport rugby club emerged in the early 1920s. They were a middle-ranking side in the Manchester area, but disappeared in the 1930s. They are best remembered for two incidents; on one occasion the team were getting changed in the open-air on a pitch next to a railway line when a passenger train stopped a few yards away. The passengers were horrified to see a collection of half-naked men and reported the incident to the police. The club had much explaining to do.

The second incident came after they lost 45-0 to Wilmslow. A Stockport member rang the local paper and erroneously reported the result as 45-0 to Stockport. Wilmslow were not amused.

The third Stockport club emerged in the 1950s as Davenport RUFC. They had modest roots and initially changed in a cycle shed. Yet within a decade Davenport had built a fine, two-storey clubhouse and were amongst the top sides in South Manchester. Davenport grew to rank with the best in Cheshire, and their annual sevens, the Glengarth, became the most prestigious in the North West.

League rugby damaged the Glengarth Sevens because clubs were loath to release players for friendly matches. Davenport also declined in the 1980s but recovered.

The club changed their name to Stockport RUFC. In 2006 they were North 2 West Champions and reached the final of the Intermediate Cup, where they met Morley. They are currently in National Two (North).

THORNTON CLEVELEYS

"Please remember that we all have to go to work on Monday – including the opposition."
William Gervase Beckett

THE NORTH OF the Fylde had rugby teams in the 19th century, but none survived for long. The area had strong connections to the rugby stronghold of Widnes through the influx of chemical workers from south Lancashire to Thornton Alkali Works (which eventually become part of the giant ICI Company).

There is a reference to two local teams – the Cockle Hall Rangers and the Bourne Hall Turnip Loupers – playing a game on 3rd September 1887. (The Bourne Hall club appears to have been connected with Thornton Alkali Works). A NU match between Thornton and Fleetwood is recorded on 6th May 1897, although no further mention is made of these two sides. A Blackpool club also existed, but they, along with Fleetwood, enjoyed little success, and both languished at the bottom of the NU leagues. In 1900-01 Blackpool became Thornton Rangers without changing their fortunes.

Rugby in Thornton Cleveleys resurfaced in 1927 when two rugby enthusiasts, Arthur Diggle and Stan Forber, had the idea of forming a club. They contacted likely players, including Harry Paynter, a former Northumberland player who had played for the defunct Fleetwood side. He had also played at the highest level with Plymouth Albion. A meeting was held at Baines School, Poulton, presided over by Mr. J.J. Jagger. Harry Paynter was the first secretary and captain. The patrons were Tom Silcock (a feedstock millionaire) and Lord Stanley (heir to the huge Derby Estates). E.F. Lutyens, the world famous architect, was the first president. He is often credited with designing the new town of Cleveleys earlier in the century. In fact, Lutyens was only an office boy at the time, but he assisted with some of the designs. He returned ten years later and built two houses. Modern critics say he actually devoted two weeks to the task and left the real work to his staff. Lutyens had been sent to the North Fylde to reorganise the local ICI factory that had been struggling. In the 1920s, he was relatively unknown, but his reputation grew after he designed World War One memorials at Thiepval and the Cenotaph in Whitehall.

Tom Silcock provided a ground on School Road, Thornton with a car park. Lutyens performed the official opening on Wednesday, 21st September 1927. The first match should have been a Fylde Secretary's XV and the Vale of Lune Secretary's XV. Unfortunately, flooding prevented the arrival of Vale of Lune, so Fylde played Thornton Cleveleys before 200 spectators.

The original ground was a quagmire, and eventually Mr Silcock offered a site with good drainage on Fleetwood Road,

Thornton Cleveleys in 2004.

near the town's famous 18th century windmill. The opening game at Fleetwood Road came in time for the start of the 1928-29 season.

The club flourished until 1932, when the Great Depression and waning enthusiasm brought a large overdraft. 1934 to 1936 were dark days for the club; on occasions the whole team travelled on a lorry. Better times came with the recruitment of two stalwarts: Graham Beckett and John Pughe-Jones, who on occasions took the role of captain, treasurer, chairman and president.

After the war, fixtures recommenced on Easter Monday 1946, against Ashton on-Mersey and over 400 people witnessed a fine open game. Thornton won 26-8.

Thornton were a successful junior side throughout the 1960s and opened their new clubhouse with a match between Thornton President's XV and Major W.B. Howarth's XV. During this era the club produced its finest player: Tony Richards, who played for Fylde, Wasps and Lancashire. He scored 35 tries in 50 appearances for the county. He also played for the NW Counties in their victory over the 1972 All Blacks, as well as for England on tour.

Thornton Cleveleys made national headlines in 1970 when two of their players – Brian Olsen and Trevor O'Connell – were identified as ex-Blackpool Borough RL players by an anonymous letter to the RFU. Both players were automatically banned from playing rugby union.

Thornton were a popular side in the mid-20th century as the visitors could take a trip to Blackpool after the match and see the tower.

Another outstanding servant of the club was W.G. (Bill) Beckett (1941-1998), who was an excellent prop who played nearly 1000 times for the club. Beckett later became Lancashire treasurer and was closely associated with Cliff Brittle's attempts to control the RFU's professionalism.

Thornton was badly hit in the 1960s by a split that saw the Roman Catholic section of the club from St Joseph's College form their own breakaway club: Old Josephians. Thornton battled on, but were affected badly by the success of Fleetwood and Blackpool. In 1996 Thornton were runners-up in the Lancashire Vase to Birchfield of Widnes.

(Thanks to Robin Gorrie, Dr Phil Horsfield, Phil Moran, Martin Dickins, Harry, Richard & Roger Hesketh, Bill Joynson)

TOC H (Manchester)

"We are a charitable organisation, we give tries away to everybody."

THE TOC H movement was founded on the Ypres Salient during World War One by the Rev. Philip 'Tubby' Clayton. The Toc H house in Poperinge was a place where battle-weary troops could have a clean bed, a cup of tea and a quiet prayer. Thousands of war-weary soldiers were cared for in the rented house only a few miles from the battlefront. The house still exists as a museum where visitors still get treated to a cup of tea and a piece of cake.

After the war, Tubby Clayton opened a residential home to help teach young men the spiritual lessons of World War One. The organisation spread worldwide, providing help and accommodation for young people. At its peak, Toc H had 20,000 members

A Toc H rugby club was formed in 1921 in south London by Irish international Dr W.R.F. Collis, and a Manchester rugby club was formed in 1924 by members living in the local hostel. They played on Simon Field, Stenner Lane, Didsbury and got changed at the Didsbury Hotel. Toc H became affiliated to the Lancashire Union in 1929 and were soon fielding four regular teams. Despite intense competition, Didsbury Toc H continues to play in the Lancashire leagues.

TRAFFORD MV
(formerly Metrovick)

METROVICK RUFC ARE amongst the oldest surviving works clubs, having played regularly in east Manchester since 1923. The rugby club emerged from the Metropolitan Vickers Company, which provided the world with electric turbines. Metropolitan Vickers itself emerged from the Westinghouse Company, who strived to be the perfect employer, which included building a model village for the employees and their families. At its high point, the factory had 25,000 employees, including an abundance of apprentices, who provided new blood for the rugby, soccer and cricket teams.

The fledgling Metrovick rugby club was fortunate to receive financial support from the company, but anxious to assert independence. The club had a good pedigree, as amongst its founders was England trialist Dick James, who had played for Waterloo.

Their first rugby ground was one of Farmer Britton's fields near Hough End Hall, which required the players to change in a farm shed. After some years the club acquired 13 acres of ground at Glebelands Road in Ashton-on-Mersey, which eventually boasted two first-class rugby pitches and changing accommodation.

The massive MV factory suffered badly from German bombing during World War Two. But, despite the disruption, the factory kept working and Metrovick RUFC kept playing. The factory was important to the war effort as the huge workforce produced turbines and munitions, which were desperately needed.

An unusual feature of the club was the large number of colonial players who played in their colours. Players came from South Africa, New Zealand and other parts of the Commonwealth to learn the business of generating electricity. At one time Metrovick fielded only two British players in the First XV – the rest were foreigners working at the factory. Unfortunately, the foreign players soon returned home, which meant that Metrovick once had an incredible 67% turnover in players in one season. Not surprisingly with such a turnover, Metrovick have always been a junior club.

The decision of the club in its early days to establish their independence from the company became important when, in the 1960s, the parent company was consumed in a series of takeovers. Some of the new owners looked at the affluence of the rugby club with envious eyes, but they could do nothing because the founders of the rugby club had wisely secured

Trafford MV in action.

control of the team. In the turmoil of takeovers and name changes, Metrovick RUFC even had the temerity to keep the old name until the supply of apprentices became a trickle. This forced the rugby club to look outside for new talent. The name became 'Trafford MV' as membership was opened to everyone and a successful junior section was created.

The best-known player to emerge from Metrovick is Steve Diamond, a rock-hard hooker who graduated to Sale in the early 1990s, Steve made 290 appearances for first Sale FC and later Sale Sharks after the game went professional, plus appearances for England A, The North and the Barbarians. In his first full season as joint coach, with Jim Mallinder, Steve guided Sharks to second place in the Premiership, along with winning the Parker Pen European Challenge Shield, Sale's first major trophy in more than 140 years. Later Diamond was coach of the Russian national team and could again return to Sale.

More recently Ben Lloyd left Trafford MV for Sale, where he won an England U20 cap.

(Thanks to Jim Ward and Andy Searle)

TYLDESLEY

'The Bongs'

THE TOWN OF Tyldesley lies on the road from Manchester to Wigan. A 'bong' was a hill or bank. Each September, an annual fair, the Bongs Wakes week, still takes place. The town had a great rugby history, built around Tyldesley RFC.

The club was originally formed in 1879 as "The Knights of the Star and Garter" at Garrett Hall, but changed their name to Tyldesley RFC in the 1881 season when they moved to Wall Street. "The Knights of the Star and Garter" took their name from their headquarters.

The 1880s saw an explosion of interest in Lancashire rugby and Tyldesley were one of the best sides in the county. They enjoyed the nickname of 'The Mighty Bongers'. Initially they made little impact, but the catalyst to success was the poaching of James 'Buff' Berry, the Cumbrian half back, from Kendal Hornets. Berry had played for Westmorland against the Maoris in 1888, which helped him establish a huge reputation. In this age of amateurism, Berry, a poorly paid mill worker, was easily lured

south with promises of lavish expenses and a sinecure as 'mine host' of a public house. Big crowds meant Tyldesley had the funds to entice Berry and his club and county partner Billy Cross, plus other local talent.

Tyldesley suddenly became a top-class side based on a massive pack in front of Berry and Cross. They were now an affluent club, with gates often topping five figures and a fixture list including most of the leading clubs of Lancashire, Yorkshire, South Wales and the North East.

In 1892, a Lancashire Championship was formed by Broughton Rangers, Oldham, Rochdale Hornets, St. Helens Recs, Salford, Swinton, Warrington, Wigan and Tyldesley. Superficially things were blooming, but, behind the scenes, matters were starting to unravel for Tyldesley. The club needed success to balance the books, but when they won the Lancashire Championship in 1896, they still had a deficit of £180 on the year.

In 1894 Buff Berry was a spent force and was allowed to leave on a free transfer. The RFU was also looking at the strange recruitment policy that had made Tyldesley a success. Tyldesley were at loggerheads with the RFU and decided to join the NU. The move was doomed because the NU tried to discourage forward domination in favour of open back play. This was diametrically opposed to Tyldesley's strength as the original kings of forward strength.

The club's decline continued. Season 1899-1900 proved to be Tyldesley's last in the first class ranks as they finished bottom of the Lancashire Senior League. They suffered from a wholesale defection of their best players to Wigan RLFC. Debts outstripped income and relegation brought bankruptcy. On 6th April 1901, the bailiffs knocked on the door of Well Street and the remaining quality players moved to other NU clubs.

Tyldesley was reformed in 1921 as a rugby union side at Well Street and were the strongest team in Lancashire in 1923-24. They produced a number of top-class players: J. Hodgson scored 34 tries in 1921-22, F. Fearnley was a top-class full-back and Guy Wilson. In 1927 Wilson came to prominence when he scored 200 points in a season as an 18-year-old. He could play anywhere in the backs, was capped by England and became a member of the British Isles team that toured Argentina. In 1927 Wilson was reputed to have had a devastating side-step.

In 1930, Tyldesley and Kendal played a benefit match for Buff Berry, who had fallen on hard times. That same year, Dowling, the Tyldesley Captain, tried a penalty into the teeth of a gale. The ball went up into the wind and came to halt in mid-air. It dropped onto the crossbar of the goalposts, where it stayed

Guy Wilson

briefly, for a second, before dropping back into play. The referee promptly blew his whistle and signalled a successful kick.

Another golden era came in the late 1950s when Tyldesley had 51 consecutive wins and winger J. Raines scored 47 tries during the sequence.

Brian Ashton

The best known Tyldesley player of modern times is Brian Ashton. Brian was a bank clerk who played for Leigh RUFC when he was persuaded by Tyldesley stalwart Terry Alexander to join them and switch to fly-half. Ashton earned a great reputation with Tyldesley before moving to Fylde and then Orrell, who were higher profile clubs. In 1975 he was selected for England on the Australian tour but had to return home. Brian is now known as England's top coach after leading Bath (1989 to 1996), Ireland (1996-8) and England.

Tyldesley played on the same ground at Well Street for 120 years, but eventually in 2001 they moved to the superb St. George's Park. Since the advent of league rugby, Tyldesley have been a mid-ranking North West club. Season 2008-2009 was a great year for the club when they were North Lancs & Cumbrian champions and reached the final of the RFU Senior Vase.

(Thanks to Terry Alexander)

VALE OF LUNE

"Lancaster is a place possessing staid old houses."
Charles Dickens 1845

LANCASTER IS A curious city and is completely different to any other city in the North West. It has a magnificent castle overlooking the River Lune, which makes it virtually unique locally as Oliver Cromwell demolished most of the rest during the Civil War.

Lancaster's centre is remarkable for the fine, cramped Victorian houses, which – though disliked by Dickens – give the place a splendid charm of its own. Lancaster's prosperity came from the manufacture of Linoleum, a process that made owner Lord Ashton a millionaire. Ashton left a number of fine memorials to the town's faded prosperity.

Lancaster doesn't appear in the list of RFU clubs because in 1910 the local rugby unionists expressed their separation from the NU by calling their club 'Vale of Lune RUFC'. The original Lancaster RFC played from 1875 and gave Barrow RFC their second ever match.

Lancaster RFC produced some fine players – notably Jack Pinch, who won three England RU caps in 1897-98. Pinch was selected by Lancashire during an era when Lancaster were making a name for themselves by winning the RFU North

Western League in 1892-93. Around 1898, Lancaster joined the NU, but were soon in financial trouble. Lord Ashton rescued the club with a donation of 100 guineas to pay off the debts on condition the club left 'licensed premises'. Lancaster RFU changed their name to 'Lancaster Northern', but disbanded in 1906.

A local rival at Morecambe operated for a decade from 1896 as members of the NU. Morecambe RFC produced two notable players: Bob Wilson and Jack Bartholomew. Bob Wilson left Morecambe for Broughton

Jack Pinch

Rangers. He was one of the best English NU players of the era and was capped by the NU's England team. Jack Bartholomew moved to Huddersfield, for whom he made 187 appearances. He is long forgotten, unlike his nephew, the great comedian Eric Morecambe.

Vale of Lune RUFC was born at a meeting in the Phoenix Rooms, Lancaster in March 1901. The club took the unusual name to separate itself from the NU side, who were still operating. Their first official fixture, against Preston Grasshoppers, was played later in the month. The new club came together on Boxing Day 1900 when 'Jackson's Lancaster Rugbeians' lost 27-0 to Preston Grasshoppers. At the time, there was no rugby union being played by anybody else in the whole of north Lancashire.

The old Lancaster club had played on a ground near St. Mary's Church before moving to Quay Meadow. On the demise of the NU club, Vale of Lune took over Quay Meadow, where they stayed until World War Two.

The Quay Meadow ground was famous for a pronounced slope from touchline to touchline. Changing facilities varied in the early days, from tubs and buckets in nearby warehouses to a walk to the public baths, which were nearly a mile away. Vale were soon one of the best sides in the North West and in 1930-31 won 24 of 28 matches.

After World War Two, Quay Meadow was unavailable, but Vale found an excellent replacement at Powderhouse Lane (which in Victorian times had been a gunpowder factory and the home of Lancaster FC soccer team). Whilst Powderhouse Lane was three miles from the city centre, it had excellent drainage and natural spectator facilities on a high terrace overlooking the east side of the ground. The bad news was that Vale had to raise £4000 (£150,000 in 2015 prices) to acquire Powderhouse Lane.

The new ground was officially opened on the 7th September 1949, with a match between Vale of Lune and a Joe Mycock XV. Mycock, the Lancashire and England forward, began his rugby at Giggleswick School and played for Vale of Lune before playing for Sale and Harlequins.

Around this time, an attempt was made to re-start rugby league in the city. Salford RLFC played an exhibition match in Lancaster, but the move came to nothing.

Perhaps the most famous Vale player was an obscure 1950s

winger from Carnforth called Cecil Parkinson, who later turned to politics. Parkinson found greater success on the right-wing of politics than at rugby and rose to become transport secretary in the Thatcher government.

Jock Hobbs is perhaps the Vale's most illustrious player of all time. A brilliant flanker, he joined the Vale through the good offices of BBC commentator Don Mosey, who knew his family from frequent visits to New Zealand. Jock made 22 appearances for Vale in the 1982-83 season and was a huge influence on everyone there. On his return to New Zealand he became the All Black captain. In the 2002-03 season he was elected chairman of New Zealand RUFC

Powderhouse Lane may not have been Twickenham, but its natural banking could hold 5,000 spectators. This made it a popular venue for big games, including the North West v Australia game in 1980. Powderhouse Lane also hosted an odd touring match in 2005 when the England RL XIII played the Lebanon national team in a 13-a-side match.

Vale were, in the pre-professional era, astute movers in the attraction of players. They recruited well in the city, had their own junior section and made excellent use of the players available in Cumbria. The most notable was Andy Higgin, who played for the North and England U21s. In 1986-87 he set a record of 28 drop goals – a feat which earned him a place in the Guinness Book of Records. Other notable players were Sam Hodgson (Cumbria, North and England 'A'), Mark Nelson (North Winger), Steve Swarbrick (Lancashire) and Brian Bonney, who established a club record of 550 appearances. Stuart Reid began at Vale of Lune before moving to Boroughmuir and being capped for Scotland. When league rugby arrived, Vale were a force in English rugby. Three times in the late 1980s, they reached the third round of National KO Cup. Vale were Merit Table 'C' Champions in 1986-87 with seven wins in nine matches, which gave them an 83% average. Table 'C' was renamed National League 3 in 1987.

Vale remained in National Division 3 from 1987 until 1991, when they suffered a remarkable decline due to players retiring or moving to more upwardly mobile clubs, such as Orrell. Vale tumbled through the leagues, eventually bottoming out in the North West leagues.

A thriving ladies section emerged and reached the Ladies Premiership Division 1 in 2005.

(Thanks to Stuart Vernon).

WARRINGTON

WARRINGTON RUFC WAS formed after World War One to fill the void left when their predecessors, Warrington RFC, joined the NU. The original town club was formed in 1879 by ex-members of two rival clubs: Padgate RFC and Warrington Zingari RFC. The first Warrington club played on Sankey Street and were nicknamed the 'Wires' in recognition of wire-making, which was the town's main industry. The following season Warrington merged with Padgate Excelsior, and subsequently with Warrington Wanderers, and played on the delightfully named Slutchers Lane, next to the Cable Works.

In 1883 Warrington moved to Wilderspool Road, where they remained for nearly 120 years. The next season they won the 1885-86 West Lancashire and Border Towns Cup. They attracted 10,000 for a match against Widnes, and were awarded a county match in 1888-89. Warrington RFC joined the NU in 1895 and have always been in the front rank of the 13-man game.

Rugby union reappeared in 1923, but Warrington RUFC must have operated before that date because Bury played a Warrington on 22nd April 1922 at Chester Road in front of 1200 spectators. Bury won 11-5. Amongst those who played for Warrington in the match was J.R. Locker, who was eventually to become president of the Rugby Football Union.

Tom Knowles

1924 saw Warrington using a ground near Loushers Lane, but two years later they joined with the town cricket club, only to return to Loushers Lane after two seasons. The best Warrington player of the era was Tom Knowles (1908-1985), who moved to Birkenhead Park. He was capped at fly-half by England in 1931 against Scotland, toured with the British Isles in 1930 and 1936 and played 52 times for Cheshire.

The late 1940s were a golden era for Warrington RUFC, with only eight defeats in 58 games under the captaincy of R.G. Bennett and D.T. Clarke. Club members J.A. Cooper, A.G. Smith and J. Foden played for Lancashire.

Warrington produced a top-class player in the 1970s in Dave Roughley, who was capped at centre by England. Later, Phil Stansfield won North honours and was a Sale regular for a decade.

League rugby arrived at a bad time for Warrington, whose fortunes were just in decline. They worked hard and in 1997-98 (their 75th anniversary season) the club won South Lancashire & Cheshire One and qualified for the National Knockout Cup. In 2002 they suffered a body blow when the clubhouse was destroyed by fire, forcing them to move back to the local cricket club.

WATERLOO FC

A WATERLOO FC existed in West Lancashire in the 1860s, formed by pupils of Cambridge House School, Seaforth. That club did not last long, but then another school, Merchant Taylors School, produced the club we now know as Waterloo FC. Merchant Taylors was to produce some of the greatest names in Waterloo rugby, including Joe Periton and Ben Kay. Merchant Taylors initially called their old boys side 'Serpentine FC' after the road nearest their pitch, which lay between Blundellsands railway station and West Lancashire Golf Club. The owner, Colonel Blundell, asked only that the posts were removed after matches. Unfortunately, the happy relationship terminated when Blundell's gamekeeper accused the club's players of poaching. They were in fact filling in rabbit holes on the pitch, which were dangerous to the players. After this problem the fledgling club was forced into a series of moves, including a prolonged stay at Manley Road, Waterloo, which accounted for the change of name.

Waterloo are synonymous with red, green and white hoops, which were adopted in 1894. But they began with navy blue and crimson stripes, then progressed to blue hoops with white stripes before settling on the colours that made them famous.

The St Michael's Ground was opened on 16th March 1921, as 'the Memorial Ground' with a match against Liverpool. St Michael's was originally part of the old West Lancashire golf course; the modern golf course now lies to the west. The Waterloo ground became a venue for many of the North's major matches. At its peak, it held 12,000 spectators and, between the wars, had a 'tanner bank' (6d), which was popular with dockers from the nearby Seaforth Docks.

Harold Periton

Waterloo's first international came in 1923, when S.B. McQueen played for Scotland. Since then there has been a regular succession of international players and hundreds of county players. Harold Periton (1901-1980) won 21 England and 64 Lancashire caps as a flanker in the late 1920s. He remains the only Irishman to captain England. Soon afterwards Bob Foulds won two England caps whilst with Waterloo after playing for Moseley and Furness.

Watcyn Thomas captained Wales and Waterloo, but is more closely associated with St Helens RUFC. Watcyn recorded his eight years at Waterloo as the happiest of his rugby life. But it must have been a tough time for Watcyn too, as he had to supervise schools rugby at Cowley School on Saturday mornings and then rush to Blundellsands to play for Waterloo. His club colleague, Ray Bark-Jones, won two Welsh caps in 1933. At the same time, brothers Graham and Stephen Meikle were capped by England. Remarkably, both brothers scored tries on their international debuts.

Dickie Guest

The Cowley School connection provided Waterloo with Jack Heaton and Dick Guest; both had careers that spanned World War Two. Jack Heaton won nine England caps between 1935 and 1947, which was the longest international career at the time. He scored three penalty goals against Scotland in 1939 to give England a 9-6 victory in the Calcutta Cup. His cousin, Dickie Guest, played for England on 13 occasions between 1939 and 1949, and played alongside his cousin on six occasions. He also played 49 times for Lancashire.

Small and slight, tricky and nimble, Guest replaced Obolensky in the England team in 1939 and played in all England's Internationals until 1949. Waterloo were well represented at international level at this time; Bob Weighill (England), E. Bole (England) and F. Trott (Wales) were war-time caps, and Dick Uren was capped four times by England between 1948 and 1952; his brother, Harold 'Boy' Uren, also turned out for England at full-back in 1946. Dick was picked to play for the Barbarians in 1947-48, and was invited to join a Lions tour to New Zealand, but declined owing to his business commitments. Uren also represented Cheshire at golf on nine occasions between 1966 and 1968, and came to play off scratch.

At club level, much of Waterloo's post-war successes were attributed to scrum-half Gordon Rimmer, who played 78 times for Lancashire and 12 times for England and toured New Zealand with the 1950 Lions. He was part of a remarkable club side that attracted the best players from the whole North West because the England selectors always included Waterloo on their itinerary.

Waterloo's success continued with Alan Ashcroft – another product of Cowley and St Helens – who won 16 England caps as a forward in the late 1950s. He was once pressed into service on the wing for England in direct opposition to the legendary Tony O'Reilly of Ireland. He also played 52 times for Lancashire, including a match against Ulster where injuries reduced the Lancashire pack to six men, with Ashcroft playing as a one-man back row. "I didn't mind," said Ashcroft, "but next time I want three men's travelling expenses!" Ashcroft was one of the best English players of the era and a member of the 1959 Lions.

Dick Greenwood of Merchant Taylors had a short but remarkable England career, which brought him five caps. The flanker was one of the first England players to recognise the importance of fitness and organisation. An outstanding captain of Lancashire and Waterloo, he lost his England place due to an eye injury. In the early 1970s he broke new ground by moving to Italy, which wasn't on the rugby map at the time. He was Italy's top try-scorer in 1973-74. He returned to England and became national coach, but retained his links to Waterloo. His son, Will Greenwood, began his rugby at Waterloo before joining Harlequins and becoming one of England's finest centres. But, as was the case for his England colleagues Kyran Bracken, Ben Kay, Austin Healey and Paul Grayson, the lure of the big professional clubs meant only a brief playing career at Waterloo before moving south. Ben Kay, a huge lock forward, was a product of Merchant Taylors before moving to Loughborough University and later Leicester. He won 62 caps for England and played in the 2003 Rugby World Cup-winning team.

It became a sad fact that top-class players, who once would have spent a lifetime at St Michaels, were easy pickings for rich clubs in the south. Waterloo, even with its superb facilities, could only attract 1,000 spectators on a good day, whereas their rivals could attract ten times that number.

Nevertheless, Waterloo tried to keep up with their rivals. They briefly changed their name to Waterloo Drummers and had a line of real percussionists to welcome the players onto the field.

Sadly, the drummers soon beat a retreat. The club managed to recruit Tony Russ, a top coach who had led Leicester Tigers to great success, but the drain of top players meant that the club had to accept middle status in the National Leagues.

Professional rugby proved hard going for Waterloo. By 2002 they had drifted down to National Three North. They reorganised and fought their way back to National One, but lacked the big backing of many of their rivals. National One was a trial, with only three wins in 30 games. The era was memorable for the achievements of stalwarts such as David Blyth, who made 500 appearances over 20 years. It proved the start of another slump and a string of relegations followed.

WALLASEY

IT IS KNOWN from the records of New Brighton that rugby was played in Wallasey in 1870. Their records state that matches were played regularly at Claremont School in Wallasey. One match is recorded between teams from New Brighton and Egremont, and around this time J. Herron formed the Egremont Wanderers Club, which later merged with New Brighton.

The present Wallasey club started life as Egremont RUFC in 1926, with A.T.B. Rosser, A. Ingram, S.W. Mason and E.A. Wardle among its founder members. The club drew its members mainly from the Wallasey and Oldershaw Grammar Schools; indeed, in the 1930-31 season a separate Old Wallaseyans RUFC existed.

The Second World War cost Egremont their two pitches, but in 1947 the West Cheshire Golf Club offered a parcel of vacant land near the promenade, which became the club's long term home. That year the club changed its name from Egremont to Wallasey at the request of the RFU, who had received representations from Egremont RUFC in Cumberland. The club felt confusion was arising from having two clubs with the same name.

The club's close proximity to the sea has meant that the pitches are seldom frozen. This brought Wallasey its finest hour in 1981, when Leicester Tigers rang the Wirral club and asked for a match because almost every other pitch in the country was unplayable. Not surprisingly, the Tigers won easily, but Ian Booth, Wallasey's winger, scored a hat-trick of tries for Wallasey.

Wallasey are now a middle-ranking club in the Cheshire leagues. In 1993-94 they reached Round 5 of the National Junior Cup and the 1994 Cheshire Plate final. Four years later, the club won the South Lancashire & Cheshire Two title.

(Thanks to Andy Rae)

WEST PARK ST.HELENS

WEST PARK WAS formed in 1947 by Old Boys of West Park Grammar School in St. Helens at the Black Bull public house. The Old Boys had played a handful of games the previous season under the title of the Catholic GSOB. Unbeknown to the founders, their entry in the game coincided with the worst winter of the 20th century, which restricted their progress – and everyone else's. Despite the snow, West Park produced an international in Martin Regan, who played for them before joining Blackheath. He subsequently won 12 England caps between 1949 and 1953.

The next international from West Park was Tom Brophy, who attended West Park GS. Brophy developed into a top-class fly-half at Loughborough Colleges, where his elusive running made him a Lancashire regular. Whilst a Loughborough student, Brophy made his debut against France. Despite beginning with West Park, Brophy played most of his club rugby with Liverpool. As a player he had a reputation for always trying to make a break every time he got the ball. But Brophy suffered from constant changes of his scrum half partner by the English selectors – five in eight internationals. In October 1966 he joined Barrow RLFC.

West Park's first cup victory came in the 1953 Caldy Sevens, which was one of the top end-of-season competitions. It crowned a perfect season of 32 victories in 32 matches, with 584 points scored and 165 conceded.

West Park began life on a school pitch, but moved to a pitch adjoining a collection of allotments on Prescott Drive. Eventually, in 1955, the club signed a lease on the 'Red Rocks', a hillside on the outskirts of the town, though the casual visitor can neither remember 'red' or 'rocks'. Today the ground on Eccleston Hill is one of the best in the region. West Park bought the Red Rocks in 1962.

West Park grew as a club and were rewarded in 1969 when Mike Glover and Bill Lawrenson were picked for Lancashire. They were soon joined by Rob Briers, who eventually played for the North West counties and was an England trialist.

The 1970s saw West Park as serious contenders for the Lancashire Cup, although they lost to mighty Orrell in the 1973 final. This was despite the constant loss of their best players to senior clubs. Many of their best players have moved to Waterloo to play National League rugby – notably Biff Handley, Sean Fletcher and Mark Ryan. Amongst the best Park players was David Lawrenson, who moved to London and became one of rugby's top writers.

West Park reached the National Leagues after being promoted to North One in 2002 under coach Martin Jones.

WIDNES

'The wide promontory'

The industrial town of Widnes lies on the north bank of the River Mersey. Rugby and Widnes are synonymous, and a dozen league and union clubs have operated in the town. But all are in the shadow of Widnes Vikings RLFC, who were world champions of the 13-man game in 1989.

Rugby union has always played second-fiddle, although the town's Wade Deacon School produced two Lions: Reg Higgins and Pat Quinn.

The current 'Widnes RUFC' were formed as Old Widnesians in July 1959 by the old boys of Wade Deacon School. OWs were a good junior club and produced a top-class player in Eric Hughes in their second season. Eric was Lancashire's and the NW Counties' hooker. He eventually turned to rugby league, as did Tony Karelius, who set a club record of 21 points in a single match against Birkonians. OWs were always vulnerable to rugby league and lost numerous good players to the paid ranks.

Currently Widnes are one of the top sides in Lancashire with probably the most successful junior set up in the county.

(Thanks to Roy Knowles and Gordon Unsworth)

WIGAN

The Lancashire town of Wigan is one of the centres of world rugby, and Wigan Warriors RLFC are one of the great names in the 13-man code. The Warriors emerged from the original Wigan RFC club, which was formed in 1879 and operated from Dicconson Street.

Rugby had been played since at least 1858, when one 'Michael Rowney' was arrested for playing rugby football near Hardybutts. In the 1860s Henry Ackerley, the Wigan Secretary, was arrested for misappropriating funds. He told the magistrates that the illicit funds were "trifling out of pocket expenses".

A second Wigan FC emerged in 1872 and played at Folly Field on Upper Dicconson Street. Their fixture list included Southport and Warrington, but they disappeared briefly only to re-emerge and become the cornerstone of the town's sporting heritage. In Victorian times, they were dogged by financial problems for the remainder of the century. However, Wigan emerged as the top Lancashire club until they joined the NU in 1895. The club's best known player was E. Bullough, who won three England caps.

The union game was restarted in 1913 by Wigan Old Boys RUFC, which was formed by N.K. Smith, V. Bradshaw, S. Staveley and F. Booth. N.K. Smith had been a top-class centre and understudy to Cyril Lowe in the Middlesex side before becoming headmaster of Pemberton Modern School in the town. The union side soon disappeared during World War One, but reappeared in 1920 at Prospect Park, Standish in the grounds of the town's grammar school.

In 1930 Wigan Grammar School Old Boys went open, although they were still playing on the school fields at Standish.

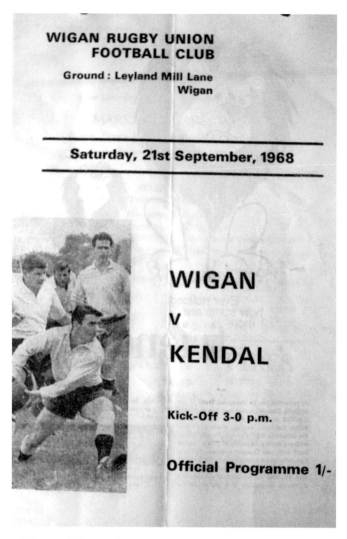

WIGAN RUGBY UNION FOOTBALL CLUB

Ground : Leyland Mill Lane
Wigan

Saturday, 21st September, 1968

WIGAN
V
KENDAL

Kick-Off 3-0 p.m.

Official Programme 1/-

Wigan OBs produced an international in the 1950s in Gordon Rimmer, who moved to Waterloo and eventually won 12 England caps. The club changed its name to Wigan RUFC in the 1970s and has been amongst the best in Lancashire since leagues arrived. Wigan were eclipsed in the 1970s by the emergence of Orrell from the west side of town. Wigan remained as a class side, although hardly known outside Lancashire. Early in the 1980s Dave Cusani played for Wigan before moving to Orrell, where he was capped by England. Their 1999 side included the ex-Orrell fly half Peter Williams, who had won three England caps earlier in the decade.

(Thanks to Chris Smith, Roy Knowles and Gordon Unsworth)

WILMSLOW

"The Knightsbridge of the north."
Andrew Rigby

WILMSLOW WAS A tiny village, best known for button making until the railway arrived in 1842 and turned this quiet corner of Cheshire into a dormitory town for Manchester. The first Wilmslow RFC was founded in 1884 and played on several grounds with varying success until disbanding in 1901. Wilmslow was reformed in 1923 on the suggestion of James Baxter, then president of the Cheshire Union. The first match of the season was against Kersal, which Wilmslow lost by seven tries to one.

The present ground at Pownall Park was taken over in 1934, and after World War Two was dedicated to the memory of 21 of its members who lost their lives in the war. The occasion was marked by Lancashire and Cheshire playing a friendly game.

Wilmslow emerged in the 1960s from a good club to one of the best in the North West and qualified for the National Junior Cup in 1972. They made national headlines before losing 18-10 to Moseley at the Reddings.

Wilmslow produced numerous county players and David Wrench (England) and John Shipsides (North of England). More recently, Josh Baxendell began at Wilmslow before playing for Sheffield, Sale and England.

One of the best amateur clubs in the North West, Wilmslow play in North 1 West.

WINNINGTON PARK

"When professionalism arrived, we paid the players and they left. Now we don't pay them and they still leave – but at least it's not cost us a fortune'."
Bob Dean, 2000

THE CLUB WAS founded in about 1908 by staff from the Brunner Mond Chemical Company in Northwich. The name of Winnington Park records an old estate on the north-west side of Northwich. Brunner Mond later became part of ICI Chemicals. After the First World War the club became part of the Winnington Park Recreation Club.

Before a move was made to Jubilee Field, matches were played on the paddock of Winnington Hall, on the north-west side of Northwich. When the club went open, a decision was taken to change the name to that of the old estate. The club was fortunate in having a rugby playing school – Sir John Deane's, Northwich – in the district, but the richest source of players was ICI apprentices.

The first international to play for Park was Leslie Haslett, who won two England caps at lock-forward in 1926. In 1930 Charles Gibson became a Cheshire regular and moved to Birkenhead Park, where he won an England trial. Other prominent players include G.H. Gibson (England trialist), D.W. Brown, R.D. Gillespie (Scottish trialists) and K.H. Jones (the 1949-50 Cheshire hooker). David Wrench began his rugby with Winnington before winning two England caps in 1964 at prop with Harlequins.

Dewi Morris was easily the finest player to represent Park. Morris was a student at Crewe & Alsager College and played for four years at Winnington in the mid-1980s, when the club was promoted from North 1 to Area League North. Welsh by birth, Morris eventually moved to Orrell. He opted for England because Wales wouldn't consider him because he played outside the principality, so when Richard Hill, the first choice scrum-half, was injured, Morris was selected for his adopted country. It was not all glory as Morris was once castigated for standing to attention for the National Anthem with his socks down.

In 1988 he moved to Liverpool St Helens, who were on the verge of promotion to National One, and within weeks he played for the North v Australia and scored the winning try. This was enough to win him selection for England against Australia – only ten weeks into his first season of top-class rugby. He became an England regular and later a respected TV commentator.

Winnington Park were 2010 Cheshire Bowl winners.

(Thanks to the late Bob Dean and 'Ollie')

WIRRAL
(formerly Old Wirralians)

OLD WIRRALIANS PLAYED their first games in 1936-37. The club drew its members from Wirral Grammar School, which is one of half a dozen great rugby schools on the Wirral. The first captain was A. Coathup, who led the side until September 1946.

The school and club produced Bob Weighill (1920-2000), who won four England caps in 1948. Weighill was a top-class swimmer as a boy and spent four years in the police before joining the RAF as a pilot in World War Two. Weighill had a distinguished RAF career and won the DFC, which delayed his entry to rugby. He played for Old Wirrallians, Birkenhead Park, Waterloo and finally Harlequins, where he won his first cap. Later he became RFU Secretary, IRB Secretary and ADC to the Queen.

Wirralians made headlines in 1972 when they won the National Old Boys Sevens.

Amongst the best players produced in recent years is Jez Ellis, who played top class rugby for Orrell. Wirral rank amongst the best clubs in West Cheshire and possess some of the best facilities in the area. In 2014, they reached National 3 North under coaches Andy McKinney and Matt Cairns. Matt began at Wirral before playing 180 games at hooker in the Premiership for Harlequins, Saracens and Sale Sharks. In 2007, Matt won an England cap. Currently Wirral field four senior teams, a ladies team and 300 juniors.

(Thanks to Steve Wood)

CHAPTER SEVEN - YORKSHIRE

"In the North of England, the game is often played in a very different spirit, and at times the anxiety to win leads to much unpleasantness."
The Field, 1882

ST PETER'S SCHOOL, York is famous for not allowing the burning of a guy on Bonfire Night because Guy Fawkes was a pupil before he attempted to blow up the Houses of Parliament. The school can also lay claim to the earliest known rugby football in Yorkshire, dating from 1850.

A decade later club rugby came to the fore in the White Rose county when there were at least six successful sides operating: Sheffield (1863), Huddersfield (1864), Hull (1865), Otley (1865), Halifax (1866) and Bradford (1866). It is known the game was also flourishing in Leeds because the city was represented at the formation of the Yorkshire RFU in 1870, and was involved in the organisation of the first ever county match when Yorkshire met Lancashire. Actually, the opposition 'Lancashire' was Manchester FC, who ran their county until the late 1870s. The 1870 Roses Match marked the beginning of the county championship, although it was another 18 years before the RFU sanctioned it officially. In the earliest days, counties were content to play each other on an informal basis.

Yorkshire players were noticeable by their absence from the first international matches, and it was 1875 before the first Yorkshire player, W.H. Hutchinson of Hull, wore the white of England. Thereafter the White Rose was well represented, and G.T. Thomson of Halifax was an England regular for five years. Later, Yorkshire's premier player was Dicky Lockwood, a brilliant attacking three-quarter, who won 14 England and 46 Yorkshire caps.

The game grew within Yorkshire, and in 1877 the 'Owld Tin Pot' (the Yorkshire Challenge Cup) was introduced to accommodate new clubs in the county. The county side benefited from the growth and they soon overtook Lancashire as the 'cock of the north'. Indeed, Yorkshire became the premier rugby county in England and were popular with visitors from other parts of the country. In 1884 Oxford University entertained Yorkshire, who had not been beaten for three years. The fixture provoked such great interest that Oxford switched the match from the Parks to Iffley Road Athletics Track because the university did not have permission to charge admission to its usual pitch.

A loose county organisation existed until the 'Yorkshire Rugby Union' was formed in 1888; previously Leeds, Bradford, Huddersfield, York and Hull had provided a five-man committee which controlled the county's rugby. Gradually, the committee had to relinquish control to an organisation representing all Yorkshire clubs. The change came at a good time as Yorkshire were county champions. Two years later Yorkshire defeated the Rest of England in an official international trial. This unlikely fixture arose because the RFU were financially embarrassed after a wrangle with the other home countries and suggested the money-spinning tie.

Yorkshire's success owed much to drawing its strength from a wider social background than the predominantly middle-class roots of the game in the south. In truth, rugby had become a game vastly more popular in the north than in the south. Club rugby in the north was underwritten by spectators, who paid their money through the turnstiles. A successful side meant lucrative gate money, but an unsuccessful side meant spectators looked elsewhere for their sport. The best way to assemble a successful side was to offer inducements to players to join your team. This was achieved by offering sinecures – such as the tenancy of a public house – or simply by paying money illegally. Many of the players were ordinary working men who simply could not afford to lose a Saturday's pay from their six-day working week. The big Yorkshire clubs eventually proposed to the Yorkshire RU that clubs be allowed to pay players for 'broken time' or time off work. The RFU, a predominately southern, middle-class organisation, said no, which caused conflict with the big Northern clubs.

There is an argument that the London-based RFU were not too bothered what happened at the other end of the country. Professionalism had been accepted by soccer for a decade, but the round ball game was dominated by North West and Midlands clubs. Soccer had a place in the south, but it was a middle-class varsity sport typified by Corinthian FC, composed of Oxbridge graduates. The chief instigator in the fight against 'broken time payment' was a Yorkshire resident: the Rev. Francis Marshall, Headmaster of Almondbury Grammar School, Huddersfield. Marshall had moved to Yorkshire in 1878 and became a leading county administrator and Yorkshire's voice on the national RFU. From 1889 onwards, Marshall sought to punish clubs that made illegal payments. The witch-hunt began with Leeds St. Johns, Bradford and Elland, but continued looking at the affairs of many clubs, large and small. Marshall stirred up such a 'hornets' nest' that children stoned him when he rode through Leeds and he received poison pen letters threatening his life. Marshall's enquiries antagonised many of his county colleagues and he was forced to seek allies in the south of England.

In Marshall's defence, English rugby was in mess in the 1890s because 'under the counter' payments were dragging clubs to the brink of penury. Players mysteriously moved clubs as they followed the money, and swapped clubs without concern. An economic recession in the 1890s piled more pressure on the clubs and bankruptcy was always hovering in the background. A Yorkshire delegation attended an RFU meeting, on the 20th September 1893, to press for players to be compensated for loss of wages, but their motion was defeated by a huge margin.

Rugby was more widely spread than soccer but couldn't command the huge crowds of association football. Rugby had ambitions to emulate soccer, but nobody could persuade the RFU to remove the financial shackles as the FA had done.

On 29th August 1895, a meeting was called at the George Hotel, Huddersfield by northern clubs to discuss their plans for the coming season. Although not officially part of their agenda, the clubs formed the 'Northern Football Union' and agreed to break away from the RFU. The signatories were Batley, Bradford, Brighouse Rangers, Broughton Rangers, Halifax, Hunslet, Hull, Huddersfield, Leeds, Leigh, Liversedge, Manningham, Oldham, Rochdale Hornets, Stockport, St. Helens, Runcorn, Wakefield Trinity, Warrington, Tyldesley, Wigan and Widnes clubs.

The Yorkshire RU was devastated because almost all their major clubs joined the rebels and the county's best players joined the exodus. The big clubs were soon joined by their smaller counterparts. The number of rugby union clubs in Yorkshire dwindled from 150 to 14. Yorkshire had been county champions six times in seven years before the Schism, but it was another 30 years before they took the title again. Lancashire, the 1891 County title winners, suffered similarly and didn't win the title again until 1935.

The Schism led to split loyalties in many towns. Where the original town club had joined the Northern Union, a new 'Unionist' club was formed only streets away. It became commonplace for a rugby league and union club to operate in the same town or village, and both claimed to be the original article. The Unionists received an unexpected boost in 1900 when the Northern Union changed its name to the Northern Rugby League and excluded a number of its member clubs who weren't considered viable. The rejected ones either disbanded or rejoined the RFU.

Both strains of the sport were, however, under pressure from soccer. The round ball game had an uphill struggle in some parts, particularly in Leeds, Bradford and Hull, where rugby was king.

Nationally, the loss of the Northern Union clubs had little impact on the far-distant RFU, but it left the Yorkshire Union painfully bruised. It even had to find new venues for county matches because the big grounds often belonged to clubs who had become part of the NU. Yorkshire matches between 1895 and 1897 were switched to Goole, Morley, Dewsbury, Castleford and the less sophisticated grounds in Leeds.

For ten years Yorkshire struggled, and their England representation almost disappeared. Things were dire in 1905, when the first All Blacks visited Leeds and humiliated Yorkshire by defeating them 40-0. But all was not lost, as the Rev Alfred Thompson of Headingley created a direct link between the county rugby union and its schools by asking the headmasters of secondary schools in the county to support Yorkshire rugby. The response led to the creation of 'Yorkshire Wanderers', a near-county side who took rugby union into schools and tried to capture the imagination of the next generation of players and supporters. It fed the roots of the axiom that every good Yorkshire RU club was fed by its local grammar school. The improvements helped good times return to the county, and in 1928 Yorkshire defeated Cornwall 12-9 in the County Championship final.

The 1930s saw Yorkshire in the shadow of Lancashire, but the rivalry fuelled the annual Roses Match, which became the highlight of the Northern Group programme, to the delight of successive county treasurers. Rugby in both counties grew so strongly that by 1976 the Roses match involved a dozen internationals. Even when league rugby pushed county rugby back into the shade, the Roses match retained an edge amongst the players and popularity with the paying public.

Yorkshire were county champions in 1987, 1994, 2000, 2001 and 2008.

BEVERLEY

'The Beavers'

BEVERLEY IS ONE of Britain's finest small cities, and rugby has a long history there. The first club was formed on the 17th September 1883 at the Beverley Arms Hotel by the Rev. William Gell, who had just left Oxford University. The Reverend became the club's first captain. The first match was a defeat by Hull Town 'A'. The first season saw ten matches against junior sides from Hull, with home matches played on a pitch behind the railway station.

In 1885 Beverley RFC adopted white jerseys with a black beaver motif, which brought them their nickname. They fielded two top class-players in E. Coulman and Gilbert Harrison in the 1880s. Coulman began at Beverley and later played for Hull Town, Yorkshire, and Richmond (alongside A.J. Gould in the Richmond three-quarter line). In 1887 Beverley persuaded Gilbert Harrison (ex-Hull and England) to join as captain.

Two years later there was an abundance of sides in the town, with names such as Rising Star, Victoria, Falcons, West End Rovers, Excelsior, Free Wanderers and Workingmen's Club. They, like the original Beverley RFC, had disappeared by 1900.

The current Beverley club was formed in 1959 as Longcroft OBs, but changed the name to Beverley RUFC in 1965. They were 1975 Yorkshire Silver Trophy winners and County Shield winners twice in the 1980s.

The club's rise to prominence began in 1996-97 when they did the double of Yorkshire Shield and Yorkshire League champions. 2000 found them in North East 2, but they fell back to Yorkshire 2 within three years.

Since then they have produced three successive promotions, built on an unbeaten home run from 2003 to 2007. They have twice reached National 3 (North) and have had some colourful imports. Vlad Ursk was a Croatian international and Head Coach and Anthony Posa was also a Croatian international, although New Zealand born.

BRADFORD & BINGLEY

"To visit Bradford – To descend into hell."

Anon, 1840

THE 1840 VISITOR to Bradford who penned the above quote was grossly unfair to the city, which once was second only to London for prosperity. Those days are gone, but it is today a large conurbation with fine suburbs. Its rugby days also have declined, but Bradford has given much to the two codes of rugby – not least the Barbarian tradition.

Rugby in Bradford can be traced back to 1866, although the first fixture list was only issued in 1872. Two seasons later Bradford RFC were undefeated in a calendar year and did not concede a single point. The following year, Bradford provided five players to Yorkshire and T.S. Tetley was selected for the England team.

The 1880s saw the first golden era for Bradford rugby with a host of top-class players – notably Laurie Hickson, Tom Broadley, Herbert Ward and W.H. Smith. They first won the Yorkshire Cup in 1884, defeated mighty Blackheath in 1886, and were comfortably the best side in Yorkshire. Bradford moved to Park Avenue in 1884 and had enough cash reserves to buy the ground for £7,000 six years later.

All was not perfect as in 1884 Wakefield Trinity complained of 'unpleasant behaviour' during a match with Bradford.

The club were attributed with several major developments in the game. In the 1880s, 'foiking' by the opposing scrum-half during a scrummage was an irritating tactic (foiking was the act of extricating the ball by kicking into the heart of the scrum in an effort to free it). Bradford developed a tactic called 'wheeling the scrum' (i.e. pushing along one side until the scrum spins 180 degrees), which stopped the opposing half-back getting near the ball.

Bradford's second development was the wing overlap, in which the three-quarters passed the ball rapidly along the back-line, creating space on the flank. This tactic was attributed to Rawson Robertshaw of Bradford, who is considered the first centre to exploit the link with the stand-off to create space for his winger to get clear.

Their third contribution was to help in the formation of the Barbarians. In 1890 Bradford hosted a party of Varsity players, led by Percy Carpmael, who enjoyed the trip so much they formed the 'Ba-Bas' as a regular touring team.

By the 1880s, Bradford was probably the strongest side in England. However, they were suspected of paying their players, and they did seem to attract quality players from far and wide. Despite big gates and fielding amateur players, Bradford often failed to balance the books, which suggests that rumours of illegal payments were accurate.

In the early 1890s, the textile industry, the town and the rugby club were hit by a financial depression. The economic downturn brought two results: the Independent Labour Party was formed in the city after a strike at Manningham Mills and Bradford RFC joined the fledgling Northern Union in an attempt to solve their financial problems.

Bradford were one of the founder members of the breakaway Northern Rugby Union. They enjoyed some success in the NU until a shortage of money forced the club to abandon rugby in favour of soccer and to adopt the name of Bradford Park Avenue FC. The soccer club played in the Football League until 1970, when they lost their league status. A replacement NU rugby side filled their ranks in 1907 as 'Bradford Northern RLFC' (later Bradford Bulls), who have been one of the pillars of rugby league.

The flag of rugby union was kept flying by Bradford Wanderers, who were joined by a new club, Bradford Rangers, in 1903. The two clubs soon amalgamated and played on the Branch ground at Shipley. Wanderers had an England RU international in Arthur Cockerham, who played for the England team in 1900.

Shortly afterwards two more small RU clubs emerged: Horton and Bradford Old Boys. Ground availability was a big difficulty for RFU clubs in the Bradford area; Horton, for instance, commenced activities at Southfield Lane, then went to Fagley and then Horton Park Avenue, and the Wanderers also played on several grounds.

After World War One, Herbert Robertshaw financed the purchase of a RU ground at Lidget Green, which was officially opened in 1919 by the Lord Mayor. The All Blacks spoilt the party to open the ground by defeating Yorkshire 41-5.

Horton & Wanderers RUFC became Bradford RUFC on the 26th May 1915. The kingpin of the side was Edward Myers (1895-1956), a product of Dollar Academy in Edinburgh, which was ironic as he was the scourge of Scots rugby in the 1920s. Like many a great player, Myers was outstanding at numerous sports. At Dollar Academy, he excelled at rugby, cricket, golf, tennis and at athletics, where he was blessed with amazing speed. Myers was first selected as an England reserve when only 17, but eventually won 18 caps between 1920 and 1925 at either centre or fly-half.

E. MYERS.

Myers became regarded as the most elusive broken-field runner of his day, but he suffered from unfair comparisons with W.G.A. 'Dave' Davies, his predecessor in the England No. 10 jersey. Davies and Myers were different types of player, but the general public wanted a new Davies rather than a Myers. He continued playing for the Bradford club long after being discarded by England.

In 1930 the British Isles touring team selected W.G. Bonner of Bradford for their tour of New Zealand. Bonner was one of an unlucky handful of players who were picked for the British Isles but never capped by their home country.

In the 1920s, a rival club emerged in the city in Old Bradfordians, who closed their doors in 1935.

Lidget Green was expanded to hold 25,000 spectators for the return visit of the All Blacks in 1935, but the ground was badly bombed during World War Two.

Bradford recovered their strength after World War Two and provided five men to the 1953 Yorkshire side and produced several internationals. Roger Pickering became the first Bradford player to captain England. Pickering played six times for England and 52 times for Yorkshire. A contemporary in the Bradford team was Geoff Cooke, who later became a highly successful England manager. He led England to a string of Grand Slam victories before returning to manage Bradford & Bingley towards the end of a great career.

The club's greatest international connection was celebrated in 1965 when the 75th anniversary of the formation of the Barbarians FC brought a visit from the great tourists. The Ba-Bas beat their hosts 47-3.

The most recent Home international player to play for Bradford was Dr. G.W. Mitchell of Scotland, who played for Bradford and Yorkshire in 1970-71 before emigrating to Canada.

In 1978 the club were relegated from the Northern Merit Table and three years later amalgamated with Bingley to form Bradford & Bingley RUFC.

Bradford v Kendal 1930.

The merger of the two clubs seemed the logical course of action. Bradford had the fixtures and the history and Bingley had excellent facilities of over 50 acres with three first-class pitches and the ability to expand and improve. A merger was agreed and completed in 1984 and two years later a new club house was constructed at Wagon Land, Bingley.

Bradford & Bingley rose rapidly in the late 1990s, being North 2, North 1 and National 3 North champions over ten years. In 2004 B&B won the Intermediate Cup 11-6 and played in National 2.

BRIGHOUSE RANGERS

BRIGHOUSE IS A mill town between Halifax and Bradford, where Brighouse Rangers RFC were formed in 1879. They distinguished themselves by winning the Yorkshire Cup in 1895, beating Morley 16-4 in the final. Their best player was Billy Nichol, who represented both Yorkshire and England at rugby union.

By the turn of the century the Rangers had joined the Northern Union. This proved an error and within two years Rangers were at a low ebb. By 1904 they were in the NU Second Division and attracting poor gates. In 1906 the Northern Union reduced the number of players in a team from 15 to 13 to help the smaller clubs, but this was too late for Rangers. At the AGM no officers could be found who were willing to carry on the club, which was virtually bankrupt. The club's effects were sold at auction at the end of August 1906. The account of the sale makes pitiful reading: 24 pairs of shin pads fetched 8p, nine ear caps 5p, 13 pairs of boots 18p, and a collection of footballs 30p. The total sale realised £110 and was used to pay off creditors.

Rangers were revived in 1913 in the Northern Union and this time a ground was available on the old pitch at Lane Head. Rangers reformed again after World War One and today are one of Yorkshire's top amateur rugby league clubs.

CASTLEFORD

THE ORIGINAL CASTLEFORD RFC was formed in 1877 and rapidly rose to become one of the north's leading clubs. They could even field a number of internationals. In 1896 Castleford won the Yorkshire Cup and provided three forwards for the 1896 England side: Harry Speed, John Rhodes and John Ward. The glory was short-lived as the coal-mining town was split when a faction within the club left to form a NU club. Speed, Rhodes and Ward opted for the NU and were unavailable to the RFU.

Despite the split, the original rugby union club remained a leading power in Yorkshire rugby in the years up to World War One – notably by winning the Yorkshire Cup on five occasions (1901, 1902, 1903, 1906 and 1908).

The cup victories were not without incident as Castleford vied with Skipton for the title of Yorkshire's top club. The two sides met in the 1903 Yorkshire Cup Final at Harrogate and drew 6-6, which forced a replay. Castleford fielded 'Long' John Taylor of England in the centre, although he was a member of West Hartlepool. Taylor had won 11 England caps with Wests and was considered one of the best kickers in the game. Skipton felt Taylor was not a genuine member of Castleford and feared (rightly) that he would dominate proceedings in the replay; Taylor scored all the points in Castleford's 6-0 win. The cup was presented to Castleford after the match, but Skipton felt robbed and protested to the Yorkshire committee, who ordered a second replay. Castleford refused to attend and the YRU awarded the cup to Skipton. Castleford made their sentiments clear by returning the cup with an extra present of 15 babies' dummies.

Castleford took revenge on the next occasion they met Skipton in the County final by winning 29-0. The bitterness lingered for many years and a fixture between Skipton and Castleford was 'always a bloodbath'.

After the Great War, schoolmaster Pat Delaney revived rugby in Castleford by introducing it to the town's grammar school. Castleford RUFC was revived and had a string of homes before moving to the site of the old Whitwood Colliery. A new clubhouse was opened in 1974.

Castleford have traditionally been amongst the county's best sides and were Yorkshire Cup semi-finalists in the 1960s. 2015 saw Castleford top of Yorkshire 3

(Thanks to Bill Thackray)

CROSSLEYANS

CROSSLEYANS RFC BEGAN life in 1923 as the old boys of Crossley School, Halifax. The school was opened in 1864 by John Crossley, who was the owner of the world's largest carpet manufacturing business. Like many old public schools, it was originally intended for orphans, particularly those born in Yorkshire to middle-class parents. By World War One, the school had opened its gates to boarders who were not orphans.

Crossley School had produced good rugby players from its foundation. In 1912 it produced Albert Rutler, who served as Lancashire's captain. Legend has it that he was a reserve at an England trial but missed his chance as he was attending to a dying spectator when summoned to the field by the selectors.

J.S. Bolton, the school headmaster, was the rugby club's first president and driving force. OCs began with a modest fixture list, playing junior clubs or the 'A' or 'B' teams of senior clubs. Season 1924-25 saw OCs undefeated as the club's reputation improved.

OCs didn't lose many matches, but one defeat 'stuck in the craw' of the new club. In 1930 OCs travelled to Fylde to play the Lancastrian club's second XV. Unfortunately Fylde First XV had no fixture, so they 'strengthened' their Seconds with most of the First XV. Fylde won 39-3, which left the visitors feeling aggrieved.

OCs grew in strength in the 1930s. In 1936-37, they were the only side to win at local rivals Brodleans, and the following year they won 21 of 27 matches.

The outbreak of World War Two saw OCs playing at North Dean, the home of Heath RUFC, when Crossleyans' home pitch at the school was commandeered for war service. That year OCs became the first local junior club to defeat Halifax, when they won 14-12 at Overden. Both sides were heavily depleted due to the outbreak of war.

OCs were becoming established in Yorkshire rugby and in 1960 they won the Yorkshire Cup in an era when the county was dominated by senior sides.

The club has produced some distinguished names. Brian Campsall played for OCs for two seasons before becoming an international referee. In 1980 OCs' most famous son, Brian Moore, made his debut as a sturdy 16-year-old. Moore played at OCs for two seasons before becoming an undergraduate at Nottingham University. Nottingham RFC were riding high at the time and Moore became their first choice hooker. He later moved to Harlequins and played for England and the Lions. But he is so much more than simply Brian Moore, rugby player; he a lawyer, author and a television commentator as well.

Jim Mallinder was another product of OCs in the 1980s. A skilful centre, Mallinder played for Sale at the top level and was also an England 'A' cap before becoming one of the UK's top coaches. Winger James Naylor also went west, joining Orrell and getting an England 'A' cap. Additionally Andrew Atkinson won an England 'A' cap, and played widely across the north of England.

Many Riaz of OC is another international who has played both rugby league and rugby union for Pakistan.

Crossley School was independent before joining the state system under the 1944 Education Act. The Old Crossleyans Athletic Club acts as an umbrella organisation and still runs the bar. Cricket and squash are also played there.

(Thanks to Richard Davies and Max Uttley)

DEWSBURY

DEWSBURY RFC WAS formed in 1875. The club rapidly produced a great player in William Stadden (1860-1906), a half-back who played eight times for Wales in the late 1880s, including in Wales's first win over England. The game in February 1890 was appropriately played at Crown Flatt, Dewsbury in the days before Twickenham became England's home. Despite a snowstorm, 4000 spectators watched the international match. It was a disaster because of heavy snow, which made the pitch practically unplayable. Arthur Gould, the Welsh captain, earned his reputation with a brilliant display of ball handling in awful conditions.

The original Dewsbury RFC went over to soccer in 1898, which prompted the formation of a NU team who played at Crown Flatt until 1998.

DRIFFIELD

DRIFFIELD RUFC DATES from May 1926, but the sport was flourishing in the town before that. It made the headlines in 1909 when the RFU President Phillip Woods was assaulted by two men whilst refereeing a match in the town. The case was dismissed because 20 witnesses refused to name the assailant.

The rugby club was founded at the Keys Hotel, Driffield by five members of Bridlington RUFC, who felt that the town of Driffield could support a club of its own.

The club's first president was Mr W. Parkinson; Club captain and vice-captain were Mr L.M. DuPre and Mr E.T. Shepherdson, respectively. The latter was also the club secretary.

The first pitch was a field owned by Albert Spencer, who allowed the site on St. John's Road to be used by the club until 1950. After that it was developed as a housing estate, now known as Spencer's Way. The Keys Hotel was adopted as the club's headquarters; the proprietor at the time was Tom Burton. The changing rooms, known as the 'Kennels', were behind the hotel and the baths were wooden beer barrels sawn in half.

The first game the club played was away against Hessle Church, and Driffield played in Hornsea's strip as their new jerseys didn't arrive in time. Driffield won that first game thanks to an Irish International, Dr. Hugh McVicker, playing for them. He had scored the only try for Ireland against England that year. He also played for Richmond and the Army. It is believed that he was with a medical practice in the town for a while, but not much else is known about him.

In the 1927-28 season, Driffield had a very good and successful side, and out of 23 matches played 18 were won, three lost and two drawn. The new club ended the season winning the inaugural Hull & ER Seven-a-Side competition.

The new club had a rival in Driffield RC, who played rugby league until 1930. When they closed down, many of their players changed codes to union.

Driffield continued throughout World War Two thanks to the RAF and Army team billeted in the area. When the war ended in 1945, work began to rebuild the club. G.H. 'Tich' Hoggard was mostly responsible for this. From the 1947-48 season there

was once again an official fixture list. A game was played against Barnsley in the Yorkshire Shield on 25th January 1947, and the score was 3-3. A replay couldn't be arranged, however, because of the terrible winter of 1947, when most of the county was covered in thick snow for months.

The season finished with only 17 matches played, of which eight were won, five lost and four drawn. At this time the team were still playing on St. John's Road pitch. When the St. John's Road ground became unavailable, games were played on a ground in Skerne Road and the teams changed at Mrs Kay's house (which is now the Woodlands Rest Home for the Elderly).

Later they changed at the Blue Bell Hotel, using the pub's changing and bathing facilities in sheds at the back. Tin baths were used, of which there were only four, so it was often four to a bath. The Skerne Road ground was very muddy in wet weather and the baths were frequently solid with mud by the time the players had finished with them.

In 1957 the club bought an old RAF Wartime Cinema, which lasted, with adjustments, for 50 years.

In 1995 the club purchased a 6.5 acre field at Kelleythorpe, but it took over five years to raise the money to develop the ground. The money was eventually provided thanks to a £530,000 lottery grant, which went towards the £875,000 redevelopment of the sports ground.

Driffield played for a season in North One. 2006-07 saw Driffield undefeated at home until late January 2007. Driffield have had many highlights in recent times. In 2000, Driffield were the top RU club in the East Riding area and reached the last four of the Powergen Cup.

The best known Driffield player is Tosh Askew, who moved to Liverpool RFC, then a top-class club. He later became England U19 coach.

FEATHERSTONE

THE YORKSHIRE VILLAGE of Featherstone was revolutionised by the opening of a coal mine in the 1860s. Men flooded into the area, followed by their families.

Initially a cricket club was formed, and in 1884 so was a rugby side called Featherstone United. The first game was a victory over a side from the village of Methley, followed by wins over two sides from Wakefield. Featherstone United folded after a couple of seasons, but a new club, 'Featherstone Trinity', emerged.

Trinity soon became established as one of the best junior clubs in West Yorkshire. In 1894 the club – by then called Featherstone – joined the West Riding League, which they won. September 1895 saw the exodus of the big Northern clubs to their own Northern Union, but Featherstone stayed with the RFU. The problem for Featherstone was that most of the strong Yorkshire rugby sides had defected and opposition in the rugby union ranks was declining. Players were leaving for better rugby.

Their best player of the era, James Metcalfe, was selected for the RFU's North v South match in 1896. Two years later Metcalfe and Featherstone decided to join the Northern Union. This decision wasn't a successful one as the club folded in 1902.

Soon afterwards a new club called Featherstone Rovers was formed, which became one of the leading lights of rugby league in the 20th century.

GOOLE

"The port in green fields."

GOOLE IS ENGLAND'S most inland port, being 50 miles from the sea. Rugby Football in the Goole area goes back to Victorian times, but street football can be traced back even further to the Middle Ages and the 'Haxey Hood' game. On Twelfth Night (6th January) each year two teams from the neighbouring local villages of Haxey and Westwood Hill would try to push their opponents and a leather cylinder called 'the Hood' back to where they began.

Goole, as an area, changed in 1820 when a canal was opened between Knottingley in the heart of the Yorkshire coalfields and Goole on the River Humber. Economic growth came with the opening of the canal, and the town became famous for ship building.

A rugby team existed in Goole in the 1880s. There are records of Goole playing Hull, a top-class side, in 1883. Goole disagreed with a referee's decision in the game and walked off.

A NU team played in Goole in the 1890s, but soon disappeared. The demise wasn't surprising as in 1898 they lost 63-0 to Oldham and 34-0 to Featherstone in NU Cup matches. The Featherstone match was remarkable for six Goole players being sent off by the referee, and another had to be carried off.

The next mention of rugby came in 1927, when the Goole GSOB were formed. They became a formidable side and attained high-ranking status in the 1950s, when Kendal's records show the Cumbrians agreed to pay Goole GSOBs' expenses if they would travel to Kendal. Goole GSOB changed their name to Goole in the 1970s and left their facilities at Murren Avenue to move to Westfield Banks in 1991.

The best players produced by the club include Oscar Sugden, who played for Yorkshire; Tony Donaghue, who played for Morley; and brothers Richard and Andrew Wilson, who played for Wakefield. In 2000, Goole were Yorkshire Shield winners. The high point of Goole's League days was North 2 East in 2000-01

(Thanks to Michael Kelly)

HALIFAX

"We welcome anyone with a smile on their face."
Graham Smith

HALIFAX IS A rugby stronghold set high in the Pennines. Rugby league has a long tradition in the town, but rugby union is still played by five local clubs. The best known RFU club is Halifax RUFC, but Halifax Vandals, Old Rishworthians, Old Brodleians and Heath (Old Boys) kept the 15-a-side code going in an area. This is surprising because an acre of flatland is a rare commodity amid the rolling Pennine hills.

The original Halifax RFC have played rugby league since the 1895 Schism and survive today, maintaining an unbroken line back to the earliest days of the sport. Rugby has been played in the town since 1873, when members of the West Yorkshire Rifle Volunteers formed Halifax RFC. The original meeting to form the club followed an advertisement inserted in a local newspaper by Sam Duckett. The result was disappointing, as only eight people turned up, and although it was decided to form a club, no one knew the rules!

It took until November 1874 for Halifax to play their first game (away to Leeds Athletic). The membership then was only 16, all of them players, but only 14 turned out in the first game.

The story of how Halifax decided (if decided is the word) on their traditional colours of blue and white is unusual. Red and black should have been the club's colours, but the London firm that was asked to supply them had not got those colours in stock. Blue and white jerseys were taken instead, and so remain Halifax's colours to this day.

The first home game was against Wakefield Trinity at Kings Cross Road. In their second season, Halifax found a better home ground at Ovenden, until they fell out with their landlords. They were obliged to move first to Savile Park and then to Hanson Lane.

Halifax quickly established a reputation amongst the best in Yorkshire. George Thomson was the first Halifax player to win international honours when he was selected for England in 1878. Other England internationals were A. Wood and Harold Wilkinson. Another England international associated with Halifax was Jack Dyson (1865-1908), who also had ties to Huddersfield RFC. A strongly-built sprinter, Dyson scored 30 tries in 1889-90 for Halifax. Outstanding performances for Yorkshire propelled him into the England team that faced Scotland. However, at the time Dyson was dismissed as a pure sprinter with 'poor hands'. He joined Huddersfield in 1895 but retired the following year to run a public house.

Halifax were Yorkshire Cup winners for the first time in 1886 after several near misses. That year they moved home again to Thrum Hall, a farm near Hanson Lane that was to become forever associated with Halifax rugby. The first big game at Thrum Hall was Halifax v the 1889 Maoris, which was an easy victory for the locals and one that encouraged the England selectors to award Harry Wilkinson his first cap. Halifax were becoming a magnet for top-class players from all over the north, which dragged the club into the 'broken time' turmoil that was afflicting Yorkshire rugby. Based at the heart of the north of England, Halifax joined the Northern Union and have been an

Harold Wilkinson scores a try for England in 1929.

integral part of the 13-man game ever since. By contrast, rugby union virtually disappeared until after World War One.

The current Halifax RUFC began life in 1919 as Saville Old Boys, which became Halifax Old Boys before the suffix was dropped. The current Halifax RUFC, as we know them today, played their first match on 8th September 1923 against Pudsey and won 19-8. There was no settled ground in the first season of the Saville Old Boys. At first it was at Broomfield, next at Spring Hall, then Friendly Fields and later still at Ovenden Cross. Finally, they moved to their present ground at Ovenden Park in November 1925. Electric lighting was installed on the ground for training purposes and Halifax became the first club in the north to have this facility.

Three-quarters Wilson Smith and Fred Adams were members of the Halifax side in the club's first golden era – the interwar years. In 1926-27 Halifax won 28 of 34 matches and three seasons later won 30 of 33. Notable players of the era were the two great half-backs, Frank Berry and Bill Flathers; international Harry Wilkinson, capped 47 times for the county between 1924 and 1931; and, lastly, Harry Eastwood, Yorkshire's hooker and captain of Halifax for eight seasons.

Harry Wilkinson's father had also been capped for England in the 1889. A tall, thin forward with a shock of blond hair, Wilkinson scored two tries on his England debut in 1929, a record that was not matched for 57 years. Wilkinson had gone to a soccer-playing school and didn't play rugby until he was 21. Wilkinson Jnr. scored 181 tries in 150 matches for Halifax. He toured with the 1930 Lions, where he was second top scorer behind A.L. Novis. He played 47 times for Yorkshire and was county President. He died in 1988, aged 85.

Another famous name to play for Halifax was W.F. Browne, the legendary Irish forward who was stationed in the area during the late 1920s.

In 1950 W.W. Wakefield opened the Standeven Memorial Ground at Ovenden Park. Dennis Standeven, who played for Yorkshire 26 times, presented the ground to the club in

memory of his father and brother. He also paid off the mortgage, on condition that the ground was used for rugby forever.

The club had another golden era, culminating in 1961-62 when they defeated Waterloo (twice), New Brighton and Swansea. Their pack alone scored 58 tries, with 22 from the front row. Halifax were strong enough to be invited to play fixtures against sides such as the mighty Cardiff.

Halifax were punching well above their weight, fielding British Lions like Phil Horrocks-Taylor and Michael Campbell Lamerton. Horrocks-Taylor began his club rugby at Halifax and won nine England caps between 1958 and 1962. A product of Heath Grammar School, he played for Halifax until he was called up for National Service. He turned down a commission because the Army wanted him to stop playing rugby. Afterwards, he went to Cambridge University. He was outstanding in the Light Blues victory in the 1956 Varsity Match, when he eclipsed the brilliant Welsh star Ollwyn Brace of Oxford.

Horrocks-Taylor was the subject of one of rugby's best known jokes; Tony O'Reilly of Ireland once explained away a missed tackle on the Yorkshireman with the comment: "Horrocks went right – Taylor went left and I was left holding the hyphen."

Campbell-Lamerton won 23 Scotland caps and was the 1966 Lions captain. Reports suggest his Lions appointment was a compromise and unpopular with the Welsh contingent. As Lions captain, Campbell-Lamerton found the abrasiveness of touring wasn't suited to his amiable, sensitive nature.

Halifax had other outstanding competitors during this era. For example, winger Malcolm Bussey scored 11 tries in 13 games before winning a rugby blue at Cambridge.

Halifax at Cardiff in 1956.

Sadly, Halifax RUFC declined, which impacted on their already modest gates. The size of Halifax's gates during the era can be gleaned from the impact of the terrible winter of 1963; the club's minutes record that, "We saved money because no gate money was lost (most of our spectators are members) and the club has saved a fortune on travelling due to the snow."

Halifax were one of Yorkshire's middle-ranking sides in the years following the arrival of league rugby. The New Millennium saw Halifax boosted by sponsorship; they rose into the National Leagues and won the Intermediate Cup. In 2003-04 they lost only two competitive matches and were promoted to National Two. Sadly, the sponsorship dried up and in 2007-08 Halifax lost nine first team members and were relegated.

When the funding dried up, the club had to accept their semi-professional status was unsustainable. An exodus of players forced the club to concede that they didn't have the playing resources to continue.

Halifax accepted that they had to start again at the bottom of Yorkshire rugby. So, in 2009, they entered Yorkshire Six, with the Second XV stepping up to fill the void left by the first team exodus. Halifax went from the greensward of the National League to playing on public playing fields and behind workingmen's clubs, but club officials feel happier with life.

HARROGATE

HARROGATE RFC WAS formed as Harrogate Hornets FC and played its first match on 16th December 1871 against Darlington, who recorded their opponents as 'Harrowgate'. The game was played on the 'Stray', which is 200 acres of common land carved out of the Forest of Knaresborough. The Hornets suffix was later dropped. The club has played a role in making Yorkshire a major part of English rugby. They were viewed as the best team in the county in the late 1870s.

The original Harrogate RFC were offered the option to join the Northern Union in 1896, but declined the opportunity – perhaps because they had always relied on public schoolboys for players, who felt more affinity with the RFU than the NU. In 1896, Harrogate FC moved to Carlow Road, which became their long-term home.

A decade later Albert Pickering was their first international when he represented England in the 17-9 defeat by Ireland in Dublin. Pickering, who had joined Harrogate from Old Dewsburians RUFC, was county captain for three seasons.

In 1914 the club split, with Harrogate FC continuing as a football club and the rugby players becoming Harrogate Old Boys RFC, who became Harrogate RUFC in 1923.

During the inter-war years, Harrogate became part of an end-of-season circuit for touring rugby teams, although the tradition had previously been only for seaside resorts. Many touring teams used the Great Eastern Hotel in Harrogate as a tour base. Successive proprietors had much to contend with. One story recalls a rugby player climbing drainpipes to reach a third floor window after being locked out. His teammates fortunately rescued him when he got stuck 30 foot above the ground.

During the inter-war era Harrogate rose in stature and vied with Headingley for the title of Yorkshire's premier rugby union club. International recognition was, however, slow to reach Harrogate players. It was 1954 before Ian King, a talented full-back, was selected by England. King kicked a penalty and conversion on his England debut but was discarded by the selectors after only three appearances.

In 1964 North Eastern Counties played Whineray's All Blacks at the Harrogate Agricultural Showground, home of the Royal Yorkshire Agricultural Show.

Perhaps the greatest of Harrogate players, Jeff Young, played for the club at this time. He arrived in Harrogate from St. Luke's College, Exeter to take up a teaching appointment in the town. He won 23 Welsh caps and played for the Lions in the first test against South Africa in 1968. Jeff also played for London Welsh, RAF and Bridgend.

Soon after Young's departure, Peter Squires emerged. Squires was the last of a breed of multi-talented sportsmen. He played first-class cricket for Yorkshire, won 29 England caps at rugby, and toured with the 1977 Lions to New Zealand. Small of stature, but blessed with devastating pace, Squires' career with England began with a try against New Zealand, when England recorded their first ever away win against the Kiwis. Sadly, his international career spanned dismal years for England as erratic selection and mediocrity bedevilled the national team. Squires stepped down from international rugby in 1979 and returned to Ripon RFC, his original club.

In 1971 Harrogate were one of the first English clubs to start mini and junior rugby. This has enabled the club to stay at the front of Yorkshire rugby and hold National League status. They have been County Cup champions on twelve occasions, and

represented Yorkshire in the 2002 County Sevens, when they emerged as champions.

Harrogate had a good competitive pedigree before the introduction of leagues, as in 1967-68 they were Northern Champions of the unofficial Pennant Merit Table. They entered the league structure in 1987 in North 1 (then the equivalent of level 5) and began a golden era of three promotions in six years. 1994 saw Harrogate reach Division Two (Level 2).

A witness to this was one of the club's best servants: Ralph Zoing. A product of Bristol's famous Colston School, he played for Harrogate from 1985 to 1999, scoring a record 1,085 league points in just over 100 appearances, and was coach for five years. Ralph attributes much of the club's success during this 'golden era' to Peter Clegg, captain and coach in the early 1990s, and Graham Sisswick, who was associated with the club for 40 years.

Besides Ralph Zoing, Harrogate has produced many top-class players: Martyn Wood played for Wasps, Bath and England; and Guy and Simon Easterby opted for Ireland at an early stage. Guy won 42 Irish caps, whilst Simon was Ireland's most capped flanker and a British Lion. The Easterby name is more familiar in horse racing – Walter, Peter and Mick were leading horse trainers. Simon progressed to Leeds via Ampleforth and Harrogate. He played for Ireland before opting to play his club rugby in Llanelli.

Currently Harrogate are the best Yorkshire side in National 2 North.

(Thanks to Ralph Zoing)

HEATH
(formerly Heath Old Boys)

HEATH RUFC IS one of the easiest clubs to find, being directly off the main road into Halifax. It is impossible to miss the club's excellent facilities at West Vale. The club was formed in 1927 by the Old Boys of Heath Grammar School, Halifax.

The grammar school itself had a formidable reputation for rugby long before the Old Boys club was formed. The school produced a string of internationals for Halifax: George Thomson, Albert Wood, Charlie Fox and Ernest Fookes. Fookes (1878-1948) was educated at Heath GS before winning 10 England caps as a player for Sowerby Bridge in the 1890s. He returned to his native New Zealand in 1900, but toured the UK with the 1905 All Blacks.

Heath GS switched to soccer for a period, but reverted to rugby union in 1927, which led to the formation of a casual Old Boys side that initially played both rugby and soccer.

The rugby club affiliated to the Yorkshire RFU and arranged a full season's fixtures for 1928-29 under the first team captain, J.G. Jackson. The club's first game was an 18-8 defeat to Halifax Vandals 'A'. They acquitted themselves well for a new club and subsequently won 11 and lost 11 games over the season, scoring 297 points against 285. Other local teams they played at that time were Caldene (Mytholmroyd), Brighouse Rangers, Elland, Halifax, Halifax Vandals, Old Crossleyans, Copley and Hebden Bridge Old Boys. Many of those early rivals have long since disappeared.

The early 1930s were a great period for Heath OBs, with victories easily outnumbering defeats. An 'A' team was formed, who beat the Old Rishworthians in their debut match in September 1930.

Heath's first pitch was at Peat Pitts, which was vacated in 1934. The players cannot have been sorry as the local paper reported on one occasion that, "The ground was waterlogged and a veritable quagmire which in one part of the field held up many movements." The report continued, "conditions were terrible, incessant and heavy rain fell throughout the first half and the ground which was heavy at the outset rapidly developed into a morass."

In 1935 Rex Fry, the club treasurer, 'pulled strings at the Town Hall' and managed to obtain the lease on corporation-owned land at West Vale, where the rugby club could operate. Changing facilities were arranged with the Bridge Inn on Rochdale Road. Heath OBs remained at West Vale until the outbreak of World War Two, when the ground was ploughed up.

After the war, Heath briefly returned to West Vale in 1949, but a shortage of players proved a continual problem. They were able to briefly persuade a local schoolboy, J.P. Horrocks-Taylor, to wear their colours. Horrocks-Taylor subsequently moved to Halifax and later Middlesbrough, with whom he was capped by England.

In April 1955, Heath OBs went into temporary abeyance, and the goalposts were sold to Longwood RLFC for £6.50 and the grandstand to Halifax RUFC for £10. After several seasons of inactivity, the club reformed and obtained a 10-year lease on a new ground.

The early 1960s were equally difficult for the club, principally because they had no changing or social facilities. The lack of a base for social efforts made fund-raising difficult, and the terrible winter of 1962-63 caused the cancellation of 13 consecutive matches. However, the new changing rooms were ready for use in October 1963, at a cost of £600. The following season saw a chink of light when they were able to field Peter Warden, who had represented Great Britain in the 400m hurdles at the Rome Olympics. The tide had turned, and the club won 29 of 35 games in 1966-67. Heath were expanding rapidly and dropped the 'Old Boys' title in 1976.

A decade later, Paul Stewart, the First XV captain, tried his luck with high-riding Wakefield. Stewart did well there and was selected for Yorkshire and the North of England.

The arrival of league rugby saw Heath in Yorkshire Division 4, from where promotion was gained in 1997-98 to Yorkshire 3 as champions. 2001–02 was a golden year: winning the Junior Cup, the Yorkshire Silver Trophy and Yorkshire Two.

HUDDERSFIELD

"The Ascot of the North"
19th century newspaper description

THE LARGE TOWN of Huddersfield sits near the highest point of the M62 motorway linking Lancashire and Yorkshire. The town has an important place in rugby history as the rebels from the two counties met at the George Hotel in 1895 to agree the formation of the Northern Union.

The first rugby club in the town emerged from Huddersfield Athletic Club. Huddersfield was known as the 'Ascot of the North' for the popularity of its athletics festivals in the 1860s. The town's athletic club subsequently expanded into cricket, rugby and football.

The first known rugby match in Huddersfield was in 1866, when Leeds played Manchester in a match designed to promote the burgeoning sport. Manchester won, largely due to their half-back, a burly ex-Rugbeian who flattened the opposition. It was 12 years before the next recorded match, when on 2nd November 1878, Huddersfield RFC played Manchester Rangers.

The following year Henry Huth, a wool merchant from Huddersfield, was capped at full-back for England against Scotland. Huth (1859-1926) was one of three brothers who represented Huddersfield and Yorkshire at rugby. Henry also played cricket for the North of England.

The following year, Ernest Woodhead of Huddersfield was picked for England in odd circumstances. Woodhead was studying in Dublin and found himself in England's colours when one of England's players was so ill with seasickness after the voyage to Dublin that an urgent replacement was sought. After the match Woodhead received his cap and the team's thanks, but he was never selected again.

Jack Dyson (1865-1908) was capped for England against Scotland in 1890. He joined Huddersfield RFC in 1885 and established a reputation as a strongly-built sprinter whose suspect handling let him down. He scored 30 tries in season 1889-90, which led to his selection for Yorkshire and England. He retired from rugby in 1896 to run a public house.

Rugby matches were played at the Rifle Field in Trinity Street and upon the amalgamation with St. John's Cricket Club, they moved to Fartown in 1879. Fartown became the permanent home of the renamed Huddersfield RFC.

The club attracted the RFU's attention again in 1893, when they were suspended for two months for enticing two Cumberland amateurs to move to Fartown. Huddersfield were in the top ranks of English rugby clubs when in August 1895, the town's George Hotel hosted the historic meeting at which 20 clubs resigned from the Rugby Football Union to create professional rugby league. Huddersfield RFC switched to the NU and became a permanent part of the Rugby Football League.

Rugby Union disappeared in the town for a decade, but it was easy for local RU enthusiasts to travel the five miles to Halifax, where the 15-man game flourished. In 1907 Halifax Rangers were struggling, so two members, Walter Scott and C. Edgar Brierley, decided to revive RU in Huddersfield. The initial meeting was held at the Pack Horse Hotel, where it was decided to form Huddersfield Old Boys RUFC. It was 1909 before the club finally took the field when they played Barnsley at Luck Lane Cricket Ground. Changing facilities were available at the Cropper Arms. Later the club moved to a pitch on Thornhill Road.

The club closed down during World War One, but re-started in 1919 at Salendine Nook. The club later took a lease on land at Waterloo, where it adopted its colours of white, claret and gold – the colours of the old, pre-1895 Huddersfield club. A member of Huddersfield OBs must have played a part in the formation of Fylde RUFC in 1919. The seaside club wrote to Huddersfield OBs asking for permission to adopt Huddersfield's colours. Permission was granted.

In 1920 Tom Bletcher and Harry Netherwood from the club played for the North. Also that year, the club came to rank amongst Yorkshire's best, and in the 1920s produced a top-class player in Clarence 'Tubby' Smith, who was an England trialist and Yorkshire regular. Smith had the misfortune to be understudy to the peerless W.J.A. Davies, which meant that he never made the national team. However, his lack of international recognition may also have been due to his mischievous nature as he was reported to be a real handful off the pitch.

Waterloo, which was opened in 1921, was constantly improved. A stand was built with changing rooms, and then the entire property was purchased for £700. This was followed in 1935 with a £350 investment in a new pavilion and bar, with ladies welcomed to a hitherto male bastion when they began the tradition of after-match tea-making.

In 1939 the club decided to drop the 'Old Boys' suffix because few of its players were the products of public schools. The change didn't occur until 1946 and coincided with a golden era of four internationals: Nim Hall, Frank Sykes, Eddie Horsfall and Ian Feddes.

Norman 'Nim' Hall was an England regular from 1947 to 1955 and perhaps the best English fly half of his generation. Hall won 17 England caps and was captain on 13 occasions. He was a wonderfully talented player, blessed with balance and a natural swerve which took him past opponents. He originally intended to follow his father by becoming a doctor, but failed his medical exams at St. Mary's Hospital. Sadly, Hall's fortunes off the field paralleled his decline on the pitch. He was reported to have fallen on hard times. Ken Shaw, a Huddersfield stalwart, held the opinion that the post-war Huddersfield side was probably the best in the club's history, and Hall was the finest player.

After Nim Hall, Huddersfield unearthed another natural talent in Frank Sykes, who won four England caps, toured with the 1955 Lions and appeared 79 times for Yorkshire, including 66 consecutive appearances. Sykes' England appearances were limited due to the competition for the wing berths from Jeff Butterfield and Peter Jackson. Huddersfield considered Sykes improved as player when he was taken under the wing of a club stalwart called Bobby Fletcher, who taught the winger much of his skills.

Another international associated with Huddersfield is Ian Feddis, the son of a rugby league professional. Feddis jnr played for Scotland in the 1960s and was a great club captain for Huddersfield. Another family associated with the club is the Cliffords, who included Lewis Clifford, the 1956 RFU President.

In 1959 the club embarked on an expansion plan to build a new pitch on an adjacent railway embankment. To fund the plan every player was told to raise £5 – a handsome sum in 1959. Over the years the club acquired more land, essentially to cater for the growing number of junior teams, making HRUFC a significant landowner and one of the few major sports organisations to own, rather than lease, its own property.

In 1966 the club sold part of its property to fund the purchase of the 26 acres at Lockwood Park. They now have a main floodlit pitch with a capacity for 1,500 spectators, seating for 500 and parking for 300 vehicles, as well as further rugby pitches and an Astroturf all-weather pitch.

On the field, the club were regulars in the Top 60 Merit Tables in the days before league rugby. In 1969 the club pioneered mini-rugby in England. They had a famous coach in Ted Wood, who later was the Durham University and England Students coach.

Since league rugby arrived, Huddersfield have been promoted three times: to North One in 1992 and 2001 and to National Three North in 2007.

The best modern player to emerge from Huddersfield is Luther Burrell, who began with the club before moving to Huddersfield Giants RLFC, Sale Sharks, Leeds and then Northampton Saints. He made his England debut in 2013 and cemented his place in the team with brave running.

(Thanks to Ken Shaw)

HULL

HULL HAS BEEN a port since ancient times, but its fortunes grew rapidly with the opening of a commercial dock in the 1750s. The opening of the dock and the proximity of the Yorkshire coalfield made Hull one of the success stories of the Industrial Revolution.

Rugby in the city goes back to 1865, when Hull FC was formed by a group of public schoolboys. The club's first ground was at Woodgates Hall, North Ferriby, but they soon moved to a ground opposite the Londesborough Arms in Selby, and later to Newland.

The founders included W.H. Hutchinson, who was the first Yorkshireman to win an England cap. A shipowner by profession, Hutchinson was educated at Rugby School and played in the final 20-a-side international match between England and Ireland at Kennington Oval. In later life, he recalled that in the sport's early days it was common during a match for players to grab an opponent by the hair.

Hull RFC were second best in the city to Hull White Star before the two clubs agreed to merge in 1881 and to move to the White Star's ground at Hall's Field on Holderness Road. White Star was the senior partner in the merger and many of the Hull members resigned in disgust. Another adverse effect of the merger was that attempts to blend the two sets of colours on a single jersey proved fruitless when the new jerseys ran in the wash. This forced the club to opt for a 'black' jersey, which later changed to 'black and white hoops'

Hull RFC thrived after the merger and had average gates of 3,000 spectators for home matches. Rugby was a booming sport in the city and Hull were able to draw players from the dozen junior clubs. Across the city, another successful club was formed in 1883 by a group of apprentice boilermakers under the title of Kingston Amateurs. They became better known as Hull Kingston Rovers

Hull RFC were promoted to the Yorkshire Senior Competition in 1893, but struggled. Around this time, the club moved to Airlie Road near the Boulevard. In 1895 Hull joined the NU and were highly successful from the outset. Despite the split, Hull FC gave donations to local rugby union charities for 30 years after their decision to quit the RFU.

Hull KR also joined the Northern Union. The antagonism between the two sides was legendary. Hull and HKR traditionally met on Christmas Day and replayed the match on Boxing Day. They remain two separate entities today.

HULL & EAST RIDING

RUGBY UNION IN Hull was revived in 1900 when Bill Cobby, a schoolmaster from Hymers School, raised a side to play a Castleford XV. The Hull team was considered a representative team and called 'Hull & East Riding RFC' to record the fact that they were representing the district. Eventually, Hull & East Riding became a regular side. They were sufficiently well regarded for J.L. Fisher and B.S. Massey to be selected for the 1904 British Isles tour to Australia and New Zealand, which was led by Bedell-Sivright. Little is known of the Hull duo, but the tour was a success, with 16 wins in 19 matches.

The club had a lean period between the wars; indeed, in the 1930-31 season they won only five of 27 matches.

The early 1950s were also sparse for Hull & East Riding. A witness to H&ER's post-war days was Les Anson, who went to Hull Grammar School (a soccer-playing school, but one that produced many excellent rugby players). An acquaintance, connected to H&ER, persuaded Les to play in the centre for a club side against Driffield, although he had never played rugby before. Les made his first team debut at hooker against a Headingley team that included two internationals. The era saw H&ER having a rough time, but they nevertheless produced an England international in centre Roger Sangwin, who won two England caps in 1964, whilst David Bell had an England trial and Geoff Moore played 30 times for Yorkshire.

The arrival of Brian Moxon galvanised the club into a revival. Moxon had won 15 Yorkshire caps whilst with Huddersfield and Headingley and helped revive Hull & East Riding. The 1960s saw H&ER record 69 victories in 89 matches over two seasons.

In the early 1970s Hull Spartan Rugby Club had merged with Hull & East Riding, and for the next two decades the club's XV were known as Hull Spartans.

Hull & East Riding have played at various locations, moving from Goddard Avenue to the Circle. The introduction of a league structure in 1987 forced the need for a senior club to own its premises and control its bar income. Two years later, Hull & East Riding had another merger, this time with Hull Ionians, and took that club's name and status in North One. Not everybody was happy with this merger and a breakaway Hull & East Riding club was formed. Hull Ionians went along with this in order to keep more clubs alive in the area.

HULL RUFC

THE MEMBERS OF the original Hull & East Riding club who were opposed to the merger with Hull Ionians formed Hull & East Riding RUFC (1989) and were given membership of Yorkshire Six. Ironically, in July 1992 H&ER (1989) themselves merged with Old Hymerians to form Hull RUFC. The new club took over tenancy of the Old Hymerians ground at Haworth Park and their league status in North-East Division Two. The colours of the new club were to be red, black and gold and the first club captain was Zimbabwean international fly-half David Walters. The first coach was former England international prop Paul Huntsman.

Hull's first game at Haworth Park was a 51-12 victory over Hemsworth. Their first league game was at home to the eventual champions Doncaster, who were defeated 8-6.

In 2001-02 the new club won 19 and drew one of their 22 league matches. That year the club recruited Gary Pearce, the ex-Wales and Lions half-back, as player-coach. The following season, Hull were third in North Two, and in 2004-05 were promoted to North One.

The final Hull RUFC game to be played at Haworth Park was on 19th April 2008, when Hull beat Westoe 27-25. The following season would see Hull playing at their new home, the Ferens Ground on Chanterlands Avenue. Ironically, the opening match at the new Ferens Ground was also against Westoe, with Hull winning 63-8. After only five seasons, Hull took their place in the newly created National Two North.

HULL IONIANS

HULL IONIANS WERE promoted to National One in 2013, but they have a long, complicated story. Hull Ionians as they exist today were formed in 1989 by the merger of the Ionians club with Hull & East Riding RFC.

The Ionians were originally formed in 1926 by a dissident handful from Old Hymerians, who met at one player's house at 37 Marlborough Avenue in Hull. The club name allegedly comes from one player's mother, a lady called Iona, who provided tea and biscuits during the meeting. This legend is rather undermined by the fact that the name of 'Ionians' echoes the Victorian habit of giving their teams the names of ancient warriors – the Ionians were perhaps the most fearsome Greek tribe in ancient times.

After playing at various venues, they leased a ground at Dunswell, north of Hull, in 1932 before purchasing land at Elloughton in February 1961. They opened a £6000 clubhouse in 1963. Initially, the buildings were rather spartan, with changing rooms in corrugated iron buildings (which later became the kitchens) and meetings held in the local hostelry. This all changed in 1963, when the Elloughton clubhouse was opened. A lounge bar and improved changing rooms were added over the next two decades. This clubhouse was demolished when the Elloughton ground was sold for house building. This funded the move to Brantingham. The great driving force of the club for many years was Les Booth, who later became Yorkshire President.

In1989 Ionians merged with Hull & East Riding, who were then in North One. The new club adopted the name of Hull Ionians and the colours were quarters of cherry red and white (those of Hull and East Riding) and the green and blue of Ionians. Unfortunately, history repeated itself when a Hull & East Riding element defected, taking the name of Hull & East Riding with them.

Hull Ionians reached the Intermediate Cup Final in 2000, but lost 14-10 to Dunstable. They had the consolation of being the first Hull side to reach Twickenham. After being a long-term fixture in North One, Hull Ionians reached the National Leagues in 2005 after a play-off victory over Kettering. Ionians were coached by a real veteran war-horse, Mick Watson, who had done sterling service across East Yorkshire. In 2009 Stephen Townend took over as director of rugby and ex-Lion Gary Pearce became head coach.

Mick Watson in action.

2012-13 proved a record-breaking season for the club. In the last match of the season they needed a bonus point win to be league champions, which they achieved in style with a 50-7 victory over Caldy, thus winning National 2 North and promotion to National 1 for the first time ever by an East Yorkshire club.

HYMERS COLLEGE

Robert Stokesby founded Hymers College in 1889. A schism among members of Old Hymerians occurred in 1926 and Hull Ionians was formed at Brough outside the city. Old Hymerians won the Yorkshire Cup in 1973, but in 1992 merged with Hull & East Riding (1989). Hymers College OBs played at Haworth Park, which became the home ground of Hull RUFC.

ILKLEY

"Wheear 'as tha binn since ah saw thee?
On Ilkla Moor baht 'at'"
Unofficial Yorkshire anthem

ILKLEY IS A delightful town in the Pennines, near the junction of the main roads from Leeds, Harrogate and Skipton. The River Wharfe runs through the middle of the town and helped establish Ilkley as a spa town in the 19th century. Ilkley was a popular centre for affluent gentlefolk who made their money in the great cities of Leeds and Bradford and wanted to escape to the fresh air of the countryside. Many of the people who moved to Ilkley were of German origin and made money in the clothing trade. Amongst the prosperous families were the Steinthals. Two of their sons, F.E and P.C. Steinthal, were top-class rugby players for the newly-founded Ilkley Rugby Club and Yorkshire.

Francis Steinthal was born in Bradford in 1886 and educated at Bradford Grammar School. In 1906 Francis won an Oxford Blue at centre, which led to an England trial in the North v South match. He was one of the most prolific try scorers of the era for Ilkley and Yorkshire. In 1913 Francis was finally selected for England in the Wales match, when he replaced F.M. Stoop. He kept his place for the 1913 France match and partnered Ronnie Poulton in the centre. Francis was then dropped amid criticism that he had shown 'a loss of pace' and 'selfishness' in the French match.

Steinthal faced a dilemma in 1914 when England went to war with Germany. Francis chose England and joined the British army. A major stumbling block was his German name, so in 1914 Francis changed his surname to that of his wife, Emeline Petrie, a well-known sculptress. He rose to the rank of army captain before being invalided out of the Army with war wounds.

Francis Steinthal wasn't the only international from Ilkley as P.F. Douty won three Scottish caps in 1929. The president of the club at this time was John Green, who had won eight England caps whilst with Skipton.

By this time, the holidaymakers were deserting Ilkley Spa, but rugby tourists still made for the Dales. The most famous visiting team to be based at Ilkley was the 1935 Australian rugby league team, who defied convention by using the rugby union ground as its training headquarters. The hospitality paid a curious dividend in 1936, when the Springboks (rugby union) team toured Australia. The South Africans were denied training facilities by the Australian rugby league authorities until Harry Sutherland, the Australian team manager, prevailed on Sydney

Cricket Ground to open its doors to the rival code. Sutherland explained that the kindness of Ilkley RUFC had set a precedent that he felt required to follow. The RFU had different ideas. In 1947 the Ilkley ground made the news when the RFU banned the visiting New Zealand Rugby League team from practising there.

Other less-famous visitors to the Pennines came for the rugby. In the mid-20th Century, British rugby made end-of-season tours to Skipton, Ilkley and Roundhay. Old Leysians, then a fine side, visited Ilkley in 1948 and spent the after match hours in the Crescent Hotel. The landlord soon tired of the high jinks and told the teams they could have one last round. "We'll have seventy pints and make it snappy," was the Leysian captain's reply.

The end of season circuit no longer includes the Dales, so Ilkley have settled down to a quieter existence in the middle-ranks of Yorkshire rugby. In 2011 the elderly clubhouse at Stacks Field was replaced with a superb new facility. It sparked a revival as in 2012 Ilkley rolled back the years when they reached Twickenham, but lost to East Grinstead in the Intermediate Cup Final. In 2013-14 they won The Yorkshire Shield and were promoted to North 1 East

YORKSHIRE CARNEGIE
(formerly Leeds Carnegie, Leeds Tykes, Headingley & Roundhay)

LEEDS CARNEGIE RUFC has a long history stretching back as far as 1878 and the formation of Headingley FC, who were later to merge with Roundhay RUFC to form Leeds RUFC.

Rugby in the city goes back even further. In 1864 an advertisement appeared in the Leeds Mercury asking potential 'footballers' to attend Woodhouse Moor. They soon attracted 500 members and 150 regular players. This club became Leeds Athletic Club, who fielded an international in R.H. Fowler.

Another club, Leeds St. John's FC, was formed in 1870 and was known as the 'Amber and Blues'. St. John's played initially at the Militia Barracks before moving to the Cardigan Fields. St. Johns restricted membership to church members, but eventually dropped the restriction and accepted all-comers. St. John's were the beaten Yorkshire Cup finalists in 1887.

Leeds St. Johns dropped the suffix in 1890 and became part of the Leeds Cricket, Football and Athletic Co. Ltd. They bought a plot of land from the Cardigan Estates, known as 'Headingley'. The new rugby club wore brown and green jerseys.

The first match played by the new club at their new stadium was against Manningham. The new Leeds club was enormously successful and had 27,654 spectators for one cup match against Halifax.

Leeds RFC joined the NU in 1895 and became one of the greatest participants in the 13-man game.

Following the usual tradition, no rugby union club adopted the city's name for a century, and the mantle of promoting the RFU game fell to three major clubs: Headingley, Roundhay and Morley. Today only Morley still play, but Headingley and Roundhay merged to form Leeds RUFC in 1992. They were reported to have raised £3.5 million by selling Kirkstall and Chandos Park.

Leeds RUFC played their first match against Hampshire-based Havant in September 1992 following the merger of Roundhay RUFC and Headingley FC. In 1996 Leeds RUFC signed an agreement to join Leeds CF&A club that ran Headingley Stadium. Two years later they were renamed Leeds Tykes under the majority shareholder Paul Caddick, who already owned Leeds RLFC.

In July 1998 Leeds Tykes became part of the world's first rugby partnership with the creation of Leeds Rugby Limited. The company encompasses Leeds Rhinos Rugby League and the then newly-named Leeds Tykes as they entered Allied Dunbar Premiership Two.

In 2005 Leeds shocked the nouveau riche of the professional rugby union when they persuaded All Black legend Justin Marshall to join them. Back home Marshall had won 77 caps for New Zealand. That year they won the National Knockout Cup, beating Bath 20-12 in the final.

The merger allowed the club to move to Headingley. One benefit of the merger was that Wendell Sailor, the outstanding Australian winger, was persuaded to play for Leeds. Sailor is considered one of the finest three-quarters produced by rugby league. He eventually returned to Australia and played in the 2003 Rugby World Cup.

Leeds' new professional rugby union club became a 'yo-yo club' between the Premiership and National One. Coach Phil Davies was the keystone of the club's time from 1996-2006. He oversaw recruitment campaigns that brought a steady stream of internationals to Headingley: Iain Balshaw, Andre Snyman, Mark Regan, Diego Albanese and Gordon Bulloch. The sad fact was that Leeds could recruit talent, but many drifted over to more affluent southern clubs. It wasn't just experienced talent that gravitated to Headingley. Brilliant youngsters like Jordan Crane, Danny Care and Tom Palmer broke through at Leeds before moving on.

Danny Care is one of a number of brilliant youngsters who have come through the ranks in Leeds.

Stuart Lancaster had been in charge of developing the young talent at Leeds. When Phil Davies stepped down in 2006, Lancaster was asked to take over. He found only seven players available with just weeks until the start of the National One season. Somehow, he found a full squad and galvanised it into a team who were promoted back to the Premiership in 2007. He subsequently became England's 2015 Rugby World Cup Director of Rugby.

In 2007 the club entered another new exciting era, with Leeds Metropolitan University taking a 51% share in the club and renaming the team Leeds Carnegie for their return to the top flight. The venture saw some of the highest attendances recorded for rugby union games at Headingley Carnegie, and brought with it some unique opportunities for both players and supporters thanks to this ground-breaking partnership. In 2014 the club changed its name to Yorkshire Carnegie to show their pride in being the county's premier rugby union side.

In 2015, Yorkshire Carnegie announced the signing of Kevin Sinfield, one the greatest rugby league players of all time.

LEEDS PARISH CHURCH

THE LEEDS PARISH Church RFC was one of the strongest Yorkshire clubs in the 19th Century. They owed their origins to the Muscular Christianity movement in the city. Unfortunately, they are best remembered for their brushes with the RFU over shamateurism. In 1887 they were suspended for professionalism, rumours of which continually surrounded the club until 1896 when they joined the NU. The club left the NU in 1901 and ceased playing.

LEEDS ST. JOHN'S

LEEDS ST. JOHN'S RFC was formed in 1870 by Mr. T. J. Ogden, who later became headmaster of Rossall School. The club took its name from St. John the Evangelist Church on Briggate, Leeds.

Like many clubs, St. Johns RFC was formed by cricketers, from the Church Sunday School, looking for something to do in the winter. The first pitch was on Carlton Hill and the first game against Wakefield Trinity.

LIVERSEDGE

LIVERSEDGE RFC WAS formed in 1877 by colliers in the Spen Valley. The club produced two early England internationals in Harry Varley and Bob Wood. Varley defected to Oldham RFC in 1892. Liversedge were founder members of the NU and Yorkshire NU Senior Champions in 1896. Four years later Liversedge merged with neighbours Cleckheaton and opted to play at Cleckheaton's ground at Whitcliffe. The club changed its name to Cleckheaton NUFC in 1902 and folded several years later.

ROUNDHAY

ROUNDHAY RUFC DISAPPEARED in 1992, when they merged with Headingley to form Leeds RUFC. They were formed in 1924 by a meeting at the Mansion House. Their first home was a field on Talbot Road, rented for 30p a week, where they played the Third XV's of bigger clubs. The following year, Roundhay rented a pitch at Bracken Edge for £2 a week and Bob Oakes, the Yorkshire secretary, sent an invitation XV to help promote the new club. In 1928 Bracken Edge was sold and the club moved to Lidgett Lane and got changed in a laundry.

In 1932 Roundhay purchased facilities on Chandos Park, which became their home for 60 years. In that first season at Chandos Park they won 28 of 35 matches.

In 1948 Jack Best, a canny full-back, became the first player from the club to represent Yorkshire. Dennis Wilkins, from Roundhay, won 13 caps for England in the period from 1951-53, playing all the Five Nations games plus one test against South Africa.

In 1950-51, 27 games were won from 33 matches, with David Stead kicking 210 points. 1954 saw the side reach the county final for the first time, when they lost 17-3 against the Royal Signals at Otley.

In 1963 Bev Dovey propped for England against Wales and Ireland whilst at Leeds University, and after a series of moves around the country returned to Leeds in 1973, where he soon captained the side.

The 1970s saw Roundhay fielding two top-class players in Keith Smith and John Atkinson. Many experts consider fly-half Keith Smith to be the best player to wear Roundhay's colours. He was an England regular for two seasons in the 1970s. But a more famous player was John Atkinson, who played in the same set of backs as Keith Smith. He joined Leeds RLFC, who were then at their zenith, and played 518 games, scoring 340 tries, a club record. He played in numerous finals for Leeds RLFC, and scored a brilliant try in the 1978 Rugby League Challenge Cup final against St. Helens.

With the arrival of league rugby, Roundhay found themselves in the upper-middle rank of Yorkshire rugby. They only gained promotion once, at the end of the 1988-89 season, having finished third the previous season in National League 4 North. In the summer of 1992 they merged with Headingley as Leeds RUFC.

HEADINGLEY

HEADINGLEY WAS FORMED in 1878 under Captain J.H. Potter, with fixtures played at Cardigan Fields. Amongst other important characters in those early days were the Platt brothers, Herbert, Sydney and Joe. The Platts were all talented players, but it was Edward Platt (who never played for the club) who steered the club towards a permanent home at Clarence Field at Kirkstall in 1902. Headingley had a wonderful playing area with natural sand drainage.

In 1903 Headingley had the honour of staging an important England trial game. This was to be followed by return visits in 1910 and 1912. At the time rugby in Yorkshire needed a shot in the arm; by 1904-05 only 14 clubs remained with the Yorkshire RFU and it seemed as though the end was nigh for rugby union in the county. The main saviour was R.F. Oakes, who was elected a member in 1901 and maintained a 50-year association with Headingley. He played only briefly, captaining the club in 1903-04, but his major contribution was in administration. Under his auspices the Yorkshire RU was built up to 108 clubs and 57 schools by 1952. He was also President of the Rugby Football Union.

Headingley RFC bought Kirkstall after World War One, and then proceeded to develop the ground and its facilities. The club's fixture list also blossomed and they were one of the top sides in the north by the outbreak of World War Two.

Rugby was suspended with the outbreak of war, but when peace came four teams were soon being fielded at Kirkstall in the traditional green, black and white strip. In the 1958-59 season the club had three county captains – Oliver Grievson (Yorkshire), J.W. Collard (Durham) and L.F. Reid (Cumberland) – playing regularly in the first team. That year Peter Thompson got the last of his 17 England caps.

The greatest name associated with Headingley RFC was Ian McGeechan, who made his First XV debut in 1965. He went on to win 27 caps for Scotland, toured South Africa with the 1974 Lions (playing in all four tests and also coaching four Lions tours), and captained Headingley, Yorkshire, North Eastern Counties, Scotland and the Barbarians. He has gone on to become one of the great coaches in the modern game.

John Spencer, who made his debut with Headingley in 1966, also went on to captain England in four of his 14 games and to tour with the Lions in Australia and New Zealand. Like Ian he has gone on to serve the game at club level, returning to his native Wharfedale, and at national level in various administrative roles.

The final great name to wear Headingley colours was Peter Winterbottom, who captained Yorkshire and England. He won 58 England caps and appeared seven times for the Lions.

Headingley played their last game at the end of season 1991-92.

LEODIENSIANS

LEEDS GRAMMAR SCHOOL opened in 1552. Its old boys, the Leodiensians, have a fine rugby tradition dating back to the 19th century. The best player produced by the school in the old days was Frank Hutchinson (1885-1960) who won three England caps in 1909 whilst with Headingley and appeared 13 times for Yorkshire. The school had already produced two top-class players in A. Yeadon, an England trialist in 1903, and Patrick Munro, who was captain for Oxford and Scotland in 1904.

The Old Boys rugby club of Leeds Grammar School dates back to 1923, when they played their first matches on the school fields at Lawnswood. Old Leos moved to a ground at Robin Hood in Wakefield in the early 1930s and changed at the Coach and Horses public house. They remained in Wakefield until the 1950s, when they moved to the LGS Old Boys sports centre at Alwoodley. Full-back David Caplan emerged from

David Caplin

the club in the early 1970s before joining Headingley, from where he was capped by England.

The school still produces fine rugby players, but the 'Old' prefix was dropped by the OBs in the 1970s. The club occupy a position in the middle echelon of Yorkshire rugby. They were Yorkshire Shield semi-finalists in 2002 after reaching the fourth round of the Intermediate Cup several years earlier. Leos won the National Junior Cup in 2003-04.

The best player to emerge in recent times was Dan Eddie, a fly half with Leeds Carnegie.

MIDDLESBROUGH

'Ayresome Grievances'
old joke

THE TOWN OF Middlesbrough is today regarded as one of the commercial centres of the North East, which belies its humble origins. In 1850 Middlesbrough was still a village; its rapid expansion came in the second half of the 19th century with the rise of the iron industry and the expansion of the town docks along the River Tees. The ICI Chemical Company then arrived, and by the 1920s there were 60,000 men working in the town.

Middlesbrough's first recorded game was in exalted company – the Northumberland club side, who died out in Victorian times. Northumberland were too strong a team to contemplate accepting a fixture with a brand new side, which suggests that Middlesbrough RFC had already established a reputation. Northumberland won easily by four goals and four tries to nil.

However, we know Darlington FC had played a Middlesbrough side on the 15th February 1873. Middlesbrough were a man short and lost by a goal to nil; indeed, the club lost all of their first three matches. Middlesbrough broke their duck away to York, who they beat by two goals and six touchdowns to nil.

Curiously, the club never played 20-a-side, preferring 15-a-side from their inauguration. These details are all we knew of the original 'Middlesbrough FC', who disappeared in the late 1870s. Another side, Middlesbrough Rovers, appeared in 1879 and played in Albert Park before moving to the Ayresome Park area. A second club, 'Tees Side Wanderers', appeared in 1881 and shared personnel with the Rovers.

Ayresome Park later became the home of Middlesbrough Football Club. The ground was jokingly referred to as a place where fans could 'Ayresome Grievances'.

The 1880s saw a great surge of interest in rugby across North Yorkshire, with sides formed at Thirsk, Ripon, Bedale, Easingwold and Barton, as well as the more successful Wanderers and Rovers in Middlesbrough. In 1892 Rovers lost their ground and the two sides merged as Middlesbrough

RC. Cruelly, soon afterwards, the combined club then lost its remaining ground and led a nomadic existence, which led to the demise of rugby in the town in 1895.

In 1920 Arthur Knott revived the club and mustered ten men to face Hartlepool Rovers. Not surprisingly, the Durham side won 27-3. Things got worse for the next match against St. Peter's School, York, when the students won 60-0. Despite this dismal beginning a complete stranger, Tom Darmand, offered a rent-free pitch and groundsmen on land adjacent to Green Land.

Middlesbrough RUFC became established in 1927 when Sir William Crosthwaite, a local shipping tycoon, raised the £1,200 to buy a ground at Acklam Park. At the time, the club had 65p in the bank. Crosthwaite himself funded the grandstand and changing rooms.

Six years later, the rugby club merged with Middlesbrough Cricket Club, which helped make Acklam Park an all-year-round facility.

World War Two saw an end to fixtures until 1945, but, despite Sir William's generosity, the club were heavily in debt from the purchase of Acklam Park. Amazingly, a local landowner, Sir Thomas Poole, left the club £2,000 in his will – an astonishing sum (equivalent to £200,000 in 21st century terms). Overnight the gloom was lifted, results improved, and top-class players joined the club. Laurie Gloag, who had won four Scots caps in 1949, was paired in the centre with Alan Towell, who was to win two England caps with Leicester and Bedford.

The most remarkable Middlesbrough forward was Jack Rowell, who moved to Gosforth and became one of the greatest coaches in rugby history.

In the 1960s, Phil Horrocks-Taylor, a wonderfully talented runner and fly-half, joined the club after winning nine caps for England and the 1963 Lions.

He was succeeded by Alan Old, who was a totally different style of fly-half, but no less effective. Old was a skilful runner, but his kicking strategy took advantage of law changes that had altered the role of the outside-half. Old won 16 England caps in seven seasons, but was never a regular for his country. He was better thought of by the Lions selectors and was part of the 1974 Invincibles tour to South Africa. Old kicked 15 of 16 conversions as the 1974 Lions beat Mossel Bay. A week later Old was badly injured and missed the rest of the tour. His brother, Chris, was an England cricketer and the two brothers played rugby together for Middlesbrough at one time.

The club's third great fly-half was Rob Andrew, who appeared at Acklam Park whilst a student at nearby Barnard Castle School. He eventually moved to Cambridge University, Wasps and Newcastle, where he became one of England's greatest ever players.

A similar story applied to Rory Underwood, a contemporary of Andrew's at Barnard Castle School, Middlesbrough and for England. Born in the town, the brilliant winger made his Middlesbrough debut in 1979. He joined the RAF and had a long association with Leicester Tigers and England with whom he won 85 caps.

Since the introduction of leagues, Middlesbrough RUFC have been regulars in North One, suffering the odd relegation but usually bouncing back.

Three brothers, James, Chris and Charlie Simpson-Daniel, began at Acklam Park. James played for Gloucester and England and Chris and Charlie played for Newcastle Falcons. A new clubhouse was built at Acklam Park and was opened by Rory Underwood and cricketer Liam Plunkett.

In 2015 the club play in Yorkshire One.

(Thanks to Don Briedon)

MORLEY

Morley is a suburb of south-west Leeds. The local rugby club was formed in February 1878 by Dr. John Haslem, the headmaster of Turton Hall College, Gildersome. Haslem, a Baptist minister, taught the rudiments of rugby to the local youth, and organised a match between them and his college boys. The youths called themselves 'Morley Juniors'.

Interest grew and the Juniors suffix was dropped. Morley RFC was born. On 9th November 1878, Morley won their first game against Dewsbury Birkdale at a pitch on Fountain Street. The club briefly played on a ground at Cross Hall Fields, but moved to Scatcherd Lane, their long term home, in 1890.

Morley first entered the Yorkshire Cup in 1889, but lost to Leeds. The following year, Morley lost to Manningham in an encounter in which the victors wore rugby boots with studs while Morley's mill lads and miners wore their working boots!

The club's first international was Harry Bedford, a local lad, who had won 12 Yorkshire caps whilst with Batley. Bedford moved to Morley in 1888, with whom he won three England caps against the 1889 Maoris, Ireland and Scotland the following year. Bedford subsequently went into the licensed trade.

In 1895 Morley were Yorkshire Second Division champions, but lost the Yorkshire Cup Final 15-0 against Brighouse Rangers at Headingley in front of 20,000 spectators. They reached the final again in 1901, but lost 20-6 to Castleford at Harrogate.

Scatcherd Lane has long been synonymous with rugby union, but the Maroons were briefly members of the Northern Union. They played their first NU game on 7th September 1897, at home to Bradford. The NU upset Morley by classing the newcomers as a junior club. The ill-feeling split Morley into two distinct clubs: Morley Northern and Morley English (RU). The situation became even more complicated when Morley Northern's best players defected to the rugby union club. This caused the NU club to fold whilst the rugby union club survived.

At the start of the 20th century, Morley RUFC produced two England RU internationals in Jack Shooter (1875-1922) and George Marsden (1880-1948). Shooter was a coal-miner who had begun work in the pits at 12 years of age. An outstanding forward, 'Snowy' Shooter won four England RU caps and 21 caps for Yorkshire between 1893 and 1900. He was nicknamed 'Snowy' because of his blonde hair. He defected to Hunslet RLFC in 1900, but played for Morley again after the Great War. 'Snowy' died shortly afterwards, precipitating a benefit for his wife and children. Unfortunately, one of the organisers ran off with the £100 raised.

George Marsden

George Marsden won three England RU caps in 1900 before switching to the NU and playing in England's first NU international, which was an interesting affair because at the time England was the only country playing the NU rules. The NU authorities created opposition by playing 'the Other Nations', which was a collection of Scots and Welsh players with NU clubs. Marsden and Shooter were able to return to the RFU ranks through a technicality: in 1902 the RFU banned anyone who played NU rugby 'sine die', but did not make it retrospective. The Morley men were thus able to resume playing rugby union.

After World War One, Marsden was reported to have moved to Blackpool and helped found Fylde RUFC. The Woodlands club marked the connection by incorporating the maroon of Morley in their colours.

Morley RUFC folded around 1909 but reappeared a decade later. At first it was proposed that an NU club be formed, but eventually a rugby union club emerged. The club returned to Scatcherd Lane, but as tenants of Morley Cricket, Bowling and Athletic Club. On 22nd November 1919, Morley met Headingley 'A ' in a drawn match watched by nearly 600 spectators.

One of the highlights of the 1919-1920 season was New Maroons v Old Maroons. The Oldies included Bobby Peel, the 64-year-old Yorkshire and England Cricketer who had played for Morley in 1884.

A curious note is that in the 1920s Morley were coached by Ben Gronow, the RL legend, which contravened RFU laws. He paid for his sins by not being listed in club photographs.

Morley grew in stature by drawing players from the local grammar school. However, they were only offered second team fixtures by the top clubs. Their stock grew rapidly when they beat Bradford in a cup match. They gained status in Yorkshire rugby and were Yorkshire Cup champions on three occasions. Their Yorkshire Cup games attracted gates of over 2000 and they had even greater support in the final of 1929, which they lost narrowly to Otley at Bradford.

Morley resumed at Baildon after World War Two and initially were a successful team. The 1960s were disappointing, but the Maroons soon regained their status as one of the best sides in the north.

In 1971-72 David Hoyland set a club record with 39 tries in season and the club had three county players for the first time for half a century. Morley reached National Two in the early 1990s, but struggled to reach the next level. After several near misses, the club slumped out of the National Leagues.

Scott Benton, the Gloucester and England scrum-half, began at Morley as an eight-year-old in 1982. He was unlucky to be understudy to Matt Dawson in the England side.

In 2006 Colin Stephens, the Welsh fly-half, took over as club coach and led Morley to the Intermediate Cup final, where they lost to Stockport. 2015 saw Morley in National 3.

NORTH RIBBLESDALE

THE NORTH YORKSHIRE town of Settle lies amongst the limestone escarpments of the Pennines, where the River Ribble begins its long journey to the sea. Settle is famous for sheep rearing and for the public school at Giggleswick. The town's rugby club is North Ribblesdale RUFC and dates from 1923.

A 'Settle RFC' existed in Victorian times. They were formed on the 28th October 1879 and were one of the best sides in the region, with fixtures against Skipton, Keighley, Bingley and Lancaster Olympic. Like so many other sides, Settle died out around the turn of the century.

When North Ribblesdale were formed, they were not universally welcomed because Skipton were 'top dogs' in the Dales and had first pick of every promising player. Also, two other clubs, Kirkby Lonsdale and Holme Wanderers, lay to the north of this splendid corner of England. The emergence of 'North Rib' and 'Upper Wharfedale' played a part in Skipton's decline.

Being off the beaten track, it was 1948 before North Rib produced their first county player in flanker Ken Davidson. That year Brian Braithwaite-Exley of Headingley did so well in an England trial he was capped, although he initially appeared in the match programme as 'A.N. Other'. Braithwaite-Exley joined North Rib in the twilight of his career.

A far more famous international player arrived at North Rib in 1996 –Keith Robinson, a 19-year-old from Waikato, New Zealand (the North Yorkshire club had links to Te Aroha Cobras in New Zealand). Duncan Brown, the match secretary, recalls: "He looked useful and could put himself about. If there was any trouble, he was in the thick of it." Eventually Robinson went home, but returned to the UK with the 2002 All Blacks.

North Ribblesdale won the 1978 Yorkshire Shield and were runners-up in 2003. Their highest league placing was in 1994, when they reached North-East One after winning Yorkshire One. The club are currently back in Yorkshire One. In 2014 Jack Walker, a product of the club, was captain of Yorkshire Carnegie.

(Thanks to Duncan Brown)

OTLEY

"The great over-achievers"

OTLEY IS A prosperous market town in the heart of the Yorkshire Dales. It is also the home of one of the great over-achievers of English rugby.

It has a special part in the nation's rugby history as the North of England XV defeated the 1976 All Blacks at Cross Green – Otley's bucolic ground. The victory was sweeter because many of the North's players (Alan Old, Steve Smith, Fran Cotton, Tony Neary etc.) had suffered at the hands of the national selectors.

Otley RFC was founded in 1870. The high point of Otley's Victorian heydays came in 1889 when they won the Yorkshire Cup, beating Liversedge at Cardigan Fields, Leeds by 4-3. Captain Fred Mudd received the trophy and the thanks of club President Harry Garnett, who was head of Wharfedale Paper Mills in the town.

The club produced two England internationals in the 1890s: Arthur Briggs (1892) and George Hughes (1896). Hughes' principal claim to fame was to have represented both Lancashire and Yorkshire at rugby, which makes him unique given the age-old animosity between the two counties.

Otley came under pressure in the late 1890s when a NU team was formed in the town. Otley NU disappeared in 1904 – a fate that almost befell Otley RUFC. The union side temporarily went out of business, but were reformed at the Wharfedale Ground in 1907 under Harold and Kenneth Duncan, with Harry Garnett as president.

Otley rose rapidly to win the Yorkshire Cup on seven occasions in the next half-century. They appeared in 13 finals and made 19 semi-finals. Although they were successful, these were also rough days. There are records of an Otley match at Skipton which "ended abruptly due to the unfairness of the visitors (Otley), who being overanxious for victory and did not conform to the rules". During the game, one of the Otley players had "aimed a deliberate kick" at one of the Skipton players. Skipton refused to continue the game, which ended in confusion with the angry Skipton supporters pursuing the Otley team back to their hotel.

The 1921-22 season was a notable one in that the club moved to their present ground at Cross Green. The final match at Wharfedale was an 'In Memoriam' match for the dead of World War One; Yorkshire beat Wharfedale XV 23-3. Wharfedale consisted of eight Otley players and seven Ilkley players.

With the move to Cross Green, the club headquarters were the Queen's Head Hotel on Kirkgate. At the back of the building were the changing rooms, including a huge communal bath that was filled by hand using buckets.

That season Otley played in Wales for the first time, meeting Mountain Ash, Cross Keys, Ebbw Vale and Aberavon. Frank Trenham won an England trial, but Frank Malir was Otley's finest player of the era. A great captain and centre for Otley, Malir was part of a great Otley team who went undefeated for three months in 1926. Malir was born in India, educated in Scotland and joined Otley in 1924 as an 18-year-old. He was a real Otley stalwart and led Otley to two County Cup victories, was capped by Yorkshire 45 times and served for many years as a club official after his retirement from rugby in 1935.

A Yorkshire regular, Malir had to compete with H.P. Jacob for an England place. First selected for an England trial in 1928, Malir had to wait two years to finally get his cap. He was one of the best centres of the era, but still had his critics. One newspaper dismissed him with the remark, "Malir is a strong runner and nothing else!"

In 1930 Malir was partnered in the England team by his club-mate, A. H. Bateman, for the away international against Ireland. Bateman was a brilliant scrummager and an England regular that season. Malir's brother also played in an England trial. Welshman Les Manfield of Otley was capped by Wales in 1939, but unlucky to miss his best years due to World War Two. His Otley contemporary, Arthur Gray, won three England caps in 1947 at full-back.

Cross Green hosted an England trial in the 1950s. Although Otley were one of Yorkshire's strongest sides throughout the rest of the 20th century, but the club was largely overlooked by the international selectors. Cross Green was, however, a popular venue for county and touring matches. The 1976 defeat of the All Blacks was the pinnacle of all the matches ever played at the ground.

One unusual recollection by a newspaper columnist of Cross Green comes from a Roses match during the 1980s. He recalls that one aged Yorkshireman spent the whole match complaining that the "gentleman of the press should be charged admission like the rest of us folks".

The 1980s saw the emergence of Nigel Melville, a wiry scrum-half, who began at Otley before moving to Wasps, where he played for England and the Lions. He subsequently became a leading coach. Paul Sampson followed the same route, playing scrum-half for Otley before joining Wasps and being capped for England against South Africa in 1998. Steve Ravenscroft also began at Otley before moving to Bradford and Saracens, from where he won two England caps in 1998. A contemporary was John Bentley. He switched to rugby league before returning to the 15-man game, where he won England and Lions caps. Off the field, Roy Manock of Otley was a leading figure in the RFU and an RFU President. An unlikely international champion was Kirk Arundale, who began at Otley, moved to Indonesia and played for his adopted country when they were Asian champions.

International rugby reached Cross Green in 1991 when it hosted a Rugby World Cup match between Italy and the USA. Italy won 30-9, but complained after the match that the grass was too long!

On the field, Otley were regarded as the great over-achievers of the National Leagues. In 2004, they reached fifth place in National One on an annual budget of £350,000 – a sixth of what some of their rivals were spending each year. They compensated by good management and sterling service by their players, notably Simon Binns, who played 124 games for Otley over six seasons, scoring 1,348 points.

The 2004-05 side, coached by stalwart Peter Clegg, included local lad Danny Care from Prince Henry's School, Otley. Danny moved on to become an England regular with Harlequins. Flanker Dan Hyde moved to the Premiership, won England 'A' honours, and played for his country in a non-cap international.

Mark Luffman, a club coach, made national headlines off the field in 2010 when the team coach was travelling on the motorway to a match. The coach driver suddenly collapsed and the quick-thinking Mark grabbed the steering wheel before a catastrophe could occur.

On the field, the decline in funding by the RFU meant a club like Otley, who relied on semi-professionalism aligned to good management, could no longer compete with fully professional sides. Otley suffered several relegations, but bounced back to National Two in 2013.

OLD BRODLEIANS

LIKE OLD ALLEYNIANS, Old Brodleians take their name from their school founder rather than from the old school. In 1684 Matthew Brodley left the funding for a school in Halifax in his will. The school, Hipperholme Grammar School, still survives in a village on the north-east side of Halifax. Rugby union was introduced to the school in 1924, replacing soccer.

OBs were founded in 1930 by Joe Houfe, the first captain, and Philip Beard and began with a game against a vastly more experienced Old Rishworthian team.

OBs were unusual in being an 'open' club from its inauguration, which allowed it to supplement its numbers with anyone available. The initial enthusiasm soon abated and interest waned. This coincided with the Great Depression, which proved a blessing for OBs, who were able to take over the superb facilities on Denholmgate Road from a soccer club that went bust. Changing facilities were also acquired in a disused stable at the Hare & Hounds Inn. Finding a permanent home proved the catalyst for a change in OBs' destiny and their fortunes revived.

The 1960s saw the club flatten the Woodhead pitch and they obtained a portable structure from a closed RAF Hospital that acted as a clubhouse. The pitch was opened with a match against Halifax RUFC.

OBs became established as one of the top junior clubs in Yorkshire. Their best known player is Charlie Hodgson, who joined the minis in 1990 and gained a huge reputation whilst with Bradford Grammar School. After three years at Durham University, he opted for a career as a professional rugby player

with Sale Sharks, where he scored 1753 points in 11 seasons. A slightly-built individual, Charlie understudied Jonny Wilkinson, but still won 38 England caps and represented the 2005 Lions. Charlie was a rugby league fan long before he ever played rugby union. A family friend invited him to Old Brodleians rugby club and his first game was for the opposition as they were short. He has also played for Saracens, Durham University and Yorkshire.

(Thanks to Freddie Holt)

RISHWORTHIAN

"Membership is open to any gentleman who doesn't put his feet on the table."
Comment by member (1934)

RISHWORTH IS A small town on the Pennine moors near Halifax. Rishworthian, formerly Old Rishworthians, were formed at the Palais de Danse ballroom in the town. For half a century membership was restricted to the old boys of Rishworth School. C.L. Johnson was the first president and E. Hirst was both the first captain and secretary. A pitch was found at South Owran and changing facilities at the Cock and Bottle Hotel. The pitch was first described as "off Pinnar Lane amid the quarries, and reached after a long walk along the road and across three or four fields". Season 1933-34 saw OR moving their dressing facilities from the Cock and Bottle public house to the more spacious Manor House Hotel.

A memorable match took place in the 1930s against Leeds Salem. One of ORs supporters, fresh from a wedding, behaved so badly he had to be locked in a hut for the duration of the match and afterwards was cold bathed into semi-sobriety.

2007 saw Rishworthians in Yorkshire 5, but they made a remarkable rise to Yorkshire 1. In 2010 Richworthians were Yorkshire 2 and Silver Trophy champions.

ROTHERHAM

"If they can find a reason to not promote us, they will."
Mike Schmid 2002

ROTHERHAM IS AN industrial town to the east of Sheffield. Traditionally it has been best known for its links to the coal and steel industries, but its rugby team have been making headlines since the arrival of National leagues.

Soccer has been played in Rotherham for over a century, but a rugby club did not emerge until 1923. Rotherham RUFC played at the town's cricket ground on Clifton Lane until 2003, when they moved to Millmoor, the town's soccer stadium, before moving back to Clifton Lane. The club owes its roots to Jack Hemsall, a local schoolmaster, who introduced rugby to Spurley Hey Secondary Modern School after World War One. Spurley Hey became the main source of players for the new club.

Rugby enjoyed great popularity in Rotherham's schools after World War Two, but Rotherham RUFC suffered because it could not get top-class fixtures. The club felt that it was difficult for a middle-ranking side to reach the elite of Yorkshire.

In the 1960s facilities at Clifton Lane were rather primitive. Rotherham had a wooden shack and training took place in the glare of the headlights of their cars, which were strategically parked around the pitch.

Rotherham were the Yorkshire Shield winners in 1973, but were ranked only 15th in the county league table when leagues arrived in 1987. A number of factors were, however, working in Rotherham's favour: from the start coach Geoff Wappett had an outstanding record of producing some of England's finest school sides. They also benefitted because their local

Geoff Wappett

rivals, Sheffield, were in decline and the club's sponsor, Mike Yarlett of the Yorkshire Windows company, was a generous benefactor.

During their eight-year rise Rotherham climbed through the leagues, losing only nine games. They were promoted in five out of the eight years. They were champions of NE1, N2, N1, Div 5 North and National Div 4 between 1988 and 1995, thanks to a mixture of Yorkshire and southern hemisphere players. They were far-sighted in their approach to league rugby, and in 1992 built a gym and a private health club.

The best-known player was David Strettle, an England winger. A talented footballer, Strettle had been on Manchester City's books before switching to rugby. Injuries blighted his early career, but he persisted and, after moving to Harlequins and then Saracens, he was restored to the England team. The other best known Rotherham player was Gareth Steerson, who moved to Exeter Chiefs and became one of Britain's top point-scorers.

Eventually Rotherham won promotion to the Premiership, where they faced bigger and better-funded clubs. The club felt the established Premiership clubs were reluctant to admit them because the facilities at Clifton Lane were judged sub-standard at the highest level. Three times promoted to the Premiership and despite twice finishing bottom, Rotherham kept bouncing back. On one occasion they won National One but were refused promotion for not meeting the entry criteria, a fact which evoked coach Mike Schmid to comment that, "If they can find a reason to not promote us, they will."

Rotherham had several changes of name during the period. They were known as Rotherham Earth Titans and Earth Titans in acknowledgement of their sponsors, before becoming Rotherham Titans. They have a long term plan to move into a community stadium with Rotherham United Football Club, with a council initiative set to come to fruition.

Currently Rotherham are yet again hot on the heels of the National One leaders.

SANDAL

SANDAL IS A suburb of Wakefield lying on the south side of the city and is famous for its medieval castle. There were several rugby clubs in the area in the 19th century, including the splendidly named 'Sandal Band of Hope RFC'.

Sandal RUFC was formed in June 1927 by Claude Beaumont, who had played for St. Helens RUFC and Wakefield RFC. Initially the club played in green and white hoops, but changed to maroon, gold and white in 1930. The choice of colours was decided because, at the meeting concerned, the committee sat at a table with a maroon tablecloth on which was placed a gold and white coloured packet of Wills cigarettes.

In 1932 Sandal won the Yorkshire Shield for the best junior side in the county. The following year they reached the County Cup final to confirm their place amongst the best senior sides. However, Sandal had to settle for the runners-up place as Otley proved too strong, winning 13-9.

Sandal had initially used Tetley Field as a pitch and the Walnut Tree public house for changing. After four years at Tetley Field, the club purchased three and a quarter acres at Milnthorpe Green for £260. The city council agreed to help by levelling the pitch. This was not exactly an act of altruism, however, as the council used domestic waste to level up the surface. The new ground and stand was opened on the 23rd September 1936, with a friendly against Headingley. Headingley's squad included F. Williams, the Wales fly-half, and the ubiquitous Prince Alexander Obolensky, the legendary England winger. Headingley won 3-0. The grandstand was opened by Major Lionel Holliday, a local landowner who later became one of the most influential racehorse owners of the 20th century.

Despite the new ground, Sandal remained at the Walnut Tree Inn until 1952, when the Silver Jubilee was celebrated with the opening of a new clubhouse.

Sandal continued to be a leading Yorkshire side throughout the next 20 years, with the highlight being a second Yorkshire Cup final appearance in 1958, losing 11-0 to Old Roundhegians. Off the field, the facilities at Milnthorpe Green were improved and now rank amongst the best in the county.

The club's improvement on the field coincided with the arrival of league rugby. The Diamond Jubilee season of 1987-88 saw Sandal in North Two and their debut in the National Knockout Cup. It was another decade before Sandal finally won the Yorkshire Cup for the first time after three final defeats.

In 1995 Sandal entered the National leagues, but were relegated in 2002. The best player to wear the club's colours must be Tim Stimpson, who won Yorkshire Junior honours before joining Newcastle Falcons, Leicester and then playing for England at full-back.

In 2005 Sandal fielded two England players: 1987 World Cup captain Mike Harrison and England centre Brian Barley. The famous duo joined Sandal after the demise of Wakefield RFC.

Currently Sandal play in North One.

(Thanks to Henry Everett)

SCARBOROUGH

A RUGBY CLUB existed in the seaside town of Scarborough in Victorian days. It is known that in 1879 a team of rugby players from the local cricket club played York in a floodlit rugby match – two huge engines powered the four floodlights. Sadly, the weather was dreadful and only 1,000 people attended. The Scarborough team were: J.Kitching, W.Sanderson, J.Kimmings, C.Wheater, H.Hare, H.Vyvyan, F.Rowntree, J.Webb, H.Vassall, R.Hodgson, E.Hodgson, G.Harrison, G.Frank and A.Jones. Harry Vassall was, of course, the great Oxford and England player. The guest of honour was Lord Londesborough, who was a great supporter of Scarborough Rugby Club.

That club disappeared towards the end of the 19th century, but reformed in 1926. The club's founder members included Joe Hardcastle, a local garage owner; John Guthrie, a London businessman; and the legendary 'Baron' Atkinson Jowett. 'Baron', as he was always known, ran the club for almost 50 years as if it were his own property.

Initially Scarborough played at the Athletic Ground, but soon moved to Newby, where they changed in a converted chicken shed.

In the 1932-33 season Scarborough reached the final of the Yorkshire Shield, captained by John Guthrie, who skippered for eight successive years. In the final Scarborough lost to Sandal 6-13.

Three years later, Dr. I. Stevenson, the team doctor to the 1935 All-Blacks, settled in Scarborough and become the team's coach. Under his guidance Scarborough became one of the strongest clubs in the county.

Scarborough rapidly produced two internationals in Peter Gedge and Robert Marshall. Gedge, who also played for Cambridge University and Edinburgh Wanderers, won a Scotland cap in 1933 against Ireland. Lock forward Robert Marshall (1917-1945) won five England caps in 1938-39, and scored a try on his international debut. Marshall was killed in action serving in the Navy in 1945.

Scarborough RUFC struggled for some years after World War Two, but the 1960s saw the club established as one of the most attractive attacking sides in the North East. The 1962-63 season was the club's finest year, with a single defeat by 6-3 at the hands of Hull & East Riding.

In the 1980s Scarborough joined the first national league system in Yorkshire Division One. The highlight of recent seasons has been reaching the semi-finals of Intermediate Cup in 2015.

In 2009, the J. M. Guthrie clubhouse opened as Scarborough provided some of the best facilities in northern rugby.

SELBY

SELBY IS A market town in North Yorkshire on the River Ouse, with a 12th century abbey church. The town prospered from the local coalfields and from its links to the paper, chemicals, glass and electricity industries.

Rugby in Selby can be traced back to the 1880s, when several clubs existed with links to local churches and a successful town club flourished. All the clubs eventually died out before World War One, but several rugby league clubs emerged. Hull FC played their home matches in Selby for a period. This was "so West Riding players had less distance to travel when playing Hull FC for away matches", which suggests there were few Hull-based players in the side.

Drax Grammar School led the way in restarting rugby after World War One when they switched from soccer to rugby in 1924. Initially rugby was restricted to an annual match played by the schoolmasters of Drax GS against the Goole club.

The present Selby RUFC emerged in November 1933 at a meeting in the town's Museum Hall. The new club adopted the colours worn by the original town club: amber and red hooped jerseys with blue shorts (they added a green ring to the jersey in the late 1940s). The club's first match was against York YMCA on the 30th December 1933, resulting in a Selby victory 6-0. Indeed, the new club won their first three matches before losing 13-8 to Morley 'A'. The earliest home matches were played at Burn Bridge, with the Anchor Inn used as changing rooms. At the end of their first season, Selby decided to move closer to the town and bought a ground on Leeds Road, which was officially opened in September 1934 with a match against 'Mr Bob Oakes XV'. The visitors won 25-8.

Inspired by the match, Selby improved and earned 21 victories the following season. Three years later, Arthur Pearson became the first Selby player to be capped by Yorkshire.

A casual club side was fielded during World War Two, who played mainly against Army and RAF sides. The full club reformed officially in 1946, but two years later a schism occurred when Old Draxonians were formed by former grammar school pupils. Six years later the two sides were united again as Selby OBs. Oliver Grieveson joined the club around this time, and eventually became an England trialist and winner of 48 Yorkshire caps after moving to Headingley.

The club received a boost in the early 1960s with the building of the massive Drax Power station, which brought new faces and prosperity to the area. Selby were also honoured with the presence of a full England international winger when John Ranson appeared in their colours for two seasons.

The 'OBs' suffix was dropped in 1966 as Selby grew in stature. They were Yorkshire Shield finalists on three occasions in the 1970s, although they lost the first two finals narrowly to West Park (Bramhope) and Rotherham. It was third time lucky in 1974, when they beat Bradford Salem 9-6 at Morley. The feat was repeated in 1982 with victory over Driffield at Hull Ionians.

The two best known names to emerge from Selby in the 1980s were Rob Latham and Diccon Edwards. Latham left Selby for Wakefield in 1987, and eventually played 14 times for the North of England. Diccon Edwards played for Leicester Tigers, Newport and Leeds RUFC. Curiously, he won a cap – for the Welsh Rugby League team!

In 2006 Selby announced a plan to develop their own players from their 400 juniors. It was rewarded with a great season in 2012-13 when they won the Yorkshire Two championship and RFU Senior Vase final.

SHEFFIELD

IT IS OFTEN thought that there are only two types of football in England: association and rugby, but there originally was a third football game, 'the Sheffield Rules', which was played in the South Yorkshire city.

Sheffield Association Football Club was formed on 20th October 1857 by Sir Nathaniel Creswick and Major Vickers. They are the first and oldest surviving organised football club. Their first recorded club football match saw them play Hallam.

In 1863 a game of soccer was played between teams representing the FA and the Sheffield clubs. Rugby was also played in the city around this time, for Sheffield RFC played Leeds Athletic, the Manchester club, Manchester Free Wanderers and Sheffield Garrick RFC.

Rugby in Sheffield must have been popular as the city provided four players – Chambers, Eyre, Johnson and Lockwood – for the Yorkshire side in the first Roses match. Interest in rugby remained, but always languished behind soccer as two famous association sides emerged: Sheffield Wednesday (1867) and Sheffield United (1889). Rugby died out in Sheffield before the end of the century.

In 1902 a new Sheffield RFC was formed by cousins Harold Willey and Billy Gray, using a pitch off Sandygate Road. Willey and Gray had learnt the game at Uppingham School. The first game of the revived club was against Nottingham on 24th January 1903, resulting in an 8-0 victory. The Sheffield team were a motley crew with "hardly two shirts alike and one player wore a scruffy fisherman's jersey". The following week Sheffield lost away to Trafford Park Rovers from Manchester due to "a bad referee".

Sheffield were quickly recognised by the county selectors and wingers Bernard Wragg and Harold Willey were selected for Yorkshire. Willey was subsequently picked for an England trial. He was an excellent player and the main driving force behind the club in its early days.

In 1911 the rugby club joined forces with the city's hockey club and other amateur organisations to form the Sheffield Amateur Sports Club. Two years later the club came under threat when a rugby league club was promoted, although the danger failed to materialise.

The sports club lost its facilities during World War One and in 1920 they purchased Abbeydale Hall. Unfortunately, the rugby club's fortunes were dire at this time. Rugby league had reappeared, but soccer was top dog throughout the city. The situation was to remain unchanged throughout the inter-war years, although the rugby club improved and eventually gained the status of a good middle-ranking outfit. After World War Two, Sheffield reached the semi-finals of the Yorkshire Cup in 1947-48.

A number of internationals have emerged from Abbeydale. None was more remarkable (or controversial) than Dr. Doug Keller. He first emerged as a member of the 1947 Australian touring team and won six Aussie caps. The doctor stayed on in Britain, took a job in a Sheffield hospital and joined the local rugby club. Keller's continuing presence in Britain was noted by the Scots selectors, who also noted he qualified

Doug Keller

Sheffield were one of the country's top sides from the 1970s until the appearance of league rugby. The team included Alan Old, David Holmes (England reserve) and Andrew and Bill Reichwald. Bill was club captain for 16 years.

The emergence of professionalism was an anathema to Sheffield, who couldn't raise money as they didn't own the bar or the ground. Six relegations have hit Sheffield, which were barely counterbalanced by two promotions. Today they play in North East One.

In 2004 Sheffield RUFC began sharing players with Sheffield Eagles RLFC, including Jimmy Pearson, Sheffield's top point-scorer for a season.

On the positive side, they can boast 400 youngsters in their mini ranks and 70 junior coaches. Amongst the club's products are Neil Briggs (Saracens) and Jos Baxendall (Sale).

(Thanks to Andrew Reichwald)

SHEFFIELD TIGERS

SHEFFIELD TIGERS HAVE risen rapidly to join the National leagues after 80 years in the shadow of the Sheffield club. Tigers were formed in 1932 and played on Concord Park in the city. Eventually the club moved to Dore Moor on the west side of the city. A pleasant spot in the summer, it is rather bleak in winter.

In the days before the mobile phone arrived, newspaper reporters covering matches hated visiting Dore Moor because the nearest public phone box was a mile away. Saturday evening newspapers wanted match reports at half time and at the end of the match. Most clubs had a committee member who did this job, but few volunteered to 'ring the papers' when they played away at the Tigers. The correspondent needed to be fitter than the players to get the news through to the evening newspaper!

The sense of bleakness at Dore Moor was worsened by the Tigers using an ancient railway carriage as changing rooms for the first 20 years of their existence.

Goodness knows what R.V. Stirling, the England captain, made of Dore Moor after his years at Welford Road. He played a few matches for Tigers whilst working in the area.

The arrival of League rugby saw Tigers as a middle-ranking club in the Yorkshire leagues. It was, however, 2005 before Tigers got their first ever league match against Sheffield RFC. The Tigers won 30-3.

It came at a time when Tigers were rising rapidly and achieved three successive promotions. The Dore Moor club had a core of former Rotherham players, including three professionals. The club chairman defended his recruitment policy, which saw five of the players employed by his orthopaedics firm: "People don't even get expenses and they are all paying a GBP15-a-month direct debit to play." By 2007, Tigers had reached their highest ever League position after three successive promotions and victory in the 2005 RFU Junior Vase.

for Scotland through his family roots. He made his Scots international debut as captain and went on to win seven caps. He left Sheffield RFC when he took a job at Guys Hospital, where he played rugby for his hospital, as well as London Scottish and Kent. In 1951 he returned to Australia and promptly announced his intention to resume playing for the Warratahs. The Australian selectors seriously considered re-selecting him until the IRB decided 'enough was enough' and introduced new rules to prevent anyone else following Keller's example. Sheffield continued to have medical connections as, besides Keller, Dr. Glyn Jones also played for the club after appearing for Wales.

Sheffield was an improving side with Keller and Jones on board. They were skippered by Bill Ransome, who was the first non-commissioned man to captain the Royal Navy rugby team. The improvements continued throughout the coming decades and in 1969-70 they saw 30 victories in 36 matches.

The 1970s saw the emergence of Alan Old at Sheffield as one of the best players in Europe. Old was born in Middlesbrough, and played for the town's club and Leicester Tigers before moving to Abbeydale. A superb fly-half, Old played for England and the Lions. He was at the helm when the North West Counties beat the 1972 All Blacks and also captained the 1976 North team who triumphed over the New Zealanders at Otley.

SKIPTON

THE FINE TOWN of Skipton stands on the road from Leeds to Kendal. It enjoyed an economic boom in Victorian times thanks to the arrival of canals and new methods in agriculture, manufacturing and mining. In its wake, Skipton's population grew from 8,600 in 1871 to 12,000 within a decade.

Ermysted's Grammar School is the district's most famous rugby school. Ermysted's adopted rugby in the 1870s and a match is recorded between the school and the local rugby club on the 26th March 1881.

There are records of football matches in the district during the 1860s between sides from the local mills and quarries. Skipton RFC itself was founded in 1874 and originally played in maroon and amber stripes until changing to cardinal red jerseys in 1889. Unlike the earliest sides in the town, most of the players were the sons of prominent families in the textile industry. The club's first captain, A. Sidgwick, came from the family who leased High Mill, whilst Algernon and Lionel Dewhurst were the sons of John Bonny Dewhurst, who owned the largest mill in the town.

Skipton's first fixture was against local rivals Ilkley on the 7th November 1874. Skipton, captained by Sidgwick, had only 13 players. Other fixtures followed, against Leeds Grammar School (loss), Burnley Rovers (win), Bradford (loss) and Otley (loss). A match against Otley at Skipton ended abruptly due to the roughness of the visitors, who were described as "overanxious for victory and not conforming to the rules". The ill-feeling between the two clubs was to resurface later in their histories.

In 1878 the club secured the use of a field at Sandylands, between the railway line and the River Aire. Previously, they had used a field on Carleton New Road. The new pitch at Sandylands was flat and, more importantly, convenient for the town's railway station, which was an important consideration with railways being virtually the only form of long-distance transport at that time.

The average number of spectators at Sandylands was modest, fluctuating between 100 and 200 depending on the opponents. An open-air grandstand was erected on the west side of the field to accommodate spectators prepared to pay an additional 3d (1p) over the standard admission price of 3d.

The club's first changing facilities were at the Craven Hotel in Craven Street, which necessitated a half-mile walk to and from the pitch. In 1889 the headquarters moved to the Old George Hotel in the High Street. Bathing facilities were two tin baths, and water was drawn from a hand pump at the corner of the field.

Skipton must have had a good reputation for they toured south Wales in 1893, playing Neath and Penycraig. The Neath match must have been rather rough. One of the Skipton team reported: "We made a good show for 20 minutes, and then the crowd sang 'Land of My Fathers' and we put the tin hat on it. We lost by 13 points."

Skipton chose to stay members of the RFU in 1895 when many of the leading Yorkshire clubs turned to the Northern Union. The club benefitted because the Yorkshire RU viewed them as one of the best sides left in their ranks. In 1897 Robert Little was chosen to represent Yorkshire, and another 25 Skipton

players were selected for Yorkshire before World War One. Indeed, four Skipton men captained the county side: G.P. Ackroyd, John Green, W. Knox and Bob Duckett.

John Green

John Knox was the first Skipton player to be capped when he represented Scotland in 1903. John Green (1881-1968) was capped on eight occasions for England between 1905-07. Green, a talented line-out player, was a product of the famous Giggleswick school in nearby Settle.

Fred Bonsor was capped by England during his days at Bradford, but also played for Skipton. Another Skipton player to win England honours was John Dewhurst (1867-1947).

Skipton appeared five times in the Yorkshire Cup final between 1903 and 1912. In the first final, they drew with Castleford at Harrogate, which led to a replay a week later at Wakefield. Skipton were astounded when Castleford selected Little Jimmy Taylor, the famous England goal-kicker, who everyone knew played for West Hartlepool. The Skipton captain protested to the referee that Taylor wasn't a bona fide member of the Castleford team. The match went ahead, with Skipton losing 6-0 with two tries by Taylor. Castleford were promptly disqualified for playing an ineligible player. The bitterness rumbled on for years and culminated in 'a bloodbath' between the two sides in 1908 as Skipton lost 29-0.

The 1909 Final against Otley at Headingley was little better as Duckett, the Skipton captain, led his team off the field after several brushes with the referee. Skipton claimed an Otley player had deliberately kicked an opponent. After the match, the Skipton supporters stormed the Otley dressing rooms.

By 1923 Skipton could boast some of the finest facilities in Yorkshire. Changing accommodation was luxurious compared to the past; the dressing rooms were lit by paraffin lamps and heated by a coke stove.

County matches were a regular feature at Sandylands. The close proximity of the Lancashire border meant the annual Roses match was a popular visitor to Skipton. In 1924, 4,000 spectators packed Sandylands for the old grudge match.

But the 1920s saw new rugby clubs being formed all over the Dales. Upper Wharfedale, North Ribblesdale and Colne & Nelson all emerged, and gradually the competition for players would lead to Skipton's decline.

The problem was not apparent in the 1930s as Skipton could still field top-class players like H.P. Crabtree, an England trialist, and 'Bunt' Horner, who represented Yorkshire on 30 occasions between 1932 and 1937. And Skipton must have been a tough and talented side in 1935 as Middlesbrough, their opponents in a Yorkshire Cup tie, finished the match with 11 men, the other four being either in hospital or receiving treatment. Middlesbrough found the experience so painful that they refused to play in the Yorkshire Cup for years afterwards.

Skipton has an odd place in rugby history – it was the first place were a contact lens was lost in a rugby match. In April 1951 they entertained Hinckley, who were on tour. Mike Smith, the Hinckley and England fly-half, was experimenting with large haptic lenses, which at one inch across were considered too large to become dislodged. But the match was halted when Smith lost a lens. After an exhaustive search by all the players, the lens was found and the game resumed.

Success was harder to find for Skipton as the decline in local industry saw youngsters leaving the area in search of work. Skipton RFC suffered from the drain and its fortunes declined. Later, the rise to national prominence of Wharfedale RUFC has also put pressure on Skipton, who have nevertheless fought back and developed first-class facilities with squash courts and a new clubhouse.

Today Skipton RFC are a good junior club in the Yorkshire leagues. They are coached by former Leicester, Sale and Leeds Prop Martin Whitcombe. By 2007 they were at their highest level since the arrival of league rugby after three successive promotions.

WAKEFIELD

WAKEFIELD RUFC OPERATED from 1902 to 1994, but rugby in the town goes back to 1873, when Wakefield Trinity, the town's most famous club, was formed. Trinity were formed on Heath Common as part of the Holy Trinity Church Young Men's Society. They had many great players before joining the Northern Union in 1895.

The most famous was Dickie Lockwood, a tiny half-back, who won 14 England RU caps between 1887 and 1895, when he defected to the NU with Trinity. Richard Evison Lockwood (1867–1915) made his début as a right-wing three-quarter for Dewsbury at the age of 16 in 1884 and rapidly established himself as a sporting phenomenon. At 19 he played for Yorkshire and England and rose to captain the English rugby union side in 1894 – the first England captain not from a public school background. Known as 'the Little Tyke', 'Little Dick' and 'the World's Wonder' – partly because of his age and also because of his diminutive 5ft 4in stature – Lockwood was brilliant in attack and deadly in the tackle, with a knack of being in the right place at the right time. An astute tactician, he was responsible for introducing the Welsh-originated four three-quarter system into the Yorkshire county team, and for popularising the tactic of running after the ball after punting it in order to put his forwards onside. No player was as famous in northern rugby, nor so symbolised the rise of the working-class player as Lockwood. He was employed as a woollen printer in a textile factory when, in 1889, he transferred to the Heckmondwike club, who paid him, it later emerged, £1 per game, contrary to rugby's amateur regulations. Although the club was suspended for professionalism by the Yorkshire

Rugby Union, Lockwood survived two investigations of the same charge. Despite having captained England earlier in the season, he was eventually barred by the Rugby Football Union in 1894 from playing in a club match after he had withdrawn from the Anglo-Scottish match because he couldn't afford to take time off work. A few weeks after the 1895 rugby schism, Lockwood joined Wakefield Trinity in the Northern Union. In 1900 his career turned full circle, however, as he returned to Dewsbury, and in 1903 he retired.

Trinity went on to become one of the professional game's greatest clubs, whereas the union club struggled for a long time after their formation in 1902. The Great War proved pivotal to the club thanks to the generosity of one bereaved family. The club was given the chance to thrive when the Kingswell Family gave the College Grove ground to Wakefield in memory of Lieut. F.A. Kingswell, who had played for Wakefield before he joined the army and died on the Western Front.

The gift of College Grove in 1919 proved the start of a new era, beginning with victory in the Yorkshire Cup. Success on the field brought the club to the attention of the international selectors; Dr. J.B. McDougall won the club's first cap in 1919 when he represented Scotland.

The next international was Reg Bolton, who won five England caps between 1933 and 1938. Bolton learnt his rugby at the Queen Elizabeth Grammar School, Wakefield, which supplied players to Wakefield (as did other schools, such as Silcoates School, Hemsworth GS and Rothwell GS). The link between the schools and Wakefield provided a conveyer belt of talent that was the envy of far bigger clubs.

Wakefield produced a string of internationals from the 1970s. Les Cusworth was the best drop-goal kicker of the era. Educated at Normanton Grammar School, Cusworth switched to Leicester Tigers and was England's first choice No. 10 in the early 1980s.

Dave Rollitt began at Wakefield before moving to Bristol University. A familiar figure with his grey hair (he went grey at 20-years-old), he was one of the great English flank forwards of the 1970s. He remained in the South West and was lost to his home county.

College Grove, home of Wakefield RUFC, in 1991

Wakefield could also field Tim Stimpson, Jon Sleightholme, Dave Scully and David Baldwin, who were amongst the best players of the 1990s.

Wakefield reached the semi-finals of the National Knockout in 1976 and were Division 3 Champions. They played glorious rugby and supplied Mike Harrison, England's first World Cup captain. But they paid the price for allowing their ambition to outstrip their means. With little support (either in terms of crowds or finance), no youth set-up and no second team, the end became inevitable once the four main backers decided that they were throwing their money down the drain.

In 2000 Wakefield were taken over by Bradford Bulls RLFC, following the successful Leeds Tykes model. The aim was to preserve rugby at College Grove by making the personnel of the two teams interchangeable across two codes. In June 2004, following relegation, the club's RFU funding plummeted. Gates had fallen to 100 and they had no assets. Many of the Wakefield players, including Mike Harrison and Brian Barley, were forced to move to arch-rivals Sandal across the city, and College Grove, one of the most famous rugby grounds, ceased to be used for rugby.

WHARFEDALE

WHARFEDALE RUFC CAN claim, along with North Walsham, to be the smallest community to field a National League team. The club draws its members from the twin villages of Threshfield and Grassington (population 2,500). Wharfedale isn't actually a town; it is a district high in the Pennines, where the River Wharfe emerges.

Traditionally, rugby players from the area joined Skipton, who were the leading club in the Dales. In 1923 Skipton's hegemony was challenged by the formation of North Ribblesdale in the north of the district and Upper Wharfedale in the heart of the Dales. A rugby side had played in Grassington in Victorian times, but died out around 1900.

Skipton retained their supremacy until the 1940s, when their rivals began to grow in stature. In 1954 Brian Hoggas won a Yorkshire cap, but it was another 40 years before they produced another county cap.

Upper Wharfedale, in particular, grew in prominence in Yorkshire rugby, but suffered from the difficulty in tracing where they were based from the parochial name. Eventually, some members decided to drop the 'Upper' prefix, which upset the old-timers. A heated debate followed before the reformers won the day in the late 1970s.

The club had already produced a top-class international in John Spencer, a superbly talented centre who won 14 England caps after leaving Wharfedale for Headingley. Spencer was closely associated with David Duckham, his international partner. He was once asked if he had learnt anything from playing alongside Duckham. John replied: "I once tried to copy Duckham's side-step and ended up spraining my ankle." He toured with the 1971 Lions before stepping down to concentrate on qualifying as a solicitor. He finished his playing days as captain of the Wharfedale 'A' squad. John has been appointed manager of the 2017 Lions.

John Spencer

League rugby arrived when the club's fortunes were on the rise, and they achieved four promotions in rapid succession. They fielded five brothers, the Vyvyans. Charles Vyvyan joined Sale, where he was picked in the back row for the North of England.

Amongst the club's players was David Lister, who set a National League record of 144 consecutive appearances until getting suspended for three yellow cards. Despite their modest roots, Wharfedale have retained National One status.

(Thanks to Mike Harrison)

YARNBURY

THE ORIGINS OF Yarnbury RUFC lie back in 1872 when a rugby side was formed at Headingley Hill Congregational Church in Leeds. They played rugby regularly until 1896, when, together with Leeds Rifles Brigade, the boys went camping to Upper Wharfedale and played the local side Grassington (now Upper Wharfedale RUFC). Following the game the team was entertained by Captain Stocks at his residence in Yarnbury, which had once been a centre for lead mining. So enjoyable was the experience that the players voted to change the name of their rugby team to Yarnbury, although it retained its close ties with the Congregational Church and Leeds Rifles. This close liaison with the Rifles is represented by the powder horn incorporated in the club crest.

It was around this time that there was a dispute within Yarnbury, causing some members to go their own way, and they formed Headingley RUFC (1878). It is said that Headingley took the best jerseys (green, white and black) and Yarnbury had to change colours to blue, white and black. Yarnbury moved to a new pitch at Meanwood and then on to Butcher Hill, with changing facilities of no more than "cold water and a bucket".

Yarnbury have survived into the 21st century and ran five senior sides in the 1990s, plus 120 juniors. In 2014 the club reached the final of RFU Senior Vase. They lost 20-13 to Newent from Gloucestershire but were promoted from Yorkshire One.

In 2011, Yarnbury's Bob Hood was appointed coach of the England Counties U20s team.

YORK

YORK RFC BEGAN in 1868 with no money and no permanent home. The club was founded at Mrs. Scott's house opposite the Knavesmire by Robert Christison, who was one of three rugby-playing sons of the passenger manager of the North Eastern Railway. Robert played for Durham in 1875, whilst his two brothers, Sandy and Bill, were in the Yorkshire side in direct opposition. The Christison brothers had learnt rugby at St. Peter's School, York, where the game had been played since 1850 – the earliest recorded rugby in the North of England. Robert Christison is recorded as having scored the club's first try.

The new club called the 'York Amateurs' had a succession of pitches, including one situated on the bank of the Ouse, and was prone to be flooded in winter. Eventually, the club persuaded the racecourse authorities to let them have a permanent home opposite the grandstand.

York's first important match was against Hull FC, led by H.H. Hutchinson, the England international. York lost heavily, which was a habit that took them three seasons to leave behind. The first win was against York Training College – under soccer rules!

York improved around 1876 when they recruited Charlie Wood from St Peter's School. Wood was a brilliant half-back who once scored six tries in a match against mighty Bradford.

Despite the club's success, or maybe because of it, York drifted into financial turmoil. They continued to switch pitches and had brief spells at Wiggington Road and Poad's Fields on Clarence Street.

In 1883 York merged with local rivals, York Melbourne RFC, which kept rugby going in the city. This coincided with the club nearly becoming homeless when local residents pressed for them to be evicted from Clarence Street amid complaints of drunkenness. The local opposition was eventually thwarted, but not before they had persuaded the club's landlords to increase the ground rent to 50p – a punitive sum for an amateur club.

In 1887 York signed A.E. 'Compo' Thompson, who was the best forward in Yorkshire. In 1891 he moved to Sunderland and played for Durham.

The 1890s saw the club fielding a top-class half-back pairing in George Grace and Harry Hayes. The duo helped carry York through the difficult years when the Northern Rugby League was formed. York eventually switched to the NU. They won the NU North Eastern Second Division in 1900-01 and were promoted to the NU First Division after beating Liversedge in front of 3,000 spectators. The rugby league side continues today as York Knights.

Several small RU clubs, including York Spartans and York & North Riding emerged in the city. These two clubs merged to form York RUFC. The club was highly successful after World War Two; they built up a strong fixture list, and were twice the winners of the Yorkshire Shield in 1949 and 1964. York were a presence in the Shield for many years, and were winners again in 1981 and twice runners-up in the 1970s. Since the leagues emerged, they have won several North East titles and briefly played at North Two level.

(Thanks to Gordon & Sylvia Prentice)

CHAPTER EIGHT - DURHAM

BLAYDON

'Ah me lads, ye shud only seen us gannin',
We pass'd the foaks upon the road just as they wor stannin';
Thor wes lots o' lads an' lasses there, all wi' smiling faces,
Gawn alang the Scotswood Road, to see the Blaydon Races.'
Geordie Anthem

BLAYDON IS A town on the Durham side of the River Tyne, a couple of miles upstream from Newcastle. The town is world famous for its horse races, although the horses haven't graced the turf since 1915. The fame is owed to a Victorian song, 'The Blaydon Races', that was written to promote the racetrack. The local rugby club originally played on the inside of the racecourse for a number of seasons before the Great War.

Blaydon RFC dates from 1888, when there were a dozen other rugby clubs in the city of Newcastle. The club was originally called 'Blaydon Star' and their first known game was on the 29th September 1888, against Benwell Juniors. The club grew rapidly due to the expansion of the local mining industry and within a decade were amongst the top north-eastern clubs, with fixtures against Rockcliff, Northern and West Hartlepool.

Blaydon maintained steady progress in the years before the Great War, winning the 1904-05 Durham Junior Cup and sharing the Durham League title with Winlaton.

Besides the racecourse, the club used a ground at Stella Hall, which was probably unique because it lay in two separate counties. The right wing of the pitch was on the Northumberland side of the border, while the left flank lay in Durham. It was therefore possible for even the most unfit rugby player to cover parts of both counties during a match.

The Stella Hall ground was leased from the Stella Coal Company, who employed hundreds of miners, including colliery manager Bob Williams, who was one of the earliest Blaydon players to win representative honours. Appropriately, he won four Durham caps and two Northumberland caps in the 1920s.

In 1929 Sammy Miller signed for Salford RLFC from Blaydon RU. He began at Aspatria, but moved to Blaydon. Although he made 312 appearances for Salford RLFC, he was never capped in either code.

Blaydon resumed rugby after World War Two with an unbeaten season, and were able to field a greater player in Martin Donnelly (1917-1999). He came over to England with the New Zealand cricket team and served as a tank commander in North Africa before entering Oxford University in 1945 to read History. At Oxford he played quite remarkable Varsity cricket as well as rugby. During the 1946 cricket season he scored six centuries, and in 1949 he got a double-century against England in the Lord's Test. In 1947 he was capped for England rugby.

As a rugby player he was primarily associated with Oxford University and Blackheath, but he also represented Blaydon on an occasional basis.

In 1948, the Stella ground was the subject of a compulsory purchase order and a new ground was found at Crowtrees near the River Derwent. In the late 1950s they were a strong side, and in 1958-59 they lost only four of 33 games. The club continued to make progress and reached the Durham Senior Cup Final in 1973, losing 14-0 to Hartlepool Rovers.

Blaydon's best known player of the era was Steve Gustard, a burly winger who played for the club for four years before moving to Gosforth and becoming part of their championship years. Gustard also captained Northumberland to the 1982 County Championship title. Amongst his other achievements was representing Spain. He was picked as 'a ringer' for Spain whilst working as a student in the country and even scored seven tries in one match.

More orthodox internationals were Steve Bainbridge and Mickey Skinner. Bainbridge won 17 England and Lions caps in the 1980s. A 6ft 7in lock-forward, he began as a Blaydon colt before moving to Gosforth, Waterloo and Fylde. He was an outstanding lock forward, but prone to on-field indiscipline – notably he was sent off twice in fifteen months, which cost him his England place.

Mickey Skinner was one of the best loved characters of modern rugby. He, too, began as a Blaydon colt before joining Blackheath and Harlequins. He was 28 when he won his first England cap, but was a regular in the 1991 World Cup side. An abrasive flanker, Skinner always seemed to have a helpful word for opponents and referees alike. Mickey made his Blaydon debut at 17 before moving to Kent with his work.

Another great Blaydon character was Dave Guthrie, who was club captain for 15 years as Blaydon rose from North One to National One in the early part of the 21st century. Paul Gustard began at Blaydon before joining Leicester and becoming a successful coach.

Blaydon reached National One in 2009 and were Intermediate Cup runners-up in 2001.

DARLINGTON

THE TOWN OF Darlington is renowned for engineering, construction and telecoms industries. It owes much of its fame to the building of the world's first passenger railway in 1825.

Rugby arrived in Darlington in the 1850s, when it was played at the local grammar school. The town's rugby club is the oldest in the North-East, dating from the 18th October 1863. The club was formed at the Green Tree Inn in Skinnergate by the local cricket club, who decided to play rugby football in the winter.

The cricket and rugby clubs lost their home on Park Street, but were rehoused on the site of Feethams Cricket Ground.

A series of fund-raising ventures were organised, including a football match between Durham School and the grandly named 'All England XI'. The fund-raising ventures paid for the levelling of the Feethams ground and for the building of a new pavilion. Rugby fixtures were, however, few and far between as Durham School and Richmond (in Yorkshire) were the only other local sides. Later matches in the decade were arranged with Harrogate and Rochdale.

Darlington pictured in 1883.

In 1871 Darlington hosted the first match between Durham and Yorkshire. The two teams met again for the first official match at Darlington on the 6th December 1873. Durham fielded seven Darlington men, including Tom Watson, who was club captain for 14 seasons and England's top sprinter.

Things were primitive, even for county players; they had their post-match bath in an old tub behind the local pub. On one occasion, the Darlington captain found a bunch of celery in the murky waters. The celery appeared soon afterwards on the dinner table.

Darlington continued to host the Durham county matches during the 1870s and provided the backbone of the county team. Amongst their county men was John Lowthian Bell, who won an England cap at half-back in 1878.

Another international from Darlington was Frank Pease (1864-1957). Pease belonged to the fabulously rich family who had hired the unknown Robert Stephenson to build the first railway. He was capped by England whilst playing for Hartlepool Rovers, having left Darlington because the rugby club had begun to decline with the creation of a soccer section. Eventually soccer took over the sporting interest of the town, and the rugby club became a shadow of its former glory.

Darlington retained some significance in rugby ranks as James Huggon, a Scotland international, joined the club around the turn of the century after graduating from the Queen Elizabeth Grammar School in the town.

Following a period of decline in membership because of the First World War, the club gained new strength in the 1920s and 1930s, producing a series of top county players, including the late G. Tarn Bainbridge (a former club president).

Darlington's best player of the 1920s was Billy Patrick, a half-back who suddenly joined Northampton. He was unlucky as the Saints were in hot water for recruiting players from other clubs and the RFU began to suspect illegal payments. Patrick then signed for Bradford RL, but never played for the first team. He tried to resume as a rugby union player, but was banned for life by the RFU.

In 1929 the club president, Arthur Feetham, gave a ground to the rugby club at Lingfield. Between the wars, the club's ground was in Hundens Lane, before moving to Lingfield Lane in 1962, then to Blackwell Meadows in 1994.

In the early 1950s Darlington fielded an international in Iain Cordial, who had won four Scotland caps when with Edinburgh Wanderers. One of his teammates was Malcolm Stringer, who won the Mr. Universe bodybuilding title.

Other players of renown were two Darlington schoolboys, D. Freeman and R. Sutherland, who played for the North East Counties against the 1954 All Blacks. The tourists won 16-0. B.A. Pledger of Darlington was unlucky to be Durham understudy to Stan Hodgson, the Lions hooker.

The best Darlington player of the 1960s was Barrie Stoneman, who played for Darlington GS and Durham County before joining Richmond and winning an England trial.

The move to Blackwell Meadows has helped Darlington to produce its own youngsters. They did well in the early 2000s and were North One champions in 2003 before drifting back to Durham & Northumberland One. Darlington celebrated their 150th anniversary in 2013-14.

DARLINGTON RUGBY FOOTBALL CLUB

THE FIRST HALF-CENTURY

1863 ~ 1914

by Bob Jackson

DARLINGTON MOWDEN PARK

DARLINGTON MOWDEN PARK RUFC can proudly boast the best rugby ground outside the top of the National leagues. Their ground is the 27,000 seater Northern Echo Stadium, previously home to Darlington Football Club. The soccer club's misfortune in losing their home coincided with Mowden Park's search for a new home after selling their own ground.

Darlington Mowden Park began life as the old boys of the town's Queen Elizabeth Grammar School. The headquarters of the club was on Victoria Road in the city centre. Plans for a ring road forced the club to sell their Victoria Road headquarters. An opportunity arose to buy a ground near Mowden Park housing estate. The grammar school had closed its doors in the 1960s, which forced the club to go 'open' in 1968,

The club was traditionally one of Durham County's senior clubs, with fixtures against the big Hartlepool clubs and Durham City. But Mowden Park were in the doldrums in the mid-1980s, which led to being placed in N&D One in 1987. Since then Mowden Park have climbed to the National leagues. Perhaps their finest hour was losing narrowly to mighty Harlequins in the last 16 of the National Knockout Cup.

The best players from the club have been Brian Stoneman, Tom Catterick (Newcastle Falcons), Alex Gray (London Irish) and Mike Ellery (England Sevens). A short-term link up with Newcastle Falcons meant that some famous players have made brief appearances for Mowden Park, notably Geoff Parling, Phil Dowson and Toby Flood. Stand-off Toby Flood didn't impress one of the locals, who didn't rate him at all and said so. Less than a year later, Flood won the first of many England caps.

Perhaps the most significant player to wear Mowden's colours was Kevan Oliphant, who arrived in the 1990s with the club in the Northern League. Oliphant provided 331 points in one season to be England's top scorer. He teamed up with his ex-West Hartlepool teammate Dave Mitchell to form a brilliant coaching team who took Mowden to four successive promotions.

In 2012 Mowden sold their Yiewsley Drive ground, after 40 years of occupancy, to move to the Northern Echo Arena soccer stadium. In the same year they reached National Two and National One in 2014.

(Thanks to Kevin Keeligan)

DURHAM

THE CRADLE OF rugby in Durham County is Durham School, where the game has been played since 1850. Amongst the earliest players were the Crombie Brothers, who introduced the game to Edinburgh Academy, thus beginning a massive legacy to Scottish rugby. Since 1855 an annual match between Durham School and Edinburgh Academy has taken place.

In 1876 the Durham RU was formed by representatives from Houghton-le-Spring, Durham University, Bensham (later Gateshead Fell), Westoe, Sunderland, Stockton and Darlington. The 1895 Schism proved a blessing to Durham

Durham pictured in 1893.

because there was 100 miles between the county and the heart of the breakaway – a long way in 1895. The NU did make attempts to start a rival league, and even formed a NU team of Durham and Northumberland players. Eleven of the 19-man squad came from the South Shields NU club, but it proved a fruitless exercise.

When the RFU denied access to Lancashire and Yorkshire international players, Durham proved a realistic alternative, especially since Durham were entering a golden era. In this period Durham won the title of champion county six times (once jointly with Devon), were runners-up the four remaining seasons, and Northern Group leaders each year. They scored 740 points to their opponents' 293.

The era saw three Durham men change rugby in other parts of the north: Bob Oakes, Bernard Oughtred and John Todd. Between the wars, Oakes was a major driving force at Headingley and with Yorkshire, Oughtred helped re-establish rugby in south Cumbria after the Great Schism and Todd formed the Derbyshire RU and created the successful Blackwell club in the 1920s.

Durham were a major force between the wars, when they could call upon the services of Carl Aarvold and a host of other fine players from Durham School. But they also relied on working-class players as well as Old Dunelmians, but they were hit hard by the Great Depression of the 1930s. Mining and shipbuilding were two of North East's biggest employers, and they were devastated by the depression. In 1931 there were 175,000 people out of work in the county (when unemployment benefit was 35p per week). Many men followed the Jarrow marchers and walked to the south and midlands in search of work. In 1934 Carl Aarvold played in a charity match in St. Albans that was designed to raise money for the Durham Distress Relief Fund. Only World War Two solved the problem of unemployment in the North East.

The combination of miners and Varsity types in the Durham side did have its amusing side. Middlesex RU officials noted their horror when, following a match against Durham, the northerners regaled their hosts with a repertoire of 'earthy songs', which didn't meet with their hosts' approval

Carl Aarvold worked hard to restore Durham's fortunes on the field. After World War Two, Durham struggled, but produced some great players in Mike Weston, John Dee, Sam Hodgson, John Ranson and Garath Archer.

DURHAM CITY

DURHAM CITY FC were formed in 1872. In 1888 they won the Durham Cup. They were an excellent side, but were behind Hartlepool Rovers (who beat them in the 1889 final). That year City met Northumberland RFC (now defunct), who were put to the sword, with City crossing the Northumberland line 15 times.

The first famous player to emerge from the club was Dr. H. Brooks, who went to Australia & New Zealand with the 1888 British Isles team.

In 1911 Bill Coulson won an England trial, and three years later Alfred Maynard played for England in their Grand Slam season. At the outbreak of war Maynard joined the Royal Navy, but was killed on active service in 1916.

After World War One, Durham City established themselves as a first-class side. Season upon season, they were hard to beat. In 1930-31 they won 24 of 28 games; the following season it was 19 of 23; and in 1935-36 it was 20 of 27.

One youthful observer of the era was Carol Rolling, whose father, George S. Shaw, was City's fixture secretary and first team linesman. George had an important role in the team's tactics, especially when it came to supporting the club's best player – Tom Danby. Tom was a teacher and a dual England international at rugby union and rugby league, despite being 'very short sighted'. A top-class goal-kicker for Durham City, Tom relied on George as linesman to wear a white overcoat that enabled him to locate the goalposts for penalties and conversions. Danby later moved to Harlequins, won an England cap and in 1949 joined Salford RLFC. He was quickly picked for Great Britain RL for the 1950 Australia tour.

A golden era for City came in the late 1950s with three international: Stan Hodgson, John Ranson and Mike Weston. Hodgson played top-class rugby for 40 years. He came from a family who were long associated with Durham City. His early days saw him compete with Eric Evans, the England captain, for England's hooking jersey. Eventually he broke through, and even made the 1962 Lions team, but broke his leg in the early stages of the tour. As a rugby nut, Stan would play anywhere at any time. But since he was a teetotaller, he skipped the Calcutta Cup post-match banquet to go home and play for City the following morning. Ranson began at Durham City, but won an England cap whilst associated with Rosslyn Park. Weston represented the 1962 Lions. He began at Durham School and was associated with City from his early teens. Possessing a great long stride, he never looked hurried in the fly-half position. In the England team, he played out of position at centre. His playing career was also blighted by knee problems.

City had an association with the University of Durham, which saw brief appearances by great players from the university, such as Will Carling and Phil de Glanville.

The 1960s saw Durham City possess a superb fixture list, which they retained until the introduction of leagues. Despite being placed in National 4, City were astute enough to opt out of professionalism. The decision cost them their prized nationwide fixtures, but they still thrive today at Hollow Drift in Durham/Northumberland 1.

(Thanks to Carol Rolling)

Mike Weston

GATESHEAD
(formerly Gateshead Fell)

GATESHEAD FELL WAS formed in September 1907 as Bensham RFC and played at High Teams Forge in Bensham. By 1921 the club had enough players to run three teams. That year the AGM decided to change the name to Gateshead Fell.

The club moved to a new ground next to Low Fell, before moving to their current ground next to Gateshead Fell Cricket Club, which they bought from Lord Northbourne in 1925 for £4000 (a huge sum for a small organisation). Eventually, part of the ground had to be sold for housing.

After World War Two, Fell converted a disused air raid shelter into a clubhouse. This was replaced by a new building 1953, but the grandstand burnt down in 1957. That year the ground was levelled and the club had to play at the De La Rue on Team Valley Trading Estate.

Over 22 Fell players have played for Durham over the years, including G. Hunter (31 appearances). Gateshead Fell were defeated finalists in the 1956 Durham Challenge Cup final.

The most famous player to play for Fell was Alan Tomes, who played twice for Scotland in 1976 whilst with the club. Alan, a giant lock, had attended Heathfield GS in Gateshead. He is most commonly associated with Hawick RUFC, from where he became a Scotland regular and was picked for the 1980 Lions.

The club merged with North Durham and the combined club was renamed Gateshead RFC.

HARTLEPOOL
(formerly Hartlepool GSOBS)

THE EXACT FOUNDING date of Hartlepool Old Boys is uncertain, but it was either 1891 or 1893. The club's founder was Dr. A.E. Morrison. He had played previously for Hartlepool Rovers and assembled a side from members of the town's Boys Brigade.

Their first recorded match was a victory over Stranton Parish Church. Several weeks later, the OBs lost to Hartlepool St. James. One of their earliest players, Bob Poole, played for Durham and was rapidly enticed to Hartlepool Rovers. That led to him winning an England cap against Scotland in 1896.

A split occurred at the club in 1894, which saw most of the members of the Boys Brigade – a teetotal organisation – going their own way because the OBs sold alcohol after matches. Despite this setback, the OBs were becoming a real force and won the Durham Junior Cup.

Bob Poole rejoined his old club, where he became a central figure and led them to become one of the top junior sides in the North East. Poole departed to the Northern Union in 1902, but left a team with some top-class players. Sam Irvin (1880-1939) toured the West Country with the OBs and liked what he saw. Indeed, he promptly joined Devonport Albion, who were possibly the best team in England at the time and certainly the most cash-driven amateur outfit in the RFU. Albion got round the amateur rules by offering jobs in the dockyards. Irvin was capped by England at full-back in 1905, but poor old Sam was blamed for England's worst ever defeat by Wales. He was described as "having no ability in tackling or kicking" and rapidly joined Oldham NU club.

Harold Havelock began with the OBs before moving to West Hartlepool and Hartlepool Rovers, where he won three England caps in 1908 before defecting to the professional ranks. Havelock was noticed when Hartlepool Rovers hosted the North v South England trial and he was immediately promoted to the England pack.

The GSOBs were officially classified as a senior club in the Durham rankings from 1902 until 1906, but decline set in, and although they produced some good players, they never regained senior status.

In 1925-26 the OBs were reunited with the Boys Brigade, but the merger only lasted a couple of seasons.

OBs produced the occasional good player in the ensuing years – notably W. Gillespie, who won an England trial in 1930. Gillespie played for the North East against the 1927 Waratahs, but the strength of Rovers kept the OBs in the shade.

In 1970 Mayfield Park became the new HQ, which claimed to have the highest goalposts in the North East.

HARTLEPOOL ROVERS

"Our hallowed Friarage. it is like Kew Gardens and a gentleman's lawn rolled into one."
WL Oakes 1883

THE 21ST CENTURY finds Hartlepool Rovers as a middle-ranking club in Durham/Northumberland 1. As such, it is hard to believe that Rovers were once one of the top ten sides in English rugby, with a history of 30 internationals and 42 Durham County Cup victories.

Rovers were formed in 1875 by C.A. Harrison, O.K. Trenchman and E.C. Jobson as Hartlepool Albion. They became Rovers in 1881. Their first ground was at Love Lane, which was rented from a timber merchant. When they merged with Hartlepool RFC in 1883, they gained possession of the Friarage Ground. In 1887 the Friarage hosted the Maori tourists, which saw Rovers lose narrowly.

Rovers fielded 26 internationals between 1887 and 1925. In 1887 Rovers were honoured when Frank Pease (1864-1957) was picked by England for the Ireland match in Dublin. Pease was from a wealthy local family. Tall and fair-haired, he was educated at Harrow. W.H. Towers represented Wales that year as well.

Fred Alderson arrived at Friarage in 1889, via Durham School and Cambridge University, and made a huge impact by adopting the Varsity way of playing with four 'backs'. He won six England caps and was captain on his international debut. Curiously, he never captained Rovers. In 1892 Alderson cited a Tudhoe player, John Duffy, for violence on the field and persuaded Rovers to boycott the 1893 County Cup final because Tudhoe insisted on picking Duffy. Rovers beat Tudhoe 15-3 the following year and were champions another ten times over the next two decades.

Fred Alderson

The visit of the first Barbarian touring team in 1890 saw Alderson, Pease, F.C. Lohden and W. Yield represent their home side. Alderson was one of Carpmael's first touring partners in 1891, but he chose to play for his home club against the BaBa's in their first ever match.

Frederick Lohden joined Rovers from Durham School. He was a bit of a rover himself and had a few sojourns abroad. He was picked for England in 1893, but could not play due to a family bereavement. He based himself in London for most of his life.

William Yiend epitomised another strand of local life; he learnt his rugby in the town and worked on the railway. He was capped by England in 1889. Bob Poole and J.H. Jewitt won England caps whilst with Rovers, but both defected to the Northern Union in 1903.

Despite the defections, Rovers continued to produce England internationals, such as Francis Boylen (1908), Harry Coverdale (1910) and Arthur Dingle (1913). Scrum-half Coverdale was unlucky as his career coincided with that of the legendary Cyril Kershaw. Dingle was educated at Durham School and Oxford, where he won a Blue and was selected for England.

Fred Chapman, the scorer of the first try at Twickenham in an international.

In 1911-12 Rovers set a world record of 860 points in a season, scoring 209 tries, a record that stood for 50 years. Their kingpins were Arthur Doyle and Fred Chapman. Chapman (1888-1938) was the scorer of the first international try at Twickenham. He, like so many other great Rovers players, moved South in pursuit of a life outside rugby.

One forgotten Rover ho merits a mention is Dr. W.A. Robertson, who never won international honours for his country but played for the 1910 British Isles team.

This era also; produced the man who is indelibly linked to rugby in the region: R.F. 'Bob' Oakes. He captained the club in 1899-1900 before moving to Yorkshire. He played for England on eight occasions and was later RFU President. He went on to organise an annual Yorkshire v Hartlepool Rovers match.

Success continued for Rovers between the wars, when they regularly provided ten players for Durham and took the County Cup on five occasions from 1922 to 1926. They dominated North East rugby between the wars, but suffered during the Great Depression when the best young players left the area. One example was Barney Hudson, who signed for Salford RLFC from Rovers. A miner, Hudson joined Salford to escape the pit. Salford got him a job in an engineering factory and had his talented services for 20 years.

In 1931 Cliff Harrison, aged 19, made a brilliant scoring debut for England against Ireland. He began with the Boys Brigade before joining Rovers. Unfortunately, he dislocated his shoulder after his second match and was never selected again by England.

Rovers lost the Friarage in 1939 after 50 years when the government decreed that school pitches could not be sub-let during the wartime emergency. After the war, Hartlepool Council blocked a renewal of the lease. Fortunately, Rovers raised enough money to buy a pitch on Easington Road, which was called 'the New Friarage'.

Rovers continued to produce international players – notably Tom Peat, Albert Agar and Johnnie Dee. The latter won two England caps at centre in 1962 and became the club's only Lion when he toured South Africa.

Between 1968 and 1981, Rovers won the County Cup on 12 occasions, and in 1970-71 scored 209 tries to equal their previous record.

The post-war years saw the emergence of a local rival in West Hartlepool. The two clubs met each other on Boxing Day in a fierce local derby, and the golden rule was that players never moved between the two clubs. The rivalry with West Hartlepool continued until the advent of professionalism in 1987.

Wests chose the brave new world of paying players, whereas Rovers decided their modest gate could never fund such a venture.

Rovers lost their best players, and (heaven forbid) John Wrigley switched to Wests and went on to represent the North of England. Shorn of their best players, Rovers tumbled down the leagues into Northumberland and Durham One. Decline may never be attractive, but Rovers recognise that to have tried professionalism would have meant financial suicide.

HOUGHTON

HOUGHTON RFC WAS founded in 1873, and its founders were closely associated with the subsequent formation of the Durham County RFU. P. Junor of Houghton was chairman of the county's preliminary meetings in early October 1876. Junor had been chosen to play for Scotland in 1873, but his work for the local brewery prevented him from playing. He was never selected again.

Three years later, J.T. Todd of Houghton captained the county XV and was elected to the county committee, subsequently becoming county president. In 1885 he became Durham's first county representative on the RFU. Much interest surrounds the idea that this J.T. Todd was the same man who founded the hugely successful Blackwell RFC in Derbyshire in 1919. Both men share a name, were approximately the same age, had a love of rugby, were RFU officials, and came from the North East. It is safe to presume the J.T. Todd

J.T. Todd

of Houghton was the same J.T. Todd of Blackwell.

Houghton produced a total of 18 county players between 1873 and 1888 as they strove to be the premier club in the county. They were the first winners of the Durham Challenge Cup in 1880-81, beating Sunderland by three tries to nil. The following year Houghton lost in the final to Westoe by one try to nil. Their only other cup final appearance was in 1891, when they lost to Hartlepool Rovers by two goals and a try to nil.

During the 1939-45 War their field and facilities were used by the army.

NORTH DURHAM
(merged with Gateshead in 1998)

NORTH DURHAM RFC were formed in 1876 by members of Gateshead Cricket Club. The club has many claims to fame, not least for having produced the first captain of Wales: Rev. Charles Newman (1857-1922).

Newman was a founder member of Newport Athletic Club in 1875 and played in the first rugby match for the town. He was elected to be captain for the season 1882-83. The "Rev. Charlie" as he was known won his Blue at Cambridge in 1882 and later played for Durham. He played in the first Welsh team, as full-back in 1881 and went on to win ten caps (mainly at half-back), including six as captain. Newman was short, thickset but powerful and a very elusive runner, having the ability to run through a whole team. He was the first man to introduce the true passing aspect of rugby to South Wales. Floodlights were used for the first time in Wales when Newport played Cardiff in 1879. The light was not as good as it might have been and Newman noticed that the Cardiff players were watching the man rather than the ball. The next time he had the ball he told O.M. Rosser to run across the field when he pretended to pass. The Cardiff players were still following Rosser as Newman scored and was leaning against the upright waiting for them to realise their mistake. On taking his degree he was ordained and posted to a parish in the north of England, where his

North Durham Rugby Football Club,
1876 :: 1926
"JUBILEE" DINNER.

1876

AND LIKE

STILL RUNNING.

COUNTY HOTEL.
NEWCASTLE-ON-TYNE.
NOV. 13TH. 1926.

subsequent life was spent. Newman was hardly a lucky player for Wales as they won only one of his ten internationals. He had better luck with North Durham as they were winners of the Durham Senior Cup in 1883 and runners-up to Hartlepool Rovers the following season.

As well as Newman, North Durham also had a top-class player in Jack Showery, who was an England reserve in 1885 and won 33 county caps.

The first England international from North Durham was John Hall, who won three caps in 1900. Little is known about Hall except that he also played for Gateshead Institute, Hartlepool Rovers and Blackheath.

We know far more about Joseph Brunton (1888-1970), who was North's second England international. He won three caps in England's Grand Slam season of 1913-14 before World War One ended his international playing career. He served with distinction in the Great War, winning the Military Cross. After the war he joined Rockcliff RFC, and later became an international referee and an RFU President.

In 1929 North Durham returned to Prince Consort Road after nearly half a century of playing at various grounds, and they remerged with North Durham Cricket club in 1936. Two years later, the rugby club regained the Durham Challenge Cup.

The post-World War Two years saw North Durham in decline. However, George Grace, who also played for Ryton and Coventry, managed to win 35 caps for the county and was an England trialist.

Down the years, 50 North Durham men have won county caps. The most recent was Tommy Unwin, who played prop for Durham County from 1963 to 1972, making 51 appearances. Although relatively small for a prop at 14 stone, Unwin's athleticism, power and strong scrummaging won him an England trial. He captained North Durham for a record five seasons.

The redevelopment of the town of Gateshead in the final decades of the 20th century caused North Durham RFC to enter a period of decline, and in 1998 they merged with Gateshead Fell as 'Gateshead'.

STOCKTON

STOCKTON IS AN industrial town on the River Tees famous for engineering, chemicals and the steel industry. Stockton RFC were formed in 1873, but details are sketchy. We know that the club supplied five players to the 1874-75 Durham County side who played Yorkshire at Darlington and later at Leeds. In total, six Stockton players represented the county in the 1870s and 1880s before the club went into abeyance. Their swan-song was a game against the 1888 Maoris, which resulted in a big win for the visitors.

The club operated from Parkfield, near Bowesfield Lane, where they remained until 1914. Little is known of the early years and the club went into abeyance from 1914 and 1923. Dr. John Brydon revived the club with the help of several friends and managed to recruit 33 potential players. A field was found off Station Road in Norton at the cost of £10 a season and the

Royal Hotel became the headquarters and changing rooms. The opening match was a 3-0 home victory over Middleborough 'A'. In 1925-26 John Sladden became the first Stockton player for half a century to represent the county.

The club's biggest problem was the distance between the Royal Hotel and the Norton Showground. They tried erecting a tent for players to get changed in, but eventually decided to buy the Norton Showground and erect a changing pavilion.

The new facilities were opened in 1931 with a match against a Durham XV. The good times did not last and the ground was sold to developers in 1933. The club finally vacated Norton Showground three years later and moved to Eaglescliffe and then Preston Cricket Ground.

History was repeated in 1939 as the club found itself with no home and only a handful of players. The club closed its doors until 1945. Eventually, a permanent home was found at Norton Cricket Club, which preceded good times on the field when Charles Tealey, a big winger, became a county regular.

One of the club's greatest moments came in 1964, when Stockton reached the final of the Durham Senior Cup. They lost 20-6 to Durham City, who were one of the best clubs in the region at the time.

Arthur Chapman was the best Stockton player of the 1960s, playing for Durham and English Universities before moving to Rosslyn Park, where he had an England trial.

In the early 1970s, the club received a set-back when Grangefield Grammar School, its principal feeder school, was closed. They sought to fill the gap with junior rugby, which was comparatively rare at the time.

Stockton had links to Norton Showground going back to 1923. At one time, there were grandiose plans to develop it as Durham County's home ground, which included even a railway station for trains to deposit spectators. The plan never happened, but the showground was developed into a fine ground.

The club's best-known players of recent times were David Cooke and Steve Hackney. Cooke was a brilliant winger who was England's top try-scorer in 1992 after moving to West Hartlepool. Hackney began at Stockton before moving to Leicester Tigers, where he was a reliable and talented three-quarter on the fringe of the England squad for a number of seasons.

The best player to be produced by Stockton is the huge lock Geoff Parling, whose father taught at Grangefield School and was a player and referee at the club. Geoff played for them from the ages of 12 to 16, when he won a scholarship to Durham School and signed for Newcastle Falcons. He played 116 times for the Falcons before moving to Leicester in 2009. In 2011, he made his debut for England and was one of the stars of the Lions in Australia in 2013.

SUNDERLAND

"The Mack'ems – We mack em' (ships) You tack em."

SUNDERLAND IS A town legendary for its devotion to soccer, but in the late 19th century the club were frequent suppliers of rugby internationals to England. Sunderland RFC was formed in 1873, six years before the town's soccer club and they were the first club to win the Durham Cup.

Henry Kayll of Sunderland was one of the first internationals. A wealthy landowner, Kayll won an England cap in the 1878 Calcutta Cup match. One of six rugby-playing brothers at Sunderland, Henry Kayll's other reason for entering the history books was as the first athlete to pole vault over 11 feet when he set a world record in 1877.

Dr. Howard Marshall played for Sunderland after winning a single England cap in 1893. Marshall had earlier toured South

Sunderland in action in 1937 at their Ashbrooke ground, which has been their home since 1887.

Africa with the 1891 British Isles team. Marshall later wrote several updates of the Rugby Football book by his namesake, the Rev. Frank Marshall.

Other internationals from Sunderland were Dr. Alan Ayre Smith (1876-1957), who went to Australia in 1899 with the British Isles team; Arnold Davison; and Rev. Francis Poole, who won three England caps in 1895 whilst with the club – the same year he took holy orders. Norman Cox won a single England cap in 1901 after distinguishing himself with Durham

Sunderland didn't produce any further internationals, but they did give the RFU an influential President in Eric Watts Moses. He was an official on the 1950 Lions tour to New Zealand, which brought home to him that English rugby suffered due to lack of coaching and organisation at any level. On his return, Moses organised the earliest coaching in English rugby, pursuing top coaches such as Carwyn Jones and John Elders. He was RFU President from 1945 until 1950.

Since 1887, Sunderland RFC have played at Ashbrooke.

WEST HARTLEPOOL

THE FIRST WEST Hartlepool club existed briefly from 1875 until 1880. Four years later the club was reformed and were highly successful for 20 years, winning the Durham Senior Cup. They were the backbone of the Durham side which won the County Championship on five occasions between 1900 and 1909.

Wests produced seven internationals during this era. The best was 'Long John' Taylor (1876-1951), who won 11 England caps between 1897 and 1905. Taylor moved to Hartlepool from Castleford, where he first won acclaim for his goal-kicking.

Another remarkable Wests international was Harry Havelock, who won three England caps in 1908. Havelock was one of those rare sons of Hartlepool who played for both Rovers and Wests, a swap that did not endear him to either side. Havelock joined Hull RLFC, which ended his availability to Wests and England.

The 1905 All Blacks played a Combined Hartlepool XV at the Old Friarage. The All Blacks won 63-0 and the match resulted in a famous journalistic error. The reporter reported, "They were all backs", which was meant to record that all 15 Kiwis could handle like three-quarters. The newspaper sub-editor thought it was a spelling mistake and adjusted the piece to mention 'All Blacks' – a name that stuck.

The collapse of Wests in 1908 due to financial problems was sudden and spectacular. The club's home, the Victoria Ground, was taken over by a new club, Hartlepool United RFC.

Wests reformed in 1919 under the Rev. Bertram Jones, the rector of Hartlepool. The reformed club had an odd habit of hanging a carved wooden monkey from the crossbar during matches, echoing the legendary execution of a monkey in the town during the Napoleonic Wars.

Wests greatest player emerged in 1925 in the spindly shape of Sir Carl Aarvold, one of the greatest three-quarters of all time. Aarvold was England's captain on seven of his 16 appearances. In 1930 he became the first Englishman to lead the Lions to victory in New Zealand. Aarvold later became a High Court judge.

In 1965 Wests moved to Brierton Lane, which became their famous home ground. Undoubtedly the finest players to grace Brierton Lane were the Whetton twins from New Zealand. Alan and Gary played for Wests in the mid-1970s as youngsters seeking experience. Alan won three All Black caps in 1983, whilst his brother won 58 caps from 1981 to 1991.

In 1983-84 they won the Northern Merit Table with 32 wins and four draws in 43 matches.

Wests were becoming the town's premier club as Rovers declined. They acquired a fine team in time for the establishment of leagues in 1987. They could field an excellent side, with two North of England locks in John Dixon and John Howe, top English try-scorer in David Cooke, and a brilliant fly-half in John Stabler (who had joined from Rovers).

Under the support of Phillip Yuill, a local builder, the club reached the top division, but struggled against sides with greater facilities and bigger pockets. But even the disappointment of relegation was eclipsed by the death of John Howe during a match against Morley.

Wests fought their way back by recruiting Mike Brewer, the All Blacks flanker, as club coach. He was aided by Steve Vile, an excellent Australian fly-half. Brewer took Wests back to the First Division in 1998, but history repeated itself as the club were rapidly relegated.

Today Wests play in North One East – a long way from their Premiership days.

North of England lock-forward John Howe, who sadly died on a rugby field during a match against Moseley.

WESTOE

"South Shields is beset by much ignorance and many moral evils through the want of school accommodation."
Government inspector's report in 1853

IN THEIR EARLIEST days, Westoe RFC were an unusual combination of a pit team and the products of a local grammar school. The club takes its name from Westoe Higher Grade School, which opened in 1893. The club was founded in 1875 and was one of several on the south side of the River Tyne. Westoe had its first county player in 1887, when G. H. Thompson played for Durham. There are records of the club losing to Durham University and Durham City.

The town of South Shields was a booming port at the end of the 19th Century, and its success was displayed by the local rugby club, South Shields RFC. The club were Durham Champions in 1895. They defected to the NU in 1901, but rapidly decided to re-join the RFU and then 're-defected' in 1902 when the NU started a North East League. Soon the club was in financial trouble and closed their doors.

Westoe RFC emerged in the ashes of South Shields. In 1909 Westoe fielded Dr. F.E. Chapman, who had an England trial before moving to bigger clubs and winning eight England caps. In 1920 G.S. McIntyre of Westoe played in the Varsity match, and in the 1930s William Anderson and James Waggott had England trials.

The 1930s were a golden era for Westoe, with six Westoe players represented Durham in 1937-38. Also J. Waggott was a Welsh trialist, and W. Anderson had an England trial.

In 1953 the local school changed its name to South Shields Technical School for Boys, which horrified the headmaster, Bill Lucas, but the school continued to provide players for the club. Westoe were a good side at the time and won the Durham Cup.

The local mine, one of the deepest in Britain, closed in 1986, which meant Westoe had to rely on its youth section for players. It has worked well as Gareth Archer and David Wilson began at Westoe and moved on to play for England.

Katie McLean was captain of the England Ladies Rugby team. Katie is a prolific goal-kicker who played in the 2010 Women's World Cup.

Westoe won the Intermediate Cup and reached National Two, but were relegated in 2013. Today the club is multi-faceted, with rugby, cricket and squash.

(Thanks to David Barnes)

CHAPTER NINE - NORTHUMBERLAND

"The further North, the keener the spirit."

BLYTH

NOT A GREAT deal of information is available about the initial formation of Blyth in 1921. It is known that they were one of several Northumberland clubs established in the early 1920s, which were usually driven by men who had experienced the game in the forces during World War One. We also know that one of the main figures behind the initiative was Norman Jackson, who played at a high enough standard to warrant a county trial. Norman captained the club in its early seasons.

The club opened its first season in September 1921 with a match against newly-formed neighbours Seghill, which was won 20-0. The first recorded team list is from the match against Low Fell a month later, and it included N.W. Nicholson and Bill Morrison, who later gained a county trial. Bill was from a local farming family who provided the playing pitch near Cowpen Colliery.

Given the economic conditions of the North East at this time, it is hardly surprising to learn that the club was subject to considerable ups and downs. Bill Hickey, a player from those years, later recalled that the players would meet up before the start of the season and that fixtures would be arranged according to the numbers available and likely strength. Some years there were insufficient players to form a team, so no fixtures were arranged and the players drifted off to play elsewhere before trying again the next season. On other occasions there were enough players to warrant the fielding of a second XV. There seems to have been a constant exit of players, understandably given the employment problems of the 1920s and 1930s in the North East. Bill's own brother, Sid, emigrated to Australia, where, ironically, he became a leading state rugby administrator. It was in these circumstances that the club faded away in 1937.

It was nearly a quarter of a century later before the Blyth club re-emerged. That it did so is credited to several people. Two were former players, the club's original captain Norman Jackson and Peter Daley, an outstanding forward from the 1930s who had gone on to enjoy success at Rockcliff. They were joined by Bernie Cranmer, a Lancastrian rugby fanatic who stayed in Blyth after wartime service in submarines, and by Sgt. Eric Potter, an Army recruitment officer in the town. Together with other former players the group managed to rent facilities and to recruit players – quite a number of them native to Blyth, but who had learned and played the game elsewhere.

The first season in 1961-62 was a resounding success, with enough players to produce two XVs and both winning well over half of their matches. This flowed over to the next season when a colts side was formed. On-field success led to a stronger fixture list, which nearly proved fatal to the young club. Older players did not feel up to harder games and the younger ones lacked

the experience to cope. The result was a slippery slope of lost players and losing teams, one fuelling the other. By 1969 few of the pioneers remained and the club struggled to field even one side. Saturday lunchtimes for the stalwarts were spent scouring the streets of Blyth for players to make up the numbers, rather in the style of a press gang. The lack of a settled HQ did not help hold the club together either.

Perseverance paid off. Within two years the club was turned around, helped by the superb half-back partnership of Tim Viard and Denis Reynolds, who linked with some uncompromising forwards. Results picked up, so that in 1971-72, 28 of 37 games were won, with 1044 points being scored in the process – a record which would stand for 40 years. The following season the club won their first trophy in the form of the Northumberland Junior Shield. Two years later the Junior Cup was captured and the club was able to field four sides. Furthermore, in 1974 the club amalgamated with Blyth Cricket Club, gaining the longed-for clubhouse. This was followed two years later by an on-site pitch. The premises have since been extended twice to provide one of the best facilities in the North East today.

Also in the early 1970s, a group of players established a youth section, adopting the recently introduced mini rugby as a means of providing the game to youngsters who played only soccer at school. This led to a Colts XV being organised once more. These initiatives, taken up in the long term by Max Proud and others, went on to provide a constant stream of players, with the result that Blyth first XV has invariably consisted of 90 per cent or more home-grown players.

By the 1980s on-field progress had slowed as established local clubs were reluctant to grant first XV fixtures, so Blyth had to look further afield. This involved travelling, but it meant that the players could hone their skills against the likes of Kendal, Penrith, Edinburgh Wanderers and Middlesbrough. The reward for this enterprise came with the establishment of leagues in 1987, which saw the club placed in Durham/Northumberland Division 1, above several of those other clubs which had previously refused fixtures. This placing was justified when Blyth won promotion to NE2 in the league's first season, a position they held for the next nine years.

However, the club went into a decade of slow decline, subsiding to mid-table in Durham/Northumberland's lowest league. Their former success faded in the memory, probably due to their continuing to prefer the old and trusted members instead of blooding the club's young players. This was only reversed when former colt Tony Smithson returned to the club and captained the first XV for a record six successive seasons. Helped initially by coaching input from Newcastle Falcon's All Black forwards Joe McDonnell, and then Carl Heyman, the team achieved promotion twice in four seasons in 2009 and

2012. The latter season saw a new record of 1113 points scored in 24 league outings. Tony's term ended in 2014 with the club well placed in D/N 1 and a victory in the Northumberland Senior Plate.

Sadly, none of the 1961 founders remain to bask in the club's success. However, a considerable debt is owed to the three members from that time who have each given five decades of unbroken effort to the club: Jim Bell, who joined in 1962, had filled nearly every official office, plus a few unofficial ones; Stuart Bainbridge (1964) was secretary for 28 years (followed by 15 as Northumberland RU secretary); and Alan Heinzman (1966) served as Chairman for 26 years and is still active as club treasurer.

BORDER PARK

BORDER PARK HAS good claims to be the most unique club in England. Set in the heart of Kielder Forest, only a stone's throw from the Scottish border, this far-flung outpost of the game enjoys a setting second to none deep in Northumberland's wilderness territory.

The club was founded in 1961 during a period when several clubs were established in the county. Although the club was set up by local rugby enthusiasts, the very sparse local farming community meant that its existence was only made possible by the influx of workers from the Forestry Commission. The club's original clubhouse and pitch were remarkable. The clubhouse was a remote old railway building left after the demise of the single track cross-border branch line from Hexham to Riccarton. It could only be approached by driving along an embankment, part of the old track bed. This sounds harmless enough until departure was experienced in a coach in the pitch black of Europe's darkest skies when the driver had been carried away by the post-match celebrations. This without mentioning the section which had to be navigated in reverse!

The stone clubhouse was little changed from the time of its Victorian construction, with facilities to match. The small bar was interesting in that it lay on the route from the upstairs changing rooms to the downstairs communal bath. In true Victorian tradition visiting ladies averted their eyes. The pitch lay below on the valley floor, giving the impression of a huge natural amphitheatre.

Sadly, this unique ground was lost because of the damming of the valley to form Kielder Water in the 1970s and is now under water. The club was re-housed near to Kielder village with more modern, but less charismatic, facilities.

One of the club's founding fathers was Alex Simmons His work for Border Park was accompanied by a forthright and partisan loyalty. Many a referee found his efforts supplemented by comments and 'advice' from Alex shouted at volume and then amplified by the surrounding hills. When the club qualified for representation on the Northumberland RU committee, Alex duly became Border Park's spokesman. Finding the first meeting somewhat snooty and unwelcoming to a member from a tiny junior club, Alex went along to his second and under 'Apologies for absence' announced that he apologised for being present but that Border Park were here to stay.

Given its position and catchment area, Border Park has never had any pretentions to greatness. Instead, the traditional rugby values of a hard game on the pitch followed by a full evening's conviviality were established early and continue to the present day. The club flourished in the 1960s and 1970s, even stretching to a second XV for many seasons. Several good players were produced and encouraged to develop their game at Tynedale, the nearest major club, albeit 30 miles away down the North Tyne valley. These players invariably returned to their roots afterwards and helped support the club.

Latterly the club has struggled. The establishment of league rugby in England made life difficult as Border Park's location meant that participation in that system would have imposed impossible travel demands. For a time the club played in the Scottish Border Leagues, but this was not sustainable either. This meant that the club reverted to friendly fixtures against club 2nd and 3rd XVs. This worked for a while, but in recent years teams have not always been willing to travel, leaving Border Park a succession of away games with long gaps between home fixtures.

To the credit of players and officials alike the club soldiers on and even provided the President of Northumberland RU a couple of years ago in the shape of Tom Richards. Rugby would be a much poorer game were clubs like this to disappear.

(Thanks to Stuart Bainbridge)

MEDICALS

'The problem with medical students is they aren't content with being great doctors – they also have to be great rugby players'
Miles Kington

IT IS A popular misconception that only the hospitals and medical schools of London have produced successful rugby sides. Medicals RFC are a rugby club based in Newcastle-Upon-Tyne who originally drew their players from students and staff of the University College for Doctors and Dentists. The rugby club was founded in 1898 as Durham University College of Medicine – odd because the college was based in Newcastle, some 30 miles north of Durham. They were even members of the Northumberland RU.

Durham College of Medicine became Medicals in 1937 as they tried to make clear they were the first Medical school to run an independent rugby side, as opposed to a hospital or university.

The club has produced four internationals: Dr. Frederick Chapman (1888-1938), Reginald Armstrong, Dr. Stephen Peel and W.D.G. (Derek) Morgan, who won seven England caps.

Chapman also won seven England caps and is best remembered as the man who scored the first international try at Twickenham. He moved around as he won his England caps with Medicals, Northern, Westoe and Hartlepool Rovers. His international career spanned from 1908 (when he toured with the British Isles to New Zealand) to 1914. He went on to become a popular RFU President. Medicals is unique in having produced two other RFU Presidents in Derek Morgan and Danie Serfontein, who played for the club.

Derek Morgan

Chapman was the brother of Herbert Chapman, who was the first recognisable soccer manager, winning First Division titles with both Huddersfield and Arsenal.

Armstrong won a single cap at prop in 1924 against Wales. He was the first doctor to identify foot and mouth disease in humans during the 1967 epidemic. Dr. Stephen Peel won a wartime England cap.

The club's most recent triumph was winning the 1995-96 National Junior Cup after overcoming an original entry of 512 clubs. Medicals are now an open club.

(Thanks to Simon Hart)

MORPETH
(formerly Morpeth Old Edwardians)

MORPETH IS AN attractive market town 15 miles north of Newcastle. There are records of rugby being played there in the 19th century, but the present Morpeth RFC dates from 1947. They were founded as 'Old Edwardians' in 1948 by old boys of King Edward VI Grammar School, Morpeth.

Unfortunately, another Old Edwardians already existed in Birmingham, and in May 1950 the club became Morpeth Old Edwardians. They retained the name until 1970, when they became Morpeth RFC. The club played on the school playing fields until 1954, when they moved to Grange House Fields.

MOEs were regular Northumberland Cup finalists from 1965 to 1982, although they always were second best to mighty Gosforth – then in their prime.

The early 1970s were the first golden era for Morpeth. In 1972 David Pringle of Morpeth was an England reserve against the All Blacks. The next year Brian Keenleyside joined Morpeth from Rockcliff. One of the best-known Northumberland players of all time, he played for Morpeth for nine seasons.

Morpeth made local headlines at the end of season 1973-74 after they qualified for the National Knockout. The Morpeth team was made up of local lads who suddenly had the chance to face the great and good. They overcame Neatherall of Cumbria, then Stockwood Park from Luton, which brought a third round fixture against mighty London Irish. Irish fielded four internationals, but were still beaten. Their next visit was to the 'Rec' at Bath, where Bill Hewitt, the Morpeth fly-half, found himself opposite John Horton of England. The awful weather proved a great leveller and Morpeth won 13-9 to reach the semi-finals.

The semi-final was against Rosslyn Park, as Bill Hewitt recalled: "They were enormous. Andy Ripley, Neil Mantell – both England players – plus Lionel Weston, the international scrum-half. We hung in until half-time, but they got on top in the second half."

The club did not kick on after their golden season, but two of Morpeth's stars went on to play at a high level: Brian Keenleyside played for British Police, and Alan MacMillan won an England 'A' cap. The rest of the lads stayed together as Morpeth and the club have remained a middle-ranking North East side.

The best player to wear Morpeth colours was Toby Flood, who began at Ainwick before briefly appearing for Morpeth as a stepping stone to Newcastle Gosforth, Leicester Tigers and England.

(Thanks to Bill Hewitt)

NEWCASTLE FALCONS

NEWCASTLE FALCONS ARE today the premier club in the North East of England. They have been in the vanguard of professional rugby since its advent, and have pioneered the development of outstanding youngsters, including the peerless Jonny Wilkinson. But until the 1960s, aspiring young players in the North East looked elsewhere for rugby. Percy Park, Northern, Rockcliff and Durham City were viewed as the top clubs for Geordie talent.

Newcastle Falcons emerged from the old Gosforth RFC, which could trace its roots back to 1877 when the club was formed by W. Farr and a number of ex-Durham schoolboys. Their first ever match on the 3rd November 1877 was against Northern RFC, one of the city's other great clubs.

Gosforth played at Ashburton Meadows before merging with Northumberland RFC and taking over that club's ground behind Gosforth High Street. The combined club ran into financial problems in 1894, but survived by selling their goalposts. They went on to win the North East Second Team competition in 1905.

They lived in the shadow of the established clubs for most of their formative years, but still produced two internationals in George Robinson and Alastair Smallwood. Smallwood was educated at Newcastle Royal Grammar School, where he established an outstanding reputation as a brilliant three-quarter. After playing for Northumberland, he went up to Cambridge and then joined Leicester. A teacher at Uppingham for 35 years, Smallwood still holds the record of seven tries in one match when the Tigers put Manchester to the sword in 1922. Henry Robinson (1885-1948) also won an England trial whilst with Gosforth in the 1920s.

Gosforth began to establish themselves after World War One. They won the 1928 County Cup, beating Percy Park 5-3 in the final. In 1951 they plunged £10,000 into a huge new ground on the Great North Road. Sadly, the massive outlay meant that the club had to wait four years before they completed the move. The brave new venture paid dividends when great names joined the club.

The first great name to be associated with Gosforth was a gawky Scots student called Arthur Smith from Cambridge University. Smith was a brilliant winger who eventually won 33 Scotland caps and was the Lions captain in 1962. Another Newcastle University student was prop Ray McLoughlin, who won 40 Ireland caps and toured with the 1966 Lions. It was a tremendous coup to recruit two Lions to what was previously a modest provincial side.

Gosforth established themselves as the North East's premier side by dominating the Northumberland Cup from 1960 to 1993.

From a tiny band of workers, two far-sighted men emerged: Martin Millican and John Fenwick, who drove the club forward. Behind the scenes Fenwick started quietly working on the fixture list. Blackheath Harlequins, London Scottish and Richmond all came to Gosforth, or Gosforth went to them.

In the 1970s Gosforth produced an amazing team composed of local lads and talented players who moved into the area. They included Roger Uttley, who was studying in the city. Roger eventually won 23 caps, captaining England on five occasions. He was blindside flanker with the unbeaten 1974 Lions to South Africa, then became England coach and manager. Unfortunately, Uttley's England days were ruined by the ludicrous selection policy which saw him as the 17th England captain in 13 seasons.

He wasn't alone in being messed around by the selectors. Peter Dixon went on two Lions tours, but was never an England regular, winning only 22 England caps. Malcolm Young won 10 caps in the twilight of his career, but was ignored in his prime even though he was a prolific goal-kicker and outstanding scrum-half. In the season 1972-73, Dixon's father, who was born in Keighley, played for Skipton. Educated at St. Bees, Dixon moved on to Yorkshire Schools, England Under 19s and Cumberland and Westmorland. Richard Breakey played for Scotland.

In 1976 Gosforth won the National KO Cup with a great team: Young, Dixon, Jack Rowell, Colin White, Steve Gustard (an England trialist who played for Portugal), Terry Roberts, Duncan Madsen, Richard Breakey, David Robinson and the Patrick brothers, Brian and Harry.

Gosforth improved from 1975, when Jack Rowell, a huge lock-forward, took over as coach. Roger Uttley says, "Robinson, Dixon and myself ran the training sessions, but Jack was the ringmaster."

When Rowell left for glory with Bath and England, Mike Mahoney took over. Gosforth attracted big gates for important games, but played in front of a few hundred for lesser matches. Fly-half David Johnson never won an international cap, but was an outstanding player. He made his debut for Gosforth as

Malcolm Young, Roger Uttley and Peter Dixon.

a 14-year-old and played into his 40s. He later recalled: "We'd get thousands for cup matches, but there were so few spectators for some games that I knew the Christian names of everyone on the terraces."

In 1983-84 prop Colin White won four caps despite having lost three fingers in a forestry accident. Tiny by international standards, White was a part-time SAS soldier.

Gosforth remained a force throughout the 1980s and managed to attract top players, particularly Scots such as Jim Pollack.

In 1990 the club changed its name to Newcastle Gosforth and abandoned the traditional green and white-hooped jerseys in favour of black and white, the colours associated with the city's football team. A schism occurred and an independent Gosforth RUFC emerged.

The arrival of professionalism in 1995 found the Newcastle Gosforth club in Division Two and in dire financial straits. Salvation came in the form of a soccer man: Sir John Hall, the chairman of Newcastle United FC, who set up 'Newcastle Sporting club' to run the football and rugby clubs.

Hall acted quickly by recruiting Rob Andrew, the England fly-half, from Wasps as the club's new director of rugby, despite his youth and inexperience. Andrew had links in the North East through his days at Barnard Castle School, from where he went to Cambridge University and won rugby and cricket Blues. After a season at Nottingham RFC, he joined Wasps, with whom he played eight seasons. He rapidly made his England debut, but came in for some rough treatment in his first match against France. He eventually won 70 England and 13 Lions caps, which included three Grand Slams, and he played in the England team who were runners-up in the 1991 Rugby World Cup. After retiring as a player, Andrew was director of rugby at Newcastle from 1995 to 2006 before joining the Rugby Football Union as elite director of rugby in August 2006.

When he first arrived at Newcastle, Andrew looked north of the border, signing two top Scots players: Doddie Weir and Gary Armstrong. Tony Underwood, the flying England winger, arrived at the same time.

Rob Andrew and Sir John Hall.

(1,246 in 97 matches). He holds the records for most penalty goals (255), most points at a single ground (650 in 42 matches at Twickenham) and most drop goals in a career (36).

In 1999 Sir John sold the Falcons to businessman Dave Thompson for a 'nominal' sum. In the Premiership, Falcons have enjoyed middle-rank status, but their greatest success has been producing players such as Jonny Wilkinson, Toby Flood, Matthew Tait and Jamie Noon. Toby Flood was understudy to Jonny Wilkinson at both Newcastle Falcons and England before moving to Leicester Tigers in 2008.

Flood came through the Falcons' Academy and made his England debut in 2006, but had to wait four seasons to become a consistent selection. Jamie Noon was the sturdiest of the England pair that came through the academy. He made his Falcons' debut in 1999 and toured North America with the 2003 England team. He was an England regular during the 2005 Home International season.

Later the Falcons signed three ex-rugby league stars who had all begun in the 15-man game before signing for rugby league clubs. The lifting of barriers against professionals playing rugby union meant that Pat Lam, John Bentley and Alan Tait could play for Newcastle. Perhaps the most audacious signing was Va'aiga Tuigamala, the legendary All Black centre. Tuigamala had been part of Wigan RLFC's great years before joining Newcastle. The deal cost Newcastle £200,000 a year – a huge sum for either code.

The Falcons also recruited a number of lesser-known names, notably Jonny Wilkinson from Fareham. Wilkinson's career was to bear an uncanny resemblance to that of his mentor, Rob Andrew. Both were small, tough fly-halves who were outstanding goal-kickers.

The club's approach to recruitment made many enemies in rugby as John Hall and Rob Andrew targeted top-class players from other clubs in a manner unheard of in rugby.

Newcastle was the first fully 'professional' club in the world. Hall and Andrew saw the club earn promotion from the National Two to the Premiership in 1995. The following season they became English champions at their first attempt. The season after that Newcastle didn't play in Europe as English teams did not take part in the Heinekin Cup, but they did go on to the National KO Cup final against Wasps. They lost, but won the trophy in 2001 and 2004.

The 1997 Lions selected five Newcastle men for the South African tour and the club reached the semi-final of the new European Cup. They could field a team of stars in Peter Walton, John Leslie, Doddie Weir, Stuart Grimes and Gary Armstrong, who were all Scotland internationals. Jonny Wilkinson made his debut as a teenager and was the youngest England player for 70 years when he was a shock selection by Clive Woodward for England. Wilkinson was only 18-years-old, having just played for England Schools. He was picked at fly-half against Australia when they lost 76-0. But things got better. He inspired England to win the 2003 Rugby World Cup, which earned him the freedom of Newcastle. Jonny was a consistent source of points and was second on England's all-time points-scoring list

Matthew Tait

Noon, like Toby Flood, had to wait until the end of the decade to confirm his place as an England regular. He moved to Brive, the French club, in 2009. Sadly, Newcastle also saw Martin Corry, Garath Archer, Geoff Parling and David Wilson move to other clubs.

Despite having one of the best development programmes in the Premiership, Newcastle looked abroad for talent. Legends such as Mark Mayerhofler and Carl Hayman arrived at Kingsholm Park.

In 2012-13, they had a brief sojourn in the Championship, but emerged as runaway winners and returned to the Premiership under England legend Dean Richards.

NORTHERN FC

NORTHERN WERE FORMED in 1875 in the Newcastle suburb of Elswick. Originally the club drew their players from the products of Durham School. There are records of Northern losing to Edinburgh University in 1879. The Scots outfoxed the Geordies by playing with half-backs – an innovation at the time.

Northern fielded a dozen internationals in the years before World War One. The first internationals were Edward Emley and P.H. Morrison, who played for England in 1890. Later in 1890, the two Scott brothers were both capped, as were the three Gibson brothers a decade later. The Gell brothers were also capped.

In 1895 Dr. Herbert Dudgeon played for Northern, although he was more closely associated with Richmond. First capped by England in 1887, Dudgeon went on the 1901 British Isles trip to South Africa. He was badly injured on tour, but recovered to play again. He wasn't the first Northern player to represent the British Isles as George Gibson went on the 1899 Tour (but was never capped by England).

Arthur Wilson began as a Northern player before attending Camborne School of Mines. He played for the Mining College and Camborne RFC, which brought him to the attention of the Cornish selectors. In 1908 he played for Cornwall in the Olympic final against Australia. Australia won 32-2, but it encouraged the English selectors to choose Wilson to play for England against Ireland. He was killed at Passchendaele in 1917.

Northern retained their strength after World War One, and in 1924-25 the club won 22 of their 25 fixtures. The string of internationals continued with Dr. Reginald Armstrong, William Alexander and John Hodgson. Dr. Armstrong also played for Medicals RFC. Hodgson, an Old Rugbeian, went to New Zealand with Prentice in 1930. A big forward, he moved to London with work in 1930.

1937 was a memorable year for Northern when they became the first team to win at Kendal and the club purchased McCracken Park.

After World War Two, Northern still produced internationals. J.L. Baume was a captain in the Northumberland Fusiliers. He was an outstanding prop and his exploits for Northern and the army won him an England cap in 1950. The last international to represent the club was Feldlim Mcloughlin, who was capped by Ireland.

The rise of Gosforth in the 1970s pushed Northern into the shadow. Both Colin White (England) and Jim Pollack (Scotland) played at McCracken Park before moving to Gosforth and winning international caps. Scots legend Scott Hastings also briefly played for Northern before returning to Scotland. Henrie Le Roux followed the pattern too before playing for South Africa.

England's Grand Slam full back, Dr. Jonathon Webb, began at Northern before moving to Bristol University, from where he joined Bath and won 33 England caps. David Rees was a brilliant winger who began at Northern before winning England caps whilst with Sale.

The continual drain of young talent to richer clubs meant Northern had to accept middle-ranking status. In 2010 they were promoted to North One East under the coaching of Gosforth legends Jim Pollack and Colin White, and were Intermediate Cup runners-up to Old Reds.

PERCY PARK

"Someone said that England have become predictable. I take that as a great compliment."

Don Rutherford

PERCY PARK IS the oldest surviving rugby club in Northumberland. The actual date of Park's foundation is not known, but Percy Park Terrace, their first home, was built in the late 1860s by the Duke of Northumberland. The Duke must have been a rugby fan because, during the building work, he created space for a large field where he allowed rugby football to be played.

The first captain was Mr. J. Stanley Todd, who fixed the date at which an organised group played rugby football on the Percy Park field as 1872.

Few facts about club activities until 1880 are available because the honourable secretary (if honourable is the right word) lived in 'digs' and absconded without paying his rent to his landlady. The landlady refused to surrender his property, including the club's minute book, until the club paid the outstanding debt. As the club declined to pay, the minute book was never recovered. We do know that, around this time, the skull and crossbones motif was added to the plain black jersey, which gave way to black and white hooped jerseys in 1884.

In November 1880, Percy Park met their local rivals Northern FC for the first time in terrible weather. T.H. Morrison, the Park skipper, objected to the game being played as the weather was so bad. Northern refused to cancel the match, which they won easily as Park were two men short.

Percy Park led a nomadic existence after leaving the Terrace. Around 1880 the club moved to Collingwood Monument Fields, which overlooked the harbour; then they moved to Asylum Lane (now known as Mariners' Lane). Records show admission was charged at Asylum Lane; on one occasion 6s.9d. (33p) was taken at the gate, as well as a fake penny.

In 1884 the club moved to Hazel Avenue, south of Preston Cemetery. The owner of the land was evidently an opportunist, for there was a clause in the tenancy agreement that if the club won the County Cup the farmer was to receive an extra 50p. He received his reward in 1886 when Percy Park won the Cup, defeating Elswick.

By 1887 Percy Park were playing on the North Shields Cycling track. The following year the ground played host to the first Maori touring team, who played a team chosen from the Percy Park, Tynemouth and Rockcliff clubs. The combined team lost narrowly to the Maoris. Percy Park had better fortune in 1895, when they became the first North East club to defeat the Barbarians. The victory coincided with their first season at Preston Avenue, a ground with which they were to become associated in the 20th century.

The following season Park were honoured when G.C. 'Tot' Robinson (1876-1940) was capped by England. The fastest winger of the era, Robinson scored a try in seven of his eight internationals. Tot also toured South Africa with the 1896 British Isles team and later was an RFU President.

In February 1902, Peter Hardwick, a hard-working forward, became the second Park player to be honoured by winning eight caps for England.

The first Northumberland and Durham leagues was created around the turn of the century, and although Park disliked the idea of leagues, they were champions in 1904-05. In the late 19th century they lived in the shadow of Rockcliff, but they dominated the pre-World War One years.

The Great War took its toll and the club were slow to recover. On 3rd January 1920, a revived Percy Park RFC arrived at Hartlepool OBs with just five players. Amazingly, Hartlepool took pity on their struggling rivals and a match of some description was played.

Eventually, Park regrouped and produced two great wingers between the wars. Billy Wallace began his rugby with Percy Park before spending six seasons with Leicester. He was never capped for England, but won a Lions cap against South Africa in 1924. Carston Catcheside was perhaps the greatest player ever produced by Park. Catcheside grabbed six tries in his first four internationals, and he scored in all his England trials and internationals. He eventually finished his international career with 13 tries and a drop goal. He made his name with a 100-yard break to score the winning try when England beat Ireland at Ravenhill in 1924. Catcheside was promptly sick on the pitch.

Catcheside was an elusive character who once submitted an expenses claim to the RFU that read: 'Fare £2/19/11d. Toilet 1d. Total £3. Travelling expenses submitted by Carson Catcheside to cover cost of Newcastle-London trip whilst on England duty'. Catcheside had 'rounded up' the fare by a single penny to make £3. The RFU Treasurer was not amused and subtracted the penny.

On another occasion, Catcheside and a teammate arrived from an away match in Newcastle city centre late one Saturday night. The two couldn't get home without transportation, so were stranded. The teammate, however, worked in an upmarket furniture shop in the centre and suggested the store had plenty of beds on display. Using the teammate's key, the duo went to bed in the store. Catcheside rather unwisely chose a bed in the front window, where he was disturbed by a passing policeman in the morning. Despite this escapade, Catcheside went on to become a High Court judge.

SENIOR CUP FINAL
April 12th, 1924.

Park's 50th anniversary was celebrated in 1925 with a match against Leicester. The result was a draw 5-5. The following year the great W.J.A. 'Dave' Davies of England played in several matches for Percy Park whilst stationed with the navy on the Tyne.

The 1930s saw a golden era for Percy Park under the great half combination of Telford Moralee and Tony Baker. Telford made his First XV debut in December 1933 and played into the 1950s. As a scrum-half he was strong, courageous and inventive. He gained 38 Northumberland caps, captaining the side on many occasions, despite missing seven war-affected seasons. He was travelling reserve for both English trials in 1949-50 at the age of 34. He also played in the combined Northern Counties XV against the Kiwis. Moralee forged a brilliant partnership with Tony Baker, who himself played 32 times for Northumberland. With Moralee and Baker at half-back, Park enjoyed a successful period that included winning 25 of 28 matches in 1937-38 and winning the 1939 Northumberland Cup the following season.

After World War Two, S. Peel played for England against Wales in one of the victory internationals. Five years later, Ronald Macdonald of Park was capped for Scotland and went to New Zealand and Australia with the Lions.

Closer to home, Percy Park guaranteed their future by establishing a limited liability company – Percy Park Memorial Ground Ltd., who bought Preston Avenue.

During the late 1950s Park's fortunes waned, although the first XV won the County Cup in 1957 and 1958. At this time, W.G.D. (Derek) Morgan (although his primary allegiance was to Medicals) was vice-captain. A big, strong No. 8, Morgan was both mobile and an intelligent reader of a game. He was unique in being the only English pack leader who spoke with a definite Welsh accent. After nine consecutive England caps, his career was prematurely ended by a severe knee injury.

The 1960s saw Park at a low ebb, but they produced an outstanding full-back in Don Rutherford, who was capped for the county on 14 occasions. Don Rutherford was first picked for England against Wales in January 1960 whilst with Percy Park. He was also a member of that season's unchanged, all-conquering English side. After an indifferent game against the Springboks the following year, he lost his England place and had to wait five years before being recalled. He later toured Australia and New Zealand with the Lions. Sadly, a broken arm during the Lions tour curtailed his playing career. Rutherford's best football was played when captaining Gloucester, where he demonstrated the value of an attacking full-back in the days when the role of full-back was kicking for touch or receiving a sodden rugby ball in his own 25. Rutherford's analytic appreciation of the game's techniques and tactics earned him the position of the RFU's first coaching administrator.

Ron Tennick was club captain 1965-68. An England trialist in 1970, Ron went on to become a top RFU Coaching Administrator.

In 2012 they reached the National leagues for first time. The following year they won the Northumberland and the Senior Cup.

ROCKCLIFF

WHITLEY BAY IS a holiday resort on the coast only a few miles from the hurly-burly of Newcastle-Upon-Tyne. Whitley Bay became a popular dormitory town for businessmen from the city with the opening of the railway in the mid-19th century. Rockcliff took its name from a district of Whitley Bay. A rugby ground existed in Victorian times near the High Point Hotel on the north-east side of the town.

The original Rockcliff rugby club was formed on the south bank of the River Tyne in the 1870s. They disbanded in December 1882, with the remnants of the team joining Percy Park as 'the Second B', which roughly equates to a fourth team. Rockcliff were soon reformed in 1887 in the adjacent suburb of Cullercoats. Over the next 30 years, Rockcliff were ranked amongst the best sides in Britain, winning the Northumberland Cup on seven occasions between 1890 and 1902, and providing three players for the England team in 1893.

Many of the originators must have been experienced players, because Rockcliff lost only one match in their first season and persuaded the Northumberland county authorities to admit them to the Senior Cup. They reached the Senior Cup semi-final in the club's second year and were champions the following season. Success in the Senior Cup brought Rockcliff's players to the attention of the England selectors.

Amongst their first great players was John Greenwall (1864-1942), who won two England caps in 1893. He is a man who ranks amongst the greatest Northumberland players, with over 100 county caps; indeed, Greenwall was the first player to receive a Northumberland cap from the authorities. His brother, William, was also a good player. W.N. Greenwell was a Denstone product who played for Oxford, was capped for Northumberland and Midland Counties, and was an England trialist. Greenwell later taught at Denstone and emigrated to South Africa in 1904.

Little Billy Taylor was an England contemporary of John Greenwall and Tom Nicholson. Despite coming from a remote corner of the kingdom, Taylor was England's fly-half for most of the 1890s, during which time he won 14 caps. Taylor joined Rockcliff in 1886 and rapidly made a reputation as an outstanding goal-kicker. He represented Northumberland against the 1889 Maoris, and was noticed by the England selectors. He was a complete sportsman, as he played cricket for Northumberland and became a professional golfer after retiring from rugby.

Little Billy Taylor

Since most of the Yorkshire and Lancashire clubs were denied to rugby union after 1895, the RFU looked to clubs like Rockcliff for replacements. Rockcliff were at their zenith as Stan Anderson, Tom Nicholson, Fred Bell and Tom

Simpson were also capped by England, and the club supplied seven of the Northumberland team who won the County Championship. Tom Simpson was considered the best winger in English rugby in the 1900s, when he won eleven England caps. He was so highly regarded that the Northern club took great pride in having flattened Simpson in one derby match against Rockcliff.

Rockcliff were invited to South Wales in 1896 and established a reputation in the principality, which enabled them to visit Llanelli, Newport and Swansea. Invitations to play Gloucester, Northampton and Bristol soon followed. The club were attractive opposition and able to persuade the top clubs to travel to Whitley Bay. Swelled by success, Rockcliff obtained a new ground at Whitley Park.

Rockcliff were fortunate to pick up top-class players from the working-class areas of nearby Wallsend. However, their recruitment in Wallsend so enraged the locals that the Wallsend club defected to the NU.

In 1905 Rockcliff suffered a series of setbacks when they lost their ground at Whitley Park and a group of their best players moved to the NU, including Tom Owen (who played for Wigan for a decade). The club eventually found a replacement ground at Hillheads and celebrated by regaining the Northumberland Senior Cup in 1909. At this time, Alfred Kewney became the club's seventh international. Kewney eventually won 16 caps after joining Leicester.

Joe Brunton (1888-1971) was Rockcliff's last international of the era. In 1914 he broke into the England team that won the Grand Slam, which was unfortunate timing as only weeks later war broke out. He spent the next four years in the mud of wartime France instead of the greensward of England. He never won another international cap, but was a referee and RFU President in 1953.

Rockcliff RFC never fully recovered from World War One, although in the 1920s they had victories in the Senior Cup and the Junior Cup on four occasions. Indeed, Rockcliff were the Junior Cup champions 14 times. They could still field seven sides, composed largely of shipyards workers, but internationals were restricted to Harold Whitley and M. Robson in the 1930s.

World War Two proved another hurdle for Rockcliff. The club entered 1946 with a handful of players and the Hillheads ground in a dilapidated state. Rockcliff re-established themselves, but suffered because they were unable to attract schoolboy players from the district. A boost eventually came with an influx of players from King's College, Newcastle, which later became part of Newcastle University.

Rockcliff produced a quality player in the 1960s in Brian Keenleyside, who played for the Whitley Bay club before joining Morpeth. Keenleyside was one of seven Rockcliff players who were capped by Northumberland in 1965, a period that saw Rockcliff reach their first County Cup final for 40 years.

The best Rockcliff player of the era was prop Andy Cutter, who came through Whitley Bay GS. He began at Rockcliff before playing for Gosforth, Wasps and Harlequins. His spell at Gosforth included consecutive National KO Cup final wins.

Most recently, another Rockcliff player to follow the same path was Paul Van Zandvliet, who propped for Newcastle Falcons when they were Premier League Champions.

Later, Rockcliff merged with their arch-rivals Whitley Bay to form Whitley Bay Rockcliff.

SEGHILL

'Dinna gang near the Seghill mine
Across the way, they stretch a line
To catch the throat and break the spine
Of the dirty blackleg miner.'
Geordie Folksong

SEGHILL IS A mining village 13 miles north of Newcastle. The local rugby club emerged in 1921 as a colliery side. The club were run by (or, more correctly, ruled by) mine owner Major Martin Walton-Brown.

The Major was a millionaire mine owner who, like several others of their ilk, had curious views about amateurism. Brown ran the club and the small village with a rod of iron. He recruited 'miners' based on their rugby-playing ability, and they arrived from all over the North of England and Wales.

Seghill quickly rose to prominence thanks to the major's recruitment campaign. Only four years after formation, Seghill won the Northumberland Senior Cup in 1925. They repeated the feat in 1929, 1930 and 1932.

A famous story concerns one 'amateur' player who got a trial with Huddersfield RLFC in the 1930s. Brown heard that the player was travelling by train, so he rang up Newcastle railway station and got the stationmaster to announce on the tannoy that the player should go to the stationmaster's office. The player duly arrived and was handed the phone. On the other end of the telephone was Brown, who offered the player a choice between Huddersfield – meaning instant eviction from his tied cottage – or returning to Seghill. He chose the latter.

In the 1920s, Seghill had plenty of fine players for bigger clubs to examine. Winger Tom Berber and forward William Wallace had England trials, and another England trialist, 'Bumley' Little, suddenly appeared at Seghill in 1928. Their forward, O. Kaiser, was a regular for Northumberland for a decade.

Fly-half Tom Kenny managed to get past Newcastle Station in 1933 and signed for Salford NUFC.

Seghill retained their rugby tradition after the mines were nationalised in 1948. The club has never regained their prominence, although they reached the Senior Cup final in 1968. In the 1960s, Seghill had a great colts side, but sadly many moved to more fashionable and bigger clubs. One was Keith Richardson, who moved to Gloucester and was later a successful coach.

Today Seghill play in the Durham and Northumberland leagues.

TYNEDALE

TYNEDALE ARE TODAY one of the north's top sides, but they have been around since 1884 when we know they played (and lost) to Northern. They won the Northumberland Cup in 1887, and were regular winners until 1948. Then they had to wait 44 years before regaining the trophy (principally due to Gosforth's dominance).

Their greatest claim to fame is that they were the first English side to win on the Scotland Sevens circuit in 1893. Around this time, W.G. Bailey of Tynedale played for Durham.

Between the wars, Tynedale were a middle-ranking club in the North East and the backbone of the Northumberland county side. In 1936 A. Brogden, the Tynedale stand-off, was picked for an England trial. In 1946 William Rutherford repeated the feat. Rutherford was one of the best players in the North for many years.

Two Tynedale players of the 1970s finally won international caps after leaving Tynedale. Scrum-half Malcolm Young played at Tynedale for a season before moving to Gosforth, where his talents as a mobile No. 8 and goal-kicker bought him 10 England caps. Prop Rob Cunningham played for Tynedale before moving back to his native Scotland, where he was a Scotland reserve on 20 occasions. Tynedale were emerging from the shadows and were regular County Cup winners, which bought prominence in the National KO Cup.

In 1993 fly-half John Fletcher of Tynedale toured Canada with England. In 2012 Rupert Harden moved to Gloucester, where he was picked for England

A new century saw Tynedale rise from National 3 to National 2, where they were unbeaten at home in 33 matches. In 2009 Tynedale reached National One.

CHAPTER TEN - NOTTS, LINCS & DERBY

*"I saw my first rugby game last week. I am impressed by what
a thick skinned type is required to be a rugger player."*
Letter to the Derby Daily Express 1922

DERBYSHIRE

THE DERBYSHIRE RFU was originally formed in 1920 by a small group of enthusiasts from the Chesterfield area. The first president was John Todd, who had helped create Houghton-le-Spring RFC and had played for Durham. Todd was one of the richest coalmine owners in the Midlands and had played a leading role in the formation of both Chesterfield RUFC and Blackwell RFC. To generate interest, Todd had arranged an exhibition game between an England XV and Durham County at the Recreation Ground, Chesterfield, which attracted 8,000.

The clubs affiliated to the DRFU in 1922 were Burton-on-Trent, Chesterfield & District (later to become two separate clubs: Chesterfield and Blackwell), Denstone College, Mount St. Mary's College, Hayfield, and Trent College. The Derby club was affiliated shortly afterwards. By the end of the decade, Ilkeston, Old Baileans (Matlock), Old Mannerians (Bakewell), Swadlincote and Buxton were all members of the Union. The Thirties saw the spread of the handling code in Derbyshire and new clubs were formed, including Ashbourne, Derby Tigers, Derby Borough Police and Old Dronfieldians (now Dronfield). Ashbourne was unusual because it was still the home of the ancient game of street football

In 1926 the Nottinghamshire, Lincolnshire and Derbyshire RFU was formed for County Championship purposes, and since then Derbyshire men have continued to play a prominent role in this organisation, both on and off the field. Indeed, in 1927-28 Derbyshire provided an average of nine players for each NLD match.

Amongst the county's earliest and greatest players was Prince Alexander Obolensky (1916-1940), who fled his native Russia at the time of the revolution. He played for Chesterfield in the early 1930s after a spell at Trent College. The prince went on to become one of the legends of English rugby.

Prince Alexander Obolensky in action.

ASHBOURNE

'The Cathedral of the Peaks'
1950s advertisement

ASHBOURNE IS ONE of the few places where street football survives today. The town authorities have made many attempts to ban the game, most notably in 1860, but it still survives. The game is played on a field three miles in length that includes hedges, ditches, streams and other obstacles. The opposing teams, 'Uppards' and 'Downards', represent the upper and lower parts of the town (that is to say those who live 'up north' or 'down south' of the Henmore Brook). Each team defends a mile and a half of territory on either side of the starting area. The goals at Sturton Mill and Clifton Mill are three miles apart. The goal scorer must tap the ball three times on the mill wheel of the opposition. A scorer gets to keep the ball if he crosses the opponent's line and a new ball is thrown into the fray. The match ends at 5pm on Shrove Tuesday.

The ball is still made in the traditional way as a leather casing filled with cork shavings. The game is started when a celebrity throws the ball into the air. Amongst the celebrities who have started the game down the years was King Edward VIII, who started the mayhem in 1928. Edward caused more mayhem on a wider field nearly a decade later by abdicating.

Thirteen years earlier, the Ashbourne game had been in doubt because so many local men were away on war service. The game went ahead and there was even an away match. The Ashbourne Territorial Regiment were stationed in Braintree in Essex and unavailable in Ashbourne on Shrove Tuesday. They kept up the tradition by playing street football on the Braintree streets. This produced the headline in the local paper: 'Furious Football Fun. A game even the Kaiser can't stop'.

Ashbourne RUFC was formed in 1932 by Major C.F. Ball, the headmaster of Queen Elizabeth's Grammar School in the town. The previous year, Ball had introduced rugby to the school and even persuaded Derbyshire to play a county match against Staffordshire on the school playing fields. Derbyshire's try scorers included Prince Obolensky.

The club have been supporters of Derbyshire rugby ever since. Their best known players are David Heath, a DRU President, and Josh Redfern, who won England Counties honours.

Ashbourne currently play in Midlands 2 and recently were Intermediate Cup quarter-finalists.

BAKEWELL MANNERIANS

BAKEWELL WAS ORIGINALLY the ancient capital of the Peak District and is famous for the bakewell tart.

The town's rugby club began as 'Mannerians' and was formed in 1928 by Dr Ian Macdonald, headmaster of Lady Manners School, Bakewell and a young teacher called Dr Reg Harvey. The club played on the school playing fields. The original team actually had a Latin name of 'Tum et Nunc' (meaning Then and Now) and was composed of pupils, teachers and ex-pupils of the school. 'Tum Nuncs', as they were nicknamed, eventually became Old Mannerians RUFC. Their first game was against Buxton RUFC, but it was 1930-31 before a full fixture list was established. The following season the new club were undefeated. The best player of the 1930s was George Dunlop, who played for NLD in 1936.

The early 1950s saw OMs as one of the top sides in the East Midlands, despite fielding only one XV. The following decade saw OMs still as a major force, with Mick Marvin, Bob Winthrope, Jeff Pearson, John Pearce, Trevor Gratton and Terry Green all playing for Notts, Lincs and Derbyshire. Mannerians were four times winners of the Derbyshire Sevens and reached the final of the Loughborough Sevens.

A number of OM players moved to bigger clubs. John Pearce, Tony Robinson, Nick Asquith, Denzil Bowyer and Andrew Hall played for Nottingham and Terry Green had two seasons with Moseley.

The 1970s were disappointing and it was 1987 before things improved. This coincided with changing the name from OMs to Bakewell Mannerians to reflect the club being a part of the town. Initially fortunes in the leagues were not good, but the early 1990s brought success under club chairman Mick Webster and skipper Denzil Bowyer. The club won NLD4 in 1991-92, followed by NLD3 the subsequent season. A league restructuring promoted them to NLD1, where the club stayed for three years until relegated in 1994-95.

Currently BM play in Midlands 2.

BLACKWELL

IN THE LATE 1990s, a piece of history was re-enacted when Sir John Hall, a Geordie millionaire, had a vision of establishing top-class rugby in the North East. This dream had previously been realised 70 years earlier, when another Geordie millionaire, John L. Todd, tried to establish rugby in the tiny Midland town of Alfreton.

Don't worry if you've never heard of Alfreton or Todd; you would have to be a pensioner to have heard of Todd's 'professional' experiment, which had the briefest time in the headlines before disappearing into oblivion. Alfreton is an unlikely setting for a sporting experiment, being a small ex-mining town between Chesterfield and Derby. Todd and his attempt at joining rugby's elite provides a salutary lesson for today's rugby millionaires.

Todd promoted a grandiose sporting dream that was always doomed to failure. Blackwell RUFC had money, facilities, enthusiasm and great players, but it lacked real rugby roots. Having said that, Todd himself had a real rugby pedigree. He founded the Houghton-le-Spring rugby club in 1873 and was Durham county captain for three seasons. A 1925 report says Todd had played for Scotland in the old 20-a-side days, but this is uncertain. It is a fact that a 'J. Todd' played for Scotland in 1873, but John L. Todd was not a Scot and served the English game all his life, including being a leading RFU member during the Great Schism of 1895.

Ironically, Todd's next public appearance came at Blackwell in 1920, when he promoted an exercise that bent the amateur laws to a greater extent than some of the clubs he had helped expel in 1895. Certainly English rugby union needed a boost in 1920, for the Great Schism, the popularity of association football and World War One had decimated the amateur rugby game. Todd emerged from the Great War as the major coalmine owner in the North Midlands, with over 1000 employees working at nine pits centred on the tiny Derbyshire village of Blackwell (pop. 400). The village consisted of four streets of terraced houses, one pub and a unique sporting complex.

Blackwell village was overlooked by Todd's mansion. From his front room he could watch the colliery-wheel bringing coal to the surface and also survey the streets for work-shy miners. For all his sporting altruism, Todd was a Victorian tyrant. If an employee spoke out of turn, he knew he would be sacked and evicted from his company house. Wilf Heywood was one of Todd's miners. In his old age, Wilf remembered walking down the street one afternoon when the large bewhiskered mine owner appeared and harangued him for not being down the pit. Todd was wrong, for Wilf had been sent home legitimately, but Todd knew everyone in the village and what shift they worked.

Todd prided himself on what he saw as the God-fearing folk of Blackwell. He once remarked that it was a 'sinless village', which caused the national press to try to dig up some local scandal. He was used to getting his way, but that wasn't always the case when he was dealing with people who weren't reliant on Blackwell Colliery for employment. He had helped form both the Derbyshire RFU and the Chesterfield RUFC in 1919, but the club committee weren't beholden to him. A dispute blew up when Chesterfield had trouble finding a regular pitch. Todd wanted them to move five miles south to Blackwell, but the club declined, possibly because of the travelling, but more likely because they knew that Todd would then be their lord and master.

Todd couldn't understand Chesterfield's reluctance because the Blackwell facilities were the best in the Midlands, with

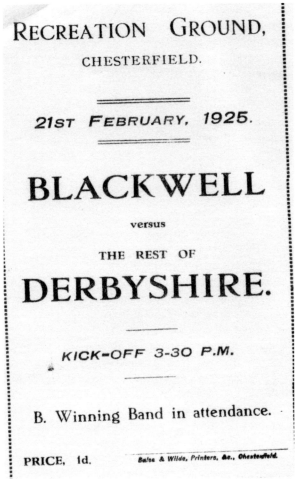

RECREATION GROUND,

CHESTERFIELD.

21ST FEBRUARY, 1925.

BLACKWELL

versus

THE REST OF

DERBYSHIRE.

KICK-OFF 3-30 P.M.

B. Winning Band in attendance.

PRICE, 1d.   *Bates & Wilde, Printers, &c., Chesterfield.*

TWOPENCE EACH.

RUGBY UNION FOOTBALL.

DERBYSHIRE COUNTY

VERSUS

YORKSHIRE !

ON THE BLACKWELL CRICKET GROUND,
ON WEDNESDAY, OCT. 24th, 1923.   Kick-off, 3.45 p.m.

| DERBYSHIRE COUNTY. | YORKSHIRE. |
| Colours : Blue Jerseys. | Colours : White Jerseys. |

BACKS :

W.R.H.Pooler (St. Mary's Hospital) 1—G. Harnall (Wakefield)

THREE-QUARTER BACKS :

D. Armstrong (Blackwell)   2—C.H.Holliday (Bradford), Capt.
G. L. Nicholson (Blackwell)   3—W. Smith (Halifax)
R. B. Meikle (Blackwell & Coventry)   4—F. J. Adams (Halifax)
N. R. Pooler (Blackwell and   5—W. F. Burke (Rotherham)
St. Mary's Hospifal)

HALF-BACKS :

A. Eyden (Burton)   6—R. Burgess (Leeds University)
J. H. Stone (Burton)   7—J. H. Lumby (Bradford)

FORWARDS :

Dr. Stokes (Ilkeston)   8—R. W. Tolson (Wakefield)
W. J. Keeley (Derby)   9—J.N.BrynWilliams (Rotherham)
A. M. Watt (Burton)   10—C. Smith (Keighley)
K. B. Smith (Burton)   11—D. Smith (Bradford)
C. G. Beddows (Burton)   12—W. C. Bateson (Bradford)
J. S. Fletcher (Blackwell)   13—L. K. Hogsett (Headingley)
A. Beresford (Blackwell)   14—E. Burke (Bradford)
R. Fenn (Blackwell)   15—H. L. Proctor (Headingley)
Referee : W. H. Wheeler, Leicester.
Linesmen : C. E. Averill and R. F. Oakes.

SCORING : Try, 3 pts.; Goal converted from a Try, 5 pts.; Dropped
Goal, 4 pts.; Penalty Goal, 3 pts.

Points in the Game.   Illegal :

Knocking on or Forward.   Passing Forward.
Putting Ball unfairly in a Scrummage.
Lifting Feet before the Ball is in the Scrummage.   Playing Off-side.

hot water baths (a luxury in 1920), changing rooms, a covered stand and a walled pitch around a lush rugby and cricket area. Todd had already persuaded the county cricket authorities to play Derbyshire cricket matches in the village, and the county's record partnership for the ninth wicket was set at Blackwell.

If Todd couldn't get his team locally, there were plenty of rugby players available in Wales, where the wartime promise of 'a land fit for heroes' sounded hollow to soldiers who came home to find unemployment or low wages. Todd sent agents to the Welsh coalfields to recruit 40 miners, who were either big forwards or talented backs. None were internationals, but several were Welsh trialists. Bill Hale from Abertillery was regarded as the best hooker in Glamorgan, George Hoyle was a brilliant fly-half, and Leslie Richardson was to become the Midlands' top flanker.

Work for the 'rugby-miners' of Blackwell consisted of a soft job on the surface and time to train. The easy jobs were not on offer to non-rugby players, which generated ill-feeling between the newcomers and the locals. Todd targeted anyone who threatened his expensive imports. When Welsh winger Giles was involved in a fight in the local public house, The Blackwell Hotel, Todd immediately sacked Giles's adversary and had his private police force evict the local man's family.

Action on the Blackwell rugby pitch got underway in 1923 when the new team, with its enormous pack of Welsh forwards, immediately dominated local rugby, losing only five of 26 matches and scoring 511 points and conceding 100. The established rugby powers were perplexed about the whole

experiment, not least because they didn't even know where Blackwell was!

Todd fought hard to overcome those who stood in the way of his rugby dream. He persuaded the county sides of Durham and Yorkshire to play Derbyshire at Blackwell, where the impact of the new side can be gleaned from ten of Derbyshire's XV being Blackwell men.

The mine owner financed his team's rise up the pecking order by the simple expedient of accepting away fixtures regardless of the travelling time and cost. Few other clubs could afford to spend money on such extravagances as travelling and hotels, especially as it bent the rules on amateurism.

By 1925 Blackwell were one of the best sides in England, with an astonishing record of one defeat in 27 matches, and that was only a 13-12 loss against Headingley, who had a team of internationals and county players.

The late 1920s were a success story as Todd got the fixtures he wanted against the cream of English rugby. The portals of Coventry, Bedford, Cheltenham and Newport opened to the tiny Derbyshire club. In 1926 mighty Blackheath, the oldest open club in the world, entertained one of the newest sides.

Nothing, it seemed, could stop this new force in English rugby, which eventually had 100 regular players and a pioneering youth squad. Then, in March 1929, Todd died and it became apparent that Blackwell had everything except roots. The First XV players were all imports and the locals were more interested in soccer. Superficially, Todd's death made no difference, but the business empire had passed to Arthur Ellis, Todd's son-in-law, who was a soccer fan with no wish to continue pumping money into rugby.

Blackwell carried on for five more years with its top-class fixture list and recorded wins over giants such as Coventry. Then, in 1935, came a bombshell when Ellis replaced the rugby posts with soccer posts. The rugby club closed down and the players drifted off to other districts.

Today only the superb Blackwell soccer ground betrays a distinguished history in the sleepy Chesterfield suburb. The pits and the terraced houses are long gone and only a handful of old-timers can recall another era when 'the sinless village' was headline news.

When Blackwell disbanded, their available funds were presented to the county organisation and used to help other clubs.

BURTON-ON-TRENT

'The Crofters'

THE TOWN OF Burton-On-Trent (pop 50,000) is associated with two words: Bass and Brewing. In the 1880s a quarter of Britain's beer was brewed in Burton.

In 1870 the Bass Brewery was one of the biggest employers in Burton and it was a group of brewery workers who formed the rugby club on 5th October of that year. Initially Burton RFC operated from the local cricket club using 'the Sheffield Code of football', but they switched to the RFU laws in 1876. Their earliest fixture list had some familiar names, but many of their opponents disappeared long ago. The club stayed at the cricket club until 1888, when they played at a series grounds usually associated with the beer trade. They operated at the Crescent Brewery Ground until 1896, when they moved to the Ind Coope ground. Three years later Burton moved to Marston's ground. Their nomadic existence came to an end in 1910, when they moved to Peel Croft in the town centre, which became their long-term home.

Initially Burton played in black and red stripes, but in 1875 they switched to blue and chocolate hoops. This proved unsatisfactory when washed, so a white jersey with a black hoop was adopted.

1880 saw Burton vying with Moseley for the title of Midland club champions, and they won the Midland Counties Cup in 1883. They repeated the cup victory five years later, beating Leicester.

In 1886 Burton on Trent declined to send players to the Midland Counties trial as they were engaged playing Cardiff. They then confirmed their strength by defeating the Maori tourists. The tourist's manager said afterwards that Burton were one of the best sides in Britain. He also blamed the quality of the Burton ale for his team's lack-lustre display.

Burton were also doing well locally as, in 1898, Burton took two records from a brilliant Denstone School team; they were the only team to beat the school and the only side to cross Denstone's line.

Burton's success brought a first England cap for Frank Evershed, who had won a mighty reputation with the

Midland Counties team; indeed, Evershed was the first Midland Counties player ever to be capped. He eventually made ten appearances for England, moved to London and joined Blackheath. He was from a famous rugby family and his brother was already an established player.

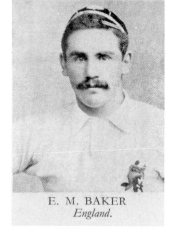

E. M. BAKER
England.

Other internationals from Burton were John Robinson (1872-1959), who won four England caps in the 1890s, and the Reverend Edward Baker (1874-40), who won seven England caps in the same era.

The club was a major force until 1900, when interest in rugby in the town declined, thereby forcing a merger with St. Modwens, the other rugby club in Burton.

Good times returned in the 1920s when defeats were a rarity. 1926 saw victory over Swansea as Burton produced a side to rival their 1890s team. They remained a force in Midlands rugby until the 1960s, when the town and the rugby club suffered from the decline of the brewing trade.

Mergers and takeovers became an integral part of brewery life. Household names such as Ind Coope disappeared and even mighty Bass Beer became a part of a multi-national conglomerate. Without the resources of yesteryear, Burton have had to rely on local youth. The rugby club have spent most of their days 'yo-yoing' between Midland One and Two, but currently Burton play in National 3 Midlands under coach Steve Smith. In 2009 Burton Colts reached the final of the National Colts tournament.

CHESTERFIELD

CHESTERFIELD LIES TEN miles south of Sheffield, but the two places are completely different. Sheffield is the archetypal northern city, whereas Chesterfield is classed as a Midland market town, complete with a twisted spire on the parish church.

Rugby was certainly played in North Derbyshire in the 19th century, but few facts are known about the teams involved. The modern history begins in 1919, when a brief announcement in the Derbyshire Times invited anyone who might be interested in forming a rugby club to a meeting in the Station Hotel, Chesterfield. The meeting gave birth to Chesterfield & District RUFC.

One of the founders was John Todd, a local mine owner. The club played for two years at Mr Todd's Blackwell Colliery, some five miles south of the town, until a schism occurred in August 1922. Todd formed a separate club called Blackwell RFC, whilst Chesterfield moved back to the town. The Chesterfield version of events was that Todd was an autocrat who wanted to rule the roost. Rather than submit, the Chesterfield members opted to form as a separate club. The Blackwell team were packed with Welsh rugby players who had been specifically recruited for Todd's mine at the owner's personal expense, whereas Chesterfield RFC preferred to rely on local people.

Initially Chesterfield played at the High Fields before moving to Brampton. The team changed in a stable behind the Terminus Hotel and bathed in two halves of a beer cask. Their fixture list was composed almost entirely of school and college sides, indeed anybody who would give them a game. The earliest fixtures were at Mount St. Mary's College, Spinkhill, Sheffield University, Worksop and Burton Grammar School. The Chesterfield players were warned by the captain that when playing schoolboy sides, they ought to "play by the book". Ironically, many of the schoolboys turned out to be bigger, stronger and faster than the Chesterfield adults.

In the mid-1920s the club was able to purchase its present ground at Stonegravels for £1,600, a trifling amount in modern terms, but a fortune to a new club. Money was a problem, not least because 10% of the club's income was swallowed up by the cost of sending telegrams to players advising them of their selection. Telephones were strictly the preserve of the rich.

Local rugby did receive a boost in 1928-29, when an England XV played a North Derbyshire XV at Chesterfield FC's Saltergate ground in front of 28,000 spectators. The North Derbyshire side were named 'Reverend Ewbank's XV' after a well-known local cleric. Buoyed by the famous visitors, Chesterfield RUFC hardly lost a match that year. The Chesterfield squad was now so strong that it provided most of the Derbyshire county side that beat County Durham 20-0 at Blackwell.

One of Chesterfield's most famous players in the early years was Glynn Davies. Born in Swansea, Glynn played for Bryntawe as fly-half before joining Chesterfield in the 1923-24 season. He eventually became established as a Derbyshire regular, playing 46 times for the county.

As the club became established, Chesterfield obtained most of their fixtures from the Sheffield area and were even able to find regular fixtures on a Wednesday afternoon. The side was selected from local people who did not have to work on 'Early Closing day'. This is a peculiarly northern and midland tradition where shops closed early on the day before payday because everybody had spent up and trade was quiet.

The most famous player to wear Chesterfield's colours was Prince Obolensky, who played for Chesterfield in the early 1930s whilst a pupil at Trent College. Even as a schoolboy Obolensky had an amazing reputation and was viewed as unstoppable in schools' rugby. The Prince went on to star for Derbyshire, Oxford University and England.

CHESTERFIELD RUGBY CLUB

the first 50 years

Another top-class youngster was Bill Thompson, who played in the first Three Counties trials in 1926 while still at school. He tells the story of how the old Derbyshire team first turned out wearing Lincoln Green shirts. After a match at Leicester, the shirts came back from the laundry tinged blue, and that's the colour they've remained ever since. Thompson left Chesterfield for Leicester and played in a British Lions trial at Peterborough. However, he was considered to be too young and too light to make the Lions team. He did earn the consolation of being named reserve for the East Midlands side.

Clarence 'Gillie' Gilthorpe, who began with Chesterfield as a 15-year-old, won 2 England wartime caps whilst with Bedford. In 1932 he joined Wasps, who converted him from a prop to a hooker. A regular member of the Notts, Lincs & Derby team, in the 1937 season he played in the England trials and was selected as reserve hooker. In 1939 he was invited to join the Lions party to tour South Africa, but had to decline because his employers, the Air Ministry, refused him leave of absence. He was subsequently selected to play for England against Scotland, but dropped out with injury. He finally won England honours during the war, when a handful of internationals were organised.

In 1952-53 Chesterfield acquired its first clubhouse on the ground at a cost of £300. This was a successful time for the club under flanker Derrick Drabble, who was a regular for the county. Winger Ben Broadhead was a key member of the side at this time. He holds the distinction of being one of Chesterfield's most capped county players, with 26 Derbyshire appearances to his credit in 14 seasons. During this time he captained the county twice.

The most successful period in Chesterfield's history began in the 1970s, when they were Derbyshire's premier club. They won the new Derbyshire Knockout Cup in 1974 and later the Three Counties Cup.

The giant Fran O'Neill, six foot one and 16 stones, was one of Chesterfield's biggest influences during the early 1970s. Fran, a loose-head prop-forward, skippered Derbyshire when they won the North Midlands title (the Six Counties pennant) for the first time in 1976-77, and he also played a key part in Chesterfield's years of Derbyshire Cup supremacy.

Currently Chesterfield are in Midland 4 under the name of Chesterfield Panthers. They have a good record in producing talented youngsters; hooker Ross McMillan began with the club before moving to Northampton and Bristol, and Charlie Davies began in the Juniors and stepped up to play for Stade Francais, London Wasps and England U20s.

DENSTONE SCHOOL

RUGBY HAS BEEN played within the confines of Denstone School in Derbyshire since at least 1877, when a school rule was passed that all fellows who refused to play rugby were to be 'gated' (i.e. restricted to school premises). The first external encounter for the school team came that year against Newcastle High School, resulting in a "draw slightly in our favour". The match is remarkable as both Denstone's half-backs collapsed with cramp.

Denstone soon established a reputation as a good rugby school and three pupils, A. Sulley, W.N. Greenwell and E.M. Baker, were offered trials on their arrival at Oxbridge merely because they had learnt the game at Denstone. Sulley failed to win a Rugby Blue at Cambridge, but later played centre for the Midland Counties and was an England trialist. Greenwell had a similar career, but Baker proved an England regular. He partnered F.A. Leslie Jones at Oxford as a centre and the duo were selected as the England centre pairing in 1895. Baker was an England regular from 1895 to 1897 and was regarded as one of the best three-quarters of the era.

An annual match against 'Old Denstonians' became a feature of school life, but it wasn't until 1898 that the First XV overcame their elders.

Dr. Walter Bensemann

In 1903, Old Denstonians had a tour of Germany, which was arranged by the mysterious Dr. Walter Bensemann, who was teaching at Denstone. Bensemann was the organiser of the first England v Germany soccer match and was later unmasked as a suspected German spy (see: Old Birkonians). The following year Old Denstonians toured France and, on the way home, played mighty Richmond in London, losing 11-5. Bensemann was responsible, of course, for organising the tour.

Another inveterate traveller associated with Denstone was N.F. Humphreys, who played his rugby with Durham City and was part of the 1910 British Isles team to South Africa.

The 1920s began with a star in the school ranks, when Mark Sugden emerged as a superb scrum-half. Sugden had a brilliant dummy, which mesmerised opponents. He showed his consummate class in 1921 when he inspired Denstone to a remarkable season, with 15 wins in 20 matches and scoring 629 points whilst conceding only 151. Sugden made his debut for Ireland in 1925 and was a permanent fixture until 1931, during which time he won 28 caps. Sugden was unusual for a scrum-half because he was tall and slightly built. He had a superb pass allied to a tremendous sense of timing.

Denstone had trouble in finding any other player of Sugden's stature, but in 1927 they produced Pat Davies, who was capped for England whilst with Sale. In 1933 T.A. Kemp, a centre, led the First XV as a prelude to captaining England. Several years later B.M. Cunningham, an Old Denstonian, was selected by England against Wales in a services international.

Rugby at the college recommenced in 1945, with the First XV playing the Old Denstonians. The college had a great record in the late 1940s, playing a mixture of leading public schools and the second XVs of the top Northern club sides.

The 1950s saw former pupils figuring prominently at Oxbridge. L.D. Ashcroft and R. Green represented Oxford, whilst R.W.W. Dawe and D.G. Jones appeared for Cambridge.

The school resumed a Christmas tradition of having a pre-Christmas tour of London. Many of the leading public schools also headed for the capital, and the annual Denstone v Blundells fixture was one of the most attractive.

Two remarkable years were 1966, which saw Denstone unbeaten all season, and 1973, which was the college's centenary with a special match in the presence of the venerable Dr. Tom Kemp. Also that year the college produced Alastair Hignell, a top-class full-back and cricketer, who played 170 cricket matches for Gloucestershire. He won 14 caps for England whilst with the Bristol club. He later became a fine broadcaster and journalist.

Alastair Hignell

DERBY

A 'DERBY MATCH' is a commonly used phrase that describes the hostility of two local sides meeting in a sporting contest. The original Derby match was a game of street football played between the massed ranks of young men of two parishes, St. Peter's and All Saints, in the city of Derby. The original game began in the market place and ended with the participants in either the River Derwent or Morledge Brook. It was played annually during the daylight hours from Shrove Tuesday to Ash Wednesday and was famous for violence. Drunken participants turned the event into a riot. The match was decided when someone scored a goal, but as the 'goalposts' were three miles apart it was a relief to all concerned. The game was prohibited in 1846, but the name 'Derby' remains. The spirit of the old football game lived on through association and rugby football.

The round ball was preferred by the local public schools of Repton, Trent College and Derby School, whereas rugby was more popular with Derby Grammar School and Spondon School.

Rugby had its following with half a dozen clubs in the city, notably Derby Wanderers, Derwent Rowing Club, Derby St Andrews, Ockbrook Church Union and Derby Trinity. There was great concern at this time about serious injuries; in the match between a Birmingham team and Derby Wanderers, Mr. Wilcox of Birmingham was "collared" by Mr. Champion of Derby, who 'accidentally' fell on Wilcox and broke the Birmingham player's neck. In 1876 one local club suffered one death, two broken legs, two broken collar bones, one internal rupture and one case of a chest injury.

A side called Derby RFC operated in the city in the 1890s, and it seems likely they had been playing for a few years previously because their name occurs in other clubs' fixture lists. We know that a Derby side played at the Arboretum and won six of seven fixtures, but they were reported as being "rather rough". The first Derby RFC disappeared soon afterwards.

Rugby re-emerged in 1922 in the form of Derby Tigers RUFC. Just as little is known of the Tigers, but they provided the nucleus of the current Derby RUFC, who emerged in 1949. Derby RUFC were playing on Markeaton Park, but moved to Kedleston Road in the late 1950s. The club purchased a sectional building from the RAF at a cost of £75 and transported the sections on lorries to Kedleston Road. The county organisation helped with a donation from the Blackwell Fund. The gift funded an annex at Kedleston Road called 'The Blackwell Room'.

The years following World War Two were great days for Derby. In 1949-50 the club won 21 of 37 matches, their best season for 18 years.

Dr. Karl Mullen

In 1953 one of the greatest names in rugby played for Derby, Dr. Karl Mullen. He had led Ireland to two Triple Crowns and captained the 1950 British Isles. Mullen worked at Derby Royal Infirmary and played for Derby at Kedleston Road.

The 1983-84 season was believed to be the best season in the club's history, when they won 30 of 35 games and drew only two. The team achieved 20 unbeaten matches in a row, set a home record run of 18 unbeaten games, scored 119 tries and conceded only 29. They drew 3-3 with Paviours of Nottingham in the Three Counties Cup final, but Paviours, as the away side, were declared the winners. Derby have a good record in the Three Counties Cup, with title victories in 1979-80, 1986-87 and 1995-96.

The club's record for appearances is held by Sean Jennings, who played 533 times for the club, scoring 3,882 points. In June 2002, Derby RFC moved from Kedleston Road to their new clubhouse and grounds at Haslams Lane.

The best-known senior player from Derby in recent times is Alan Dickens, who moved to Northampton Saints and Saracens. His father was the rugby club's president.

The club are middle-ranking in the Midlands leagues. They won NLD Cup in 1996 and were runners-up in 2009, but were relegated from National 3 in 2013.

The club could at least take consolation in Jonathan Joseph, who played for Derby colts before moving to Millfield School and joining Bath. He went on to become the most dazzling English centre of his era.

GRIMSBY

'The Blues'

THE ORIGINAL GRIMSBY RUFC was formed on 2nd December 1885. The first match was a defeat against a side from Hull. In 1910 a NU team was formed in Grimsby, but soon disappeared. Rugby union emerged in January 1923, when a team was formed at the Ship Hotel in the town. The first match was a 31-5 defeat away to Gainsborough and the first home match was on the Fairfield Scartho, when Grimsby beat Gainsborough 62-0.

Dr. W.M. Dobson played for Grimsby in the early days. He had won three Scotland caps and was later a president. They have fielded a number of other internationals: Philip Dunkley, who played in the Obolensky match, and in 1935, Charles Beamish, a former Irish international, played for the club. Many of Grimsby's earliest players were ex-public schoolboys working in professional jobs in the area.

In 1931 Grimsby found a permanent home at Fairfield Scartho, where they stayed until World War Two, and they finished the 1930s as one of the best sides in the county. After World War Two, Grimsby played for 12 years at Barretts Recreation Ground, which had no bathing facilities. In 1950 Pop Dunkley started organising training nights to raise the club's standard. Eric Macklam was a leading player and later NLD President. In 1962 Grimsby left the mud of Barretts Rec for a new ground at Springfield Road. The ground was opened with a match against Headingley.

Grimsby are still playing at Springfield Road. They are currently sharing facilities with the splendidly named 'South Humber Rabbitohs', no relation to the Australian NRL champions 'South Sydney Rabbitohs'. Grimsby are currently playing in the middle-ranks of Midland rugby.

HOPE VALLEY

"Sheffield's answer to the Lake District."
local joke

FORMED IN 1979 following a public meeting, Hope Valley RUFC originally played their home fixtures at Hope Valley College, before a 10th anniversary fixture against Derbyshire President's XV saw the opening of the club's own facilities at Hollowford Road, Castleton.

Hope draw their players from Sheffield, Chesterfield and the Valley itself. They traditionally acted as a feeder club for the local senior clubs, most notably Sheffield RUFC, where former Valley stars Mark Rodgers and Paul Oldridge were established names. Ian Dommitt played fly-half for Notts, Lincs & Derbyshire in 1996.

KESTEVEN
(formerly Bourne)

RUGBY CLUBS IN South Lincolnshire led a precarious existence until 1947, when a club was formed at Bourne. Clubs had briefly played in the area before that date, but few survived. Bourne RUFC themselves had a difficult entry into the world because after only ten matches of their debut season the worst winter of the 20th century arrived and brought a premature end to the season. The founders, Derrick Smith and Warwick Purchase, reasoned that Bourne wouldn't survive unless they broadened their horizons and their catchment area. They renamed the club Kesteven RUFC in the hope of attracting players from the whole district and the main town of Grantham. Fortunately, they were able to recruit a few ex-servicemen who had played rugby whilst in the forces.

The club's earliest fixtures were against RAF sides plus a few local clubs. The shortage of petrol meant away fixtures in far-distant Nottingham (30 miles) were a rare treat. The first home pitch was a farmer's field at Stoke Rochford on the Grantham Road. Despite the odds, Kesteven became a formidable side and suffered only four defeats in season 1952-53 under captain Ray Coleman.

They moved to the school pitches at King's School, Grantham at a time when one Margaret Roberts was at the girls' grammar school. She later became Mrs Margaret Thatcher.

The rugby club bought six acres at Wood Nook in 1958 and purchased an old hut for changing.

Two famous players have worn Kesteven's colours over the years. Ken Wilson propped for Kesteven before moving to Gloucester, where he won an England cap in 1963 and then joined Oldham RLFC. Air Vice-Marshall Larry Lamb was a fine player for the RAF and an occasional three-quarter for Kesteven in the early 1960s. He achieved greater fame as one of England's finest and most recognisable referees. Lamb combined an RAF career with refereeing to such an extent that he sometimes arrived at rugby grounds in his uniform. He once arrived at Coventry in uniform and was told by the gatekeeper that "fancy dress night is next Saturday".

Today, Kesteven have local rivals on their doorstep, including Bourne RUFC, who resurrected the name.

NEWARK

NEWARK RUGBY CLUB will be familiar to anyone on the Kelham Road driving from the town to Mansfield. Its spacious pitches and clubhouse have hosted many county games. The town is also famous for Magnus Grammar School, one of the leading schools in the area.

It was the Rev. Henry Gorse, headmaster of Magnus Grammar School, who organised the club's formation in 1919. A previous Newark RFC had existed in 1891, when they played Nottingham and won 8-0. Several other matches were played, but the club soon disbanded. Gorse had banned all other forms of football at the school in 1911, insisting that only rugby union be played in winter.

From 1921 to 1922 Newark RUFC played on the playing fields of the grammar school. They moved to the cricket club for eight years and used the Royal Oak on Castlegate as changing rooms. From 1930 to World War Two they played at Muskham Road.

The Kelham Road ground was bought in 1947 and opened in 1950 with a fixture against Leicester Tigers. An army hut was erected in 1964, but electricity was not supplied until 1968. Catering was primitive, but gradually things improved for the ground and it became one of the best in the Midlands.

Newark has produced many famous players; George Cullen played for Leicester and England and Peter Pulfrey played 173 times for Leicester in the 1960s and was in the East Midlands team that played the 1969 Springboks.

Dusty Hare first emerged at Newark before moving to Nottingham RFC and later Leicester. He made his England debut in 1974 and was a regular for a decade. He didn't make an instant impact on rugby, being a permanent fixture in Newark Seconds for three seasons, as well as being a regular with Notts county cricket club. He eventually moved on to Nottingham RFC, became a 300-points-a-year full-back, and scored two tries for England Under 23 against Japan in 1973. He made his England debut against Wales in 1974 and enjoyed the stop/start existence of his teammates until the 1980 Grand Slam victory.

Dusty Hare

John Wells, a product of Magnus Grammar School, broke into the Newark First XV in 1981 and was part of the side that won the 1982 Notts Cup. He moved on to Loughborough University and Leicester, for whom he played nearly 400 times. He also appeared for England against Italy in a non-cap international. Later he was head coach of England.

Other players from Newark include Greg Tonks of Northampton and Tom Ryder of Glasgow.

NOTTINGHAM

"Everybody has heard of Nottingham Rugby club but nobody knows where it is."
Simon Beatham, 2005

IN THE 19TH century, the city of Nottingham grew rapidly, thanks to its coalfields and its lace-making industry. The Birkin Family were one of the city's wealthiest lace families as well as the driving force behind the city's rugby club.

The first recorded rugby game played in the city was a Nottingham v Derby Wanderers match in January 1876. Most of the Nottingham players were ex-pupils of Rugby School. Nottingham RFC were formed in 1877 by an Old Rugbeian called Alick Birkin, who had just come down from Rugby School. He contacted some of his friends to see if there was any interest in organising matches. Birkin was only 16 years of age at the time, but found enough support to establish a club.

Reports suggest the original Nottingham RFC struggled for several seasons in the late 1870s and went into abeyance for a time around 1882.

Birkin was captain of Nottingham for seven years. He was succeeded by his brother, Leslie, who held the job for 11 seasons. The Birkin family were to be associated with Nottingham RFC from 1877 to 1956. Another member of the family, Harold Birkin, formed the Notts, Lincs & Derbyshire RU in 1926, with Lump Cartwright as Vice President.

The club suffered badly from the 1895 Schism because many of their most attractive opponents joined the NU. Indeed, interest reached such a low point that the club struggled to field a single side, despite playing local second-rate teams. It was a temporary situation for, despite their problems, Nottingham produced an England captain in Vincent 'Lump' Cartwright (1882-1965), who was another Old Rugbeian. Cartwright made his England debut during his years at Oxford University, where he was a contemporary of Adrian Stoop. He eventually won 14 England caps and galvanised Nottingham into a force in regional rugby by leading the club to victory in the 1906 Midlands Cup.

Cartwright was unlucky to be England captain when the national team was struggling. He was also an England contemporary of J.E. Greenwood, who lived much of his life in Nottingham and was a director of Boots the Chemist, one of the area's biggest employers. Curiously, Greenwood never played for the city club, or even mentioned it in his autobiography.

Nottingham's next international was one of the game's all-time greats: Prince Alexander Obolensky. The Russian Prince attended Trent College in the city and found time to play for both Chesterfield and Nottingham. Obolensky entered the realms of greatness in 1936 when, on his international debut, he scored two tries in England's first ever win over the All Blacks. Indeed, it was England's only victory over New Zealand until 1984. The All Blacks were lucky; the following year Obolensky put a Brazil XV to the sword by scoring 17 tries in 80 minutes, one every seven minutes. Obo was the son of a Russian Prince who fled Russia in 1919. He attended Trent College, Nottingham

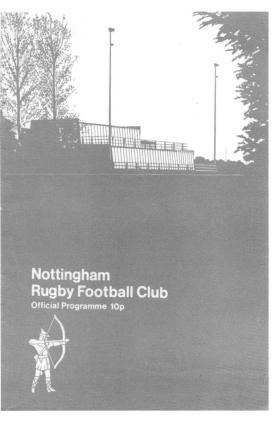

and Brasenose College, Oxford. Quiet and reserved off the field, he wasn't well regarded by some of his England teammates, who saw him as a pure sprinter who lacked rugby skills. He was still a Russian national when he made his England debut. King Edward VIII was not amused and raised the issue with the Prince, who then took British citizenship. He pioneered athletic boots that were based on running shoes, unlike the heavy cork-studded boots that rugby players usually wore. He joined the RAF in 1939 and was killed in an aeroplane accident on 29th March 1940.

Subsequent internationals were John Pallant, who was capped by England in 1967, and Dusty Hare, who made his debut for England against Wales in 1974.

Nottingham were a good side at the time, but in the space of 15 years they rose to rank in the top eight of the Senior National League, a remarkable achievement and a triumph for the club's philosophy of support for the new league system.

They produced two remarkable coaches in Dai Roberts and Alan Davies. Dai Roberts left to become the Canadian coach, while Davies took Nottingham to the semi-final of the 1984 National KO Cup. Alan Davies established a reputation as one of Britain's top coaches and later became the Welsh national coach.

A host of fine young players played in Nottingham green in the 1980s and 1990s: Rory Underwood, Rob Andrew, Dorian West, Brian Moore, Richard Moon, Steve Hackney and Neil Back all went on to international success, but sadly for Nottingham, it was with other clubs. Leicester Tigers were the big attraction for Notts players and became the irresistible magnet for a crop of future internationals who made the short journey to Welford Road, only 20 miles down the M1.

Nottingham managed to hang on to some other fine players, such as Chris Gray and Gary Rees. Gray, a dentist from Edinburgh, became a top-class Scottish lock, but kept his association with Nottingham. As did Rees, an England flanker, who continued to turn out for the Greens as they tumbled down the leagues in the 1990s.

Between 1989 and 1991 Simon Hodgkinson collected 14 England caps and amassed 203 points, including a new record of 60 in the 1991 Grand Slam campaign. Bristolian Hodgkinson appeared for the Green and Whites, including one season as captain, until he left for Moseley in 1993. He returned to Beeston in 1995, playing for another two seasons.

The 1980s saw Nottingham punching above their weight, and when leagues arrived in 1987 they had six players in the England team and were regularly in the quarter and semi-finals of National KO Cup. They were riding high, but decline set in, which wasn't helped by the onset of professionalism. By 1997 Nottingham were struggling in National Two and gates fell to 500. The decision was made then to sell the ground and look for a new site within the city boundaries, but this proved a torturous process.

On the field, the low point came in 2002, when Nottingham, to avoid relegation, had not only to win at Stourbridge but also hope that other results went their way. They won with a last minute penalty, but had to wait 30 minutes for news to permeate through that other results had fallen favourably. Better times came in 2004 when coach Simon Beatham led Nottingham to promotion to National One.

On 29th April 2006, after 102 years at Ireland Avenue, Nottingham moved to the Lady Bay Sports Complex. Unfortunately, Bay wasn't ready, and a temporary home was found at Meadow Lane, home of Notts County soccer club. They eventually played at Meadow Lane from 2006 to 2015.

2007-08 was a successful season as they finished level on points with second-placed Exeter Chiefs, one of the wealthiest clubs outside of the Premiership.

Nottingham has established links to New Zealand. Kiwis Gary Delaney and Craig Hammond were outstanding servants, and All Black legend Ali Williams arrived at Nottingham in January 2011 to recuperate from a serious injury. He played four times for the club before returning home and helping New Zealand to win the Rugby World Cup. In 2009 Notts scrum-half Tim Usasz played for the USA in the Churchill Cup.

Nottingham have also figured prominently in English international ranks through Sam Vesty, Dan Cole, Billy Twelvetrees, Tom Youngs, Dan Coles and Alex Corbisiero, who all played for Nottingham whilst learning their trade with Leicester Tigers.

Tom Youngs played 55 times for the Green and Whites over three seasons between 2008 and 2011, scoring 15 tries. Youngs was turned from a centre to a hooker during his time at Nottingham, and after just one full season back at Welford Road, he made his England debut against Fiji and received a call-up by the British & Irish Lions.

Nearer home, David Jackson holds the record for most league appearances for a Nottingham player. He made his senior debut in 2000, having been with the club minis since he was six years of age. In 2013 Tim Streather was voted the Championship's player of the year.

.

NOTTS POLICE

THE NOTTINGHAM COUNTY Constabulary was formed in 1840, but the city of Nottingham had constables before that date. Nottingham City Police was formed in 1936. At its peak in the 20th Century the city had 1700 policemen and cadets who played football, rugby and cricket.

In the early 1960s, long before the days of the amalgamation of police forces, the former Nottingham City Police played away to either Leicester City or the Leicestershire Constabulary. The match would invariably be at one venue: Victoria Park, Leicester.

Victoria Park is a huge council park with changing rooms on one corner. If you were last out of the changing rooms when playing there on a dark afternoon in winter, you could lose your way. Similarly, if you ever had to leave the pitch and make your way back to the changing rooms, you might never arrive. You could not see the playing area from the changing rooms, and neither could you see the changing rooms from the pitch. To make matters worse, the home side had to carry the posts from the pavilion and erect them on the pitch, so hopefully they knew where to put them.

One winter's day, Notts Police played Leicester City Police on the Park. The home side ran out of the changing rooms in the drizzling gloom (no lights in those days) and trotted for what seemed to be about a mile to the pitch. Notts kicked off immediately and at the first scrum realised one of their second row was missing. They convinced themselves that he would eventually find the ground and pressed on regardless with 14 men. But the missing man did not arrive! Notts returned to the changing rooms, which were in complete darkness. After a lot of searching and swearing, the groundsman was located and opened up. As the doors were unlocked and the lights put on, there was the missing player, fast asleep, sitting in a hand-basin with just his shirt on ...and everything else immersed! He had apparently tried to apply Elliman's Athletic Rub to the base of his spine with one hand whilst holding the bottle with the other. Because he was trying to hurry, the 'lotion' ran down between his bottom and beyond with painful consequences! The only way he could get any relief was to "get some water around the affected area", and obviously the best way was to try and hitch onto the edge of a hand-basin and turn on the taps. After achieving this manoeuvre, and as the burning and stinging were subdued, the lights went off and the place was locked up. He was in total darkness. He had been on early shift for six consecutive mornings, and because of the darkness, the warm soothing water and his tiredness, he promptly fell asleep. The missing lock played on for Notts Police for many more seasons, but is best remembered for the incident in the Victoria Park hand-basin.

(Thanks to Malcolm Gough)

MODERNS
(Nottingham Moderns)

MODERNS BEGAN LIFE in 1956, when a group of 15-year-old school-leavers from the Cottesmore Boys School formed their own side called Nottingham Moderns RFC. The club played on public parks for 20 years before undergoing rebranding as Moderns, which coincided with a move to Wilford Lane. The original members included Doug Scott, the legendary mountaineer who was the first man to climb the South West face of Mount Everest. He was also a successful author.

Better known for rugby were Geoff Read, who joined Nottingham, and Brian Hall, who moved to Leicester Tigers. Other players who won representative honours include Roger Brumby for Jamaica, Mike Burke, who won over 50 caps for the Arabian Gulf, and Alan Pearson, who emigrated Down Under and played for Western Australia against England and the All Blacks.

Moderns have won the Three Counties Cup and the club have also reached the semi-final of the Midlands Club Championship.

PAVIORS

PAVIORS ARE THE old boys of High Pavement School, which was formed in 1788 for the education of Unitarian children. The original building was in the lace market of Nottingham. In 1895, the school moved to Stanley Road, Forest Fields.

The former pupils rugby club was formed in 1922 as High Pavement Old Boys Rugby Club, who wore a maroon and green strip. In 1927 a split occurred within HPOBs and some members left to form Nottingham Casuals.

Two years later, the club went open. HPOBs were to lead a nomadic existence. They played at Ireland Avenue, home of Nottingham RFC, on the school playing fields in Strelley, at Highfields, in Melbourne Park before, in 1958, finding a permanent home at Dale Road, on the top of Carlton Hill.

The best known Pavior is Anthony Wharton, who played for Nottingham and became RFU President in 1977.

Paviors have traditionally been dependant on their minis and juniors. In the 1980s, the club won the Three Counties Cup on three occasions and qualified for the National KO Cup, including reaching the Fourth Round.

The club have spent their league years towards the top of the Midland Leagues.

SKEGNESS

'Skegness - a beard-shaped promontory'

HI-DE-HI WAS A television comedy about a seaside holiday camp set in the 1950s run by a mysterious Mr Joe Maplin. The madcap comedy was fiction, but, in fact, Skegness RUFC owes its roots to the real-life Joe Maplin, a larger-than-life Skegness resident called Billy Butlin, who invented the holiday camp in 1936.

Butlin stopped serving the needs of holidaymakers when World War Two broke out and switched to serving the army at the camp in Skegness. As he was feeding the soldiers, Butlin realised that when the emergency was over, he could convert the army camps to cater for peacetime holidaymakers. When the soldiers left Skegness army camp, he bought the place, redesigned it and persuaded families to buy his organised holiday world of chalets and packaged entertainment.

In the TV series, Joe Maplin recruited some odd types as camp managers, notably Jeffrey Fairbrother, a university don who had fallen from grace at university. This wasn't fiction because Butlin actually recruited some of his managers on the same basis, including Des Scaife, a rugby player at London Irish, who took over the Skegness camp. Amongst Scaife's innovations was organising the Billy Butlin Rugby Cup each Easter for visiting rugby teams. The cup ran from 1950 to 1956.

Scaife is believed by some people to have founded Skegness RUFC, but others dispute this. He is also said to have founded the Irish Wolfhounds (the Irish Barbarians), but other people disagree with this version of events too. They give the founders of Skegness as Mr. J.A.C. Baker-Beall, the local bank manager, who was assisted by G.R. Bell, T.E. Pearman and Melvin Moffatt. The inaugural meeting, held at the Links Hotel in Skegness, was on 24th February 1949. Veterans who had played wartime rugby in the services were also among the founder members. This was a case of third time lucky for rugby in Skegness, as two other clubs had been founded in 1924 and 1934 respectively, but neither had lasted more than three years.

The 1949 club had a strong First XV and a competent 'A' XV during the next three or four seasons. Probably the biggest contribution to rugby football in Skegness came from Mr G.R. Bell. As a founder member, he played in the backs until 1951 and later served as a Three Counties referee. Bell handled the majority of the club's home matches for over 20 years.

From 1950 to 1956 the club promoted the seven-a-side tournament of the Lincolnshire Rugby Union, in which Scaife was involved. This was an Easter Monday fixture, and when the event was moved to Lincoln, the Skegness club held its own tournament for two more seasons.

From 1971 until 1985 the club's headquarters were at the White Hart, Burgh-le-Marsh, where rugby players from all over the county enjoyed the hospitality of the landlords, Rob and Caroline Watson.

Since 1987 the club has been running a very successful veterans tournament in September every year, with teams participating from all corners of England. The junior section of the club was started in 1990, but didn't survive past 1995. Happily, it was restarted in 2003 and has progressed to become a thriving part of the club.

In 1985, with the co-operation of the Indoor Bowling Club, the club built its own premises at Wainfleet Road Memorial Playing Fields on land owned by East Lindsey District Council. Crucial financial help was given by Bateman's Brewery and the Sports Council, and many of the members contributed their time and skills to the actual construction work. The clubhouse was then extended in 1995 and partly refurbished in 2004.

CHAPTER ELEVEN - WEST MIDLANDS

*"Birmingham is a city where its inhabitants work as if they must
get rich by evening and die the next day."*
Alexis de Toqueville (1835)

THE CITY OF Birmingham is the heart of the West Midlands. It is a remarkable city by any standards and was a beehive of industry before James Watt opened a foundry in 1796, which sparked the Industrial Revolution and saw the city's population rise from 56,000 to 200,000 in 50 years. Besides commerce, the city's other great strand is non-conformism. This puritanical streak and a large Methodist population earned Birmingham the nickname of the 'Holy City'. It is little wonder that it became a centre for migration by Welsh non-conformists throughout the 19th and early 20th Century. Every rugby club in the city has its smattering of Welsh names and many of its greatest rugby players were first or second generation Welsh. One of Birmingham's innovations was welfare for workers – although, in the best non-conformist tradition, it was strictly limited to teetotallers.

The earliest club matches date from the early 1870s, when the mighty Newport played Edgbaston Crusaders, who were described as possessing the best pack in the Midlands. The pre-eminence of rugby in the region was doomed from the moment that an obscure match was played in 1874, when Aston Villa, a club formed by a Methodist church, met Aston Brook St. Mary's at Perry Barr in a mixed match of 45 minutes rugby and 45 minutes of 'Sheffield Association Rules'. Aston Villa decided that they preferred 'Association' and created huge interest, as did another side called 'Small Heath', who became Birmingham City FC. The man in the Birmingham streets decided that they preferred the round ball game to rugby, which became the preserve of the middle classes. Rugby became associated with the public and grammar schools. Their influence was so strong that eight of the area's 25 clubs were Old Boys clubs. Moseley were the region's top side, but Old Edwardians FC were once their serious rivals and Midland Counties Cup winners in 1889-90. It was, however, Moseley who were perennial challengers for the title of the best club in the Midlands against big East Midland clubs such as Coventry and Leicester. The three sides dominated the Midland Counties Cup, which was the unofficial regional championship. This competition fell out of favour after World War One and was abandoned in 1926.

The composition of Midlands rugby had fragmented long before the cup was confined to the bank vaults. The Midlands Counties RFU had been formed in 1879 and originally controlled the whole region. They kept control for 50 years, and even defeated an attempt to found a professional 'Midland Union' in 1897 alongside the Northern Union. The existence of MCRFU irked the individual counties, who were keen to enter their own side in the County Championship, and they felt their players weren't getting a chance in the regional side. In 1920 the differing interests of the constituent counties brought an end to the Midland Counties RFU.

The disintegration of the senior body saw the formation of four new bodies: the East Midlands RU, Warwickshire RU, Leicestershire RU and the North Midlands RU. The East Midlands was based around Bedford and Northampton, Leicestershire drew from the city of Leicester, whilst in theory the North Midlands stretched from Birmingham to Stafford and Derbyshire. In practise, the 26 constituent clubs in the North Midlands RU were based largely on Old Edwardians RFC, who were a major force in the city and region.

All the Midland counties benefited from the influx of Welsh rugby players, particularly in the years between the wars. Hard times in the Welsh mines forced thousands of mineworkers to seek employment in the factories of the Midlands. Later the region benefited from rugby playing students studying at the local universities and teacher training colleges.

Moseley remained 'top dog' in the West Midlands until the 1990s. Unfortunately, Moseley's attempts to thrive in the professional age brought their downfall, which coincided with the rise of other clubs such as Birmingham RFC, Stourbridge and Dudley Kingswinford. Despite the changes, the region's Old Boys clubs survive and provide a backbone to rugby in a football-mad area of England.

ALDRIDGE
(formed when Old Centrals and Witton merged in 1998)

M. JONES, THE Headmaster of Central Secondary School, Suffolk School, Birmingham, formed Old Centrals in 1913. Jones, who had played for Llanelli and was a Welsh trialist, had switched Central School from soccer to rugby the previous year. Old Centrals (or Central Secondary OBs as they were originally known) played their first game against the school on 11th October 1913. OCs won the match 11-8. The following week Old Cents played Aston Old Edwardians 3rds at home but lost 19-3. This was one of only three defeats in that opening season (Old Dixonians won 5-3 and Handsworth won 6-0) when the highlight was a remarkable run of 15 straight wins. Home matches were played at Penns Lane on a ground rented from a local butcher.

It was five years before the club could enjoy a second season due to World War One. Fixtures were usually played against local second teams until excellent results brought the right to First team rugby. A move saw fixtures played at Dads Lane, Stirchley, followed in 1924 by a move to Gospel Lane, Hall Green, where they remained until 1939. The following season, OCs lost 7-0 to Newbold-on-Avon in the Midlands Counties Cup final, and the following season Harry Dare was selected for the new North Midlands side.

The years after World War Two saw OCs playing at Metchley Lane, Harbourne and going from strength to strength, winning the 1951-52 North Midlands Sevens. In 1954-55 the club were unbeaten all season with figures of P23 W19 D4 L0. Behind the scenes the committee acquired a ground at Streetley with a clubhouse added in 1956. The Streetley ground was officially opened by Peter Robbins followed by a match between Old Centrals and Combined Birmingham Old Boys. Results in the following years were modest, although OCs became a renowned sevens side. It was the 1970s before OCs established themselves in the 15-a-side game under Dave Harris (ex-Coventry). 1970-71 saw results of P31 W28 D1 L2 F634 A172.

The 1990-91 season saw the club reach the quarter-finals of the National Junior Cup, but generally the arrival of league rugby saw Old Centrals struggling for new players as the old school had ceased playing rugby and had even been renamed Central Byng Kendrick School. New blood eventually arrived with the merger with Witton.

WITTON

Witton was founded in 1918 and played out of the GEC Magnet Club, where they remained until 1982. The following three years saw the club operating from Ansells Club, Birchfield, Aston Old Edwardians and eventually Perry Barr Park. The arrival of league rugby saw Old Centrals struggling for new players. The loss of the Perry Barr pitch in 1998 led to a merger with Old Centrals. The club operated from Sutton Coldfield and changed their name to Aldridge. The new club's colours were agreed as maroon, gold and black hooped jerseys and a badge of a raised arm holding a bolt of lightning.

(Thanks to Dave Hemingway)

ASTON OLD EDWARDIANS

AOEs, THE OLD boys of King Edward's School, Aston, are one of those great clubs who once challenged the big city clubs. The club was formed in 1889 by W.O. Bailey and Ted Beasley. The school played soccer until 1894, when H. E. Scott, an old Pauline, became games master and introduced rugby. Aston King Edward's soon became a fine side and one of the best schools in the region.

The club began playing at Holford Drive but subsequently moved to Perry Hall. Eventually AOE's bought a pitch at Perry Common, which was dedicated as a memorial to the 123 AOE old boys who died in World War One.

The club's greatest era was the years after the Great War. In 1922-23, AOE's recorded wins over some of the region's bigger clubs, including Coventry, Moseley and Burton. That season, they provided eight players for the North Midlands team who reached the final of the County Championship. AOE's lost to Gloucester in the North Midlands Cup when the trophy represented the club championship of the entire region. Two of the team, R. Baker and H.E. Markwick, had England trials.

During World War Two, AOE combined with Camp Hill OE; a link recalled in the annual "Teddy Parker" Cup game played ever since by the two clubs. Teddy Parker was one of the great rugby administrators in Birmingham and devoted a lifetime to serving the game.

In the 1970s, playing membership was opened to all-comers and the first Sunday Colts sides were established at the club. 2002-03 saw still greater success, as the 1st XV were champions of Midlands 3 West (N), won the North Midlands Cup for the first time and were Greater Birmingham rugby club of the year. The club were boosted around this time by an influx of players from the defunct Erdington club. The following year, AOEs retained the North Midlands Cup.

In 2006 Gary Street, ex-AOEs, was appointed England Women's coach and led the national team to win the 2014 Women's Rugby World Cup.

2014 saw AOEs playing at Sunnybank Avenue and competing in Midland 2.

BARKER'S BUTTS

BARKER'S BUTTS RFC takes its name from Barker's Butts Lane in Coventry. The club was originally based at Meriden, but moved to Keresley and later to Pickford Grange Lane. Barkers was formed in 1945 from the ashes of a works side called Daimler RFC.

During the 1960s Barkers Butts struggled to get fixtures with the better sides in the Midlands and had to look elsewhere. They ended up travelling further afield to take on teams such as Hemel Hempstead and Sedgley Park.

The introduction of the Warwickshire Cup in the 1970s allowed Barkers Butts the chance to humble some of the area's more established clubs. And when the leagues were introduced there was some consternation over the placing of Barker's in Midlands One.

Barker's Butts traditionally had links with a number of secondary schools within the city of Coventry, including King Henry VIII, Bablake, Woodlands and Finham Park. But the decline in schools rugby in the 1970s forced Barker's to look internally for players and they were amongst the first in Warwickshire to organise colts rugby.

The first international to emerge from Barkers was Huw Davies, who also played for Stourbridge. He played 151 times for Barker's in National One and played 21 times for England.

Their finest son is Neil Back, the feisty flanker, who began at Barker's in the 1980s before moving to Nottingham and Leicester Tigers, where he was a prolific try scorer. He made his England debut in 1994 and eventually became part of the legendary back row of Hill, Back and Dallaglio. They were the

BROMSGROVE

Neil Back, who began his rugby career at Barker's Butts.

BROMSGROVE WAS THE principal town in the West Midlands during Saxon times. It may have lost its pre-eminence, but it is an attractive suburban town to the south of Birmingham. One of its most famous assets is the famous Bromsgrove School, which has produced many fine rugby players. Bromsgrove School had links with Rugby School as John Day Collis, their headmaster from 1843 to 1867, had studied under Thomas Arnold.

Bromsgrove RFC was formed by a meeting on 25th September 1872 at the Corn Exchange. The first game took place on the 12th October1872. Sadly, the end of the club's first season saw a fatality when Charlie Haywood, a thirteen-year-old player, was injured and subsequently died, when, as the local paper reported, "he cannoned against Phillips with such violence that he is now in a precarious and insensible state."

The club was jinxed, as in December 1892, Rev. G. H. Knight of Bromsgrove School died as a result of injuries sustained in the Worcester v Bromsgrove match. Knight fell on a ball during a Worcester dribble and was kicked in the head.

A luckier product of the school was William Bunting (1873-1947), who played for the town team before moving to Moseley and Richmond. Bunting won nine England caps at centre. Bunting had hardly played outside Bromsgrove School when he was picked for England. He was considered one of the best three-quarters of his era and could play anywhere in the back line. After Bromsgrove, Bunting attended Cambridge University. He made his England debut in 1897 and was the star of the England win over Scotland.

Bunting then dropped out of the international reckoning for a season when he took a teaching appointment at Bromsgrove School. He eventually resumed playing for the town side, which was described by one newspaper as "a small local club". He was back in the England team in 1899 and joined Richmond shortly afterwards. Bunting kept up his links to his old school and organised the annual Old Bromsgrovians dinner.

Despite Bunting's presence, the town rugby club struggled because several other sides were operating locally, such as Bromsgrove Unity and Crusaders. They, like the town team, disappeared in the early 1880s.

Soccer arrived in Bromsgrove in the early 1880s, and soon a dozen association football clubs were playing regularly. Bromsgrove RFC reappeared in 1888 but disappeared again eight years later despite Bromsgrove School playing the oval ball game in winter.

By October 1895, rugby in the county of Worcestershire was languishing. A meeting was held at the Golden Cross Hotel in Bromsgrove which decided to amalgamate the town club with Worcester RFC. The merger never came to pass as Bromsgrove wanted to complete their pre-arranged fixtures before any action.

The 20th Century saw Bromsgrove as a prosperous, middle-ranking Midlands club. Local opposition was rare as they were for a time the only club in Worcestershire, although a rival side called Bromsgrove Crusaders operated in the town in the early 1920s.

cornerstone of the England team who won the 2003 Rugby World Cup. Supreme fitness allied to a tireless work rate made Back a stand-out performer in international rugby – but not before he silenced his critics. He struggled to shake off the widely held notion that, at 5ft 10in (1.78m), he was too small for an international flanker. It was during the Lions 1997 tour to South Africa, however, that the rugby world started to appreciate his true worth: he made a decisive contribution when he came on as a replacement during the series-clinching win in the second Test. Later, he toured Australia with the Lions in 2001, helped England to the Rugby World Cup in 2003 before exiting after the Lions' 2005 tour to New Zealand.

Another member of the victorious England team in 2003 was Danny Grewcock MBE. He also began at Barker's before playing for Coventry, Bath, Saracens, England and the 2001 Lions to Australia. Danny was a tough, uncompromising character who occasionally upset the authorities.

Since then, Barker's have produced more top class players: Leon Lloyd (Leicester), Jim Hamilton (Gloucester and Scotland), Andy Goode (Worcester, Saracens, Leicester and England) and Tom Wood (Northampton and England).

Despite its reputation for producing great players, the club have been middle ranking in the Midlands leagues with an occasional foray into the National leagues.

The second international to appear for Bromsgrove was Peter Kingston, the Moseley and Gloucester scrum-half, who appeared for the club in the early 1980s. Kingston was the England scrum-half on the 1975 Australian tour. Jordan Crane, a future England international, began at Bromsgrove and moved to Colston's School, Bristol

In the 1970s Bromsgrove became the first British team to tour Russia when they played Moscow.

In 2001, the club reached the quarter-finals of the Intermediate Cup and have steadily risen through the ranks to reach National 2 North by 2012.

BIRMINGHAM & SOLIHULL
(Pertemps Bees)

BIRMINGHAM HAS ALWAYS been a soccer city, with three major clubs, Aston Villa, Birmingham City and West Bromwich Albion, who have all pushed rugby into the shade.

Rugby has been played in the city since the 1870s, but Birmingham RFC was only formed in 1911. They had no ground initially and had to play away every week. Few of the team were experienced rugby players as most were ex-soccer players. Birmingham RFC finally found a home pitch at Windermere Road when another club, Moseley Harlequins, disbanded. That pitch was used until the Great War and was replaced with pitches at Warwick Road, Tyseley and later York Road.

The York Road days were amongst the most successful in the club's history, with fixtures against Llanelli, Northampton, Guy's Hospital and Waterloo. Unfortunately, York Road was sold for greyhound racing, which forced Birmingham back to Windermere Road. The change led to a decline in the fixture list and a severe financial crisis in 1927. Birmingham nearly went out of business and had to lodge with Camp Hill Old Boys, a move that enabled them to survive.

Perhaps the finest player to represent Birmingham was Ivor Jones (1901-1982), who played as a youngster for the club and the North Midlands whilst studying in the city. In 1923-24 Jones captained both club and county and held the club try record with 34 in a season. He later returned to Wales, where his achievements were prodigious. He won 16 Wales caps between 1924 and 1930, played for Llanelli from 1922 to 1938 and was club captain for eight seasons. He toured Australia with the 1930 Lions, where he was selected at flanker but played in every position in the backs, including an entire test match at scrum-half.

After World War Two, Birmingham RFC moved to Edgbaston Cricket Ground, the home of Warwickshire cricket. They remained at Edgbaston until 1967, when they moved to Portway on the Evesham Road. The time at Edgbaston was well spent as Birmingham pressed for first-class status and regularly supplied players to the county side. A club record was set in 1966 when Tim Smith, the Birmingham flanker, scored four tries in 23 minutes against the City Police.

The club were in Level Seven when Leagues arrived in 1987, but rose rapidly and had reached National One after 15 years. In 1989 they changed their name to Birmingham & Solihull. The club then played the most audacious card in their history by changing their name to 'Pertemps Bees' RUFC. Pertemps Ltd is a famous employment agency that was founded by the mother of an ex-Birmingham player called Tim Watts. The club heard that Tim had taken over the firm and asked him for help. The RFU were not amused by Pertemps' commercialism and banned other member clubs from following suit. This was a controversial step as Harlequins had already renamed themselves as 'NEC Harlequins', and works sides such as Kodak, Racal Decca and British Aerospace had existed for generations.

Things worked better than everyone thought as 'the Bees' challenged for promotion and reached the semi-finals of the 2004 Powergen Cup. They lost to Newcastle Falcons but had taken the scalp of mighty Wasps, the 2004 European Champions, in the quarter-finals.

In 2006, Bees were saved from relegation from National Division One by a league reorganisation. They were relegated in 2008 but bounced straight back.

Amongst the most famous players who played for Birmingham & Solihull were Craig Chalmers, the Scotland fly-half and Steve Brain, the England hooker. The club's best-known coach was another England international in John White.

In 2014, Birmingham won one of the oddest games in rugby history when they beat Preston Grasshoppers 18-17 in the 101st minute. The officials played 21 minutes of injury time (thought to be a record in a match with no serious injuries), which gave Birmingham the opportunity to kick the winning penalty with the last play of the match.

Birmingham pictured in 1923.

SOLIHULL
(merged with Birmingham RUFC in 1989)

SOLIHULL OPTED FOR rugby rules in August 1884. The town of Solihull is a leafy suburb to the south-east of Birmingham. Rugby in Solihull has always been split between Old Silhillians RFC, who draw their players from Solihull Grammar School, and Solihull RUFC. The two sides met annually on Boxing Day in the Wedgebury Cup, named after a local publican.

Solihull RUFC have produced a number of top-class players in hooker Steve Brain, winger Martin Hale and full-back Chris Gifford. Brain was an abrasive hooker with Coventry and Rugby Lions in the 1990s and played 13 times for England. Hale, a product of Solihull School, moved to Moseley in 1964 and was capped by England against South Africa. A phenomenal try-scorer, Hale got 48 tries for Moseley in 1967-68. Gifford appeared for both Coventry and Moseley and represented England against Argentina in the 1970s, when caps were not awarded because the Pumas weren't recognised as first-class opposition.

The club also produced a famous name in Ian Duncan-Smith, who was leader of the Conservative Party from 2002 to 2005. Duncan-Smith played fly-half for Solihull Colts in the early 1970s. Legend has it that he was an accomplished number ten, which is about as close as he ever got to number 10 Downing Street.

Solihull kept their identity after the merger with Birmingham and even reappeared as a separate entity in 2000. The new side were effectively Birmingham & Solihull Thirds and have provided a league platform for many fine players. They rent a ground from the senior club and have won three successive promotions.

(Thanks to Dave Radburn)

CAMP HILL

CAMP HILL KING Edward Grammar School is another of the King Edward VI Grammar schools in Birmingham. The school was opened in 1882 in the suburb of Camp Hill on the west side of the city. An old boys association was formed the following year, although a rugby section came later. Several old boys of Camp Hill proved outstanding players for other sides before CHOEs were established, notably P.O. Patterson, an English trialist. A number of other old boys played for Moseley.

Birmingham in action.

To help establish a rugby club from Camp Hill OEs, a match was played in 1885 between the school and an old boys side. The curious scoring of olden times is shown by the match being drawn despite the Old Boys scoring nine touchdowns to one.

The first outside fixture arranged by Camp Hill Old Edwardians was in 1888 against Five Ways Old Edwardians, but the weather prevented any play. In October 1893, Camp Hill beat the Aston Old Edwardians at Thompson's Nurseries.

The first captain of Camp Hill OEs was F.M. Wharton, who played for Warwickshire, the Midlands and Cornwall. Camp Hill's first ever try-scorer was Teddy Parker, who also captained Camp Hill for 18 seasons.

Initially, CHOEs played at Showell Green Lane before a move was made to Wake Green, which could only be reached by train. In 1898 C.A. Fentiman joined the school and formed a formidable half-back partnership with Harry Gibbs for the Old Boys that helped the club establish a fixture list, including Leicester, Rugby, Nuneaton, Burton and Moseley. Camp Hill were unusual in adopting the idea that the team's forwards should play in fixed positions, whereas in other teams, members of the pack scrummed down where they wanted. It was another 50 years before England adopted fixed forward positions.

The years before World War One were a struggle for Camp Hill as young, inexperienced players were forced into First XV action. 133 CHOBs died in the war, but a rugby side at Wake Green was raised again in 1919 under the captaincy of Teddy Parker. The outstanding player of the era was winger E.F. Odell, who played for the Midland Counties at rugby and Leicestershire at cricket. Odell missed an England trial at rugby due to injury.

F.S.D. Stephenson was one of OE's finest sons. He made his debut for CHOEs in 1908 and played regularly until 1950 when he took up refereeing.

In the early 1920s Camp Hill gained notoriety for inconsistency. Their form dipped during the mid-1920s and it was only at the end of the decade that a good team emerged. Unfortunately, Wake Green was lost, but a pitch was bought at Haslucks Green Road, Shirley for £1138. The move to the new ground sparked a remarkable run of 35 wins and one draw in 36 games from April 1933 to November 1934.

In the mid-1930s Camp Hill lost only 36 of 147 games with nine drawn. The most prolific point-scorer of the era was Dennis Harris, who was captain in 1933-34, CHOBs greatest season with 27 games won of 28. The following season Camp Hill played their first ever game in London, beating Saracens 18-3.

The late thirties saw Camp Hill with an outstanding record, and they claimed their first international in W.E.N. Davies, who, although Birmingham born and bred, was three times capped for Wales in 1939 whilst playing for Cardiff.

A student-based team kept the club going throughout World War Two. In 1940-41 they lost only four of 25 games, including winning by 14 points to 13 over Gloucester at Kingsholm.

After the war, they were strengthened by the arrival of two experienced Welsh players, Sid Harris (Neath and Swansea), and Ken Bayliss (Bangor University and Pontypool), both of whom were masters at Camp Hill School. The arrival of new blood from the school gave the club a great end to the decade, which couldn't last and the Fifties saw decline.

Camp Hill have had many home grounds over the years. They left Bartley Green in 1961 and moved to King's Norton. In 1974, they sold the King's Norton ground and moved to a larger complex at Hopwood, near Redditch, on the south side of Birmingham.

The King's Norton era produced Camp Hill's greatest players: Keith Fielding and Paul Gibbs. Keith Fielding was one of the quickest players in rugby history. His try-scoring was legendary with Camp Hill, Loughborough University, Moseley and England. He switched to rugby league in the early 1970s and became an outstanding success.

Paul Gibbs is largely forgotten but was a remarkable player. He began at Camp Hill but emigrated to Australia, where he earned the remarkable honour of playing for the Australian national team despite being a Pom.

Players such as Fielding and Gibbs are rare, but they have since produced numerous players for the North Midlands and Greater Birmingham. Today the club accept their position as a middle-ranking club in the Midland leagues. They dropped the OE suffix in 1971. In 1980, they qualified for the National Knockout Cup, where they met Broughton Park who had several internationals.

The 1990s saw Camp Hill as Birmingham's top-ranking junior club. Their best-known player was Ruan Maclean, who won Scotland A honours.

(Thanks to Oscar Twiby)

COVENTRY

COVENTRY IS THOUGHT of today as an industrial city, but at the start of the 19th Century it was a small Midland town built on the ribbon trade. Everything about the city changed with the invention of the bicycle and later the motorcar. The new industries led to a spectacular growth in population. The city grew from 21,000 in 1800 to 335,000 by 1970.

Coventry RFC was formed in 1874 by members of Stoke Cricket Club. The first match took place at Allesley Park College. They soon moved to the Old Bull Fields, which later became known as 'the Butts'. The new club made an enormous impact and were undefeated in their first two seasons and only lost one match in their third year.

Coventry are the first recorded club to play with four three-quarters when they used the tactic in an 1883 cup tie against Stratford. Two local schools, Warwick School and King Henry VIII School, pioneered the tactic, which was adopted in 1884 by Cardiff to accommodate F. E. Hancock, their brilliant three-quarter.

Coventry won the Midland Counties Cup in 1891, which was the regional club championship, and held the title for four years. They soon established an excellent fixture list that included many of the best London clubs. Their most famous players, of those early days was an elusive winger called Harry Ratcliff and the Rotherham brothers, Alan and Arthur, who were the backbone of the team. Alan Rotherham won 12 England caps, whilst his brother Arthur won five. Alan was the first great half-back to use the ploy of out-running the opposition without passing. Sadly, he later committed suicide.

The success of Coventry brought criticism from the RFU and their Midland rivals. It was rumoured they were enticing players from other sides to join them with illegal payments.

Coventry were involved in a plan to create a Midland Union based on the Northern Union. They even organised an NU match against Runcorn at the Butts in 1910, which they lost 15-3 in front of 3,500 spectators. The NU experiment was short-lived as the RFU suspended them but stopped short of banning the club altogether. The truth was that Twickenham had learnt a bitter lesson from the 1895 Great Schism and were reluctant to repeat the same problems, especially as a NU League had been formed in the South West. Two events saved the day for everyone: Coventry's NU results were terrible (they lost 102-0 to Leeds, conceding 24 tries in 80 minutes, including eight scored by F. Webster) and then the outbreak of World War One drew an end to the brief excursion into blatant professionalism.

Coventry lost the Butts during the Great War and struggled to find a regular home when peace returned, but they at least returned to the bosom of the RFU in March 1919 with a match against the touring New Zealanders. They lost 13-0, and then met them again, losing 47-0.

Behind the scenes, their cause was being helped by Bablake Grammar School switching from soccer to rugby. Bablake would eventually provide many fine players to the city club. Other boosts were the formation of the Coventry and District RU, which helped co-ordinate the game across the area, and the acquisition of the club's permanent home at Coundon Road in 1925.

The outstanding Coventry player of the period was Dickie Pemberton, a fly-half who understudied W.J.A. Davies for England. Pemberton had to make do with Midland Counties caps rather than the full prize. Jimmy Giles (1912-1967) won six English caps at fly-half a decade later; he captained Warwickshire to the County Championship and was a member of the 1938 Lions tour of South Africa. Giles's finest hour was playing as an emergency centre in the Third Test against South Africa when the Lions won 21-16.

The Coventry forwards of this era were awesome, notably the three Wheatley brothers: Harold, Arthur and Neb, who were all coalmen by profession. The trio were a handful for any referee, or opposing pack. Gerald 'Beef' Dancer of Bedford recalls: "The game was harder in those days, but we never had raking or use of the boot. Games with the Midland clubs were real wars. I remember the Wheatleys from Coventry. One of them, Neb, used to frighten me to death just looking at him. He was huge and real ugly, but you know we all got on well after the game and, on England trials and the like, we used to stick together. We liked London clubs even less than we liked each other." Neb must have frightened the national selectors because he never won a cap, whereas Arthur won five and Harold received seven. Arthur and Harold played together three times for England. Truly Coventry's forwards of the period were a difficult breed. It is recorded that one was once sent off for smoking during a match. The referee explained, "It wasn't so much the smoking, it was when he asked me for a light."

George Harriman was an England trialist in 1933, but never made the final 15. It's doubtful he worried greatly about it as he finished his working life as Managing Director of BMC, the UK's premier motor company.

Coventry, as a city and as a club, suffered during the Great Depression and in 1932 two of their best players, R.S. Roberts and A. Gascoigne, defected to Rugby League.

Despite the dark economic clouds, the late 1930s were the second great era for Coventry when they established a senior club record of 73 unbeaten matches between 1935 and 1937. Great beneficiaries were Warwickshire, whose success invariably coincided with high points in Coventry's history. During season 1938-39 Warwickshire won the County title with a side including nine Coventry men.

Although the Coventry area suffered terribly during World War Two, the needs of the city's industries meant there was sufficient manpower for the rugby club, who were able to continue throughout the emergency; indeed, Coventry were undefeated from 1942 to 1945.

Success continued after World War Two, with Ivor Preece as the kingpin. The Coventry fly-half was called up by England in 1948 when the nation's fortunes were at a low ebb. Preece brought stability and eventually won 12 caps and toured with the 1950 Lions. Ivor Preece was the last player to score a drop goal whilst it was worth four points. Ivor's son Peter won the same number of England caps in the 1970s and scored a record 32 tries for the club in 1971-72.

The next great player from Coventry was Peter Robbins, who was a loose forward who adopted the role of creator rather than destroyer. He attended Bishop Vesey Grammar School in Sutton Coldfield, where he was an outstanding athlete. Robbins graduated to Oxford University, where he was awarded a rugby blue for three successive seasons and was Oxford captain in 1956-57. He helped reorganise Oxford rugby from also-rans into worthy Varsity champions, which led to his England debut in 1956.

Robbins earned a huge reputation, but missed the 1959 Lions tour after breaking a leg playing for the Barbarians. Legend has it that he blotted his copybook with Oxford and England by throwing a double bed out of a ninth floor window on a Varsity tour to South Africa. Nobody was hurt but Robbins had developed a reputation as a loose cannon. Despite his foibles he later became a highly successful businessman but died young.

A contemporary of Robbins was a three-quarter who ranked with the best in the game's history: Peter Jackson. One of the greatest of wingers, Jackson was a rock-like defender (only two direct opponents scored against him in a decade of England caps), but his attacking skills defied imitation. In 20 games for England, Jackson scored 22 tries, and he scored 19 tries on the 1955 Lions Tour (only one less than the legendary Tony O'Reilly). He was described as the best England wing of the century. He suffered the inevitable droppings that

Peter Jackson

Bert Godwin, pictured right.

plagued all England players of the era, but was restored for the 1963 season, in which England again carried off the Home Championship.

Jackson's retirement coincided with the emergence of David Duckham, who became a national hero. People who knew nothing of the sport agonised over England's ill-use of his unique attacking talent. An outstanding schoolboy sprinter, Duckham arrived at Coundon Road in 1967 from King Henry VIII School and Old Coventrians. Despite national prominence, Duckham was readily available as a cashier at a Coventry branch of Barclays Bank. He ranks amongst the most attractive figures in English rugby history. He won 36 England caps during one of England's many troughs. A brilliant winger, he won four Lions caps in 1971 and set a record of six tries against West Coast Buller during the tour.

Coventry were one of Britain's finest and most attractive sides in the 1960s and 1970s, but backs like Jackson and Duckham relied on tough forwards. Phil Judd won 22 England caps at prop between 1962 and 1967. He also set a club record of 425 appearances for the First XV. Generally, Coventry's players were poorly rewarded by the England selectors, despite them having justifiable claims to be the best club side in England. Herbert Godwin won 11 England caps and toured with the 1962 Lions.

An urban legend surrounds this period in Coventry's history. A party from the club toured Spain in an era when few Spaniards spoke English. The rugby lads regaled the local bars with the rugby songs familiar to players of the era. A Spanish radio station heard the team and were told they were 'Old English folk songs', which was true. Folk music was at the time gaining worldwide popularity. They tape-recorded the folkists, blissfully unaware of the material. It was only when the programme was broadcast on Spanish radio that the authorities became aware of the nature of the material – from the outrage from English speaking listeners.

Back home, Coventry were frequently shown on television, and their players were amongst the best known in rugby, none more so than a young Fran Cotton, possibly the best prop forward of the era, as demonstrated by his appearances for the 1974 Invincible Lions.

Geoff Evans and Peter Preece were picked for England between 1972 and 1974, but then rejected. Even David Duckham was rejected in the mid-1970s as the England selectors indulged in an aimless pursuit of success. The most prolific point-scorer in English rugby at the time was a Coventry player, Peter Rossborough, who won only seven England caps but amassed over 2000 points and scored 100 tries for his club.

Coventry were amongst the first English clubs to use a club coach when they appointed George Cole in 1974. At the time they were riding high, but things slipped away. By 1978 Coventry were in dire straits following a mass exodus of talent: Tim Barnwell (to Leicester), Fran Cotton, Roger Creed, Adam Dunning (to Sale), and John Gray and Keith Fairbrother (to Rugby League).

They won the National Knockout Cup in successive seasons in the early 1970s and they continued to be a powerhouse in British club rugby into the next decade, but were unable to sustain success when League rugby arrived in 1987. Then, in the 1980s, local rivals Rugby Lions emerged to challenge Coventry's dominance. Coventry were relegated from Division 1 as Rugby's fortunes rose, based on ex-Coventry players such as Art Malik, Steve Brain and Eddie Saunders.

There was little to attract spectators, or big-name players, to Coundon Road after one brief season at the top level. For the rest of the 20th Century, Coventry were respectable denizens of National Division One and Two.

In 2004, Coundon Road was sold and the club moved to Butts Park Arena.

David Duckham and Tony Gray

DUDLEY KINGSWINFORD

DUDLEY KINGSWINFORD IS a side who operate on the west side of Wolverhampton, where the industrial expanse of the Black Country gives way to the rolling countryside of the Severn Valley. DK were originally formed as Harper Bean works team in 1920. Harper Bean Ltd later became Bean Industries and were subsequently absorbed by Garringtons and GKN.

Harper Bean RFC became Dudley RFC in 1922 and changed their name to Dudley Kingswinford in 1928 when the Club moved to Penzer Street.

Their first North Midlands player was J.L. ('Jack') Fellows, who played 19 consecutive championship games between 1924 and 1928. Other Midlands players over the years included Woodall, Bridgeman, Cutler, Trevarthern and Hopkins. Perhaps the finest player to represent Dudley Kingswinford was Cliff Watson, a blacksmith at Round Oak Steel Works who learnt his rugby at the club. Cliff saw an advertisement in a Sunday newspaper for a "strong lad to play rugby league" and wrote for a trial. He moved to St. Helens and eventually captained Great Britain RLFC. Another famous name from Dudley Kingswinford was Ken Pattison, who became one of the world's top referees in the 1970s.

The best known DK player is scrum-half Shaun Perry, who came through the club's junior ranks before moving to Coventry and Bristol. Perry made a handful of England appearances between 2006 and 2008. His career was handicapped by a string of injuries that prevented him consolidating his place as England's regular number nine. Perry is remembered at Dudley Kingswinford as having impressed everyone as a rooky colt on his first night at training by dictating tactics to players twice his age. He continued working in a full-time job until joining Bristol.

DK have always prided themselves on developing local talent. In 2001, they were Midland One champions and reached National Two North. In 1999 they reached the Intermediate Cup final.

The previous year, one of their players won £4.2m on the lottery. He is reported to have underwritten the club in recent seasons.

EARLSDON

THE COVENTRY SUBURB of Earlsdon has a distinguished history, not least because Frank Whittle, the inventor of the jet engine, was born in the area. Earlsdon RFC are the third oldest club in the city of Coventry. The original Earlsdon RFC was founded in the 1890s by Earlsdon Wesleyan Methodist Church but closed in 1900. Several years later, Earlsdon Boys Brigade reformed the rugby club. Initially Earlsdon RFC were a modest side. They improved considerably after World War One and played First XV fixtures against the best junior sides in Coventry.

Neil Back, the England and Lions flanker, began with Earlsdon, but subsequently joined Barker's Butts, Nottingham and Leicester. Their best known modern player is prop Carl Rimmer of Exeter Chiefs.

Earlsdon were promoted to Midland 2 in 2014.

(Thanks to Jack Carnall)

EDWARDIAN

"King Edward's School: an imposing and smoke begrimed stone pile, slap in the middle of the city."
Victor Downie

EDWARDIAN RFC WERE originally the Old Boys of King Edward's School, Birmingham. The club were one of the top sides in the Midlands until World War Two and the school was hugely influential in the region's education system.

The school could trace its origins to King Edward VI, who was one of the most remarkable figures in educational history. Despite dying young, he left a remarkable educational legacy in Birmingham. Edward came to the throne in 1548 and inherited a huge financial legacy from the sale of church land during the Reformation. The young king decided to use the money to found a series of schools across the Midlands; the most important of which was King Edward's School Foundation in Birmingham. The school grew in reputation and by 1889 was viewed as a model educational establishment.

The school authorities were asked by the local authority to organise the setting up of Birmingham's other grammar schools. The result was a series of King Edward Grammar Schools at Aston, Camp Hill and Five Ways modelled on the original King Edward's Grammar School. All the schools produced famous rugby sides who carry the 'Old Edwardians' name.

The original school building was on New Street in the heart of the city. The establishment seems to have been a bit grim. Victor Downie was a student between the wars: "Visits to the bog (toilet) carried the risk of premature demise. We were made aware that the great city stands upon the River Rea which was used by local factories for dumping inflammable material. The bog was set above a tributary of that far from mighty river. A casually dropped match was likely to cause an explosion."

The school began playing rugby in the early 1870s and a casual rugby side was formed by Old Boys to meet the School XV on an annual basis. The first side was officially formed at a meeting on the 26th June 1882 in the Governor's Room at the school. The founding father was Paddy Adams, who had been playing for Gloucester. Old Edwardians thus became the first Old Boys side outside of London.

The Old Boys rugby team had originally operated from Edgbaston using the Warwickshire Cricket Ground. They rose rapidly through the ranks of Midlands rugby and won the Midland Counties Cup in 1890 beating Burton-on-Trent in the final.

In the 1890s Old Edwardians had a nationwide fixture list, which included a variety of sides including Leicester, Swansea and Runcorn. Other teams weren't so impressed to be visiting Old Edwardians. In 1896 Bath complained about a nightmare journey through "an endless succession of suburban streets".

The outstanding sporting product of King Edward's School at this time was Bernard Oughtred (1880-1949), who played briefly for the club before moving back to his native Hartlepool, where he won six England caps with the Rovers club, but lost his place after he was blamed for the defeat to Wales in 1902.

Dr. Edward Assinder played for England in 1907 as the right centre. Assinder later became a top-class amateur golfer.

F.J. Breedon, Assinder's Old Edwardians wing partner, was a formidable competitor who was an England reserve and set the club's long-time record of 39 tries in a season. In 1913-14, another OE, Harold Harrison (1889-1940), won four caps whilst with United Services Portsmouth.

The club can claim to have been the backbone of the most unusual England international side of all time. The 1900 Olympics were held in Paris and the records show, "A French Rugby team overcame German and British Contingents to win the gold medal", which isn't the full story. The 1900 Olympics were poorly organised and not helped when the RFU refused a request to send an English XV to compete. The RFU pointed out that, at the time, French rugby was of a modest standard, the Olympics were a new idea and the France v England match was scheduled to be played on a Sunday. Eventually, an Old Edwardian player, with connections, persuaded the RFU to let him raise a team. The RFU dictated that the team had to fulfil their club commitments on the Saturday before the match and all the team had to be back in time for work on Monday morning. On Sunday, October 28 1900, the England XV lost 27-8 in front of 10,000 spectators. The side included H.S. Nicol, J.G. Wallis and V. Smith of OEs. The team were weary from playing the previous day and travelling on the overnight train to Paris. At least they took the Olympic silver medal. The British press were hostile to the team and branded them a disgrace, which was rather uncharitable.

OEs played at Kings Heath but 1925 saw the club playing at a greyhound track with a rugby pitch in the middle. Before that Old Edwardians played in Selly Oak and changed in a public house where the bathing facilities were half beer barrels filled with cold water.

In December 1926, Old Edwardians were awarded an England trial by accident when it was decided their ground could cope with more spectators than Moseley. OE's nomadic existence continued with occupation of a ground at Wheelers Lane, Kings Heath, followed by a move back to Edgbaston Cricket Ground. In 1959 a permanent home was found at Streetsbrook Road, Solihull.

In 1948 a sensational newcomer, Peter Jackson, helped OE record home and away victories over Moseley. Jackson was picked for an England trial in 1950 whilst with OEs, but had to join Coventry before he won a cap. Eventually he won 20 caps for his country between 1956 and 1963 and won Lions caps in 1958. At the same time, Brian Wightman won five England caps whilst with Moseley and Coventry after beginning his club rugby with OEs.

Times were changing, forcing the club to go open in 1968 as the post-war educational reforms saw the traditional supply of new talent falter. Results improved and in 1971-72 a record 27 victories were recorded, including the North Midlands Cup. The renaissance did not last and in 1977 the OE name was replaced by Edwardian FC.

In 1984 they played in OBs Merit Table and in 2011 were Junior Vase Finalists.

ESSINGTON

ESSINGTON RUFC WAS formed in 1997 by the merger of Wulfrun RUFC and Rubery Owen RFC. Wulfrun was formed in 1963. The Wolverhampton side enjoyed 20 years of success, and even produced a great player in Nick Jeavons, who was one of the game's outstanding England and Lions flankers. At the start of the 1980s Wulfrun were running four sides, but within a decade that had dwindled down to two.

Rubery Owen was an ex-works side. The Rubery Owen RFC had begun life in Walsall, where the company were the town's biggest employer. Their fortunes had faded as the supply of apprentices from the factory dried up. Initially a merger between the two clubs was blocked because Staffordshire and North Midlands RFUs could not make up their mind which county the club belonged to.

In 2009 Essington were Midland Six champions.

FIVE WAYS OLD EDWARDIANS

THE RUGBY CLUB with the oddest name is probably Five Ways OEs. The name comes from the club being the old boys of Five Ways King Edward's School in the centre of Birmingham.

The club was originally called Five Ways Grammar School Old Boys RFC and was founded on August 25th 1892 by the brothers Charles and Percy Bryant. The club had a long list of home pitches: Church Avenue, Harborne; Court Oak Road, Harborne; the School playing field at Portland Road; and Lordswood Road until, in 1934, they moved to Masshouse Lane.

Despite the school's links to Birmingham, the Club joined the Coventry and District RFU, who selected P.E. Bryant and J.W. MacIlwaine to play for a District XV who defeated mighty Coventry 10-0 in the 1895-96 season. In the 1901-02 season the Five Ways Second XV was unbeaten in club games, winning 11 and drawing 2, and scoring 179 points to their opponents' eight.

Eventually Five Ways entered the Midland Counties Cup competition, and on several occasions reached the third round. By the season of 1903-04, the club had made such progress that their fixture list included Burton, Leicester Stoneygate, Nottingham, Nuneaton, Rugby, Stratford and Wolverhampton.

Paul Gibbs became Five Ways' first international when he played for Australia against Scotland in 1966 at Murrayfield. Gibbs attended King Edward's Birmingham, but played for FWOE before emigrating to Australia in 1961.

The best player who played for Five Ways (and the first to win an England cap) was Keith Fielding, who went to the Grammar School before winning England junior honours and moving to Moseley and Loughborough University. He was picked for an England trial after three matches for Moseley. His England debut came in a game where England recorded their biggest win over France for 55 years. He later moved to Rugby League.

The club's best-known member is Peter Grace, who represented the Midlands and contributed hugely to rugby in the area.

In 2000, Five Ways were in North Midlands 1 but subsequently have slipped down the leagues.

KIDDERMINSTER CAROLIANS

THE WEST MIDLANDS town of Kidderminster is famous for carpets and its football team, Kidderminster Harriers FC. The Harriers were once a successful rugby union team despite starting life as an athletic club in the mid-1870s. There were several other rugby clubs in the town, including the Choir and a Kidderminster RFC.

The 'Harriers' had six very happy seasons playing rugby. They even provided two players, C. Barton and P. Goodwin, who in 1875 played for the West of England against Oxford University. In those far off days, the West of England encompassed any player of talent from Cornwall to Kidderminster. In 1884 Kidderminster Harriers got through to the 2nd Round of the Midland Counties Cup. Harriers switched to soccer shortly afterwards.

It was not until 1923 that rugby returned to Kidderminster when a town club was formed. They made rapid progress and W.E. Richardson of Kidderminster was the North Midlands hooker when the region lost to the second All Blacks touring team 40-3 in 1924, and T.L. Winwood from the club played for the North Midlands against the 1931 Springboks.

In 1937 another rugby club emerged in the town called the Old Carolians, who were the Old Boys team from King Charles the First Grammar School. The 1939-45 war saw the Carolians cease playing, but the Kidderminster club played on throughout the conflict. Carolians reformed in 1948 and, for many years, the annual Derby between OCs and Kidderminster was the highlight of the season.

The two sides had talked of an amalgamation and, although there were opponents in both camps, the merger eventually came to pass in 1969. The new club became Kidderminster Carolians RFC.

In the leagues, KCs were runners-up in North Midlands One in 1996-97 and undefeated champions the next year. Promoted to Midlands West Two, they were fourth in 1998-99, and then took the title the next time around. Kidderminster improved in the late 1990s and have been in the top North Midlands divisions. They were twice semi-finalists in the Junior Vase in the early 1990s.

The best known Kidderminster Carolian player in recent times was Neil Lynas, who moved to Moseley and was capped by England U21s in 1990.

(Thanks to Brian Gittins)

LEAMINGTON

"A pleasant town of abundant trees and un-faded Regency architecture."
Anon 1880

RUGBY PLAYERS (AND everyone else) down the ages owe a debt to Leamington, which was the world centre of the sanitary appliance industry in the Victorian era. Each year, inventors of sanitary devices headed to Leamington to put their appliances on display. The spa town was flushed with success in the 19th Century when royalty came to take the waters. Emperor Napoleon III lived in Leamington to escape "the madness of London".

Leamington Rovers RFC played for several seasons during the 1870s and were one of the earliest sides in South Warwickshire. Interest waned and the game was dormant throughout the district by 1900.

Rugby was played in the town during World War One when Dover College, one of the great rugby-playing schools, was evacuated from the South East. After the college left, a casual rugby side operated in Leamington in the 1920s, which led to the formation of Leamington RFU on 14th April 1926 by the Deputy Mayor of the town, G.W. Hawkins, who became the first President. A curious aspect of the formation was that several people involved with the new club had participated in the unsuccessful attempt to establish 'Northern Union Football' in Warwickshire before World War One. The matter was noted by the RFU, but not pursued. Leamington soon found a full fixture list against local junior clubs, including a certain Worcester RFC.

Leamington found life difficult, especially when two rival clubs emerged: Old Warwickians RFC and Old Leamingtonians. The three clubs talked about merging, but nothing ever seemed to happen, although OLs and Leamington played on adjacent pitches at Victoria Park in the town.

Leamington had the services of an international in 1949 when scrum-half A. Kelso Fulton played for the club whilst he was working locally as a doctor. He played briefly before returning home and being capped by Scotland in 1952 whilst with Edinburgh University.

Another international association came in 1951 when the All Blacks used Leamington's ground to train prior to the ABs v Midlands match.

In 1958, Leamington produced a genuine international in Keith Savage, who began in the First XV as a schoolboy and starred for Leamington when they won the 1961 Coventry Sevens. He later played for Northampton, England and the Lions. Other internationals associated with the club are Peter Preece (12 England caps) and Frank Wilson of Ireland, who played for several years whilst working in the area.

In 1968, Leamington finally got their own ground, which was christened 'Moorefield' in honour of Pip Moore who had done much to get the club on its feet. The ground was formally opened with a fixture against a Warwickshire XV.

The best-known players in recent times have been Craig Luxton (Harlequins and England U21) and Laurence Boyle (Leicester, Oxford University and England U21). Recently a couple of stalwarts, Alex Carroll and Matt Dale, played for Wales in a Touch Rugby World Cup.

The 75th anniversary season of 2001-02 was memorable as Leamington were Midland 1 (West) champions. The club made the record books in 2011 when it organised the world's biggest scrum, with 361 played involved.

Leamington RFC First XV

MALVERN

"Follow me lads, I'm right behind you."

Shaun Lancett

MALVERN IS FAMOUS for many reasons. Elgar, the great composer, lived here; Malvern College is a leading independent school and the town rugby club has been highly successful in recent times.

Rugby football was played in Malvern in the early years of the 20th century. The Club in its present form came about in 1934, when several of the town's worthies held an inaugural meeting at the Lyttleton Rooms to ratify the formation of Malvern RUFC.

Malvern RUFC began by playing around the Three Counties, then expanding to the Greater Birmingham area. MRFC became an established fixture for many teams, including the United (second XVs) of Gloucester, Cheltenham, Moseley and other top-class clubs of the time. Locally there was the 'Templars Trophy', where Malvern competed against other local sides like Tewkesbury, Evesham, Pershore and Ledbury.

The 1990s and 2000s were a golden era for Malvern. They were champions of North Midlands One (1994-95), of Midlands West One (1998-99) and of Midlands Two West (2000-01). The climb saw Malvern rise from the North Midlands league to reach Level 5 for several seasons in National 3 Midlands before

falling back to the Midland leagues. They were the Junior Shield champions in 1994 beating Old Hamptonians 8-6.

The best-known players to appear for the club are David Llewellyn (Wales), Ping (China), Bo Kristoffson (Sweden) and Tim Streather, who began at Malvern before joining Nottingham and Saracens.

MOSELEY

"The club who came back from the dead – twice."

John Beale

MOSELEY WERE ONE of the great English rugby sides of the 1900s who fell rather from grace at the end of the century. They were formed in October 1873 by members of the Havelock Cricket Club, who rapidly adopted the red and black colours that were to be inextricably associated with the club.

Initially, Moseley played both codes of football but settled on rugby. The club left the Havelock ground for St. Paul's Road, Camp Hill, but later moved to the Reddings. The first match played at the Reddings was a win over Leicester on the 6th October 1880. They were unbeaten from 1879 to 1882 over 54 matches, scoring 118 tries and conceding only seven.

The 1880s saw Moseley record two great results. In 1886 they beat Cardiff and in 1888 recorded the first defeat of the New

Zealand Maoris on their tour. The club's most famous player was full-back Fred Byrne, who won 13 England caps and was considered the best three-quarter in the Midlands.

Moseley were so strong they effectively composed the Midland Counties team in its earliest days and, as a club, dominated the Midlands Counties Cup with seven title wins in thirteen years. They also dominated Birmingham rugby and played an annual fixture against a Combined Birmingham Old Boys XV. This fixture was regarded as a blatant piece of player poaching and clubs like Old Edwardians boycotted the fixture.

In 1900 they provided four players J.H. Birtles, C.P. Deykin, M.W. Talbot and F.C. Bayliss for the England team who played France in the Olympic stadium. The Moseley Wanderers, as they styled themselves, were awarded the silver medal in the rugby section of the 1900 Olympics.

The most famous Moseley name to wear England colours was Peter Cranmer, who won 16 caps and was part of the England back line in the famous 1936 win over the All Blacks. Cranmer was born in Acocks Green in Birmingham. He first attracted attention at Oxford University and was quickly picked for the England team against Wales in 1934. The level of organisation in international rugby, in those far off days, can be gleaned from the fact that Cranmer and Ronald Gerrard of Bath were paired in the centre. At dinner the night before the match, Gerrard told Cranmer he didn't fancy playing opposite Claude Davey of Wales, who took a great deal of stopping. Cranmer suggested he and Gerrard swap places without consulting the selectors, or even the captain. They took the field in changed positions and helped England beat Wales. Cranmer kept his place for 16 consecutive England internationals between 1934 and 1938. His place in rugby history was guaranteed when he played in the victory over the 1936 New Zealand side and scored a drop goal. Cranmer also found time to play for Warwickshire County Cricket Club from 1938 to 1947.

Moseley were Birmingham's pre-eminent club throughout the 20th Century and drew talent from all over the area: Tom Pargetter (from Stratford-on-Avon), John Finlan (Old Salterians), Martin Cooper (Wolverhampton), Jon Webster (Walsall), Sam Doble (Wolverhampton) and Nigel Horton (Kings Norton) all moved to the Reddings before establishing themselves in the England team.

Two top-class internationals were lost to the paid ranks in the 1970s. Mike Coulman arrived at Moseley from Stafford and established himself as one of the best prop forwards around, winning nine England caps. He joined Salford RLFC in 1968. Keith Fielding, from Five Ways Old Edwardians, arrived at Moseley from Loughborough Colleges, where he had gained attention by scoring 11 tries in the 1970 Middlesex Sevens. Fielding won ten England caps between 1969 and 1972, but he followed Coulman to Salford RLFC and became a rugby league legend.

Despite these losses, Moseley still provided four players, Doble, Webster, Finlan and Cooper, to the 1971 England Centenary team.

In 1972 the Reddings saw the Midland Counties score a famous victory over the All Blacks. Moseley provided eight of the winning team. Midland Counties West may have been a rather contrived combination, but Moseley were also the backbone of the Warwickshire side who lost the 1972 County Championship to Gloucestershire at Twickenham.

At the time the club could field seven internationals and competed with Coventry for the title of West Midlands champions. They had reason to celebrate in 1973 when they played Fiji and the Barbarians in their Centenary year and won both matches. In 1976, they also took the Anglo-Welsh Trophy for the best results in a curiously organised merit table for the top sides on both sides of Offa's Dyke.

Moseley's facilities were, at the time, good by rugby club standards but behind the best. In 1985, they appointed a Commercial Manager, Greville Edwards, who had previously pioneered perimeter advertising. Edwards hired a portacabin as a 'hospitality suite' and introduced the idea of match sponsors. It was a million miles from Royal Ascot, but Edwards raised nearly £400,000 in his years of innovation.

The arrival of league rugby found Moseley slipping behind their rivals, who had bigger bank balances. Leicester, Northampton and Rugby were the premier sporting establishments in their own vicinity, whereas Moseley suffered because soccer is the major sport in the city of Birmingham and rugby was always a minor attraction. They found it increasingly difficult to attract international players in competition with their rivals in a market ruled by the chequebook. They were placed in the highest league in 1987 and held their own for four seasons until relegation occurred. They were a good side, but strictly Division Two with crowd attendances to match.

Moseley were striving to be part of the brave new world: trapped between its past and its future. Some members weren't too sure about the change. In 1993, they announced a switch from their traditional red-and-black hoops to rugby league style jerseys. The club committee were so horrified at the prospect that they had a whip round to buy a new set in the old colours.

The following year, the club tried to fund their professionalism by selling the Reddings whilst keeping the lease. The first professional club went into administration in 1998 and a second club struggled on for four years to achieve financial stability.

An offer came to take the club to Oxford, which proved the catalyst for a consortium of Moseley members to fight to keep the club in Birmingham. The club survived in Birmingham under its own name in National Division One and even won the new National Trophy in 2009.

On May 6th 2010, Moseley bade farewell to the Reddings with a match against Worcester, who were now the leading club in the West Midlands and who fielded many ex-Moseley players. The Reds and Blacks are still in the city and now installed at their new home at Billesley Common.

In 2008, Moseley came to an agreement with Gloucester for dual-registration for youngsters. One of the first was Henry Trinder, who went on to play for England.

NORTH MIDLANDS

THE NORTH MIDLANDS RFU emerged in 1920 from the demise of the old Midland Counties Union, which had represented the whole region since the emergence of county rugby.

'North Midlands' originally defined an area covering Greater Birmingham, Derbyshire, Staffordshire and Worcestershire. It became something of a misnomer in 1926 when Derbyshire joined Notts and Lincs to form a new 'county'; then, in 1964 Staffordshire broke away. Their place was taken by the contiguous counties of Herefordshire and Shropshire.

The new North Midlands side reached the County Championship final in 1921-22 after winning the Midland Group, but lost 19-0 to Gloucestershire at Villa Park. Results in subsequent years were disappointing, but at least they had lucrative fixtures against the 1924 All Blacks, 1927 Waratahs and the 1931 Springboks. All three matches were lost.

The North Midlands weren't blessed with great stars, but at least Peter Cranmer (England) and Gwyn Bayliss (Wales) made themselves available. Bayliss was a full-back more associated with Newport and Wolverhampton.

A real star appeared in 1948 with the emergence of Old Edwardians winger Peter Jackson. In 25 games for North Midlands, Jackson scored 20 tries, including five in one match against Leicestershire.

The 1950s were a depressing period for North Midlands, although two of their captains were recognised by the England selectors – prop Geoff Vaughan (Old Luctonians) played in all three England trials in 1954 and number eight Brian Wightman (Camp Hill OE and Moseley) became North Midlands first 'home-produced' cap in 1959.

The long-awaited renaissance materialised in 1964-65 when, captained by flanker Don Abbey (Old Centrals and Moseley), North Midlands were joint top of the group with Warwickshire, who, however, won the play-off. From this North Midlands XV, winger Martin Hale and prop Mike Coulman (both Moseley) were subsequently capped by England, scrum-half Bob Lloyd-Jones (Stourbridge and Moseley) was travelling reserve for Wales and winger Keith Hatter (Old Dixonians and Moseley) and hooker Don Lane (Moseley) had England trials.

The availability of floodlights brought renewed interest in Midland County rugby in the 1960s as mid-week fixtures meant more top-class players were available. Fly-half John Finlan (Old Salteians and Moseley), winger Keith Fielding (Five Ways OE and Moseley) and lock Nigel Horton (City Police and Moseley) played together for England in 1969.

Midland Counties (West) made history in 1972 when they beat the All Blacks at Moseley. Seven North Midlanders – Malcolm Swain, John Finlan, Les Smith, Nigel Horton, Ian Pringle and John White (all Moseley) and Trevor Corless (Birmingham) – were in the victorious side.

The upturn in North Midlands' fortunes arose because Moseley were at their zenith. Besides the contribution from the Reddings, the North Midlands had leaders in Corless and Mark Keyworth who both played for England. The reward came in 1977-78 when they finally reached the County Championship final for the first time since 1922, coincidentally against Gloucestershire. Fortunately they won 10-7.

SHREWSBURY

"Football is a game more fit for farmboys and labourers than young gentlemen."
Samuel Butler (Headmaster of Shrewsbury School 1798-1836)

SHREWSBURY RUFC WAS founded in 1908 and can claim to be the oldest rugby club in Shropshire. There was an earlier Shrewsbury RFC, who were a highly-successful club as there are records of Burton-on-Trent playing Shrewsbury in 1871-72. Little else is known of the Victorian club beyond that they followed so many of their contemporaries into oblivion.

The current Shrewsbury side owe their origins to an animated conversation in the now demolished George Hotel in the city between Freddie Richards, Bill Jones and a Mr Deakin, which resulted in the group raising a side. They rented a farmer's field at Sutton for a fixture against Stratford. The match result has been lost, which may not be a bad thing as Stratford were a good side at the time.

The club didn't stay long at Sutton before playing at a number of grounds, including Upper Road in Meole Brace, Longden Road and at a borrowed pitch at Shrewsbury School. Eventually, in 1946, they 'settled' at West Midlands Showground, off the Berwick Road. The 18 years spent at the Showground were instrumental in putting Shrewsbury on the rugby map, both in playing and financial terms.

Geographically Shrewsbury were well placed and able to attract fixtures from the Midlands and the North West. They established an excellent fixture list, including Birkenhead Park, Orrell, Stourbridge, Walsall, Winnington Park, Wolverhampton and Worcester. By 1959, Shrewsbury were a leading side in Shropshire and helped start the county union.

The best known player associated with Shrewsbury RUFC is Haydn Mainwaring, who had been a distinguished full-back for Swansea and Wales. He was working in the area and delighted the club by playing for several seasons in the twilight of his playing career. Mainwaring has a place in rugby history because of one tackle. During the 1961 Barbarians v South Africa game, Mainwaring produced a try-saving tackle which denied the Springboks the honour of being unbeaten on tour. It was described as 'the tackle of the century' at the time.

Shrewsbury's playing successes formed a sound basis for fundraising and the club was able to purchase its own ground at Sundorne Castle, build a clubhouse in 1964 and erect floodlights in 1968.

Rugby success is cyclical and the heady times of the Sixties gave way to topsy-turvy results in the subsequent decades. The introduction of league rugby found Shrewsbury in North Midlands One, but latterly they slipped into Midlands West One.

SHREWSBURY SCHOOL

THE FAMOUS OLD school of Shrewsbury is noted for its support of Association Football, which isn't surprising given that it had its own ancient football game called 'Dowlings' which was played into the late 19th Century. Dowlings prohibited handling of the football. It was originally an informal activity and did not become a recognised school sport until Dr. Kennedy became Headmaster in 1836, and he provided a field for the game to be played on Coton Hill. One of his successors, Dr. Butler, considered the game "only fit for butcher boys" and removed it from the curriculum.

In 1877 the school adopted association football. Dowlings' however, continued for a decade before being totally replaced by the new game.

Despite its association with soccer, Shrewsbury School produced two outstanding rugby internationals. John Hirsch (1883-1958) attended Shrewsbury before emigrating to South Africa and playing for the Springboks, whilst Claude Davey of Sale and England ranks amongst the greatest centres of all time.

SHROPSHIRE RFU

ALTHOUGH THE SHROPSHIRE RFU was officially formed in 1959, a Shropshire Wanderers side played Hereford in 1873 under the laws of rugby. It took another 36 years later for club rugby to be established: Shrewsbury Rugby Club was founded in 1909, followed by Ludlow (1933), Old Whitchurchians (1936), Newport (1946), Telford (formerly Wellington Hornets) in 1960, Bridgnorth (1962), Oswestry revived (1976) and Market Drayton (1980).

By 1959, Shrewsbury were the leading county side, and with the help of their secretary, Ted Paulett, the seeds were sown to start the county union. Clubs were invited to forward names for consideration for a trial game against Shrewsbury.

Shropshire looked around for their first full game. They were offered a 'friendly' against the great county side from Gloucestershire, which was politely declined for obvious reasons. F.J.D. (Doug) Thompson of Whitchurch eventually settled for North Wales, who Shropshire overcame 13-5, with tries by John Burgess (2) and Martin Thouless, and Peter McGowan kicking two conversions.

The side was: E. Bowen (Shrewsbury), G. Acton (Ludlow), B. Watson-Jones (Newport, captain), C. Lewis (Ludlow), J. Burgess (Newport), A.W. Kerr (Harper Adams Agricultural College), A.J. Hern (Ludlow), M.H. Thouless (Newport), Sam Eccleston (Old Whitchurchians), J. Hollins (Newport), P. McGowan (Shrewsbury), A.J. Gibson (Newport), Duncan Wood (Shrewsbury), M. Rainsford (Newport), and R.N. Hern (Ludlow). During the season Shropshire used 29 players. In the last two games of the season, Clive Ashby, a South African at Harper Adams College, played for the county. He went on to play for Wasps, Barbarians and England.

The first season ended with two wins and two losses plus a draw from the five outings. The following season all games were won and in the next year Ian Beer (Cambridge, Harlequins and England and headmaster at Ellesmere College) appeared three times but never actually played for a Shropshire club. Tony Gladdy joined Sam Eccleston in the county side in the second season.

In the early 1960s the county struggled, achieving only one win in four seasons. The players of this era included: S.C. Lister, E.G. Mackereth, K. Byers, R. Bland (Shrewsbury), P. Hood (Ludlow), P. Bromley (Wellington Hornets), P. Mellor (Whitchurch), R. Turner (Bridgnorth), G. Malpass, J. Burgess, D. Brotherton and M. Talbot (Newport).

The Birmingham Post Six Counties Championship was formed in 1972 by Shropshire, Worcestershire, Herefordshire, Derbyshire, Greater Birmingham, South Warwickshire and North Warwickshire, which brought a revival of enthusiasm and interest in the county scene. The new competition brought a new meaning and challenge to each game, with the winners receiving a pennant and a barrel of beer – this proved sufficient incentive to the competitive spirit of the players. Shropshire had to wait until 1978-79 to grab the Six Counties honours. The next season the county again took the title.

Shropshire county rugby never reached these levels of success again, and of the 24 games played between 1980 and 1984 only four wins were recorded. The advent of the league system in 1987 brought greater demands on players, with the ambitions of clubs and players over-riding their county commitments. A devalued six counties programme was reduced to three and national league players ceased participating.

(Thanks to Sam Eccleston)

STAFFORD

STAFFORD IS A North Midlands industrial town with a rugby club dating back to 1876. The first game was a victory over Newport (Shropshire). Down the years, the club have played at a variety of grounds, including Rickerscote Road and Silkmore Lane, before moving to their Newport Road ground.

The club's finest era was the 1960s, when a number of internationals represented the club. The best home-produced player was Mike Coulman from Risingbrook School. A mobile prop, Coulman won nine England caps whilst with Moseley in the mid-1960s before joining Salford RLFC in 1968, where he added three Great Britain caps to his list of honours. He was a policeman who won sporting honours at rugby, boxing and athletics.

During this era, Stafford attracted three other internationals: Andy Hancock and Peter Larter of England, plus the giant Scotland lock Peter Stagg. Hancock played for Stafford for three seasons in the early 1970s, while Peter Larter had a spell with the club. In the days before player registration, Larter joined Lichfield from Northampton, but the Saints would ring Lichfield occasionally on a Friday night to 'borrow' the player back.

Currently Stafford play in Midland Five West (North)

STOURBRIDGE

"Stourbridge is too grand to be part of the Black Country."
Paul Collins

STOURBRIDGE IS A sprawling town on the North West side of Birmingham which is famous for glassmaking. It owes much of its importance to its place on the ancient main road from London to Holyhead.

The first Stourbridge RFC was founded in 1876, but like the majority of rugby clubs in the area, it didn't last long. They were however the first side to play Coventry at the Butts in 1880.

Stourbridge re-emerged after the First World War and made rapid strides as the social base of rugby football expanded beyond the public schools, which had originally supplied most of the players.

1933-34 was an outstanding season for Stourbridge, with only three defeats in 26 matches. The list of Stourbridge players who have represented the North Midlands is long and distinguished. Their first Stourbridge representative was Ronnie Bird, who was later captain of Worcestershire CCC.

The rugby team originally shared premises with the local cricket club at Amblecote, before moving to leafy Stourton on the outskirts of the town. The superb facilities attracted the attention of the England selectors, who used Stourton Park for 'get-togethers' in the days of amateur rugby. In 1979 England switched a training session to Stourbridge when Coventry was waterlogged. 2,000 people took the opportunity to watch the floodlit training session.

In the 1980s, Stourbridge produced two top-class players in Peter Shillingford and Huw Davies. Shillingford was a massive

Huw Davies

lock who played for Moseley and a number of other Midlands clubs in a 20-year career that included several England trials. Davies was more fortunate and eventually won 20 England caps.

At the advent of league rugby, Stourbridge lost only six times in two seasons and were 1989 North Midlands (North) champions. In 1993, they reached Round 4 of the National Knockout Cup, where they lost to Orrell.

Well-known players who have played for Stourbridge include Kevin Whitley, who captained the club in 1998 after playing for Canada, and, in 2010, Springbok international Thinus Delport as player/coach

It is fair to say Stourbridge's golden days have come in the 21st Century when they spent eleven years in National One, competing against better-funded clubs. They were relegated to National Two in 2012, but have been up with the contenders for a return to National One ever since.

2006 saw a cautionary tale when Stourbridge player James Lloyd Jones hurt his neck playing for the North Midlands at Twickenham. He treated the neck pain with paracetamol for six months and carried on playing. Unable to shake off the injury, he went to see the doctor who diagnosed a broken neck! He never played again.

STRATFORD-UPON-AVON

THERE IS NO clear date for the founding of Stratford-upon-Avon RFC, but we know that a side from the famous old town competed in the South Midlands from the 1880s. Stratford rapidly became one of the top sides in the region.

The first known captain was Archie Flower, who had won a Rowing Blue at Cambridge and who narrowly missed a Rugby Blue. Flower was appointed captain in 1887 and led Stratford in a narrow defeat by Coventry at Christmas of that year. The following year W.H. Harrison played at three-quarter for the Midland Counties against the Maoris.

The first international associated with Stratford was Rev Richard Cattell (1871-1948), who began his career with the Warwickshire club. Cattell won a Rugby blue at Oxford before joining Blackheath, with whom he won seven England caps at half-back.

By 1900 Cattell was gone (to Moseley) and rugby in the town had virtually disappeared, principally due to the rise of soccer and the effects of the Boer War. Even the club's ground was lost as support dwindled down to a handful of enthusiasts who could only organise a few fixtures.

When the Boer War was over, Stratford re-established their place in Midlands rugby. In 1907-08, they won the Midland Counties Cup, beating Nuneaton in the final, and provided four players to the region's team. The best known Stratford player of the era was Ronny Rose, a full-back who played for the Midlands against the 1905 All Blacks.

Before World War One, Stratford offered visiting players a night's B&B at the Swan's Nest for 50p. The hotel owner was a keen supporter of Stratford. His 'ham-and-egg' teas were renowned throughout Midland rugby. You could eat as much as you wanted for 8p!

Sadly, the 1920s saw Stratford back in dire straits when a schism divided the club. The Old Boys of King Edward VI School, Stratford (whose pupils included William Shakespeare some 350 years earlier) broke away from the town club. Contemporary accounts suggest the public schoolboys considered the town club to be "too rough" for their liking. Whatever the reason, a once top-class side became two second-class clubs.

It was 1946 before the two sides reconciled their differences. The re-united club decided to purchase Peacecroft, the town's home ground. They needed a clubhouse and heard Old Edwardians of Birmingham were disposing of their clubhouse. They sent a party to dismantle OE's pavilion, which was moved lock, stock and barrel to Peacecroft.

The Bards continued to produce good players who usually migrated to bigger clubs. In 1948, Doug Kear was capped by Gloucestershire but limited his top-class playing opportunities by staying at Stratford and declining the chance to join Coventry.

Tom Pargeter began at Peacecroft before joining Moseley and Coventry and winning three England caps in 1962.

More recent honours have gone to Stratford members: Nathan Webber (England A), Howard Stanton (British Virgin Isles), Richard Grey (Scotland U18) and Adam Jeffries (England U18).

Tom Pargeter

TRINITY GUILD

TRINITY GUILD RFC was formed in 1898 by members of the Young Men's Bible Classes at Holy Trinity Church, Coventry under the unlikely title of 'Trinity Guild Young Men's Guild and Bible Class RFC', which was rapidly changed for obvious reasons to Trinity Guild RFC. The original title of Trinity Guild refers to the Guild of Coventry Merchants formed in 1364. Later the Guild were to play an important part in running the city.

The first secretary, Mr Alfred Odell, was a product of King Henry VIII School, which is one of the top rugby schools in Coventry. The school was to prove a fertile recruiting ground for Trinity Guild players.

The original colours were navy blue but were replaced with claret, old gold and blue in 1900. The new club improved rapidly and soon had fixtures against some of the best Midland sides, notably the Old Edwardian clubs. Gradually Guild were amongst the top sides in Coventry and in 1912 got a fixture against the mighty town club, losing 28-3. The fixture continued between the two sides until 1932, but invariably ended in big defeats for Guild.

Guild's first ground was at Kingfield, but the ground was lost to building in 1919. Alfred Odell found a field adjacent to Coundon Road Station, with an old cowshed which acted as a home changing room. An elderly lady caretaker filled half a dozen baths with a couple of inches of cold water, topped up with a kettleful of hot water. By contrast, visiting sides had the comparative luxury of using the facilities of the old Grammar School, which was a mile away.

The early 1920s were a bad time for Trinity Guild. In 1923-24 they won only six matches. In an attempt to restore their fortunes, the club adopted a youth policy and improved results followed. They also lost the ground at Coundon Road Station and had to share with Barker's Butts, followed by the use of a field at Allesley Old Road opposite the Maudsley pub, and then a move to the Memorial Park. The facilities at Memorial Park included running water straight from the local brook and sanitation arrangements were similarly basic.

Alfred Odell died in 1941 after half a century of service. Four years later the club reformed after the Second War with a meeting at the Globe pub. The Memorial pitch was gone and even the old Grammar School was no longer available. A field was found on Bennetts Road, Keresley, complete with cow shed with cows.

The Memorial Park became available again for 1947-48, and was a vast improvement on Bennett Road. A Nissan hut was acquired and the club joined the RFU, having previously only been affiliated through the county union. It took another 20 years before a new clubhouse was opened in 1968. The club's 70th anniversary in 1969 was celebrated with a match against a Warwickshire XV.

Perhaps the best player produced by Trinity Guild was Jim Broderick, who made his debut at the Trinity as a 13-year-old before playing over 350 times for Coventry.

In 1999, Trinity celebrated their centenary with a match against Warwickshire. Currently the club play in the Midlands leagues.

(Thanks to John Collings)

WALSALL

WALSALL ARE A remarkable club because they have fielded a string of internationals despite their middle-ranking status. The club was formed in 1922 and has always had a long connection with Welsh exiles through the West Midlands Sports College, a Walsall-based teacher training college. The college operated on similar lines to Loughborough Colleges and St. Luke's Exeter. Today WMSC is part of the University of Wolverhampton.

The best player to come from the college who appeared for Walsall was Terry Cobner, who captained Wales and the Lions in the 1970s. A contemporary of Cobner for Wales and Walsall was Paul Ringer, an abrasive flanker who is best remembered for being sent off in the 1980 England v Wales game, an incident that presented the Whites with victory and, ultimately, the Grand Slam.

Other Welsh caps who briefly appeared for Walsall were local boys Rupert Moon and Colin Charvis. Moon was highly regarded in English rugby before joining Llanelli and qualifying for Wales by residence. Colin Charvis migrated to Wales and eventually became Wales captain and a Lions flanker.

Apart from the training college, the club's other source was Queen Mary's Grammar School, which produced Jan Webster, winner of 11 England caps around the late 1960s. Webster began as a soccer player with Aston Villa before playing scrum-half for Walsall, Staffordshire and Moseley. He suffered at the hands of the England selectors but played in the team that beat New Zealand in Wellington in 1971 – the first away international victory over the All Blacks by a Home country.

The best-known player at Walsall in recent times was Richard Mills, a durable fly-half who topped the English point-scoring charts in the early 1990s. He scored over 2,500 points for Walsall, including 28 tries, 375 conversions and 477 penalties.

JAN WEBSTER

A curious international was Luis Crisculo of Argentina, who briefly appeared for the club in 1990s.

In 2002 Walsall were unlucky to be relegated from National 3 North after the RFU decided, on previous results, they would have been relegated if the foot and mouth epidemic hadn't disrupted the season. They dropped into Midland One and, briefly, into Midland Two.

WASPS

"We needed to find a 365 days a year income for Wasps."
Derek Richardson

WASPS EMERGED IN 1867 from a schism within Hampstead FC (later Harlequins). William and Fred Alford had a disagreement with William Tichener of Quins, which caused a contingent of Hampstead players to leave and form Wasps.

All the founders were old boys of Merchant Taylors School. Fred and William Alford, R.S. and H.G Brown and J & A.S. Sarl. The Alfords were medical students at Middlesex Hospital (later University College Hospital). The club's first meeting was held in the Alford's house at Haverstock Hill, followed by another meeting at Eton and Middlesex Tavern. Wasps were invited to the inaugural meeting of the RFU, but their representative went to the wrong hostelry.

In 1879, Dr J.M. Biggs was the first international to play for Wasps when he played for England at The Oval in London. Another prominent early Wasp was G.H. Harnett, who instigated the Kent County Cup. He later managed the 1908 British team which toured New Zealand and Australia.

Wasps led a nomadic existence until 1923 when they moved into Sudbury. Between the wars, Wasps ran 14 sides, with selection carried out weekly in an upstairs room of the Shakespeare Inn on Regents Street. The first team captain always sat at the head of the table.

R.M. Sawyer was First XV captain from 1926 to 1935 – the first golden era for Wasps. He played 301 consecutive games for the First XV. In 1923-24, the club won 20 of 24 matches; in 1929-30 they won 24 of 30, and the following season they were unbeaten, winning 28 and drawing two of 30 matches and scoring 530 points. In 1930-31, the club won 28 of 30 – only Catford Bridge and Sidcup got pointless draws. Despite being ignored by the England selectors, Wasps were the best side in London in 1936-37. They could, however, boast two of the best Welsh players of all time in Vivian Jenkins and Harry Bowcott.

The club carried on after the outbreak of World War Two. In November 1940, a German bomb spoilt the post-match celebrations. Besides blowing out the clubhouse windows, a large crater appeared in the corner of one of the pitches. The following Saturday, Wasps played St. Mary's Hospital – bomb crater and all.

After the war, Wasps finally began to provide internationals, beginning with Patrick Sykes, who achieved seven England caps at scrum-half between 1948 and 1952. Under Sykes' captaincy,

Ted Woodward, John Herbert, Peter Yarranton and Andy Hurst all won international caps.

When Peter Yarranton took over as captain, he led Wasps to 26 wins in 35 matches, allowing the Sudbury club to reclaim the title of London's best. Peter Yarranton had a 50-year association with Wasps despite arriving at Sudbury with zero rugby experience. He is reputed to have told a club official that he was 'a scrum-half' as it was the only position he knew. Four years later, he won the first of five caps.

Two of the best scrum-halves of the era were Clive Ashby and Dick Kent, who competed for the club's No. 9 jersey. Ashby was understudy to Dick Kent. The club was bemused when the understudy Ashby was picked for England and Dick Kent was never selected. At the time, Ron Syrett was a tough flanker who won 11 England caps.

Unfortunately the club's fortunes declined in the following decade as many of their players retired at the same time. Fortunes improved in the 1970s with the recruitment of a host of top players, notably Tony Richards, Ken Moss, Roger Uttley and Nigel Horton. They were augmented by All Blacks Mark Taylor and Kim Fawcett. Uttley captained England and was first choice flanker for the 'Invincible Lions' of 1974.

In the two-year period between 1983 and 1985, eight Wasps players represented England: Maurice Colclough, Nick Stringer, Huw Davies, Nigel Melville, Andy Dunn, Rob Lozowski, Mark Bailey and Paul Rendell. Later in the decade, the club had Kevin Simms, Fran Clough, Jeff Probyn, Dean Ryan, Chris Oti and Steve Bates all picked for England.

England representation reached its peak in May 1989 when Rob Andrew captained England against Romania, David Pegler captained the England B side against Spain and Steve Pilgrim captained the under 21 team against Romania. All the teams won that day. Later, Steve Pilgrim was banned sine die by the RFU for having a trial with a rugby league club. The RFU described the lifetime ban as Pilgrim's own fault as he had disqualified himself by contravening regulations.

Wasps entered the professional era in great shape with an excellent blend of youth and experience, including the young Lawrence Dallaglio, who was developing into a world-class flanker. The teenage Dallaglio left Ampleforth and was looking for a club. He opted for Wasps because they were at the top of Level 1. He chose well.

In 1996-97, Wasps won the first championship title of the professional era and the National KO Cup under the ownership of Chris Wright of Chrysalis Records. They changed the club name to London Wasps.

Chris Wright fought hard to put Wasps in the vanguard of the Premiership. He appointed Warren Gatland as coach from 2002 to 2005, with Shaun Edwards, a rugby league legend, as his assistant. Gatland was later to become Head Coach of Wales and the British Lions.

Wasps proved the best team in Europe. They won the Premiership play-off title, but had to survive high drama in the European Cup final. Against a Toulouse team of high quality, the Wasps lived on scraps and scored on virtually every trip into Toulouse territory. The French turned the screw in the closing stages and levelled the score in the last minute. Wasps hung on grimly. Rob Howley, the great Wasps and Welsh scrum-half, pounced on a French mistake to snatch victory for Wasps. Champions of Europe, but only just.

They won the Heineken Cup in 2003-04 and 2006-07, the Anglo-Welsh Cup in 1999, 2000 and 2006 and the Aviva Premiership in 1990, 1997, 2003, 2004, 2005 and 2008.

When Warren Gatland returned to New Zealand, the legendary coach Ian McGeechan replaced him as Wasps Director of Rugby. McGeechan led the successful Lions tours to Australia in 1989 and South Africa in 1997 and the honours continued to roll in. The star names continued to play at Adams Park: Kyran Bracken, Phil Vickery, Simon Shaw, Matt Dawson, Rik Flutey, James Haskell and a surprising name in Serge Betson, an iconic French flanker. Serge admitted he was astonished how thorough Wasps did their match preparation. At the same time, the club has produced outstanding young players such as Joe Launchbury and Joe Simpson for England.

In 2008, Chris Wright stepped down, having led Wasps to eleven trophies in eleven years. Today the club is owned by businessman Derek Richardson. At the time, Wasps still played at Sudbury, which wasn't suited to big crowds. At first Wasps played at Loftus Road, QPR's ground, but later moved to Adams Park, the home of Wycombe Wanderers FC. They bought a stake in the Ricoh Arena in Coventry, but obviously there was a huge problem for long-standing supporters who had a near 200-mile round trip to home matches. The club

The Ricoh Arena

said that at Adams Park they were losing £3million a season. Within months of moving in, Wasps were selling out their new 32,000-seater stadium. The razzamatz of match day and a top-class team rapidly won the hearts of local rugby fans.

(Thanks to Melissa Platt)

WHITCHURCH

WHITCHURCH (POP 8,934) IS an old country town situated in the northern part of Shropshire on the Welsh border. The original rugby club was Whitchurch Old Grammarians RFC, which was formed in September 1936 for former pupils of Whitchurch Grammar School (founded 1550). The driving force was Johnnie Johnson, the maths master at the school, who joined the staff in 1926 from Totnes in Devon and produced the first school team in season 1931-32. The Old Boys XV captained by Eric Lewis, a local estate agent, played their first fixture on 24th October 1936, defeating Shrewsbury 20-6.

The club reformed after the war in 1947 and changed their name to Old Whitchurchians. They produced an England trialist in Peter Davies, who scored a try in the 1947 trial at Birkenhead Park but never made the national team.

In the 1970s the club started their dominance of the Shropshire scene by winning their first ever county cup, a process they repeated on twelve further occasions, with complete dominance in the 1980s. The county floodlit trophy (now lapsed) was gained in 1971, 1986 and 1987.

The traditional link with the Whitchurch school, now Sir John Talbot's Technical College, sadly diminished, whilst at the same time there was an influx of players from schools such as Heber School at Malpas. With the changes, a decision was made to change the club's name to Whitchurch RFC, although the school's Talbot emblem was retained.

In 1987 Whitchurch were placed in North Midlands I of the Courage leagues and an official club coach was appointed in 1988-89. The last game of the season in April 1991 brought promotion to Midlands II West, and 1992 they were admitted to the newly-formed Midlands Two League. In 1997-98 an undefeated league season brought promotion to National League Two North. This position was maintained for four seasons, but cruelly, after 10 victories and a draw from 26 league outings and pressure from northern clubs coming down, Whitchurch dropped back to Midlands One along with three other teams.

They won the North Midlands Cup in 1997 (beating Worcester 18-17) and again in 1999 (Stourbridge 19-15), being the first ever Shropshire club to reach the finals.

Whitchurch still proudly run four senior fifteens and have a side competing successfully in the Lancashire/Cheshire senior Colts league, and themselves organise an under 19 tournament. A thriving mini, junior and colts section have been running since 1975 and attracts over 200 youngsters, who vie for dressing rooms with a strong Ladies XV, started in 1992, on Sunday mornings.

A large, well-furnished clubhouse with four adjacent pitches completes a very successful and ambitious set-up at Edgeley Park, Whitchurch.

In 2005, the club were switched from the Midlands to the Northern leagues.

WOLVERHAMPTON

OFFICIAL RECORDS SHOW Wolverhampton RFC was born in the Star & Garter pub, Victoria Road, Tettenhall in 1875 with a meeting attended by G Walton-Walker, his cousins Harry and Frank Walton (the first captain), Charles Mander, William Underhill and brothers Edward and Arnold Crane. The Waltons, Mander and Underhill were all Old Rugbeians.

This is contradicted by Harry Walton's 1937 account of events. Walton recorded that he, his brother and Mander had already organised a team in 1874, which played at Riches Street cricket ground. Certainly WRFC were playing the following season and Mander and Walton laid out the rugby ground the following year.

The original ground was a cricket ground near the Halfway House pub on the Tettenhall Road. Playing with 20-a-side, Wolverhampton's earliest opponents were Kidderminster, Stafford, Coventry and the local grammar school. Fixtures were also played against Tettenhall College, who also supplied players for the new club.

The club was firmly rooted in leafy Tettenhall, where they laid down firm roots at Daneshill Road, despite a brief spell at the old Racecourse.

Wolverhampton played in the 1884 Midland Counties Cup and, by 1897, were an outstanding side that comfortably defeated Aston OE in the first round of this competition.

The first notable player to emerge from WRFC was Arnold Crane, who won Midland Counties Honours in 1882-83 and became RFU President. The 1890s saw WRFC as a major force, with Rev E.M. Baker (Oxford U & England), Rev A.H. Colville (Oxford U), W. Attlee (Cambridge U) and C. Hamilton-Shaw (Moseley & England), although they all are usually associated with other larger clubs.

Wolverhampton RFC were being pushed into the shadows in the years before World War One by the emergence of Wolverhampton Wanderers Football Club, who became one of the giants of the round ball game.

Between the wars, the club welcomed such names as Jim Timmis and Gwyn Bayliss. Timmis played for the Midlands against the 1924 New Zealand team, the 1927 Australasians and the 1931 Springboks. Jim was the best of five Timmis brothers who all played for Wolverhampton; he played 37 times for the North Midlands. Bayliss joined Wolverhampton in 1934 from Pontypool with a single Welsh cap, although he was Welsh reserve on 15 occasions. He was an elegant full-back with a languid approach to the game.

In the mid 1930s, the fixture list included Handsworth, Pontypridd and Ebbw Vale, as well as old adversaries such as Stoke, Walsall, Burton and Stafford. In 1935-36 they won 20 of 23 games.

World War Two saw WRFC disband, but a club called Wingfoot RFC played occasionally. They were mostly employees of the Goodyear Rubber Company, who were one of the district's largest employers.

The immediate post-war years saw WRFC going well and they were able to field A. Dorward and J.L. Allan of Scotland. The club bought the Castlecroft Road ground, adjacent to the famous Wolverhampton Wanderers soccer training ground and where they still play, finally leaving Danescourt Road in 1950. Three Nissan huts were erected as changing rooms and a clubhouse was built with a £30,000 contribution from Ansells Brewery. The ground was opened on 25th November 1950 (the 75th anniversary) with a match against a Staffordshire President's XV, which was won 6-3.

The Castlecroft purchase was ultimately a great success but left the club parlous for some years and money was unavailable for other work, such as pitch or clubhouse improvement. Despite the hard times, the club kept up good performances on the field and produced a number of players who won honours, notably Jim Cooper (Lancashire), Gerry Jones (Staffordshire) and Ron Bowen (North Midlands).

The new clubhouse was officially opened in September 1962 with a match against a Gwyn Bayliss International XV, who fielded many of the best players of the day, including Phil Horrocks-Taylor, Trevor Wintle, David Perry and Peter Robbins. The result was a defeat 25-6.

The 1960s were a time of great success as good young players emerged from the local schools. In 1961-62, 32 of 43 matches were won despite a poor start to the season. At the end of the decade a string of top-class players passed through Castlecroft en route to Moseley, including Martin Cooper and Sam Doble. Cooper, a leggy kicking fly-half, won five England caps whilst with Moseley but had his first England trial whilst with WRFC. Sam Doble, a tall full-back, was amongst England's best in that position until he died of cancer whilst in his prime. His death generated real sadness in the game and was commemorated with a televised charity match at Moseley, which featured all the best British players.

Doble (later of Moseley and England) once got to Exeter and found he'd forgotten his rugby boots. He tried several pairs of boots before eventually taking the field in his shoes. He still kicked immaculately, including a 50-yard penalty.

Sam Doble

When the Courage leagues were born, Wolverhampton found itself in Midlands Division One. The Staffordshire Cup was finally won in 1988, but the following season the team was relegated to Division Two. At the end of the 1991-92 season, the club was promoted into Midlands Division One again. Since then the club has fallen back somewhat due to financial pressures in the professional era. In 1998-99 they were relegated to Midlands Division 2. They are currently in Midlands 3 West.

WORCESTER WARRIORS

"There is nothing magic about the word Leicester or Gloucester that gives them a divine right to the best players."

Cecil Duckworth

WORCESTER IS A cathedral city on the banks of the River Severn. In the 19th Century, the city had two rugby-playing schools in Worcester Royal Grammar School and the King's School. King's adopted its own version of football in the 1860s using a round ball. Their game was based on charges by the heaviest boys and bore a strong resemblance to rugby. King's soon switched to rugby and were a major force in Midlands rugby until 1892, when they switched once more to soccer. The Royal Grammar School's headmaster was the Rev. Francis Ele, an old Rugbeian, which accounts for that school's long-term preference for rugby.

Amongst the founders of Worcester RFC was Walter Goodall George (1858-1943), one of the foremost athletes of the 19th Century. Goodall George held the world mile record for half a century. He married the daughter of the owner of Royal Worcester Porcelain.

Worcester RFC played their first match on the 8th November 1871 when they lost to Worcester Artillery. The city's rugby club prospered and two of their players, A. Bailey and C. Grindon, appeared in the 1875 West of England side that played Oxford University. The club also had three representatives in the 1877 West of England side that played 'South Wales'. The Welsh national side was only granted a fixture against the West in the early days and had to wait until 1882 to meet the full England team.

The first international to play for Worcester was John Robinson (1872-1959), a Cambridge Blue who had played four times for England. His claim to fame was that he had to wait ten years between the first two caps. Another top-class player to appear for Worcester was R.G.T. Coventry, an Oxford Blue.

Worcester drew their fixtures from local clubs such as Evesham and Bromsgrove, with an occasional match against such sides as Coventry Seconds. The club must have been well regarded as three of their players appeared for Midland Counties in November 1892.

In the 19th Century, Worcester RFC had at least three different home grounds before settling at Pitchcroft on the Racecourse in 1894, with the Northwick Arms acting as a changing room. Two years later, the original Worcester RFC disbanded but reformed in 1908.

After the Great War, Worcester reformed and established themselves as one of the best sides in the West Midlands and secured fixtures with Coventry, Moseley and Gloucester. They were not, however, viewed as being their equal and relied on other good local sides for normal fixtures.

The club's first golden era began in 1929-30 when they won 23 of 26 fixtures, followed by 23 of 29 the following season and 27 wins in 30 matches in 1931-32, which was exemplary. During the twenties the club had several players with first-class backgrounds: H.K. Evans (Cardiff & Bristol), F. Youd (Cheshire), C.F. Walters (Neath), F. Williams (Glamorgan) J.N. Poynder (Devon & Lancs), M. Averill (Bristol), Rev. J.T.B. Evans (Navy), W. Hughson (Pontypool) and A.P. Atkins (RAF & Ireland).

Worcester, at this time, had a reputation for hospitality that exceeded their facilities: their pitches were often mud heaps and the public houses they used for changing were basic. A picture of 1930s rugby comes from an old timer who recalled playing against Worcester when they operated on the racecourse and got changed in the cellar of a pub next to the river. In the days before refrigeration, the beer was kept cold by the public house having a stream that ran through the cellar, which cooled the beer barrels – and everything else. Unfortunately the cellar often got flooded. The muddy rugby players made the best of the flooded cellar by stripping off after matches and bathing in the filthy freezing waters of the pub basement.

In 1956, Worcester found a permanent home at Bevere. The new pavilion was opened by the RFU President and the First XV played a Mickey Steele-Bodger XV. The home side won 10-5. The outstanding player of the period was Cyril Waters, who won a record number of caps for the North Midlands side.

Worcester RFC left Bevere in the early 1970s and opened a splendid ground at Sixways, just off the M5. Despite excellent facilities, they initially struggled to come to terms with the new league structure and even finished bottom of Midland Two (West) in 1987-88, but after that were promoted seven times in nine years.

1994 was the height of National Lottery fever. Even if you couldn't win the big prize, the Lottery Fund could provide handsome aid to sporting organisations. Worcester set their ambitions on a million pound indoor sports centre. The club approached Cecil Duckworth to help. Duckworth had just sold his famous central heating firm. Worcester and Duckworth persuaded the Lottery Fund to donate £1.3 million. Mr. Duckworth was hooked and saw potential in the modest Midland One Club and its equally modest support, which barely reached three figures. He took an enormous gamble by transforming Sixways into one of the best rugby grounds in Britain, with a capacity for 10,000 spectators.

With such massive backing and superb facilities, Worcester were able to attract some of the best Birmingham-based players, such as Steve Lloyd and Mark Linnett, who had been part of England squads. Top-class players and coaches gravitated to Sixways, attracted by the quality of the organisation and the facilities. Les Cusworth and Geoff Cooke held the reins for a time as the club progressed upward.

John Brain took over as Head Coach in July 2001 after 20 years at Gloucester. He remained at Sixways until 2007 when he moved to Bristol. When he arrived, Worcester had just won Division Two and, in 2004, they reached the Premiership winning 26 of 26 games in Division One.

Chris Pennell scoring in the Greene King IPA Championship final.

The transitory nature of promotion to the Premiership, with its stock of regular clubs, augured badly for Worcester. They entered the Premiership with some fine players: Pat Sanderson and Andy Gomarsall of England, Thirius Delport of South Africa, plus an international selection of talent. The captain was Ben Hinshelwood of Scotland. The arrival of Pat Sanderson, the England flanker, seemed risky for the player's international ambitions. He shouldn't have worried as he ended Worcester's season as England captain for the Churchill Cup in North America.

Worcester survived season one in the Premiership with some comfort, but season two saw them at the bottom of the table. Brain was replaced by Mike Ruddock, who had led Wales to the 2005 Grand Slam, and defensive guru Phil Larder. They survived again and they shocked world rugby by signing Rico Gear, the All Black scoring machine, who was not only a New Zealand legend but the top try-scorer in New Zealand domestic rugby. Also incoming was Hugo Southwell of Scotland, and flanker Tom Wood emerged from within the club and, although he moved on, he was one of England's future stars.

Worcester ignored the odds and, whilst in the lower half of the table, they regularly avoided relegation and were finalists in the 2007-08 European Challenge Cup, losing to Auch of France. They continued to recruit big name internationals, such as Aussie Chris Latham. They also signed some of the best English talent in Matt Kvesic, Matt Mullen and Andy Goode, who all went on to England honours.

CHAPTER TWELVE – EAST MIDLANDS

AMERSHAM & CHILTERN

THE SOUTH BUCKINGHAMSHIRE towns of Amersham and Chiltern were relatively slow to become commuter towns. Only in the early 1920s did London business people realise the quality of life in the Chilterns, which sparked a boom in house building.

The first known rugby match in the area was in 1915 when two sides from the Royal Engineers played a match at Chesham Cricket Club. The match was organised to raise the £14 needed to clear the debts of the cricket club.

Nine years later, a meeting was called in Chesham Bois to try to establish a local rugby club. The founding fathers were Ernest Halton and his three sons, plus Eric Ainsworth-Redfern, Dennis Richardson, Charles Penny and Bertie Side. This being done, the new club still had to come to terms with being the only club in the whole district.

The first match was arranged for Boxing Day 1924, away to Berkhamsted OBs at Berkhamsted School. The OBs, who were vastly more experienced, won 28-0.

After the match, Teddy Tyrwhitt-Drake and Mr. E. Forward, a landowner of the Pineapple public house on Amersham Common, offered the use of the field behind the public house together with use of an old cow shed adjacent to it as changing rooms.

Amersham's second match was away to RAF (Halton) at Wendover and ended in another defeat; this time losing 21-0. The following week A&C lost to UC Hospital 28-0. It was, however, fourth time lucky as A&C recorded their first win by defeating an Old Merchant Taylors XV by 11-3. Winger R.B. Middleton had the honour of scoring the club's first ever try.

They took out a 35-year lease at Weedon Lane, Amersham in 1929 where a pavilion was erected. Over the next ten years they regularly fielded two or three teams.

Amersham and Chiltern rapidly assembled a fixture list composed of junior sides from some of London's finest. The club won six of their 14 matches that first season.

They had a famous member in the 1920s when Geoffrey Roberts KC turned out for the club. In his youth he had been an Oxford Blue at rugby and tennis and was capped at rugby by England in 1907 and 1908. Later Roberts was a prosecuting lawyer during the Nuremberg Trials of German war criminals.

A more recent international is Josh Lewsey, a product of Watford GS and the club's juniors. He moved to Bristol RFC and London Wasps. He won 55 England and three Lions caps. Alan Simmons also moved to Wasps and played for England at prop.

A&C's Under 17s reached the semi-final of the National Plate in 2010-11. The senior side can claim that they were the only Buckinghamshire side in the National leagues.

(Thanks to Roger Cook)

BEDFORD

"Bedford isn't so much a sleeping giant, it's one in a coma."
Frank Warren

BEDFORD IS AN ancient but progressive town some 50 miles north of London. The town is famous for John Bunyan, a local preacher who wrote 'A Pilgrims Progress'. Its famous son of modern times is Budge Rogers, a classically-talented rugby player who was one of the most recognisable sportsmen of the 1960s and 70s. Rogers began and ended an illustrious sporting career at Goldington Road, a spacious ground with ageing facilities just off the main road to Cambridge. It has to be said that the main road is considerably flatter than the rugby pitch, which had a famous slope.

Bedford takes its colours from the Light Blue of Cambridge and Dark Blue of Oxford. In theory, Bedford lies equidistant between the two great centres of learning, but in practice Cambridge is much nearer.

Bedford RFC was formed in 1886. From the start the two great sources for players were Bedford School and Bedford Modern School. It has to be said that Bedford, as a town, has a high number of private schools. Bedford School was always the most exclusive, whilst the Modern School was also a select grammar school and a million miles from a secondary modern school.

Bedford won their first match 10-3 against Olney, a local village side, and soon made an impact on English rugby when their 1893-94 side had a 100% home record.

The first great name to play for the club was Basil Maclear. He was a brilliant rugby footballer and cricketer, indeed, he first came to prominence when he was Bedford Grammar School's top bowler for the 1897 and 1898 cricket seasons. His selection for the Ireland rugby team was curious. He was born in Portsmouth and considered, and rejected, by the English selectors, but it was for Ireland that he excelled. He made his name in an Ireland v Scotland match when he

Basil Maclear

was targeted by Bedell-Sivright, the legendary wild man of Scots rugby in the 1900s. Maclear was in full flight when the Scot stood in his way. The two collided at full tilt. When the dust settled, Bedell-Sivright was prostrate on the floor and Maclear was touching down for a try. Maclear was killed in World War One. One newspaper said merely, "Maclear was a good footballer before the war" – hardly overstating his achievements.

1911 saw Bedford produce another star in Dick Stafford, a teenage giant who played for the Bedford club at 15 years of age and had won four England caps by his premature death at 19.

Jumbo Milton was another teenage forward for Bedford and England. Indeed, the club had a reputation for big forwards, which is curious as Bedford claim to have invented the scissors move amongst its three-quarters. Certainly, of the five Lions produced by Bedford, three were backs, beginning with Tony Novis, an army officer who played for England and was in the 1930 Lions squad.

But it is big, tough forwards that one associates with Bedford. The most unusual was Gerald 'Beef' Dancer, who was selected for the 1938 Lions tour of South Africa despite never winning a peacetime England cap. (See Bedford Athletic)

B.J. McMaster was another Bedford player who won an England cap in a wartime international. He was selected again in 1943, but sadly he died on active service only days before he was due to report for the match.

Ray Longland was an outstanding forward after joining Bedford from Olney, but subsequently joined arch-rivals Northampton.

All these great players were eclipsed in Bedford mythology by D.P. 'Budge' Rogers, who was one of the best forwards in rugby history. He played 34 times for England in the 1960s and broke W.W. Wakefield's record as England's most capped player. He played two tests for the 1963 Lions and made 485 appearances for Bedford – his only club. He was the kingpin of the 1969-70 Bedford side who were unofficial champions of England and Wales, winning the Sunday Telegraph Pennant that year and finishing second the folloing year. Budge ended his career as a 35-year-old by leading Bedford to victory in the 1975 National Knockout Cup, beating Rosslyn Park 28-12 in the final.

At the time, Bedford could field a host of internationals: Jacko Page, Jeremy Jannion, Billy Steele, Tony Jorden, Neil Bennett, Bob Wilkinson and Derek Wyatt. Alan Lewis, an inexperienced and uncapped scrum-half, was even selected by the 1977 Lions in New Zealand.

A sad event took place in 1967 when international Danny Heam was paralysed after making a tackle for the Midlands against the 1967 All Blacks.

Bob 'Jumbo' Wilkinson is certainly the most televised Bedford player of all time. It was a tradition that the Barbarians always fielded an inexperienced youngster in even the biggest match. Jumbo was the recipient of the invitation from the Barbarians to play the 1973 All Blacks at Cardiff Arms Park. The match produced one of the greatest moments in rugby history. The BaBas counter-attacked from under their own posts; the ball was flung from player to player before Gareth Edwards dived over the New Zealand line. Wilkinson played a crucial part in this try and the attacking move has been shown hundreds of times on television, but hardly benefitted him because the England selectors ignored his talent until 1978.

In 1974 Bedford produced a great Lion in Billy Steele. A Scotland international, Steele brought brilliant speed to the Lions wing for the 1974 Invincible Lions in South Africa. Another great Bedford winger was Derek Wyatt, who scored 145 tries for the club in 152 games over five years.

League and professional rugby came a decade too late for Bedford. When the game went professional in 1995, they had just been promoted to Level Two, where they finished bottom and only avoided relegation because of the RFU's restructuring of the leagues.

The club was bought by Frank Warren, a boxing promoter with no previous involvement with rugby. Frank earned high praise for his efforts to breathe life into Bedford, but to no avail. "It isn't so much a sleeping giant, as one in a coma," said Warren, whose Sports Network Group pumped millions of pounds into the club. He tried to revive Bedford by recruiting Paul Turner and Geoff Cooke as a management team. The duo had previous history of success, but the move didn't work at Bedford despite signing a host of famous players, including Jeff Probyn, Martin Offiah, Norman Hadley, Rudolf Straueli and Junior Paramore. Frank Warren's experiment lasted just 14 months.

Warren, however, seemed to enjoy the involvement at Goldington Road and became a popular figure with the players and supporters. Sadly, he had no choice but to try to sell the club. But to whom? Selling an impecunious rugby club proved difficult – as did life at Goldington Road.

The oddest event in Bedford's history came one evening several years later, when regulars in the bar heard noises in the upstairs offices. They climbed the stairs and found a stranger trying to open the club's safe. It transpired that the safe-cracker had been hired to steal the deeds to the Goldington Road ground. He never revealed who hired him, but the obvious perpetrator was unaware of one salient fact: the ground didn't belong to the rugby club and is owned by an ancient health trust and couldn't be sold. The supporters discouraged the master criminal by buying him a drink, which was how the plot came to light.

More welcome visitors were players such as Andy Gomarsall (England), Gareth Rees (Canada) and Derwyn Jones and Mike Rayer (Wales).

Sadly, the team declined. Not surprisingly, the supporters wearied of such attempts to acquire Goldington Road and in 2000 decided to buy the rugby club for themselves. A meeting was held on the pitch and it was decided to raise £600,000 to return the club to its origins. The money was raised in shares and the club renamed Bedford Blues RFC. Since then the club has been run by volunteers and the generosity of Jeff Irvine, a local builder.

Future internationals who have appeared for Bedford include Mauritz Botha, Karl Dickson, Dan Cole, Tom Youngs, Owen Farrell and Billy Twelvetrees, who all played for the club before their international careers took off.

Bedford have come close to glory in recent years. In 2006, they reached the National Knockout Cup final, but lost to Harlequins, and in 2013 Newcastle Falcons pipped them to promotion to the Premiership.

BEDFORD ATHLETIC

BEDFORD WAS A military town at the beginning of the 20th Century. Amongst the units based in the town was the Royal Army Medical Corps. The regiment consisted mostly of volunteers who drilled on Bedford Modern School field and had their own rugby section which played on Bedford Park.

They played their first game on 30th September 1905, losing to Kempston 'A' 9-3. Most of the 'Rams' were young working men who had not been to rugby-playing schools and had learnt the game with the Volunteers. The Rams played fixtures against sides such as Bedford Grammar School, Bedford Wanderers, Luton and Olney.

In 1908 the Volunteers became the Territorials. The change required members to enlist for a longer term of service, which discouraged many volunteers. Eventually, the local RAMC headquarters moved to Luton, which spelt the end of the rugby section. The last match played by the Rams took place on 1st April 1908, when they drew 3-3 with Northampton St. Giles.

The end of the military connection did not prevent the former players reforming as a civilian club. An inaugural meeting was held at the Kings Arms, St. Mary's on 16th April 1908. Why the name 'Athletic' was adopted is not certain, but a Bedford Athletic soccer club had existed locally in 1904. Bedford Athletic RUFC's first ground was opposite the Park Hotel, Kimbolton Road, and their jersey colours were to be black and white, as an alternative to the RAMC's red jerseys. According to a founder member, someone said, "We are like a lot of old magpies, so why not black and white?"

Athletic were coached by Basil Maclear, an Irish international, who had captained Bedford. Maclear was actually English, but had served as an army officer in Ireland and qualified for the Emerald Isle. He was killed at Ypres in 1915.

After World War One, rugby in Bedford was in a difficult position. The best players could join Bedford RUFC, which was revived in 1920, but the only other rugby club in the town was Queen's Works, which did not accept members who weren't associated with the company.

Two young men A.E. Sharman and H.F.G. Tucker, who had just left the Bedford Modern, were refused admission to Queen's. They resolved to reform the Athletic, although the new Bedford Athletic Rugby Club had no connection with the pre-war club. The old Athletic club was largely composed of working class non-rugby lads, whereas the post-war Athletic was mainly ex-pupils from Bedford Modern which was one of the leading rugby-playing public schools.

The original Kimbolton Road pitch was extremely rough "preventing anyone from running", whilst bathing facilities at the Park Hotel consisted of half barrels serving as baths (little wonder that many preferred to turn up in kit).

1921-22 was a successful season, but the demands of Bedford RUFC saw Athletic losing its best players to the town team. Many fine players appeared for Athletic, notably A.H. 'Jamie' Greenwood and R.C. Brumwell, who were both England trialists and members of the famous 1930 Midland Counties XV, the only side to beat the South African tourists. Iowerth Evans, a Welsh international, finished his playing days with the Athletic, whilst N.L. Dudley-Ward was a Welsh trialist.

SERVICES INTERNATIONAL—SCOTLAND versus ENGLAND
At Murrayfield, Edinburgh, on 26th February 1944

ENGLAND
Reading from Left to Right—(Back Row) L/Cpl. E. Ward, Sq./Ldr. J. Parsons, Cpl. J. Mycock, Schoolmaster J. B. Doherty, F/Lt. R. G. H. Weighill, Cpl. G. Hudson. (Middle Row) L.A.C. J. Lawrenson, Lt. G. Hollis, Cfn. J. Stott, Capt. R. E. Prescott (Captain), Cpl. R. J. Longland, Sgt./Instr. R. L. Francis, Sgt. G. T. Dancer. (Front Row) F/Sgt. I. Dustin, Lt. P. R. Hastings.

'Beef' Dancer in one of his appearances for England in a wartime international.

The following season saw Athletic rent a ground owned by Mr. A. Cave behind the Fox and Hounds in Goldington Road, where the club remained until 1925. They then managed to rent a corporation ground on Newnham Avenue, although they still used the Fox and Hounds for changing.

Gerald 'Beef' Dancer first appeared for Athletic in 1928 after leaving Bedford Modern. He played for the Barbarians and toured with the 1938 British Lions in South Africa. Beef was the club's first British Lion, although he never won a peacetime England cap (he played for England in wartime matches). He was a late replacement for the 1938 British Isles party, but played in all the test matches. The journey to South Africa took two weeks and the party were away for five months. Beef played in 20 out of the 22 matches. He later remembered "There was a profile of me in a South African magazine that painted me as a right villain. On my passport on the way out, I wrote 'cauliflower ear' in the section where it wanted 'distinguishing marks'. On the way back, the boys said I wouldn't be let in because I'd grown another one. It was really rough, but I enjoyed the games."

Beef later ran a pub in St Ives, where he became friendly with boxing promoter Andy Smith and his stable of boxers, which included Joe Bugner, who later fought for the world heavyweight title twice.

After World War Two Athletic reformed and played at Barker's Lane. In 1950 a 'new' office of Fixture Secretary was created. The new office went to Ron Cox, who was to serve Athletic and the East Midlands for half a century. In 1953-54 Arthur Marshall, who had begun with the Athletic, was RFU President

In 1959 the pitches at Newnham Avenue ground were developed by the Corporation as a running track. They provided a pavilion and a new pitch for the rugby club in Russell Park, whilst a further pitch was rented at Fenlake Meadow.

By 1960 the Athletic was believed to be the largest club in the Midlands, with six sides, colts and youth teams. A large proportion of new members were still Old Bedford Modernians. About this time, John Cooley, who began with Athletic Fifths, went on to play for the East Midlands and was an England trialist.

In 1972, Athletic had a part in the establishment of the National Knockout Cup when the East Midlands RU were asked to organise a competition to produce a local representative to take part in future rounds. Rushden and Higham emerged as local champions, beating Athletic in the final as Northampton.

A decade later, Athletic finally won the East Midlands Cup, beating Peterborough in the final. In 1995 they won the Intermediate Cup, beating Stroud 29-25 in a wonderful final.

In 2010 the club received an email from an unknown South African player looking for a club in Britain. The player was Mauritz Botha, who later moved to Bedford Blues and then Saracens. He played ten times for England.

Athletic have played in National 3 and were Midland One Champions in 2013.

BEDFORD SCHOOL

BEDFORD SCHOOL HAS produced 16 internationals, three British Lions, 29 Barbarians and 21 Blues.

It is impossible to say when rugby football was first played at the school. There is, however, a report from 'Bell's Life in London' of a match between Bedford Grammar School and Christ's College Cambridge, played in 1870. Later that decade inter-school matches were being played against Bedford County School, Perse, Kings School in Ely, St. Paul's College, Stony Stratford and Magdalene College School, Oxford. It is also known that a match was played against a 'Town XV', which the School lost by 'three rouges to one'. From 1878 matches were frequently played against Bedford Rovers, who in 1886 joined forces with the Bedford Swifts to form the Bedford Town club.

The man who first put Bedford School on the map as a leading rugby school was the remarkable E.H. Dasent, coach from 1884 until 1909.

In 1903 J.G. Milton, a member of the XV, played as a forward in all three international matches for England. In 1906 the East Midlands back division consisted mostly of Bedford School boys. Dasent's methods certainly produced internationals. P. Christopherson, captain of Oxford, was the first, playing for England in 1891. In 1906 C.E.L. Hammond, later to captain his country, played with J.G. Milton against Ireland, in whose ranks was the legendary Basil Maclear. Maclear had left the school in 1898. P.G. Jacob, F.H. Palmer, C.H. Milton, F.G. Brookes, E.L. Chambers, H.H. Vassall and S.W. Harris also played for England during this period. Vassall and Harris were both British Lions.

D.P. 'Budge' Rogers was Bedford School's greatest player; he was capped 34 times for England, and was a British Lion and Barbarian. The best-known Bedford Modern player in recent times is Martin Bayfield, who won 34 England caps in the 1990s before becoming a television presenter.

HIGH WYCOMBE

THE BUCKINGHAMSHIRE TOWN of High Wycombe was once the furniture capital of Britain. Some of the greatest names in the furniture industry operated from the town: Parker Knoll, G. Plan and Ercoll. The townsfolk of High Wycombe have worked with wood since the Middle Ages. The men were known as the Bodgers, who cut down trees and made chair legs, which they took to the town where the women made chair seats from reeds.

It is therefore appropriate that a piece of local furniture should give the key to early rugby in the town. A member visiting Wales found a Victorian octagon tablet marked as being presented to the town clerk of High Wycombe by the rugby club on the occasion of his marriage in 1891. Previously it was thought that rugby began in High Wycombe in 1929.

A small number of clubs existed in Buckinghamshire, including the first High Wycombe side, in 1891. They applied for use of Rye Mead as a ground, but local byelaws prohibited rugby being played on its precious greensward. The rugby club got round the problem by renting a pitch from the local cricket club, who insisted on half the gate money. What the landlord cricketers didn't realise was that there weren't enough rugby clubs in the locality to generate a fixture list – never mind a piggy bank. The original club did well in its first season but then died out.

Rugby didn't reappear until 1929, when Old Wycombiensians RFC was formed by a group from the local Royal Grammar School. OWs played on a pitch loaned by the Royal Grammar School and entertained afterwards at the Flint public house. This arrangement existed until 1947, when the club moved to Redford's Sport Ground, Totteridge, with post-match refreshment at the Black Boy, Terriers. The local council eventually offered land adjacent to Kingsmead as a clubhouse and the use of land for two pitches. The original clubhouse was built over a period of four months by club members out of a second-hand war office building and was opened on the 25th November 1949. This building was extended several times to accommodate the five regular Saturday sides.

The influx of non-RGS players led first to the name being changed to Wycombiensians, and then, in 1962, to High Wycombe RUFC. Around this time the club produced several internationals. John Woodward won 15 England caps between 1952 and 1956. He began with Old Wycombiensians before moving to Wasps. Although a big man, he was incredibly quick. This path to Sudbury was also trodden by Ron Syrett (11 England caps) and Clive Ashby, whose exploits attracted the attention of Wasps and England. More recently, Christian Wade, a product of RGS High Wycombe and the club juniors, moved to Wasps and made his England debut in 2011.

For five years from 2009, Premiership rugby was played in the town as London Wasps moved to Adams Park, home of the local soccer club Wycombe Wanderers, before they moved to Coventry in 2014

HINCKLEY

HINCKLEY IS A market town 16 miles north of Leicester previously famous for the hosiery trade. Rugby School is only 13 miles away and the game was played in Hinckley from 1880 onwards. The town's MP at the time was an old Rugbeian called Albert Pell, who introduced rugby to Cambridge University.

Records about the club, however, are only available from October 14th 1893, when a match is recorded against Nuneaton Crusaders at George Croft. Hinckley lost by one try and five minors. A second match (and defeat) was recorded a fortnight later against Nuneaton Albion The first victory came in November 1893 against Westcote Albion. A visit to Stoneygate in December 1893 proved difficult as the Leicester side won by two goals and six tries to nil.

Hinckley's second season was more successful as the new club played in the Leicestershire Combination against Second XVs of more established clubs. Reports are rare for the following ten years. Hinckley were in the third division of the Leicestershire Combination.

The Palmer family played a major part in Hinckley's efforts throughout the 20th century. Ron Palmer played 592 games, Phil 424, Ralph 404 and Arthur 322. Ron Palmer scored over 2000 points and also turned out for Leicestershire, Nuneaton and Leicester.

A famous son of Hinckley RFC was international golfer Guy Wolstenholme, whose father, Harry Wolstenholme, began as a soccer player before switching to the oval game. The club was greatly helped in the 1920s when Hinckley Grammar switched from soccer to rugby. Hinckley became a major force in the 1920s, losing only 14 times at home in nine years. On April 1st 1932 Hinckley beat Saracens 14-3

In the mid-1930s they were unbeaten for over a year and included Charles Bloxham, who won an Oxford Blue. In 1936-37. Their statistics were P34 W29 D1 L4 P467, with two players having international trials and 12 playing for the county. There was still a place for improvisation, however, as on a trip to Stafford the driver fell ill. One of the players took over and drove the bus home. Unfortunately the police stopped the bus and the driver was fined £1.

Hinckley were slow to recover from World War Two, but the club was gifted a ground at Coventry Road by Arthur Tansey and the Palmer Brothers, which became home to Hinckley RFC, Hinckley Cricket Club and the town's ladies hockey team. The cricket, rugby and a new soccer team moved to Leicester Road in 1967.

The most famous player produced by Hinckley was M.J.K. (Mike) Smith, whose father had been a member of the rugby club. Mike attended Stamford School and St Edmund's, Oxford, where he became the only man to hit three centuries against Cambridge in Varsity cricket. At Oxford, Smith formed a brilliant half-back partnership with Onilwyn Brace. Five weeks after the Varsity match, Smith was capped for England against Wales directly opposite Brace. M J K Smith was the last Englishman to win cricket and rugby international caps. He played 147 games for Hinckley, was captain for three seasons (1956-59) and skippered the Leicestershire county rugby team. He retired from rugby in 1959 aged 26 to concentrate on cricket.

Hinckley won the county cup four times in the 1970s, which brought qualification to the National Knockout Cup. On February 9th 1973 they played local giants Leicester in the last 16 of the cup and only lost 16-4. Obviously, their best players have progressed to the Tigers, notably David Bird (285 appearances for the Tigers), England B winger Barry Evans and legendary No. 8 Dean Richards, who was called up by England for the game against Ireland in 1986 and was a regular for eight seasons, winning 48 caps.

Domestically, Mick Reeve broke the Hinckley try-scoring record with 186 tries in December 1986 and the club were Leicester League Division One champions in 1991. In recent season, Hinckley have risen from Midland 2 to National 3.

KETTERING

KETTERING IS A MIDLAND town notable for its unusual architecture of ironstone and red brick. A Kettering rugby club was formed in 1871 by the Rector of Barton Seagrave. The original club played under Uppingham Rules, but four years later adopted RFU rules. Despite the lack of a permanent home, the new club established a reputation as the premier junior club in the East Midlands.

The four Mobbs Brothers of Kettering were noted rugby players in the town, as well as being employed in the shoe trade. The brothers developed a football boot for themselves which gradually was adopted across the region. Rugby players preferred long bullet-shaped studs, whilst soccer players used smaller studs. Both codes relied on a nail down the centre to keep the stud in shape. Unfortunately the cork studs soon wore down, leaving a raw nail that could inflict great damage. It was this problem that they solved.

Edgar Mobbs was the best known of the Mobbs brothers. He played 179 times for Northampton and five times for England. A Saints legend, Mobbs was killed in action in July 1917 at Zillebeke during the Third Battle of Ypres while attacking a machine-gun post.

Between the wars, Kettering was one of many clubs who benefitted from Welshmen moving to the Midlands in search of work. Ralph Bainbridge moved to Kettering in 1938 and was First XV captain for five successive years in the 1950s, recording a 52-match unbeaten run in that period.

Kettering were East Midlands Cup champions for six successive years from 1975-81. They currently play in Midlands One East.

LEICESTER TIGERS

LEICESTER TIGERS HAVE had their ups and downs but are probably the most successful rugby club in European rugby. Certainly their support, history and record of internationals are unique in English rugby and, despite the rise of the local soccer club, they have a unique place in the heart of the locals that is only rivalled in the British Isles by sides like Gloucester, Cardiff, Swansea and Munster.

Leicester has a history of street football, but organised club rugby dates from 1869, when St. Margaret's United and Leicester Athletic were formed.

The Tigers were formed on the August 3rd 1880 at the George Hotel – though not the same George Hotel that 15 years later gave birth to Rugby League – that being in Huddersfield. The George Hotel, Leicester also gave birth to Leicester City FC from the merger of Leicester Societies, Leicester Amateur and Alert football clubs.

Leicester was a hotbed of rugby with 20 different sides. In 1887, there was enough interest for a knockout competition, called the Leicester Junior Challenge Cup. This loose amalgamation eventually gave way to the formation of the Leicestershire Rugby Union in 1890, when Belgrave St. Peters, Leicester Crusaders, Wimbledon, Leicester Rovers, Nelson, Oadby, Leicester Swifts, South Wigston, St. George's Guild, Ashby-de-la-Zouch, Leicester and Stoneygate came together.

The Tigers' first match was against Moseley at Belgrave Cycle Stadium on 12th October 1880, resulting in a draw. This was a splendid result because Moseley were one of the strongest teams in the Midlands. The result augured well as the season's figures of P30 W19 D7 L4 were highly creditable against experienced but local opposition.

The second season proved a tougher test as 'parish pump' sides were replaced by the cream of Midland Counties rugby. Around this time, the club adopted chocolate and gold hoops, which is thought to be the origins of the Tigers' nickname, although anyone assuming it refers to the famous white, red and green hoops displays an alarming lack of knowledge about the animal world. Chocolate and gold were the colours of the Leicestershire Regiment, who were also known as the Tigers.

In September 1892 Leicester took the lease on a ground at Welford Road, which was officially opened with a match against a County XV. To engender interest in local rugby, the county organisation introduced a league, which only lasted two seasons. Although the Tigers refused to enter the league, they were the principal beneficiaries because they were able to attract the best players in the city to their colours.

The Tigers were soon an established side. Club and county were soon at odds because the Tigers felt the LRU was primarily conceived as an organisation for junior rugby and the Tigers were not a junior club. Initially relations between the Tigers and the Leicestershire RU were convivial. The severe winter of 1893 stretched the Tigers' finances to its limit and the county stepped in to organise a benefit match, which kept them afloat.

A decade later, matters were less convivial. The county union had initially agreed to 'lend' players to the Tigers to form an 'A' team. Matters became unpleasant when the Tigers began cancelling 'A' fixtures without consulting the county. The bitterness led the Tigers to refuse the use of Welford Road for county matches.

The Tigers, in conjunction with eight local clubs, organised the LFC Alliance, whose job was to organise local rugby to promote the Tigers. The Alliance eventually disappeared in 1940.

The dispute with the county didn't worry Leicester because they saw themselves as the area's premier club, who, from the mid-1890s, began to dominate the Midland Counties Cup. They eventually opted out of the Midland Cup completely after winning the trophy seven years in succession.

Despite this success, Leicester were only moderately successful on the national stage until the involvement of Tom Crumbie, a local businessman who proved the catalyst that moved the Tigers into the front rank of English club rugby. Under Crumbie's control, 30 Leicester players were to win international caps in 20 years. A canny operator, Crumbie looked far and wide for rugby talent – everywhere, it was said, except for Leicester!

Tom Crumbie

Even in the early 1900s players mysteriously commuted from as far as the North East to play for the Tigers at a time when the RFU was trying to root out covert professionalism from the game. Crumbie held the post of club secretary for 33 years and earned a reputation for bending the laws relating to both amateurism and the impartiality of referees. He made a point of meeting referees straight off their train. He welcomed the officials with a lift in his car, a meal in the evening and a bed at his home.

Crumbie did his best for Leicester and the club became a magnet for talent. It seems fair comment that despite the rumours, the RFU weren't interested in 'opening a second front' in the Midlands after the internecine battles with the Northern Union from 1895 onwards. He had money to play with because by 1925 Leicester had 8,000 members and large gates.

In 1908 the Tigers were denounced by Moseley for 'sham amateurism' after three Leicester players were accused of playing for the Tigers although they were on the books of NU clubs. The Tigers evaded punishment because the players had signed with NU clubs before the 1901 ban on players being paid. Formal proceedings were instigated, but the RFU decided there was no evidence to support professionalism. The RFU investigated Leicester over T. Smith, J. Jackson, S. Matthews and F. Hardyman, all ex-NU players. All were classed as professionals, but Crumbie got the decision overturned. So great was Crumbie's impact on Leicester that when he died in 1928, the club built a new stand and named it after their secretary.

Certainly Tom Crumbie and Leicester proved a formidable ally to the RFU in the years when the North's best talent was unavailable, and they produced England internationals in the years before World War One, notably John Miles, George Keeton and Will Penny, but also players who had won international honours with other clubs gravitated to Welford Road: Richard Cattell (Moseley), Ted Jackett (Redruth), A Brice (Cardiff), William Yiend (Hartlepool Rovers) and Mark Morrison, who led the 1904 British Isles side. Leicester's rise was mirrored by the selection of three Tigers to join the 1908 British Isles tour to Australia and New Zealand: Tom Smith, F. Jackson and T. J. Jackett.

Welford Road

In the 1920s, Leicester were competing with the best club sides in Britain – sometimes with unusual results. In 1923 they played away to Swansea and drew the match with a try in the final moments. The referee blew for full-time and wrongly refused to allow the conversion to take place. After the match, Leicester successfully appealed to the RFU and it was decided to settle the dispute by sending two Leicester players back to Swansea, the following week, to take the kick. 2000 Swansea fans turned up simply to see the conversion taken. The Tigers missed the conversion, to the jubilation of the crowd.

Relations with the county must have been better in 1927 as the Tigers made up the entire Leicestershire XV who played the Waratahs, the predecessors of the Australian national side. Four years later, Leicester formed the backbone of the awkwardly named 'Leicestershire and East Midlands XV' who beat Benny Osler's Springboks 30-21 in front of 25,000 spectators at Welford Road. The victors were led by Leicester and Irish legend George Beamish.

The 1920s saw Leicester fielding four of the greatest players of the era: W.W. Wakefield, Alastair Smallwood, Harold Day and Leo Price. Wakefield was working in the Midlands after leaving the RAF. Smallwood is largely forgotten, but won 14 England caps on the wing during the golden era of English rugby in the early 1920s. A talented musician, Smallwood worked at nearby Uppingham School for over 30 years. Day was the best English goal-kicker of his generation and was one of the earliest examples of the philosophy of "taking a field with a brilliant goal-kicker and then finding 14 other blokes to make up the numbers".

Day is best remembered for two unseemly incidents. In 1920 Lowry of Birkenhead Park was included in the England XV against Wales and even featured on the team photograph, but then Lowry was told he was dropped in favour of Day because the Leicester player was more suited to the heavy underfoot conditions. Later Day was involved in a wrangle when he played for East Midlands although he lived and taught in Essex, played cricket for Hampshire and played for Leicester on Saturdays. North Midlands successfully argued that Day actually lived in Leicester.

Leo Price (1899-1943) was one of the best forwards of the inter-war years. He was a Boy's Own character: war hero and top-class at rugby, cricket and hockey. He won four England caps, scoring two tries. In 1922 Price played for England at rugby and hockey on successive Saturdays. His caps were shared between Tigers and Richmond. A schoolmaster by profession, he taught at Uppingham and Christ's Hospital before becoming headmaster of Bishop's Stortford College. His most famous exploit was attempting a drop-kick for England against Wales. The drop goal was so misdirected, he managed to recover the ball and dive over for a try.

Four Leicester players – Douglas Kendrew, Bernard Gadney E.S. Nicholson and Prince Obolensky – played in the 1936 England team who beat the All Blacks 13-0, the whites first ever win over the New Zealanders.

Kendrew arrived from the new Woodford club in Essex. A brilliant player at schoolboy level, whilst at Uppingham School he was a late replacement for W.W. Wakefield's XV to play Woodford, where he impressed so much he was recommended to Leicester. His meteoric rise saw him capped by England and the British Isles within months of arriving at the club. He later joined the Army and rose to become Brigadier General and later promoted to Major General in 1957. He was also Governor of Western Australia from 1963 to 1973.

Bernard Gadney, a scrum-half, surpassed even Kendrew's achievements. He was the first Leicester player to captain England and led England to the Triple Crown in 1933-34 and to their first victory over the All Blacks in 1936. The

Bernard Gadney

following year, Gadney became the first captain of a British Isles team to tour Argentina. He lived to be 91 and was revered as the 'grand old man' of English rugby and the last survivor of the 'Obolensky match'. As a scrum-half he was described as being "as slippery as an eel".

Gadney was one of a handful of Englishmen (or any other nationalities), who, until modern times, could claim to have been on the winning side against both the All Blacks and the Springboks. He was one of seven Leicester players to play in the Leicester & East Midlands XV who beat the 1931 Springboks by 30-21 at Welford Road.

Today the 1936 England victory over the All Blacks is uniquely identified with Obolensky, but it owed much more to an earlier defeat of a Leicster & East Midlands XV by the All Blacks. The Leicester players lost that day but surmised that the New Zealanders were vulnerable to a strong scrummage and, in the England match, stunned the New Zealanders by dominating the fight upfront. Obolensky did the rest and got the glory; Kendrew, Gadney etc. did the work and were completely overlooked.

After the Second World War, there was a general feeling that Leicester were amongst the best in England, but they were behind the Welsh clubs, who had a better grasp of fitness and organisation. The Tigers tried to improve in many ways, including abandoning Tom Crumbie's elitist notions of nationwide player recruitment and started looking closer to home by establishing a second team as a focus for the city's best local talent. The club did, however, undertake some exotic fixtures, including drawing 6-6 with the Romanian national team in 1956.

A famous outsider arrived at Welford Road in 1958 in Tony O'Reilly, who was one the greatest players of all time. He was a remarkable player and person. Capped by Ireland and the Lions, as a teenager, he was a winger in the Obolensky mould who later became an incredibly successful businessman, including becoming UK Managing Director of Heinz Foods, the world-wide food manufacturer. O'Reilly only lingered at Welford Road for two seasons, but, as the world's most famous rugby player, he guaranteed a big crowd whenever or wherever he played.

The 1960s saw the Tigers as front rank but not special. The turning point came in 1966 when Chalkie White was appointed coach, though his role was not formally recognised in the days of amateur rugby in case it was misconstrued as 'professionalism'. White, a Nottingham schoolteacher, was superficially an odd choice because he had been a journeyman scrum-half for Camborne. However, he proved to be an outstanding success. He never got the job of England coach, but had two future England coaches working under him at Welford Road in John Elders and John Elliot.

White was ably supported by Graham Willars as club captain. They and the management team were able to steer the Tigers into an excellent position of strength, just as in the early 1970s English rugby emerged from 80 years of inertia. The first step was the establishment of a National Knockout Cup, open to the top sides and county cup winners. The re-organisation of the club meant that the Tigers had a fine young team at a time when the Cup was gaining popularity and they reached

National Knockout Cup winners 1979.

five finals in seven years and won three consecutive titles. They beat Moseley 15-12 in 1979, London Irish 21-9 in 1980 and Gosforth 22-15 in 1981.

At the time, the Tigers could field some of the best players in Britain, notably Paul Dodge, Peter Wheeler, Clive Woodward, Steve Redfern, Garry Adey, Les Cusworth, Nick Youngs and Dusty Hare. It was no coincidence that the 1980 England Grand Slam team included four Leicester players in Wheeler, Dodge, Woodward and Hare.

And yet, as well as the stars, Leicester possessed a battery of top-class clubmen who also were great servants: Steve Kenny, Barry Evans, Tim Barnwell and John Duggan.

In 1982 White left and half the Tigers team retired. In a final flourish Leicester's 'golden generation' were the backbone of the England team who in 1983 finally recorded a second home win over the All Blacks, echoing events in 1936. Like many other clubs they faced the inevitability of rebuilding without suffering a trough.

The next change was the arrival of league rugby, which the Tigers took in their stride. They kept the ethos of an elite club side long after other clubs had lost it in pursuit of success,

SIX LEICESTER PLAYERS IN THE ENGLAND XV v NEW ZEALAND AT TWICKENHAM, NOVEMBER 1983. LEFT TO RIGHT: DUSTY HARE, NICK YOUNGS, PETER WHEELER, LES CUSWORTH, PAUL DODGE AND CLIVE WOODWARD

principally because they moved seamlessly into league rugby and professionalism using the same type of people as in their amateur days, be they players, coaches or administrators.

Fortunately the arrival of League rugby coincided with a new crop of youngsters who were emerging at Welford Road. The talisman of the new team was local policeman Dean Richards, who was to become one of the finest ever Leicester and England players. To support him, they were able to recruit a host of stars who would become the backbone of the England team of the 1990s, notably Martin Johnson, Austin Healey, Rory and Tony Underwood, Neil Back, Graham Rowntree, Richard Cockerill and Darren Garforth. The last three were known as the 'ABC Club' as the Tigers clung to the tradition of using letter to denote players rather than numbers.

Tigers were landed with the complaint of being "too forward orientated", but became more expansive in the 1990s.

In 1987-88 they became the first official English club champions when they won National Division One, later renamed the Premiership, but it proved a false dawn as arch-rivals Bath emerged and dominated English club rugby for a decade.

When Dean Richards retired, his place as Leicester and England leader went to his team-mate Martin Johnson. The huge lock proved a Tigers and England captain in the mould of Wakefield and Richards. He emerged from local junior rugby, had a spell in New Zealand (where he was selected for their Under 21s) and came home to become a national icon. His precord reads: played for Leicester when they were the Premiership champions in 1999, 2000, 2001, 2002; two European Cup wins, 84 caps for England, with 39 as captain, including the 2003 Grand Slam season; played in three World Cup teams, with two as captain, including the crowning moment of a great career when he was the England captain lifting the 2003 Rugby World Cup in Australia.

Much of Leicester's strength had come from promoting from inside Welford Road, but in 1997 they looked externally with the appointment of Bob Dwyer, the coach of the Australian team that won the 1991 World Cup. He was a great success, but the formula ultimately didn't work as a series of foreign coaches came and went with mixed fortunes. Eventually, in 2009, the club appointed ex-hooker Richard Cockerill as coach. A fiery character, Cockerill surprised his critics by proving a successful leader.

Perhaps the surprise was the club's policy of external recruitment when it had a tradition of promoting internally. Dean Richards, John Duggan, Ian Smith, Graham Willars, Clive Woodward, Joel Stransky, John Wells, Martin Johnson and Graham Rowntree had all coached with success after playing for the Tigers.

The Tigers had also looked to recruit the best of the Midland players, but acquired some gold dust with veterans from the Southern Hemisphere finishing their careers at Welford Road, notably Josh Kronfield (New Zealand), Rod Kafer, Pat Howard (both Australian) and the Springbok stars Van Heerden and Joel Stransky.

At home, the Tigers produced two further England captains after the retirement of Martin Johnson in Martin Corry and Lewis Moody.

Corry replaced Johnson as England captain, but was unlucky as England's fortunes spiraled downward. At least in 2007, he was an integral part of the Leicester team that almost achieved 'the impossible treble' of the English Championship, the National Knockout Cup and the European Cup.

Moody was a worthy successor to Corry. The blonde flanker won 71 England caps over a decade and appeared five times for the Lions. At club level, he played in the Tigers' European wins. Sadly, his career was blighted by injuries, but he bounced back to lead his country in 2011.

In recent seasons the Tigers have confirmed themselves as the biggest club in England, with 13,000 season tickets sold every year. They have also provided a conveyer belt of talent: Tom Croft, Ben and Tom Youngs (England and Lions), Dan Cole, Louis Deacon, Manu Tullagi, Dan Hipkiss, Jordan Crane, Toby Flood, Billy Twelvetrees (England) and Gordon Murphy (Ireland).

The Tigers in action.

LEIGHTON BUZZARD

THE NAME OF Leighton Buzzard has got nothing to do with birds. Leighton means a 'farm in a clearing', whilst Buzzard is a corruption of 'de Busard', the local landowners.

The game came to the town in March 1922 when Bedford Athletic took two sides over to Cedars School; the first time that the game had been played in the town. Later a trial match between Bedfordshire and Northamptonshire was played at Leighton Buzzard as a 'missionary' match.

A Leighton Buzzard rugby club existed from 1934 to the Second World War. It was, however, the 1950s before the club reformed. A steady stream of youngsters emerged through Cedar Grammar School and from people moving to the area.

Stewart Maxwell was one talented player who moved to the area and joined the club. A superbly-balanced runner, Maxwell had played for New Brighton and the North Western Counties, and, indeed, had scored two tries for the 1972 NW Counties side that defeated the All Blacks at Workington.

Other distinguished players include John Davidson, who moved onto Moseley, Leicester and Oxford University, George Ellis, an Olympic rower, and John Surgay, who had been with Northampton.

Leighton Buzzard have risen into the higher levels of the Midlands leagues in recent years.

LETCHWORTH

LETCHWORTH GARDEN CITY – the first of its kind, with Welwyn a close runner-up – was founded by Ebenezer Howard as a Quaker Foundation, one of whose tenets is total abstention. As a result, Letchworth had no permanent home, neither pitch nor clubhouse, and led an even more nomadic existence than the majority, being compelled to play on a variety of sites in surrounding villages where no such prejudice existed, notably Norton of the Three Horseshoes.

Their first match was in late 1924 against RAF Henlow, with an unrecorded outcome. In 1926, arrangements were made to use the playing fields of the Norton Primary School, which in turn led, in 1931, to the use of the pitches of Letchworth Grammar School.

The 1931 and 1936 seasons each produced 100 per cent records. Then came the outbreak of the Second World War, during which the club managed to remain active, merging with the Tabulators' Company (the forerunner of ICL), whose rugby activities ceased post-1945.

Letchworth recorded their first international player in the immediate post-war years in the person of Geoff Kelly, whose death they were saddened to have to record, especially as he had not long previously been voted their first life member.

It was in 1956 that they finally moved to their present headquarters at Baldock Road, where they run a range of senior teams and lively youth and mini sections.

Currently Letchworth play in London 1.

LICHFIELD

THE CITY OF Lichfield (population 30,000) is most famous for its cathedral, Dr Johnson and David Garrick. Its rugby club are one of the oldest clubs in the Midlands, being originally formed in 1874. The earliest Fixture List is dated for the season 1876-77 and includes games with Burton, Derby, Birmingham Crusaders, Atherstone and Tamworth.

Lichfield RFC originally had 40 members and had its headquarters at the Bowling Green Inn. The ground was listed as being one quarter mile from Lichfield Station. Records of the early years and the early part of the century are very few, and there are no traces of reports or photographs for this period. There is no trace in the RFU records of any reference to the Lichfield Club until 1914. Operations were suspended until the 1920s when the club reformed using the Goat's Head Hotel on Breadmarket Street as headquarters and the local cricket club ground as a pitch. More pitches were needed as players returned from the forces and several teams were playing every Saturday. These were found in Beacon Park, Walsall Road (now Bartlett's farm) and Old Burton Road.

It was in the next 30 years that the Lichfield Club really developed into the strong and virile club it is today. Membership was to greatly increase and fixtures strengthened, while many of their players were to be selected to represent their county of Staffordshire.

In 1954 the Club moved to a new ground by the hospital and shared premises with the Lichfield Cricket Club, where it was to remain for a number of years. To celebrate this move, a Lichfield XV played the county side, a game which Staffordshire won 9-3.

Lichfield became a serious force in Midlands rugby in the years after World War Two and over 20 players have played for North Midlands and Staffordshire. The finest was perhaps Mike Davis, the England lock and 1980 Grand Slam coach. More recently, the club's fortunes have faded, but it did produce England 'B' centre Stuart Potter, Nathan Jones and Lol Davies for Leicester and one year did very well in the Pilkington Cup before going out to Bath.

Ken Job – The Iron Man – did not get an England cap, but what a great job he did for the North Midlands, Moseley and Staffordshire before coming back to play for Lichfield. Other Lichfield players have played senior county rugby over the years, include Ken Webb, Eric Fairgrieve, Mick Pyatt, Brian Ivey, Bernard Malin and Mick Bowen.

A milestone in the club's history came in 1961 with the purchase of the present ground in Boley Lane, the first time they had ever owned their own premises.

In 1983 Lichfield had the honour of being the last surviving junior club in the National KO Cup, losing to Harlequins and then losing to the same opposition the folloing year.

In 2014 Lichfield were top of Midlands One (West) and Emily Scarratt of Lichfield Ladies was England Women's player of the year.

NEWBOLD ON AVON

NEWBOLD IS A village, near Rugby, situated between the River Avon and the Oxford Canal. The club was founded at the Boat Inn, which was run by William Gamble, who had a relative who was bursar at Rugby School.

The first recorded match for the new club was on 17th November 1894 against Napton Rovers, resulting in a defeat 3-0 (a try to nil). A fortnight later they played their second (and last) game of the season, losing 9-0 (two tries and a drop goal) to Rugby Star.

Things improved in 1895-96, with three wins and a draw from eight fixtures. In 1898-99 cup success came to Newbold, when the club beat Rugby Star in the final of the Coventry & District Junior Cup. Two years later, Newbold regained the cup, beating Hilmorton. Three years later, they were local league champions and won the Midland Daily Telegraph Cup.

Cup successes continued into the 20th Century, although the 1909 cup final victory over Rugby Old Boys was notable for a massive brawl involving both teams and the crowd.

In 1911, Newbold tried to advance themselves with fixtures against the big boys of Midland rugby. Unfortunately the big cats of Leicester beat the village side 65-0. Other results were better, with victories over Belgrave, Five Ways Oes and Oadby.

Newbold has produced numerous good players down the years, but most migrated to the bigger clubs in Rugby, Coventry and Northampton. Jack Tomes was an outstanding part of Newbold's early success, but he made a mistake by joining the short-lived Coventry NU team in the days before WW1. It cost him his future in rugby union, although he persisted with the NU and he eventually won an England RL cap.

The 1920s were notable for the RFU applying restrictions on the few remaining cup competitions and insisting on 'friendlies', which didn't impede Newbold's progress. In 1921, they were sufficiently strong enough to play Rugby Lions in front of 5,000 spectators. The golden era continued until 1926 and a string of Newbold players went on to glory. In the early 1920s the club produced eight county players and a wing-forward, C. Harris, who gained an England trial whilst with Coventry.

A newspaper cutting dated February 1925 records: "Year after year this little village of 600 turns out two teams. The first fifteen are unbeaten at home and have only succumbed to Nuneaton and Rugby away from home. The reason of their success is that every member of the team is on the ball. Their pertinacity throws their opponents off the ball."

Decline came with the 1930s, although they made some impact on the Midland Minor Cup, but good seasons were few and far between. A curiosity is that Newbold continued to organise benefit matches for ex-players who could not work due to ill-health, although this contravened RFU laws on amateurism.

It was 1950 before Newbold acquired its first clubhouse, an old army hut, which was fitted out by the members with baths, all for £500. Previously the club had used a variety of the local pubs. In 1956 a new ground was opened with two full-size pitches. Three years later, Newbold unveiled a new £11,000 clubhouse, and in 1965 a new stand was erected.

In the 1960s, the four Webb brothers played for Newbold. Bill, Jim, Dick and Rodney were regulars for the village before moving to bigger clubs. Indeed, many of Rugby Lions' side hailed from the Newbold club. Rodney Webb won 12 England caps between 1967 and 1972. His brother Dick emigrated to Australia and toured Europe with the 1966 Wallabies.

In the late 1960s, Newbold produced 6ft 8 in John Lacey, who moved on to Rugby, Northampton and Coventry and represented England.

The most famous son of Newbold is hooker Richard Cockerill, who played for Newbold before joining Coventry and then Leicester. He took over as acting head coach of Leicester in 2009 and guided them to the Guinness Premiership title, but a week later they lost in the final of the Heineken Cup to Leinster.

Newbold currently play in Midland Two. They are great cup fighters: In 2011 they reached the RFU Senior Vase final and, in 2014, reached the Midlands semi-final of the Intermediate Cup, where they drew both legs but lost on the away draw rules.

NORTHAMPTON

"Northampton is like a corner of Wales transplanted to the Fens. Everybody is related to someone who plays rugby – or went to school with someone who played for the Saints."
Mike O'Brien 2007

NORTHAMPTON IS A city rooted in rugby. Franklin's Gardens, the home of the rugby club, is probably the town's most famous building, alongside the Barclaycard offices. It is only a few yards from St. James Church, whose curate, the Rev. Samuel Wathan Wigg, founded the rugby club in 1880, hence the club's nicknames of 'the Jimmies' or 'the Saints'. Originally the Saints were not the town's premier side. This honour belonged to Unity FC, who gave the St. James outfit a hammering when they first met. However, towards the end of the 19th Century, Unity and St. James merged to produce a single club, Northampton St. James, who were capable of taking on the country's best sides, including Leicester and Harlequins. The 'St. James' suffix disappeared in 1897.

An unsavory series of events occurred in 1897, two years after the Great Schism, when Northampton RFC were suspected by the Welsh RU of 'enticing' Welsh players to the East Midlands. In fact, the illegal payments were made, but luckily no action was ever taken

In 1899 Northampton had its first Lion in Blair Swannell, who toured Australia. Swannell also went on the 1905 Lions tour. He was never capped for England, but played for Australia against New Zealand, despite his reputation for indulging in the rougher side of the game.

Harry Weston was the club's first international in 1902, representing England in the 18-3 defeat by Scotland at Blackheath. Weston, a farmer from the village of Yardley Gobain, was never recalled, but his son Billy, also of Northampton, was capped 16 times for England at wing-forward between the wars.

Edgar Mobbs

In 1905 Northampton played the touring New Zealand team, but lost 32-0. The previous Saturday a youngster called Edgar Mobbs had made his debut. Mobbs rapidly established himself as a top-class back, winning seven England caps and becoming the first Saint to captain his country. Mobbs was immortalised for his bravery during World War One when he raised his own corps, D Company, 7th Northamptonshire Regiment, which included many local sportsmen. Sadly, only 85 of 400 volunteers in 'Mobbs' Army' survived (they were also known as *Mobbs' Own*). Mobbs himself was killed at Passchendaele in 1917, leaving a legend that he inspired his men by leaping out of the British trenches and kicking a football into No-Mans-Land. Mobbs' memory is commemorated by an annual match between the Barbarians and the East Midlands and there is a bust of him on the War Memorial in Northampton.

Another war hero was Freddie Blakiston, who played 17 times for England during the Whites golden era under Wavell Wakefield and Dave Davies. Blakiston was the forerunner of a dozen Saints who won England honours between the wars.

Two Saints, Ray Longland and Billy Weston, were in the England pack who defeated the 1936 All Blacks in the Obolensky match. Ray Longland was automatic front-row selection for England from 1932 to 1939. He was first noticed by the selectors when he played for the East Midlands & Leics XV who defeated the 1931 Springboks – one of only a handful of defeats for the South Africans on British soil.

Between the Wars, the gates at Franklin's Gardens were the biggest in English rugby. It was rumoured as much as £400 was being taken for some home matches, which rivalled even the best-supported Welsh sides.

The club stepped up another level in the mid-1930s when Gordon Sturtridge, an Australian international, joined the club and brought a level of antipodean polish in an era when coaching was unheard of.

The most unusual player to ever appear for the Saints came in 1942, when Bill Fallowfield, a rugby league player on war service, came to the area and played for the Saints. Bill was later Secretary of the Rugby League and a staunch opponent of the RFU.

Another remarkable name to appear for the Saints was Michael Green, author of Coarse Rugby. Green is probably the only reporter who covered a match he played in. He was detailed to cover a second XV game at Franklyn's Gardens whilst working for the local paper. The Wanderers were a man short and drafted in the scribbler as an emergency winger. When word got out, Green expected to be sacked. In fact, he got promoted.

After World War Two, Northampton were a rugby town, with a dozen junior clubs in the vicinity acting as feeder clubs.

Northampton established themselves as the powerhouse of East Midlands rugby with a Who's Who of English talent: Don White (15 England caps, 1947-1960s), Jeff Butterfield (26 England caps and six Lions caps), Ron Jacobs (29 England caps), Dickie Jeeps (24 England and 13 Lions caps), Frank Sykes, Louis Cannell, Phil Taylor and Bob Taylor. Butterfield, Jacobs and Jeeps were all captains of England. A popular saying was "that if you were good enough for Northampton, you were good enough for England".

Another Saint as Yorkshireman Jeff Butterfield, who attended Cleckheaton Grammar School and was a devout Bradford Northern RLFC supporter. He modelled his elusive running on the Bradford rugby league stars and scored three tries in his first Yorkshire trial and two tries on his Yorkshire debut. His career, however, was dogged by hamstring trouble.

Don White was a great character. A local joke was that, as a player, White sailed so close to the wind he was reckoned to have been born a foot offside. England's first coach, he was recruited specifically to prevent the 1969 Springboks from humiliating the old country, but White led England to victory against the Springboks – the country's first victory over the old enemy since 1913, although he upset the RFU, who decided 'squad training' for England was unsporting, and it also cost several thousand pounds a year. White stepped down in 1972, a sadder but wiser man.

In the 1970s and 1980s Northampton produced top-class players such as Rodger Arneil (22 Scotland caps) and Gary Pearce (35 England caps), but local rivals Leicester and Coventry ruled Midlands rugby.

The turning point to better things came when the club committee was overthrown in 1988 by a group of rebels. The new regime led the Saints to the Division 2 title and the semi-finals of the National Knockout Cup. They revolutionised the club by appointing Barrie Corless as a soccer-style manager and importing Wayne Shelford, the All Black skipper, as player/coach. Talented newcomers also arrived at Franklin's Gardens, such as Martin Bayfield of Bedford, Paul Grayson from Preston Grasshoppers, Ian Hunter from Windermere and Tim Rodber from RAC.

At the outset of professionalism the club was bought by Keith Barwell at a time when rugby clubs were suffering terrible financial problems. Barwill, a local businessman, was the pivotal figure who piloted Saints through 20 turbulent years and bought a steady hand to the tiller.

Northampton again became one of Britain's finest sides, and in 1991 they reached the final of the National Knockout Cup, losing in injury time to Harlequins. The following season the Saints would have won the First Division title but for an end of season defeat.

When Shelford returned to New Zealand, the club appointed the legendary Scotland and Lions coach Ian McGeechan as his replacement. McGeechan made the Saints a major power in European rugby with brilliant youngsters such as Matt Dawson. Dawson began as a junior with Marlow RFC before moving to the famous rugby school, RGS Wycombe. He was picked for England at under-16, under-18, and under-21 levels before joining Northampton in 1991. He first came to prominence as a member of the England team who won the

1993 World Cup Sevens, but he had to wait until 1995 for his full debut. Dawson became first choice scrum half on the 1997 Lions tour to South Africa and was a pivotal figure in England's orld Cup triumph in 2003. After retirement from rugby, he became a top television entertainer. He was a regular on A Question of Sport, but was also popular on Strictly Come Dancing.

1997 saw Saints sign Pat Lam from Newcastle Falcons, Argentinean hooker Freddie Mendez and South African World Cup 1995 winner Garry Pagel. All three were instrumental in helping Saints secure second place in the Premiership and a first-ever European cup place.

The highlight of the era was in 2000 when Northampton defeated Munster to win the Heineken European Cup and in 2002 Saints ended Leicester Tigers' five-year unbeaten home record.

Ian McGeechan left in the 1999 season to take over the Scotland national side, but success continuedIn as they qualified for the Heinekin Cup regularly and recruited players such as in 2005 Carlos Spencer, the former All Black full-back. On the downside, they were relegated in 2007-08, but bounced back the following season under head coach Jim Mallinder and in 2009 they won the European Challenge Cup, beating Bourgin in the final.

The club provided the backbone of the 2012 England squad, with eight Saints players picked by Stuart Lancaster. They included Dylan Hartley, a sparky hooker who lost his Lions place after a sending off in the 2012 Premiership Final.

Saints are currently one of the best sides in Europe, with internationals such as George North of Wales, Lee Dickson, Luther Burrell, Tom Wood, Dylan Hartley and Courtney Lawes, all England regulars.

(Thanks to Mike O'Brien and Tom Richens)

NUNEATON

'The Nuns'

NUNEATON RUGBY FOOTBALL Club was founded on 5th November 1879, at a meeting held at a local hotel: the Newdegate Arms. This hotel was to play a significant part in the evolution of the club for the first quarter of its life, as it provided the ground to play on – the Newdegate Arms Field – together with the dressing rooms and bathing facilities until the outbreak of war in 1914. The population of Nuneaton town was approximately 14,000 at the time, and has risen to 78,000 today.

In Nuneaton at the end of the 19th century, the game was being played regularly by small clubs named 'Albion', 'St Mary's', and 'Hartsill'. The first recorded Nuneaton game was against Tamworth on 7th February 1880. Nuneaton were wearing their chosen colours of a jersey of navy blue with the clubs initials, which were picked at a meeting held on 25th January 1880. They changed again on 11th September 1881 to a black jersey with a red sash. They again changed to black and red hoops in 1900.

Carlos Spencer

Tom Power was selected in 1881 to play for Midlands Counties against Middlesex at the Oval, London, thus becoming the first Nuneaton player to achieve county honours.

Fixtures were arranged only weeks in advance and appear very unbalanced, with Leicester, Bedworth and Allesley (Coventry) amongst the competition. In the late 1880s and early 1890s there was a struggle for survival through lack of players. In 1890 Nuneaton Town Football Club disbanded and amalgamated with the strong St Mary's team, re-naming both clubs 'Nuneaton St Mary's'. They played under that name until the 1892-93 season. A second XV team was formed during this time, and Rugby, Nottingham, and Northampton appeared on the fixture list.

In 1900 one Harry Cleaver became a player with the club. This was the start of an association to last until his death in 1968. During his active service with the club – first as a player, then club captain, secretary and finally president from 1950 – Harry did much to develop both the facilities and the playing staff and, to his credit, was instrumental in the foundation of the Warwickshire RFU, becoming president in 1938-39. In 1951 the English Rugby Football Union honoured him when he became their president.

By the outbreak of World War One, Nuneaton RFC had established a very creditable reputation within rugby circles through their fixtures and also performances in the Midland Counties Cup competition. It was at the outbreak of war that the Newdegate Arms Field became earmarked for building and the club lost their ground.

In 1919, under the direction of Harry Cleaver, a ground-sharing arrangement was agreed with Lichfield Brewery Co. Ltd. and Nuneaton Cricket Club for a pitch behind the New Inn at Attleborough. It was also this year that Nuneaton paraded its new colours, adding a white hoop, giving rise to the red black & white jersey which is still in use today. In 1920 the cricket club moved to another site, leaving Nuneaton RFC as the sole tenant.

In the early years many improvements took place to make the ground one of the best in the region. These improvements became the basis of negotiations for the purchase of the freehold from the brewery, which was achieved in 1930. In recognition of his sterling work for the club, the ground became known as the Harry Cleaver Ground – the name it carried until the final game on 30th November 1995.

Between the wars, Nuneaton continued their playing success, notably winning the Midland Counties Cup in 1921-22 and 1923-24. Players who were prominent at that time were J. Farndon, F. Warren, J. Bates, W. Merry, A. Andrews, A. Horton and G. Randle. The second XV was revived in 1923, and in 1929 the 'Old Boys XV' became Nuneaton Saracens XV.

Ground improvements continued up to the outbreak of World War Two, when normal playing arrangements were curtailed. However, the club continued to operate throughout the war by providing games for the forces, universities, and hospital sides.

The club's first international was the legendary W.S. (Wally) Holmes, who joined the club in 1944 as a wing-forward and played second row for Warwickshire and front row for England. He won his first England cap on 21st January 1950 and went on to represent his country 16 successive times. During his career he also appeared eight times for the Barbarians, took various Midland honours, and represented Warwickshire on 32 occasions.

The team improved, and the record from 1947-54 was as good as in any period in the club's history. The 1949-50 season was notable for ground attendance records being shattered when they took the scalps of Coventry, London Irish and Saracens, followed by a historic eight days towards the end of the season when they defeated Leicester, Northampton and Coventry.

During the whole of this period Don Sproul, an outside-half and outstanding kicker, captained the team. His ability was recognised by 35 selections for Warwickshire and the Midlands, and he had two Scottish trials.

The club celebrated its 75th anniversary in 1955, when all living players of the Midland Counties Cup-winning team attended, along with the trophy.

Following this period - dubbed 'the Golden Years' - other outstanding players continued the run well into the 1960s and 1970s. J. Davies (400 games), K. Stokes, R. Jenkins, M. Ford, T. Temple (400 plus games) and D. Maltby were all regular Warwickshire players. The period culminated in a match against Cardiff (with future Welsh stars of the 1970s in the side) on 19th December 1969 to celebrate Nuneaton's 90th anniversary and to christen their new floodlights.

There were many other remarkable Nuneaton players. Colin Duncan, son of Ted, was a Cambridge Blue. Other fathers and sons included 1950s Gale and 1960s Masser, and the sets of brothers who all played a major part in Nuneaton's success that continues today. From 1879 onwards the following sets of brothers were legends within the local sporting scene: 1880s Rowbottom, Parsons; 1890s Drakeley, Jebbetts, Brownson, Merrys, Warrens Paling, Cox, West, Atkins; 1900s Bacon, Clarke, Orton, Turnbull, Hutt, 1920s Venn, Streather, Wood, Cramphorn; 1940-50s Holmes; 1970s Hudsons, Lord; 1980s Savage, Masser; 1990s Sharp, Mitchell, Pearman; 2000's Gibson, Marshall, Southwell, Vupinola (Tonga).

Nuneaton has always found players and administrators who follow the Harry Cleaver tradition. From 1945 until 1987 a further administrator emerged in Aeron 'Taffy' Thomas, who continued to rebuild not only Nuneaton RFC, but also the local rugby scene in Warwickshire and the Midlands. Taffy led most of the improvements and held the positions of secretary (1964-76), chairman (1971-84), president (1980-86). Locally, he was a founder member and president of the Nuneaton District Union, and was instigator and first chairman of mini and junior rugby in Nuneaton. He also fought a battle with the RFU to ensure that Nuneaton would be included in the first class clubs association, and was president of Warwickshire RU from 1980 until 1982.

Nuneaton's tradition of setting the pace was further enhanced by the demise of school rugby in the early 1970s. The club was one of the first to recognise this problem for up-and-coming rugby players. Under the guidance of Thomas, Doug Hulme and other officials and players of the club, they embarked upon a program to introduce and encourage mini and junior rugby. This early initiative has paid off, with this section of the club growing in depth and strength and they established an enviable reputation and honours of its own. Since its inception in 1973-74, national honours have included: Gareth Mitchell (England Colts, 1988-89), Graham Rowntree (under-16s, 1986-87), Boulstridge, Goode and Grindle (under-16s, 1996-97), M. Needham (Great Britain Colleges, 1998) and P. Littlehales (RFSU 'A', 1998).

Graham Rowntree continued to represent England at all age groups, obtaining his full England cap in 1995-6 against Scotland. He moved to Leicester, for whom he played 398 times. He won 54 caps for England and was twice capped in tests by the Lions. He has become a leading coach for England and the Lions.

Steve Carter achieved a first when he played for England Students Rugby League side, winning the Students' World Cup in 1989.

Nuneaton fly-halves have dominated the county teams, and in 1988-89 season, in all county age groups, all fly-half positions were occupied by Nuneaton players. R. Massey (county captain), W. Masser (under-21s), S. Burns (under-18s), L. Thomas (under-16s) and G. Mitchell (Colts) were all products of Nuneaton's mini and junior system. The mini and junior production line continues into its 40th year. In addition, the ladies XV was formed in 2002-03, with a squad strength of 20 players and a full fixture list.

The centenary year of 1979 produced various events throughout the season, including a black tie club dinner held at the Co-Op Club in Nuneaton, with over 300 members and guests attending. The fixture list that year contained 46 matches, including six Welsh games, one Irish, 10 senior clubs, the RAF, and Minneapolis from the USA, plus their normal club fixtures. Unfortunately, Nuneaton's record for the season was: P46 W18 L26 D2. Terry McCarthy was club captain and played every match.

The 1980s saw many changes within the structure of rugby football in general, and for Nuneaton they were not to the club's best advantage. On the basis of their merit table performances, they were placed in Division 3 of the Championships. Nuneaton remained in the lower leagues and were relegated from Division 3 to National League 4 North, then down to National League 5 North. Further restructuring of the leagues (such as the introduction of the Premier League) put Nuneaton into National 3 North. In 2003 Nuneaton won their league and promotion to National Division Two.

In the National Knockout Cup, Nuneaton had two good runs, one in 1989-90, when they were beaten at home by Saracens in the third round, and in 1999-2000, when they reached the fourth round, but lost against Northampton.

Nuneaton's Colts team of 1987-88 was one of the best sides in the Midlands, and possibly the country, and an excellent season culminated in G. Mitchell winning an England Colts cap and the team becoming Warwickshire County Champions for the first time in the club's history. They won the County Championship for the second time in 1991-92 season.

Darren Garforth joined the club in 1988 from Coventry Saracens and played for Nuneaton from 1988 to 1991. Although he had England trials during his stay at Nuneaton before joining Leicester, he was eventually selected for England, playing 25 times and winning six Barbarian caps. Darren retired from premier rugby in March 2003. Appreciating his time at Nuneaton, Darren came back, filling the position of player/coach and assisting Nuns in their push for further promotion.

With the development of the senior sides and the continued expansion of the mini and junior section, the Attleborough Road facilities became stretched to the limit. A decision was taken to look for a new home where they could accommodate their playing membership on one site without having to play on various grounds around the town. Attleborough Road would be sold off, and with grants from the Sports Council, the proceeds would finance a new site identified at Liberty Way. This site is 1.5 miles from the old ground and covers an area of 50 acres, as opposed to the five acres at the old ground.

In 2014 the Nuns were top of National 3.

(Thanks to Eric Ballard)

OADBY WYGGESTONIAN

OADBY WYGGESTONIAN has to be the most unwieldy name in rugby. They were formed by the merger of two old clubs – Oadby and Old Wyggestonians – in 1971.

Oadby RFC was formed in 1886 by members of Oadby Sunday School Cricket Club on the outskirts of Leicester. The Black Dog, a local pub, became the club headquarters and a field off Wigston Lane was the home pitch. Oadby must have been a good side as they defeated Stoneygate on the 9th February 1889. The euphoria didn't last, as Stoneygate won the return match by a large margin. The official formation of the club was in 1890 by a group led by Tom Blackwell.

Any delusions of grandeur at Oadby were crushed in 1891 when they were omitted from the Leicestershire RU's new Senior League. This forced them to play in a 'junior cup' competition and to find friendly matches. Oadby reached the Junior Cup final in April 1893, but lost to St. Leonards. The club's improvement was recognised by the county, who promoted the first XV to the Senior Cup. They rapidly reached the Senior Cup final, but lost to Leicester 'A'.

The rapid rise encouraged Oadby to enter the prestigious Midland Counties Cup in 1896, and that year three Oadby players were invited for Midland County trials, whereas only two Tigers were selected. None of the trio were, however, selected for the Counties side. It was a high-watermark, as Oadby went into decline and were struggling in the Junior Cup within five years. This was despite them establishing a steady supply of talented boys from the local school.

In 1896 the club were embroiled in an unpleasant dispute when it was alleged a Belgrove Rovers player had been offered 20p to throw a match against Oadby. The case was never proved, and eventually the county union lost interest in trying to show anyone to be guilty.

Oadby got a better press with the selection of Sam Matthews for the Midlands against the 1905 All Blacks. Matthews had begun with Oadby before joining the Tigers and winning an England trial.

Around this time, Oadby reached the semi-final of the LRU Senior Cup, which proved one of the oddest matches in rugby history. Oadby and Aylestone St. James, their opponents, arrived to find no goalposts at the venue. A spade was found, holes were dug, and the posts dropped in. Not surprisingly, the posts were far from vertical.

One of the posts fell over during the first half, but the situation was saved when a spectator offered to hold up the offending post! This worked well, until torrential rain proved too much for the heroic spectator, who walked away and the post fell over. The referee decided enough was enough and abandoned the match. Oadby won the replay, but lost in the final to Fosse Road.

The club gained strength in the years before the Great War, culminating in 1912-13. That season they were the local champions, winning all three local cup competitions, including the Rolleston and Senior Cups.

The 1920s began well for Oadby with two junior finals – both lost. Yet within a couple of years they folded due to loss of interest. It took another decade before 2000 spectators saw the revived club play another match at Uplands Road Park, their new home. The reason for the huge crowd was that the opposition was an all-star XV led by Douglas Prentice, the Tigers captain.

Doug Norman

Inspired by the match, Oadby were able to borrow Doug Norman, a famous player for Leicester and England, to help the club become established. Oadby did well and won 17 of 25 matches that season. Later Doug Norman became club president.

Oadby were associated with another international in the 1950s, when Mike Wade came through their juniors, but departed for Leicester, with whom he was capped.

Old Wyggestonians were the old boys of Wyggeston Grammar School. Before OWs was established, the school had produced Percy Lowrie (1888-1956), who played for Leicester and England. The school preferred soccer in the 19th century, although a Wyggeston RFC operated briefly in the 1890s.

Rugby came to Wyggeston Boys School in 1920 with the appointment of Thomas Kingdom as headmaster of the school. An old boys rugby section was formed in 1921 that played on Victoria Park. The club's founders were G.R. Eaton and C.D. Parker. The first match was not a success, as the new club were crushed 35-0 by Leicester Barbarians. Some reports put the score at 60-0!

Results improved when enough players were found to field two teams, and Old Wyggs were regarded as a top junior side by 1930, when they fielded four XVs, plus a 'Thursday half-day' side.

In 1935 the OW Association bought an eight-acre ground for cricket and rugby in Oadby for the princely sum of £2,000. The rugby ground was christened on the 14th September 1935 with a 10-6 victory over Olney.

OWs lost the Oadby ground during World War Two, but managed to field one team. 1945 saw several Old Wyggs come to prominence: Doug Prentice and Billy Moore, who played for Leicester and were capped for England in the last Wartime Service International.

The early 1950s saw OWs field David Attenborough, who played briefly for them at flanker. He eventually joined the BBC and became one of the most famous broadcasters in the history of television.

Wyggeston Grammar School produced many fine rugby players and were regulars in the National School Sevens. In 1964 they drew Millfield School in the first round. They were taken apart by a teenage prodigy called Gareth Edwards, who was unknown at the time but became the greatest player of his era.

In 1971 an amalgamation of Oadby and Old Wyggestonian took place. The merger came about when Stuart Anderson of Old Wyggs, and Maynard Allsop and Rod Mitchell of Oadby, who all lived on the same street, got their heads together and reasoned that both Oadby and Old Wyggs could benefit from becoming a combined club.

The first match of the merged club was on the 15th September 1971, with a 17-11 victory over a local invitation XV. The essential pragmatism of club rugby was demonstrated when the First XV took the field in Old Wygg's colours, whilst the lower teams wore Oadby's old colours. The 1970s were difficult for the merged club, but things improved towards the end of the decade when they reached the Leicestershire Cup final, losing to Westleigh 10-7.

The 1970s saw OW receive a boost when Leicester Tigers asked the club to allow them to use OW's ground as a training base. This saved the famous greensward of Welford Road for matchdays, whilst in return OW had floodlights and other improvements made to their ground.

The best known OW player of modern times was Simon Povoas, who went on to Leicester and England 'B'. Currently, OW play in the Midlands leagues.

(Thanks to Denis Whitaker)

OLNEY

OLNEY IS A delightful village only a few miles from Bedford. The rugby club are one of the oldest rugby teams in the world, being founded in 1877. Their first recorded game was played on Cherry Orchard, a meadow on the banks of the River Ouse that is now the town cemetery.

In the 19th Century, Olney's arch-opponents were Bedford RUFC. Already an established side, Olney gave Bedford their first ever match at Goldington Road on 9th October 1886. Bedford won by 10-3 after Olney had opened with a goal worth three points.

The cerise and french grey colours of the Olney Rugby Club are thought to be unique. It is believed the original jerseys were a gift from the first captain at the formation of the club. Except for two short periods, when football jerseys were almost impossible to obtain shortly after World War One, the players have never worn any other colour.

The most colourful international from Olney was Blair Swannell, who was a member of the British Isles tour to Australia in 1899 and to New Zealand in 1904. He decided to remain in Australia and played for New South Wales in 1905 before being capped by his adopted country.

Olney's most famous player was Edgar Mobbs, the Northampton legend. Mobbs was one of 16 members who lost their lives in World War One. He had moved to Northampton and, at the outbreak of the war, formed the Sportsmen's Battalion. A wartime international was actually played on the County Ground, Northampton in 1915 between England and Scotland, with Edgar Mobbs as captain of the home side. The side included Jack Gillam, Ned Mann and Henry Grierson of Olney.

Olney continued to produce top-class players between the wars. The Millward family were famous rugby players. John Millward, Senior and Junior, both played for Olney, as did two other relatives – all scrum-halves. .

Ray Longland began with Olney before going on to play for Bedford, Northampton and England. His departure from Olney was contentious as his home club weren't consulted when he defected to Bedford. Bedford were censured by the RFU for improper approaches to other clubs' players.

Longland was one of a number of Olney players who moved to bigger clubs as the once proud club had to accept junior status. Others included England trialists Tommy Crouch and Roger Perkins, whilst Sam Kitchener had 19 years in Bedford's First XV. Kitchener, a man of strong religious principles, turned down a chance to play for England against France because it meant playing on Sunday.

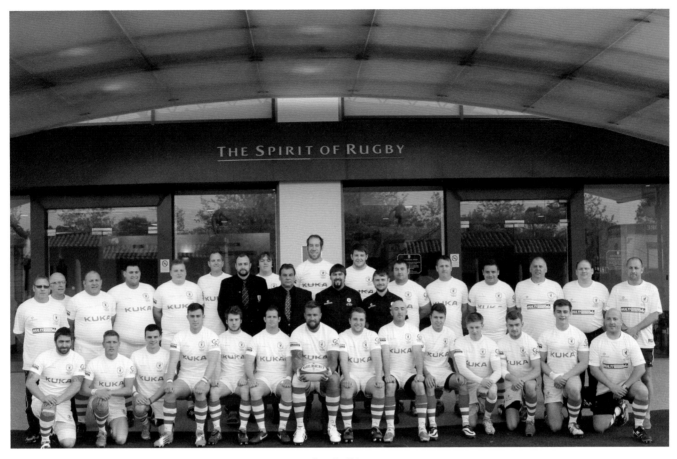

Rugby Lions

Gerald 'Beef' Dancer of Bedford and the British Lions remembered Roger Perkins with mixed feelings: "The best hooker I ever played with was Roger Perkins of Bedford... a country boy from Olney, which used to be a sort of nursery at the time for both Bedford and Northampton. We had some great times together at Northampton. I remember one year, I got Roger drunk before the Old Paulines match and we tried to bring him round with cold water. During the game, the referee asked our captain to send him off. 'Some mate you are,' he said to me afterwards."

Beef also recalled: "We once had a rough match and an opponent kept hitting Roger, who called a 'domino move'. I asked him once what a 'domino move' was. Roger told me to wait and see. At the next scrum, Roger flattened his adversary, who went out like a light. 'That's a domino,' says old Roger. 'Double six'."

For those who remained at Olney, the years between the wars reached their greatest heights in the 1934-5 season. Olney won 26 of their 34 games, amassing 711 points, with only 198 scored against. Reg Tompkins scored 40 tries as a wing three-quarter, and Alec Bell scored 30 tries in the centre.

After World War Two the local school stopped playing rugby, which reduced the club's life blood and led to the club developing its own youngsters.

Since the arrival of leagues, Olney have twice been Southern Counties North champions in 1998 and 2008.

RUGBY LIONS

"The town of Rugby should be synonymous with the very best of rugby football."

THE TOWN TEAM of Rugby have always lived in the shadow of the famous school. Relations between the two have always been good. The town's side came into existence in 1873, but a club seemed to have existed in the town before that date.

Rugby RFC must have had considerable status in the game as the first England trial match, North v South, was played on Reynolds Field, which was the club's first home. Rugby RFC suffered only one defeat in 22 matches in 1877-78, a season that included a win over the highly regarded Burton-on-Trent club. Eight years later Rugby confirmed their status by winning the Midland Counties Cup, defeating Moseley in the final. Moseley gained their revenge in the following year's final and Rugby were finalists again in 1903, losing to Leicester.

Perhaps the club's finest hour came in 1889-90, when they played the first Newport 'Invincibles' team and scored two of the three tries that Newport conceded that season.

Decline soon afflicted the town club, but hope came from an unusual quarter when L.J. Percival, son of the school's headmaster, took over the captaincy. Percival instigated a tradition that masters from the school played for Rugby RFC. Some great internationals were thus associated with the club: Geoffrey Conway (18 England caps), John Bruce-Lockhart (two Scotland caps) and Harold Kittermaster (seven England caps). Other internationals included E.H. Wynne (Scotland), H. George (Scotland), J. Hall (England), M. Bradby (England), D.G. Davies (Wales) and P. Dunkley (England). Percival himself was an England international.

After Percival, the next great instigator of change was Geoffrey Conway, who arrived in 1922 and transformed Rugby into a fine side. In two seasons under Conway's leadership the club won 51 of 74 matches. After Conway's departure, the club continued to be a force in the Midlands until the 1960s, when the club found retaining its best players difficult while in competition with other Midlands clubs, such as Bedford, Leicester, Northampton and Coventry. Top-class players such as Rodney Webb, Stan Purdy, Danny Hearn, David Powell and Eric Gilchrist played for Rugby before winning international honours at other clubs. Lesser names also won honours: Norman Marr and Eric Bates both won England trials in the mid-1970s.

The period between 1987 and 1991 marks the most successful in the history of the club. The club were a little miffed to find themselves placed in Division 4 North in 1987 at the outset of league rugby, but they rose to Level 1 in 1991. The arrival of new players, most notably Steve Brain, Coventry's England international hooker and Rugby's inspirational captain, saw the side march through the newly-created league system until it reached the very top, with promotion to Division One in 1990-91. They then slipped into Division 3, forcing a reformation of the old club as 'Rugby Lions FC' in 1995.

A happier memory was the presence of the club's finest player: Eddie Saunders, a long-legged winger. Eddie arrived from Coventry in the 1980s and scored 251 tries in 381 appearances for Rugby Lions, including scoring a club record of 39 tries in one season. He was England's top try-scorer for two seasons, but never got more than an England trial. Eddie is viewed as perhaps the best player who never won an international cap.

Mark Mapletoft was another Lions legend. He scored 1,000 points in 14 years, beginning with Rugby and moving to Gloucester, Saracens and Harlequins. Mark won an England cap in 1997.

A brief era of stability ended in 2002-03, when the club lost all 26 league games. The Lions have spent the seasons since moving up and down the national leagues. In 2011, under a new management structure, the Lions set out a five-year plan to reach the Premiership. However, after one season the club found itself out of the league structure altogether. A season of friendlies with a squad of players based around the Lion-hearted Tailenders vets side were cheered on by a very loyal group of dedicated supporters in games against other clubs only too happy to help the Lions regain their league status.

The club reformed and were readmitted to the leagues for season 2013-14, starting in Midlands 5 and gaining promotion in both seasons 2013-14 and 2014-15. They also became Midlands Junior Vase Champions in 2014 and 2015, and secured a trip to Twickenham in 2014 to play in the RFU Junior Vase Final.

CHAPTER THIRTEEN - LONDON

"London clubs are not good enough, my boy. They are all chinless wonders and medical students down there."
Michael Green's father's advice to the great rugby writer

LONDON SUBURBS

THE ANCIENT GAME of street football disappeared from the highways of London in 1580, when the Lord Mayor banned it. A version of street football was to be found in many of the schools of the city, which was remarkable considering they tended to be based round churches and space was at a premium. Eventually, most of the old schools moved to the outskirts of the city, where land was cheap until urbanisation became a factor in the 20th century.

The City of London itself had been expanding rapidly since the 18th century, due largely to the arrival of workers driven off the common land by its enclosure. Another influx came in the form of affluent young men from the provinces in search of a career in the legal or medical professions. It was medical students at the teaching hospitals who brought rugby to the city and the world. Many had been educated at Rugby School before entering Guy's Hospital, where the world's first rugby club was formed in 1843. Initially, matches were 'in-house', but soon Guy's played their counterparts at St. Thomas's Hospital.

Gradually, most of the city's hospitals formed rugby clubs and provided many of the game's best players. Curiously, the England rugby selectors regularly picked players from the London hospitals, but ignored hospital rugby outside of London. Perhaps an element of snobbery applied because, in the provinces, trainee doctors were paid a salary, whilst medical students in London were expected to live on a private income.

Almost without exception the earliest rugby players were blessed with a private income and were the products of public schools. Their numbers were small, for in 1865 there were less than 20 football clubs in London. Rugby expanded rapidly in the 1870s, and a growing number of ordinary people wanted to play the game. Some of the aspirants were neither rich nor blessed with special talent. They had little to offer the premier clubs and had difficulty in getting a game. They could only succeed by contacting old school chums and forming an 'old boys' club. The old boys clubs began modestly, but eventually became the lifeblood of the new sport. Dozens were formed, and many survive today.

The earliest old boys club in England is Old Paulines, the ex-pupils of St. Paul's School. The school originally lay within the cathedral grounds until a lack of space forced it into the suburbs. Paulines were followed by Old Merchants Taylors, Old Milhillians and Old Leysians, who all regularly produced international players from a tiny number of available players. This was extraordinary when viewed alongside the operations of the big clubs, such as Coventry, Northampton, Leicester and Gloucester, who had huge resources and could spend serious time and money pursuing the best available talent. The old boys could only draw from within their own ranks, but they were also more focused and better drilled because their players had learnt the game from a single sports teacher. Outside their ranks, few players had advanced rugby skills because few clubs taught them to newcomers; training videos and films were unheard of in those days and the RFU disapproved of writing about rugby for money.

If London was the home of rugby union in 1900, it certainly wasn't the numeric heartland, for there were only 20 clubs within a dozen miles of the centre. The small number of clubs in London during Victorian times is not surprising when one considers the population of the City of London was three times what it was in 2000. Redevelopment, the Blitz and social upheaval have seen an exodus of people to the suburbs.

The number of clubs grew to 100 by 1925 with the emergence of a new wave of old boys clubs. These came from the new grammar schools, which imitated the public schools. The new grammar school teams were also different in being more open to talented newcomers. A huge forward or flying winger could be absorbed into their ranks without any problem, whereas the old clubs clung to restricted membership.

The old boys clubs, new and old, had little influence with the traditional rulers of London rugby: the county unions of Middlesex, Surrey, Kent and the Eastern Counties. Their cosy world of county matches had unwelcome opposition in the early 1900s, when the Northern Union tried to galvanise interest in their sport within the city confines. In 1908 the NU organised the first ever test match against Australia at Park Royal, Willesden. The four London RFU counties countered with a 'London representative XV' to play the Australian RU tourists (known as 'the Rabbits', but later the Wallabies – the NU visitors had already pinched the name of the Kangaroos). London RU, with eight internationals, beat the Wallabies RU 3-0, but lost the return fixture. Their success helped to kill interest in the NU international, which attracted only 2,014 spectators.

The Northern Union repeatedly tried, but failed, to engender interest in its code in the capital. Their greatest gift to London sport has been the Rugby League Cup final, held annually at Wembley, which could attract 60,000 spectators, most from the north.

By contrast, the London RFU representative side became a serious force, despite having only a handful of fixtures each decade. They drew with New South Wales in 1927 and inflicted the only English defeat on the 1951 Springboks. But the "representative XV" were, in fact, totally unrepresentative of the city's rugby in the 20th century, which consisted of suburban clubs that often operated from council pitches.

County matches were played on Wednesday afternoons. It was argued London players never had the affiliation to their county because London was bigger than the county. The early 1960s saw the re-emergence of non-OB sides, such as London Welsh, Wasps and Richmond, after OB sides had dominated London rugby. The decline of old boys rugby in the post-war years was partially due to the fall in the population of the capital. The building of the new towns in the Home Counties led to a quarter of the population leaving London.

Today London has a steady flow of new players from New Zealand, Australia and South Africa, who head for the bright lights and have little difficulty in getting a game of rugby.

MIDDLESEX

"An acre in Middlesex is better than a principality in Utopia."
Macauley

IT HAS BEEN generally accepted that the Middlesex RFU was founded on the 15th November 1879, but several games had already been played before that date under the county name. Most of these early fixtures were at the Old Deer Park, Richmond and usually against Surrey. The first full season is, however, best forgotten because Middlesex lost all of their matches.

In 1885 the county was composed of the following clubs: Richmond, Clapham Rovers, United Hospitals, Marlborough Nomads, Harlequins, Rosslyn Park, Kensington, Old Cheltonians, Upper Clapton, Middlesex Wanderers, Saracens and Old Internationals (known today as Borough Road College).

Middlesex had improved by 1887, when they were invited to participate in a football tournament for Queen Victoria's Jubilee at the Kennington Oval. Middlesex chose a team composed almost solely of internationals for a match against Lancashire, which was lost by a try to nil.

The following season Middlesex established themselves as the unofficial county champions. In 1888-89, for reasons unknown, only one fixture was played, against the New Zealand Maoris at Sheffield Park, Sussex. Middlesex included six internationals and won by nine points to nil. In 1891 Middlesex supplied 11 members of British touring party, including the captain, W.E. MacLagan of London Scottish. Despite this honour, Middlesex went into decline and suffered nine consecutive defeats. They reversed the run with a win over Midland Counties in 1894.

Middlesex finally reached the County final in 1905, but lost to Durham on a mud heap at West Hartlepool. That year Middlesex played the first All Blacks at Stamford Bridge – home of Chelsea FC – losing 34-0. The following season they played the South Africans on their inaugural tour, losing 9-0.

The 1920s got off to a bad start with the election of the British Isles captain, R. Cove-Smith, as county captain. Because of eye trouble he was unable to play a single game. He was replaced by another great English forward, W.W. Wakefield. The club reached the final of the 1929 County Championship.

On the 14th May 1925, it was proposed that a seven-a-side competition between the Middlesex clubs should take place at the end of the season. The Middlesex Sevens became a highlight of the rugby season and endures into the 21st century as the London Sevens.

In the 1930s Middlesex successfully fought off an attempt by the Northern Union to introduce rugby league to the capital.

After World War Two Middlesex led work to expand rugby union across the county. County President Bill Ramsay organised a coaching course for schoolmasters at the Twickenham Technical College on behalf of the county. 200 people turned up. This set something of a pattern, and in later seasons an excellent coaching system evolved, with Middlesex leading the way.

1950 saw the foundation of the Middlesex School Union and the restructuring of the South Eastern County Grouping. Middlesex flourished throughout the decade, when the highlights were two county titles. The county regularly provided players to England – notably Ted Woodward (Wasps), Albert Agar (Harlequins), Brian Boobyer (Rosslyn Park), Nim Hall (Richmond), Pat Sykes (Wasps) and Doug Wilson (Met Police). The county also provided ten players to the London Counties team that recorded the only defeat of the touring 1950 Springboks.

In 1958 Middlesex provided five players to the British Lions: Doug Baker (OMT), Johnnie Williams (Old Millhillians), Tom Reid and Robin Thompson (Bath, London Irish) and Doug Wilson.

BARKING

FOUNDED IN 1930 as 'Park Modern Old Boys', the club played on municipal pitches in Barking Park until 1989, when they moved to Goresbrook. They made an excellent entry to rugby, with 16 wins from 19 fixtures in their first season.

The club came into their own after World War Two when they lost only one of 66 matches over three seasons and provided Dutchy Holland and Doug Brown for Eastern Counties. They also won the Essex Sevens in 1948 and 1951 and the Eastern Counties Sevens in 1949. The club's outstanding player of the era was Bob Whittle, who was capped by EC.

The club dropped the OBs title in 1974, as they looked to widen their image in Anglian rugby. In 1987-88 and the following season Barking won the Essex Senior Cup and qualified for the National KO Cup.

The club's success brought a squarely-built prop-forward called Jason Leonard to prominence. The teenage Leonard was spotted by teacher Mickey Eyres, who played for the club and was always looking for potential players. Leonard came through the Barking Juniors before playing for the England under-19s and moving to Saracens, who were beginning to become established in England's elite. Saracens were Division Two champions in

Jason Leonard

Leonard's debut season. He made his England debut in 1990 against Argentina and went on to win over 100 caps for England and the Lions over 14 seasons. Leonard joined Harlequins in 1991 to further his international career, which was to last 16 years and earned him a world record 114 England caps and a World Cup winner's medal. He was also the first England player for 60 years to be in four Grand Slam-winning sides. Despite being England's most capped player, he never scored a try for England.

Barking may have lost their best ever player, but they themselves rose to National Three. In the 1990s Jeff Probyn, the former England prop, became player/director of rugby in National Two South. The most recent England international to emerge from the club was Kris Chesney, who moved to Saracens in 1995 and subsequently played for England under 21s and England Sevens.

CIVIL SERVICE

THE MODERN IMAGE of a civil servant is vastly different from the role in 1863 when Civil Service FC was formed. Civil servants in Victorian times were less than 50,000 in number and tended to be recruited from 'Varsity types', usually Classics scholars with skills in Latin and Greek. This may seem curious today, but the universities were created by medieval kings to provide educated staff for the royal needs. Latin was the language of educated men, and the tradition of learning it lived on, even into the 20th century. It died out

when the demands of the welfare state dictated massively increased staff numbers drawn from a wider section of the public.

The size of the civil service itself grew exponentially as the state expanded until over a million people were employed. The London area was the hub of the organisation, which guaranteed a steady stream of new blood to the august Civil Service football club.

The Civil Service FC of 1863 drew its numbers from the higher echelons of the service. Its founder was Sir Henry Truman Wood from the Patent Office, who was secretary for 35 years. The new club even sent a delegate to the first meeting of the FA in 1863.

The club formed a soccer section, which provided six players to the Scotland soccer team who played England in the first international. The soccer side have remained a staunch amateur organisation – in the 1890s they refused to pay their annual subscription to the Football Association for fear of impinging their amateur status – and it saved money.

The Civil Service FC were also represented at the founding of the RFU in 1871. Civil Service FC were a force on and off the field and had a fixture list to rival the best. They soon had two England internationals in JE. Bentley and W.W. Hewitt, although they had divided loyalties with other clubs.

D. Evanson was CSFC's best player of the era and was capped five times by England. He eventually was persuaded to move to Richmond, who, along with Blackheath, 'borrowed' Civil Service's best players.

The borrowing problem grew so bad that CSFC were forced to abandon fixtures for 1878-79 because the available players were not up to scratch. It seemed the end of the club was nigh, until hard work from the Post Office players saved the day. The club recovered and in 1885 defeated Paris at Dulwich. It was the first visit by a French rugby team to England, although the French team were composed almost entirely of English-born players. Civil Service visited France in 1902, and defeated Racing Club of Paris 27-0.

The next international to appear for the club was T.S. Kelly, who won 12 England caps around 1900 and played for Lancashire, Middlesex and Devon. The most famous player to appear for CS was Matthew Mullineux, who captained the second British Isles team in 1899. Mullineux was a remarkable man, but not a remarkable rugby player. Educated at Cambridge, he qualified for CS until taking Holy Orders, at which point he moved to Richmond. He was never capped by England, nor even won a trial, and he only appeared in one of four test matches for the British Isles in Australia. Mullineux had little time for rugby in the years leading up to World War One as he served as a naval chaplain. He won the military cross during the Great War and worked prodigiously after the war to commemorate those who fell. He organised the first pilgrimages for families to Flanders and Gallipoli in the early 1920s and was one of the organisers of the Menin Gate at Ypres to commemorate the war dead. He finished his days as vicar of Marham in Norfolk and is remembered as the champion of the war casualties.

J.F. Brown, a contemporary of Mullineux, captained CS before moving to South Africa, where he developed rugby in the region.

CSFC kept its fixture lists between the wars, and regularly fielded nine sides on a Saturday. Its finest fixture list came in 1923, when it celebrated the game's centenary with nine matches against Rugby School and all the other surviving clubs – including Guys and Blackheath – who had attended the 1871 RFU formation.

Their grounds included Wimbledon Common, Raynes Park, Old Deer Park, Richmond Athletic Ground, Kensal Rise and Duke's Meadow, Chiswick.

After World War Two Civil Service reclaimed their status and unearthed another international in C.G. Woodruff, who moved to Harlequins and won four caps.

Besides the Saturday fixture list, the club also organises a Civil Service representative side, who play the RAF, Royal Navy, Army and the United Banks XV.

CLAPHAM ROVERS

CLAPHAM ROVERS FC had a brief but distinguished rugby history. Rovers played both codes of football and won the FA Cup in 1880. The rugby section were among the founder members of the RFU. Their best-known member was Seymour Whalley, who helped found the London Society of Referees.

The club played on Clapham Common and fielded a string of England players and trialists: R.H. and L. Birkett both played for England. R.H. was capped by England at both codes. He was the father of Jack Birkett, the famous England international centre. Other internationals from Rovers were Charles and Henry Bryden, Dr. A. Allport and C.H. Coates. J.E. Taylor played for Rovers before moving to India and captaining the Calcutta club, who donated the Calcutta Cup to the RFU.

Clapham Rovers rugby section disbanded in 1895 and many of the players moved to Brighton RFC.

(Thanks to P.M. O'Keeffe)

CROYDON

RUGBY WAS PLAYED in Croydon from the 1860s, notably at Whitgift School and by Old Whitgiftians (which was a closed club). The first rugby club in the town was Oakfield FC, which existed from 1867 to 1874. The best-known member was C.J. Rothney, who organised the presentation of the Calcutta Cup to the RFU.

The first Croydon RFC emerged in 1877, but lasted only a season. The second entity, which had a first-class fixture list, was formed in 1879 and survived until 1896. It emerged from the ashes of North Park Whitgiftians. Despite the change of name to Croydon, it still attracted boys leaving Whitgift School and the officials were usually OWs. Croydon eventually disappeared with the establishment of Old Whitgift FC. The club's best-known player was Sir Charles Cleveland, who was an excellent forward at Oxford, and was capped by England in 1887. In later life he was head of the British Secret Service and helped to frustrate many enemy activities.

Croydon appears to have reformed around 1900, but was soon wound up, as were local rivals Norwood FC and Selhurst Wanderers. The only surviving clubs in the area were Sutton, Streatham and the London & Westminster Bank.

In July 1910 an appeal was made to reform the club specifically for locals who played rugby but were not old Whitgiftians. A ground was found on Mitcham Common and Frank Chamberlain, an OMT (Old Merchant Taylors), was captain and for many years the driving force. A fixture list was created, beginning with St.Mary's College and largely made up of local college sides.

Croydon adopted the borough arms for its badge, and the Earl of Pembroke was elected president. Amongst the earliest members was full-back H.M. Rushworth, who is described as having played in a blazer over an old rugger jersey.

The current Croydon RFC was formed from the merger of Shirley Wanderers and Old Croydonians. Shirley Wanderers (formed 1956) were a nomadic side who operated from the Shirley Poppy public house. The poppy grows in the neighbourhood and was adopted as the club badge. Old Croydonians RFC ceased playing in 2001, but were persuaded to join the Wanderers as Croydon RFC.

In recent seasons Croydon have played in the Surrey leagues with their most recent highlight being in 2012 when they were semi-finalists in the Junior Vase.

EALING

"The Queen of the Suburbs"
19th Century quote

THE SMALL AGRICULTURAL town of Ealing has undergone major changes since 1838, when the Great Western Railway opened a station at Ealing Haven (now called Broadway). Initially, Ealing was a backwater, until it was transformed into a dormitory town by Henry Austin, who specialised in developing the outskirts of London, before moving to America in 1872. It was the arrival of the underground railway in 1880 that brought the biggest change as the population rose from 5,000 to 30,000 in 20 years.

Ealing RFC played their first match on 6th November 1869, beating Hanwell College by two goals. Their early fixtures were sporadic and the next recorded match was a draw with Harlequins in November 1870. A report in The Field magazine states that a game had taken place in which ten Harlequins defeated nine-man Ealing at Tufnell Park. Little wonder that 20-a-side matches were soon dropped in favour of XVs.

Legend has it that Ealing sent representatives to the Pall Mall meeting in 1871 that established the RFU. The Ealing delegates met a party from Wasps on the way and the two groups preferred a few convivial drinks to attending the meeting. Unlike many of those represented at the Pall Mall restaurant, Ealing survived and were officially founded in October 1871.

The club had a variety of home grounds in the early days. They began on Ealing Common and then wandered to Mill Hill Park, West Middlesex Polo Club, West Ealing, Drayton Green, Perivale, Alperton and eventually to Gunnersbury Park, which was the property of the club's first president, Leopold de Rothschild.

Their time at Gunnersbury Park saw the club running six regular sides. But World War Two cost Ealing their home and they lived hand to mouth by sharing facilities with Barclays Bank and later UCS Old Boys. However, in 1958 the council leased the club a ground on Horsenden Hill. The era began badly, as the new clubhouse was prone to being flooded by sewage. But it was still an improvement on their old home at the Ballot Box pub, where two ancient iron baths where shared amongst 30 players and the referee.

Ealing's most famous son arrived in the 1950s. Michael Green was a Fleet Street journalist who made his Ealing debut for the thirds wearing leather shoes because he had forgotten his rugby boots. The referee saw Green's hopeless predicament and agreed to swap his footwear with the ex-Leicester man. He joined Ealing under odd circumstances. A relative of Green's had played for Osterley RUFC, a club that was near Ealing. He took the tube to Ealing and signed for the local club, which, he thought, was Osterley and went home. He had actually joined Ealing. Green compiled the rugby results for the Observer newspaper and steadfastly refused to include Harpenden's rugby results in the paper because he was once kicked by a Harpenden player.

Green eventually put his opinion about real rugby, in rather rough terms, to Chris Brasher, the sports editor. In summing up, Green commented: "95% of rugby in England is played by people without a full team, people who vomit all over the pitch, people who don't know the rules – not the golden wonders of Twickenham." Brasher then told Green to write an article about life at the bottom. Gradually, this article became the book The Art of Coarse Rugby, published in 1957. To date Green's books have sold over a million copies.

The limelight that directed towards Ealing helped them prepare for their centenary when Harlequins renewed the fixture from 1870 and the first XV celebrated the season with only five defeats in 31 matches. The arrival of league rugby in 1987-88 saw Ealing as champions of London One, and they were Middlesex Cup champions on three occasions.

Since 1999 Ealing have seen much change. That year they moved to Castle Bar and became 'Ealing Trailfinders' in support of their sponsors. The club were National 1 Champions in 2013.

ESHER

ESHER WAS A sleepy backwater community in Surrey until improvements to the ancient A3 road transformed the small village at the foot of the South Downs into a busy dormitory town for London. The Kingston bypass opened in 1923 and was one of a series of new arterial roads constructed by London County Council in the years after World War One. The population of the village grew rapidly as commuters moved into the area.

Esher RUFC was formed in 1923 and within six years was running six XVs. The number rose to eight teams by 1939. Amongst the first players was Aubrey Downey, who was the reigning English 880 yard champion at the time. Downey's family were to be associated with the Surrey club for many years.

The club went into suspension during the war, but in 1945 development was started at the ground in Molesey Road in Hersham, and soon a new clubhouse had been built. Adjoining land was later bought and the ground, with its seven pitches, is now the largest belonging to any club in England. At times Esher fielded 13 sides, plus schoolboy XVs during the Christmas and Easter holidays.

Esher soon established a high-class fixture list with clubs on both sides of the Welsh border. Several players represented the club at the top level: George Jenkins was a Welsh trialist, Bill Downey captained Cambridge University in 1957, P.T.C. King represented the Barbarians and Hampshire, Frank Booth was a notable player who moved to Leicester and became a renowned coach, and Ken Wilmshurst was the British Olympic captain in 1956.

The club became one of the best and highest-scoring sides in Surrey in the 1950s, with 633 points accumulated in 1953-54. The best known captains of the era were Ian Brackenbury, who was first XV captain for four seasons, and P.J. Osborn, an England trialist.

One Esher captain made headlines of the wrong kind in the 1960s when he upset the authorities on an end of season tour of Jersey. The Esherman attributed his misbehaviour to reacting to a barman who turned a soda siphon on his party during a "quiet night's celebration".

The 1970s were a golden decade for Esher. The first XV were runners-up in the Surrey Cup on two occasions, but stepped up a level to win a hat-trick of County Cup wins.

Following major refurbishment to the club, Esher became popular hosts for touring teams. In the 1960s they entertained several Argentinian clubs and defeated both the Zambian and Spanish national teams.

Other sides at Esher were less successful – and proud of it! The club's veteran side were called the 'Expendables' after a John Wayne war film. Esher's Expendables had their own laws e.g. 'Forwards should be able to run 15 yards without assistance', 'backs should be able to run 30 yards without oxygen', 'players who are unavailable for selection are asked to notify their captain by kick-off on match day', and 'members are asked to pay their annual subs at least once every four years'.

The most famous Esher player is John Inverdale, the TV commentator, who was a top-class full-back. John also served on the board of the club. Other well-known players include Robbie Shaw, who won two USA caps, Chad Erskine (ex-Rotherham) and Irish international Rob Henderson. On the coaching side Mick Schmid and Kris Chesney have been with the club and ex-England internationals Peter Winterbottom and David Pears have helped to keep the club in the third level of English rugby.

In 2007 Esher made the headlines because of 4,000 Parakeets that were living wild in 50 huge poplar trees. The birds were made homeless when a tree collapsed on top of an ambulance. This forced the club to cut down the 100ft poplars and to plant smaller ones.

GREAT WESTERN RAILWAY

RAILWAYS WERE AT the forefront of technology in the 19th century and they played a significant part in the formation of the sport. Rugby in France began with the Southern Railway's team at Le Havre, where Mr Longstaff – their agent – formed a side who played against ex-patriot Britons. Today GWR RFC are unique in being the only railway side to keep their name and identity long after the railway company disappeared. Their rivals, Midland and Scottish Railway and Southern Railway RFC, disappeared long ago.

The heyday of GWR rugby was during the inter-war years, when railway rugby was a serious force. This wasn't surprising, as over 50,000 employees worked for the railway companies and they were reinforced by a steady stream of apprentices who provided new blood to the rugby sides.

GWR RFC was formed on 5th March 1927 as a one-off side for a match between the London GWR depot and their Bristol counterparts. The Bristol side were unbeaten for three years, largely due to the mud heap of a pitch they possessed behind the locomotive sheds. The London branch, however, won in Bristol and started playing regularly. Their cause was aided by Welsh players transferred to Waterloo following the 1926 general strike. The Anglo-Welsh links were maintained for many years by a series of representative matches between GWR London and their South Wales team, which often included internationals.

'Railways international' matches were arranged with sides drawn from the Welsh, French and Irish Railways. Home for the English matches was GWR's headquarters at Castle Bar near Ealing. The pitch was far from perfect, as it was covered in flint that cut the players. The problem was solved when the local schoolchildren were enlisted to collect flint as part of a geology study.

GWR was a players' club with its own traditions. Players were expected to buy opponents tea and beer, which upset the large Welsh element, who thought it an extravagant waste. Another tradition was to give presents to players on the eve of their wedding. The club minutes records one occasion when "It was the Chairman's pleasant duty to present some silly bugger with a gift on the occasion of his marriage, though it was inconveniently during the season."

The most famous player associated with GWR was W.W. Wakefield, the England Grand Slam captain who coached the club in the early 1930s. He accepted the role during a spell as a paint salesman and found the railway an excellent customer in return for a few hours at Castle Bar. 'Wakers' even brought Harlequins to Castle Bar. Quins beat GWR by 44-3.

The post-war years saw GWR with a good fixture list against the second teams of the capital's top clubs. However, a civil servant called Dr. Beeching proved a tougher opponent than any Welsh international. Beeching was hired by the government to save money. He axed many railway lines, stations and depots in a search of economic salvation. Thousands of railwaymen were made redundant and the mass hiring of apprentices was a thing of the past. GWR lost their new blood and lost most of their best fixtures.

The privatisation of the Railways in 1996 saw the end of Castle Bar as GWR's home ground. The facilities were sold off, but fortunately the club were able to hire a pitch from the new tenants.

HARLEQUINS

"Keep it simple – do it quick."
A.D. Stoop

THE WORD 'HARLEQUIN' originates in the French 'Hellequin', who were devils of medieval legend. Gradually, the word came to refer to clown-like figures of the bygone theatre. Today the word is principally associated with the upper-crust rugby club who have been one of the top sides of English rugby for generations.

Quins originated as Hampstead FC. They were formed by William Tichener in 1866 and initially played on Hampstead Heath before moving to Finchley then Highbury. They kept the Hampstead name for seven years until a change to 'Harlequins' reflected the fact that their members hailed from all over the city.

Legend has it that the consensus of members wanted to keep the 'HFC' badge on the jersey and the existing motto 'Nunquam Dormio' (I Never Sleep). This decision is supposed to have been taken after a night on the town culminated in an informal meeting under a lamppost in Hampstead. It was also decided to change the old colours of black and gold to the quartered colours that were to become famous.

Quins were present at the RFU formation and provided a player – P. Wilkinson – to the first England team. Wilkinson, however, listed his home club as 'the Law Club'.

The first official Harlequins to be capped were Herbert Sibree, who joined from Kensington, and William Leake, who played half-back for England in 1891. Quins grew in stature so quickly that within a decade the RFU was accused of favouritism in the selection of England players.

Quins' major source of player recruitment was from schoolboys identified when their 'A' team played the first XVs of public schools. The aim was to establish good relations with new talented players. So, not surprisingly, the vast bulk of Harlequin players were public schoolboys. In the 1890s Harlequins established a link with Rugby School, which produced some of the greatest names in their history, notably Adrian Stoop and Ronald Poulton-Palmer.

In 1900 Quins were invited to send a team to play Rugby School, where they encountered the school's 'boy wonder', Adrian Dura Stoop, who was bound for Blackheath FC. Quins persuaded the elegant fly-half to join them and changed the future of rugby. Stoop was the first player to realise that there were huge advantages available to a team if the ball could be moved quickly. Adrian Stoop first came to prominence at school as a brilliant gymnast, and he believed that a half-back had to possess a gymnast's attributes to make the grade. Stoop turned the role of fly-half into the pivot of the whole team whilst he was still an Oxford freshman. He separated the roles of the two half-backs into the scrum-half, who beavered away around the

Above: Adrian Stoop, and below in later years.

scrum, and the fly-half, who waited for a quick ball to attack the opposition. Stoop loved nothing better than running with the ball in hand, and he rapidly became a favourite with spectators for his attacking flair.

The Times newspaper attributed the boom in London rugby to Harlequins – and Mr. Stoop. Not everyone was impressed, however; when England opted for the all-Harlequins back-line of Stoop, Lambert, Sibree and Poulton-Palmer, one critic remarked that the national team were opting for "mere handball".

Off the field, Stoop was amongst the first to discourage players from using cigarettes and drinking alcohol during the playing season. Love him or hate him, there was so much more to A.D. Stoop than rugby. In later life as a selector he used to write to young players that had been capped for England, telling them where they could improve their game. In his private life, Stoop was a faith healer. In 1951 he resuscitated P.D. Cleavor of Harlequins, who had been concussed. Stoop put his hands on him and Cleaver regained consciousness.

Harlequins and Stoop helped pull English rugby out of the slough that had dogged it since 1895. In 1909 Stoop was the first man to catch a ball in a Twickenham international. Wales kicked off and Stoop caught the ball and kicked ahead. Bert Solomon recovered the ball, ran 40 yards and fed Fred Chapman, who touched down for the first international try at the RFU headquarters.

Despite their success, Quins led a nomadic existence, playing at Hampstead (1866), Chiswick Park (1883) and St. Thomas Hospital Ground (1896). Then, in 1909, Harlequins agreed a deal with the RFU over what one critic described as "the pretentious and costly area" at Twickenham. The fact that Quins played their home matches at Twickenham meant the stadium was used for more than just internationals. The first ever match at Twickenham was an unexpected 14-0 win over Richmond. Despite the doom-mongers, Quins thrived at Twickenham, and even began to make a profit. The RFU reacted by upping the rent charged to their tenants.

World War One took the life of numerous Quins, none more mourned than the peerless Ronnie Poulton-Palmer.

After the war, Stoop continued to play and made occasional appearances into his fifties. His place at fly-half passed to another great, W.J.A. Davies, who was also associated with the Royal Navy. Davies had an unsatisfactory entry to English rugby; he lost his ticket as the England party travelled to the match. He couldn't show it to the buffet car manager and had to miss his meal. The RFU Secretary, Charles Marriott, was not amused and insisted Davies sit next to him for the rest of the journey.

In April 1924 Quins played the USA in a 'friendly' prior to the Americans contesting the Olympic Games in Paris. The USA were the reigning Olympic champions. J.M. Currie of Quins broke his leg in the opening sorties as the Americans played gridiron in contrast to rugby. Quins were still successful, winning 21-11. The USA retained their Olympic title, beating France 17-3 in the final. The only other entrants were Romania.

Harlequins' success was cemented in the 1920s with great players such as 'Jenny' Greenwood, Archie Gracie, Dave Davies

Above: Ronnie Poulton-Palmer, who died in the Great War, and below, W.J.A. Davies.

and Wavell Wakefield. Flying Officer Wakefield was in charge of RAF recruitment at Uxbridge and used his office to select talented younger players for the RAF and Harlequins, his Saturday club. The Quins were certainly adventurous; in 1923 they became the first rugby club to fly to a match when they took a plane to Cologne to play the British Army.

W.W. Wakefield was the first modern British forward. He was incredibly quick and strong and took a lot of stopping when he got the ball in the opposition 22. Wakefield took Cherry Pillman's techniques of the pre-war era and developed them for the three back-row players who worked as a team. He also perfected the 'quick heel' from the maul and scrum. W.W. was perhaps the first English forward who had all the skills of a three-quarter. This was the legacy of years of rugby training at Sedbergh School near Kendal. Born in Beckingham on the 10th March 1898, Wakefield was the son of a fine player whose injury had denied him an Oxford rugby blue. His father was also one of the first men to fly an aeroplane in 1902. W.W. attended Cambridge after serving in the Navy and Air Force in World War One. He joined Harlequins and made his England debut in 1920. Eventually, he played 31 times for his country, missing only two internationals in seven seasons. He became England captain in 1924 and reorganised the team.

There can be no greater tribute to Wakefield than that of the All Blacks modelling their forward play on the England team of the early 1920s. At the time, the Scotland forwards were famous for their ruthlessness, particularly when dribbling. The Scots were accused of kicking any player in their path, which usually intimidated sides like England. Wakefield brought an end to the intimidation by fair means or foul (as the situation needed).

Sadly, the 1924 England v All Blacks game proved an anti-climax because England were in decline. The New Zealanders proved too good for England in a violent match, which saw Cyril Brownlie of New Zealand become the first international player ever to be sent from the field. On the field, W.W. was no angel. He once admitted biting Jimmy Clinch of Ireland, who was choking him. Clinch rapidly released his grip and never took offence. Wakefield played on until the 1930s, although he was too old for England duties. He prospered off the field, becoming Swindon's MP and receiving a knighthood in 1944.

After Wakefield's retirement, Quins were fortunate to possess a great captain in centre Bobby Davies, who made them the best London club of the era. His courage on the field wasn't so surprising as he took a sojourn from school as an 18-year-old to fight on the Western Front in World War One. He was immediately captured by the Germans and spent six months in a prisoner of war camp before being sent back to school.

Colin Laird of Quins holds the distinction of being the youngest ever player to pull on an England shirt. The fly-half was a mere 18 years and 134 days old when he made his debut during England's 11-9 victory over Wales at Twickenham on the 15th January 1927. He went on to make ten appearances for his country (scoring five tries) and was an ever-present in the side when England won their sixth grand slam in 1928.

Amongst the most famous Harlequins of the inter-war years was Douglas Bader, but although he was offered a trial by the club, it's unclear if he ever wore the famous jersey. He had a reputation for recklessness – on and off the pitch. He was seriously injured in a flying accident and lost both his legs. but refused to be written off and was back in the cockpit for the Battle of Britain. He was captured by the Germans – wooden legs and all – and became a national hero and a major film was made about his life. But even Bader's friends admitted he was a difficult person to live with.

Despite their success, Quins did not like playing at Twickenham, and in 1937 they made the first steps to finding a home of their own, away from the empty stands. "Depressing" was Adrian Stoop's description of their life at HQ. Stoop even talked to the MCC about Quins moving to Lord's Cricket Ground in Central London. That project, however, came to nothing, but eventually in 1963 the club bought a ground a mile west of HQ named the 'Stoop Ground' in honour of the great fly-half.

Harlequins were a major part of English rugby after World War Two, with four internationals in the 1947 England side: Mickey Steele-Bodger, Jika Travers, Joe Mycock and Bob Weighill. Five years later Quins provided 14 players to the trials of the Home Counties and eleven for England. The year after that Quins fielded six England players.

Harlequins' domination of South East rugby continued into the 1950s. England, however, suffered several lean years and looked for new talent. They selected ten new caps, including the Harlequin second-row partnership of John Currie and David Marques. All but one of Marques' 23 caps for England between 1956 and 1961 were won alongside Currie. Marques played 11 seasons for the Quins, one of them as club captain, and 18 games on the 1958 Lions tour, including tests against Australia and New Zealand. After retiring from rugby he crewed for GB in the America's Cup yacht race.

Quins made history in 1958 when the first penalty try ever was awarded to Leicester against them at Twickenham. Curiously, the referee awarded the penalty try for an incident that occurred 30 yards from the Quins try line.

The most unusual Harlequins international is Jeremy Spencer, who had been a ballet dancer before concentrating on rugby. Spencer had wonderful balance and an inch-perfect pass. Not surprisingly, he didn't linger long at the top with comments such as, "I can pee further than my rivals can pass" attributed to him. Spencer moved to France and helped develop players such as Fabien Pelous, the great French captain.

Robert 'Bob' Hiller was Quins best-known player of the era. Playing full-back, he won 19 England caps between 1966 and 1972. He captained England in seven internationals and scored 138 points, an England record at the time. He went on two tours with the British and Irish Lions – to South Africa in 1968 and to New Zealand in 1971.

Harlequins were always open to innovation, and in 1974 the club recruited All Black Earle Kirton as a coach who continued the philosophy of running rugby. Subsequently, they recruited Mike Davies, who was to lead the England team to the 1979-80 Grand Slam. Subsequently, they brought in great players from down under, including All Blacks John Salmon, John Gallagher, Zinzan Brooke, Troy Coker from Australia and Andre Voss from South Africa.

Will Carling, above, and Chris Robshaw, below – two of Quins' England captains.

Harlequins produced two great England captains in Peter Winterbottom (58 England caps, 1982-1993) and Will Carling. Carling was perhaps the most notable Harlequin of modern times and was a surprise selection as England captain in 1988. His reign coincided with a golden era and he led England to the Rugby World Cup Final in 1991, losing to Australia. He played for Harlequins from 1987 to 2000 and his international career ran from 1988 to 1997, including 59 appearances as captain. He captained England to three Grand Slam titles and was a member of the British Lions tour of New Zealand in 1993.

Quins made a great contribution to England's 1991 Rugby World Cup team, including Carling, Brian Moore, Paul Ackford and Mickey Skinner, who were amongst the highest profile names in British sport.

England went a step further at the 2003 Rugby World Cup, with Quins to the fore through Will Greenwood and Jason Leonard. Season 2004-05 brought Quins back to reality when they were relegated to the Championship. The club bounced back under England legend Dean Richards as director of rugby. Richards acquired some great players. Andre Vos, the ex-Springbok captain, led Quins back to the Premiership. Andrew Mehrtens, the All Black fly-half, arrived to bring experience, but it was lesser known New Zealander Nick Evans who had a longer-term effect. Although Evans won 16 Kiwi caps, he was a virtual unknown. He arrived on a three-year contract rumoured to be worth a million pounds. He was a sound hand at the tiller, and indeed 2012's Premiership Player of the Year. Two talented youngsters also arrived in Mike Brown, who established himself as England full-back, and Ugo Monye, who played for England and the Lions.

Quins and Richards were headline news in 2009 when an ugly incident occurred in the quarter-final of the Heineken Cup. Quins were accused of using a blood capsule to simulate a blood injury to a player. The 'bloodgate' cheating allowed Quins to replace the 'injured' player with a player who had already been substituted. The fall-out caused Dean Richards to resign, the physio and player to be banned, and the club to be fined a reported £259,000.

Richards was replaced by Irish international Conor O'Shea and the club has since created an outstanding academy structure, and, in view of events, new disciplinary rules on and off the field.

Quins produced a string of internationals; indeed, nine Quins were in the 2012 England party to South Africa. Kingpin of Quins and England sides in the current era is Chris Robshaw, a tough back-row forward. A product of Warlingham RFC, Robshaw went to Millfield School before joining Quins at 18 years of age. He made his England debut against Argentina in 2009, the same year he was Premiership Player of the Year. In 2011 he captained Quins to 14 successive wins on the way to the Premiership Championship and was promptly selected as England captain– the most inexperienced for 30 years. A great leader, he was, amazingly, overlooked for the 2013 Lions party amid accusations of anti-English bias by the Lions' selectors. Experts suggested Robshaw was overlooked because the selectors didn't want a proven leader in the squad who might challenge their selected leaders.

KINGS COLLEGE HOSPITAL

KINGS COLLEGE HOSPITAL RFC are one of the few survivors from the 1871 Pall Mall meeting that gave birth to the RFU. C.M. Madden and C.E. Pope represented the club, which was formed in 1862 by the Medical Department of the college.

The club helped form the Hospitals Cup in 1874 and had their captain, W.J. Penny, selected for England. Despite their part in the formation of the Hospitals Cup, Kings College Hospital were always amongst the also-rans, due mainly to a shortage of players. Life was tough for London Medical students, who didn't receive a penny in grants during their student days or as newly-qualified doctors.

KING'S COLLEGE SCHOOL OBs

KING'S COLLEGE SCHOOL, Wimbledon is one of Britain's leading rugby schools. The school dates back to 1829 and was founded by the University of London on the Strand in Central London as a junior department of King's College.

1897 was a momentous year for the school as it moved to leafy Wimbledon and the first rugby match against a casual old boys XV took place.

It took ten years for King's College School Old Boys to be officially founded by a group led by F.E. Laughton and J.D. Casswell. The club's first golden era was the early 1930s, when they won 39 of 51 fixtures over two seasons.

The 1950s were a great era as King's College School Old Boys produced a string of top players, including Chris Winn (England. Rosslyn Park, Surrey and Sussex), Robin Davies (Oxford University, London Welsh and Wales) and Gordon Bendon (Wasps, Surrey, Eastern Cos, Middlesex and England). They ranked amongst London's top OB clubs, but, needless to say, the best players gravitated to the top clubs.

In 1956 the club moved to a new ground at Kingston Vale. Eight years later they shocked the established club rankings by reaching the final of the Middlesex Sevens – the pinnacle of London club rugby before leagues and cups returned.

The school and club together produced Rickie Bartlett. Bartlett began at King's before moving to Harlequins and then playing for England. When he was reprimanded for being the slowest fly-half in English rugby history, he quipped: "and the slowest in the Home Counties too".

In 1983 King's College School Old Boys won the Surrey Cup and found themselves in the London OB's Merit Table.

LONDON IRISH

"Irish Breeding is more important to a horse than a human."
Freddie Maxwell, 1963

LONDON IRISH ARE the youngest of the three great London Exiles clubs, being formed in 1898 by a group of distinguished Irishmen living in the capital. The founders included Edward Carson, who later was one of the most controversial figures in Irish history as leader of the Ulster Unionists during the partition of Ireland.

The oval ball game has a long and distinguished history in Ireland; indeed, soccer was virtually unknown in the South until the 1880s, and it still is second best in parts of the island to this date. So, given the enormous migration of Irish people to England in the 19th century, it isn't surprising that an Irish Exiles club emerged in the capital.

London Irish's first game came on 1st October 1898, against Hammersmith at Herne Hill. Irish won 8-3. The presence of Louis Magee in the Irish side brought enormous kudos to the club. Magee played 27 times for Ireland, four times for 1896 Lions in South Africa and was one of the greatest Irish players of all time. He was also a great commuter as he also played for Bective Rangers in Dublin despite living in London. Little wonder he joined London Irish. Part of the raison d'etre for forming London Irish was the Irish RU wanted a team in London to be their representatives, with the aim of fast-tracking selection from the club to the international side. But things didn't work out as planned and London Irish frequently complained of being neglected by the Irish selectors.

In 1904 they lost their ground at Herne Hill and for a spell had no settled home. After an exciting entry to the scene, the club's fortunes waned and only modest players made themselves available due to the lack of a permanent home. They eventually found one at Norbiton.

The years after 1914 were doubly disastrous for London Irish, owing to the Great War and the Troubles back in the old country. 'The Troubles' split Ireland into two countries – the Irish Free State and Ulster – creating animosity for generations. Back home, the Irish national rugby team opted to stay as a single entity in which politics was never allowed to interfere with playing rugby. The same situation applied to the London Irish club, and it remains so to this day. Orangemen mixed with Free State men without a cross word being spoken. At official dinners, the toast was always to 'the Queen and the Irish Republic'.

The blend worked, as between the wars Irish emerged as a top-class club with a string of great players. George Stephenson was one of the finest centres of the 20th century. He won 42 Irish caps in the 1920s and was Ireland's most capped player and the top try-scorer. The same era featured Jamie Clinch (30 caps), Eugene Davy (34 caps) and George Beamish (25 caps). This international recognition was remarkable as the Irish selectors rarely bothered travelling to England to watch players. A situation developed where a top-class Irish player who won honours back home and then moved to England was always likely to get the nod over any Irishmen who only played in England. One obscure Irishman who evaded recognition was Spike Milligan, the legendary comedian, who played in the club's junior teams in the late 1930s. Irish also had a scrum-half at the time called Danaher, who made a few people laugh. His party piece in matches was to clamber directly over the scrum and to jump on top of his opposite number. Whilst hardly sporting, and rather dangerous, it wasn't strictly illegal until the authorities banned the practice.

In 1931 Irish finally bought a permanent home at Manor Lane, Sunbury, which they purchased for £1280. The new home was christened with an 8-8 draw against London Welsh.

The first match after World War Two was against London Scottish at Blackheath (Sudbury was requisitioned by the authorities). Irish lost that day, but quickly recovered and celebrated their 50th season in 1948-49 with only nine defeats in 30 matches. Irish fielded some remarkable players at the time. Father Tom Gavin was the first priest to play for Ireland. John Daly and Des O'Brien were an integral part of Ireland's first Grand Slam in 1948. The O'Flanagan Brothers were part of that small band that won international caps at two sports; Kevin and Michael were both capped by Ireland at rugby and soccer. Kevin was a regular for Arsenal at soccer. Outside the first XV, Irish's second XV was nicknamed the 'Wild Geese' in honour to the exiled Irish soldiers who fought in the Low Countries in the 17th century.

Irish fell away in the early 1950s, but their cause was helped when they were given a seat on the Irish RU Council, which allowed them a voice in selection. At the same time the British and Irish governments signed an agreement that allowed free access for citizens between the two states, which led to an influx of Irish workers to England, and London in particular. The rugby club benefited from an increase in players and supporters.

The club became a conveyer belt of great names. 1954 saw the debut of Andy Mulligan, one of the game's greatest scrum-halves, fresh from winning a double blue at Cambridge, and in 1955 Robin Thompson captained the Lions in South Africa.

London Irish had a prolonged temporary stay at Blackheath due to lack of money to develop Sunbury. They only returned to Sunbury in 1959, but it soon became a little part of Ireland behind the leafy avenues of West London. On 9th September 1959, Sunbury reopened with a match between K.H. Chapman's XV and a combined London Irish, Scottish and Welsh XV. That season proved memorable, with open running rugby led by captain Andy Mulligan.

Despite the remoteness of Sunbury, the club developed a reputation as one of London's best watering holes. Indeed, part of the traditional problem with London Irish was that socialising was as important as rugby. Fitness was not a great concern. The big name players could swan in and out of Sudbury without the selection committee having any control. Famous visitors on match days included Spike Milligan, poet Louis MacNeice, plus actors Richard Harris and Peter O'Toole.

This laissez-fare attitude wasn't epitomised by all the great London Irish players. C.M.H. 'Mike' Gibson was one of the greatest rugby players of all time. Fit and fast as a greyhound, Gibson won 69 caps for Ireland and the Lions between 1964 and 1977 to become the most capped player of the era. His durability was remarkable and he played on a record fiveLions tours.

A change to 'professional amateurism' came in the late 1960s, when Ken Kennedy revolutionised Sunbury from a traditional drinking outlet into an athletic club. In 1977-78 Irish won the London Merit Table and reached the 1980 John Player Cup Final (they lost to Leicester). At the same time Sunbury was turned into one of the best grounds in British rugby, with its rows of plastic seats – green, of course.

Since the introduction of league rugby, London Irish have always been amongst the top clubs. They have striven to compete with the high rollers. For a brief spell in 1995, they tried to return to their Irish only roots, but have generally competed for the best talent – on and off the field.

The 1990s saw Irish fielding some brilliant players, such as Jim Staples and Simon Geoghegan, and having some top-class coaches like Dick Best, Hika Reid and Clive Woodward. Irish threw off the mantle of the 'fun club extraordinaire' and became worthy members of the Premiership.

The club played at Sunbury until 2000, when, determined to attract bigger support, they moved to the Madejski Stadium in Reading, whilst the amateurs stayed at Sunbury,

Since the move Irish have paradoxically produced a string of English internationals, notably Delon and Steffan Armitage, Marland Yarde, Nick Kennedy, Paul Hodgson, Topsy Ojo, Alex Corbisiero and Riki Flutey. Non-English stars have included Conor O'Shea (Ireland), Thomas Castaignede (France), Oliver Magne (France) and James O'Connor (Australia). Rikki Flutey is one of only two men in history to have played for and against the British Lions. He played against the Lions in his native New Zealand before moving to Britain.

Sadly, Irish have suffered, more than most, from their best young players moving to richer clubs in England and France.

Marland Yarde, ironically one of London Irish's England internationals.

LONDON SCOTTISH

"The history of Scotland is one of theology tempered by homicide."
Ivor Brown

LONDON SCOTTISH ARE the oldest of the capital's exile clubs. The club was formed in April 1878 as an association for 'London Scotsmen'; indeed, a number of the founders were members of the London Scottish Regiment. Many of those in attendance at Mackay's Tavern on Ludgate Hill were also members of St. Andrews Rovers, a soccer club that was open to all nationalities. St. Andrews soon disappeared, but the new rugby club adopted their colours of blue jerseys, white knickerbockers and red stockings.

London Scottish's first match was played on Blackheath Common against Ravenscourt Park and was won by Scottish by a large margin. The second match was a defeat at the hands of Queens House. The club did not stay on the common, or anywhere, very long, with brief stays at Lillie Bridge, Fulham, Clapham Junction, Hampstead and Old Deer Park. They eventually found a permanent home in 1894 as co-tenants with Richmond FC of Richmond Athletic Ground.

LS undertook their first tour of the 'old country' at Christmas 1880, which cemented relations with the international selectors. W.E. Maclagan was the club's first international. He was also associated with Edinburgh Academicals, but won 20 of his 25 caps whilst with London Scottish. He captained the first British Isles team to tour South Africa in 1891. A first-class defensive three-quarter, Maclagen had great kicking ability.

Maclagen was part of the best back-line in club rugby across London, which helped Scottish become the capital's top side. In 1886 only Richmond, Cambridge University and Blackheath could beat the exiles. A couple of seasons later LS offered second team fixtures to good sides such as Upper Clapton, who could field three county players. And by 1894 Scottish were the backbone of the Scotland team that trounced England in the Calcutta Cup.

Everything seemed perfect, but it was an illusion. Six years later the first XV won only four matches all season. However, relief came in the shape of an Edinburgh schoolboy named K.G. Macleod, who made an immense impression, despite playing only occasionally for the club between 1905 and 1908 whilst at Cambridge University. Macleod, one of Scotland's finest ever backs, was invited to play against Wales at Inverleith in 1903 as a 15-year-old, but was refused permission to play by his headmaster at Fettes. Macleod left Fettes that summer to go to university, and the SRU took advantage and played him against New Zealand in November 1905 when he was only 17. Macleod played with his brother for Scotland, but the brother's early death caused K.G. to give up the sport.

It was a good era for both Scotland and their exiled brothers, as London Scottish supplied ten players to the national team in 1906-07 and the following season the club had 14 members capped. It was a bone of contention in Scotland that the WRU actively promoted London Welsh as the place for Welsh exiles to aim for, whereas the SRU were lukewarm in their support for London Scottish.

The last weekend of the 1913-14 season has poignant memories for Scottish, as they fielded four teams, out of whom 44 players were killed in the Great War.

There was no competition for the club's greatest player of the inter-war years; it was Ian Smith, who was known as 'the Flying Scotsman'. Smith came from Winchester School, where soccer was the preferred sport. Despite his total inexperience at rugby, Oxford University selected him for a rugby blue based on his brilliant sprinting ability. Smith was so fast, only H.P. Jacob, the England international, could keep pace with him. Smith eventually won 32 Scotland caps and was picked for Cove-Smith's Lions to tour South Africa in 1924.

TOP ROW: 1. D.WRIGHT. 2. C.C.TAYLOR. 3. G.OLDING. 4. T.G.H.JACKSON. 5. A.I.WATSON. 6. R.B.BRUCE LOCKHART.
CENTRE: 1. J.D.NIVEN. 2. R.W.DUNN. 3. K.H.S.WILSON. 4. K.I.GEDDES (CAPT) S.C.A.OGILVY. 6. R.W.F.SAMPSON. 7. G.W.THOMSON
BOTTOM: 1. B.M.McKENZIE. 2. D.M.WHYTE. LEFT INSET: R.AITKEN. RIGHT INSET: N.C.CHARTERIS

In 1935 the club fielded J.R. Page, who was a New Zealand fly-half.

After World War Two, London Scottish kept their special status, with six members being capped for Scotland. They included the remarkable Doug Keller, who was selected as Scotland captain despite having played for Australia on their 1947 tour. Keller caused consternation after he returned and tried to re-qualify for Australia. The IRB clamped down and decreed players could not play for more than one international country. They were worried that Keller would emulate his predecessor A.C. Wallace, who played for New South Wales before playing for Scotland and then returning home to captain Australia in 1924.

Success continued into the 1960s and the best season in the club's history was 1964-65; they were defeated only twice in 30 matches. Later, they won five successive Middlesex Sevens finals, and also provided six players who were the backbone of the Scotland team that held the 1964 All Blacks to a 0-0 draw.

In the 1960s the club could field three Scotland captains: Stewart Wilson, Ian Loughland and Mike Campbell-Lamerton.

Two great characters stand out from this era: Frans Ten Bos and Alistair McHarg. Frans Ten Bos, who arrived in Britain in 1940, became the most successful captain in their history, but his Dutch origins were a stumbling block to his international hopes. Unlike his predecessor Keller, Ten Bos had had to prove he had Scottish blood before being selected by the SRU. Alistair McHarg was the greatest London Scottish character of the 1970s. An eccentric lock-forward, he ignored every known coaching tenet by appearing virtually anywhere in his back-line in the hope of charging at the opposition with the ball under his arm. McHarg won 44 Scottish caps, but mysteriously was never picked for the British Lions.

Other great players of the 1970s included Mike and Alistair Biggar, Alan Lawson and Ron Wilson, who all gave great service to their club and country.

London Scottish were a 'nearly' club in the National Knockout Cup; they were runners-up in 1974 and have the best KO Cup record of any side in the capital. The low point was losing 13-3 to virtually unknown Orrell, which evoked the comment from the London Scottish captain that "to lose was bad enough, but on a layby off the M6 was worse". Despite this setback, they were usually near the top of the London Merit Table and later the National leagues.

They were quick to embrace professionalism in 1995 – perhaps too quick. The club only had 23 professionals and 2,000 spectators, insufficient for a tough 30-match season or to fund replacements.

Funds ran out in 1999, which made them a target for takeover bids. One Scottish businessman tried to lure them to Edinburgh – a move blocked by the SRU. Bristol and Leeds were accused of trying to take them over, purely as a mechanism to ensure Premiership status. That year London Scottish reformed as an amateur club in Herts & Middlesex Division 1. They had been demoted nine leagues after ceasing to be professional. Sadly, Richmond had hit hard times as well, which brought a return of the two sides back to the Rec.

By 2009 London Scottish had returned to National One and the brink of the Premiership. Great modern names associated with London Scottish are Kenny Logan, Phil Godman and French legend Serge Betsen.

LONDON WELSH

"Wales is in the main a peasant nation. Landed aristocracy in Wales is alien to Welsh culture, Welsh national ambitions and aspirations."
Wick Powell (1929)

LONDON WELSH MUST rank as the most influential club side of the 20th century. The decade between 1965 and 1975 saw the Welsh national team pre-eminent in Europe and their 'London Office' were leaders, integral in everything that changed British rugby in the final quarter of the century.

London Welsh RFC started on the 26th June 1885, at a meeting held in the Anderson's Hotel in London. They began at the top with a team containing six internationals. They weren't the first Welsh Exiles team in the capital, as a side composed of Medical and University students from the principality had played a few games three years earlier.

It was 24th October 1885 before the club took to the field for the first time against London Scottish at Walthamstow. The first London Welsh team included A.J. 'Monkey' Gould, who was the game's first superstar. Gould was only an occasional player for London Welsh. Indeed, he seems to have played for half a dozen different clubs during his career. He even played against his teammates when they embarked on a Christmas week tour of South Wales that same year. London Welsh's matches against Swansea, Newport and Cardiff became part of Welsh folklore, but they were viewed as city slickers by the Welsh public, who loved nothing better than booing the exiles. Swansea and the trialists were beaten, but there were narrow defeats by Newport and Cardiff.

Sadly, the success of the first season was a flash in the pan, as they won only one game in the next two seasons. But, despite the results, Welsh had four players picked for Wales: A.J. Gould, C.G. Taylor, E.P. Alexander and R.P. Budworth. W.H. Thomas was picked for the British Isles team to tour Australasia.

With hindsight, Welsh had adopted too strong a fixture list from a standing start. They were popular visitors with spectators, but they didn't at the time have the resources to match top-class sides. Things got so bad that the club disbanded for a year. However, the Welsh Rugby Union recognised that having a focal point for exiles in London had much to offer the national team. So the WRU urged Welsh players living in the capital to join London Welsh and promised to 'fast-track' the best players into the national trials. They also donated £50 a year to club funds.

To reciprocate, London Welsh showed their colours by restricting membership to "Welshmen, those of Welsh descent and those who had played for a Welsh club".

The WRU kept their word, and London Welsh blossomed into one of the best sides in the city. Players were regularly picked for Wales and seven past and present players made it into the 1908 Lions team.

London Welsh loved to attack, but their forwards were a tough outfit. An occasion is recorded when Welsh visited Bath and upset the referee, the home side and the supporters with their rough-house tactics. Eventually the referee sent one Welsh forward off, precipitating a walk-off by the whole London Welsh team. Eventually the London Welsh officials persuaded their fourteen back on to the field, where harsh words were exchanged with the referee and Welsh walked off again – this time for good.

Welsh played their matches at the Oval and various other London grounds. However, from 1919 onwards, with the exception of one short period, all home matches were played at Herne Hill, described by one writer as "slightly less hospitable than the North Pole". They moved to Old Deer Park, Richmond in 1957, which is a fabulous venue, overlooked by the picturesque pagoda in nearby Kew Gardens.

Re-establishing the club after World War One was a difficult task until Capt. Geoffrey Crawshay, a wealthy businessman, began a recruitment campaign at Oxbridge that produced a steady stream of talent into London Welsh's ranks and rapidly changed the club's fortunes.

Perhaps the club's best player of the era was Wick Powell, a scrum-half. Powell was not like any other scrum-half of the time; he was huge, energetic, tough as nails, but most of all unpredictable. It was said that Powell's teammates had no idea what he would do next, never mind the opposition. Powell won 27 Welsh caps, but eventually fell out with Welsh and joined Northampton as a forward. He made such an impact at the Saints that Wales asked him for a Welsh trial in the back-row.

The Oxbridge connection helped make London Welsh one of the great sides of the 1930s, famed for their attacking varsity rugby. This is the more remarkable because Welsh did not have a proper home ground of their own at the time. When they moved to Old Deer Park, the new home was opened with a match between the club and a Welsh XV. The internationals won 17-8 in front of 7,000 spectators. The ground inspired London Welsh and they became one of the most glamorous sides in rugby in the next 25 years.

Great rugby names such as Bryn Meredith and Carwyn James turned out, but off the field there were star-studded names too. Richard Burton, the legendary film star, had been a regular figure in the bar before he became famous. His marriage(s) to Elizabeth Taylor was/were front-page news. Burton even took his new wife to Old Deer Park and is quoted as ordering "a pint for me, and a half of whatever Elizabeth is drinking". His relationship with Elizabeth Taylor was turbulent, but Burton kept his friendship with the club until his death in 1984.

The arrival of John Dawes from Newbridge transformed London Welsh from a great social club into a top-class rugby club. Dawes and his vice-captain, Roger Michaelson, saw that rugby was changing and that interchangeability between forwards and backs was the way forward if British rugby was to compete with France and New Zealand. The days when pedestrian forwards could walk from scrum to scrum were over. Fitness and mobility were to replace fatness and monotony.

Welsh gathered a talented team that epitomised the new breed: John Taylor, Terry Price, Tony Gray, Jim Shanklin and Mike Roberts were good internationals, but they were eclipsed by four giants of the game: John Dawes, Gerald Davies, Mervyn Davies and J.P.R.Williams.

John Dawes OBE, who joined London Welsh as a player in 1963, was a superb leader and the catalyst during a golden era when crowds of 5,000 relished dazzling performances from outstandingly gifted players. He was also skipper of the successful 1971 British Lions, London Welsh having an amazing seven representatives in the squad.

Gerald Davies was a complete three-quarter: fast, intelligent and brave. Mervyn Davies (no relation) was the finest no.8 of his generation. He was huge at 6ft 6 ins, an outstanding loose-forward in attack and defence, and mature beyond his years. He walked into the Welsh international team in his first season of senior rugby and stayed for a decade. Davies was capped 38 times, winning two Grand Slams with Wales and three Triple Crowns. He also went on the victorious Lions tours to New Zealand in 1971 and South Africa in 1974, playing in all eight tests. Having been appointed captain of his country in 1975, Davies was widely expected to lead the 1977 Lions squad. But at the age of only 29 his career came to an abrupt and unhappy end. In March 1976 he was playing for Swansea in a Welsh Cup semi-final against Pontypool at Cardiff when he suddenly collapsed on the pitch. He had suffered a brain haemorrhage.

Even 'Merve the Swerve' was overshadowed by Dr. John Williams from Bridgend, known universally as 'JPR'. He would figure in anyone's list of the best ten rugby full-backs of all time and was a supreme athlete. He won the juniors at Wimbledon as a tennis-playing teenager, before becoming the most capped rugby full-back of his time. Highly intelligent, Williams was nevertheless brave to the point of foolishness. His crash tackle on a French winger in full flight saved a certain try and won Wales the 1976 Grand Slam. The worst thing one can say about

JPR was that he set a standard that has been hard for Welsh full-backs to live up to since his retirement. JPR had joined London Welsh from St Mary's Hospital in London, where he qualified as a doctor in 1973, the year before his second Lions tour. He didn't travel with the 1977 Lions because it was reported that he was told to 'buckle down' and focus on his career in surgery by his consultant. He became a fellow of the Royal College of Surgeons in 1980 and retired from international rugby the next year.

The 1970s were a golden age of Welsh rugby, and few Welsh teams took the field without their share of stars from the London office. London Welsh were unbeaten at home from 1967 to 1971 under John Dawes, and in 1970-71 recorded a sequence of 18 straight wins. In 1971 they provided the Lions with six members on their epic victory series in New Zealand: JPR, Gerald Davies, Mervyn Davies, John Taylor, Geoff Evans and Mike Roberts.

Welsh rugby, both in the principality and in London, declined in the 1980s. Pinpointing one reason is impossible. Two principle factors were the drying up of the post-war conveyer belt of talent from the grammar schools and talent from the valleys succumbing to the attraction of the money available by 'Going North' to rugby league.

London Welsh were enormously attractive opposition, but they were in decline with the arrival of league rugby, and by 1994 had slumped to Division 5 South. They bounced back to Premiership 2 in 1998. Two years later London Welsh requested permission to join the Welsh National League, which was rejected by the RFU. They were an ambitious Championship club, but suffered because the RFU wanted the Premiership open only to clubs with grounds that could hold 12,500 spectators, which Old Deer Park couldn't. The club were surprise Championship winners in 2012, but were told they didn't have the infrastructure for the top league. They took the case to court, which to everyone's surprise, they won. Initially they accrued enough points to stay up, but disaster struck when they were found to have fielded an ineligible player and were docked hard-won points. Sadly, relegation then became inevitable. 2014 saw London Welsh back in the Premiership.

London Welsh provided a remarkable six players to the 1971 Lions squad.

MARLBOROUGH NOMADS

MARLBOROUGH COLLEGE OPENED in 1843 for the free education of the sons of clergymen out of respect for the parsimonious salaries paid by the Church of England. The sons of laymen could attend, but had to pay. The game of rugby arrived at Marlborough in 1852 with the appointment as headmaster of Dr. Cotton from Rugby School.

Although Marlborough had only been open for nine years, it was a hot-bed of poaching, trespass and bad behaviour. Cotton reformed the teaching syllabus and organised a programme of games. He justified these games as a way of keeping boys out of mischief and inside the school grounds. He encouraged his pupils to spend time and money on "wholesome" recreation. He also appointed young, enthusiastic games players as masters, and then inculcated the Rugby School system of 'muscular christianity'.

In 1864 Marlborough College played Clifton. Records note the match was marred by "ill feeling over hacking" and the two schools didn't replay the fixture for many years.

Marlborough School produced 34 internationals between 1871 and 1926, including four of the first England team: F.W. Mills, Harold Freeman (one of the founders of the Oxford University RFC), W.B. Fletcher and A.B. St. George Hammersley. Only a handful of the college's internationals were exclusively associated with the Nomads, notably Harry Vassal and Leonard Tosswill.

Marlborough Nomads FC were originally raised as a team for a one-off match against the school in 1868. The match became an annual fixture for 40 years. Nomads were the first genuine old boys club. They soldiered on despite being based in London, 100 miles away from their alma mater. On the upside, London-based Nomads were able to attend the RFU inaugural meeting at the Pall Mall restaurant.

Initially, the Nomads played on Blackheath alongside 'the club', an arrangement that continued until Blackheath FC moved to the Rectory Field. Subsequently, Nomads lived up to their name by playing at Dulwich, Surbiton and Stamford Bridge.

Apart from the heroes of the first international, the best known Nomads included William Mortimer, who was a triple Cambridge blue at rugby, cricket and hockey. He was a Nomad regular for many years, but also played for Blackheath, the South, Kent and England. He also represented the university at hockey. Frank Mitchell was another triple Cambridge blue, who played cricket for both England and South Africa. He gained six rugby caps for England as a forward between 1895 and 1896 and played in goal for Sussex. He captained his university in both these sports against Oxford. Sydney Morse (1854-1929) was one of Nomad's earliest captains and played for England from 1873 to 1875. Morse was a great favourite of Queen Victoria's and demonstrated the new-fangled gramophone to the monarch in 1897.

In 1898 Nomads were a match for every other club in the capital. They lost their unbeaten record to Blackheath in a brutal match in which their opponents were condemned for their lack of sportsmanship. Two years later Nomads were one of the best ten sides in Britain, good enough to play the Sussex County XV. Their fixtures against Richmond were regarded as one of the best in the capital (the other was London Scottish v Harlequins).

Yet no club in rugby history declined so rapidly. It started in 1908-09, which was a truly awful season with barely a win. The following season they conceded thirteen tries to OMT. Soon afterwards, they were crushed 59-0 by Oxford University. Anything Oxford can do, Cambridge can do, and in March 1911, Nomads were hammered by the Light Blues. Urgent meetings were called by Nomads officials and, within a few weeks, they disbanded and advised their players to join Rosslyn Park. So ended the history of one of the finest sides in the early history of the game.

METROPOLITAN POLICE

POLICE RUGBY HAS been one of the casualties of the 21st century. Today chief constables are primarily concerned with efficiency, balancing the budgets and keeping bobbies on the beat. There is little tolerance for policemen injured on the rugby field.

How different it was in days gone by, when police rugby was one of the major parts of the English game and Metropolitan Police RFC was one of England's top sides.

Policemen were archetypal rugby material, because in Victorian times brawn rather than brains was the criteria for 'recruitment'. The Home Office in the 19th century wanted big men who could intimidate criminals, rather than the reverse.

Metropolitan Police RFC arose from an invitation in 1923 for a friendly match between the Newport Police and their London counterparts. The London police weren't stupid and arranged a series of friendlies against teams that posed less of a threat than the Gwent men. The first match was a win over London University XV, followed by a defeat by London Dental Hospital. The Newport fixture eventually went ahead, both home and away, with narrow victories for the Welshmen.

Met Police established a good fixture list in the late 1920s, mostly against the better London clubs. The first two seasons of the 1930s saw Met Police win 46 of 50 matches.

Amongst the earliest Met players to attract attention was Harold Bailey, an England trialist in 1935. Arthur Rees went one better, winning 13 Welsh caps in the 1930s. Later he became a chief constable.

The Mets major success came in 1938 when they took the Middlesex Sevens, beating the cream of British rugby talent.

World War Two saw the boys in blue with more to worry about than rugby; indeed, it took almost a decade before resumption in 1948. The reformed club included forward Dyson Stayl Wilson, known as 'Tug', one of the Met's finest players. Wilson eventually won eight caps for England between 1954 and 1955, and he played for the 1955 Lions. Wilson was a small wing-forward who was born in South Africa. After he retired from rugby and the police, he sailed around the world in a yacht.

The post-war fixture list contained most of the old London elite. A regular fixture from the pre-war years was against the Paris Police, which continued until the 1970s, with the

English side usually winning. The Met might not have had the best players, but they had the biggest. In 1956 they fielded Vic Streeter, who at 6ft 6 ins was the biggest rugby player in England. The 1960s was a golden era for the Met, with defeats few and far between.

Success continued into the 1970s, with the Met supplying a number of players for the South Eastern Counties. The best known was hooker Tony Boddy, who represented Middlesex, won an England trial and toured South Africa with the England party.

In 1983 a new boy joined the Met from Plymouth, Paul Ackford. He was never a household name during a remarkable rugby career, which saw him rise to England and Lions status. His eventual second-row partnership with Wade Dooley was one of the greatest in English and Lions rugby history and included the 1991 World Cup Final. Ackford began his career with the Met, but eventually left the police behind to join the Daily Telegraph. On the field, he led the Met for a season before joining the star-studded rota at Harlequins. He was replaced by Martin Bayfield, who by coincidence was an England lock who later also joined the media.

Another famous name to have a brief spell with the Met was John Gallagher, from Askeans. Gallagher emigrated to New Zealand and produced hitherto unnoticed skills as a full-back, which led to a meteoric rise to All Black status. He returned home to join Leeds Rugby League Club.

A brief flirtation with National League Three eventually saw Met Police drop into National 4 (South), where they enjoyed mid-table status. But a new era in English rugby had dawned, and the new National Knockout Cup saw the Met reach the quarter-finals before losing to mighty Bristol.

Gradually the Met's traditional fixtures, against the best London old boys' clubs, were falling away and being replaced by new fixtures against club sides in both England and Wales. Despite having 20,000 policemen to select from, the Met had to cope with uncertainties over selection and the fact that rugby was being changed by greater intensity, fitness and coaching; all this at a time when the demands of the police service were also increasing. The first signs of semi-professionalism were making the recruitment and retention of talented players increasingly difficult.

In 2000 Met Police dropped out of London 1 and all their results were expunged for the season.

The Met can still mix business with pleasure. In 2007 the first XV were staying at a Cardiff Hotel when a thief burgled their rooms. He was rapidly apprehended by some huge rugby players.

OLD ALLEYNIAN

"Anyone who says his schooldays were the happiest of his life must have been pretty miserable afterwards."

J. E. Greenwood

IT IS EASY to be confused by the background to Old Alleynian FC, who are the old boys of Dulwich College in South-East London. They take their name from Edward Alleyne, a 16th

century actor who founded Alleyne's School. In the 1850s Dulwich College separated from Alleyne's School. Dulwich adopted rugby, whilst Alleyne's chose soccer.

Rugby was played at Dulwich College as far back as 1859, and there are records of St. Paul's School playing an informal OAs side in 1872. Certainly, the college were regularly playing schools at rugby in the 1870s, but without an old boys club the former pupils tended to join Blackheath, Harlequins or other London clubs such as Streatham (where in 1897 the entire side was composed of Old Alleynians).

At this time Dulwich College were generous benefactors to the area. In 1885 the school governors presented part of the common to public ownership to prevent it being developed by property speculators. Much of the donated land was used for golf, tennis, football and rugby.

Two OAs who figured prominently at this time were C.M. Wells, who was one of the best half-backs of the era, and Robert Baines, who founded the Rosario club, the first rugby club in South America.

The college had a busy fixture list and played 19 games in 1884-85, including against Richmond. The following year the college's first and second XVs played Harlequins I and II on equal terms. Quins were led by W.R.M. Leake, who taught at Dulwich College and had played for England.

In March 1898 Leake contacted former OAs that he thought might be willing to play rugby on a regular basis. Several months later R.M. Everett, who was only 18-years-old, offered to set up the club. In September the new club played Croydon III XV. OAs first captain was Lindsey Smith, who had played for Lennox, Surrey and the Barbarians.

OAs found a pitch at South Norwood Park, but the only washing facilities were at the local lake and involved breaking the ice in winter. South Norwood was decidedly unsuitable, and over the years OAs moved to Elm Grove, Sydenham (1902), Cavendish Road, Merton (1903) and Horn Park Farm, Lee (1904). In 1905 six-and-a-half acres of land on the east of College Road were handed to the Alleynian RFC.

In 1906 the original changing rooms were built. They were considered some of the best in London, with basins, baths and running water. There was also a small room where soft drinks and refreshments could be served.

By 1905 OAs could field five sides and had been the first club to tour Germany. Soon afterwards they visited Paris and defeated Stade Francais.

One of the earliest members was J. 'Birdie' Partridge, who was one of the most remarkable rugby players of all time. He played for South Africa in 1903, was an England trialist and also played for Newport, Blackheath, and Pretoria. He also helped to found the Army RU.

Dulwich College established a link to the Oxbridge clubs. Fortunately for those OAs who were not academically-minded, Oxford's head of maths also looked after the first XV at rugby and ranked ability as a rugby player above algebra.

The strength of OAs rugby is demonstrated by the 1913 Varsity Match, when five OAs took the field. W.D. Doherty, J.E. Greenwood and Cyril Lowe appeared for Oxford, while David Donald and Eric Loudoun-Shand appeared for Cambridge. All eventually became internationals, despite the outbreak of the Great War. Doherty won seven Irish caps, J.E. 'Jenny' Greenwood won 13 for England.

In 1913 there was a shock when J.E.Greenwood, an established England forward, chose Alleynians over one of the top sides. 'Jenny' later confessed to a wealthy friend that OAs had bribed him to join "a second class club with a muddy pitch" by paying his university debts. He shouldn't really have had any student debts at all because he was the grandson of W.W. Deloitte, founder of Deloitte, Haskins & Sells, the world famous accountancy firm. Greenwood played in three varsity matches before graduating and taking a job as a trainee accountant. He soon tired of book-keeping and so returned to Cambridge and re-joined the rugby team. He served with distinction in World War One, then immediately joined Boots the Chemist as a director despite, as he admitted, having done barely a day's work in his life. He served Boots for 40 years, whilst also leading a full and active life. J.E. wrote an entertaining autobiography, but his writing couldn't compare with his fellow OA, novelist P.G. Wodehouse, who was a great supporter of Dulwich rugby and who had acted as rugby correspondent of the Old Alleynian magazine.

OAs were, between the wars, one of London's top sides. Ken Stark was first capped by England in 1927 and won nine successive England caps. T.E. Priest and A.F. Heppenstall won England trials before Eric Whiteley played full-back twice for England in 1931. Tragically, John Farmer, the OA & Surrey hooker, broke a fingernail in a match, developed tetanus and died in three weeks. This was, of course, in the days before penicillin.

The club, particularly the forwards, were at their zenith in the early 1930s and were able to enhance their fixture list. They retained their position into the 1950s, despite a small, light pack. They could produce top-class players, notably Ian Coutts, who won two Scotland caps, and R.D. Barnett, who emerged as a brilliant centre. However, retaining players was a problem because the pitch was a mud heap with a slope. OAs recognised the problem and began a campaign to improve facilities.

Two famous Old Alleynians: who went on to England honours: Danny Cipriani (above) and Nick Easter (below)

OAs eventually had to accept that the days were gone when they could attract, or keep, fixtures against the first-class clubs. They found a home in the middle-ranking clubs of the South-East and competed in the county and national knockout cups. They have produced some great players, including Andrew Mullins, David Flatman and England international fly-half Danny Cipriani, as well as two England forwards, Nick Easter and Andrew Sheridan.

They won the 1991-92 Surrey Cup after losing in two previous finals. It was a golden season that culminated in winning the London Two title to establish themselves as the premier OB side in the capital – and all this with a team of pure amateurs and a 'closed' status that meant every member was an old boy of Dulwich College.

The good times could not last because OAs were competing against clubs that embraced semi-professionalism. After several relegations, the treasured 'closed' status was surrendered in 1995. They were rewarded in 2003 when they won the National Junior Vase at Twickenham with a team including 13 OAs.

OLD BLUES

"The products of Christ's Hospital are imperfectly schooled but admirably educated."
Sir Richard Lodge

CHRIST'S HOSPITAL (WHICH is actually a public school) gave many things to England, but the term 'old blue' is one of the most famous. The school was founded in 1553 for orphans, who wore blue coats. This was the origin of the colours for Oxbridge sporting honours. The dark blue of Oxford is from Christ's; the light blue of Cambridge is from Eton.

It grew to become one of the most famous schools in the world, not least for having produced the poets Samuel Coleridge and Charles Lamb. Sir George Rowland Hill, the first RFU secretary, was another old boy.

The 'Old Blues' rugby club (an old boys' club) was founded in November 1873 for a match against Christ's Hospital 1st XV, on a field in Palmer's Green. The school won. The OBs stayed together and played about 12 games a season, with reasonable success.

In November 1874 the school adopted the RFU code of rules and the Christ's Hospital Football Club was formally inaugurated. The school was allowed to play at Lambeth Palace by special permission of the Archbishop of Canterbury.

The OBs club went into abeyance in 1882 after a game against Rosslyn Park, in which the Old Blues captain, S.H. Welsh, suffered a heart attack and died. After that the members lost interest in the game and the club became just for meeting and drinking until 1893, when the club was resurrected by a few stalwarts. The first game was (again) against Christ's Hospital 1st XV, but this time the old boys won.

In 1898-99, under J.G. Donaldson's captaincy, the club came well to the front and three teams were put on the field. The first team played 19 matches, winning 17 and only losing one (the very last of the season), with an aggregate of 344 points to 20.

The first Old Blue international was S. Reynolds, who moved to Richmond and gained England international caps in 1900 and 1901.

In 1902 the school moved after 350 years in Newgate Street in the City of London to a vast acreage of green fields at Horsham. Some Old Blues players were determined, despite the exodus of the school from London, to retain their spirit. Consequently, in the decade before 1914 Old Blues RFC established its reputation as a first-class club through its rare strength and depth. This is illustrated by the results from seasons 1907 to 1911: played 98, won 68, lost 25, and drawn five.

Four teams turned out regularly in 1909-10 and five teams from 1911-12 onwards. The fixture list had been gradually strengthened, and at the outbreak of war the club was one of the best in London. Certainly, its playing membership was flourishing; 148 Old Blues played for the club in 1913-14 and the total membership was 314.

After World War One Old Blues soon re-established themselves, and in 1921-22 they won 20 of 25 games. In 1922 an unofficial merit table of 40 London clubs existed. Royal Naval College (Greenwich) were champions with 87% and Old Blues were second with 85%. The merit tables were basically flawed because everybody's fixture list was different, but in an age without league tables any yardstick was better than none. A better measure of their excellence is that the Old Blues were the only club to defeat Camborne in 1926-27.

Old Blues produced an England international during World War Two: D.L. Marriott, and P.C. Delight was an England trialist in 1954. At this time, though, Old Blues had to settle for being a middle-ranking club.

The opportunity arose in 1982 to sell their Fairlop ground at a price which seemed to be lower than its real value, yet it would suffice to buy the present ground at Motspur Park in Surrey and pay off the bank overdraft. So there was naturally a great deal of worry over the decision which had to be taken. And yet the choice was not too difficult: the club were certain to face a miserable demise if they stayed at Fairlop, while Motspur Park, only some 30 miles from Christ's Hospital, could be made the base for a better future.

Despite a greatly enlarged playing membership and steadily improving results, in the ten years following the occupancy of their new home it became apparent that they held a surfeit of land, yet, the efforts and generosity of certain members notwithstanding, there were forever insufficient funds to be able to provide a decent clubhouse for members and guests. Accordingly, it was agreed that the club should sell one half of their grounds to King's College School and to join with their Old Boys to create a new semi-detached pavilion. This building was opened by the then President of the RFU in 1993 and is expected to provide magnificent facilities for players and supporters alike for many years to come.

Recent seasons have brought successive promotions from Surrey League One to London League 2 South (National Level 6). They have been victorious on four consecutive occasions in the Central Division of the Combined London Old Boys Merit Table and have won their annual cup competition. Additionally, they have twice gained entry to the national cup competition, on one occasion losing narrowly to Blackheath.

OLD CRANLEIGHAN

CRANLEIGH SCHOOL OPENED in 1865. Rugby was late coming to the school as it was only introduced in 1916. An old boys soccer team from the school operated in the 1890s.

Rugby was introduced by the then headmaster, Rev. Herbert Rhodes. Although himself an Oxford soccer blue, Rhodes had the foresight to engage L.C. Gower, nominally as a teacher of mathematics, a subject of which he understood precious little. Charles Gower had been invalided out of the army, having been wounded in the German East African campaign, and, whatever his academic shortcomings, was very soon to become a legendary coach.

Charles Gower

Within a year, the first XV were beating all the school sides by a distance, including 136-0 (20 goals and 12 tries – remember, only three points then) against the previously unbeaten KCS Wimbledon. A contemporary later noted that the boys had always believed that they were robbed of the then record victory score (138-0) when the game stopped five minutes early.

The hardest of taskmasters, Gower had his team practising every lunchtime, and his creed was to win the ball and spread it ever wider. "The simple things done well, and at top speed, the perfect giving and taking of passes, incessant backing up, and relentless pressure", as E.W.Swanton was to later write of Gower's style.

By 1920 the first XV lost only to a very strong Harlequins 'A' 13-15. This team included three future internationals, of whom the best was perhaps H.P. 'Jake' Jacob, who won a hat-trick of Oxford rugby blues. England chose him against Wales on the wing even though he was a centre. England won 17-9, and for the next match, a 14-3 victory against Ireland, Jacob was moved to centre, where he set up a try for Len Corbett before then scoring three tries himself against France. Jacob was only capped once more, against France in 1930, when he was teaching at Cranleigh School. He was a housemaster at Cranleigh for 16 years before becoming headmaster in 1959. He played club rugby for Blackheath and Old Cranleighans and represented Kent. But his coaching helped Cranleigh produce three more internationals: Frank Reynolds and Robert Carr for England and Con Wallis for Ireland. Another pupil, Stanley Couchman, toured South Africa with the 1938 British Isles party and subsequently became president of the Rugby Football Union.

An occasional Old Boys side began to function in the early 1920s, but it was not until 1928 when the current Thames Ditton ground was purchased (10 acres for £2500 and a like amount to build the clubhouse) that the OCs really began to make their mark. On the back of some remarkable results, and with the good work of the fixture secretary, an aspiring journalist

H.P. 'Jake' Jacob

Alan Key

called E.W. (Jim) Swanton, the fixture list grew to include the premier teams in England, including Bath, Bedford, Bristol, Coventry, the London exile sides, Moseley, Northampton, Sale, Swansea, and Wasps.

Swanton became one of the best known sports writers and broadcasters of the century. The archetypal English gent, whose philosophy was "that to lose with grace is better than winning without honour" reflects a bygone age. Injury forced him to run the line at Sale in 1935. He antagonised the home crowd when he disallowed a try for 'foot in touch', which the partisan home supporters firmly believed was a perfectly good try. He survived unharmed, until one occasion at Bristol when a lady supporter took her umbrella to him and the local police escorted Swanton from the pitch for his safety.

Between the wars, Rugby was the only English School that produced more internationals. Success continued through the 1930s with a string of internationals: Alan Key (England 1930-33), Maurice McCanlis (England 1931 and who also captained Oxford University at cricket), Maurice Bonaventura (England 1931), Clive Wallis (Ireland 1936), Jeffrey Reynolds (England 1937-38), Robert Carr (a virtual unknown when capped by England in 1939) and Stanley Couchman (a big, quick forward who kicked goals). L.S. Leroy, who was perhaps the most gifted of all Cranleigh footballers, left for Canada, where he was to play for the national side, never playing in an English season.

The 1938 Lions tour to South Africa was remarkable as three OCs were invited to join the party: Jeffrey Reynolds, Stanley Couchman and Cyril Sutter. Reynolds was first choice fly-half until sustaining serious injury, while Couchman (later to become President of the RFU) was one of a handful of players to play for the British Lions without winning a cap for England. Suter, sadly, was unable to travel because of business commitments. Another OC who could well have achieved international status was Reynolds's scrum-half V.A. Cox, who was badly injured at the wrong time. Returning to play hockey while recovering, he was capped for England in that sport.

In the early 1930s OCs had a first-class fixture list, but it wasn't enough for the England selectors, who asked Alan Key to move to Harlequins to further his international chances.

OCs were a match for everyone. In 1937 they beat Fettesian-Lorettians and Swansea. Perhaps their finest win was defeating Coventry at Coundon Road when the Midlanders had the best pack in England.

The war brought this golden era a close. With the ground requisitioned and nearly all the players serving King and country, rugby was off the agenda. The records show that in 1944, from a school with some 350 boys at that time, 1150 Old Cranleighans were serving in HM Forces, with 80 killed, 16 missing and 63 made prisoner, while 50 military awards and decorations were won and 63 mentions in dispatches.

Old boys rugby was never going to be the same after the war. The OCs continued to produce a number of good players, with Jeffrey Clements capped for England in 1958, while Andrew Wright had a final England trial and Robin Whitcombe was a fine fly-half in the 1960s.

H.P. Jacob retained his links with the club as second master, and for a period was interim headmaster of Cranleigh, but times were changing and the pre-eminence of rugby football in

Gower's day was becoming unfashionable. With games taking a lesser profile and fewer leavers joining the old boys, it had to be accepted that the OCs were no longer a match for some of the stronger provincial sides. Even worse, in common with other old boys sides, it would have to accept non-Old Cranleighan players.

The best-known OC sportsman of modern times is perhaps David Westcott, who combined occasional appearances as scrum-half for the old boys with top-class hockey, captaining the Great Britain team to an Olympic Bronze in 1984.

In the 1990s, with the aid of lottery and other funds, the OCs spent £850,000 in enhancing their Thames Ditton base, which is now widely acknowledged as one of the most attractive venues on the circuit, with the OCRFC maintaining a level in Surrey Division One.

OLD LEYSIANS

OLD LEYSIANS RFC operated from 1877 to 1960. The club was formed by old boys of Leys School, Cambridge.

The school was opened in 1875 and only had 150 pupils, whereas other public schools had three times that number. Yet within a decade, Old Leysian RFC was formed at a meeting held at 68 Holland Road, Kensington. On Saturday 29th December 1877, J.C. Isard, the householder, entertained several school friends (L. Waterhouse, J.B.M. McArthur, J.M. Richards and E.S. Whelpton) with the notion of forming an old boys side in the capital. Unlike some of the other public schools, Old Leysians were sparse in number and only 15 players were assembled.

Fixtures were difficult to find at first, but OL found opposition amongst the other fledgling OBs clubs in London. There was nothing unusual in their story until 1882, when OLs went on their first tour to South Wales, where they somehow contrived to arrange fixtures with Cardiff and 'South Wales' (a precursor of the Welsh national side). OL were disgusted to arrive in the principality to see press reports lambasting Cardiff for "engaging with a fourth rate London club". The OL were angry at this dismissal of their chances and were fortunate to win the toss and to play the first half with a howling gale at their backs. OL scored three touchdowns and held on in the second half, when Cardiff were expected to cut loose. It was easy to dismiss the Cardiff victory as a 'freak result', but a month later OL defeated Cambridge University by two goals and two tries to nil. That season Isard, McArthur and co. won 20 of 26 games.

OL were a power in English rugby, and in 1888 defeated mighty Blackheath at the Rectory Field.

International honours were slow to arrive, but in short order six OLs won international honours for N. Spicer, J.E. & L. Walker, A. Spicer, D. Green and G.L. Lloyd. Lloyd captained Wales in 1902.

OL played exclusively in the capital. They began in Wormwood Scrubs, then moved to Balham (1879), Paddington (1889), Stamford Bridge (1891) and Elsham (1901).

1909-10 saw Leysians in magnificent form, which culminated in a 17-9 victory over Harlequins, who were considered the best team in England at the time. This was not a case of a weakened

Quins simply fulfilling a fixture, as they fielded the Stoop brothers, John Birkett and some of the best players of the day. Two years later OL won 20 of 22 matches.

Besides their success, the curious aspect of OL was that their 200 members lived all over southern England, and the rugby section assembled every Saturday, with many making long train journeys. OL's was limited to two sides by sheer shortage of numbers, but still were one of the best clubs in London. In dire emergencies, OLs would wire the school to request a couple of boys be despatched, post-haste, to London for the afternoon. This practice was banned altogether by the RFU in the 1970s.

In 1950, Old Leysians were forced to abandon their first-class fixture list and to adopt the status of a side that played only half a dozen matches a season. Ironically, around this time, Leys School produced Geoff Windsor-Lewis, the top-class Welsh three-quarter, who was forced to join London Welsh for regular rugby.

OLD MERCHANT TAYLORS'

"It appears Old Millhillians' define success as simply beat OMT."
The Times 1910

FOOTBALL HAS BEEN a part of the curriculum at Merchant Taylors' School since the 16th century. Indeed, one headmaster, Richard Muncaster, wrote in 1581: "Football... is great helps, both to health and strength. Strengtheneth and brawneth the whole body, and by provoking superfluities downward, it dischargeth the head, and upper parts, it is good for the bowels, and to drive the stone and gravel from both the bladder and kidneys."

Rugby football at MT dates from 1859, when a match was played in Hackney between the school and Royal Naval College, New Cross. Little is known of the encounter except that neither side had much idea of the laws. In the circumstances, it isn't surprising that for the next two years the school played soccer.

Rugby at MT School became established in the mid-1860s. The old boys of MT gravitated to Wasps or other London clubs; indeed, Wasps RFC was formed in 1867 by six OMTs. John Bentley, an OMT, joined the Gypsies and played half-back for England in the first two internationals. Subsequently, the Taylor brothers, both OMTs, played for England. Their club association was with Blackheath.

Around this time Merchant Taylors' School moved from Suffolk Lane to Charterhouse Square. In 1882 Les Gunnery, a pupil, called a meeting in the school library, which led to the formation of 'Old Boys Cricket and Football Club'. Bolstered by talent from the school, OMTs improved steadily to rank against the best sides in London.

OMT's status was recognised in 1901, when they defeated mighty Cardiff. Also that year Nigel Fletcher and John Raphael were the first OMs capped directly from the club. Fletcher won four England caps as a forward between 1901 and 1903, while Raphael, born in Belgium, was an all-round sporting great, excelling at rugby, cricket and golf. He was one of the best three-quarters of the era before World War One and won nine England caps in four years. Blessed with great natural talent, Raphael was also noted for sulking when things didn't go his way on the rugby field. He was a superb all-rounder, who later captained both Oxford University and Surrey at cricket and was one of the highest-scoring batsmen in Varsity history. He led the England rugby team on their unbeaten 1910 tour of Argentina and also found time to play top-class golf as an amateur. He was killed in action in 1917.

Jack Will was another OMT who had won seven Scotland caps but was killed in World War One. Other OMT internationals of the era were Cyril O'Callaghan MC, who won seven Irish caps, and William Cheesman, who won four England caps as the scrum-half partner of W.J.A. Davies.

Like most Victorian clubs, OMT led a nomadic existence. They began on the school fields at Brondersbury, before moving to Stamford Bridge (later the home of Chelsea FC) and then to Old Deer Park as co-tenants with Rosslyn Park. In 1922 they opened their new ground at Teddington with a match against Rosslyn Park, who had been their first ever opponents. The Lord Chancellor, Viscount Cave, made the official opening. Fifteen years later the club moved to Croxley Green near Watford.

OMTs resumed rugby immediately after the armistice and gave a debut to one of OMT's greatest players: Dr. Ronald Cove-Smith. Cove-Smith had played for various hospital sides before the war and had to complete his punctuated education at Cambridge before becoming OMT, England and the British Isles captain.

Largely forgotten today, Cove-Smith was one of the greatest England forwards and captains. He locked England's scrum from 1921 until 1929, which was a golden era for the Whites. He appeared on the winning side for England on 22 of 29 appearances. He captained his country on seven occasions, including a precious Grand Slam, and led the 1924 Lions to South Africa. He later became one of the first players to write his autobiography.

Domestically, Cove-Smith led the OMT side for six seasons that saw them ranked amongst the best sides in Britain. The good times reached into the 1930s, when Fred Huskisson emerged as a top-class England forward. He made his name on England's inaugural tour to Argentina in 1936 and kept his place until the Second World War ended international rugby.

Ronald Cove-Smith (with ball) as captain of England's 1927-28 Grand Slam team.

The mid-1930s saw OMTs as the best OBs club in London. In 1935-36 they defeated Harlequins, the best open club in London, and took London Scottish's home record.

OMTs declined in the post-WWII years, as they restricted entry to genuine old boys, which put them at a huge disadvantage alongside the 'open clubs'. Overall, OMTs results were respectable, but could not compare with the 1920s and 1930s. This was despite the emergence of Douglas Baker as England's fly-half. He won four caps in 1955 and toured South Africa with the Lions. Baker was a stalwart of the club throughout 1950s, despite being the first top-class player to use contact lenses, as he was very short-sighted. In those days contact lens were not tiny pieces of filament, but lumps of hard plastic. Baker once asked his optician: "Will they come out playing rugby?" To which the optician replied: "Only if your head comes off." This technical innovation proved a nightmare on the 1955 Lions tour, when replacement lenses had to be sent from London by post, which took weeks.

An integral part of OMTs history was tours, and they were among the first clubs to tour the Pacific islands. Indeed, they took great pride in being the first English team to play in outposts like the Cook Islands.

In 1992 OMTs won the European Clubs Sevens, their first piece of silverware since the Middlesex Sevens in 1937. Another international honour occurred in 1991, when OMTs hosted a match between the Combined London Old Boys and the Soviet Union.

OMTs entered league rugby in 1987 in London 2 alongside old friends St. Mary's Hospital and Woodford.

OMT have the unusual status of being a long-standing member of Middlesex, but playing their home matches in Hertfordshire. Indeed, their ground at Durrants is often used for Hertfordshire County Cup finals. The club have produced two RFU Presidents: E. Prescott and M.F. Waters.

OLD MILLHILLIANS

"Old Millhillians are representative of the great non-conformist middle classes to which this country owes so much."

Dr. S.T. Davies, 1924

IT IS UNTHINKABLE in the 21st century that the British & Irish Lions would pick a scrum-half pairing from a middle-ranking club side, however distinguished the club's history. But this happened in 1930, when the legendary tourists looked to Old Millhillians for their half-backs.

OMs are one of the most remarkable clubs for representative honours. Four OMs have represented the British Isles (W.H. Sobey, R.S. Spong, A.F. Todd and J.E. Williams), nine members have played for England, two for Scotland and one for Wales. Additionally, nearly 100 have played county rugby.

Old Millhillians are the products of Mill Hill School, which was founded in 1807 and owe their origins to a Past v Present match at Mill Hill School that took place annually in the 1870s. The 'Past' players decided to establish a regular side. R.J. Wells, the 1878 Past captain, was the first skipper, with C.W. Cunnington as honorary secretary. The most surprising aspect of the club's formation was that they would play, in their words: "Rugby Union until the club is sufficiently strong to play Association as well."

OM's first club fixture was in October 1879 against the long-forgotten 'Union FC', which was lost. OMs began playing on Battersea Park, before moving to Hendon, where they stayed until 1890. The club established a good fixture list against the new wave of old boys clubs in the capital. In 1886 they played and defeated mighty Northern in a match refereed by Rowland Hill. They also made history around 1890 when they toured France and played Racing Club of Paris, one of the first visits to France by an English club. In 1887 OM had produced an England international in J.H. Dewhurst, who won four caps. It was a moment of glory before the club closed its doors due to a lack of numbers, though there was sufficient interest to retain the Present v Past match.

This proved a temporary demise anyway, as OM reformed in 1903 and resumed their first-class fixture list. Almost immediately they had T.W. Pearson capped for Wales.

OM played in Finchley after they reformed and until they moved to Southgate. There they stayed until 1926, when they had the wisdom to buy Headstone Lane (Harrow).

The school suffered badly from World War One, with 183 of its former pupils killed. It was 1919 before OM were revived with a match against the school.

Roger Spong

Wilf Sobey

Mill Hill School produced a quite outstanding crop of players in the early 1920s, with Roger Spong, Wilf Sobey (England and Lions), T. Lawther (Scotland), Pritchard, John Anderson (Scotland), plus half a dozen other players who won blues or county honours. With such a strong team, OM were able to advance their fixture list to one of the best in England. Wilf Sobey and Roger Spong were the half-backs of this remarkable team. The partnership continued for OMs, England and the Lions (on the 1930 tour of New Zealand). Spong was described by George Nepia as "a near genius. He was quick, lively and courageous". Sadly, Spong was never robust and he developed knee problems. His career was ended by injury in the first match of the New Zealand tour. Sobey had a more durable physique and played club rugby into his 50s, content to play junior rugby for OMs long after his international days were over. Spare a thought for Charles Wiggins, who understudied Sobey for many years without winning great honours, although he was a fine leader for the club.

Two other fine players of the era deserve mention: T.H.B Lawther and Peter Howard. Lawther won a rare honour when he became one of a handful of Scots who were picked for their country even though he played for OM – this honour was usually reserved for exiles playing for London Scottish or the Army. OMs had so much talent in the late 1920s that they won 63 of 71 fixtures over three seasons.

Peter Howard (1908-1965) played for Oxford University in 1930 and 1931. He was capped eight times for England and was captain in 1931. He won a silver medal in the four-man bobsleigh at Cortina in 1939. A noted author and playwright, he was the leader of a religious organisation called Moral Re-Armament (an international moral and spiritual movement). He also was unfortunate to miss selection for four Lions tours in the 1930s due to injury.

Part of the reason for the club's success was the excellent facilities at Headstone Lane, which were, however, a long way from Twickenham. A pavilion was erected in the late 1920s, but no bar existed because the club did not have a drinks licence. The club gave away beer, but it expected members to make an annual donation towards the brewery bill.

OM were popular competitors in the Middlesex Sevens, but in 1939 they withdrew from the competition when it emerged the application by United Services had failed to arrive. OM felt Services deserved their place and they stepped down to allow Services to be substituted in.

After World War Two OM merged with Old Haileyburians due to a shortage of players, since most young men were in the services and school leavers were needed for national service. Eventually OM reasserted its strength, and in the 1950s were the best old boys' side in the South East. Bridgwater & Albion were rather aggrieved to lose to OMs, as they only lost two games all season.

The club continued to produce players and administrators for the country. W.D. Gibbs (1955) and Bill Ramsey (1971) were RFU Presidents. The school produced another vintage crop of players in the early 1950s, which fed through to the rugby club and enabled OM to retain its top-class fixture list. The two top players were John Roberts and John Williams, the latter became one of the last players from an old boys club to win an England cap in 1955. Bill Ramsey was a great captain of OM in the 1930s, before becoming a leading RFU fixture secretary and president.

Season 1958-59 was one of the best in the club's history, with victories over Bedford, Saracens, Wasps and Rosslyn Park, but time was against OM and the other old boys sides, who could not keep to the level of the big city clubs. In truth, top-class rugby could not be maintained, however good the link to the old school.

In 1978 OM celebrated their centenary with a match against an International XV.

Despite the decline in old boys rugby, in the final quarter of the 20th century OM were still able to be involved in the London Merit Table in the years leading up to the foundation of leagues.

Currently OMs play in Herts-Middlesex One.

One of Old Paulines' successful inter-war teams.

OLD PAULINES

"Sooty imps who flit to and fro in the gloom of the grille behind the choir of St. Paul's."

Anon (1770)

ST. PAUL'S CATHEDRAL is one of London's greatest landmarks. What is not widely known is that the cathedral housed a school from 1509 until 1877. St. Paul's School has a famous list of old boys, including Samuel Pepys, the Duke of Marlborough and John Milton. The growth of the city led St. Paul's School to move to Hammersmith. Old Paulines were well-known at Oxbridge for arriving with bronchitis, a legacy of the city smogs.

It is thought that rugby was played at St. Paul's from the 1850s. They sent two youthful representatives to the inaugural meeting of the RFU in 1871. The Old Pauline RFC was founded in 1871, which makes it the oldest surviving old boys club in the world. And there are records of St. Paul's School itself playing Old Merchants Taylors' at Primrose Hill in the same year, which makes that fixture amongst the oldest surviving school matches.

The OP inaugural meeting came in November 1871 at the Cathedral Hotel in the churchyard. A ground was rapidly found at Battersea and club colours of chocolate and magenta adopted. The club's earliest fixtures included many of the sides who had helped form the RFU, including Richmond, Wimbledon Hornets and Flamingoes. The following season the club played 23 fixtures when St. Bart's Hospital, Guys and Harlequins were added. The St. Bart's match was memorable

for Old Paulines being six men short of the customary 20. They had a fragmented start to their history because many of their players were away at Oxford and Cambridge and matches were restricted to the university holidays.

Many of the finest varsity players had learnt their rugby at St. Paul's. The 1899-1900 Old Paulines team is considered to rank amongst the best in the club's history, containing five rugby blues, including R.O. Schwarz. It proved a false dawn, as soon afterwards OP struggled to survive as a rugby club and needed reviving in 1910.

Reginald Oscar Schwarz played in one Varsity match for Oxford at half-back. He played his club rugby for Richmond and made his international debut against Scotland in a match played on 11th March 1899, at the Rectory Field, the home of Blackheath at the time. He was dropped, but recalled the following year to play Wales and Ireland. He played cricket for Middlesex and after moving to South Africa for Transvaal. He returned to Britain with the touring South African sides of 1904 and 1907, and was a Wisden Cricketer of the Year in 1908. During World War One, Schwarz served with distinction in East Africa and France. He attained the rank of major and was awarded the Military Cross. He died of flu seven days after the armistice.

OP were a serious force between the wars, with fixtures against the best England and Welsh sides. In 1924 R.J. Hilliard played for England against the All Blacks. They were fortunate enough to reap a rich crop of talented players from the school, who were coached by I.M.B. Stuart, the Irish international.

During World War Two OPs merged with Old Cranleighans on a temporary basis until 1945.

Paulines maintained their senior status into the 1950s, when, like many old boys sides, it became increasingly difficult to compete with the big town clubs as their entire playing strength came from a single source. But, despite a decline, Paulines settled into good quality rugby against other old boys sides in the capital.

In 1971 they had pride of place at the centenary celebrations of the RFU, being one of only eight surviving founding clubs. They also produced a great international in Peter Stagg, who was one of Scotland's finest ever forwards, winning 28 caps between 1965 and 1970. Stagg went on to Oxford and eventually joined Sale.

Today Old Paulines are a famous name in the mid-ranking Home Counties leagues.

OLD WHITGIFTIANS

WHITGIFT SCHOOL WAS opened in 1596 by Dr. Whitgift, the Archbishop of Canterbury, who founded a number of alms-houses and grammar and middle schools. Rugby was introduced to the school in 1870. Six years later North Park Whitgift FC was formed for old boys. In 1879 the OB club went 'open' and changed the name to Croydon FC. The club kept a tradition of appointing an Old Whitgiftian as captain.

In 1901 a second Old Whitgiftians was formed with D.J.G. Lawson as captain. They won 15 of 17 games that first season, with two draws. A ground was found in Thornton Heath by S.E. Sachs, the first honorary secretary. The founding of the new club led to the demise of the Croydon club.

OW quickly established an excellent fixture list and were 1905 Surrey Cup champions. Two years later P.P. Phillips received an England trial. Four years after that OWs moved to Addiscombe Road.

The club lost 40 members in World War One.

Results were reasonable throughout the 1920s without being spectacular. In 1929 the lease on Addiscombe Road expired, which necessitated a move to Croham Road and included moving the club pavilion. They also celebrated when Peter Brook was the first OW to win an England cap.

In 1931 a new pavilion was opened in memory of A. Brodie, a former Whitgift headmaster. Peter Brook won three England caps and Basil Ellard Nicholson (1913-1985) was capped twice for England. Nicholson was also picked for the 1937 British Isles team, but missed the tour due to injury.

At the outbreak of World War Two OW moved in with Old Mid-Whitgiftians and, eventually, a shortage of numbers led to the formation of the 'Mitres' – an amalgamated side – for the duration of the war.

After the war OW joined forces for several seasons with Old Alleynians, as both sides couldn't raise full teams on their own strength. World War Two took its toll on OW, and in 1948 Peter Brook unveiled a war memorial to those who had fallen.

In 1948 M.F. Turner became the third OW to be capped when he appeared twice for England. Turner was honoured with the club captaincy in the half centenary year of 1951-52 and surpassed expectations with figures of P28 W21 D5 L2, which was marginally better than the previous record season of 1932-33, when the figures were P31 W23 D2 L6. Amazingly, Turner and the first XV produced the superb figures and then finished the season by winning the Surrey Sevens.

After these great heights, subsequent seasons were a return to realism, but Ian Beer, an OW who had captained Cambridge University, won two England caps.

The school were fortunate in the 1950s to recruit Welsh international Gerwyn Williams as director of PE. He was an early product of Loughborough College before later becoming the first official Oxbridge coach and later a Blackheath coach and his new methods benefited both school and the OW.

The OW's greatest successes came in the 1960s, both at the 15-a-side game and in sevens. They reached the finals of the Middlesex competition at Twickenham in six consecutive years, a record for a junior club.

OW's best-known player of the 1970s was Alan Wordsworth, who began with the club before playing for Cambridge University and England.

In recent years, with the introduction of league rugby, the club has once again become open to non-Whitgiftian membership. Recent seasons have seen mixed results, but they won the Surrey One League Championship in 1994-95.

In their centenary season of 2000-01, their colts won the Surrey RFU Under-18 Championship, and in 2002-03 they won the Surrey RFU Shield. More recently, in 2007, the OWRFC 1st XV won the Surrey Shield, their league and the Wanderers also won their league.

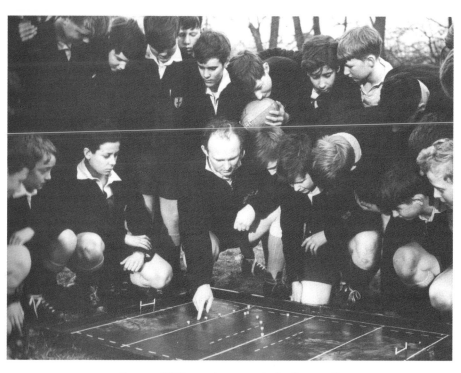

Gerwyn Williams gives a tactical talk to pupils.

PARK HOUSE

PARK HOUSE FC has its roots in a rugby club which was formed in 1883 by the Rev.G. Mallows Youngman, curate of St Alfege's Church at Greenwich, for the youth of the parish. Their first game was on 22nd February 1884 and was a heavy defeat by a club called Eagle. By the following year, under the captaincy of H. Bridel, the club had acquired a list of fixtures based around south-east London.

The club continued, but adopted the name of Park House in 1888, when the Rev. Mallows Youngman opened a gym at Park House, 1 Upper Park Street in Greenwich. The club colours were black and red, the red being restricted to the collar and cuffs of the jerseys.

By 1892 the fixture list contained many names still familiar today, including the Honourable Artillery Company, UCS, St Mary's Hospital, Saracens and Jesus College, Oxford. The highlight of the season was 13th February 1893, when the first French team visited England. Park House boosted their chances with the services of W.F. Carpmael of Blackheath. 3,000 spectators saw Park House victorious, winning by two goals and two tries to one try. That year the club joined Kent County RFU.

The club won the Kent Cup three years in succession (1897-99) and a special medal was struck by the Kent RFU to commemorate the feat. At that time the club had four teams being regularly fielded. There were two moves, first to Vanbrugh Field at Maze Hill (where Saracens were beaten 5-3 before a crowd of 1,500 spectators), followed by a second move to Kidbrooke Road. Previously that season in December Racing Club of France had been beaten 17-6 in Paris. The fixture list continued to improve, and regular games were played with many of the teaching hospitals, Wasps and London Irish.

The club continued to move southwards, to Bromley Road, Catford, at an annual rent of £20. Spectators were charged threepence, but ladies and boys entered free. The posters with a list of fixtures were put up by groundsman Tomlinson as part of his duties. Unfortunately, the club began to decline as bigger clubs poached their best players. Park House responded by persuading the RFU to make a rule that players couldn't move clubs unless they paid their subscriptions at their old clubs.

In the 1920s Park House rented two pitches at West Wickham whilst they got changed at the Railway Inn. Five years later, they moved to Baston Farm, to the north of Hayes.

The outstanding Park House player of the period was F.E. Parnacott, who was captain from 1928 to 1936 and a Kent regular. In his first season, Parnacott led the club to the county cup final, where they lost to RN Chatham.

On 24th May 1945, the club was reformed following the war using a temporary ground at Rookery Lane, Bromley Common. However, only one XV was fielded, and that with the help of Old Dunstonians. After a season at Rookery Lane, they returned to Barnet Wood Road in September, 1947.

In the early 1950s a very close association was formed with the Royal Naval College at Greenwich, whose members were made eligible to play for Park House. This link brought an influx of US Marines, who brought a taste of American football to the sport.

The most famous player to appear for Park House was Denis Thatcher (husband of Margaret), who played for Park House in the 1950s.

The new clubhouse was officially opened on the 7th October 1973 by Miss Mary Mallows Youngman, the granddaughter of the club founder. Or, so it seemed. In fact, it was a hoax perpetrated against the club president, as George Mallows Youngman died a bachelor.

Park House currently play in London 3 (SE)

RICHMOND

"We were happy to be a friendly and laid back club and to live on past glory."
Tony Hallett, a club stalwart and ex- RFU secretary

RICHMOND RFC WAS founded in 1861, which makes them one of the oldest clubs in existence. The club are so close to the roots of rugby that many Old Rugbeians joined the club as one of the few places in the world where club rugby could be played. For Old Rugbeians in the 1860s, the choice for club rugby was Ravenscourt Park or Richmond.

Edwin Ash, one of the founding fathers of the RFU, is credited with forming Richmond FC at a military academy in the area. The club's first recorded match was against arch-rivals Blackheath in 1864 (actually the only other club in the city) and did much to galvanise public interest in the capital. The next recorded match is against the Royal Naval College, New Cross.

The club began playing on Richmond Green, although it was prohibited by a local by-law in 1867. They were forced to leave the Green for Old Deer Park after a fracas in the crowd. Richmond stayed for 17 seasons at Old Deer Park, before moving to the Athletic Ground at Richmond in 1889. For most of their history, they have been co-tenants with London Scottish.

In 1871 Edwin Ash called the inaugural meeting that created the RFU following Scotland's challenge to England to play a rugby international. Not surprisingly, Richmond were represented by D.P. Turner in the first England team, and since 1871 over 100 Richmond men have played for their country.

Ash was the first RFU secretary, four Richmond men were on the first RFU committee, and two Richmond men – E. Carleton-Holmes and E. Rutter – helped draft the laws. Carlton-Holmes was the club captain at the time and was asked to pick the Richmond colours. He saw a squad of Belgian troops in the city who were carrying a red, gold and black flag, which he described as "warm and comfortable colours", so gold, red and black became forever associated with Richmond.

Links were rapidly established with young men from the best public schools (Rugby, Uppingham, Wellington etc.), who gravitated to Oxford and Cambridge Universities and were then persuaded to join Richmond in the city.

In the 1880s Richmond included some of the most innovative players in the game, including E. Temple-Gurdon, who is credited with being the game's first specialist front-row player. Previously the front-row was simply composed of whoever arrived first. Unlike modern players, front-rows stood up in the scrum because bending down was an open invitation to a knee in the face (and still is!). Temple-Gurdon is credited with being the first brave soul who risked his good looks by crouching to look for the ball's entry to the scrum. His contribution was initially unwelcome, being condemned as "hardly under the category of fair football". Fair or unfair, 1886-87 saw Richmond unbeaten and probably the best side in Britain.

The turn of the century found the club still a leading and major force in the game, although many of its early rivals had fallen by the wayside. Richmond could have also disappeared, but Temple-Gurdon quietly funded Richmond when financial pressures threatened his club.

On the 11th November 1905, Richmond played the first All Blacks. The club held the New Zealanders very well through fine tackling, and it was not until late in the game that the speedy and innovative New Zealand team got on top and won 17-0.

On 4th October 1909, the meeting with arch-rivals Harlequins provided the first match of the Rugby Football Union's new ground at Twickenham, the Quins winning 14-10.

The outstanding Richmond player between the wars was the Rev. Peter Brook, who could effectively play in any position on the field, except hooker. He retired at the outset of World War Two, but travelled with the first XV as a spectator for many years. In 1951 Brook went to watch Bristol v Quins and found Quins were a man short. He thought nothing of coming out of retirement to guarantee Quins had a full team.

Richmond were a major force in the 20th century because they maintained their links to the major public schools and varsities. This was boosted by accepting players from South Africa, the best-known being Tommy Bedford, who won 25 Springbok caps in the 1960s. Other top-class internationals included Chris Ralston (1974 Lions and 22 England caps) and Peter Kininmonth (22 Scotland caps).

In 1961-62 Richmond had a wonderful centenary season, with 21 wins in 33 matches, a club record culminating in a narrow defeat to a RFU President's XV. Three years later they broke new ground by playing two matches in Spain as part of British Industry Week.

Richmond have many other claims to fame: they have had players represent all the Home Countries, Argentina, India, Italy, Japan, South Africa and the USA. They were also amongst the first clubs to form a Ladies Section (1987), a junior section and a veteran's team called 'the Heavies' (1960s).

The club has won the Middlesex Sevens on nine occasions and were the leading English club side as recently as 1974, but by 1992 the once top club had dropped into National Three.

Rugby was changing and their pre-eminence in London had been overtaken by Wasps and Harlequins. No longer could the varsity sides be relied on for international talent. The game in general had become more professional and fewer internationals were public school products who lived in London.

Salvation seemed to arrive in Ashley Levett, an international financier who took over Richmond and pumped millions into the club. They rose rapidly from Division Three and left their traditional home for Madjeski Stadium, Reading. Levett recruited top internationals to Richmond's ranks, such as

Scott and Craig Quinnell, Ben Clarke, Dan Luger, Adrian Davies and Allan Bateman. Season 1998-99 began brightly for Richmond in the Premiership, with six wins from their first 10 games. But fortunes changed, and the end of the season saw the club win only one of their last six fixtures as the club went into administration. One suggestion was that they merge with London Irish and London Scottish into a unified London side, but they preferred to form a new club called 'Richmond Amateurs' and apply to join the leagues at the very bottom. This meant Richmond meeting teams to whom they once offered 'Extra B' fixtures. But they proved you can't keep a good club down as they recorded 70 unbeaten league fixtures.

The shock of seeing one of the game's greatest clubs reforming at the lowest strata of league rugby caused panic amongst old giants with new debts. Many clubs formed 'satellite clubs' who would start at Level 11, but rapidly rise against modest opposition. If a financial crash occurred, the old club could assume the identity of their satellite club and avoid the ignominy of playing on public parks. Sadly, Richmond had to learn the hard way and begin at the bottom.

Coached by Brett Taylor, Richmond rose in the early 2000s from Level 9 to National Three South on their return to the National leagues. It must have been an interesting experience for middle and low-ranking clubs to be welcomed to the famous surroundings of the Athletic Ground, especially in 2005 when ex-Springbok captain Bobby Skinstad played for Richmond. The unfamiliar opposition was probably too busy defending, as Richmond set a world record of 83 league games without defeat. By 2012 Richmond had reached National One.

ROSSLYN PARK

ROSSLYN PARK IS A real geographic location in Hampstead, but is famous only for rugby. Rosslyn Park takes its name from a stately home, Rosslyn Lodge, which in the mid-1860s was developed for housing. The club emerged from the old boys of Highgate and Mill Hill Schools, who had a cricket club. In 1879 the members met in the Roebuck Hotel, Hampstead and decided to create a rugby section.

The existence of Hampstead rugby club (later Harlequins) meant that another name had to be chosen. Rosslyn Park RFC was the choice, with O.N. Harcourt as captain. The first honorary secretary was C. Hoyer Millar, who was to be the doyen of Park for half a century. Millar secured a pitch opposite Fleet Road School in Hampstead, with the White Horse Tavern acting as changing rooms. Park's first fixture was a home win against Belsize Sefton. The first season saw eight wins and three draws in 16 matches, which led to better fixtures.

Originally, Rosslyn Park adopted dark blue jerseys with a large Maltese cross, but within a year the club switched to the red and white hoops that they have retained. The earliest matches were with hospital second teams and against long forgotten sides such as Belsize, Victoria, Hornsey Rovers, Orion, Reindeer, Falcons, Bloomsbury and Walthamstow.

Park were fortunate in establishing links with many famous schools, notably Mill Hill, Uppingham and Bedford Grammar School. They and the Bedford club established a long-standing link that enabled players to turn out for either club, depending on where they were currently domiciled.

In 1890 Park were granted a fixture with mighty Oxford University, who fielded six internationals and, unsurprisingly, won by three goals and two tries to one goal. Two years later Park became the first English team to tour France when they played Stade Francais in Paris. The British ambassador treated both sides to a post-match meal of champagne and sandwiches.

Back home, Park underwent the usual catalogue of grounds endured by all London clubs in the 19th century. After leaving Hampstead they played at Gospel Oak, Gunnersbury Lane, and Old Deer Park, before acquiring a home in Acton in 1896.

At Acton, the club's form dipped, with only seven wins from 54 games after the turn of the century. Misery loves company, and even the great Marlborough Nomads club was struggling. Eventually, after several drubbings, Nomads closed down, but

encouraged their surviving players to move to Rosslyn Park, which gave Park a timely boost.

The first international to play for Park was G.C. Lindsay, a three-quarter who had played for Scotland from 1884 to 1887. Three years later Rosslyn produced the first home-bred international in E. Bonham-Carter, of the famous Liberal political family, for England. Bonham-Carter played for Oxford University on the occasion of the first ever fixture between Park and the Dark Blues. Percy Carpmael of Blackheath also played for Rosslyn in the match.

Alec Todd toured South Africa with the 1896 British Isles team before moving to Blackheath. He was killed in World War One. Ted Hunt, who played for Park, won five Irish caps. Men of lesser rugby talents, but who were famous in other ways, played for the club, including Gerald Du Maurier (father of Daphne) and Alec Waugh, the novelist.

Middlesex Sevens winners in 1954.

In 1911 Park broke new ground by touring Austria and Hungary, and their fortunes improved in the dark years before World War One.

Rosslyn Park remained joint tenants with OMT at Richmond until 1922, when the old boys side moved to Teddington. The club grew in strength between the wars and by 1928, they were regularly fielding 11 teams. In the 1930s they had their first England and Lions player in Ernest Unwin, who won four England caps and toured with the 1930 Lions to South Africa.

Park could field a real star in Bev Chantrell, who had won England honours with Bristol, his home-town club. Chantrill was one of the best players and goal-kickers of the era and an outstanding acquisition for Park. The Bristol club were far from happy that Bev suddenly moved to the capital, and their local newspapers suggested he had been enticed away by the offer of a job in the city. Park's outstanding player of the era was Oliver Fulljames, a brilliant centre who scored dozens of tries, but who was never selected for England.

The most famous player associated with Rosslyn Park was undoubtedly Prince Alexander Obolensky. He arrived in England as a baby from Russia and made his name playing for Oxford University against the 1935 All Blacks, which catapulted the unknown winger into sporting legend. The legend was enhanced when he scored 17 tries in a single match as an England XV slaughtered Brazil whilst on a rugby tour of South America. But who was Obolensky? Educated at Ashe Prep School and Trent College, he was described by a contemporary as "melancholy, with straw coloured hair and a slightly, stooping run". He was aggressive in possession and difficult to stop in full flight. Brilliantly quick with incredible acceleration, he was prone, however, to put on weight when not in training, and he dismayed the England selectors by his propensity to appear at the start of the season looking decidedly tubby.

Despite his fame, Obo was written off as a flash in the pan within a year of his greatest moment. Amongst his critics was King Edward VIII, who was upset that a Russian national was selected for England – obviously he was unaware that overseas players had represented all the international sides since the inception of the game. After a few barbed comments from the King, Obo promptly took British citizenship.

In 1937 he briefly rediscovered his scoring touch, but the England selectors couldn't depend on him to stay fit for matches. In 1939 they persuaded him to move to Leicester and even delayed picking the England team to see if he was match-fit. Unfortunately, he was unavailable due to being hospitalised with a dog bite – obviously he wasn't fast enough to outrun the dog. He graduated from Trinity College in 1939 and joined the RAF, and he even played two wartime internationals during the 'phoney war'. Sadly, he was killed when his aeroplane struck an obstruction whilst landing, a tragic ending to one of the greatest careers in rugby.

Rosslyn Park has been associated with the National Public Schoolboys Tournament since 1939. Twickenham had previously hosted the competition, but was requisitioned for the war effort. Park volunteered their services and saw the event grow into one of school rugby's premier events, especially after the 'Public' was dropped and the name changed to 'National School Sevens'.

Rosslyn Park's rise to first-class status came in the 30 years after World War Two. In the 1950s they could field an all-international back-line, with J.V. Smith, Brian Boobyear and Christopher Winn of England joined by George Phipps of Ireland. Boobyear went to Oxford in 1948, where he won a cricket and rugby blue. At Oxford he played in three Varsity matches, all on the winning side, which brought him an England debut against Wales. He went on to win nine caps in the next three seasons, catching the eye of the selectors for the tour to South Africa in 1951. He scored the only points in a 3-0 victory against Ireland the following year.

In 1957 Rosslyn left Old Deer Park after 63 years when they moved to Priory Lane, Roehampton.

Andy Ripley in action.

The club became national news in the 1970s when they could boast one of the greatest characters in rugby history, Andy Ripley. The 6ft 5ins flanker was a world-class 400-metre hurdler, which made tackling him a nightmare. He simply hurdled the opposition and was totally unpredictable in attack. He prided himself on showing initiative and flair at a time when the game, particularly in England, was mired in defensive confusion. Ripley won 24 England caps between 1972 and 1976 and was a member of the 1974 Invincible Lions to South Africa. The fans loved him, but the England selectors wanted a more defensively-minded player. Eventually, Ripley was discarded by England, having fulfilled a fraction of his potential. A talented writer, he was hero-worshiped at his publishers, where the young ladies were in awe of his charisma. Curiously, he was famous as much for his success in TV's Superstars, in which sports stars competed against each other in multi-discipline events. Although an amateur competing against professionals, he was a match for all-comers. Ripley's philosophy was exemplified in 1985 when he captained Major Stanley's XV against Oxford University. His team talk consisted of asking the players to each tell a joke. Sadly, Andy died in his 50s, but not before he had written several brilliant books on the experience of dying with cancer.

Another Rosslyn Park maverick was Oliver Reed, the film star and legendary drinker. Reed was a decent flanker in the junior teams, being described as "unstoppable but with terrible ball handling". He would host huge drinking sessions at Roehampton, which continued afterwards at his home. One club official suggested: "Reed wrecked the team, but saved the club through subsidising the bar." His generosity was legendary. On one occasion the club got a huge, unexpected maintenance bill, which Reed quietly paid without telling anyone.

In the 1970s Park produced several internationals: Lionel Weston, Neil Mantell, Charles Kent and John Scott. The last two players had decent careers in the England side, but Weston and Mantell were discarded in their prime.

Charles Kent was 40 years ahead of his time. Today the influence of Samoan players as crash-ball specialists in the Premiership is an integral part of the game. Kent pre-dated that tactic with no subtlety; he got the ball in mid-field and, whereas Ripley might hurdle over the opposition, Kent just tried to smash his way to the try line. Initially, he was successful, but eventually opposing sides anticipated him and he lost his novelty and his England place.

John Scott was a more durable and long-lasting proposition. A huge flanker, Scott was fortunate to join England as Bill Beaumont's 1980 Grand Slam side was being assembled. He eventually moved to Cardiff and won 34 England caps.

Park were twice finalists in the National Knockout Cup, but lost in both finals.

Since the inception of leagues, Rosslyn Park has been in the top-50 English sides. They continue to produce top-class players. Alex King, the England fly-half, joined Rosslyn Park in 1993 before joining Wasps and enjoying a long and successful career. It was his misfortune to be a contemporary of the great Jonny Wilkinson, and his England chances were limited to the great man's spells of injury. Nick Easter was educated at Dulwich College and originally played for Rosslyn before moving to Orrell and Harlequins. He was first capped for England in 2007 and played 47 England internationals. Danny Cipriani followed Nick Easter in joining Park from Old Alleynians before moving to Wasps and Sale.

In 1999 Park played in League 1 with a team of part-timers. The loss of the annual RFU Grant led to relegation from NLD2, but they survived. Currently the club play at level 3.

ROYAL INDIAN ENGINEERING COLLEGE

THE ROYAL INDIAN Engineering College at Cooper's Hill near Staines were a leading cricket and rugby side of the late 19th century. Established in 1871, the college taught public works, engineering, science, maths and Hindustani to ex-public schoolboys between the ages of 17 to 19 who were going to work in India. They had formidable fixture lists. They played the MCC at cricket and played rugby against Oxford University, Richmond and many of the leading clubs.

The RIEC closed its doors in 1906. The official reasons were the cost of running the college and the changing requirements of migrants moving to India.

SARACENS

"Saracens have held their own against the clubs on their fixture list although they are a side comparatively unknown to those who think only of famous organisations."
An Essex Newspaper 1937

IN THE 21ST century, Saracens are amongst the top club sides in the world, with a roster of famous names from home and abroad. However, this is a modern phenomenon as they were considered just below the best for most of their long history.

Saracens were founded in 1876 by former pupils of the Philological School, Marylebone (the school later became St. Marylebone Grammar School). The inaugural meeting was held at the Café Monaco on Shaftsbury Avenue in central London.

Legend has it that the name was selected out of rivalry with an existing North London club called the Crusaders. Saracens' first watering hole was the Eton and Middlesex Hotel on Adelaide Road, which was also frequented by the Old Merchant Taylors' rugby team. Unsurprisingly, Saracens first game was against OMT at Woolwich, which resulted in a Saracens win by two goals to nil. Oddly, the two teams did not play each other again until 1961.

Saracens wore their famous black jersey with a red star and crescent from the start. They swapped to red, white and black hoops in 1894, but re-adopted the old colours in 1935.

They began to emerge as a force in London from 1878, following their merger with the Crusaders. In 1882-83 they won 16 of 19 fixtures and were unbeaten three seasons later, when they conceded only one try all year. By 1890 they had a top-class fixture list, including all of the hospitals, Wasps, London Scottish and London Welsh.

Although Saracens were formed in deepest Middlesex, their nomadic existence enabled them to be involved in the formation of the Essex County Union. This odd state of affairs followed moves of home from Woolwich, Walthamstow (1885), Crouch End (1893), Tufnell Park (1894), Crouch End again (1895), Southgate (1904), Muswell Hill (1920), Southgate again (1923), Winchmore Hill (1927) and Cockfosters (1939). Unsurprisingly, with no settled home, the club found it difficult to attract big crowds.

It was during the sojourn at Walthamstow that Saracens helped form the Essex Union, and although they didn't geographically stay long in the Eastern Counties, their players have always supported Essex and the ECRU.

The move to Bromley Road, Southgate was ill-starred. Initially, the new pitch was too close to the nearest road and upset pedestrians and motorists alike when the ball strayed out of bounds and landed on the highway. Worse still was the inaugural match against Wasps, which coincided with the declaration of war on Germany in 1939.

Saracens kept going during the war by raising sides from locally-based servicemen, and they were in brilliant form by the end of the hostilities. The season of 1946-47 saw them lose only one match and they were unbeaten at home for two seasons.

Previously Saracens had been a good side without being top-class. Now they began to attract the attention of international selectors. J.H. Steeds became the first Saracen to be capped

The Mayor of Southgate kicks off a charity match at Saracens in 1935.

directly from the club. Two years later tough flanker Vic Harding joined the club and brought new methods that improved their fortunes. Contemporaries included Eric Warr and J. Wallace from New Zealand, G.M. Elliot (who represented GB in the Olympics) and Norris McWhirter, the editor of the Guinness Book of Records. McWhirter, an Oxford blue, ran for Scotland and GB as well as playing county rugby for Middlesex whilst with Saracens.

In the 1960s, Saracens produced a remarkable England international in George Sherriff. Sherriff was a massively-built amateur boxer from the East End who turned up at the ground to move a load of timber. A Saracens representative suggested he play for a local junior club and monitored his progress. Within a few months, they reclaimed his services, this time as a first team rugby player. Sherriff made his England debut only four years after the timber incident. He was one of the last internationals who could play anywhere in the pack.

Saracens were a rising force. They were runner-up in the 1958 Middlesex Sevens and regular winners at the Middlesex County Cup. 1967-68 was a record season, with 27 wins. In 1977 they reached the semi-finals of the National Knockout Cup.

The arrival of league rugby saw Saracens as a small, friendly club with a good team in a quiet backwater of suburbia. But good things were stirring at Bramley Road as they never stopped improving, and, in the late 1980s, had a fine, young team that included Jason Leonard, Dean Ryan, Ben Clarke and Tony

Diprose. Sadly, some left Bramley Road to win international honours. Saracens had found the knack of unearthing brilliant youngsters, including Richard Hill from Salisbury, who laboured under the yoke of sharing the same name as the contemporary England scrum-half.

In 1994, Saracens gave the job of head coach to Mark Evans, a rare unknown who rewarded them with promotion to the top division. They also acquired a backer in Nigel Wray, who was to be the club's major benefactor.

Suddenly, Michael Lynagh, the world's no.1 stand-off, arrived thanks to Wray's generosity. He was joined by France's Phillippe Sella, the world record-holder for international appearances. They were augmented by Tony Daly of Australia, the youthful Kyran Bracken and three Irish internationals: Richard and Paul Wallace, plus Paddy Johns. The ultimate piece of recruitment was the arrival of Francois Pienaar, the 1995 World Cup-winning captain from South Africa, as player-manager.

The big names meant the club had no future at little Bramley Road, and in 1997 a move was made to Vicarage Road soccer ground, home of Watford FC. Vicarage Road was a world away from Southgate, with a ground capacity of 20,000.

Away from Watford, Saracens won their first ever cup in 1998, when they defeated Wasps in the National Knockout Cup final at Twickenham, but they struggled afterwards. In 2006 Saracens recruited Eddie Jones, the coach of the 2003 Australian team.

Nigel Wray passed the ownership of the club to a South African consortium, who bought in nine top-class South African players under ex-Springbok captain Brendan Venter. The club also played and defeated South Africa 24-23 in a friendly. The greatest name to arrive was Rugby World Cup winner John Smit, who had won 111 Springbok caps.

Looking closer to home, Saracens produced Owen Farrell, who at 17 was the youngest ever player in the English professional RU game. He made his England debut in 2012 alongside brothers Mako and Billy Vunipola, and Brad Barritt, Dave Strettle, Mouritz Botha, Matt Stevens, Alex Goode and Chris Ashton were recruited from Northampton.

All were remarkable players, but in 2011 Saracens forward Hayden Smith moved to America to play American football for the New York Jets, where he played for them six times

In 2013 Saracens moved to a £20m stadium at Barnet Copthall, renamed the Allianz Stadium, and had gates of 23,000 by 2014.

STAINES

STAINES RUFC WERE formed in 1926 and enjoyed a nomadic existence until it found a permanent home at 'the Reeves' in Hanworth, taking its name from post-war president George Reeves. Staines had originally played on a cricket ground at Ashford. Though reluctant to move outside the Staines boundary, the club's 130 playing members and seven weekly fixtures forced the move three miles east to Hanworth. There is a sprinkling of players with recent representative experience: Robin Hall (Berkshire), Terry Bowen (Sussex) and Josh Beattie (Middlesex).

In 1948, the club were the first in Middlesex to form a colts team and the first to organise minis in 1973.

Chris Sheasby

In 1970 the club reached the finals of the Middlesex Sevens and were four times winners of the Middlesex Merit Table. Amongst their finest products were England captain Lawrence Dallaglio and Terri Siwek, who played for England Ladies.

In recent seasons, some famous names have appeared for Staines. Chris Sheasby and Nick Greenstock both played for Wasps and England before joining Staines. In 2005 the legendary Fijian star Waisele Serevi played for the club. That season Staines reached the semi-final of the Intermediate Cup, but lost to Westoe.

STREATHAM - CROYDON

"Croydon is a conceptual anachronism. It has the feel of a Midlands manufacturing town in the midst of dormitory suburbs."
Anon, 1950

RUGBY BEGAN IN the South London suburbs of Streatham and Croydon in 1867, when Oakfield FC operated. Oakfield lasted until 1874. A local rival, Streatham FC, lasted for a single season in 1871, whilst a third side, Streatham Park, also known as Lewin Rovers RFC, ran out of funds. Two Croydon clubs came and went: the first in 1877, whilst the second lasted for 16 seasons from 1879 and had fixtures against Richmond, Blackheath and many of the top Welsh clubs.

After the demise of the earliest Streatham clubs, the game was continued by Thurlow Park FC, who were formed by schoolboys from Dulwich College. The club was called Thurlow Park because its first ground was off Thurlow Park Road in West Dulwich, although they later moved to Greyhound Lane, Streatham. The club's fortunes were at their peak in 1889-90, when not a single game was lost. In 1891-92 fortunes declined after a move to Hyde Farm, Balham, where the changing rooms were so poor that it was difficult to retain fixtures and members left the club.

Around 1893 Alfred Mitchell called a meeting of members of Thurlow Park and the old Streatham Park clubs to form Streatham RFC. The new club decided to adopt the Thurlow Park colours of cardinal red.

The new Streatham club used the Greyhound Lane ground and began by running three sides. They practised passing on Streatham Common, but struggled when dark fell. If moonlight was lacking, the ball was wrapped in a large white handkerchief to aid identification. Every Thursday evening there was a club run from the Pied Bull to Thornton Heath Pond and back, and on Sunday afternoons there would be a club walk.

The first match against Charing Cross Hospital was won by a substantial margin, and Streatham went on to win the Surrey Cup, which was in its third season. Season 1894-95 saw the team score 447 points against 21 by their opponents, and again the Surrey cup was won, as it was the following year also. The club's achievements earned improved fixtures, but progress was slow.

The only player to gain international recognition while at Streatham was W.V. Butcher, who played for England against Scotland at Richmond on 21st March 1903. Butcher, who was a scrum-half, gained six further England caps over the next two seasons, the next three while he was playing for Bristol and the final three while he was playing for Richmond. In 1904 he was partnered at fly-half for three England games by Patrick Handcock of Richmond, who had the previous season been his Streatham partner. Hancock's move to Richmond to try to gain an international cap had been severely criticised in the sporting press. Both Butcher and Hancock appear in the Streatham team photograph of 1903-04, along with J.T.Sharland, one of the club's Surrey players who went on Bedell Sivright's tour of Australia and New Zealand in which 16 matches were won out of 19 played. Other internationals from the club include C.W. Greenall and A.L. Goodall, of whom little is known.

Streatham lost their pitches during World War One, but a lease was obtained on the old Croydon Cricket club in Front Road, Thornton Heath. Although the lease was renewed the following season, the ground situation remained precarious until £6 was paid down on the option of buying it. This was done with the co-operation of the local cricket and tennis clubs. A limited company was formed and an issue of shares was made. A house adjoining the ground at 159 Brigstock Road was bought in 1921 and transformed into a clubhouse, complete with tea-room, bar, bath and showers, a great improvement on the changing accommodation which had been in use at the Prince of Wales public house in Brigstock Road for the first two years. The clubhouse was extensively redesigned in 1957.

Between the wars rugby union in the area was threatened by the emergence of a rugby league club, confusingly called Streatham and Mitcham. The 13-a-side club's only memorable achievement was signing George Nepia, the legendary All Black full-back, at the end of his career. Streatham and Mitcham only lasted two seasons before disbanding in February 1937. Rugby league resurfaced after World War Two with the brief existence of a Mitcham RLFC.

Streatham could also claim a famous name amongst their ranks: James Callaghan. At the time, he was a youthful beanpole second-row who worked for the civil service. He subsequently went into parliament and became prime minister from 1976 to 1979.

After World War Two the club produced A.J. Hendrickse, who won an England trial in 1963. A decade later Streatham produced an England tourist in flanker Steve Callum, who toured Australia with England in 1975. Prop Jeff Probyn played for Streatham-Croydon for nearly four seasons at the end of the 1970s, before representing England for the first time six years later at the age of 31 while a member of Wasps.

A distinguished captain of the club was Dudley Wood, an Oxford blue who later became secretary of the RFU for many years. A kindly soul, when one Fijian team competing in the Middlesex Sevens took to selling souvenirs outsides his office at Twickenham to raise funds, he emerged, asked what all the noise was and simply said, "Seems a strange way to spend Saturday afternoon", and left them to it.

In 1964 Bernard Utting, a long-standing member, encouraged the club to change its name to Streatham-Croydon RFC with a view to strengthening its links with the developing borough of Croydon.

1971 saw the club's centenary, culminating in a fixture with the John Players Cup holders, Coventry. Streatham-Croydon won the Surrey cup in 1973-74 and 1974-75, beating Esher in the final on both occasions.

In the 1980s S-C bought an expensive set of jerseys, which made their debut against a famous old club. Afterwards, S-C were dismayed to find six brand new jerseys had departed with the opposition. They wrote to the opposition, who were horrified and called a meeting of their first XV. The club chairman quietly said: "You shouldn't have pinched the shirts, now if you were guilty please wrap them up and leave the parcel plus £1 postage in the dressing room after Saturdays match." The club chairman went into the dressing room after the match. He was shocked to find nine S-C shirts and £9!

When the league structure was introduced in the 1987-88 season, Streatham-Croydon were placed in Division 2 South. Unfortunately, the club were relegated to London 1 for the next seven seasons, and were relegated to London 2 South in 1994-95, where they stayed for three seasons. A series of relegations saw them drop to Surrey 2 for season 2001-2002.

(Thanks to Colin Belcher, John Brookes and Alec Gritton)

TWICKENHAM

TWO EVENTS HAVE probably transformed the village of Twickenham more than any other. First, the railway arrived in 1849 and brought Victorian commuters, which changed the centre of the village to the St. Mary's area. The second change was the building of the RFU's new stadium in 1909.

Rugby had existed in the village since 1867, when the 'young gentlemen' from Wellesley House Academy established a fixture list. The academy side managed to keep going for three years before some event led to their fixture list being taken over by a new side. The newcomers date from 1873, when an advertisement appeared in the local press seeking "boys with a maximum age of 17, the sons of gentlemen only, to form a football club".

The village had several existing clubs, such as 'Twickenham Proper', 'Twickenham Seconds' and the 'Young Men's Friendly Society'. But eventually a single Twickenham RFC emerged that played on Twickenham Green.

The club nearly disappeared in 1893, when a meeting was called at the Prince Blutcher public house. The agenda was dominated by a proposal to abandon rugby in favour of soccer. Eventually, the meeting voted for rugby by 21-13 and decided to switch from black jerseys to red and white hoops.

In February 1900 Twickenham RFC helped the Boer War effort by bidding £5.50 for a soldier's button.

In 1908 Bernard Mesley signed for Salford RLFC from Twickenham RU. He had previously played for Oxford University and the Civil Service. His league career was interrupted by World War One.

At that time Twickenham RFC were a middle-ranking club on the London old boys' circuit, but they soon entered a golden era. The club appeared to have become an old boys' centre for Sherbourne Public School. A number of talented products of the school played for Twickenham in the years up to World War One. Christopher Stanger-Leathes was the best-known. He also played for Northern FC in Newcastle and won an England cap in 1905. Other internationals of the period were Francis Stone (one England cap in 1914), Colin Hill (two Scotland caps in 1912), R. Jones (one Wales cap) and Leonard Tosswill.

Tosswill (1880-1932) won three England caps in 1912 before leading a busy life. A product of Marlborough, Tosswill gave up rugby for journalism and became one of the first radio sports commentators. He was closely involved in 'Rugger' in the 1920s, which was the first national rugby magazine. Tosswill seems to have had a close affection for the Twickenham as he included features on the club.

The club moved to nearby Hampton in 1914 and were allowed to keep their ground during the subsequent war as the Armed Forces also used it for rugby.

Twickenham continued to be a middle-ranking club between the wars, but without the famous names. With Richmond and Harlequins only a short journey away, the club's best players left in search of success, including Ray Dudman and Everton Davis, who joined Harlequins. Everton Davies also played for England.

Twickenham can point to two fixtures that stand out in the club's history. In 1967 the RFU granted their neighbours the singular honour of playing the centenary match on the hallowed turf of the RFU Stadium, when the famous invitation side, the Penguins, provided the opposition. And in 2002 they achieved their finest hour when they won the Middlesex County Cup after a century of entering without success.

Terry Claxton began at Twickenham. The big prop was a regular for Middlesex and London in the 1970s.

(Thanks to Jim Peters)

UCS OBs
(University College School Old Boys)

RUGBY WAS PLAYED at University College School from 1872. The first old boys side, called 'Paulatim RFC', was formed by John Ely and R.S. Hall, who placed a notice in the school magazine. 57 members agreed to join, and the first match was against Marlborough Nomads at Surbiton on the 6th October 1892. The Nomads won by two tries to nil. Three fixtures were played that season, with the best result being a draw against the school XV.

Paulatim RFC struggled from the start. Problems with a home pitch meant they agreed to play all matches away from home. At the end of the first season, Paulatim changed its name to UCS OBs. In an attempt to establish itself, the new club launched an appeal that raised £3.50. Eventually, £21 was raised to fund the hiring of a ground at Mill Hill Park. The earliest matches were played at Gospel Oak before moving to Willesden and then Action Hill.

In 1902 the club moved to a farm field at Osterley, but the changing facilities were a half mile walk from the ground. That season UCS OBs won 20 of 24 matches.

The club continued to grow, and in April 1904 played Stade Francais at Richmond in front of 3,000 spectators. Although they lost 8-0 to France's premier side, UCS OBs considered themselves the best OBs side in the capital. The best-known UCS old boy was a good player, but better-known as an administrator. Emile de Lissa ran the Barbarian FC for 23 years after Percy Carpmael stepped down.

In 1909 UCS moved to Greenford, but results were disappointing, a situation that continued until they moved back to Osterley in 1913.

After World War One, UCS retained their pre-war fixture list. Results improved, as did the new sides on the fixture list, notably Rosslyn Park, Northampton and Gloucester.

In 1922 the club bought their ground, using a limited company to raise the necessary funds. Success followed, and in 1927 they fielded an international when Colin Bishop (1903-80) commuted between the OBs and Cambridge University. He later joined Blackheath and won a single England cap against France.

UCS OBs began that season away to Cardiff, which became a regular fixture. Defeats to Cardiff were the norm, but the club's esteem was boosted.

Major Johnson was a UCS OBs stalwart for 30 years. His greatest claim to fame was that in 1931 he organised the first rugby match in Sweden, when a team of Royal Marines met a side of Swedes.

Rugby resumed at UCS OBs in 1945 at Osterley. The war years had disrupted the flow of talent, and it was only the mid-1950s before results and playing numbers improved as UCS OBs fielded six teams.

1959-60 was the best season since the war, when the club reached the final of the Middlesex Sevens. But, like all old boys clubs, UCS were losing their first-class fixture list and the distance between the school based in West Hampstead and the rugby club based in Osterley was a problem to old boys joining the rugby side. In 1979 UCS OBs left Osterley for West Hampstead.

The centenary was celebrated in 1992-93, the highlight being a match against the Combined London OBs XV.

UPPER CLAPTON
(Epping Upper Clapton)

UPPER CLAPTON FC was formed in September 1879 by Percy Barber, A.H. Ashmore and W. Sewell Singer as Orion FC (also known as Upper Clapton Orion FC) and formally became Upper Clapton FC on 11th March 1882.

Under captain F.H.W. Jenoure, the new club began with great success. The first recorded match was 29th November 1879, which saw a large win over Walthamstow Harriers. Many of their original opponents are long gone, notably Rangers, Stonebridge and Croydon Clifton.

Clapton faced OMTs at Willesden Green on 30th December 1882. That game ended in a clear-cut win for Clapton by three goals and two tries to nil, but the return match at Clapton on the 17th March 1883, the final game of their first season, was, according to Taylorian magazine, "particularly fast and well contested and resulted in a win for us by one goal and two tries to one try although we were minus three men."

The original colours of Upper Clapton were blue, but 1882 saw a change to black and amber halves. 13 years later a change was made to black and amber hoops. In 1900 red and white hoops were adopted.

The first ground was Rumbal's Field, Spring Hill, which was left in 1892-93 and the club moved to Clapton Cricket Ground in Millfields Road. A decade later Millfields was lost, and a new ground was found at the Elms, Walthamstow.

The first recorded UC player to win representative honours was George Sparks, who represented Essex from 1885-1892 after moving from Saracens.

An early Upper Clapton team.

The beginning of the century saw three-quarter John Raphael appearing for UC before moving to Old Merchant Taylors', for whom he won nine England caps. 1903-04 saw UC in dire straits. The results on the field were poor and the new ground at Elms hadn't worked out. A move to the Uplands, Walthamstow was undertaken, followed by a spell at Tottenham Park, White Hart Lane, Tottenham.

White Hart Lane was lost to housing after the Great War, which precipitated a move to Salisbury Hall, Highams Park, Chingford. The situation was still bad, and the club wavered on the edge of closure for several years. The club moved across the park in 1921 and gradually things improved, but that season of 1920-21 had been their worst, with results of P18 W0 L17 D1. Despite the appalling results, several members won honours for Eastern Counties, and one county player, R.B.Price, had an Irish trial with Ulster.

In 1926 UC found a home at Bush Park, Enfield, adjacent to the tube station. But the sum of £2000 had to be found – a fortune in the 1920s. That year UC joined the Middlesex RU following their change of ground.

They appeared four times in the final rounds of the Middlesex Sevens, the last in 1974. Probably their greatest achievement as a club came in the 1980-81 John Player Cup, for which they qualified by reaching the semi-final of the previous season's Middlesex Cup competition. In the first round they beat Woodford 13-4 and in the second they beat Crawley 18-0, before losing honourably to Bristol 3-22 in the third. Upper Clapton have produced one full international: George Mackie (Scotland) in 1975. They also produced two England under-23 internationals in Steve Jackson and Steve Callum, and numerous county players, mainly for Eastern Counties.

WESTCOMBE PARK

WESTCOMBE PARK RUFC began life as Blackheath's 'other club'. They started playing in 1904 and held their meetings at the Green Man Hotel in the village. The club was founded by Dudley Roughton in conjunction with the Rev. W.T. Money and several others. Rowland Hill, the RFU Secretary, was closely involved in founding the club.

The club took its name from a small park on the village. In their early days the club played on Blackheath itself, followed by a move to Roger's Farm, Kidbrooke, near the old Kidbrooke Aerodrome buildings. In 1914 they moved their grounds to Harrowfield Farm, Eltham. The majority of the members in the club were drawn from the boys from Christ's College, Blackheath, and the Roan School.

They had a superb season in 1911-12, when they won 19 of 22 matches.

During World War One Cecil Sewell, a member of the club, won the Victoria Cross.

Westcombe reformed in 1919, but struggled to pick up the threads, sharing Sidcup's ground before moving to Shooter's Hill. They stayed there until 1937, when they moved to Craven Road, Orpington, followed by a move to Goddington Lane as part of Orpington Sports Club.

The only international associated with Park is Joe McPartlin, a Scotland international who spent a season at Orpington in the 1950s.

Westcombe Park began the league system in the middle-ranks of London One South, which became a springboard to National League success. Ironically, it was the arrival of coaches Chas Chapman and Danny Vaughan from Blackheath which sparked the good times.

In 1997-98 Park had a record season, with 32 wins in 33 matches, including 15 league wins. In 1999 the Orpington-based side were promoted to National 3 and in 2001 to National 2 South.

The club's best-known player is Derek Coates, who was the top goal-kicker in their National League team. Coates moved to Blackheath, kicked 368 points in his first season, and scored 1000 points in four seasons.

The club's annual Mini-Festival brings 2000 young players to Goddington Dene each year.

WIMBLEDON

THE EARLIEST RECORD of a Wimbledon Rugby Football Club is from Bells Life on the 4th November 1865, recording a match against the Richmond club. The game was played on Saturday, 28th October 1865 and Wimbledon lost by two goals. On the 2nd December 1865, a further report appeared in Bells Life of a game played on the 25th November 1865 between Wimbledon and the Civil Service College. Wimbledon won by two goals.

During 1866-67 games were played by the club under such titles as 'Brakenbury's Wimbledon' (after the name of the captain) or 'Wimbledon Wonders' against Charlton, (which they lost by one goal) and Ravenscourt Park (lost by two goals). In 1868 the title 'Wimbledon Hornets' was adopted by the club. This name and date is confirmed in the Football Annual published in 1872.

During 1870 the secretaries of the Blackheath and Richmond clubs issued a joint letter to the leading London and suburban rugby clubs calling a joint meeting to consider the formation of a Rugby Football Society. The meeting was held at the Pall Mall Restaurant at the corner of Pall Mall East and Cockspur Street on the 26th January 1871 and was attended by the captain of Wimbledon Hornets (Leonard Maton, an Old Rugbeian), together with representatives of 19 other clubs. All the clubs represented at the meeting were enrolled that evening as 'original members' of the Rugby Football Union. The captain of Wimbledon Hornets was nominated to the executive committee and played a major part in the drafting of the union's code of rules. The work progressed slowly until Maton broke a leg, which gave him ample time to draft the Rules of the game as played at Rugby School. The rules were accepted by the RFU without any great comment. Maton was later honoured as the third President of the RFU.

Hornets were a valued member of the union, not least because they had over 100 members, a huge number in 1871. Games were played on Wimbledon Common and the Rose and Crown public house was used as headquarters. In January 1871, in a match against the Harlequins, the club was heavily defeated 37-0. However, in February the tables were turned and the club were the winners. During this season nine matches were won and four lost. The 1872-73 season produced a remarkable record of 14 drawn games out of 21 matches, with four won and three lost. Throughout the 1870s and early 1880s they maintained strong fixture lists.

Hornet's first internationals were H.J. and J. Graham. The latter won a single England cap in 1875 against Ireland, whereas his brother won four caps. Another Hornet selected for England was G.L. Lockton, who missed the honour due to injury.

The club's best player was Arthur Pearson, an Australian by birth and the first to win an international cap (eight years ahead of C.G. Wade). A great goal-kicker, Pearson played for England for four seasons.

At the start of the 1875-76 season the club became known as the Wimbledon Club, dropping 'Hornets' from its title. However, the connection was maintained by their second XV title of 'The Hornets'. During this period they rented two pitches at Bradbury, Wilkinson's former ground. Players then made for the Cambridge (Shannon Corner) or to the Raynes Park Tavern.

For a time the club shared the Conservative Club at Wimbledon Park, but this came to an end owing to objections to the noise and singing on Saturday nights!

One of the biggest problems facing the club in this period was one of recruitment of members, as local schools which played rugby – KCS, Rutlish and Wimbledon College – had their own old boys clubs. The club managed to maintain three teams for most of the time, but these dwindled to two by 1939. The club was fortunate in obtaining a number of old boys from St. Mary's College.

Wimbledon had always suffered from the lack of a permanent ground. It was the 3rd October 1959 before they finally found a permanent home. The first home game was played against the U.S. Navy. By the 1961-62 season, the club was fielding five XVs and the first few seasons of the 1960s were particularly successful.

It was another 25 years before the dream of a clubhouse finally materialised. In 1987 the club moved to Beverley Meads, just off Copse Hill, which coincided with the advent of leagues, with the first XV being placed in Surrey 2 in the first year of the leagues, something that upset the club, who thought they merited higher status. They were Surrey 2 champions in 1989-90 and recorded three straight promotions, eventually reaching London 2 South, where they have stayed (with a few hiccups) ever since.

CHAPTER FOURTEEN – KENT & SUSSEX

"It is injurious to a man to become a professional. He gets out of the way of work and loses valuable time. When too old for football, he finds difficulty in finding employment."
Rowland Hill (1892)

KENT

THE KENT COUNTY Football Club, as it was first known, was composed of a few Kentish clubs around the metropolis led by the famous Blackheath club. After the first two or three successful years, interest in the county began to wane. Kent passed through a rather depressing period, and it was mainly through the energy of George Rowland Hill, the first to be knighted for services to the sport of rugby union, that recovery began. And it was thanks to Hill, George Harnett, and a few other stalwarts that the county survived and flourished. Representative matches were arranged in the outlying districts, such as Ashford, and these stimulated greater interest in the county's representative XV.

Season 1896-97 was a memorable one in the history of Kent Rugby, when the county of the White Horse defeated Cumberland in the final of the championship at Carlisle. For the first time since the start of the competition in 1889, the supremacy of the northern counties, Lancashire and Yorkshire, had been checked. Included in the Kent team that season were seven internationals and five future England caps – no small wonder that Kent won all six matches.

Seven years later Kent again reached the final, but in a desperate struggle at West Hartlepool the championship title went to Durham by a single point, a dropped goal to a try. In the following season, B.C. Hartley led a brilliant side, which bristled with internationals, and for the second time Kent won the coveted title when the same counties again met in the last stage. In 1924, Kent were runners-up to Cumberland, and then three years afterwards again brought the title south when F.W.R. Douglas led the team to victory over Leicestershire, captained by F.D. Prentice, later secretary of the Rugby Football Union.

Lean years befell the county in the early thirties, but happily the decline was of a short duration, and in 1937 it reached the county semi-final, but lost to Gloucestershire, the ultimate winners. The county's activities on the field were suspended during the war years, but the administration was kept alive and it was not difficult to restart when hostilities ended and the game could resume. In these post-war years, Kent was fairly consistent, earning a place in the 1950 semi-final. After Kent's win in 1927, it was another sixty years before the county reached another final, losing 16-6 to Warwickshire.

ASHFORD

ASHFORD WAS THE cradle of rugby in the Kent countryside. The London-based clubs thrived from the earliest days of rugby, but the game struggled to lay down roots elsewhere. The game in Ashford began in 1881 with a match between the new club and an Ashford Grammar School XV. The game was repeated a year later and the town club won by five tries to nil. Initially Ashford played on a pitch near the Cradle Bridge, but moved to the Victoria Ground by 1885. They led a nomadic existence, including occupying the old golf links at Kennington.

Little else is known of rugby in the town until 1887, when the county were asked to arrange a match to promote rugby 'in the sticks'. The Kent RFU promoted a match in Ashford between a Metropolitan XV and a team from the outlying areas. Despite this match, interest declined and the game died out in the town. It briefly reappeared in the 1900s with a match between Ashford and Kennington in London.

Ashford led a desultory existence and occasionally ceased to play regularly. Indeed, the club was reformed for the fourth time in 1936 by Sir Charles Igglesden, the founder of the Kentish Express newspaper. In 1936, Ashford RFC joined the RFU and celebrated with a victory over Hastings and Bexhill 'A' and subsequently flourished until the outbreak of World War Two.

They reformed in 1946 and shortly afterwards suffered one of the oddest injuries in rugby history. On the 30th November 1946, under captain R.J. Howard, they were due to play Whitstable. At the time, Ashford played on a farmer's field and Howard cleared some cattle from it; unfortunately they included a bull, which attacked Howard, breaking his leg. It was no consolation to him that Ashford won 11-8.

The club established itself as one of the leading Kentish sides after World War Two. Initially they muddled through with temporary pitches until a member, G.H. Kynaston, provided a ground, known as Kinney's Field, in 1959. 20 years later, Kinney's Field was commandeered as it lay in the path of the M20 motorway.

The club had a long association with the Toucan. This dates from the liberation of a large advertising sign by three members attending the Isle of Thanet Ploughing Match. The bird has since decorated the Ashford clubhouse.

The early 1960s saw Ashford enjoying a golden era, losing only 19 of 81 games over three seasons. The uncertainty over the loss of the ground affected Ashford in the 1970s. However, in 1980, they moved to Bybrook, north of the town. Currently they play on Canterbury Road, Kensington.

The only international associated with Ashford was flanker Peter Bell, who after moving to Blackheath represented England against Ireland in 1968. Bell had appeared in six England trials before receiving a cap.

2014 saw Ashford enjoy successive promotions up to London 2 (SE).

ASKEANS

"I find it laughable the suggestion that Askeans are paying players when I spent Monday night trying to find the money to pay our rates bill."
Graham Terry, Chairman, Askeans RFC, 1990

Askeans were originally the old boys of Aske's Hatcham School. The school switched from soccer to rugby in 1925 and an annual School v Old Boys rugby match was played for many years, beginning on 18th December 1926 when M.R. Soper led a team of Old Askeans against the School XV.

Initially OA played at distant Gunnersbury and it was the end of the 1928-29 season before regular matches were played on the Kent RFU ground at Oak Lodge, West Wickham, followed by a move to Kidbrooke, where the club's facilities were limited but results on the field were excellent. The club bought three army huts, one for the home team changing room, one for the visitors and the third was the bar. There was no running hot water in any hut; just zinc baths filled by hand with two players to a bath. The club carried on in this manner until the onset of World War Two.

The highlight of the 1930s was when E.W. Cassidy became the first player from the club to represent the county. He was selected at No. 8 for Kent in 1934.

Resumption after the war came on 9th February 1946 when Old Askeans played Old Haberdashers on the school field. Kidbrooke was returned to the club in October 1949 and it was in that season that Dick Hills won the first of his Kent caps.

Askeans greatest claim to fame must date from the post-war era when they twice reached the final of the Middlesex Sevens at a time when it was dominated by the capital's big sides. They lost to Harlequins in 1955 and to the same opponents in 1974. During this time, Old Askeans regularly ran seven teams and provided many players for the county side.

Decline came in the early 1970s when the club broke away from the Old Boys' Association and formed an open club, Askeans RFC. To counteract decline, Askeans set up a link with two local Catholic grammar schools: St. Joseph's RC College and St. Mary's. A member at the time flippantly suggested that the club benefited from "blending the public school ethos with the feisty toughness from the Catholic boys".

The finest player to emerge from St Mary's and Askeans was John Gallagher, who achieved little of note in Britain but blossomed after emigrating to New Zealand. The ginger-haired full-back quickly established a reputation as a brilliant All Black and eventually switched to rugby league in 1992 with Leeds. His career took a nosedive when he published an autobiography, entitled 'The World's Greatest Full Back', a title

John Gallagher

that came to haunt him as he failed to make an impact in the 13-man game.

Askeans' fortunes rose rapidly in the late 1970s. In season 1977-78 they set a new record win of 150 points to three over Bredgar in the first round of the Kent Cup. The club began to attract top players, even acquiring an All Black in Greg Cooper, plus several other internationals in Lion Stewart McKinney, Tony Bond, the England Grand Slam-winner and doughty England prop Jeff Probyn, who was in the Rugby World Cup final programme as an Askean.

When leagues arrived, the club was placed in National Four, but they were unable to maintain their previous success. They found themselves competing against clubs who would book two nights in a hotel for away matches, whereas Askeans had an early rise, a five-hour drive to an away match, 80 minutes rugby and then a weary journey home.

A period of homelessness accelerated the decline, which culminated with the club drifting down to Kent 1.

BECKENHAM

THE FIRST BECKENHAM RFC existed in 1874 but soon folded. They reformed briefly in 1884 and played on Kelsey Lane. Move forward ten years and there was another restart when 25 enthusiasts led by Dr. R.M. Randell, a former captain of Guys Hospital, reformed the club. The founding meeting was held at Church House in the town. The club secured the loan of a pitch behind the Three Tuns Hotel in Kelsey Lane. The first match was against Brockley on 8th December 1894 – result unknown. The club's colours in those days were red and white vertically striped, with blue shorts and stockings. In 1899 the club moved to Haggers Field, behind Beckenham Hospital, paying an annual rental of £10 per year and using the George Hotel for changing.

In 1907-08 the club started to make definite progress and Rosslyn Park and London Irish appear on the fixture list. In the same season a second ground was obtained in Abbey Lane for the use of junior sides.

The first decade of the 20th Century saw the club fielding some splendid players. The backbone of the pack was the three Stagg brothers, John, Roland and Harold, whilst another forward, William T. Cave, played for England and the British Isles after moving to Cambridge University and Blackheath.

Unfortunately the retirement of these players signalled a period of decline and in 1910 Beckenham lost 80-0 to Old Whitgiftians. The club were down to a single team by 1912 and closed during World War One and remained in abeyance until 1924, when it was reformed by a few locals, including Dr. Randell and E.G. Loudon-Shand, the Scotland international.

A ground was found behind the Flower House in Southend Road at a rental of £30 per season. The first match saw a win against Old Dunstonians 'A'. The club colours were changed to blue and old gold, with blue shorts. That season the 1st XV won 16 out of 21 games, while the 'A' XV won 13 of 21.

In 1926 the club obtained the leases of two pitches on the Nest Anglo Sports Ground at Elmer's End for an annual rental of £50. Three sides were now being fielded and the club's captain, A.H. Wright, was selected for Kent.

The late 1930s were a golden era for Beckenham and in 1937–38 they lost only three of 29 fixtures, whilst the Second XV lost only four of 27.

Bombing during World War Two saw both the pitches and facilities badly damaged. Those were austere days when materials were in short supply – indeed, it took eight years for the grandstand to be rebuilt. One has to make the best of one's circumstances and Beckenham caused a stir by hiring a trawler to transport a touring team to France to play an exhibition match in Calais. The players were required to sleep on the deck.

James Robertson Justice

Beckenham had a link to showbusiness because, being only 13 miles from London, it was popular with the showbusiness set. In the 1920s, James Robertson Justice was a regular before becoming one of Britain's leading actors. In the 1950s, Tony Hancock, Maurice Denham and Johnnie Craddock played for the rugby club. Denham and Craddock were serious players; Hancock less so. Johnnie's wife was the legendary Fannie Craddock, TV's first cook, who did the post-match catering. Old-timers recall she specialised in serving cucumber sandwiches which were hard and curled up.

The best known players produced by the club have been Matt Hankin and Elliot Daly of Wasps. Since the introduction of leagues, the club have hovered around National level 6 (London 1 South). Today the club is totally amateur and struggling against semi-professional sides.

BETTESHANGER & DEAL
(Betteshanger Colliery Welfare RFC)

THE ISLE OF Thanet had four coal mines until recent times: Snowdown, Tilmanston, Chilston and Betteshanger. The last named was the youngest and largest of the four. It opened for production in 1927 and was the last to close in August 1989. The pit was manned from the outset by miners from all the older mining areas of Great Britain, including a good number from South Wales. They brought with them a passion and love for the game of rugby, getting together to start a rugby club in season 1932-33.

The first playing ground was a field rented from a local farmer at the nearby village of Northbourne. In 1936, the then 'Bettershanger Miners Welfare scheme' was given a ground by the mine owners Pearson Dorman Long, three miles from the Colliery.

Two notable players who represented the club in this era, were the first club skipper Ted Cox, who had formerly played first-class rugby with Cross Keys. The second was Derek Dent, who also skippered the side and who had previously played for Fylde.

The club reformed in 1948 and shortly afterwards became an open club. In 1989, at the time of the colliery closure, the club was an even mix of miners and non-miners. The club were Kent Division Two Winners in 1987-88 and 1995-96 and four times East Kent Floodlit Cup inners.

In 2005 Betteshanger merged with Deal RFC in London 3 (S).

BLACKHEATH

"What Hambledon is to cricket, Blackheath is to rugby."
Anon

BLACKHEATH FC WAS formed in 1858, which makes the club the fourth oldest in the world. The club's founder was L.P. Seuer, son of the French master at Blackheath Proprietary School. Rugby had been played at the school from the early 1850s and a number of the pupils helped form the first Blackheath team. Originally there were two rugby clubs on the heath: BFC and the Hockey & Football club. Blackheath FC drew many of their players from Rugby School, but played according to the Blackheath club rules.

From the start, Blackheath FC was at the heart of the sport. R.M. Peter of Blackheath started the Wanderers club in Dublin, which helped form the Irish Rugby Union.

On 26th October 1863, a meeting of 11 London football clubs, including Blackheath, was called to discuss the formation of a 'Football Association', which would co-ordinate the way the game was played across the country. Blackheath, who wanted to retain hacking, quit the organisation. They objected to the FA's centralised authority, but, ironically, seven years later proposed the formation of a Rugby Football Union in 1870. The club attended the inauguration of the RFU in February 1871 and are unique in attending the founding of both the FA and the RFU.

The Stokes Brothers, Lennard and Frederick, were the first great players from Blackheath. Frederick (1850-1929) was captain of England in the world's first international when they played Scotland at Raeburn Place on the 27th March 1871. On that famous day, he was accompanied by B.H. Burns, C.A. Crompton and C.W. Sherrard of Blackheath. He was better known as a cricketer in his day and was one of three brothers who played rugby for Kent.

Lennard Stokes joined the England team two years after his brother stepped down. He eventually won 12 England caps between 1875 and 1881 as a half-back. His achievements included playing in the first internationals against Ireland (1879) and Wales

Lennard Stokes

(1881). Lesser known was that Conan Doyle allegedly based the character of Dr. Watson in the Sherlock Holmes stories on Lennard Stokes. He was the sport's outstanding back of the 1870s and Blackheath's captain for five years from 1876 to 1881, during which time he scored 56 tries. Blackheath lost only six games during Lennard Stokes' tenure as captain.

Other prominent early members were Arthur Hill, who joined from the Gipsies and later captained London, Dr. Robert Henderson (1858-1923), who played for England from 1882 to 1884 and later was physician to King George V and William Burnett, who was club skipper from 1862 to 1866. Burnett emigrated to New Zealand and helped organise the 1889 Maori tour of Britain.

Blackheath may have been the best known club in South East London, but they were just one of many clubs on the Heath. On a busy Saturday, there might be 20 matches in progress. Blackheath eventually choose to play on Richardson's Field before moving to the Rectory Field in 1882 when Richardson's Field was bought for housing.

On 19th February 1881 Blackheath hosted the first England v Wales match. The day's organisation left much to be desired by modern standards. Both sides met at the Princess of Wales pub near the Common, got changed and then trekked half a mile to Richardson's Field. Wales lost by seven goals, six tries and a dropped goal to nil. The match had one bizarre moment when Lennard Stokes' huge pass out to the wing was disallowed as 'unsporting'.

The most prominent Blackheath member of the England side who played Wales was Harry Vassall, who was rugby's first great innovator. Vassal built a formidable powerbase at Oxford, which established the Dark Blues as one of the most successful sides in Varsity history. Curiously, Blackheath later established a link to Cambridge University and had first pick of their players.

Blackheath were one of the first clubs to play foreign sides. Around 1890, they played Racing Club of Paris, who, legend has it, wore berets throughout the whole match.

After Vassall, the next great Blackheath player was H.T. Gamelin (1878-1937). Gamelin was a tall, rangy full-back whose greatest days came during a trough in England's fortunes. A brilliant player, he was only in a winning England team on four occasions in 15 matches.

Gamelin was, however, eclipsed in sporting mythology by another Blackheathian, Charles Burgess Fry, the most famous English sportsman since Dr. W.G. Grace. Fry won Oxford Blues at cricket, athletics and soccer and scored 30,000 first-class runs at cricket. He played in an FA Cup Final and was a soccer and cricket international. A brilliant sprinter and wing three-quarter, Fry missed his Oxford Blue at rugby due to injury but was a reserve for the North v South trial.

That was Fry's public persona; the truth was less glamorous. He was a world-class self-publicist, once describing himself as having "the finest mind at Oxford", despite admitting to a complete lack of ability at Maths and English. Fry did barely a day's work in his life, managing by living on his friends and his sporting reputation. In 1920 he was offered the throne of Albania, but the Albanians rapidly changed their mind when they found out he had no money. His reputation took a nose-dive in the late 1930s when he promoted Adolf Hitler as a paragon of virtue.

Percy Carpmael was prominent at Blackheath and with the RFU, in 1890, he organised a 'scratch' side to take on the might of northern rugby. Described as the 'Southern Nomads' and 'a Blackheath XV', Percy's team of friends became the Barbarians.

Blackheath had a more fragile arrangement with Swansea They only once played the Welsh club away and Swansea offered "half the gate", but Blackheath refused and asked for a lump sum. The match took place in 1896 and Blackheath were horrified to find a full house at St. Helens. Blackheath officials changed their mind and asked for half the gate, which Swansea refused. Blackheath declined to travel to Swansea for the next four decades unless half the gate was offered, which it never was.

Playing for Blackheath was a huge honour. Froude Hancock, the Somerset and England forward, travelled 400 miles each week to represent the club.

In 1898, six Blackheath players captained their counties: J. Fegan (Kent), C. Dixon (Middlesex), C. Wilson (Surrey), F. Mitchell (Sussex), E. Fookes (Yorkshire) and H. Finlinson (Eastern Counties).

Until the founding of Twickenham, Blackheath regularly hosted the England v Wales game. Custodian of the pitch throughout the era was Jerry Weaver, who was groundsman from 1860 to the outbreak of World War One. He said in 1911: "The play (in the 1860s on the Heath) was rougher than now but all the players were sportsmen."

One young man who was "rougher than most" was Charles 'Cherry' Pillman (1890-1955), who could be considered the greatest Blackheath player of all time. Pillman is credited as the first British open-side flanker who followed the tactics of the 1905 All Blacks. Pillman was quick and skilful enough to play at fly-half for the 1910 Lions in South Africa. He won two Lions and 18 England caps before breaking his leg in the 1914 Calcutta Cup match. He was the star of a great Blackheath team that won 22 of 28 matches in 1913-14. The 1919-20 team, led by Pillman, surpassed their predecessors by losing only two of 25 matches.

No less an authority than Rowe Harding, the great Welsh scrum-half, attributed the end of Wales's golden era to Pillman. He wasn't a forward; he wasn't a back, Pillman was a wrecker. Until he arrived, the three-quarters had plenty of time to move the ball away from the forwards; Pillman saw his role as arriving in the middle of the three-quarters before they could safely mount an attack or kick for touch.

Blackheath just before the First World War,
with Charles Pillman standing left.

Off the field 'Cherry' Pillman, an Old Tonbridgian, was a solicitor. He won the MC in World War One. In later life, he was a brilliant golfer, but his later years were overshadowed by the loss of both his sons in World War Two.

The Pillman era was a golden era for Blackheath, when the club could field ten internationals and one season lost only one game – and that to Newport. The club had some great characters: Frank Mellish, a South African, Harry Coverdale was a tiny fly-half and fine goal kicker alongside B.S. Cumberlege (England) and A.K. Horan (Ireland). Coverdale played for England from 1910 to 1920.

The 1919 Blackheath team included another all-time great in winger Cyril Lowe, who won 25 consecutive England caps and scored 18 tries – a record that stood for 65 years. Lowe was a triple Cambridge Blue before becoming an RAF fighter ace with nine kills in World

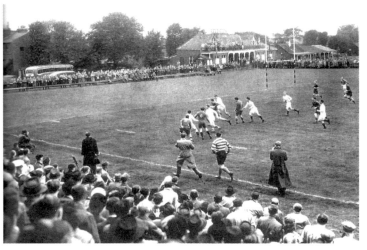

Above: Blackheath playing Racing Club de Paris in 1928, and below, a game at the Rectory Field in 1951.

African who was passing through London when World War One broke out. He joined up and won the MC. Later he played for Blackheath and won six England caps before going home and being capped by South Africa. Mellish later was manager of the superb 1951 Springboks who won all five European internationals.

Stan Harris won two England caps besides being the South African boxing champion, won the Wimbledon Mixed Doubles, played in the Davis Cup and was a world ballroom dancing champion. Whilst Harris was living in South Africa, the Lions toured the country and suffered an injury crisis. They called up Harris for two Lions caps.

Another Lion from Blackheath was Carl Aarvold (1907-1991) who captained the British Isles in three tests. Aarvold also captained England six times and won 15 caps. He guided Blackheath to their most successful season in 1932-33, when they won 30 of 39 matches.

War One. He was a pure athlete; swift and elusive in attack, yet brave and devastating in defence. Lowe and his team-mate Cyril Kershaw were part of the first great era of English rugby in the 1920s when four Grand Slams were won.

Kershaw, who won 16 England caps, is forever associated with W.J.A. Davies as the England half back pairing. If Davies was sheer magic, his scrum-half partner was a tough customer who played as a fourth back-row forward alongside Voyce, Conway and Wakefield – a formidable trio in any company. He represented the UK in the 1920 Olympics at fencing. Curiously, he was often criticised by purists for ruining three-quarter play by playing the percentages and kicking too often.

Davies and Kershaw came out of retirement to play in the 1923 Centenary match at Rugby School. Cyril Lowe had also retired from top-class rugby but, although he asked to be selected, was ignored.

One Blackheath player who missed these golden years was E.J. Blake Bludden. BB was imprisoned in Russia in 1914 and only managed to escape eight years later. He was one of the best-known players at the Rectory Field throughout the 1920s.

More famous players at the Rectory Field in the 1920s included Frank Mellish and Stan Harris. Mellish was a South

Between the wars, Blackheath could claim to be amongst England's best, although their team on international Saturdays was below strength. They were certainly the favourite side with the newspapers and got more press coverage than any other team in England.

The Rectory Field was lost for the duration of the World War Two and the club struggled to recover during the post-war years. Eventually it regained its strength and made national headlines with the Rugby Festival of Britain in 1951, when 8000 spectators saw a match under 1862 laws, followed by an international invitation match involving the cream of the Home Countries and French players.

The Fifties and Sixties saw Blackheath as an attractive side, but they were increasingly unable to attract the star names in direct competition with Harlequins and Wasps. They also suffered from the emergence of Charlton Athletic soccer club in the locality. Also, the Oxbridge connection was gradually falling into a decline which continued into the 1960s when Tony Jorden became their last British Lion. The club still produced internationals, however, in Mike Campbell-Lamerton, Peter Wright and Jorden.

Season 1967-68 proved the best for 35 years, but it was temporary relief. A decade later, they finished bottom of the London Merit Table, although they regularly qualified for the National Knockout Cup as Kent Cup champions.

League rugby saw Blackheath in National League Two and fielding one of the game's greatest characters: Mickey Skinner. He began as a Blaydon colt before joining Blackheath and Harlequins. Skinner was 28 when he won his first England cap, but was a regular in the 1991 World Cup side. An abrasive flanker, Skinner always seemed to have a helpful word for opponents and referees alike.

The 1990s saw Blackheath establishing links to New Zealand. A string of All Blacks arrived at the Rectory Field: Hika Reid, John Schuster and John Gallagher were all legends, but a virtual unknown took over as coach in 1997. Graham Henry brought innovations, but was hardly a household name. He took over as coach to Wales (1998-2002), British Lions (2001) and New Zealand (2004-2011), including leading the All Blacks to the 2011 Rugby World Cup.

Blackheath have climbed up and down the National leagues. In 2009 they were in National One.

The club celebrated their 150th Anniversary by renewing the fixture against Richmond; this fixture is the oldest club match in the game's history.

BRIGHTON

BRIGHTON RFC WAS founded in 1882. Their greatest player was John 'Jack' Birkett, who played for the club and Sussex in the early 1900s before being spotted by Harlequins and being persuaded to head to the capital. Birkett won 21 England caps between 1906 and 1912 – an incredible number when England only played three or four matches a year. He was a swift, big back who saw direct running as a mighty weapon, whereas his England and Harlequin teammate Ronnie Poulton-Palmer relied on elusiveness to outwit the opposition. Try-scoring ran in the Birkett family as his father, Reginald Birkett, had been England's first try-scorer in 1871 and Jack was the first man to score a try at Twickenham when Harlequins played Richmond in the inaugural match at the great stadium in 1909. At the time, he was never short of critics. One wrote: "Birkett is too full of himself"; another said he was "the worst best centre in international rugby due to always hanging on to the ball too long and missing passes". Yet another critic described him as "tackling well occasionally".

Brighton were a great side between the wars. In 1926-27 they had the best results in Britain, with 26 wins in 28 matches; the following year they won 23 of 26, and in 1929-30 won 22 of 27. They also produced Jim Renald, who also moved to Harlequins, where he became one of their best players of the 1930s and was an outstanding full-back for the RAF. Another top-class player was Frank Mitchell, a big forward who attended Brighton College before graduating to Cambridge University and winning an England cap. A fine forward, Mitchell was also a first-class cricketer.

Brighton's best player of the post WWII era was C. MacDonald, a Scotland international stand-off who was Brighton's best player in the early 1950s

For much of their history Brighton were nomadic. Between the wars, they had one pitch on Preston Park and used the Clarence House as a watering-hole. The main room of the Clarence had an illuminated cartwheel hanging from the ceiling. The parting of the ways came after an incident where a player was debagged and his trousers hung from the cartwheel. Despite this incident, the club somehow persuaded Sussex CCC to let them use the County Cricket Ground as a pitch, but only when the cricket season ended. Brighton moved on to Preston Park in 1950 before they acquired the use of Withdean Stadium (home of Brighton and Hove Albion until 2011)

In the 1950s, Withdean was a mud heap which was far from ideal for rugby. Led by Masefield Baker, they resolved to obtain a better ground and found a pitch at Horedean, which was shared with the Sussex Police. A perfunctory clubhouse was erected, which coincided with the government announcing that a new road was to go through the site. So Brighton lost Horedean, but received handsome compensation, which facilitated the purchase of a new clubhouse and ground at Waterhall, near the Devil's Dyke.

Since the arrival of leagues, Brighton have been one of the best clubs on the South Coast. In recent seasons the club has gone through a golden era, winning the Junior Vase, the Intermediate Cup and the Senior Vase under the direction of England Under 21 coach Neil McGovern. They currently play in London South One. The best players seen at Brighton in recent seasons have included Gary Halpin (Ireland) and Harry Leonard (Scotland).

BROMLEY
(Catford Bridge)

"I knew army life was getting boring when I became nostalgic for Catford."
Spike Milligan

BROMLEY RFC CAME into being in 1964 when an ancient old club, Catford Bridge RFC, changed its name. The team had begun in Berlin Road, Catford, but moved to Bromley in 1903.

A Catford Bridge team operated in Victorian times, drawing players from St. Dunston's College in Catford. The club's greatest claim to fame is that they were the first team to face the All Blacks on the inaugural tour of 1888. Legend has it that Catford RFC had been formed in 1886 and became a major force in Kent rugby. They were Kent Cup winners on six occasions between 1900 and 1914, when they were only challenged by army and navy sides. The club had excellent facilities on Berlin Road, which could hold 2,000 spectators.

Their fortunes took a dive when the old boys of St. Dunston's College set up their own club. The magnitude of the loss can be gleaned from the fact that the 1906 Kent Cup-winning side were almost entirely composed of Old Dunstonians.

Catford produced two notable players between the wars in H.E. Wilkins, a top-class forward for Kent, and R.W. Smeddle, who was capped by England. In 1936, they celebrated their golden jubilee with a series of matches against 'old contemporaries', beginning with Guy's Hospital.

Twenty years later, the club opened their new clubhouse with a match against a Kent XV. Eight years later they changed their name to Bromley.

Bromley's youth development system produced two Irish internationals in Paul Collins, who played for Munster and Ireland in the late 1960s, and Jim Staples, who was one of the best full-backs of the 1990s. Other top-class players from Bromley include Josh Lewsey, who played as a Junior, and Mike Friday, who joined Bromley from Wasps when player/coach of the England Sevens team.

In 2002, Bromley reached the final of the Junior Vase, only to lose to Heath of Halifax, but gained consolation by winning the Kent Junior Cup and by becoming Kent One Champions.

(Thanks to John Marriott)

BURGESS HILL

BURGESS HILL WAS formed in 1962 by two players from the Haywards Heath club and a lady called Miss Fisher, who ran the local youth club. Miss Fisher played a crucial role as she persuaded the local council to provide a pitch and posts. The pitch had originally been intended to be a cemetery.

The club struggled to find a permanent home until someone offered a disused chicken house owned by a farmer whose son played for the club.

Despite being known as the club that operated from a chicken hut, Burgess Hill grew rapidly. Eventually three sides were fielded regularly and the hut was replaced by a second-hand wooden building purchased from the local water board.

Sadly, the boom ended and the club could only raise one XV. Worse still, in 1987, the clubhouse burnt down. It was rebuilt and the club recovered and now play in the Sussex league. In the late 1980s, they won the Sussex Plate.

CHARLTON PARK

IN THE 1850s, Charlton was a village on the south east of London that was populated by well-to-do people who commuted on the new railway system to the City . There were two rugby-playing schools in the area: Blackheath Proprietary School and High House School in Charlton Park. Blackheath Proprietary School produced the 'Old Blackheathens' side that became Blackheath FC. High House School is less well-known, but introduced rugby to the syllabus in 1856. They too produced an Old Boys side called 'Old Charltonians FC', which operated on an occasional basis until they were formerly established in 1894. Club records, however, go back to 1863. Another side called 'Charlton FC' operated from 1866 until 1891, but lived in the shadow of Blackheath. The demise of Charlton FC coincided with the official formation of Old Charltonians FC. There were at least two other local clubs, Charlton Park RFC and Charlton Rangers RFC, but they soon disappeared.

OC's early matches were played on the school playing fields, whilst the changing rooms were in The Swan Hotel in Old Charlton. The club had to be content with playing the second teams of the major local clubs – Sidcup, Catford, Bromley, Park House, Beckenham and Mitcham, along with extinct sides such as Manorway, from Lee, and Royal School of Mines.

The first official match of Old Charltonians appears to have been on the 23rd November 1894, when they beat Lewisham by "one drop goal from Dawson to one try". They had to wait another two months for their next game against Upper Clapton 3rds, which ended in a Clapton win by one penalty goal and two tries to one goal. The following games were cancelled because of frost, which covered the Thames in ice from shore to shore for the first time for 50 years.

The original club attracted players from Woolwich Barracks and the link to the Barracks provided Charlton Park with two of its three golden eras. The years before the first war had Park riding high, but everything came to halt in August 1914.

The club officially adopted the name of Charlton Park RFC in 1920. They did well and in 1939 were running five teams. South East London suffered terrible bombing during World War Two, and when the club was reformed, life was difficult. Park muddled through for 20 years with a single team until they broadened their horizons by establishing links to local colleges.

Gradually Charlton Park grew in numbers and entered the leagues on an upswing. In 1992, they reached their highpoint by winning promotion to National Four (South). Park never had any illusions that their amateur club would survive the competition of wealthier rivals and they returned to the London leagues.

Park has never attracted big stars. Two first-class players to play for them were Billy Bushell, who later played for Harlequins, winning an England cap, and Doug Hursey, who captained Kent.

Hale and Pace were stars in another era of life who played for Park. Norman Pace was a gifted fly-half at second team level, whilst Gareth Hale is remembered as a willing forward in the lower teams. Hale and Pace eventually swapped South East London for the West End and comedy fame.

In 1999, Charlton Park were reported to have bought Askeans old ground and, for a time, shared training facilities with London Bronchos RLFC. The club currently play in London 2.

CROWBOROUGH

CROWBOROUGH RFC OWES its origins to a couple of youngsters, Geoffrey Cornford and Roland Hill, who decided to form a rugby club at Christmas 1936. Both had played rugby at their school in Lewes The two youngsters wrote to the Kent and Sussex Courier proposing the establishment of the club. The following month, the Courier reported: "Mr F.U. Mugliston, ex-Gloucester, presided at a meeting that decided to form a rugby club using a pitch on Beacon Road whilst the Blue Anchor pub was used for washing and changing. A couple of matches were arranged against Cranbrook RFC who were already an established side."

When the new season opened, in September 1937, 'Mickey' Barnes had virtually become manager, as well as coach and referee. The first match was played against Sussex Yeomanry,

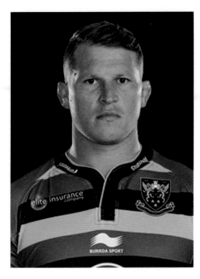

Dylan Hartley

who won by 40-0, but Crowborough won their next home fixture, against Hastings & Bexhill A, by 14-8. That season they won 12 matches, lost ten, and drew one against Wasps.

The best player who played for the Crows is Dylan Hartley, the England hooker. Born in New Zealand, Dylan met Dave Pass, the head coach of Crowborough RFC's Colts side, and was looking to come over to England. The club helped Dylan to enrol at a local college whilst he played for Crowborough Colts. He was selected for England Under 16s and ultimately joined Worcester's academy and then Northampton Saints.

Crowborough currently play in London 2 South East.

DOVER

THE EARLY HISTORY of Dover RFC is linked to Dover College, the famous public school that was founded in 1871. A Dover College old boy later recalled that Dover RFC had its roots in the scratch sides raised by timber merchant Fred Finnis to play the college. Dover College's 'private rules' were used and there were twelve men a side.

A meeting was held in the local cricket club pavilion on 22nd October 1873 to formally start a club, and a practice game was later held at the cricket ground on 12th November. A match between Dover College and Dover RFC was reported in 1877, with the college winning by one goal and one try to three tries. Further Dover RFC matches were recorded in 1870s against Dover Valley and Avenue RFC, a side composed of employees of Southern and British Railway. The original Dover RFC ceased playing fixtures in 1887, largely because the Dover College connection had dried up.

An 1899 newspaper cutting reports a match between Dover Rugby and the West Riding Regiment, which was played at the Athletic Ground. Dover lost by one drop goal and one try to nil. Later that year, Dover Town played both Thanet Wanderers and Dover College. The club's colours in those days were light and dark blue. The club became known as Dover FC by 1903, but seems to have led a sporadic existence. It reappeared briefly in 1909, but was entirely composed of Dover College masters and boys, plus officers from the local garrison. October 1911 finally saw the sad demise of the Old Boys' XV.

Around the turn of the 20th Century, Dover School produced its finest rugby player in A.D. Stoop, who moved on to Cambridge University and Harlequins. Rugby at Dover College was so strong that an Old Doverian side survived in London until 1939.

Apart from the college, no rugby was played in the town until 1925, when Dover College master Allon Ewart and the bursar T. Guthrie Morgan advertised for other enthusiasts to form a club to start the following season.

A ground was secured from the corporation at Elms Vale, which was uneven and during the week was used for cow grazing, and so before a game volunteers had to remove the cow dung. Black and amber were the chosen colours, as a tribute to the original club.

For the first year the playing record reads P15 W5 L7 D3 F67 A128. Names on that first year's fixture list included Tonbridge, Thanet, Worcester College, Oxford and Club Athletique, Paris. An unbroken run of seasons followed until 1939. In the second season the club was fortunate in having the services of Vivian Jenkins, a schoolmaster at the College who was a Welsh international full-back and later Rugby correspondent of The Sunday Times.

In 1929 the club moved to a pitch at the Danes.

July 1946 saw Allon Ewart, together with Dickie White, Freddie Maher and a few old players revive the club after the war. After this revival, thecClub enjoyed what was probably its best playing season, in 1949-50, achieving almost a 90% winning record. In 1950 Dennis Shuttleworth (ex-Roundhey, Headingley and Combined Services) played for Dover prior to winning two England caps. The fifties saw the success of the club fall away, but Sam Simmonds, who began with Dover Grammar School, received an England trial.

The 1960s saw the club field a famous name in Jeffery Archer, a youthful PE teacher who was teaching at Dover College. Little is known of his Dover RFC days, but he was an England international sprinter and must have been highly effective at club rugby level. Archer left the area when he became a politician and later a successful author. His only other venture into rugby was refereeing the annual Parliamentary rugby match between Labour and Tory parties.

The military garrison in Dover was reduced in the post-war years and Dover RFC suffered, as did the rest of the town. Dover has an unusual problem because many of the nearer rugby clubs lie 20 miles across the Channel in France. Oddly, the club have had few, if any, French players.

The arrival of rugby league in 1987 found Dover in decline. Eventually they took a decision to rely on a talented colts team and were handsomely rewarded. The year 2000 saw them languishing in Kent Three, but they were subsequently promoted five times in the next decade, reaching London Two. They also reached the last eight of the RFU Senior Vase in 2008.

(Thanks to J.D. Thomas and R. Biggs)

ELTHAM CHISLEHURST
(Eltham, Old Elthamians)

ELTHAM RUGBY HAS a place in rugby and cinema history, through its association with one of the greatest exploits in Olympic history. Eric Liddell was a top-class sprinter and rugby player who was educated at the School for the Sons of Missionaries in Blackheath, which became Eltham College, producing the old Elthamians RFC, which became Eltham RFC.

The original school was a bastion of muscular Christianity. As such, it was a fitting place for the education of Liddell, who was born on the 16th January 1902 in China, where his parents were missionaries. The family returned to Britain in 1908 and sent Eric to the school. Eric's arrival coincided with the Sons of Missionaries School leaving Blackheath for Mottingham and adopting the name of Eltham College. Half a dozen of the old boys had formed a team called the Old Elthamians, which made a promising debut, beating Sutton 'A' 38-0 on the 27th January 1912.

After World War One, OE briefly fielded two of the greatest names in rugby history: Liddell and Archie Gracie. Liddell (1902-1945) played seven times for Scotland, scoring four tries. His exploits on the athletics track inspired the film 'Chariots of Fire'. The film tells the story of two Olympic gold medalists: Harold Abrahams and Liddell. The Scots flyer refused to compete in the 100 metres final because it was scheduled for a Sunday, which offended his religious principles. This left the door open for Abrahams to win gold. Liddell switched to the 200 metres, which was held later in the week. He won a gold medal on his competitive debut over the distance. Remarkably, Liddell won the event at the Stade Francais, where he made his international rugby debut a year before. He never played rugby again and returned to China in 1925, but kept running. Legend has it that he was still one of the world's top sprinters and could have represented Britain at the 1928 Olympics. In 1932, he was inducted as a minister of religion. He was interned by the Japanese during World War Two and died in a prison-of-war camp in 1945. His portrait, with his haunting eyes, hangs in the Scottish National Gallery.

Archie Gracie, like Liddell, was the son of missionaries. He was born on the 15th October 1896 in Sri Lanka and sent by his parents to Eltham College. He captained the school rugby team for five years and the cricket team for six. Gracie played for the Eltham College First XV at thirteen years of age and appeared briefly for OEs, but he played his best club rugby with Harlequins and Headingley. He proudly described himself as "Eltham, Harlequins and Scotland". In 1921 he received his first cap from Scotland as a centre against France; he was to be capped again on a further 12 occasions, the last against France in Paris on 1 January 1924. His best-known international was against Wales in February 1923 when, playing with Liddell, he scored the winning try.

Gracie served in two World Wars, winning the Military Cross in 1917. He was a master of the surprise attack. He reacted quickly to a gap appearing in the opposition backs, or a player being out of position. A brilliant sprinter, he was also a brave defender when called to stop a forward charge.

Liddell and Gracie may have moved on but OEs continued to flourish. Old Elthamians produced a string of other internationals: N.L. Evans, E. Fahmy and S.R. Smith. Nevill Evans won five England caps in the 1930s at prop, but was more closely associated with the Royal Navy. Ernest Fahmy was

another winger in the mould of Eric Liddell. He was Chinese-born, but played rugby for Scotland. Stephen Smith, who began with OE's, was capped at scrum-half by England whilst with Richmond. His career was blighted by serious illness.

The club used the school pitches until 1934, when they moved to a ground on Eltham Road, where they remained until the Second World War. After the war, the ground was taken over for development, which precipitated a return to the school pitches.

In more recent times, prop Andrew Sheridan played for OEs before moving to play for Sale Sharks and becoming an England regular.

The advent of leagues saw Eltham playing in the London Old Boys Merit Table. The club reached National 3 in 2012 after being runners-up in London One South. In 2014 their colts were finalists in the RFU National Colts Cup.

THE GIPSIES

THE GIPSIES FC were founded in 1868 by three 'old Tonbridgians', F. Luscombe, J.A. Body and W.J. Parker. In 1872, they were one of the three top clubs in the county; whilst Luscombe and C.J.B. Marriott were leading members of the RFU. The club was disbanded in season 1883-84.

GRAVESEND

THERE ARE RECORDS of a Gravesend club playing in the 1880s. The Kentish club enjoyed the distinction of being one of the first English clubs to meet a team from France. During the season 1885-86, the Paris club came over and in their fourth and last match in eight days lost to Gravesend by a try to nil. That same year, Park House RFC's records showed that they played on Blackheath against Gravesend.

The present Gravesend club was founded in 1921 in Dartford as the Darenth RFC and played regularly in Dartford until the end of the 1929-30 season. In 1930-31 the headquarters were moved to Gravesend and the title became Darenth (Gravesend) RFC. In 1937 the name was again changed to

Gravesend (Darenth) RFC. After the war the suffix (Darenth) was dropped.

In 2010 Gravesend reached National 3 (SE) after several decades towards to the top of the London leagues.

MAIDSTONE

IT IS KNOWN a rugby match was played between Maidstone and the local grammar school in 1874, but there were reports of matches in the town from the late 1860s. It was however 1880-81 before a local club was formed. At this time their earliest opponents included Harlequins, London Scottish, Rosslyn Park and Richmond.

The club's first Kent County players came in 1885, when K. McAlpine and C.P. Disbrowe played against Middlesex. McAlpine was the driving force behind the club and when he stepped down in 1888 the club fell into abeyance. Walter Day (Hon. Sec.) and W. Harding Bensted (captain) revived the club in 1893 at Postley Fields. The club moved to Little Buckland the following year and to the Athletic Ground in 1895.

The next season the colours were changed from dark blue to Kent grey and maroon. It was found subsequently that on being washed the grey turned into a dirty white, so red and white stripes were adopted. These remained the colours until 1928, when a thin black stripe was introduced between the red and white.

The outbreak of the Boer War caused another hiatus in Maidstone rugby that lasted until 1905. Sutton Valence School had kept the game alive in the district whilst the local grammar school played soccer. 1913-14 was a very successful season, with ten of the first 11 matches won and 321 points scored against 48.

The club benefited from 1932-33 onwards as a result of the county adopting a policy of holding a County Championship home match away from the Rectory Field. Maidstone hosted the Kent v Eastern Counties match. Although the visitors won by 22-9, the game proved such a financial success that the club hosted further county matches over subsequent seasons.

Rugby union in the town found that an unusual rival appeared in 1983 when Maidstone United soccer club organised a rugby league club called Kent Invicta RLFC. 1,815 spectators saw the first game, but only 510 paid to see the second match. The experiment soon collapsed and Invicta moved across the Thames to Southend before disappearing.

Maidstone's second team reached the finals of the Middlesex Sevens in 1979.

In 1989 Maidstone were coached by Alistair McHarg, the legendary Scotland lock forward.

MARTLETS

MARTLETS WERE A Sussex invitation side which played from the Withdean Stadium during the 1950s and 1960s. They were picked from the best players in the county and operated mainly on Wednesday evenings under floodlights. They managed to persuade many of the best London sides to travel to the coast.

(Thanks to Peter Rumney)

OLD BRIGHTONIANS

'And Eton may play with a pill if they please,
And Harrow may stick to the Cheshire Cheese,
And Rugby their outgrown egg,
But here is the perfect game of a perfect sphere'
Brighton College song

OLD BRIGHTONIANS ARE one of the few surviving closed clubs in English rugby. They were formed in the 1920s for the old boys of Brighton College public school (founded in 1845). The college was unusual in admitting foreign boys. William Dawson, the headmaster from 1906 to 1933, was once asked why he admitted foreigners. He explained that he took two years fees in advance as surety for good behaviour: "They're all highly sexed, and it's only a matter of months before they sleep with a maid. Then out they go."

The Old Boys only play a handful of fixtures due to the high incidence of Brighton College students going on to university and most matches now take place when students are home from university.

Brighton College had recruited Ernest Hammett as rugby master shortly before OB was formed. Hammett (1891-1947) won eight Wales caps. Amongst his earliest recruits was Peter Hordern (brother of actor Michael Hordern), who appeared occasionally for the OB before appearing four times for England and playing for Newport, Gloucester and Blackheath. Hordern went on the 1936 Lions tour to Argentina. He also played for Sussex & Hants against the All Blaccks and toured Argentina with England in 1937. He is best remembered for accepting a bet from Prince Obolensky. The bet was made at an official dinner where Obo was irritated at an arrogant politician. Hordern was dared to squirt tomato ketchup over the politician, a request he carried out, which caused a row!

The OB played an annual match against the School XV. The tradition continued until 1966. In 1936 they played Old Elthamians and decided to play regularly every Saturday.

The best-known recent products of Brighton College was Alex King, the Wasps and England stand-off. King was unfortunate to be understudy to Jonny Wilkinson.

OLD DUNSTONIANS

ST DUNSTAN'S COLLEGE was founded in 1446 when King Henry VI ordained that a grammar school be formed in the Church of St Dunstan in East London. The school's second site was in Lewisham, where the school was situated from 1632 to 1888 when the school moved to Catford.

Initially the College played both football codes before association was abandoned in 1893. Four years later an abortive attempt was made to field a St Dunstan Old Boys team and a fixture was played, and lost, against Norwood.

Old Dunstonians are the fifteenth oldest English Old Boys club, being founded in 1903. That year a reformed St Dunstan OBs was fielded against the College XV. The fixture became an annual match and led to a meeting on 20th June 1903 to officially form an Old Dunstonians RFC. The founders were

W.U. Ross and the brothers H.W. and A.E. French.

Around this time, G. Davidson played for ODs having previously represented Ireland and played for the 1902 British Isles team to South Africa.

The first ground was a farmer's field at Whitefoot Lane, Southend, with H.W. French elected captain. The first fixture was against Beckenham on 23rd September 1903, resulting in a 27-3 win for ODs. Subsequently ODs won their first five fixtures and only lost to Surbiton 1st XV. ODs had a remarkable first season with figures of P20 W12 D0 L8 against some good quality teams.

The third season saw some famous names on the fixture list: Wasps and Saracens were beaten and a draw gained with St Marys Hospital. In 1907 the club moved to the old City of London ground outside Beckenham Hill, followed by a move to a ground near Whitefoot Lane. Unfortunately the 1912-13 season was terminated abruptly when T.M. Wilson died as a result of a spinal injury.

The First World War saw ODs enlisted as G. Company of the County of London Regiment Territorial Force. Unfortunately G. Company was disbanded after heavy losses at the Battle of Loos in 1915 and the survivors conscripted into other units. 233 Old Dunstonians died in World War One, including Lieut. Frederick Johnson, who won the VC but fell at Cambrai. The fallen are commemorated with a memorial at the English Church in Yypes.

The club reformed in May 1919 using a ground at the back of the Tigers Head in Southend Lane. Results went well, with a playing record of P23 W17 D0 L6. The good work continued the following season when they won the first 12 games, including victories over Saracens and London Irish.

1922-23 saw the club transformed into Old Dunstonians Sports Club Ltd., which allowed the purchase of six acres of open land on Beckenham Hill. A multiplicity of sports existed under the banner of the sports club: cricket, swimming, tennis etc., but rugby was the kingpin.

The new ground was opened on 14th April 1923 by Sir Rowland Hill, followed by a match against Old Alleynians, which was lost 12-6. 1923-24 saw an excellent season when H.F. Gill led the side to 16 victories in 23 matches.

Easter 1930 saw ODs on tour in Holland, where they played Delft University (lost 8-0), Eindhoven (lost 8-0) and Amsterdam(won 8-0).

The 1930s saw ODs' finest player in his prime. Wing-forward N.A. Bromage made his first team debut in 1932. A brilliant goal-kicker, he gained 36 county appearances, but missed being picked for England due to injury when the selectors called. He had an England trial in 1939. He was nicknamed 'Egg' because of his bald and pointed head. He was the club's points record-holder for a season with 144 and held the record for most career points with 1355, including 62 tries. Bromage also held the record for a match with 28 points against Old Stortfordians in 1946, including two tries, five goals and four penalties.

ODs were temporarily groundless during the Second World War and were forced into sharing the Midland Bank's facilities at Beckenham. The old clubhouse was destroyed by bombing.

Bromage and G.F. Morgan, an outstanding pre-war wing threequarter, were central to rebuilding the club in the post-

war years. Revitalisation came gradually, and by 1948 the club was fielding five sides.

In its first 50 years, ODs provided five players for London: J. Batty, F.G. Hutchinson, J.S.H. Drysdale, N.A. Bromage and N.K. Macrae-Gibson. 33 represented Kent, including Bromage, who played 36 times, F.A. Haines played for Hampshire and Y. Kirkpatrick for Surrey.

1957 saw the purchase of a new ground at Langley Park, site of the former Barclays Brewery, and the abandonment of Beckenham Hill. The club celebrated its diamond jubilee in 1962 at Langley Park, Beckenham by playing Combined OBs.

The introduction of leagues saw ODs placed in London 3, where they have remained with just a brief interlude ever since. In 2004 they reached the last eight of the Junior Vase.

SIDCUP

SIDCUP WAS A little village in Kent until the London to Chatham line was established in 1866. The railway changed the village into a commuter town. Sidcup Rugby Club was formed in 1882 on a field adjoining the cricket club at Crescent Farm. A full fixture wasn't established until 1884.

Sidcup RFC grew rapidly and attracted the best players for some miles around. Old Dunstonians joined Sidcup until ODs was formed in 1903. We also know the 1892 annual general meeting of the Kent RFU was interrupted by G.H. Johnston (Sidcup) complaining that his club had been ignored in the selection of the county teams. W.Denman, the county secretary, amicably smoothed things over by explaining that it was no easy task to pick 15 players out of about 60 names submitted.

The rugby club grew, as did the tow,n between the wars and fielded an international in the 1920s in William Prattern, who was capped for Scotland in 1927.

Sidcup became a regular finalist in the Kent Cup from the 1930s and saw improvement begin under the inspired leadership of John Evans in the late 1950s. In 1960 the club made its first appearance in the Middlesex Sevens finals at Twickenham.

An outstanding performer of this era was outside-half Billy Bushell, who contributed 402 points in 1971-72 before departing for Harlequins and England. Andy Hancock of England fame played for Sidcup in 1965.

In the 1980s Sidcup became a founder members of the Seven Counties Merit Table, which was largely the brainchild of the club president at that time, Chris Latham, who remained chairman of the table committee until its demise in 1993. Under the leadership of Roy White and Steve Price, Sidcup enjoyed considerable success, finishing top of the table on a number of occasions. The advent of the Courage leagues in 1987 saw Sidcup placed in Area League South – the equivalent of the present National Division 4 South. They also won the Kent Cup again.

During the 1990s, with the ever-increasing pressure on players, Sidcup had slid through the London Divisions 1 and 2 south to London 3 South East. Their pride for many years has been that the majority of its 1st XV players have been 'home-spun', having graduated from the Sidcup youth teams, notably Irish international Jim Staples.

Sidcup Sports club, who own the ground, and Sidcup FC share the current facilities at Crescent Farm with Sidcup Cricket Club and Crescent Lawn Tennis club.

THANET WANDERERS

THE EARLIEST KNOWN game of club rugby in Thanet was a match between Margate and Herne Bay in the late 1870s. Margate may have been good at rugby, but they were poor at maths, as, after the match, it emerged that their team had 12 men to Herne's 16. Despite the defeat, Margate FC was formed in October 1878. Unfortunately, the club played widely across the county but folded after five years. Their main source of fixtures was the Canterbury area, including the wonderfully named Clergy Orphan School.

Margate's only player of note was A.P. Bligh, who was noteworthy for entering the scrum backwards to protect his shins.

In October 1886, the old Margate club was reformed as Thanet Wanderers FC by H.T.B.Hodges. The 'Football Club' suffix was appropriate as they played both codes. Amongst the soccer club's fixtures was a match against (Woolwich) Arsenal, who went on to bigger things. The Thanet soccer club disappeared in 1887.

The rugby side's first fixture was against Ashford at Canterbury on the 19th March 1887. There were only nine clubs in the Kent RFU at the time, and seven were London-based, but Wanderers found matches with school and army sides.

Thanet Wanderers lived up to their name in the early days, using seven different grounds.

It was 1900 before Thanet came to the attention of the national selectors when A.F.C. Luxmoor won two England caps. Luxmoor also played in Kent's 1897 County Championship-winning side.

In 1898, Thanet Wanderers were badly hit when Chatham House School stopped playing rugby, which deprived Wanderers of their main source of players. The loss proved devastating and Wanderers went into abeyance. An attempt at reviving the club took place in 1909, but the old-time enthusiasm had gone.

Thanet were eventually reformed in 1922, but it was a slow process and it was 1928 before a regular home was found at Bakers Farm in Ramsgate. The club remained at Bakers Farm until 1985. Finding a permanent home helped Thanet establish a club record of P24, W21, D1, L2 in 1928-29. This achievement was eclipsed when the 1937-38 side were undefeated in 20 matches.

In 1931, Thanet broke new ground with what they called a French tour, which was actually a visit to Boulogne. The post-war years were difficult, with Bakers Farm unavailable due to government requirements, but the area was growing economically, which bought new blood to the club.

The club's 75th anniversary was celebrated with a match against Kent and a grand dinner. The dinner ended in chaos when some of the 'guests' tackled the hotel's revolving door, which propelled it onto the street. It was followed soon afterwards by the hotel's grand piano.

Results in the 1950s were modest and it was 1965 before there was cause for optimism and interest from the county selectors. Thanet won three successive victories in the East Kent Sevens, and in 1968-69 posted the remarkable statistics of P34, W29, D1, L4.

The club's best player of the era was Bernie Farrell, who played over 300 games and also played full-back for Cambridge University and Kent. Thanet teams of the mid-1970s almost emulated that glorious year, but the 1980s were mediocre.

Since the arrival of leagues, Wanderers have been in the top London leagues. They have done well in the RFU cups. They won the 1996 Intermediate Cup, beating Doncaster 21-13, and their colts were National Colts Cup finalists in 2014.

TONBRIDGE–JUDDIANS

THE TOWN OF Tonbridge in Kent has three famous schools: Tonbridge, Judds and Skinners. The first two schools produced separate clubs in Tonbridge RFC and Old Juddians, who eventually merged in 1999.

Tonbridge School has produced many fine rugby players since it adopted rugby in 1870. Before that time, it had its own game of school football called the 'gutter game', where the school team played the rest on a gravel playground. A gutter along the wall was used to steer the ball.

Tonbridge RFC arose from the ashes of a short-lived Tunbridge Wells RFC, which was formed in 1903 but moved to Tonbridge due to their Tunbridge pitch being prone to flooding. The club changed their name to acknowledge their new home and established a link to the famous public school.

The link provided Tonbridge with John Hubbard, who was capped by England in 1930. Hubbard is best remembered for wearing gloves. He was asked to join Blackheath, but failed to impress the selectors at the Rectory Field when he insisted on wearing gloves in the rain. Hubbard argued it improved his ball handling, but he was summarily returned to Tonbridge. Later he moved to Harlequins.

Tonbridge were amongst the best sides in Kent until the 1980s, but leagues arrived at a bad moment for the club. They slipped out of the upper London leagues and struggled to return to their former status. Good times came after relegation from London SE in 2008. They bounced straight back, scoring over 1,000 points in the next season. Eventually the winning run saw three successive promotions, including a 50-match consecutive winning streak and reaching the semi-final of the Intermediate Cup.

Tonbridge merged with Old Juddians in 1999.

WORTHING

"The most unpredictable side in Sussex Rugby."
Anon, 1961

THE CURRENT WORTHING RFC was formed by old boys of Steyne School in 1920, but a club existed in the 19th Century. In 1892, the original club hosted county matches at Beach House Park. The Sussex county side was composed of players from Worthing, Brighton, Hastings and Crawley.

After reforming in 1923, Worthing persuaded Brighton to give them a fixture, which resulted in a 26-3 defeat by the established club. The club had a succession of home grounds in the 1920s, beginning with a farmer's field at Upper Brighton Road. This was followed by a move to West Worthing (1923). The club left that ground in 1926 after a young player suffered a cut that led to tetanus and his death. In 1927, Worthing moved to a pitch at Castle Road, West Worthing.

By the end of the decade, things were looking up for Worthing RFC, but rugby in Sussex was in a poor state. Once again, Worthing players were an integral part of the county team and Worthing were honoured with the Sussex v Eastern Counties match in 1934.

After World War Two, Worthing resumed and merged with Old Azunians, a separate side formed by old boys of Worthing High School. Off the field, Worthing were fortunate to have the coaching services of Charles Gower, the legendary Cranleigh School rugby master.

In 1977 the Castle Road Ground was sold and a new one purchased at Roundstone Road, Angmering. New facilities were built and officially opened by Dickie Jeeps.

Worthing were slow to recognise the value of the rejuvenated county cup and had to wait until 1983 to be Sussex Cup champions.

1985 was a golden year for the club, with the First XV winning 26 out of 31 matches, the Sussex Merit Table, Sussex Cup and the County Sevens. This brought qualification for the National Knockout Cup, where, under coach Peter Greenwood and captain Jody Levett, Worthing did well but eventually went out to London Scottish, who were one of Britain's best sides at the time.

Two years later, with the introduction of leagues, Worthing were placed in London Two (South). Since 2002, they have made incredible progress from London 3 to reach National 1 in 2013 after beating Stourbridge in the play-offs.

The club's best known players are Graham Childs, who progressed to Wasps and Bath in 1990, and England international Joe Launchbury, who made his Worthing debut at 19 years of age in 2011 before moving to Wasps and becoming one the world's best lock forwards.

Joe Launchberry

CHAPTER FIFTEEN

DORSET, WILTS, OXFORD, BERKS & HANTS

DORSET & WILTSHIRE

THE FIRST RUGBY played in Dorset & Wilts dates from 1846, when the Rev. Charles Thomas Penrose joined Sherborne School from Rugby School and introduced the game. Fifteen years later, another great public school, Marlborough College, adopted the sport.

The first known senior club was Dorchester, who were formed in 1871, but ever since then, the twin counties had a serious rugby problem as there were too few centres of population to form clubs and fill a fixture list. From the earliest days, D & W clubs had the problems of a small population and large travelling distances, which left them with stark choices. They could either play minor fixtures against other local sides (which didn't engender interest) or look elsewhere to the bigger clubs of Bristol, Bath, Exeter and Yeovil. A Catch 22 situation developed because if you didn't have a steady source of local playing talent, you couldn't get good fixtures and poor fixtures didn't attract new players. Despite the drawbacks, a handful of clubs were formed in the county between the wars and some services sides emerged from army bases around Salisbury Plain.

Dorset & Wiltshire in action against Surrey.

The Dorset RU was formed in 1931 (a Dorset county side had existed briefly in the late 1870s) and its Wiltshire neighbour in 1934. They merged in 1939, which enabled them to enter the County Championship, but the outbreak of war intervened.

Dorset joined the County Championship in 1934. They won three of their six matches, including a match with the long-forgotten Coastal Command XV. Three years later, Dorset defeated the Home Fleet, which fortunately Hitler never managed in the ensuing war.

By the autumn of 1946 the Dorset Union and the Wiltshire Union had re-formed and the first meeting of the amalgamated Dorset & Wilts RFU took place in December 1946. In July 1947, the Dorset & Wilts RFU was admitted to the County Championship by the RFU before being granted Constituent Body status in April 1949. In the 1953 season Dorset & Wilts were rewarded with a quarter-final place. They held their own, but had to wait until 2010 before they won the Shield Final, beating Leicestershire 36-26 at Twickenham. They retained the Shield the following season against Surrey.

Many fine players have represented Dorset and Wilts over the years: Angus Cameron (Scotland), G.C.Phillips (Ireland) and Alexander Watt (Scotland), who played his first test for Scotland in 1947 whilst doing his national service on Salisbury Plain and joined Salisbury RFC in an attempt to stay fit. Salisbury were unconvinced about the newcomer's credentials and played him in the Third XV. Seven days later, Watt played for Scotland. Ian Beer captained D&W during the 1950s despite playing his club rugby in London. He captained Cambridge University, Harlequins and Old Whitgiftians. Beer was later Headmaster of Harrow School.

(Thanks to Arthur Bowden)

BERKSHIRE

THE FIRST GAME of Rugby Football played in Berkshire was at Wellington College, who were one of the founding RFU members. Wellington College was founded in 1853 as a monument to the Duke of Wellington and the school traditionally had strong military connections.

The first clubs in the county were Berkshire Wanderers (now Reading 1898) and Thames Valley (now Maidenhead 1922), whilst school sides appeared at Reading School (1900), Radley College (1914), St. Bartholomew's Grammar School, Newbury (1915) and Pangbourne College (1918).

A regional side for Berkshire, Buckinghamshire, Oxfordshire and Wiltshire was formed in 1923 but proved unwieldy. Eight years later, Berkshire broke away to form a separate county union after the Berkshire Wanderers club called a meeting at the Wheatsheaf Hotel in Reading. The clubs represented at the inaugural meeting were Windsor, Reading University, Thames Valley, Old Redingensians, Reading School, Newbury Grammar School, Douai School, Newbury and Berkshire Wanderers.

Representing Reading School was D. Gwen Francis, a Welsh international, who due to work commitments had been forced to reject a place on a British Isles tour. In November 1930 Francis brought a Welsh International XV to Reading to play a Reading XV consisting of players from Berkshire Wanderers and Old Redingensians. The match was played at Palmer Park and was intended to engender interest in rugby union in the county. The visitors won 10-6.

The RFU took a dim view of the Berkshire breakaway and refused them a place in the County Championship. Berkshire's first match was against Sussex on 20th January 1932 at Reading. They also played Surrey that season, and in 1932-33 they met Middlesex and Oxfordshire. Berkshire had to struggle on until 1948 before being admitted to the county championship in the South Eastern group. In 1950 Berks were moved to the South Western group and later to the adjacent Southern Group.

In 1953 the Southern Group that played the All Blacks included five Berkshire players, whilst James Murphy-O'Connor was capped for Ireland during the season. Murphy-O'Connor was a prodigious goal-kicker. He and Berkshire together made headlines when they brought him over from Dublin for three matches at a cost of £50.

In the 1954-55 season, Berkshire won the Southern Group but had to wait another 16 years before regaining the title.

In 1966-67, Reading RFC approached the county for permission for five clubs to compete against each other for a Trophy donated by friends in memory of David Cairns, ten times 'capped' in the County Championship for Berkshire. This received due approval and so started the series of matches between Reading, Redingensians, Windsor, Maidenhead and Newbury for the 'Cairns Trophy', which became the county cup and was dominated by Maidenhead and Reading.

HAMPSHIRE

THE HAMPSHIRE RUGBY Union was formed on 23rd March 1883 by Trojans RFC, who were closely supported by United Services Portsmouth. A letter was sent to every club in Hampshire asking them to send a representative to a meeting in Southampton. Letters went to Southampton Rovers, HMS Marlboro, Fareham, United Services, Royal Academy, Southsea FC, Harlequins, Southampton Hornets, Winchester Training College, Alresford, Victoria's, Ryde Rovers, Newport FC, Lymington and the Navy.

The first county match saw Hampshire play Devonshire on a friendly basis. The county had already played three trial matches against Trojans, Portsmouth and Southsea Victoria. In 1884 Hampshire played Sussex. The following season county matches were played against Kent at Blackheath and Sussex at Worthing.

Hampshire joined the RFU, but their membership lapsed on 28th May 1888. Although the county organisation had become defunct, Trojans organised a county cup with a trophy presented by Tankerville Chamberlayne MP, the president of Trojans. By 1891, the county cup itself lapsed because only three clubs competed, and this at the fag end of the season.

Trojans kept the county flag flying, but the county accounts were £22 overdrawn and only a donation of 10/6 (52p) (presumably by Trojans or one of their officials) allowed membership of the RFU to be reinstated. Funds were raised when a Portsmouth v Hampshire fixture was played at the North End ground. 2000 attended.

The county gradually prospered. A junior league was formed in 1896 and the following year the county won Group B of the South Eastern Division. However, the county was heavily dependent on Services clubs and when the Boer War came, it saw the Hants RFU cease to function from 1901 and also contributed to the temporary demise of Trojans, but both organisations later revived.

In 1908 Trojans and United Services reformed the county association (with help from Eastleigh FC and Southampton) and in 1910 they re-affiliated to the

Dudley Kemp

RFU. In 1911 Hants joined the South West Division, but immediately a dispute broke out on who had first claim on players, club or county.

In 1910 Aldershot hosted the Hampshire v Devonshire match, but it would seem that military precision was noticeably absent for the match was described as "an organisational failure" and left HRFU £50 in debt.

In November 1924 Hants acquired the rights to play the All Blacks at Fratton Park at a cost of £200, payable to the RFU. George Nepia's All Blacks won 22–0, but the day was a great success. The event made a profit of £576, of which £27 was sent to East Midlands RFU in payment of the 1900 debt.

Rugby grew throughout the county in the 1920s, with 25 clubs affiliated, and in 1926 Hampshire were county finalists and in 1933 they were County Champions by defeating Lancashire 18-7 at Dean Court, home of Bournemouth FC. The feat was repeated in 1936 under the captaincy of H.G. Owen-Smith.

The 1930s were a time of great success for Hampshire. From 40 matches, 30 were won and two drawn. Internationals included Jamie Clinch, Tuppy Owen-Smith, Victor Pike, Horsy Browne and Dudley Kemp. The last named became an inspirational figure in local rugby and a leading RFU administrator.

Hampshire's fortunes revived in the late 1980s when they reached the semi-finals of the County Championship.

BOURNEMOUTH

BOURNEMOUTH IS A wonderful seaside town, but something of a rugby outpost due to the distance from the big cities. The original town rugby club played at Meyrick Park in 1893 on land owned by the council. Amongst the earliest players was H.H. Morris, who scored 38 tries in 1893-94. The club seemed to have travelled widely in the early days, as H. Willet, scored six tries against St. Thomas Hospital in London in February 1907; a feat equaled by A.D. Heard, against Hampshire Wanderers in November 1908. To encourage rugby in the town Bournemouth played a Dorchester & District XV at Meyrick Park in 1910.

Bournemouth RFC became part of the Bournemouth Social Club in 1929, sharing facilities with cricket and hockey teams. The club produced two famous rugby figures in Douglas Harrison and Dudley Kemp. Harrison played for Dorset and Wiltshire, before becoming one of the pioneers of schools rugby. Dudley Kemp was capped for England v Wales in 1935 and later was RFU President. He also had a long association with the Trojans club of Southampton. Another international to play for Bournemouth was Jim Pook, a Scots international who turned out for the club in the 1950s.

Between the wars, Bournemouth were regular winners of the West Dorset Sevens and had their own Sevens competition. Also, the club frequently hosted county matches, but on occasions matches were switched to Dean Court, the home of the town's soccer club, which held 20,000 spectators. In 1934 Bournemouth hosted the Hants v Gloucester semi-final. A hard frost put the game in jeopardy until someone noticed a mobile tarmac heater outside the ground. The heater went on to the pitch and worked a treat as the ground was softened and the match played.

Bournemouth itself had an excellent side in 1936-37 when they won 25 of 29 fixtures. The club's best-known player of the era was hooker Jerry Pike, who was a rugby legend in his native Devon before moving.

A long-forgotten player at the club was Ronald Hicks, who had played for the club before joining the RAF in 1939 and being captured during the fall of France. He wasn't a great rugby player but was a leading light in the legendary escape from Stalag Luft III, the German prisoner-of-war camp, immortalised in 'The Great Escape' movie.

In 1989, Bournemouth sold their ground at Northbourne and moved to Poole. Minis and Juniors were well established by this time and the club produced another international in Andy Long, who joined Bath and played for England against Australia in 1997.

The club produced a remarkable player in Mike Pope, who broke club records with 31 points in a single match and reached 100 points in his first 11 matches.

In recent seasons the club have risen from South West One to National 2 South under coach David Dunn before falling back to National 3 in 2014.

HAVANT

HAVANT ARE A Hampshire side who in the 1990s achieved wonders from modest resources to reach the National leagues and become the backbone of their county side.

The club was founded in 1956, but it was 1973 before they produced their first county player. Two years later they fielded an England international in 'Big Jim' Syddall, who hailed from Lancashire but was studying in the area. Jim was joined by Graham Jefferies and Mike Chalk in the Hampshire team.

Bournemouth 4th team

The club quickly recognised the value of the county cup as a stepping-stone to national prominence, as victory brought automatic entry to the National Knockout Cup. They won the Hampshire Cup 12 times in 20 years.

The club were keen to build a solid base and by the 1980s were fielding five teams, a Colts XV and a Veteran's XV (The Mariners), giving them the largest player base in Hampshire.

Havant's history of league memberships saw a rapid rise from Area League One in 1987 rising to National 2 in 1997.

(Thanks to Bill Sugden)

ABBEY

ABBEY RUFC WAS formed in 1956 by Reading players who had nowhere to play when Reading scrapped their junior section. The new team played in the town park and operated from any public house that would welcome them. In 1971, Abbey bought 22 acres of ground. This provided room for three pitches and a clubhouse.

At the outset of league rugby, Abbey were placed in South West Two. They stayed in the same division until 2005, when they were promoted to South West One.

DORCHESTER

THE FIRST REFERENCE to rugby in Dorchester was on 9th Nov 1871, when the Dorset County Chronicle & Somerset Gazette recorded that two Dorchester teams had played a drawn game on Poundbury on the previous Thursday afternoon. The Dorchester team was selected by T. Coombs (Treasurer) and G. Andrews (Hon. Sec.). George Andrews (1848-1894), a solicitor, was captain. He was regarded as a brilliant dodger. Dorchester's subsequent fixtures that season were played against Dorset County School from Charminster, Weymouth College, Sherborne School, Evershot and a Navy Officers team.

For their second season, Dorchester operated from Poundbury. The club's first notable player was H.A.Tudor, who became an Oxford Rugby Blue. Dorchester were comfortably the best side in the area, but, due to the remoteness, they rarely travelled outside the county.

The club became associated with the Sherborne School, which had already established a growing reputation as a leading rugby school. Old boys of the school gravitated to the Dorchester club on a regular basis.

The first Dorchester RFC seems to have slipped into abeyance around 1877.

The city team briefly reappeared before World War One, but it was September 1934 before a new club called 'West Dorset RFC' was formed at the Antelope Hotel in Dorchester. The title was intended to attract players from the area rather than just the town, and to avoid confusion with East Dorset, who were an established side. Two well-known players were involved in establishing the new club: Oxford Blue C.R. Wordsworth and Irish International I.M.B. Stuart. The latter had written

Dorchester in action against Bradford on Avon.

one of the first books on rugby coaching. A ground was found on Weymouth Avenue at a rent of £3 a year. Their first match was against the Royal Tank Corps at Bovington when the army side won 15-0. With so few other sides in the area, the club was heavily reliant on Army and Navy sides for fixtures.

West Dorset closed their doors in 1939 and never reappeared, as Dorchester RFC emerged from its ashes. They were reliant upon players from the Thomas Hardye School in the town. The new club played on the Recreation Ground. Clothing rationing, in the wake of World War II, meant the new club had problems getting kit, but the Hampshire RFU helped out by sending 30 clothing coupons to help purchase jerseys.

They had a boost in 1949 when club regular Bob Hook persuaded his brother to help the club. Bill Hook, the Gloucester and England full-back, brought a Gloucester XV to play Dorchester.

The early 1950s were golden years for Dorchester when the club could provide a third of the County XV and won the vast majority of their fixtures between 1954 and 1958. In season 1955-56, they won a record 19 out of 28 games. Around this time, Brian Dibben of Dorchester played 28 times for Dorset and Wilts.

The club were boosted when the Atomic Energy Authority opened an establishment at Winfrith in 1959 that brought new players to the club. By 1961 the club had the strongest fixture list in Dorset and, at the end of the season, arranged a match against Oxford University.

Dorchester had operated from the Rec since their inauguration, but now they moved to the Depot Ground, where a second-hand pavilion was purchased to complement two pitches. Outstanding players for Dorchester have included an international in prop Brian Keen, a product of Hardye's School who went to Newcastle University, where he was picked for Northumberland and England, and Frank Dike, a Dorchester legend as he hardly missed a game and was captain over nine seasons.

2009 saw Dorchester as D&W 1 (South) champions and promoted to Southern Counties South.

In 2013, the rugby club was used for casting of a new film of 'Far from the Madding Crowd', the classic novel written by Dorchester's greatest son, Thomas Hardy.

HENLEY HAWKS

"It's all about selling tickets."
Tony McArthur

Clive Woodward's first coaching appointment was with Henley.

HENLEY HAWKS RFC have a piece of rugby history as in 1990 they offered the post of coach to the youthful Clive Woodward at a time when the ex-England player had no pedigree as a coach. Clive had just returned from Australia, and was looking for a step into league rugby. Thirteen years later, he led England to the Rugby World Cup – a far cry from the local rugby club in the Oxfordshire town of Henley, which is more famous for its rowing regatta.

Prior to Clive's appointment, Henley wasn't renowned for rugby. The original Henley RFC operated from 1927 at a ground at Dry Lea. The ground was commandeered by the army in 1939 and the club went into abeyance. The club was reformed in 1954 by several old boys of Henley GS, as Old Henleiensians. A pitch was obtained on Lion Meadows from the Royal Regatta committee and the Rowing club was used as changing rooms.

The club won the Oxfordshire Cup three times between 1979 and 1985 and found themselves in the South West League at the inception of leagues. Clive Woodward moved into the area in 1990 after a successful playing and business career in Australia. Down under, he developed a version of the oval ball game, which contrasted to the traditional English game, with its emphasis on the forwards winning the ball and the backs using it.

His coaching worked for Henley, who won South West Two and promotion to the National leagues via five promotions in nine years. Woodward moved to London Irish in 1992. Tony MacArthur, an ex-London Welsh fly half, took over as Director of Rugby and led 'Henley Hawks' (as they had been rebranded) to National One.

A second side emerged in the town, called Henley Wanderers, which merged with the Hawks in 2008.

The Hawks remains a members club, with 600 members, including the players who must pay their annual subscriptions to play. The Hawks remain in the National leagues.

MARLOW

THERE ARE RECORDS of a Marlow RFC playing High Wycombe on the 8th February 1913. Marlow won 13-0 that day. The present club was formed in 1947 by a group led by a local farmer, Roy Banberry, and a publican, Gerry Mason. The first match was against Old Wycombensians on a pitch at the Royal Grammar School, High Wycombe. Marlow, led by Fran Francis, won.

Marlow's first official game was against London Airport RFC. Home matches were played at Sir William Barlase School, whilst the Cross Keys pub acted as headquarters. 1948-49 was the club's first full season with 17 wins in 24 matches.

Marlow spent the 1950s sharing facilities with the local Hockey Club where they played on an adjacent field known as Pound Lane. In 1962, the rugby club agreed to lease ten acres of land at Riverwoods and, a year later, they played their first match at the new ground – a win over Newbury 2nds. 1973 saw the club unveil its new floodlights with a match against an International XV.

In 1981, the club were on television when Pierre Villepreux, the French coach, gave a coaching clinic to a party of British coaches.

Marlow had been one of the original 14 clubs who formed the Buckhamshire County RU in 1949. Twenty years later they were amongst the entrants for the inaugural Bucks Cup, which brought qualification for the winner into the National KO Cup. Marlow won the cup seven times and qualified to face the likes of Bath, who they met in 1980. Needless to say, Bath won, but only 30-6.

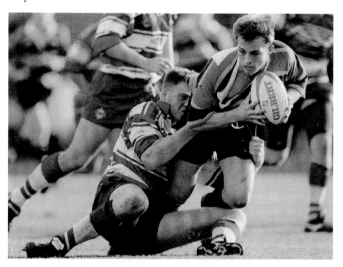

Matt Dawson, Marlow's most famous ex-player, in action for Northampton.

The best known Marlow players are Paul Burnell, a durable prop who won 41 Scotland caps, and TV celebrity Matt Dawson, who won 77 England and seven Lions caps whilst with Northampton and London Wasps. Another famous Marlow name was Peter Trunkfield, who became RFU President.

NEWBURY

THE ORIGINAL NEWBURY rugby club was formed by Herbert and Charles Whittaker, amongst others, in 1928. Newbury drew its players from two schools: St. Bartholomew's and Park House School. At that time games were played at St. Bart's Grammar School. It was not until 1932 that the club found a permanent home at Pinchington Lane, but members had to wait until 1958 for a clubhouse to be built on the site.

During season 1938-39, Newbury lost four out of 25 games. Two of their best-known players were David Thomas, who won 17 Berkshire caps, and Ian Balding, the famous horse trainer, who played for the veterans. Balding had played a record 32 times for Dorset & Wilts and won an Oxford Blue. Newbury had a link to Oxbridge rugby that lingered into the 1990s.

Transformation came to Newbury in 1972 when the M4 motorway was opened. New technology revolutionised the area, which became the British Silicon Valley. Newbury RUFC grew with the district and won the Berkshire Cup three times between 1979 and 1992. They were regular competitors in the National KO Cup and reached the 5th round in 1996-97, losing 26-21 to Leicester Tigers. In the leagues, Newbury rose from South West 2 to National 2.

Terry Burwell, ex-Leicester, became director of rugby in 1989. Later Newbury recruited Keith Richardson the ex-Gloucester, Harlequins and England A coach.

Their fortunes were further improved when they sold their Pinchington Lane ground and moved to Monks Lane. The windfall financed the building of a superb sporting complex, with five pitches and three bars plus conference facilities.

Newbury reached National 1 in 2005 and began the season with a win over mighty Harlequins. In 2007 they reached the Championship but suffered four successive relegations.

The 2008 recession hit the club hard, seeing reduced sponsorship and support. As the club struggled to break even, they lost many of their best players. By 2014 the club had drifted down to South West 1.

It hasn't been all gloom as their colts reached the National Colts Plate final.

The best-known player to emerge from Newbury was Tyrone Howe, who represented Ireland and the Lions, and in 2008 Tom Tombleson was picked for England Sevens.

(Thanks to Peter Simmons)

OXFORD

NO RUGBY CLUB lives more in the shadows than Oxford RUFC, who share a name and city with the 'Dark Blues' of Varsity rugby.

The club was formed in 1909 by a legendary rugby name, Alfred St. George Hamersley (1848-1929), who played four times for England in 1874 and was England's second-ever captain after Fred Stokes. Hamersley had a full life. A lawyer by profession, his early career saw him in the Army, which included a spell in New Zealand where he founded and captained Canterbury FC (later Canterbury Crusaders). His protracted journey back to England included time off in Vancouver, where he inaugurated rugby in Canada whilst acting as legal advisor to the Canadian Pacific Railway. He returned to England and became MP for mid-Oxfordshire. Whilst standing for Parliament, Hamersley proposed the formation of Oxford Nomads RFC.

The great man was too old to play rugby himself, but recruited eighteen players who were later joined occasionally by the peerless Ronnie Poulton-Palmer, perhaps the greatest rugby player of the pre-WW1 Years.

They changed their name to Oxford RFC between the wars. Their best-known player from this era was another local man, Bernard Gadney (1909-2001), who won 14 England caps at scrum-half.

Perhaps Hamersley had hoped that 'Town & Gown' would form an alliance, but it never came to pass. The odd varsity player appeared for the city club, but a nexus was never formed. Additionally, Oxford suffered because a dozen small clubs existed in Oxfordshire without one club becoming the focus, as in Leicester or Northampton.

In the 1950s, Oxford was a good middle-ranking club who could get fixtures against Coventry, Bath and Pontypool. When the Oxfordshire County Cup was formed in 1970, the city club were dominant with ten wins.

In the 1960s they fielded two internationals in Wright at outside-half and Parsons in the second row.

In the 1990s, Tim Rodber, a huge England flanker, joined Oxford from Petersfield before going on to a great rugby career with England and the Lions.

In recent times, Oxford have suffered from the rise of local rivals such as Maidenhead and Newbury.

(Thanks to Tubby Tyrrell)

READING

THE OLDEST CLUB in Berkshire is Reading (formerly known as Berkshire Wanderers), which played its first game on 24th September 1898. The driving forces were the RFU, the Rev. William Eppstein and Roger Walker. The RFU were keen to form Berkshire Wanderers as they wanted a rugby presence in the Home Counties. The Rev. Eppstein was headmaster of Reading Grammar School, where he introduced rugby.

There are records of Wanderers playing Redhill & Reigate and Oxford University A that first season. The club's first Wanderers player to win county honours was T.H. Olivey, who played for Hants in 1901.

Reading got a boost when D. Gwyn Francis, a Welsh international, was employed as a schoolmaster at Reading School. Francis organised an exhibition match between a local XV and a Welsh international side.

Berkshire Wanderers operated from the cricket ground on Kensington Road, but in 1948 they moved to Holme Park. In 1956 the club was renamed Reading RFC. The Diamond Jubilee was celebrated with a match between the club and a London XV organised by Peter Yarranton, who played for England and who joined the club when he lived in Reading.

In 1966 the club were running six teams every week at Home Park, Sonning. They were Berkshire Cup winners in 1969-70, 1985-86, every year from 1987-88 to 1990-91 and in 1993-94.

At the arrival of leagues, they began in South West 2 but were subsequently promoted to National Three. Throughout the 1990s they established a reputation as a 'Yo-Yo' side. They had a famous coach in Alistair McHarg and produced an England international in Eval Umda, who won two England caps. By 2014 the club were playing in SW1 East and are a friendly amateur club.

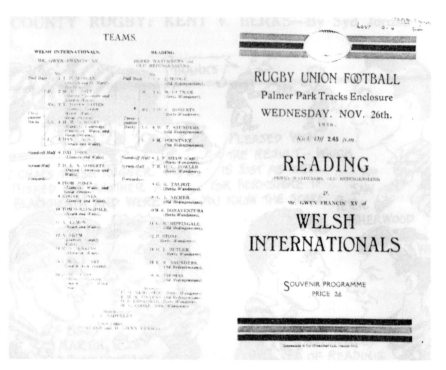

OLD REDINGHENSIANS

'The Rams'

REDINGHENSIANS WERE FORMED in 1924 by the old boys of Reading Grammar School The club is closely associated with T.J. and D.H.Easby, who were the organisers of the Berkshire Sevens competition. Denis Easby became Redingensians captain in 1951 before becoming the RFU President. The club were early converts to junior rugby, which was started by Peter Evans in 1971.

They began their league rugby in Southern Counties and struggled in the early 1990s. In 2007, OR were playing in SW1 but reached National 3 SW under Mike Tewkesbury (coach), formerly of London Irish. The club's best-known player was Tim Bell, who moved to Harlequins where he played in a John Player Cup win.

SALISBURY

"I up and down the town, and find it a very brave place. The river goes through every street; and a most capacious market-place."
Samuel Pepys

RUGBY IN THE lovely city of Salisbury began in the 1870s with Salisbury FC, who played both Union and Association. The round ball won as the club went over to association fully in the late 1880s.

Rugby reappeared in 1911, but folded in 1913 when the treasurer absconded with the funds. After the Great War, another attempt was made to reform the city club, but the city fathers would not allow "such a rough game" to be played within the city boundaries. An unlikely home was found in 1923 at Norman Court, the home of Washington Singer, a fabulously wealthy heir to the Singer sewing machine empire. Indeed, the new club adopted Singer's racing colours for the club jerseys.

In the city in the 1930s there were several other smaller rugby clubs, notably Old Wordworthians. The wartime Salisbury side drew largely from the army based on Salisbury Plain. The connection brought Irish hooker Victor Pike to the club. Although from Tipperary, Pike was most closely associated with the British Army. He was one of three brothers capped by Ireland; indeed, he scored the winning try in the 1931 Irish win over Scotland. Later, he represented Hampshire in two championship wins (1933 and 1936). During World War Two, Pike was chaplain-general to the Eighth Army in North Africa and Hon. Chaplain to King George VI and Queen Elizabeth. He left the Army in 1960 to become Bishop of Sherborne whilst continuing to live in Salisbury.

After the war Salisbury used the Cathedral Hotel as HQ. Three outstanding players of the era were Paul Pudge, the club captain, A.G.M. Watt and Angus Cameron (17 caps), who captained Scotland. Gordon Scott was a doctor in the RAMC who won six Scotland caps in the 1947-48 season.

The mid-1960s saw Salisbury as a successful club with the county's top goal-kicker in John Labbett, who scored 220 of Salisbury's 600 points in 1964-65. The club record is held by scrum-half Kenny Porter, who made his 500th appearance in 1984 whilst accumulating 2,500 points.

The greatest player to play for Salisbury was Richard Hill. He played his first game for the club at Saracens in 1993 and made his England debut four years later. He made such an impact that he was selected for that year's Lions tour of South Africa. The English back row of Hill, Neil Back and Lawrence Dallaglio came together on tour and became a fixture for six years, culminating in England's World Cup win.

Salisbury RFC

Mike Brown, a brilliant full-back, began at Salisbury before moving to Melksham RUFC and Harlequins. He became an England regular from 2007.

Salisbury are South West 2 (East) regulars despite slipping briefly into the Southern Counties league.

SHERBORNE SCHOOL

"Our public schools may be rough places, but they are a fit nurse for the boys who became great men."
Homer

RUGBY FOOTBALL ARRIVED at Sherborne in 1846 when the Rev. C.T. Penrose arrived as headmaster from Rugby School. It was, however, another 20 years before the game became established in the school calendar. By 1868, the school could boast a First XV v Old Shirburnian XV match.

Amongst the earliest players was H.T. Twynam, who became the school's first international.

Sherborne's First XV played matches against sides such as Clifton, then the premier club in the South West. The school could also claim a string of internationals in W.F. Evans (Oxford University and Wales), J.B.W. Buchanan (Dublin University and Ireland), R.T. Finch (England) and T.A. Rees, who played in Wales's first international against England in 1881.

The school and its rugby declined in the latter years of the century due to an ugly legal dispute that created terrible publicity. The club's first inter-school match proved a disappointment when they were beaten comfortably by Cheltenham College. Sherborne rallied and eventually established a first class fixture list, including St. Paul's, Clifton College and Dulwich.

1897 brought an upturn in Sherborne's fortunes when G.M. Carey, an old boy and England international, was recruited as a games master. He proved a valuable asset, not least, because he played regularly for the First XV though being well over 30 years of age. Carey, who taught at Sherborne for 30 years, is generally considered to be the inspiration for Bull in Alec Waugh's novel 'The Loom of Youth'. Bull was the archetypal English public school master, producing brave young men for the Empire.

The pre-war years saw Sherborne produce two Lions in Christopher Francis Stanger-Leathes (1904) and D.F. Smith (1910), who both gained England caps.

The Great War saw sport relegated to a minor role in school life; indeed, rugby was not played in 1918 due to "food shortages".

The 1920s saw rugby restored and there were several highlights: the foundation of an old scholars team 'the Pilgrims' and the recruitment of Harold Kittermaster as a teacher. Kittermaster had played stand-off for England on several occasions. Sadly, the 1920s also saw the early death at 55 of G.M. Carey, who had galvanised Sherborne rugby.

A.H. Trelawny-Ross was appointed games master and produced remarkable results, with 38 wins from 49 schools matches. Trelawny-Ross was a leading writer on educational matters.

Nick Greenstock was educated at Sherborne and joined Wasps in 1995. He later played for England.

SWINDON

THE RUGBY MEN of Swindon consider themselves different from the rest of the Dorset and Wiltshire county set-up because Swindon is an industrial town whereas the rest of the twin counties are rural.

Rugby in Swindon has existed since the 1870s, when 'Swindon Rangers' were a top-class club who operated mainly against sides from the Bath area. Swindon Rangers played against Bath twice in the season of 1875-76 and in 1883 they played and beat Gloucester.

The Rangers closed their doors in 1895 after a 61-0 defeat by Bath. They did, however, leave a legacy in Glasgow in Rangers Football Club, who took their name and playing kit from the Wiltshire side. Glasgow Rangers were formed in 1872 by a group including Moses McNeil, who had heard of an English rugby team called Swindon Rangers who played in white socks, white shorts and white shirts with a blue star on the breast. The Glasgow club adopted blue and white colours. They went on to legendary status in Scottish football, whereas Swindon Rangers soon vanished, although the present Swindon Rugby Club emerged from their ashes.

Alec Lewis

Any grievances that Swindon RFC harbour about their status must have been amplified in 1909 when they had the dubious honour of being the first team to miss playing at Twickenham. In those far off days, the newly-opened Twickenham stadium was shared between England and Harlequins. At the outset, teams who played Quins' second team were rewarded with 80 minutes on the legendary greensward before the authorities decided only Harlequins First XV could play there. Second team matches were switched to Fairfax Road, Teddington – and Swindon were the first club that missed out on playing at Twickenham.

One Swindon player who did play at Twickenham was Alec Lewis. Lewis was one of the most remarkable sportsmen of his era. He missed sport in his early 20s because of World War Two. He survived being blown up by a mine and was an accomplished soccer player who even represented Swindon Town FC in his youth. In his late 20s, he was persuaded to play in the backs for the town rugby team. He proved a brilliant convert to the oval ball game and subsequently attracted the attention of mighty Bath, with whom he won 10 England caps, a remarkable achievement for someone who took up rugby so late in life. Percy Chambers was another top-class Swindon player of the era. A big forward, Chambers joined Newport and played against the All Blacks.

In 1970, Swindon moved to Green Bridge Road, which sparked the club's golden era with a number of top-class players appearing in the club's colours: Jim Glover (Barbarians, Bristol), Terry Keirle, John Jackson and Roy Matthews (Bath), and Kelvin Neill (London Irish).

In 1983 Swindon had their finest hour when the club drew Blackheath in the National KO Cup. They have also produced some good players and two top-class referees in Steve Lander and Ross Mitchell. In the 1990s, the club received a visit from Mike Luke, who failed to impress as first team hooker and was picked as Third XV winger the following week. Luke, however, preferred joining Harlequins, with whom he played for Canada.

TROJANS

THE TROJANS CLUB of Southampton rank amongst the oldest in the world. They were formed in 1874 and played at Porters Mead, which is now called Queens Park on Queens Terrace (by the Dock Gates). In 1884 the Club donated the sum of two guineas towards the purchase of the proposed Cricket Ground in Bannister Park and played rugby there until 1897, when they moved to the Freemantle Ground, Stafford Road before moving to Northlands Road in 1905.

Trojans were entirely responsible for the formation of the Hampshire RFU on the 27th March 1883. They sent a letter to every club in Hampshire asking them to send a representative to a meeting in Southampton. In truth, there were few clubs around and the new county association was run by Trojans, who continued as the driving force behind Hampshire until 1900, when they temporarily disbanded for five years due to a shortage of members.

Trojans were a good side in the 19th century and produced internationals in Charles Wooldridge and C.E. Chapman. Wooldridge, a product of Winchester School, eventually won seven England caps between 1882 and 1885, although he is normally associated with Oxford University and Blackheath. Wooldridge was part of Harry Vassall's Oxford team. C.E. Chapman was a Trojans member who was capped for England in 1884 whilst a student at Cambridge University.

Two other Trojan internationals who were also associated with other clubs were A.J. Gould and James Peters. Arthur 'Monkey' Gould was the first great rugby superstar. He won 27 Wales caps and was a rugby gypsy who played from London to South Wales. At the end of his career, he wrote a newspaper article in which he briefly touched on playing for Trojans in the late 1880s and also turning out for Portsmouth RFC. Gould is also remembered for causing a huge rift between the RFU and the Welsh RU. The WRU gave him a benefit in the shape of a £700 house. The measure blatantly broke the laws governing amateurism and caused vexed relations between the RFU and the WRU for several seasons. Peters (1880-1954) briefly appeared for Trojans before joining Plymouth Albion, with whom he won five England caps.

1889-90 was a low ebb for Trojans as interest in rugby waned in the area. Trojans arranged no fixtures; indeed, there was no rugby at all in Southampton. The reason was that the Boer War took away thousands of young men, in a military and naval area, to South Africa.

Trojans were revived by 1905 and immediately picked up the reins of their earlier glory. In 1908 they easily beat United Services, who were then a top side. Things weren't so good in 1913 when they travelled away to Old Alleynians, but found three of their players had been "lost in transit", leading to a 31-0 trouncing.

Trojans could produce their own talent, such as Tracey Fowler, who was an England trialist in 1914, and H.A. Haigh-Smith (1884-1953). Haigh-Smith never won an England cap but was 'Hon. Sec.' of the Barbarians for 30 years. He was the only Hampshire selector from 1925 to 1939, during which time the county won two county titles. He was also an international touch judge for 20 years and was manager of the 1938 British Isles team.

Dudley Kemp won an England cap at flanker in 1935 after leaving Trojans for Blackheath. Kemp later became one of the most respected officials in England and Hampshire rugby.

Between the wars, Trojans had a first-class fixture list, including London Irish, OAs, HAC and Wasps.

Trojans had several home grounds between the wars. In 1923 they played at Wide Lane, Swathling. In 1929 they bought Bannister Court, a former greyhound, speedway and racing circuit. A pavilion was erected at a cost of £1500 and officially opened with a match against Saracens. The referee was the famous international 'Tuppy' Owen-Smith.

Swathling was sold in 1945 and the club played at Northlands Road and then the City Sports Centre, Southampton before, in 1953, they bought 23 acres of land at Stoneham Park for £1,205. On 27th December 1960, the pavilion was officially opened by A.T. Voyce, the RFU President.

Trojans remained a force in the post-WWII era, but their best players had to join bigger clubs to get noticed by the England selectors. James Hetherington, a former Trojan, was one of the best full-backs of the 1950s, winning six England caps whilst playing for Northampton.

Kevin Andrews began a distinguished career with Trojans in the early 1960s before moving on to Burton and Leicester. An England trialist, Andrews played 191 times for the Tigers and captained the Barbarians twice.

The 1970s saw Trojans fielding two ex-England players in Gerry Redmond and Derek Prout. Redmond won an England cap in 1970, whilst Prout won two England caps in a distinguished career with Northampton and Redruth. Prout was appointed Trojans coach in 1976.

Since 2000, two juniors have emulated their illustrious predecessors. In 2001 Tom Allen played for England under 18s, whilst six years later, his brother, Anthony, who had begun with Trojans, moved to Gloucester and Leicester. In 2006 he made his England debut against the All Blacks.

The advent of leagues saw Trojans placed in the London leagues. They were Hants 1 champions in 2010 and were promoted to London 1 South the following year.

UNITED SERVICES PORTSMOUTH

DURING THE FIRST half of the 20th Century, US Portsmouth were amongst the top British clubs and the backbone of the English rugby team. Their annual match against Devonport Services was an unofficial trial for the Navy side.

At the time, the Royal Navy ruled the waves and in 1900 its manpower exceeded 250,000. Curiously though, US Portsmouth RFC, at its peak, ignored 90% of the available Navy manpower because they weren't officers, and for nearly a century selection for the US Portsmouth club was restricted to officers based in the area, including army officers as well as naval officers. In fact, nearly all the club's players were naval lieutenants.

The club joined the Hampshire RFU in 1882; indeed, the first Hampshire county match was played at the United Services Officers' club in Portsmouth, with Lt. Crampton of the club being amongst the match organisers. Permission for the match to take place came from H.R.H. the Prince of Wales, who attended the match.

In 1898 Capt. James Shaw of USP was capped by England as the club recorded 24 wins in 29 matches against other service and South Eastern sides. The following season, they lost only one home match – to mighty Newport. US became a major side in the years leading up to the 1914-18 war and the navy blue backbone of the England team.

In 1907 United Services provided England with Walter Lapage and Admiral Sir George Hamilton D'Oyly Lyon, who were a great defensive pairing for US and England. Lapage came to prominence when he scored two tries in a North v South match. He eventually won four England caps, scoring two tries. D'Oyly Lyon was a great rugby full-back and also a great naval figure. He was joined by a succession of top-class players: A.Warrington-Morris, Norman Wodehouse, E.J.B. Tagg, C.A. Bolton, F.E. Oakley, S.F. Cooper, H.C. Harrison,

Africans, the best being Abercrombie, who was also a fine batsman for Hampshire as well as a top-class rugby player. In 1911-12 C.T. O'Callaghan and J.S. Brown played for Ireland whilst with US.

Despite providing internationals for every test match, US Portsmouth had an awesome record at club level. 1910-11 was the annus mirabilis as they defeated the cream of British club rugby, even mighty Cardiff. The Welshmen got revenge the following season but struggled to win regularly at Portsmouth. US Portsmouth also supplied players to the new Royal Navy side that had, since 1906, played a regular fixture against the Army. All this was achieved entirely from the officers ranks based in the Portsmouth area.

In 1912, a newcomer made his debut for US, W.J.A. Davies. He entered Pembroke Dockyard as an apprentice and won a cadetship to Greenwich College to study naval construction. He served in World War One and rose in rank to become Assistant Director of Warship Production. Davies eventually won 22 England caps and was the first great English fly-half. His half-back partnership with Cyril Kershaw helped England win the 1921 and 1922 championships. In 1923, along with Kershaw, he came out of retirement to play in the Rugby School Centenary match, and the following year led Harlequins to victory over the United States on the eve of the 1924 Olympics. USA subsequently won the Gold medal, beating France in the final.

Kershaw (1895-1972) was the scrum-half who passed the ball to Dave Davies for US Portsmouth, the Royal Navy and England. He won 16 England caps. A captain in the Royal Navy and the son of Sir Lewis Kershaw KCSI, he was never on a losing England side, his worst experience being a drawn game with France in 1922. He retired from international football after the Grand Slam season and holds the record, along with W.J.A.Davies, of 14 half-back appearances as a pair. He also fenced for Great Britain in the 1920 Olympics in Antwerp and was an able cricket and hockey player.

Between the wars, N.C. Browne (1927), H. McVicker (1927), J.W. Forrest (1928), W. Elliot (1931) and N.L. Evans (1932) won international honours. The roll call of internationals continued after WWII with D.T. Wilkins, J.W. Clements, N.O. Bennett, N.C. Browne, J.W. Forest, J.N. Davidson, K. Ross, J.T. Hodgson, J. Grieve, G.R. Hoskings and D. Vaughan. By the 1950s, US Portsmouth were a good side but a long way from the days of Kershaw and Davies.

The best known modern player is Commodore Jeff Blackett, who went on to become chief disciplinary officer of the RFU and a judge. In recent seasons, US Portsmouth have played in Hampshire One.

WEYMOUTH

WEYMOUTH RUFC ARE a modest Wiltshire club who once included one of rugby's greatest ever players, but kept it quiet. The first Weymouth club was formed by Messrs Scudamore and Andrews, two ex-Dorchester players, at Christmas 1871. There are records of Weymouth playing Dorchester at 'the Cemetery', a ground behind the town cemetery, in February 1872. A Weymouth College RFC also existed, but in 1880 switched to soccer.

George Hamilton D'Oyly Lyon

N.A. Wodehouse, A.H. McIlwaine and F. Wilson, whilst half a dozen more US players had England trials. Norman Wodehouse (1887-1941) was the archetypal Royal Naval forward. He gained 14 England caps between 1910 and 1913, scoring two tries. The outstanding lineout specialist of his era, he played for the Royal Navy team from 1909 to 1914. He captained England on six occasions, including the whole of the 1913 season, where England claimed an elusive first Grand Slam. During WW1, Wodehouse served in the RN, including fighting at the Battle of Jutland. After WW1, he became a naval attaché and is credited with preventing Portugal entering the Spanish Civil War. He was an Aide de Camp to King George VI and was presented with the Companion of the Order of the Bath in 1939. At the outbreak of WWII, he was appointed as Admiral in charge of Gibraltar before retiring from the Royal Navy as a Vice Admiral. He promptly returned to sea duty with the Royal Naval Reserve, working on Atlantic convoys. A long way from his battleship days, Wodehouse was killed serving on an unarmed merchantman that was sunk by a German submarine.

US was unique amongst English clubs in supplying players to the Scotland national team at a time when even London Scottish felt overlooked. Louis Greig and Cecil Abercrombie were Scotland regulars in the years before WW1. Indeed, in 1911 Scotland fielded three US players against the South

The original Weymouth RFC disappeared from RFU records around the end of the 19th century before reappearing in 1923. Their best-known player of the 1920s was a nippy scrum-half called Charles Forte, who became Britain's most famous hotelier, founding the Forte Posthouse hotel chain. A dapper figure, Forte was rumoured to have a fortune worth £100million. When Weymouth RUFC needed money they wrote to Sir Charles asking for donation. He sent them £25!

In the 1930s, the club played on a pitch on a disused aerodrome before moving to White Road and on to a municipal pitch. In the 1980s, they bought a 50-year lease on a pitch at Monmouth Avenue, but subsidence bedevilled the club. At this time, Weymouth suffered badly when their Dorchester-based players left to join the reformed Dorchester club and the two sides soon became rivals.

By the late 1930s, Weymouth had recovered and won 22 of 26 matches in 1937-38, including being unbeaten to New Year.

The club had a famous player on their books in the 1970s when a tall, balding Ministry of Defence policeman called 'Brian Brown' asked if he could train with them. Despite being 48 years of age, Mr Brown was greased lightning. He could run through any tackle. He was asked to play for the club in a local sevens tournament. Weymouth won and Mr Brown scored 27 tries in the afternoon. Picked for the club First XV, he proved far too good for any local side.

Eventually an eagle-eyed spectator spotted that the flying machine was Brian Bevan and the RFU wrote to the club asking why Weymouth were playing a rugby league player. Not just a player but perhaps the greatest ever. Bevan had been a champion sprinter in his native Australia. He had played stand-off for New South Wales at rugby union before becoming the greatest try-scorer in the history of British rugby league, with 796 tries in his career. 1954-55 was his high point with 63 tries. He remains a legend at Warrington RLFC, where 16,000 spectators attended his farewell appearance for the town club. Bevan arrived in the south when he took a job at Portland Naval Base. The great man must have been aware that all rugby league players were banned from playing rugby union. This was a rare golden era for Weymouth, who won 30 out of 35 matches in 1973-74.

Currently Weymouth play in Dorset & Wilts 1. Recently they had to relay the pitches to accommodate the town's new park-and-ride facility.

Weymouth (in blue) in action against Dorchester.

CHAPTER SIXTEEN - CORNWALL

"It's a miracle anyone paid good money to watch the first match – never mind the replay."
The Bristol Evening Post commenting, in 1954, on the fact that Gloucestershire, Somerset, Devon and Cornwall were so obsessed with winning the forward battle that scoring was secondary. This led to an extraordinary number of draws in county matches between the four and replays were a frequent occurrence. The Post felt entertainment was secondary to local pride.

THE CORNISH GAME of hurling contains many of the aspects of street football, except kicking of the ball is not allowed. In hurling, a ball is thrown through the air at Shrovetide. The game survives today at St. Columb Major and St. Ives. Hurling preceded rugby in the county and was well organised on parish lines. The arrival of rugby killed hurling.

Rugby has always been pre-eminent in the Duchy, which is one of a handful of counties without an association football league club. The local mining industry at the time boomed due to technological change. 340 mines were operated in the county, mainly extracting copper and tin, and more than 40,000 miners worked in the industry.

Sadly, in the final quarter of the 19th Century, a great depression swept away the Cornish mining industry. Rugby retained its pre-eminence, but many miners emigrated to Australia and South Africa. They took rugby with them, together with a curious talent for mauling the rugby ball (retaining possession by holding the ball tightly in one's arms and passing it to team-mates who carried on the procedure). Cornwall miners developed enormously strong arms by climbing the vertical rope ladders that linked the mine face to the surface every day. This could involve 500 feet of ascent and descent, which, not surprisingly, gave the miners incredible strength in their upper bodies, which proved to be an asset on the rugby field. The art of mauling became an integral part of the Springbok game due to the émigré Cornishmen.

1908 was the golden year of Cornish rugby, beginning with victory over Durham in the County final at Redruth. That Cornish side was the best county side in England, and also the finest county team that England had produced since the Great Schism. Cornwall were so good that the RFU invited them, as a team, to represent England in the 1908 Olympic Games in London. Actually, the 1908 Olympics attracted only two rugby teams: Australia and England (aka Cornwall). France cried off at the last minute, whilst Scotland and Ireland didn't even reply to the invitation.

The 'final' was played at Shepherds Bush on a pitch that was adjacent to a swimming bath. A net was placed alongside the bath's edge to stop players falling into the water and mattresses piled along the other touchline to stop players coming to grief on the concrete. A cycle track bisected the rugby pitch. Australia won 32–3. Cornwall officials claimed the Australians played in running spikes. The allegation was not proven. The match was so disorganised that some of the Australians declined to attend the medal ceremony.

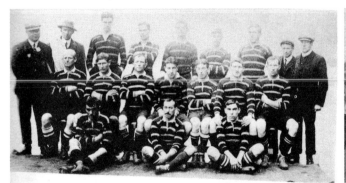

The Cornwall team which contested the 1908 Olympic final, pictured left, and action from the final with Cornwall in the hooped jerseys.

The rugby league attempted to restart rugby league in Devon and Cornwall with a series of exhibition matches in Penzance, Camborne and Falmouth, but interest was fleeting.

Cornish county rugby declined in the 1920s as the Duchy suffered an economic depression, from which it had barely recovered when the Great Depression of the 1930s struck. Young men had little choice but to look abroad or up country for employment. Cornwall had always suffered its best players moving 'up country' to earn a living. The mining industry was almost defunct by 1945, but Cornwall's rugby players kept the affiliation, as witnessed by this tale from Berkshire:

The 1954-55 season saw Berkshire win their group, beating Sussex, Oxfordshire and Dorset & Wilts and drawing with Hertfordshire. This qualified them for the quarter-final against Cornwall at Redruth with its legendary 'Hell Fire Corner'. It was a bad moment as the English selectors had just dropped three great Cornishmen: John Kendall-Carpenter, Vic Roberts and John Williams. The trio tore the visitors apart as an answer to the England selectors. As the expression goes, "Hell Fire Corner hath no fury worse than a Cornishman scorned!"

John Kendal-Carpenter grew up in Penzance. In 1946 he started playing for Penzance and Newlyn and then won a Blue at Oxford University. He made his England debut in 1951 in the front row of the scrum. He was perhaps the outstanding English forward of the era and a great captain for club, county and country.

Despite producing great players, Cornwall had to wait until 1991 to regain the County title, despite being regular South West Group winners and three beaten final appearances. Part of the problem, as the Bristol Evening Post commented, was that the County final was secondary to local bragging rights over Devon, Somerset and Gloucestershire.

Cornwall's victory over Yorkshire in 1991 at least guaranteed a full house at Twickenham as 40,000 Cornish supporters made the 300-mile trip to cheer on the county. The supporters were christened 'Trelawney's Army' after their favourite bishop, who defied the king in the 17th Century. Trelawney's army have made the journey seven times, but won on only one occasion.

1972 saw a sad piece of history when the last ever game between two Cornish mining sides took place. St. Day Mine played Wheal Jane Mine, which marked the end of a century of rugby between miners.

CAMBORNE

CAMBORNE RFC WAS formed in the autumn of 1877 and the club played Penzance in their first ever match on the 12th November that year. The visitors won by three tries in front of 600 spectators. It was another two months before Camborne again took the field, defeating Rosewarne Militia.

Redruth were Camborne's local rivals and the two sides met, for the first time, in March 1878. Redruth squeaked home by a single touchdown.

Camborne drew its playing strength from the Dolcoath Mine, which was the largest, deepest and richest mine in Britain. Many Dolcoath miners emigrated to the new mines of South Africa in the late 19th Century, including Fred Rodda of Camborne, who was regarded as the best forward in Transvaal.

Back in Cornwall, the derby matches against Redruth were the highlight of the rugby calendar. Redruth always triumphed until 1909-10, when Camborne overcame their rivals by 8-6 on the way to winning the Cornwall league. They retained the title the following year without conceding a try. Camborne were at this time playing on the local Recreation Ground, which was opened to celebrate Queen Victoria's Jubilee in 1898.

The 'Rec' was a considerable improvement on a previous ground, where, during Redruth matches, the two sets of spectators would stand on waste piles opposite each other and pelt the opposition supporters and referee with stones. In December 1899, the Cornwall RU visited Camborne to discuss the harassment of the referee in the Redruth match where a section of the crowd were "hooting, bustling and throwing stones at the referee". A Mr Buddle of Camborne was named as the instigator. He was alleged to have called the referee "a dirty cheat".

Apart from disciplinary infractions, Camborne was too far off the beaten track to bother the RFU selectors. Some fine players played for Camborne, notably Gerald Gordon Smith of Thanet Wanderers and Kent and F.S. Jackson, who toured Australia and New Zealand with the 1908 British Isles team. Despite the infractions, the Cornwall selectors liked Camborne, which they viewed as a lucky ground.

John Collins, Camborne's first international.

Rugby was the premier sport in the area and, at one time, there were a dozen junior sides operating locally, including 'Camborne Unemployed' RFC – a truly unique name in rugby annals. In 1911 Harry Launce signed for Salford RLFC from Camborne who were then Cornish club champions. He made 263 appearances for the NU side.

Camborne were arguably the best club in the South West in the 1920s, when they produced a string of county players and 'the Rec' hosted county matches. 'The Rec' had one sad honour; it hosted a number of benefit matches for the relatives of men killed in local mining tragedies.

Camborne, in the hoops, against Redruth in 1955, one of Cornwall's fiercest rivalries.

Camborne's success attracted unwelcome attention when four of their best players were enticed north to join rugby league clubs. 1922 was a golden season with 27 wins from 28 matches and only 62 points conceded. The following season, Camborne played an incredible 48 matches against all the best England and Welsh sides, losing only 11.

Each year, Camborne were honoured with a fixture against Capt. Crawshay's Welsh XV, which was effectively the Principality's best team.

Seven Camborne men represented Cornwall in the 1924 match against the second All Blacks, which was played at the Rec. The All Blacks won easily, but Camborne reigned supreme in the South West throughout the 1920s.

Cornwall had always been well regarded by the RFU because of its mild climate in the winter. Regardless of how frozen the rest of the country was, an England trial in the Duchy could go ahead because of the mild climate. In 1948 the RFU brought one of its trials to Camborne. Four years later, the international selectors finally smiled on Camborne by picking one of the club's players for England.

Despite their success, only one member of the club had been selected for international honours. John Collins won three England caps in 1952–53 after being on the fringe of honours for some years. He made his Cornwall debut in 1947 and became a county regular. In 1951, Collins was an England trialist and reserve before making his debut against Scotland. Injury ended his rugby career the following season.

The playing record of Camborne was undistinguished in the years following World War Two, brightened only by John Collins's international appearances. Less well known was Chalky White, a scrum-half who moved to Leicester and became one of the top coaches in English rugby. During Chalkie's playing career at Camborne, the club met the United States marines rugby side.

The best known rugby player to wear Camborne colours was Jeff Butterfield, the England and Lions centre, who played for the club and county whilst on National Service at Bodmin. Other notables to wear Camborne colours include G.Harris, an England trialist in 1957.

Perhaps the most famous person to appear for Camborne is famous for being eaten by a rubber fish. Robert Shaw was a fine wing three-quarter in the post-war years, before moving to London to become an actor. He did well on British television and eventually moved to Hollywood in pursuit of film stardom. Shaw appeared in the 'Sting', 'Battle of Britain' and in 1975 he starred in 'Jaws', which at the time was the biggest grossing film ever. Shaw played the part of a salty sea dog who was eaten, along with his boat, by the rubber shark.

In 1977, Camborne celebrated their centenary by winning the reintroduced Cornwall County Cup. In recent seasons they were 2003-04 Western Counties Champions and currently play in South West One.

CAMBORNE SCHOOL OF MINES

IN MODERN BRITAIN, mining is one of the smaller industries, but there was a time when things were very different. It has, however, always been a dangerous pursuit and the need for training has been apparent to everyone involved.

The Miners' Association was formed to train miners. It was founded in 1859, when training was part-time, but in 1870 full-time students were admitted. That training scheme led to the formation of the School of Science & Art, which eventually became the Camborne School of Mines in Cornwall. Here 500 trainee mine managers, officials and miners were housed and educated. There were other 'Schools of Mines' up and down the country.

In 1877, a rugby team from the Camborne School of Mines was playing but little is known of their activities. It is thought this side ceased to exist because the School wouldn't meet the costs, which led to an exodus of school players to nearby Camborne RFC.

The present club was formed in June 1896 by a meeting at the school. A subsequent meeting appointed H. Tilden Wright as captain and G.W. Johnson as Hon. Sec. The first game at Penponds is recorded as taking place on Monday 17th October 1896, against Penzance with 2000 spectators present. The result is not known, but a report suggested "the students should keep in better training", which suggests their fitness left much to be desired.

One of the earliest players was E.C. Litkie, who quit school prematurely to join the Klondike Gold Rush and was eventually killed in the Boer War. His last known words were, "Why did I leave my little back room". Honest words, if hardly the stuff of Boys' Own magazine.

For a small club, CSM had some remarkable players: P. Sherwell captained the 1907 South African cricket team and Gerald Gordon-Smith became the first Cornishman to play rugby for England. it was, however, two brothers who made CSM famous. C.H. and J.G. Milton arrived at CSM in 1905 and both were capped for England. J.G. 'Jumbo' Milton was originally a member of the Bedford club. He made his England debut as a forward against Wales at Leicester in 1904 and was capped twice more that season whilst with Bedford. His final two caps came whilst he was playing for Camborne School of Mines. C.H. also played for the Bedford club, but was capped for England against Ireland in 1906 while at Camborne Mines. The Milton family is unique in the history of English rugby since the father also played for England at rugby and captained the South African cricket team.

1905 saw CSM capable of matching Cornwall's best, including Falmouth, the county champions. CSM finished second in the Cornwall League and had seven of their players in the county side. A.J. Wilson played for Cornwall when the county were the English representatives in the 1908 Olympic Games.

Camborne School of Mines team

CSM went into decline after the great players graduated from the school. In 1909, they merged with four other mining colleges in Redruth and Penzance. The new conglomerate was called the Cornwall School of Metalliferous Mining. Referees and fixture secretaries will have been relieved in 1946 when the school reverted back to CSM.

The change of name brought a revival of interest from the selectors. Robert Kennedy won three England caps in 1949. Another old boy Len Thomas emigrated and helped to establish rugby in Canada and Malaysia.

CSM currently play in Cornwall 1. They play the Royal School of Mines from London each year in the second oldest varsity match in the world. 'The Bottle Match' dates back to 1902 and sees the two mining schools play for a three foot tall tin beer bottle.

CORNISH PIRATES
(formerly Penzance & Newlyn)

"Rugby mergers are the only form of marriage where it is positively advantageous to marry someone who knocks you about."
Hazel Oakes

THE OLD GAME of street football was played in Penzance on St. Goulder Common into the 1880s. Rugby football arrived at Christmas 1870 when a match was played on Madron Hill between Mr. W. Borlase's team and a side from the newly-arrived Eastern Telegraph Company. Borlase, a pupil of Marlborough School, raised a team of public schoolboys who were home for the holiday. Six years later, Penzance RFC was formed.

The first notable player to emerge from the club was Tom Peak, a half-back who was a county regular for almost a decade from 1883. It was 1909 before Penzance got their first international in Barrie Bennetts, who was also a member of the England team who made the first tour of Argentina. In later life, Bennetts was the local coroner.

The Newlyn club was formed in about 1894 at the southern end of the town by fishermen and quarry workers. There were several sides in Newlyn, including the Chiefs, who are best remembered for having once played Redruth with seven men – eight short. Penzance played at the St. Clare ground on the northern approach to the town, whilst Newlyn's pitch was on St. Golder's Hill, overlooking Newlyn Coombe.

Newlyn RFC were Cornwall Junior Cup champions, but in 1897-98 were disqualified for fielding an ineligible player. They took the Junior Cup title the following year without any problems. The club temporarily disappeared until 1904 due to a recession in the local fishing industry.

Penzance RFC and Newlyn RFC were two sides that didn't get on too well. Indeed, hostility amongst the rival supporters was so great that the local police banned matches between the them from 1929 until 1932. And yet fourteen years later the two clubs merged. Relationships had begun to mellow during the late 1930s. After World War Two the two sides decided to amalgamate and on the 22nd September 1945 a new club – Penzance & Newlyn RFC – played its first match against Guy's Hospital on the Mennaye Field. The field is sited perfectly with one half of the pitch in Newlyn and half in Penzance. The decision to merge in 1945 was brought about by a shortage of manpower following the war. Amongst the earliest members of the merged club were John Kendall-Carpenter, Vic Roberts and John M. Williams, who were all capped by England. Vic Roberts was a small flanker who attracted attention after some brilliant performances for Cornwall. He scored a try on his England debut and was a member of the 1950 Lions. He won his first cap with Penzance & Newlyn but later joined Swansea and Harlequins. Williams won two caps in the centre in 1951, but Kendall-Carpenter was one of the great forwards of the era. He won 23 caps between 1949 and 1954 and captained every side in which he played.

After the merger, the Pirates became one of England's premier sides and were often the backbone of the Cornwall side. In 1962 they provided the county with six players: Alvin

Brian 'Stack' Stevens

player-coach. Under Moseley, the Pirates rose six divisions in seven years, eventually reaching National One, making them Cornwall's number one club.

In 2005, Evans took another step towards his dream of having a Premiership club from Cornwall when the club were rebranded as the Cornish Pirates. Pivotal to the team was Gavin Cattle, who for seven years was skipper. Under Gavin's leadership the Cornish Pirates won the EDF Energy National Trophy at Twickenham in 2007 and also emerged as the first winners of the British & Irish Cup in 2010, beating Munster in the final. The Pirates also reached the qualifying round of the RFU Championship in both 2011 and 2012.

The best players to appear for the Pirates have included Will James (Wales), Matt Hooper, Jack Nowell and the brothers Tom and Luke Cowan-Dickie. Jack Nowell and Luke Cowan-Dickie, who had both progressed to Exeter Chiefs, were members of the 2015 England World Cup squad.

Cornish Pirates had a brief spell away from Mennaye Field from 2004 to 2010, but are currently reported to be looking to build a top class stadium in Cornwall as a centre of excellence. They are unique in celebrating the annual St. Piran's Day's by placing a giant Cornish pasty behind the goalposts to celebrate the county's favourite food and rugby side.

FALMOUTH

FALMOUTH WAS A busy but isolated port until the railway arrived in 1863. Being out on the South West Coast, large steamships began calling there to connect with the rail network. Before the opening of the railways, it took four days to travel from London to Cornwall; the railway reduced the journey to eight hours. Twelve years later a new docks system was opened in Falmouth to link boat and train passengers and establish an express service to London. The process worked two ways, as the town became a popular holiday resort for rich city dwellers.

Falmouth RFC was formed in 1873 by public schoolboys, whose families had holiday homes in the holiday town or were local gentry who sent their sons 'up country' to the top schools. There were half a dozen other clubs in the town at the time, such as the Docks, Albion, Church Institute, Working Men's Club and 'One and All'. In October 1891 Falmouth Albion merged with the town team. Interest was so great that funds were raised to buy 'the Recreation Ground', which became the centre for sport and the town club's home.

The Falmouth club was described as typically Cornish in its early days, play being more rugged than stylish and featuring powerful forward exchanges. By January 1884 four Falmouth players were in the Cornwall team.

The success of the Cornwall county team in 1898 brought Edward John Jackett to the attention of the England selectors. Jackett was a brilliant full-back who gained 13 England caps between 1905 and 1909. He also played for the 1903 British Lions and for Transvaal against the 1908 Lions. In 1912 Edward switched to NU with Dewsbury. He was prone to nervousness in the early stages of a match, but he usually recovered to play well. Besides his rugby exploits, John Jackett was also a professional cyclist and an artist's nude model. He

Williams, Brian Stevens, David Mann, Jimmy Glover and Gerald Luke. Brian 'Stack' Stevens had a career that spanned two decades. He was never capped whilst with Penzance & Newlyn and had to move to Harlequins to get England recognition He won his first England cap in 1969 and held down the loose head prop's jersey until 1975. His finest hour came in 1971 when he was one of a handful of Englishmen invited on the legendary Lions tour to New Zealand and Australia.

In the 1950s, the Pirates twice managed to defeat Cardiff, then the best side in Britain. They were amongst the most adventurous clubs when it came to fixtures. In 1959, they defeated Milan, but lost to the touring San Isidro side from Argentina in 1963. Eleven years later, the Pirates defeated the Spanish national team. One wag observed the Spaniards had won on their previous visit to Penzance: in 1595 when the Spanish navy had sacked and burnt the town.

The Pirates became a huge attraction, with 9,000 regular spectators in the 1960s, but the arrival of league rugby found them in the South West Leagues.

The most significant event of the 1990s was the return from Kenya of Richard Evans, who resolved to help the Pirates regain their prominence of bygone years. Evans helped to fund the recruitment of Kevin Moseley, the Welsh international, as

John Jackett

was one of the few men sued for breach of promise. In 1898 he became engaged to a young lady from Portscatho and a child was born out of wedlock, but Jackett found himself in court when he refused to do the decent thing.

Jackett was a member of a family who were associated with Falmouth for nearly a century. His brother Dick never won an England cap but had five England trials.

Other internationals from Falmouth were Raphael Jago. (1882-1941), who won five caps (but is more closely associated with Devonport Albion RFC), and James George, who made three England appearances in late 1940s.

In the very early years the club played at several sites – Seafront Gyllyngvase, Belmont and Quarter-Mile Lane, which is now Tregenver Road. However, around the turn of the nineteenth century a group of Falmouth businessmen and sportsmen formed the Falmouth Recreation Ground Company and built the Recreation Ground on its prominent position overlooking the harbour. It was then that the rugby club occupied its 'new' base as a tenant and where it has remained ever since. During this time the ground had hosted many County Championship matches and also two England trials in 1954 and 1968. The RFU liked to play in Cornwall because the mild climate reduced the chance of frost and snow preventing play.

In 1933 the club had the opportunity to purchase the ground but, because the necessary finance could not be raised, it was then purchased by Falmouth Borough Council, who continued to rent it to the rugby club. When local government was reorganised in 1974, Carrick District became the owners and continued to rent the ground to the club before finally granting them a 50-year lease.

Over its long history, Falmouth Rugby Club first won the county team championship in 1900 and since the end of the Second World War the players were champions again in 1956 when Bill Bishop captained the side. Bill Bishop was a Cornish rugby legend who represented the county on the RFU from 1976 to 1995.

The arrival of leagues came at a bad time for Falmouth as their playing strength was in decline and they slipped into the Cornwall leagues.

HAYLE

HAYLE RFC WAS formed in 1877 by a group of local foundry workers in collaboration with Edmund Hocking, who had played the game at Cambridge University. Hocking was a brilliant goal-kicker who led Hayle to a ten-year undefeated record. Hocking, with his varsity background, was an exception amongst the foundry workers, who were a rough bunch with a

reputation for toughness on the field. Ironically the club's motto is 'Gentle in Manner, Forthright in Deed'. From the early days, the highlight of the playing year was annual Boxing Day fixture against St. Ives for the Bay Shield.

In 1902 the foundry closed, which led to hard times for the town and its rugby club. The young men of the town drifted away as unemployment grew and Hayle rugby suffered. Bad times continued into the 1930s, but at least the club had its first England trialist in W.H.Taylor.

After World War Two, the club was revived by Ron Baumbach and results began brightly with 20 wins in 30 matches in 1946-47. The club's best known players were David Inch, who played 350 First XV games, and Terry Munglas, who won an England trial in 1965. The club suffered another blow when a by-pass was built that crossed the pitch. This caused a change of pitch layout, but Hayle bounced back and, at one time, were ranked second to Penryn in Cornwall.

In 2009 Hayle played in the Cornwall & Devon league after being relegated from Western Counties West.

LAUNCESTON

THE COUNTIES OF Cornwall and Devon are separated by the River Tamar. The market town of Launceston (pop. 11,700) is the most easterly community on the Cornwall side of the border. Rugby has been played in this farming community since the 1880s. The first verified record is of a match between Launceston and Holsworthy in 1889. Little is known of the game in Launceston until the present club was formed on 15th October 1948 at a meeting in the Guildhall called by Spencer Toy, Gordon Reeve, Eric Smith and Arthur Venning. Toy, who was headmaster of Launceston College where he introduced rugby to the curriculum, organised a team for an inaugural match against Venning's XV.

Launceston's first official match was against St. Columba of Plymouth at Herdon, which they lost 25-3. The jerseys were theoretically navy-blue, but in reality were comprised of eleven soccer shirts, plus four oddments.

The Cornwall RFU helped the new club by holding a county trial at Launceston. The club reciprocated by acquiring an old army hut for use as a changing room and placing hay bales as spectator viewing facilities. The previous tenants of the hut had been prisoners-of-war.

Many local people worked in naval facilities, but the decline of the Royal Navy in the post-war years hit the Launceston area badly and the rugby club suffered and gates dwindled. In 1960-61 the club had only five wins in 28 games. Struggling on and off the field, the club even considered a merger with Plymouth Albion, which did not happen.

The club left Herdon in 1969 when the ground was sold to David F. Smith Ltd., who subsequently became the club's long-term sponsor. Initially they played on a corporation pitch before acquiring a ground on the banks of the River Tamar.

Launceston have produced a number of top-class players, notably Derek Prout (Northampton and England), Roger Spurrell, who became a legend with Bath, and Graham Dawe. Dawe is one of the most remarkable hookers of all time. He

Derek Prout

first came to national prominence in the Launceston side of the early 1980s when they won both the Cornwall Cup and the Cornwall Merit Table, which promoted the club into the Cornwall South West league. He joined Bath, who were at that time on the threshold of greatness, and won eight Cup finals at Twickenham and was capped by England, including playing in two World Cups. He retired in 1997 but was coaxed out of retirement by Sale, despite the 800-mile round trip to Manchester. He stayed at Heywood Road for two seasons before becoming a coach at Plymouth Albion. All this was in addition to working full-time on his cattle farm in Milton Abbey.

The club entered the league structure in South West Two and eventually rose to National Two South.

(Thanks to John Fry)

MOUNT'S BAY

MOUNT'S BAY RFC were the shooting stars of Cornwall rugby. They emerged in September 1999 using Penzance & Newlyn's facilities. Their first match was against Falmouth 'A'. They finished that season by winning Cornwall 2. It was the first of seven promotions and the 2007 Intermediate Cup title in eight years. In April 2008 they reached National 2 with Ricky Pellow as Director of Rugby. Ricky took over from Calum Osborne, who was coach from 2003 to 2007. Mount's Bay began to suffer from travelling the length and breadth of England. They closed their doors in 2009.

PENRYN

'The Borough'

PENRYN (POP. 6,812) PRIDES itself on being a contender for the smallest town to have produced a first-class rugby club. The town lies on Penryn Creek, a drop-kick away from Falmouth, their arch-enemies.

Rugby arrived in Penryn in 1872 with the return of a native from up-country. John M. Thomas arrived back in the town after working in London, where he played for Blackheath. Thomas found the old game of

street football was still being played in the town using a bundle of rags wrapped in sailcloth. The participants were quarry workers, bargemen and fish porters. He suggested that the rag ball was replaced with a leather encased pig's bladder. Thus was born Cornwall's oldest club.

J.M. Thomas captained the new club in its first season. From the start, Penryn were a power in West County rugby. From the outset, their fixtures with Redruth were an integral part of the Cornish rugby calendar. The 1886 encounter between the two clubs is considered the shortest game in rugby history. The referee abandoned the match after three minutes when both teams became embroiled in a massive fight.

This is mining country and a recession at the start of the 20th Century brought hard times to the local mines and to Penryn RFC. In the 1911–12 season the club were on the point of closing when the Falmouth club closed down (they reappeared later). Penryn were able to buy the Falmouth jerseys for £5 and, with the help of some of the Falmouth players, were able to carry on until the outbreak of World War One. Another factor was that Dr. L.B. Hopper arrived in the town. He was an Oxford Blue and an England international and his enthusiasm and drive ensured the club's survival up to the outbreak of the war.

After the war, Penryn became the champions of Cornwall and the second team took the junior title. A succession of talented young players arrived at the club, none more admired than George Jago, who was the best three-quarter in the region. He was unlucky never to have earned an England cap.

THE FREEMAN OF PENRYN

ONE of the great open-side wing-forwards to emerge after the last war was sturdy, thick-set V. G. (Vic) Roberts, a native of Penryn, Cornwall, who was first capped for England in 1947 and gained 16 caps in all.

Now a Barbarians' selector, Roberts has captained his club, county and country. He made 43 appearances for Cornwall, his last being at Coventry in 1958 when Warwickshire dashed Cornish hopes of winning the County Championship.

In the 1962-63 season, at the age of 39, he turned out for a Harlequins XV against Eton. Although a regular Harlequin player in his day, he is thought of in Cornwall as a Penryn man.

Harlequins, Civil Service, Cornwall, Barbarians, England and the Lions have all claimed him, but nowhere is he

VIC ROBERTS

remembered with such affection as his home club, Penryn.

This small Cornish granite town (pop. 4,830) maintains the proud tradition of being the smallest borough in the country to boast a first-class Rugby XV. So deep is Penryn's interest in the game that Vic Roberts was made a Freeman of the Borough in September 1956, the year of his last game for England.

Now a Chief Customs Officer with the Port of London Authority, he can look back with fond memories on a sparkling Rugger career.

In 1947 he scored the winning try against France, and in 1950 he was up to take a final pass from wing J. V. Smith to gain the only try of the England-Ireland match.

Roberts was a member of Karl Mullins' 1950 Lions and cherishes many happy memories of a highly successful tour of Australasia.

Falmouth Grammar School saw the start of his Rugby career, as a hooker, but he only gained his colours for Rugby as a special presentation at the school after he had achieved fame as an international.

RUGBY WORLD (April, 1964)—33

Eddie Richards was the first Penryn player to represent his country when he played scrum-half against Scotland and France in 1929 after joining Plymouth Albion. Since Eddie, five members of the Richards family have worn the club's No. 9 jersey over 60 years.

The greatest player to emerge from Penryn was Vic Roberts. He won 16 England and 45 Cornwall caps over a decade. Roberts followed the familiar road of moving 'up country' to achieve national selection, playing most of his rugby with Harlequins. His hometown later rewarded him with the Freedom of the Borough.

Subsequent England international to go 'up country' from Penryn were Ken Plummer (Bristol 4 caps), Roger Hosen (Bristol, Northampton 10 caps) and Chris Martin (Bath 4 caps).

Penryn had clubhouse problems in the 1950s and had to operate from the Fifteen Balls public house until a new clubhouse was opened on the Memorial Ground.

Penryn consider their teams of the 1960s and 1970s to be the best in their history. They did well in the National Knockout Cup and dominated the Cornwall Cup. They were county cup winners on four occasions between 1967 and 1980, tied in 1969 and were runners-up twice.

Unfortunately Penryn were in decline when leagues arrived in 1987 and could no longer attract the gates of earlier seasons, even for matches against Falmouth.

The 21st Century has seen Penryn on the rise, reaching National League Five, whilst off the field, the opening of the University of Cornwall brought, 10,000 youngsters to the area, many of whom the club hope will be rugby players.

REDRUTH

'Kings of the West Country'

REDRUTH CLAIM TO be the second oldest club in Cornwall (after Bodmin) and the oldest in West Cornwall. The club was formed in 1875, although a match had been played in January 1874 against Penzance.

The 1875 match, organised by a Truro solicitor H.W.Hockin, attracted hopefuls from Truro, Redruth and Falmouth, including Clifton College pupil Henry Grylls, who had a long association with Redruth. Grylls and W.M. Willimott, a Marlborough Old Boy, became the driving forces. Little is known of the earliest matches but they were played on the Brewery Leats.

The first recorded mention of a match at Redruth was in February, 1876, when Truro were the visitors. A local reporter wrote: "Redruth won the toss and chose the south goal. After a good 'kick-off' by Chilcot of Truro, the 'Red' men, for the first quarter of an hour's play, were penned in their '25'. After this, however, and for the greater part of the afternoon, they had the best of it, two touchdowns being obtained by Messers. Everett and Grylls respectively."

In 1879 Redruth became the sixth known club in the country to play by 'the electric light'. The Manchester firm of C.W. Provis, owned by a man from Redruth, lit the ground as part of a nationwide experiment. Special trains ran from Truro and Penzance and brought spectators from all over the county. It was reported that the lights were seen for miles around. In the end, Redruth won by three tries to one, the spectacle cost the club £40 and doesn't seem to have made a profit.

One of the earliest Redruth teams.

Five legends of Redruth rugby: J 'Maffer' Davey, Bert Solomon, Roy Jennings, E.K. Scott and Richard Sharp.

Beer was important to Redruth as a local brewery subsidised the player's expenses, which for a time meant the club didn't have to charge for admission. But around 1900 admission to matches was introduced at two pence. Season tickets were five shillings; players "subs" one shilling.

Redruth were too far off the beaten track for international selectors, so it was 1905 before the selectors turned the spotlight on the club. William M. Grylls, the son of the club's founder, was capped against Ireland in 1905 and would have won more caps but for his army career.

The club's second cap was J. 'Maffer' Davey, who was a remarkable individual. He won a superb reputation as an elusive half-back on the rugby field as a teenager. He played for Cornwall before the 1902 mining recession forced him to emigrate to South Africa. Davey's reputation as a rugby player preceded him to South Africa, where he quickly won representative honours. He played for the famous Mines club (the best side in Transvaal) and was almost selected by the Springboks to tour Britain. The South African selectors had to withdraw their invitation because Davey had not qualified for his adopted country. Davey returned home in 1907 and was capped by England at stand-off.

Soon afterwards Redruth gained a brilliant centre in Bert Solomon (1885-1961), who was perhaps the greatest ever rugby player from the West Country. A Garbo-type figure, Solomon walked away from fame at the height of his prominence. He spent his life working as a butcher, a tough physical profession. He began his rugby with Treleigh Rangers in 1902 before being picked by Redruth RFC. His impact was so great that he was immediately offered a county trial by Cornwall. He was a rugby-playing genius, but, like so many naturally gifted sportsmen, he played when it suited him and could be a nightmare for the club's organisers.

Fortunately the good player was more noticeable than his alter-ego and he gained an awesome record in the isolated South West, which rarely encountered 'up country' sides. The 1908 County Championship shone the spotlight on Cornwall, who had to survive a tough South West qualifying round, and meant a final against Durham. Cornwall won 18-3 and Solomon was imperious. Although one of his tries was memorable as he lost his shorts after being tackled by Durham defenders, Cornwall were champions and Solomon their golden boy. As English champions, Cornwall qualified for the

unique honour of representing the nation in the 1908 London Olympics. The West Countrymen lost the Olympic final to Australia at White City.

The England selectors wasted no time after Soloman scored six tries in the 1909 Cornwall v Devon game. His reward was a place in an England team alongside Ronnie Poulton, Jack Birkett and Adrian Stoop – as potent an England three-quarter line as any in history. England duly won against Wales but Solomon felt lost amongst his international teammates. From then on, he refused to be selected by England, or even Redruth, and returned to being a butcher in his home town. Bert Solomon was a sporting genius who never came to terms with his own talent. A shy, retiring man, he is still revered in Redruth.

Are the legends of Soloman exaggerated? Redruth secretary Ken Williams recalls a meeting some years ago with the legendary Harlequin Adrian Stoop, who played alongside Solomon in that match. He said: "Solomon was a very great player. It is a pity he didn't play more often."

Redruth's traditional derby match was against Camborne, the other top team in Cornwall. These were tough, unremitting encounters; neither side took defeat well. In 17 matches between the two rivals in the early 1920s, Redruth won six matches but never scored more than eight points, whilst Camborne won seven matches and only reached double figures twice.

The decades up to World War One had seen Redruth ranking with the best clubs in the South West, but the 1920s were disappointing. Tommy Harris was an outstanding forward for Redruth who was lured to Rugby League with Rochdale Hornets, with whom he won a Great Britain RL cap.

Redruth and the Cornwall teams were on the periphery of British rugby until the 1930s, when many of the top clubs began to visit the county for end-of-season tours. Redruth were glad to see the visitors, but suffered because they had to travel enormous distances to return the fixtures. Despite the handicap, Redruth were viewed as 'Kings of the West Country'. Between 1930 and 1936, Redruth played 248 games, won 205 and lost only 33, including victories over Cardiff, Coventry, Bristol, Bath, Swansea, Oxford University and Neath.

1935-36 was perhaps the greatest year in Redruth's history, with 37 wins in 40 matches, scoring 864 points and conceding only 101 points.

Much of Redruth's fiercesome reputation emanated from the legendary 'Hellfire Corner' of the Recreation Ground on Lower Cardrew Lane. In the distant past, the pitch had a distinct slope into the corner where the home support concentrated. Visiting players who entered the corner were guaranteed a warm reception. Today the slope has gone.

Roy Jennings, the Redruth full-back, was the key figure in the success story. He played 61 times for Cornwall and had five England trials without ever winning a full cap. He was one of the exclusive club of players who weren't considered good enough for England yet good enough for the Lions. He was selected for the 1930 British Lions tour to Australasia.

Perhaps the club's greatest forward was Bonzo Johns, who played a record 88 times for Cornwall but was never capped for England, despite nine appearances as a trialist. He played for Cornwall for 16 seasons and for Redruth for three decades.

Other Redruth men were more fortunate and were capped. They included Dr. E.K. Scott and Richard Sharp. Scott was a local doctor who is better known for his association with St. Mary's Hospital and captain of England in the Victory internationals. He was a fine all-round sportsman who was 12th man for England at cricket and played for Gloucestershire. Richard Sharp began his club rugby with Redruth in 1957 and played the season for the club before becoming the best fly-half of his era.

Redruth's greatest season was 1956-57 when they lost only six of 51 matches. The next four seasons saw them unofficial Cornish champions, but they have never overcome the huge disadvantage of their remoteness. They have retained their place in the National leagues and done well in the Cornwall Cup, with six wins between 1980 and 1995.

Phil Vickery, the huge England prop, began his rugby with Redruth before moving to Gloucester. He was picked for England after just 34 first XV games.

Since the introduction of leagues, Redruth have steadily improved and are long-standing members of National One.

SALTASH

"We'll cross the Tamar,
land by land,
With 'one and all'
and who shall bid us nay"
The Song of the Western Man – R S Hawker

FORMED IN AUGUST 1969, Saltash played their first home games at Cross Park School before Mr. Henwoods' field at Carkeel was purchased. Drainage turned out to be a problem and needed major work. The players changed at Cross Park School and used the Railway Inn, Fore Street for committee meetings and post-match entertainment, but problems with the pitch drainage continued and in 1973 the club moved to their present home at Moorlands Lane. The ground at Carkeel was finally sold in 1980.

Saltash were twice beaten finalists before eventually winning the Cornwall Junior Cup in 1982. Five years later they were the first winners of the Cornish Junior Merit Table.

On the introduction of promotion and relegation in 1987-88 they found themselves in Cornwall Division One. Promoted to the Cornwall and Devon League for the 1991-92 season, they were immediately relegated but bounced straight back in 1993-94, remaining unbeaten at the top of Cornwall Division One. They recorded an amazing 127–3 away win at St. Just along the way. The club subsequently won the Cornwall Knockout Plate, the Launceston Floodlit Cup and retained the Gary Nelson Memorial Trophy.

The re-organisation of the league structure saw them promoted once again to become founder members of the new Western Counties League at the start of the 1996-97 season.

A steady trickle of young players have played in the black and gold of Cornwall at schoolboy, colt, U21 and senior level. Some have gone on to represent the South West counties; others have made their reputations further afield, while seven home-grown Saltash players represented the Cornwall Combination side in their 19-13 victory over the Plymouth Combination at Moorlands Lane in 1994.

2008 was a great year for Saltash when they topped Cornwall 1 and won the Cornwall Junior Cup. Since then Saltash have played in the Devon & Cornwall league.

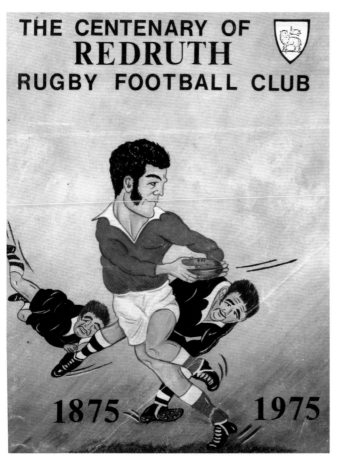

THE CENTENARY OF
REDRUTH
RUGBY FOOTBALL CLUB

1875   1975

ST. IVES

'The Hakes'

ST. IVES RFC was formed on 12th October 1889, although several other clubs were already operating in the seaside town. The 1889 side drew their playing strength from the local fishermen. They led a curious existence as they had no pitch and were totally dependent upon the fishing fleet being in port in order to field a team.

Despite the uncertainty, St. Ives survived and acquired a permanent home at Higher Tregenna in 1899. The club subsequently won the Cornwall Junior Championship and then the Senior Cup, which brought them to the attention of the county selectors at a time when Cornwall was a contender for the title of England's best. Tom 'Chicky' Wedge of St Ives was first choice scrum-half for Cornwall and eventually won 29 county caps and was twice capped by England. Wedge was a bouncy little half-back who fulfilled his contemporary Adrian Stoop's definition that a scrum-half should be half acrobat/half rugby player. 1908 was a golden years for Wedge as he was a member of the Cornwall team that won the county title for the first time and represented Great Britain in the rugby final at the Olympic Games.

Wedge was one of three St. Ives men in the Olympic team: the others were Nicky Tregurtha and Joe Treaskis. Tregurtha won 53 Cornish caps in two decades, whereas Trevaskis won 13. With so much talent, St. Ives came within a whisker of winning the Cornish Senior title in 1910, but mighty Camborne proved too strong.

Soon afterwards, hard times descended on the fishing industry and badly hit the town and its rugby club. The inter-war years saw the club boosted by two events: the local council loaned a ground to the rugby club and the sport was introduced into the local schools. In 1929 St. Ives's new pitch at the Recreation Ground was improved, a clubhouse built and it hosted its first county match. The new ground opened with a Cornwall XV v an International XV, with Cornwall featuring the peerless Bert Solomon of Redruth.

Progress continued into the 1940s and the club managed to purchase the Recreation Ground. Season 1949-50 saw St Ives winning 36 consecutive matches, with winger Jimmy Fleming scoring 46 tries. Harry Oliver was captain of St. Ives and Cornwall in the early 1950s and had two England trials at fly-half without winning a cap. St Ives were county champions in 1949-50, with Oliver setting a club record of 149 points. Also unfortunate was Tony Bone, an England reserve on three occasions, and Harold Stevens, who won an England trial in 1958 and played 60 games for Cornwall.

Peter Hendy

Barry Ninnes went one step further than so many fine St. Ives players by being capped by England in 1971. A huge lock forward, Ninnes won 24 Cornish caps before moving to Coventry, then one of England's premier sides.

Peter Hendy was another 'nearly' man who was an England trialist in 1976; at St. Ives he played 500 times and 86 times for Cornwall.

Martin Haag was a giant-sized forward who made his St. Ives debut in 1986 before moving to Bath, Penzance & Newlyn and Bristol.

Currently St Ives play in South West 2/National 3 SW.

CHAPTER SEVENTEEN - DEVON

THE DEVON RUGBY Union was formed in 1876, but several clubs had existed before this date: Tiverton (1868), Exeter (1872), Exmouth (1873), Paignton (1873), Newton Abbot (1873), Teignmouth (1874), Brixham (1875) and Torquay (1875).

In 1875 a friendly match had been played between 'a Devon XV' and Somerset at Weston-Super-Mare. Two years later, a meeting of the two counties signaled Devon's first official match as a regular schedule of county matches was agreed. By 1880, rugby was established as the leading winter sport in the county and it was only in the 1920s that soccer became widespread.

Almost every small town had a rugby team, such as Axminster, Seaton, Ottery St. Mary, Budleigh Salterton and Topsham. Other similar clubs in the county were Ashburton, Buckfastleigh, North Tawton, Plympton and Kingsteignton. All had disappeared by the Second World War, although a number have since been reformed (Topsham, Ashburton, North Tawton and Plympton).

The Devon Senior Cup was started in 1887-88 with the purchase of a trophy for 30 guineas. It was played for annually until 1932 when it was discontinued, but was reinstated in 1968.

Devon dominated rugby in the South West from 1893 to 1898 and then became a force nationally. In the years up to the First World War, Devon vied with Durham as national champions. There were a number of reasons for Devon's rise: the county possessed a number of first class clubs, notably Devonport Albion, Exeter and Newton Abbot, which were renowned for their huge forwards. The Devon pack were described at the time as "mobile and massive". The forwards were an average of 13st 10lbs each – tiny by 21st century standards but giants for 1900.

Perhaps the biggest reason for Devon's success was one club, Devonport Albion. The dockyard side 'attracted' a string of brilliant players who had often moved from other parts of the county. They can claim to have become one of the top sides in Britain in the early 20th Century. W. Spiers, D. Hollands, E.J. Vivyan, Raphael Jago and J. Peters were all top-class players who were capped by England whilst with Albion.

Devonport Albion were winners of the Devon Senior Cup on ten occasions between the cup's foundation and 1914. The Senior Cup had a variety of formats, but Albion always rose to the top. There were rumours of illegal inducements by Albion to players, but the RFU initially turned a blind eye out of fears of a second 'Great Schism'.

Devon had benefitted from the RFU's problems following the Great Schism. The RFU looked to Devon for quality players when the pick of the northern players joined the NU, and Devon forwards were the backbone of the 1906 England team who faced the All Blacks.

Ironically, the success of Devonshire rugby brought a threat from the Northern Union itself. A series of NU international matches were played in the county in 1910 and a number of Cornwall and Devonshire clubs went over to the NU, styling themselves the 'Western League'. The clubs included Bridgwater, Exeter, Teignmouth, Torquay, Newton Abbot, Falmouth, Plymouth, Redruth and Camborne.

Torquay Athletic, Newton Abbot and Plymouth were suspended for making illegal payments to players and openly advocating 'broken time' payments. Even the county treasurer was suspended by the RFU for making false statements about illicit expenses paid to the county team. The Devonshire team were all suspended, but only on a temporary basis.

Some clubs went over to the NU, notably Plymouth RFC, who became 'Plymouth Northern'. The NU fought hard to open a second front in Devon, even sending the famous St. Helens RLFC and Coventry NU to Devon to play exhibition matches. The NU invasion failed because a league structure could not be formed and the advent of the First World War directed minds and bodies to matters of greater importance. The NU attempted to pick up the pieces in 1920, but without success.

In fact, rugby union itself also went into decline and the county side was a shadow of its former self. Devonport Albion had disappeared and the Naval Dockyards were in decline. The county cup was abandoned in the 1931-32 season after several unpleasant finals where violence between the finalists occurred. It was restarted in 1968 and dominated by St. Luke's College (until it merged with the University of Exeter in 1977). Since then, Exeter and Plymouth Albion have dominated the county cup finals.

Raphael Jago

CULLOMPTON

CULLOMPTON RFC WAS formed at a meeting in July 1892 by Murray Foster, who had played the game at Teignmouth, Tiverton and Blackheath. Their first match was played at Kingsmill a few weeks later. An early fixture was arranged with Wellington, which saw the new club receive a sound hiding. Early records are sketchy, but we know that Mr A. Kerslake is recorded as the first try-scorer for the new club.

Cullompton rapidly made a name for themselves as a good Devon junior club. Figures for 1893-94 show only four defeats in 18 matches, which resulted in a fifth place finish in the Devon Second Division. Two seasons later Cullompton were winners of this division with a single defeat in 21 matches, and were beaten semi-finalists in the Devon Junior Cup.

In 1952, Cullompton were playing in Exeter but moved to Brook Meadow due to waterlogging. It was here the club celebrated its Diamond Jubilee with a drawn match against a County XV.

The following year they won the Devon Junior Cup, but within a decade the club was struggling due to lack of interest. The big freeze of 1963 saved the club because no fixtures were played for three months. By the time the snow melted interest was on the rise and Cully survived. By 1970 the club had acquired a new clubhouse. The 1970s were far more successful, with the purchase of a new pitch at Stafford Park and they won the Devon Junior Cup again in 1990.

Season 2008-09 was the most successful in their history, with victory on the biggest stage. Cullompton won the Senior Vase final, beating Tyldesley at Twickenham. 1500 travelled to support the team as jubilant captain Rob Hammett lifted the trophy. Cullompton coach Charlie Mahon had previously led Devon to Twickenham in the County Championship. Before the big win, Cully went 22 games unbeaten on the way to the Western Counties West title and only narrowly lost out to South West 1 side Barnstaple in the Devon Senior Cup final.

BARNSTAPLE '

'The Barumites'

BARNSTAPLE RFC WERE formed in 1877, but there are records of a match two years earlier between a Barnstaple XV and a team from United Services College at Westward Ho!.

United Services College at Westward Ho! also provided Barnstaple with many players. The most famous person to play rugby at USC was novelist Rudyard Kipling. He remembered life at USC as "brutal". Another old boy remembered: "The buildings were unprepossessing; the food was barely adequate; discipline was severe." The college was aimed at parents looking for a public school education on a budget. The college's curriculum was designed to prepare pupils for the Army, not for the Arts. It lived out the military life in practise and ethos.

Fixtures against the college were convenient because Barnstaple, on the North Devon coast, was isolated from the boom in Devonshire rugby, which was concentrated along the South Coast of the county.

Charles 'Nobby' Thomas

Barnstaple also found competition with rivals Barnstaple Oaks FC, who unearthed a gem of a player in Charles Thomas, but the town club soon persuaded him to join them. Charles 'Nobby' Thomas played his first game for the club at Swansea in 1892 aged 17 years. He went on to play three times for England in 1895 and, though then omitted by the national selectors, he continued to play outstandingly for Barnstaple and Devon. Local papers of the time felt Nobby was hard done by. He was an ordinary working man and a contemporary writer commented, "Sometimes performance alone does not seem to merit selection". He was a lightweight at a mere eleven and a half stone and five feet ten and a half inches when he first played for England.

Undoubtedly Thomas was the complete footballer, and later a great leader. He captained Barnstaple from 1897 to 1904 and captained Devon to win the County Championship in 1899 and 1901. With Thomas to show the way, Barnstaple won the Devon Senior Cup and in season 1896-97, were declared 'Champions of the West', losing only three of 30 games, two of which were against Llanelli and Swansea while on a tour of Wales where they travelled with a weakened team. In these games Barnstaple conceded 24 of the total of 42 points they gave away during the whole season. They scored 90 tries this season, whilst conceding only six.

Barnstaple's second England international was Sir Charles Harper, who played for the club from 1895 to 1900. He played twice for Oxford University against Cambridge and was capped by England against Wales in 1899. He and Nobby Thomas formed a fast, skilful and dynamic forward partnership for Barnstaple and Devon and yet were capped separately by England. At the age of 24 Harper was posted to the Gold Coast and later became Governor of St. Helena.

Barnstaple also had outstanding backs in M.H. Toller, H. Stoyle, W.S. Boyle and J.A. Roberts, who all had England trials. Harold Stoyle was picked as an England reserve but never got the final accolade; he joined Halifax NU in 1897.

The club's most distinguished international was Dr Alfred Fell, who had been one of a great three-quarter line at Edinburgh University. A New Zealander, Fell was capped for Scotland but just as quickly disregarded, although he was a brilliant player. The local newspaper wrote: "They do not like thee, Dr. Fell. The reason why is hard to tell". It was suggested that Fell had upset the selectors by refusing to play for Scotland against his fellow countrymen, the 1905 All Blacks. Fell was also associated with Colchester RFC.

The fortunes of Barnstaple declined after 1900, exacerbated by the cost of travelling and waning public interest.

After World War One, the club reformed and moved from the Rumsam area of Barnstaple to its present home at Pottington Road. The 1920s saw a revival in club's fortunes, culminating in two magnificent seasons: 1925-26 and 1927-28, when Barnstaple won the Devon Senior Cup, on both occasions against Brixham in front of large crowds at the County Ground, Exeter. In this period the great W.W. Wakefield had close links with the club, playing for them occasionally and coaching the side. He also brought the Harlequins club to play at Barnstaple. C.G. Pritchard was an outstanding full-back for Barnstaple and Devon in this period and was an England trialist.

The Great Depression of the 1930s hit both town and rugby club badly and Barnstaple could barely afford to run two teams. Indeed, the second XV merged with the local Grammar School Old Boys as a money-saving measure. The club reformed after World War Two in 1946 with a formidable pack of forwards, including H.A. (Bert) Jones, who played three times for England in 1950, and Ron Mabbott, a Welsh trialist. Bert Jones captained Barnstaple and Devon for many seasons and led Barnstaple to the double over Plymouth Albion and a win at Torquay for first time since 1910.

Barnstaple were a good side in 1950s, notably in season 1955–56, with 24 wins in 42 matches, and in 1957-58 when they won 33 games, beating Exeter twice and Plymouth Albion three times. Gradually the club's traditional emphasis on forward play was replaced by the backs taking centre stage, with D. Bowers getting an England trial. M.J. Blackmore, a wing three-quarter, was the club's outstanding player of this period, representing Devon at the age of 17 and having numerous England trials.

The team continued to have mainly good seasons and peaked in 1971-72 when a side led by J. Jewell won the Daily Telegraph Merit Table pennant as champions of the South West with only four losses in 39 games. The side scored 777 points that season against 252. In 1973–74 they reached the final of the Devon Cup.

The late 1970s saw a moderate decline in playing results but a big increase in membership. A third XV was formed and mini

rugby started. Off the field a new clubhouse was built and Mary Chugg became the club's president. Barnstaple soon reaped the benefit of junior rugby and the section has, since its formation, produced impressive sides. From 1985 the Devon Colts Cup was won for seven successive seasons and two colts players, Kevin Squire and Peter Bond, played for England Colts.

When league rugby began, Barnstaple were placed in South West Two. The club was promoted to South West One in 1992 and has come close to National League status in several seasons since. They also proved to be a successful cup side, reaching the National Intermediate Cup semi-final in season 1998-99 and winning the Devon Senior Cup five times between 1997 and 2002.

In 2002 Barnstaple Colts won the Devon Colts Merit Table and Devon Colts Cup and had an outstanding record of 29 wins in their 30 games.

Five years later, Barnstaple recruited Jerry Collins, who was capped 48 times by the All Blacks and captained New Zealand at the 2007 World Cup. His fierce tackling earned him the nickname of 'The Terminator'. Barnstaple coach Kevin Squire met Collins in a restaurant on his holidays and convinced him to lace up his boots for a second-string match against Newton Abbot. Collins kept hold of his second XV socks and was seen wearing them weeks later when he appeared for the Barbarians.

(Thanks to Mike Hughes)

BLUNDELLS

BLUNDELLS SCHOOL, TIVERTON, was the first school in the South West to play rugby. The school was founded in 1599 by Peter Blundell, a wealthy cloth merchant, as a school for Tiverton youths and the "children of forreyners" (outsiders). It officially opened in 1604 and moved to larger premises in 1882.

Blundells played their first rugby match on the 6th November 1868 against the newly formed Tiverton club, with the town team emerging as victors. The fixture was renewed annually until the 1930s.

Despite the first result, Blundells became the backbone of the Devon team. In 1886 the school's Old Boys played and beat the county side. In those far-off days, the school often played club sides and Blundells regularly played Exeter (until 1924), Cullompton, Wellington, Barnstaple, South Molton, Torquay and Teignmouth. Part of the reason for playing adults was the shortage of school fixtures. This isn't surprising as Blundells beat Newton College of Newton Abbot by 107 points to nil and ran up 146 points to nil the following year! In the latter match, P.J. Newby-Vincent of Blundells scored two of the tries converted 25 out of 30.

Although other schools rugby eventually became established, Blundells remained a top college side with a reputation based on the number of internationals they have produced. The first was Richard Kindersley (1858-1932), who won three England caps and indirectly was the cause of the creation of the International Rugby Board. Kindersley scored the try against Scotland in 1887 that started a dispute between the two countries that was only settled by the formation of the IRB to oversee future disputes. Kindersley eventually progressed to Clifton and Oxford.

In 1886, Blundells produced Douglas Dryden, H.C. Barnes, C. Moggridge, S. Wallis and M. Catcliffe, who were all leading rugby players of the day. Dryden played for Devon against the Maoris before emigrating to New Zealand, where he became the President of the New Zealand RFU.

Other Blundells internationals were Charles Harper (1876-1950) and Tom Kelly, who won 12 England caps with Exeter and London Devonian, and Ronald Rogers, who was chosen for the 1904 British Isles tour to Australia.

Blundells were probably the best English school side in the late 1930s when they were undefeated for two seasons. A key part of Blundell's success was the quality of the rugby masters recruited by the school, notably T.R. Jones and Graham Parker. They kept the flow of internationals with two of the game's greats in Clem Thomas (26 Welsh caps) and Richard Sharp (14 England caps).

R.C.C. 'Clem' Thomas graduated from Cambridge University before joining Swansea and Harlequins. A tough, skilful flanker, he was a Welsh regular from 1949 until 1955. He later became a journalist. Sharp ranks amongst the greatest fly-halves in the game's history. He was initially picked by England as merely a stop-gap while Bev Risman was injured, but he became a national hero. A tall, elusive runner, Sharp brought a touch of class to England in an era where the Whites were drifting into an abyss of mediocrity. He retired in 1967.

A decade later, Charles Kent left Blundells to win five England caps. Kent was nicknamed 'the Crashball Centre' because his role was to run straight through the opposition.

Blundells had a great side in 1993 when they were West of England Schools champions and National Schools runners-up.

BRIXHAM

THE 1860s WERE an interesting time in the fishing port of Brixham. The local vicar, Henry Francis Lyte, wrote a song called 'Abide with me' when he was dying of tuberculosis. The song was to become the anthem of sailors across the world and an integral part of the FA Cup final celebrations at Wembley. Ironically, Brixham was full of life at the time, with 150 trawlers and 200 apprentices in the fishing industry. Also at this time, street football was still being played at Furzeham Common.

Rugby football arrived in 1873 when the Rev. G.R. Roberts, curate to All Saints church, called a meeting at the Bolton Hotel to form a rugby club and was elected captain of the new club, whose local headquarters were on Furzeham Green. With the railways now established in South Devon and travel to and from neighbouring towns made easy, fixture lists were drawn up involving sides such as Teignmouth, Newton College and Dartmouth.

It was 1889 before Brixham had its first county player in J. Middleton, and within a decade Brixham RFC had won the Devon Junior Cup and moved to senior status. They had also moved to Great New Park.

During the 1913-14 season Brixham swept all before them, with a single defeat in 28 fixtures. Due to World War One, it was 1922 before Brixham finally won the Senior Cup in an exciting match where they beat Torquay 3-0. Brixham played in further Senior Cup finals, meeting Teignmouth at Torquay in 1930, where they lost six 6-3, and taking the cup again in 1932 with a win over nearby rivals Paignton by 5-0. As the cup wasn't played from 1933 to 1969, the club was able to claim to be cup holders for 46 years.

Between the wars, schoolboy rugby flourished in Brixham, mainly through the National School in Bolton Street. After leaving school at the age of 14, young rugby players were reluctant to give up the game and so joined the club. However, by this time, the Great Depression had hit the port hard and the rugby club began a period of struggle. In October 1933 the name of New Gate Park was changed to Astley Park in honour of Bernard Astley, who had worked wonders behind the scenes for the club.

The immediate post-war years saw Brixham under the captaincy of Jimmy Merchant. Brixham was rated as one of the strongest sides in the West of England. Mo Andrews, John Braddick, Will Coysh, Peter Greystone and Maldyn Jenkins were all selected for Devon. In 1948 the club beat Torquay Athletic for first time for 25 years.

It couldn't last as Brixham's First XV were ageing and the war had created a gap in talent. Without youth coming through, the club declined until plans for a junior set-up were devised in the late 1960s. During the 1968-69 season, Brixham colts were taking on the best and giving a good account of themselves, winning 75% of their games.

In 1978, Brixham entertained a Cantabrians side from New Zealand which was composed of ex-All Blacks, including Fergie McCormack, Bernie Fraser, Joe Morgan, Ian Hurst, Duncan Robertson, Sid Going, Lyn Davies, Alex Wyllie, Ken Stewart, Ian Kirkpatrick, Vance Stewart, Hamish McDonald, Kerry Tanner, Tane Norton and Bill Bush. Brixham lost that game 19-7. Later that season, Brixham met Torquay in the County Cup but lost 15-9.

Also in 1978 Brixham, Sidmouth and Tiverton formed the Devon Merit Table for clubs excluded from the South West Merit Table and were the winners of the Devon table three times between 1980 and 1984.

During the bad winter of 1984-85, Brixham were pleasantly surprised to get a phone call from mighty Bath, who were unbeaten by any English side for 18 months. Bath were desperate for some match practice due to frozen pitches back home, so they looked to Brixham for a playable pitch. Bath brought a team with 11 Internationals and lost 9-6! All of Brixham's points were scored by 19-year-old Sean Irvine.

In the 1988-89 season, Brixham entered the National Cup competition for the first time and won through to the third round, where they met Gloucester at home. Gloucester ran out the winners, 28-4. Since then Brixham have been in the National Cup competition on three other occasions - a record for a Devon club outside the National leagues to date.

When leagues were introduced, Brixham were placed in South West 2. Their first league match was a 12–3 victory over Newbury, but it took two seasons for Brixham to gain promotion to South West 1, followed by promotion to National 5.

In modern times, many Brixham players have played for Devon in County Championship matches and on one occasion six Brixham players played in the same game. Two players from the club have captained the county: Sean Irvine and Chris Ward. Irvine played in the combined Devon & Cornwall XV against Italy. Tony Watkinson who played for Brixham, Devon, London Irish and Oxford University and was capped at international 'B' level. Rory Jenkins began at Brixham before playing for Cambridge University, London Irish and Harlequins.

DEVONPORT SERVICES

"Squalls were driving, on a Sou'westerly, off the Hoe by kick off. The Rectory terraces were packed by a crowd officially recorded as 46 and the earth squelched as protest that it wasn't a good day for rugby."
Ian Todd (1962)

THE CITY OF Plymouth was once the home to two mighty sides: Plymouth Albion and Devonport Services. Albion played at the Rectory Ground from 1890 to 1914, a ground described as "a swamp leased from Stoke Damerel Church". The Rectory was commandeered for war service and was never returned to Albion. After World War One, the Rectory was taken over by a new side, Devonport Services RFC, who had been formed in 1912 by Flag Captain A.L. Kay.

The new club did not get chance to establish itself before the Great War began, but a RN Devon (Devonport) side filled the void during the emergency with a team composed of RU and NU players. RN Devon were so strong that they played fixtures against service teams from Wales, New Zealand and South Africa.

The new club was the first services rugby side to allow 'other ranks' to play alongside officers, which enabled them to select a team based on talent. Devonport Services were also unusual in fielding soldiers, notably the Argyll and Sutherland Highlanders, who were based at Seaton Barracks in the city. The club therefore had the cream of West Country Services talent, including internationals such as Ernie Gardner, Tom Woods, S. Kealey and Dickie Gilbert.

Devonport Services initially operated from RNE College before they acquired the lease on the now vacant Rectory Ground. The club persuaded the Navy Sports Board to fund the £6,000 needed to buy the Rectory and on 8th October 1921, they played at their new ground for the first time, defeating the Army by 10-9.

Amongst the earliest fixtures was a 15-3 win over US Portsmouth. The significant fact was that an 'all ranks' side could usually beat an exclusively officer-based club. US Portsmouth didn't like losing and were also upset to see officers and ranks mixing socially on match days.

The matches between Devonport and Portsmouth became official trials for the Royal Navy team. From 1922 onwards, the Royal Navy and Royal Marines RU donated £150 annually to help the Devonport team stay solvent. The first Devonport Services player to appear for England was Ernie Gardner, who played for his country for three seasons without being on the

losing side. He was followed by another England international in stoker Tom Woods. Stokers were the fittest men in the navy because they spent eight hours a day shovelling coal into the boilers of warships. Before World War One, warships were floating coal barges, with coal stowed anywhere and everywhere. The stokers had to shovel coal from one corner of the ship to the nearest available point to the boilers and then shovel it into the furnace. The lot of the stokers improved in 1912 when Admiral Fisher persuaded Winston Churchill, the Navy Minister, to switch from coal-fired warships to oil-burners. Consequently, the need for thousands of stokers disappeared, as did the number of lower ranks needed by the Navy.

Within a couple of seasons, Devonport became part of the fabric of England rugby, not least when the serving Navy man, Eng. Commander S.F. Coopper was appointed RFU Secretary. Coopper was educated at RNE Keyham and played his rugby in the South West. A strong-running three-quarter, Coopper had won seven England caps between 1900 and 1907. This was a strange appointment as at the time as Coopper was based in Singapore, but presumably must have been bound for home waters.

Perhaps the greatest DS player was Bill Luddington, who played for England alongside his clubmates Ernie Gardner and Freddie Gilbert. Luddington was known as 'the crusher'. He was a gigantic petty officer who acted as the ship's constable. His approach to rugby was once described as follows: "Luddington did not spare himself or anybody else in the mauls". He played

13 times for England, being ever-present during England's 1924 Grand Slam. Although he was a forward, he was also an excellent goal-kicker and he won the 1923 Calcutta Cup with a conversion from the touchline on the stroke of time. He carried on playing rugby long after leaving the Navy and was so famous he was hired by a brewery to simply tour pubs and clubs promoting their products to the adoring public. At the outbreak of World War Two, he rejoined the Royal Navy and was killed on active service in 1941.

In 1922, the Rectory hosted one of the England trial matches, which attracted 10,000 spectators. Four home players, Ernie Gardner, Freddie Gilbert, W.T. Eyres and R.G. Dobbie were selected for the trial. Gilbert was remarkable as the oldest player, to that time, to be selected for England, being 39 years of age.

Devonport Services had a reputation for producing tough forwards, such as W.T. Eyres and Barney Evans. Eyres was a journeyman forward who was never considered top-class until playing brilliantly for Devon in a county semi-final, which led to his only England cap in his 30s. He was described as "the wrong man to upset". Evans was another England international who was tiny but tough. Devonport Services also had some great Irish names in their ranks between the wars, such as Harry Stephenson, W.F. Horsey Browne and Mark Sugden.

With so many tough characters on display, it wasn't surprising that there were 'dust-ups' with some of the local opposition. In 1924, Devonport Services refused to play Plymouth Albion after problems with some factions of the Albion crowd. 'Hon Sec' Coopper had to intervene as RFU Secretary and refereed the next time the two teams met. The following year Devonport Services refused to play Penryn over hostility by the Cornish crowd. That same year A.B. Paddon, another uncompromising character, became the first Services player to be sent off for misconduct.

The 1920s were a golden era for Devonport Services, but a new decade brought decline. The club's best players were always in demand for representative rugby, which meant the Saturday side was often under-strength and continuously trying to find replacements. A deterioration in results ensued. The situation was exacerbated by the strange combination of cuts in the Navy's budget and growing international tensions between the great nations. The Royal Navy needed to focus on readiness for war rather than rugby.

Services still produced a great player in Charlie Webb, who was an England regular and a member of the 1936 England team that beat the All Blacks. An enormous lock-forward with massive hands, Webb won 12 England caps, but ironically was lost to English rugby when he was posted to New Zealand.

The Plymouth area suffered terrible bombing in World War Two and the Rectory grandstand was nearly destroyed. After the war, an appeal was raised to restore the grandstand, which was named the Luddington Memorial Stand in memory of the great player.

A famous name took over the captaincy in 1946 when David Vaughan took the helm. Vaughan was an England international during the war and one of the best known rugby players of the era. He was closely followed by Geoffrey R.d'A. Hosking (England), Alan Meredith and Malcolm Thomas (Wales), who all won international honours whilst with the club.

Lewis Jones

By 1950, the regular Navy was declining in size as the aeroplane became king. Navy rugby was saved by National Service, a leftover from World War Two, which required every able-bodied young man to do two years in the services. This saw the arrival of Lewis Jones of Wales at the Rectory. Jones was called up for the Lions tour of New Zealand along with Malcolm Thomas, who was another Devonport Services player. Thomas first played for Newport as a 16-year-old. He captained Devonport Services and the Navy, winning his first cap for Wales against France in 1949. National Service also supplied the club with Bryn Meredith, Terry Davies, Carwyn James, Derek Main, Len Copley and Fred Prosser (an England trialist). Carwyn James was a great fly-half who later became the coach of the 1971 Lions – the only British team to win a series in New Zealand.

1953 was Devonport Services' best season for decades, with a team of international stars all doing National Service. In 1956, Gordon Waddell of Scotland joined the club. He played 18 times for Scotland, was captain on five occasions and went on two British Lions tours.

Devonport Services had a tradition of fine captains, none more so than Mike Pearey, who took over when the club was in decline. Pearey was unlucky in being selected a record number of times as England's travelling reserve without ever winning a cap. A contemporary was John Inverdale, who served the club well and was the father of John Inverdale, the rugby-playing BBC presenter. Inverdale senior was responsible for the re-building of the Luddington Memorial Stand at the Rectory.

The end of National Service came in 1958 and, with it, the steady influx of conscripted recruits. Britain's rule of the high seas had come to an end. This hastened Devonport Services' decline because the club never had deep roots in the Plymouth community as its playing strengths came from being a part of the Navy.

1961-62 was a disastrous season, with only five wins in 25 games, but Mike Pearey, Fred Prosser and John Highton all won an England trial. The poor state of the Rectory pitch hadn't improved, as witnessed by a newspaper reporter covering the 33–0 defeat by Bristol: "Your correspondent would prefer to not mention the Devonport players. Some of them have played well but it was impossible to differentiate amongst them, as they were all covered in mud."

Sadly, the 1970s saw damage limitation to be the main policy as old foes beat Services. The Navy had a small fraction of its previous manpower and the drive for efficiency meant ships could no longer sit in port.

Today Services play in Western Counties West league.

EXETER CHIEFS
(formerly Exeter RFC)

EXETER CHIEFS GO back to 1871, but their first recorded match was on the 26th October 1873 against the local teacher training college that later became St. Luke's College. Exeter beat the students comfortably.

Exeter's first known pitch was 'Mr. Morrison's Field'. Subsequently, they moved to a militia area behind the city barracks, before arriving at the County Ground, which was their home for over a century until the move to Sandy Lane in 2006.

The club won the Devon Cup in 1890, but it took another 80 years before they won it again. The Cup was dominated at the time by Plymouth Albion. Exeter had to wait until the 1990s for their turn to dominate.

Exeter produced four internationals before World War One in Dr. W. Ashford, Rev. P. Nicholas, Leonard Tosswill and T.S. Kelly. William Ashford won three England caps in 1897-98. The Rev. Philip Nicholas won his Blue in 1897 as a wing three-quarter and was awarded an England cap against Scotland in 1902. Nicholas taught at All Hallows School in Exeter for some years before moving to Axminster in 1910 and is mainly associated with Honiton. Leonard Tosswill, the son of a local vicar, became Exeter's best-known international. He learnt his rugby at Marlborough College and trained to be a doctor at St. Barts before winning three England caps whilst with Blackheath. Tosswill was decorated in World War One before becoming Head of Medicine for the Ministry of Pensions, a post he combined with being a BBC commentator covering rugby internationals. He also wrote several of the earliest books on the sport. He died in 1932. Thomas Kelly, a lock-forward, is Exeter's only player to have captained England. He led the English team to a 19-0 victory over France at the Stade Colombes in Paris on the 1st January 1908. He began with Liverpool OBs and also played for Harlequins.

In the pre-World War One era, Exeter developed an excellent fixture list. It suffered a setback in 1891 when the Exeter v Swansea match was so bad-tempered that the RFU banned English clubs from playing the Welsh club. Exeter were largely spared the problems that beset other South West clubs with regards to semi-professionalism. Indeed, the club were honoured with hosting the 1898 England v Wales match and two county finals during Devon's golden era before the Great War.

In 1905, the County Ground hosted the first game by the New Zealanders, fresh off the boat after a six-week voyage from home, in front of 6,000 spectators. The All Blacks blew Devon away with a try within three minutes of the start. The match ended 55-4 to New Zealand, but left a legacy because the Devon team mislaid their jerseys en-route and borrowed the Exeter kit of white with a black hoop. After the match, Exeter RFC changed their colours to 'all black'. Over a century later, the Chiefs still play in black.

Exeter were an integral part of the first Devon side who competed with Durham for pre-eminence in the County Championship in the early 1900s. Devon were county champions in 1900 with a team that included four Exeter men: F.L. Hitt, A.E. Brock, J. Powell and C. Harper. The county reached the final the following year, which was played at the County Ground, where they lost to Durham. The two teams met again at Exeter for the 1907 Final replay, which also ended in a draw. The two sides decided honours were even and shared the trophy.

This was the high-watermark in the early history of Exeter as decline followed. Association Football became established in the city via Exeter City FC, who eclipsed their sporting rivals.

New floodlights are installed at Exeter in 1980.

John Scott

The 1920s were tough times for Exeter RFC and finances forced them to allow speedway and dog racing at their ground. They did, however, produce four England internationals in Geoffrey Roberts, A.A. Brown, Henry Ree and T.R.K. Jones. Roberts won three England caps before being called to the Bar. He moved to London and also played for Chiltern RFC. Brown, who began with St. Helens RFC in Lancashire, was a flanker who became a Devonshire regular, which brought him to the attention of the England selectors. He later became a RFU employee who toured the county's clubs teaching rugby skills. The unluckiest Exeter player of the inter-war years was Henry Ree, whose fame comes from having missed his England debut cap after injuring his toe on the eve of the match. He eventually won 10 England caps but was killed at El Alamein in 1942.

The club's best season was 1945-46 when they won 34 of 37 matches, scoring 647 points, with C.W. Ford scoring 223 points. Rugby in the city was booming, with five sides playing regularly: Exeter, Exeter Saracens, Old Heleans, St. Luke's College and Exeter University. The city side were able to draw players from the junior clubs.

Exeter's best player of the post-war years was Richard Manley, who won four England caps in 1962-63. His teammate Martin Underwood, a winger, also won five England caps in the early 1960s. A decade later, another England star emerged at Exeter in John Scott. A huge No. 8 who moved 'up country' and joined Cardiff, Scott won 34 caps and played a huge role in the 1980 England Grand Slam team. His career was cut short by an ankle injury.

Devon and Exeter rugby received a major boost when the M4 motorway opened, which made it possible for the top sides to travel to the South West. Unfortunately, it also meant the club's best players could drive to the bigger clubs, such as Bristol and Bath.

The stature of Exeter grew when they won the Devon Cup 13 times between 1970 and 1996. They also reached National One in 1997, but seemed unlikely promotion candidates until a decade later, when they built a powerful framework. In 2006 they left the County Ground to move to a purpose-built complex. They also acquired the services of some talented professionals to blend with their home-produced players and the club re-branded itself as the 'Chiefs'. The supporters became involved by dressing as Native Americans, wearing Indian head-dress and even chanting 'The Tomahawk Chop' accompanied by drums.

The Chiefs reached the final of the EDF Energy Trophy (formerly the Powergen Shield) in four of the seven seasons from 2002 to 2008, but finished runners-up on each occasion. They were promoted to the Aviva Premiership in 2010 when they beat Bristol 29-10 at the Memorial Stadium in a play-off. Kingpin was Rob Baxter, who had been club captain and coach. His family have been associated with the club for generations. Rob was voted Coach of the Year in 2012.

In 2012, the rise of Exeter Chiefs was rewarded when two of their players, flanker Tom Johnson and prop Joe Marler, were selected for England's tour of South Africa. In 2013 Scrum half Haydn Thomas played in the England v Barbarians match and Jack Nowell emerged as an English regular. The team has been led by lock Dean Mumm, who arrived from NSW Warratahs and was promptly made captain.

Now an established Premiership side, Exeter have played in the Heineken Cup, competing against the cream of European rugby clubs.

Joe Marler

HONITON

'The Lacemen'

HONITON IS A small market town in East Devon. The rugby club is the fourteenth oldest club in the county, with records going back to October 1883 when they were photographed at Budleigh Salterton on the occasion of their first match. Honiton's fourteen men emerged with a 6-6 draw.

From the beginning, the club adopted red, black and amber hoops, which were retained until the present day. Rugby flourished in the closing years of the century, with many local sides being formed in the area. In Honiton itself there were eight teams at the turn of the century: Honiton RFC (x2), Scarlet Runners, Broomhills, United Choirs, United Chapels, Allhallows Choir and Allhallows School.

Honiton's only international was the Rev. Philip Nicholas (1876-1952), a wing three-quarter who began at Monmouth School before attending Oxford University, where he won a rugby blue in 1897-98. He was capped by England against Wales in 1902 but did not let this honour go to his head. He had a brief stint with Exeter but returned to his local club and is credited with keeping the club going until the Great War. In total Nicholas was associated with Honiton for half a century.

The club had a close rivalry with another local club, Seaton. Seaton disappeared in 1914 and the survivors joined forces with Honiton's members to reform Honiton in 1919.

Various fields in and around Honiton were used during the club's history, including one off Turks Head Lane, near the present by-pass. The Ottery Moor Lane ground, later Mountbatten Park, home of Honiton AFC and Honiton RBL Cricket Club, was bought in 1920 by A.O. Morton-Moncrieff, who allowed the rugby club to play there. The club moved to Allhallows Field in 1938 to be nearer the town centre as the field became available when Allhallows School moved.

The years between the wars saw the club as a major force in Devon cup competitions. In the season of 1925-26, they reached the Devon Junior Cup final, losing 9-3 to Paignton Reserves. Honiton subsequently entered the Devon Senior Cup, but failed to make progress. The Senior Cup itself disappeared in 1931.

Derek Steele-Perkins was the club's best-known player of the era. He was a Navy surgeon and Medical Officer to the Queen. He later played for Devon, Gloucester and the Royal Navy and had two England trials without getting full selection.

The club declined after World War Two and nearly folded in 1961, when a meeting was actually held to wind up the club. Jack George and Dickie Charles saved the club from extinction. From failing to win a single match in 1960-61, they won seven in 1961-62, and gradually improved. 1967-68 was the best season for years when 21 games were won. Thirteen years later, the club won 27 games and only lost nine.

In 2010 Honiton were promoted to the Devon & Cornwall League.

Honiton centenary match 1983.

ILFRACOMBE

RUGBY BEGAN IN Ilfracombe in 1877. The present club can trace a continuous history back to that date, although records are sketchy until World War One. We know on April 20th 1895 Ilfracombe lost 21-3 to Sidmouth in the Junior Cup final at the Exeter County Ground in front of 2000 spectators.

Ilfracombe have always been a junior club who have produced a number of good players who have won England Schools and County honours. A witness to the old days is Jim Dendle, who joined the club in 1938. Jim recalls that training before World War Two centred on the public toilets in the town market. The players got changed in the toilets, which were maintained by a relative of one of the players. The team ran off for a training run whilst the relative kept an eye on the clothes.

The club had a bad time in the 1960s and dwindled down to 15 players, but it was up to three teams by 1972. They have played on a council pitch at Brimlands since 1930, but only acquired a clubhouse in 1974.

The clubhouse made national headlines in 2006 when they staged a 'Virtual Bonfire' after their annual Bonfire Night celebrations were ruined by Health and Safety requirements. The club had their celebrations around a video of the previous year's bonfire.

NEWTON ABBOT.

"Newton Abbot did us proud. The greetings were warm, everyone seemed glad to see us. For myself and the rest of the team, those were wonderful hours."

George Nepia (full-back – 1924 All Blacks)

NEWTON ABBOT'S GEOGRAPHIC importance lies as a railway junction leading to Plymouth, which is England's most westerly deep-water port. Weary passengers would alight at Plymouth after long sea journeys desperate to set foot on terra firma and catch the train easterly. Those passengers included the first All Blacks, who arrived unheralded at Newton Abbot on the 7th September 1905.

The 1935 All Blacks relax in Newton Abbot.

Few towns outside New Zealand have seen as much of the All Blacks as Newton Abbot. The connection began at the Globe Hotel. Subsequent All Blacks teams viewed Newton Abbot as a 'lucky charm' and stayed in the Devonshire town until the six-week steamship journey from New Zealand was replaced by air travel. The first All Blacks used Newton as a training base, and even played practice matches with the town team. The ABs were unknowns until they destroyed Devon 55-3 and Cornwall 41-0. They proceeded to beat the cream of Britain's rugby pride. Links were established between New Zealand and Newton Abbot that saw return visits in 1924 and 1935. Tourists from South Africa and Australia also used Newton Abbot as a base.

Newton even gave the Australian RU team its nickname. Following the success of the 1905 Australian rugby league team, called 'the Kangaroos', to the North of England, their rugby union counterparts toured in 1907-08. When the Aussie rugby union visitors arrived in Newton they were called 'the Rabbits', an awful name for a warrior breed. During their Newton Abbot visit, the Aussies ran a competition in the local newspaper to find a new name. A number of entries were received and Mac Mahon, the Aussie captain, choose 'the Wallabies', a name which has stuck ever since.

Newton are thought to be the oldest club in Devon. A club associated with the town's Rifle Volunteer Corps existed in 1867. Six years later Newton Abbot RFC were one of Devon's best sides when they were officially formed by the Rev. Townsend Warner of Newton Abbot College from a number of smaller rugby sides. Newton tended to be overshadowed by the bigger Devonshire clubs, but reached the final of the first Devon Senior Cup in 1888, losing to Tiverton. Their forwards were regarded amongst the best in Devon. The club's rise continued through the 1890s when Newton Abbot fielded H.B. Tristram, the England full-back. Tristram, who played four times for England, taught Classics and Rugby at Newton College in the town. During Tristram's time at Newton College, their Old Boys were strong enough to have played Devonshire at Newton Abbot RFC. On the strength of this match five Newtonians were subsequently picked for Devon.

Newton Abbot's next international was Denys Dobson (1880-1916), who was a regular for Devon before winning six England caps in 1902-03. Dobson is best remembered for two incidents: On the 1904 Lions tour to Australia, during the game against Western Australia, Dobson was dismissed by the referee for bad language. The Lions captain disagreed with the referee and led his tourists from the field, but they went back on to the field 20 minutes later and completed the game. His other claim to fame is his death. He was, in fact, killed by a dead rhinoceros. He was a colonial civil servant in Nyasaland in 1916 when his party was attacked by a charging rhino. The beast was shot dead but was still moving when it collided with poor Dobson. Truly a great death. When the news reached London, a team-mate remarked: "Denys always had a weak hand-off". Dobson may have gone, but Newton Abbot were perhaps the best side in Devon at the time.

In 1909, they were the first English side to beat Pontypool for a couple of seasons. They had travelled all day by train to South Wales, then when Newton Abbot asked for their guarantee (usually about £20 to cover travelling expenses), they were greeted with a huge bag full of old pennies from a sour-faced Pontypool official. The bag of pennies weighed nearly half a hundredweight.

Alf Wood, a top-class three-quarter, began at Newton Abbot before moving to Bristol and Cheltenham, from where he won an England cap. He defected to Oldham NU in 1908 and had a long and distinguished career, including winning Great British NU honours.

The summer of 1912 saw Newton Abbot sucked into the furore surrounding rugby league. An attempt was made to form a 'Western League' to play under NU rules. Later that year, several South West clubs were suspended by the RFU for promoting the NU version of the game. Newton had come close to joining the NU, but a single vote on the committee decided to stay loyal to the RFU. Newton Abbot, along with Torquay Athletic and Devonport Albion, were found guilty of breaching the laws about professionalism, whilst three Newton members were banned. F. Valley and A.A. Phillips were suspended for knowingly permitting 'broken time payments', whilst a county player called Mallett was expelled for receiving broken time payments.

The 1920s were, Newton Abbot's golden era, when they were Devon Cup winners in 1922-23, 1923-24 and 1926-27. They were rough days. Newton and Torquay Athletic refused to play each other for years after one bad-tempered encounter. And, in 1922, Newton Abbot and Paignton had serious issues. One Newton player was sent off by the referee, who upset his teammates. A few choice comments were made to the official, who sent off the whole Newton team. One daily newspaper commented: "This behaviour doesn't happen with respectable clubs". But at least the All Blacks retained affection for the town.

The club has declined since those heady days, but has produced a number of top-class players. Stuart Morris played full-back for the Barbarians, South West Counties and the South East. Another full-back was Cliff Bowen, who played for Devon from 1953 to 1959 and was an integral part of the Devon side that won the 1957 County Championship, beating Yorkshire 12-3 in the final.

An unusual venture by Newton Abbot saw an interest in greyhound racing at the ground, but this venture proved to be no great money-spinner. In 1962, Newton created a few waves because they weren't included in new South West Merit Table.

Currently Newton Abbot are a leading club in National 3 and are noted as having "a monstrous pack".

PAIGNTON

UNTIL THE ARRIVAL of tourism, Paignton was simply a fishing village. Paignton RFC dates back to 1873, when the game was played on the sea front near the Prince Regent Hotel. The original pitch was surrounded by a cycle track where penny-farthing cycles peddled away.

In 1902, the rugby club moved to Queens Park, where they shared the facilities with archery and athletics. The site had originally been a salt marsh which the local council wanted to fill. The council solved their problems with the marsh by bribing locals to dump bags of soil in it. The locals were paid the princely sum of 1d (0.4p) for each bag.

Today the rugby club share with the Paignton Cricket club, which means that all rugby matches in April are played away so that the ground can be prepared for the summer game. There is a well-equipped clubroom and bar, but the most memorable aspect of Queens Park is its splendid entrance.

Although Torquay Athletic RFC is only a mile along the promenade, Paignton's big derby was with the fisherman of Brixham. Originally there was a railway between the two ports and it was not unusual for 2,000 spectators to head for Queens Park. Most arrived on the train or on foot, but some fishermen filled their trawlers with rugby fans and sailed around to Paignton harbour.

The best-known Paignton rugby players were locally born brothers Edmund and William Woodgate, who both had England trials. Edmund was a prop and William a flanker. William played for England in 1952 as a replacement for Wally Holmes.

At the outset of league rugby, Paignton were placed in Devon & Cornwall One, but managed to rise to South West One before falling back with three successive relegations.

(Thanks to Dave Ballinger)

PLYMOUTH ALBION
(Devonport Albion, Devon Albion)

"The only true amateur is the guy who finishes last in everything."
Chris Brasher

PLYMOUTH ALBION RFC is a rugby club with one of the most remarkable histories in the game. When the club was formed in 1876 as 'Albion FC', the city of Plymouth was the beating heart of the Royal Navy, which had a staff of over 100,000 in Victorian times. Albion FC was formed by three apprentices from the Royal Naval Dockyard. The Royal Navy was, at the time, going from being a sail-based navy to a heavyweight iron-clad force which ruled the waves until World War Two.

The club's first match was against Keyham RFC, but soon afterwards the two clubs merged with the new club adopting navy blue and white as their colours.

Their other big rivals were Plymouth RFC, who were formed in 1895, and RNEC (Royal Naval Engineering College) from Manadon. RNEC played at Crown Hill and drew its players from young trainee naval artificers.

Albion renamed themselves 'Devonport Albion' as their strength and fame grew. Initially they played on Devonport Park, but in 1887 they moved to Bladderley, where admission was charged at three old pence (1p), with a third going to the landowner.

The port grew rapidly in the final decade of the 19th Century and attracted workers from 'up country'. Welsh miners particularly abandoned the coal industry for Plymouth, where there was work in the dockyards.

Devonport Albion grew along with the city and welcomed the rugby-playing miners. The club became one of Britain's top clubs in the 1890s. During this period they lost only 64 of 370 matches, despite facing long rail journeys to most away matches. One of the highlights of the era was a mid-week home fixture with Oxford University, which attracted 19,000 spectators to the Rectory, their new home.

Season 1900–01 was the high-point of Albion's success. Only Swansea lowered their colours in a season where they won 36 of 39 fixtures and scored 808 points whilst only conceding 84. By this juncture, every member of Albion's First XV was either an international or Devon county player. Albion were such a force that in 1905 they were honoured with a visit from the All Blacks, who overcame them 21-3.

Despite the long distances from the heart of the Northern Union, Devonport Albion were vulnerable to their best players being poached by northern clubs. The irony was Albion were frequently accused of illegally enticing players to their ranks. As early as 1897, the Welsh RU had investigated how D.E.

Griffiths and D. Davies of Llanelli and Rhys Lewis and J. Jones of Aberavon had all simultaneously joined Albion. The RFU were not interested in Albion's activities for two reasons: the Welsh RU's blatant testimonial to Arthur Gould, which had upset the RFU, plus the Great Schism had deeply wounded the English game and opening a new conflict on the South West peninsula was ill-advised.

In turn, Leeds NU club had approached all Albion's best players to 'go north'. The problem intensified for Albion and they lost a number of their best players in 1912, which may have prompted some Albion officials to get involved in the unsuccessful attempt to start a Northern Union league in the South West.

In the years before World War One, Albion was one of the principal suppliers of players to both England and Wales. Cliff Bowen was regarded as the best three-quarter in the Home Counties. Elliot Vivyan (1879-1935) was the club's first English international. Vivyan was a draughtsman in the dockyard who kicked ten points against Ireland in 1904, which was then a record.

Herbert Gamlin, the greatest full-back of his era, played for Albion before joining Blackheath, where he won the first of his 15 England caps.

Devonport Albion 1906

James Peters, who had won fame in the Bristol area, moved to Plymouth in 1902 and was selected for Devon and England. He subsequently joined Barrow NU and St. Helens NU. He died in Plymouth in 1954. A curious fact is that Albion awarded Peters a testimonial on his retirement in contravention of the RFU's laws.

Walter Heppell (1872-1939), Samuel Howell Irvin (1880-1936) and George Dobbs (1884-1917) also made brief appearances for England, whilst W.A. Davies played three times for Wales. William Alonso Mills won eleven England caps between 1906 and 1908. A bulky flank-forward, Mills was an inspector of shipwrights by profession. R.Gilbert won three England caps before switching to the Northern Union.

Kaiser Wilhelm and the German Navy proved a larger opponent than the Northern Union as World War One marked a watershed for Devonport Albion. The Rectory Field was commandeered by the Navy in 1914 and retained by the senior service who had a wartime side.

The original Devonport club was reformed as 'Plymouth Albion' to denote the incorporation of Plymouth RFC. Using a pitch on Beacon Park, Albion recovered and produced six internationals during the 1920s. Frank Warren Sanders (1893-1953) from Newton Abbot won three England caps, Joseph Hanley (1901-1981) won seven England caps and was described as a "big lad", Charles Gummer played against France before going to study at Birmingham University and Edward E. Richards (1905-1982) won two England caps. Greater impact was made by E.R.B. Stanbury (1898-1968), who won 16 England caps in the Cove-Smith era before moving to Bristol. Later E.R.B. was a leading RFU administrator. Robert Henry 'Bert' Sparks (1899-1984) was a local man who worked as a chargehand in the dockyards and packed down with Stanbury in the front row of the 1928 England team.

Plymouth Albion had the honour of being the first British rugby team to play a USA rugby team. The Americans were en-route to the 1924 Olympics when 15-a-side rugby was part of the curriculum. The USA were "rough and ready", as befits converts from American football. They played several games in England to familiarise themselves with the game. Amazingly, the USA team won the Olympic title in a rough match which led the Olympic committee to drop rugby for seventy years. The Americans made an impression on the Plymouth locals, one of whom commented: "Their knowledge of the laws of the game is on par with their knowledge of good wine."

Albion remained a leading side in South West rugby until World War Two, but the conflict marked the end of naval power. The years after World War Two saw the Royal Navy diminish. It no longer needed huge dockyards and Plymouth declined as a port and employer of dockyard workers. Plymouth Albion also declined. They had to compete with Devonport Services RFC, who had the pick of those rugby players who had opted to do their national service in the navy. Albion also found they were competing for the best South West players with Bath and Bristol. The M5 motorway made the big 'up country' clubs accessible for players from Devon and Cornwall.

Roger Spurrell was a player comparable with many of the great pre-war names. "A bit of a character", Spurrell did three seasons at Albion before joining Bath and becoming a legend at the Rec.

Albion fought back. In 1973-74 they won the South West Merit Table and took the Devon Cup on six successive occasions between 1983 and 1988. But their best players headed east: David Trick (Bath), Will Jones (Gloucester & Wales), Andy Reid (Bodmin, Camborne, Bath, London Wasps and Scotland), Paul Ackford (Met Police, Harlequins & England), Julian

Plymouth Albion in action in 1920.

White (Leicester & England), Dan Ward-Smith (Leicester & England), Graham Dawe (Bath & England) and Trevor Woodman (Liskeard, Bath & England). All moved 'up country' to enhance their careers.

Some fine players stayed. Ray Ellis played for the Barbarians and with David Fuge clocked up a record 487 first team appearances between 1970 and 1985.

Albion abandoned Beacon Park in 2003 after 84 years to move to a modern serviceable ground at the Brickfields, a couple of hundred yards from the Rectory.

(Thanks to David Fuge)

SALCOMBE

THE SMALL PORT of Salcombe lies on the beautiful Devon coast some 20 miles east of Plymouth. Salcombe enjoyed great prosperity in the 19th century due to fruit importation and shipbuilding. The port declined in the 20th century and tourism has become the main industry.

Salcombe RFC was founded in 1888 by the Rev. William Dowglass, who had learnt the game at Trinity College, Dublin. He soon became their best player. Being a Salcombe rugby player was tough as the post-match bath was taken in the sea – a chilling prospect in mid-winter.

The side were originally known as the 'South Devon Savages' and were a tough bunch that protected their star player. One Salcombe player decided to put an end to Dowglass being targeted by unsporting opponents. He picked up an offender and threw him into a stagnant pond beside the pitch. That settled the matter for a while and Salcombe went on to win the match.

The new club had no trouble arranging a full fixture list with teams from Plymouth, Newton Abbot and Torquay. Early matches were played at East Portlemouth behind the Church. After the games the teams retuned to Salcombe by boats for liquid refreshment. As enthusiasm for the game increased, matches were arranged with Plymouth teams, notably the Ramblers and St. Budeaux, and also with Newton Abbot and Torquay sides. Kingsbridge followed suit and there was no difficulty in finding a full winter's fixture list. After moving from East Portlemouth, matches were first of all played at the Halfway Field (originally part of Maryknowle Farm and now part of Churchill Farm) and later at the top of Batson Hill in a walled field known as 'Paddlers Field' after 'Paddler' Hannaford, who kindly loaned it to the club at a nominal rental. Paddlers Field was the club's home until 1939.

After the Second World War, Salcombe RFC acquired two large fields between Raleigh and Camperdown Roads to be used as pitches. The ground was officially opened with a fixture between the club and a Devon XV containing five England internationals.

The scoring record for the new ground was set with a fixture between the club and Old Edwardians of Birmingham. The visitors included a young winger called Peter Jackson who went on to become the best winger of his day.

SIDMOUTH

"Sidmouth is not at all grand, but comfortable and cheerful."'
Grand Duchess Elena Vladimirovna of Russia (circa 1900)

THE SEASIDE TOWN of Sidmouth lies some nine miles north of Exmouth on the South Devon coast. Perhaps its greatest claim to fame is that it became a popular resort for the aristocracy in the late 19th Century. "Escaping from their debts" was a local joke. The town was once visited by Franz Liszt, the composer, who played the piano for a soiree.

Rugby emerged around this time. There are records of rugby being played intermittently in Sidmouth from the winter of 1863. A club with 30 to 40 members was formed using the 'London Rules' and practising on Forth Field. Interest waned and the club soon died out. Another rugby club reappeared in 1880 and played a wonderful fixture on Easter Monday, dubbed 'Sidmouth Abstainers v Non-Abstainers'. The teetotallers won an acrimonious encounter. How the abstainers celebrated their victory is not known.

Rugby had, therefore, been played in Sidmouth since 1863 but it was another 20 years before a club was formed by Bingley Gibbes Pullin, who had just qualified at St. Barts in London. Pullin had led St. Barts to win the Hospitals Cup. Their first match was on the 1st November 1884 away to Exeter, who, not surprisingly, won easily.

In 1890, Sidmouth joined the Devon RU and entered the Devon Junior Cup. They won the 1895 Junior Cup, defeating Ilfracombe. Victory in this competition brought qualification for the Devon Senior Cup, which they won by defeating Devonport Albion 'A'. The following season Sidmouth retained the title, defeating Totnes at Exeter.

This was a high-watermark and the club was unable to retain its high standards. Indeed, the club barely survived but still managed to be runners-up to Plymouth in the 1905 Senior Cup final.

In 1923, the club's ground at Blackmore Field was bought by a local benefactor to ensure its long-term availability to rugby. With their own ground, Sidmouth were able to become a 'gate-taking club' and able to attract the best 'up-country' sides in front of a thousand spectators. History repeated itself between the wars as Sidmouth won the Devon Senior Cup in 1929-30, but decline followed rapidly, induced by financial problems. The debts arose from buying the pitch at Blackmore Field and adding a clubhouse.

Sidmouth re-established itself after World War Two. The golden days returned in the 1950s with three players, Geoff Ryall, Stan Baker and Pat Brown, in the Devon side, plus a losing appearance in the 1952 Junior Cup final. In April 1953 the club persuaded the mighty Swansea team to visit the Blackmore. The All Whites won 16-0.

The Devon Senior Cup re-emerged in 1968, but it was a decade before Sidmouth made the final. They lost three consecutive finals: 28-13 to Exeter, 11-10 to Tavistock and the following year to arch-rivals Honiton by the same score.

The rugby club ranks amongst the county's best junior clubs and, although the Franz Liszts of this world no longer make a bee-line to Sidmouth, music still figures in the town's pastimes. The annual folk music festival is a huge earner; certainly for the rugby club, who lease out the pitch as a car park.

(Thanks to Tim O'Brien)

ST. LUKE'S COLLEGE, EXETER

ST. LUKE'S COLLEGE, Exeter existed for 120 years but was an important part of English rugby for only a quarter of its lifetime. It began life in 1860 as the Diocesan Training College, Exeter. Although rugby football was sweeping Britain, the college principal banned the game as dangerous. References to sport at the college until the 1930s focused on hockey, in which the trainee teachers gained a national reputation. The Thirties saw the emergence, as a pre-eminent sporting figure from the college in Sir Stanley Rous, who became President of FIFA and the secretary of the Football Association. J. Ford and A.A. Brown were the first St. Luke's rugby players to win representative honours when they played for Devon.

Post-1945 developments in education saw increasing emphasis on physical education and the demand for P.E. teachers grew. The Welsh connection proved the backbone of both St. Luke's and Devon rugby. The Devon county side ranked amongst England's best in 1949 and included three college players in Derrick Morgan, Keith Maddocks and Roy Williams. Soon, no Welsh international team was complete without such St. Luke's alumni as Brian Sparks, Roy Bish, Glyn John, Gareth Griffith and Bryn Meredith, who were amongst the best Welsh players of the post-war era.

St. Luke's were undefeated by any club from Devon or Cornwall for three years from 1952 to 1955. The most famous season of St. Luke's was in 1953-54 when they scored over 1,000 points, the only time a senior rugby club had passed that milestone. The Welsh connection remained into the 1960s when St. Luke's fielded ten Welshmen. The crowd sang 'Sosban Fach' in tribute.

TEIGNMOUTH

"A fashionable watering place."
Victorian Guide Book

TEIGNMOUTH IS A famous beauty spot set amongst the red cliffs of South Devon with spectacular views across the English Channel. Teignmouth RFC was formed in 1874 and is one of the oldest in the West Country. W. Harcourt Stile, a club member, was the first recorded secretary of the Devon RFU in 1885-86, and in that season two players, W. Harwood and J.B. Styles, represented the county. The club's first international was A. O'Neill, who won three England caps in 1902 whilst with Torquay Athletic. Until 1905, the club led a nomadic existence, but since then they have played at Bitton Park overlooking the River Teign.

Teignmouth figured in the futile attempt to set up a Northern Union in the South West. In 1913 the club (and many of South Devon's rugby clubs) went over to rugby league en-bloc. Teignmouth played Torbay, under NU rules, on the 1st February 1913, but lost 20-5. Like the whole episode, Teignmouth's interest quickly faded and no club of either code existed in the town until the summer of 1914, when club officials appeared before a RFU meeting to plead that a new club with new members wanted to re-join the RFU. With the Great War only weeks away, the RFU decided to defer the decision. Eventually reinstatement came in 1919.

The club took a big step forward in 1923 when it appointed a young player, Orace Tosio, as secretary. He found a continuous stream of good players, many of whom played for Devon, and one, Frank Davey, represented England in 1931. He also improved the fixture list so that many of the top clubs in England and Wales played on the ground. George Crediford, a local farmer, was a member of the committee for 40 years at this period.

In 1963 Teignmouth were the first English side to play a Spanish side when they beat Barcelona, the reigning Spanish champions.

The 'Teigns' have three teams and a Colts XV and two pitches. Besides meeting other West Country sides, they have visited Barcelona, Dublin, Jersey and Guernsey and play in London every year on the morning of an international match. The First XV had only two full-backs in the 20 years around the middle of the century – Billy Scourfield, who played up to 1952, and Graham Nicholson, who was top scorer for 12 seasons.

Patrick Chenery began at Teignmouth before moving to Exeter and playing in France.

Mike Davis

The 1960s and 1970s saw England and Scotland benefitting from the connection to St. Luke's. Mike Davis, Graham Ansell, Peter Knight, Neil Bennett, Mike Rafter, Mike Slemen and John Scott represented England and Alan Friell became a Scotland regular.

Things came to a temporary halt in 1966 when all the college's fixtures had to be cancelled due to a skin infection epidemic breaking out.

A bigger threat was the emergence of a rival in the East Midlands, Loughborough Colleges, who could also produce great young rugby players. The 200 miles between Exeter and Loughborough provided a major obstacle in the days before motorways. The first match was in 1959 and within a decade it was the biggest student match outside Oxbridge. It became tagged the 'Apotheosis of Redbrick Rugby' and was so popular that matches were played at Old Deer Park or the Stoop.

Loughborough Colleges had grown from modest roots to become part of the brave new world of science; by contrast, St. Luke's College was suffering because the need for schoolteachers was in decline. In 1975, an announcement was made that St. Luke's was to merge with Exeter University in a money-saving measure. The merger finally happened in 1981, but not before St. Luke's played a match against an International XV including seven Lions.

TIVERTON

THE LOVELY DEVONSHIRE town of Tiverton was famous for lace-making. The lace industry was brought by the Heathcoat-Amory family, who had factories in the East Midlands but suffered industrial problems which led them to move to Tiverton. When the Heathcoat-Amorys arrived, the town was already famous for Blundells School, which was one of the leading public schools in Devon. Blundells had adopted the 'Rugby Rules' in 1870 in preference to their own football laws. Records show that schoolmasters played alongside the students for Blundells and also turned out for Tiverton RFC on a Saturday.

It was during the 1880s that Tivvy became one of the top clubs in the region. Not everything went well, as the Tiverton Gazette reported in January, 1881: "On Saturday last a match had been arranged to come off between the second fifteens of the Taunton Railway Club and the Tiverton Club, in the Cricket Field. The home team fell in and arranged themselves at the time appointed but, for some unexplained reason, the Taunton men failed to put in an appearance, and also neglected to communicate with their opponents. Much dissatisfaction was felt at this apparent lack of courtesy and after awaiting the arrival of the visitors half an hour, the Tiverton men divided themselves and played a practice match."

A 'Looker-on' wrote: "Sir, I wish to make an enquiry through your columns, which perhaps some reader may be able to answer for me. I was attracted on Saturday last to an expected football match in the Cricket Field, but, owing to the non-arrival of the opposing team, did not come off. Neither of the Officers of the Tiverton Club was on the ground, the team even being without a captain; and what I wish to know, therefore, is whether the whole affair was not a hoax? At any rate it appeared so to a good many of those who were present."

On 10th April, 1886, Tiverton defeated Exeter to win the Devon Challenge Cup (a forerunner of the Devon Senior Cup) at Polsloe Park, by two tries to nil. The club still retains the trophy.

The most famous Tiverton player of the 1880s was Dr. Arthur Roberts St Leger Pagan, a three-quarter who played for England against Ireland at Lansdowne Road in 1887. The list of Tiverton players representing Devon between 1875 and 1889 reads: B. Baddeley, H. Barnes, C. Collier, J. Collier, D. Dryden, A. Pagan, F. Greatwood, F. Herring, E. Pedler, J. Pedler, F. Pethick, Templar and H. Wallis.

A second club existed in the town in the 1890s with the emergence of Heathcoat RFC, who operated from the lace factory owned by the Heathcoat-Amory family.

Between the wars, Tiverton retained its fixture list. In 1939, Tiverton even recorded a rare victory over mighty Exeter, 6-0.

Tiverton resumed after the war in 1946 with a match against Paignton. They began colts rugby in the early 1950s and were rewarded with the first ever Devon Colts Cup in 1959. The colts were able to produce a number of England colts students: Mike Wood (England Schools), Paul Loader and John Roberts (England Students)

Since 1987 Tiverton have played in the Western Counties League.

TORQUAY ATHLETIC

'The Tics'

TORQUAY ATHLETIC EMERGED in 1886 from a merger of two small Torbay clubs: Ellacombe RFC and Excelsior FC. The new club was grandly known as 'Torquay Amateur Athletic Cricket and Football Club'. The first match took place at Plainmoor on the 30th October 1886 against St. Sidwell FC of Exeter, after which Plainmoor was lost to rugby. In 1904 the Torquay Recreation Ground Company, 'the Rec', became home to the rugby club and also other sports.

Although Torquay was a popular holiday resort, rugby in the resort was low profile, with only the annual derby against Devonport Albion meriting a mention in the national newspapers of the 1890s, although the Tics fielded the Devonshire half-backs Johnnie Davies and J. Chapman. Davies and teammate Ginger Brooking played in the 1892 South v North England trial.

Torquay benefitted greatly from the 1895 Great Schism because players from unfashionable counties, such as Devon, were selected for England to replace the NU defectors. In 1901 A. O'Neill became the first Athletic player to be selected for England. He won three caps in the forwards.

Despite their remoteness, Athletic attracted up-country sides at Easter. Amongst the visitors were top sides from Yorkshire, who took a liking to the Tics' talent, which began a curious migration from Torquay to the north, or more precisely the Northern Union. It began in 1899 when Frank Harry joined Broughton Rangers; he eventually achieved the double of playing cricket and rugby league for Lancashire. The Tics indignation at his departure was interesting because the Tics were themselves under suspicion of illicit recruiting methods. In 1899 an RFU enquiry investigated Torquay Athletic for poaching Welsh players. An Athletic official was caught red-handed trying to recruit players from the Principality and, consequently, Athletic were suspended from playing for two months. Torquay were also accused of poaching players from local rivals. Fees of £20 were rumoured to have been offered by Athletic to players from rival clubs.

In 1912, the Northern Union tried to become established in South Devon. The Devon RFU suspended officials from seven Devonshire clubs, including Billy White of Torquay. The unseemly spectre of clubs and officials conducting covert negotiations with players, and even the Northern Union, dragged on for several years until World War One intervened. Some of the expelled officials and players formed Torquay Northern RL club. Torquay Northern played St. Helens RLFC in front of 3,000 spectators at Queens Park. During Torquay Northern's brief time, the professional side even tried to share the Recreation Ground with their amateur rivals.

After World War One, the amateur RFU club restarted by hosting the January 1919 United Services v All Blacks match, the latter winning 9-0. The inter-war years were the golden era for Torquay Athletic, but they began badly when their best player, Ernie Knapman, an outstanding full-back, moved to Oldham NUFC where he won a Great Britain cap and played 208 times for his new employers. Torquay were disappointed to lose him, but nevertheless they were one of the best clubs in Britain, winning 97 of 120 games between 1926 and 1929.

A rare witness to this era is Freddie Friend, who joined Torquay in 1936 from Brixham. Freddie recalled that the Torquay RFC team did not contain a single local. The majority of the team were Welsh and the remainder were from Brixham, Paignton and Teignmouth, clubs that acted as feeder clubs – even the trainer, Charlie Pratt, was an ex-Everton footballer who had won an English championship medal with Everton in 1907. Pratt, like many others, had a 'soft job' with the council.

It was said that Torquay would never be a good side again in times of full employment. V. 'Rocker' Twose was an England trialist who moved from Wellington in Somerset, but most of the best players were from South Wales, earning Athletic the nickname 'Torquay Welsh'. In 1927 Gwyn Richards, the great Cardiff and Welsh fly-half, moved to Torquay. Richards was followed by Welsh internationals Ivor Thomas, Tommy Schofield, Ivor Bennett, and Bobby Delahey. Schofield had the honour of being the first Welshman playing outside Wales (London Welsh and Oxbridge excluded) to be capped by Wales. Delahay was the Tics captain for eight successive years and led the club to victory over Lancashire, who were on tour, in 1930.

Freddie Friend recalls: "My first skipper was Bobby Delahey, who won 17 Welsh caps at scrum-half. He played for Bridgend and Cardiff before joining Torquay in 1929 along with Gwyn Richards at outside-half. They came to Torquay because of

Tommy Schofield

the unemployment in Wales. They all worked for Vanstones Building Company. Others who worked for Vanstones were Ivor Thomas from Aberavon, a full-back, and Tom Schofield. The recreation ground was packed for every match. You couldn't get a seat in the grandstand that held 1400 spectators. We had a team full of Welsh internationals. Bobby Delahey was one of the best scrum-halves of the era. You have got to understand, life in Wales was terrible with all the unemployment. People, like the Vanstones or the Torquay Committee, found them jobs on the farms or building houses. Torquay Athletic and the Devon RFU, were run by Billy White from Torquay, who was in charge of local coal distribution and I'm sure he found jobs for a few of the lads."

Freddie made his Torquay debut against Bath without having met any of his teammates before the match. They had a First XV squad of 21 – of which nine were Welshmen and they were all outstanding or great players.

Freddie recalls: "There were four more Welshmen in the Second XV. We were known as Torquay Welsh. I played for 18 seasons without once losing my place and was captain for three seasons. I ended at 36. Despite the Second World War, I played sixteen times for the county. I lost seven seasons with being in the Forces, but played for United Services against the New Zealand and South African Forces. The average crowd for the United Services matches was 2,000. The Tics played in front of bigger crowds, up to 6,000, in the days before television. One game I have never forgotten was when every seat in the West stand was taken. The press made a lot of that. It was in March 1939 against Weston Super Mare and we took away their unbeaten home record. They boasted that they would get revenge when they came to our ground. The match at the Rec was played on a Wednesday evening and all my family came, even my mother went and I found her a seat. There were 5,000 there. It was the best I ever played for Torquay as a flanker. I received everything I expected from the Weston pack but we won 17–3. Life was different in the 1930s, the Rec was council property. Travel was always by coach. Other clubs were the same. I remember one trip to Redruth where we had a cooked meal in a restaurant by Redruth station and stopped at Liskeard on the way back. Two-thirds of our fixtures were at home. Our longest away games were Redruth, Bath, Weston Super Mare and Barnstaple. Redruth was the most hostile ground. It really could be 'Hell Fire Corner' for visiting teams."

Freddie attributes Torquay's subsequent decline to the breaking of the links with South Wales and the gradual drifting off home by players like Bob Delahey. The decline was also assisted when Gwyn Richards, Ivor Thomas and Tom Schofield all moved to Huddersfield RLFC and Rocker Twose went to Wigan RLFC.

Results were back to their best by the late 1930s when Jimmy Merchant of Torquay was the best scrum-half in the South West and one of half a dozen Tics in the Devon side. 1938-39 was the best season in the club's history with one defeat in 36 matches.

1939 saw the unluckiest ever visiting team at the Rec. On September 2nd the Australian arrived in Torquay with a full list of matches just 12 hours before World War Two was declared. The visitors had their photo taken at the Rec, visited London and went home again – undefeated. P0 W0 D0 L0.

Torquay Athletic in 1947 with Fred Friend on the front row on the left.

Torquay Athletic revived in 1946 but soon lost Ivor Edwards to Salford RLFC, but the club found a new Welsh star in Roy Bish, who was studying at St. Luke's College, Exeter.

In 1952 one of their finest servants hung up his boots: Freddie Friend retired and took up refereeing.

Torquay struggled in the mid-1950s, which led to a decline in gates. The club fought back by organising the Torquay International Rugby Festival, which kicked off in 1959 with Athletic v Milan.

Another witness to Torquay's history is Dave Godfrey, who made his Torquay debut in February 1960 against Penzance & Newlyn. Dave remembers the golden era for Athletic from 1958 to 1963 when it hosted festival week every September when top-class sides from home and abroad travelled to Torquay to complete their preparation for the new season. Leicester Tigers, Lansdowne of Ireland, Wasps, Bordeaux, plus sides from Italy and Zimbabwe played in the festival.

Torquay had great seasons, aside from the festival, but found the downside was that visiting teams who had suffered demoralising defeats tended to drift off after matches and didn't buy enough alcohol. The Tics were encouraged to adopt an unofficial policy of trying to win but keeping the opposition in the game. The opposition felt satisfied with only just losing and spent more money in the club bar.

Relations with the RFU were mixed. The festival was a great success, but the RFU took a dim view and accused the seaside club of undermining established club fixtures. But during the big freeze of 1963, the RFU could find nowhere to play their trial match until the secretary of Torquay rang Twickenham to say the Rec was playable and available. England took up Torquay's offer.

Around this time, Torquay fielded both an Irish and England international. Frank Wilson of Ireland moved to the area with a teaching appointment and played for two seasons, and local lad Mike Davis, joined Athletic as a teenager and developed into a top-class lock-forward, winning 16 England caps. Mike had an unusual background for a rugby forward: his mother was a hairdresser to the stars who played summer seasons in the resort. Mike lived down his connection with Gracie Fields to win a reputation as an unspectacular player who did the hard work and rarely allowed himself to waste time by making spectacular breaks. His career was crowned by coaching England to the 1979-80 Grand Slam.

Davis apart, Athletic were struggling and attendances were modest. They kept an excellent fixture list, but the playing side was a shadow of pre-war years. In a reversal of earlier times, Torquay's best player, John Widdicombe, left Torquay to move to South Wales with Newport.

Torquay began their league rugby in South West One, which meant swapping a fixture list with top-class up-country sides for unfamiliar names. The club continued to struggle, despite the services of fine servants such as Kevin Butterworth, who made 500 appearances for Athletic. The best player to emerge in recent times was hooker Lee Mears, who moved to Bath and became an England regular.

(Thanks to Angus Fraser, Dave Godfrey and Freddie Friend)

CHAPTER EIGHTEEN

SOMERSET & GLOUCESTERSHIRE

SOMERSET

RUGBY WAS POPULAR in West Somerset from the 1870s when clubs existed in Minehead, Wiveliscombe, Wellington and Porlock. The County Union was formed on the 7th September 1882 at the Clarence Hotel in Bridgwater and appointed a selection committee of Henry Fox of Wellington and Froude Hancock of Wiveliscombe.

In 1889, the touring Maoris recorded that the Somerset county side was second only to Yorkshire in rugby prowess, but tried to drop out of fixtures in the South West because there was more gate money on offer in the north. The RFU took a dim view and insisted the tourists fulfil their fixtures.

Somerset were county champions in 1923 and runners-up in 1935, 1939 and 1984.

GLOUCESTERSHIRE

GLOUCESTERSHIRE IS A county apart from the rest of England as it differs in terrain from the middle-class counties, such as Worcestershire, Warwickshire and Dorset that surround it. It has a rugged upland quality that is reflected in its rugby. There are spectacular hillsides and a down-to-earth approach to farming. It has some of the most prosperous areas of England, where royalty and the rich live, and it has great cities, such as Bristol and Bath, but it is also has a working class ethos, enshrined in parts of Gloucester and the Forest of Dean. It has been famous for rugby since 1881, when the county defeated a Welsh XV.

The Gloucestershire Union was formed in 1878 by J.D. Miller (Clifton) and J.F.Brown (Gloucester). They circulated a notice that a meeting was being held at the Bell Hotel, Gloucester. Only five clubs were contacted: Cirencester, Cheltenham, Gloucester, Stroud and Rockleaze. Miller brought two other representatives for Clifton. The Bristolians were from a city that originally lay in two counties: Gloucestershire and Somerset. The areas to the west of the River Avon are Somerset, whilst Gloucestershire claimed the rest.

Gloucestershire was heavily dependent on the strong clubs in Clifton and Gloucester, which enabled it to win 15 of 17 inter-county matches over its first five seasons. It didn't last, as they struggled throughout the late 1880s, but were revitalised by Hubert Boughton of Gloucester. The RFU were reluctant to give the county full county status, but in 1898 Gloucestershire were recognised as a separate entity and subsequently won the South West Division.

In 1902 Gloucestershire reached the County final, but lost to Durham. However, in 1910 they were County Champions with a team that included seven England internationals. They were now established as a major county and repeated the championship win twice more in the next decade. Arthur Hall was the outstanding player. He began as a scrum-half and partnered Adrian Stoop in the 1911 England trial, but later switched to the pack and became a great forward. Hall never made the England team, but won 44 county caps.

Gloucestershire rugby is very unusual in being composed of independent 'states' or 'combinations'. There are five combinations in the county: Bath, Cheltenham, Gloucester, Stroud and the Forest of Dean. They look after junior rugby in their area.

ASHLEY DOWN

THE FORMATION OF Ashley Down RFC is given as 1931, but two other clubs of that name had previously existed. An Ashley Down Old Boys side had played before World War One and had merged with Bishopston RFC. A second side was founded in 1921. However, a decade later is accepted as the inauguration of the club by ex-pupils of Ashley Down School.

In 1954, Ashley Down made the local papers after an unusual incident in a home match against Whitehall RFC. A maul occurred under the Ashley posts and caused a melee to form around the goal posts. The activity caused the crossbar to become dislodged. Play had to stop to discuss what to do next. As no one could replace the cross bar, the two captains and the referee agreed to guess if goal kicks had crossed the notional crossbar.

In 1965 and 1966, Ashley went twelve months unbeaten. Around this time, they produced an unusual international in fly-half Mervyn Beszat, who represented Mauritius at rugby.

In 2012 they were relegated from Gloucester One.

AVONMOUTH OLD BOYS

AVONMOUTH OLD BOYS RFC were the former pupils of Avonmouth and Portway Schools. The rugby club was founded in 1897 and described as "a vigorous side" in early newspaper reports.

Their best players of the 1930s were Bert McDonald, who played 300 matches for Bristol and was a Scotland trialist, Billy Wring, an England trialist and legend for the city club, and Derek Robinson, who wrote some excellent books on rugby. He played for Avonmouth and London Scottish before moving to the USA and founding Manhattan RFC.

Avonmouth OBs played at Weston Town Lane, but they moved to Barracks Lane in 1985. The club currently play in SW1 West. From 2003 to 2013 the club were coached by Wayne Hone, who is one of Bristol's best recent players. The best-known players produced by the club in recent years are Mike Rhodes, who played for Bristol, and Harry Hone, who moved to Moseley in 2014.

AVONVALE

AVONVALE ARE THE oldest junior club in the Bath Combination with a continuous history. The first reference to the club comes on 17th November 1883 with a game between Batheaston (later Avonvale) and Victoria FC. The honours went to the latter club, as they did for the return match two months later. The earliest pitch was on the Box Road with the Crown Inn acting as headquarters.

The club became Avonvale in 1890 – a name it retained for eleven years before opting for 'Batheaston & District FC' and then reverting back to Avonvale in 1919.

The team's form fluctuated in the 1890s with season 1896-97 the high point with one defeat in 20 matches. The following year, the first international to wear Avonvale colours emerged

in Norman Biggs, who had been the youngest ever Welsh international in 1888 at 17 years of age. After winning eight Welsh caps, Biggs played for Bath and Avonvale. He was killed by a poisoned arrow during a native attack in Nigeria in1908.

Before World War One, Avonvale were a good side and several of their best players migrated to the Bath club, notably Sam Neale and Mike Harding.

The Twenties were roaring for Avonvale with excellent results and attendances, including only 14 defeats in 78 games between 1922 and 1927. The 1926-27 season saw only 23 points conceded, including only one try, but the following decade was hard as the Great Depression hit the area badly. Avonvale and other Bath junior clubs struggled as players had priorities other than rugby.

At this time Avonvale produced its finest player, Norman Matthews, who played 43 times for Somerset, had five England trials and was first reserve when R.H.W. Sparks cried off on the morning of the 1930 Wales v England match. Sadly for Matthews, Sam Tucker, the ex-England captain, was called up and flown to Cardiff. Matthews was one of four brothers who played for Avonvale. Later, Roy Harris came close to major honours whilst with Bath and Somerset and was an England trialist.

The post-war years saw Avonvale continue to struggle, but in 1951 they managed to buy an old RAF hut to act as a clubhouse. In 1966 the local council wanted the land and ordered the hut to be vacated. They did, however, approve the construction of a new clubhouse on the Recreation Ground, which was opened in May 1971. By this time, the club was running four sides.

In 2008 the club celebrated its 125th anniversary.

BARTON HILL OLD BOYS

'The Barts'

BARTON HILL RFC was formed in 1908 by Billy Harris, a teacher at Kingswood GS and Barton Hill School in Bristol and the club drew their players from these schools for many decades.

Barton Hill School was demolished to build council flats – a very special block of council flats: Nelson Mandela House – the home of 'Del Boy and Rodney' of the TV series 'Only Fools and Horses'. Although set in East London, the outdoor sequences were filmed in Bristol.

Reports from the early 20th Century say that the original Barton Hill OB RFC possessed a huge pack that powered the club to a three-year undefeated run, which attracted huge crowds by the standards of Bristol junior rugby. There are records of Barton Hill attracting gates of over 6,000 to Eastville Park for their home games. But conditions for the players were primitive: they got changed at Bowerings factory, where the post-match 'bath' meant both teams sharing a large earthenware bread pan.

After World War Two, the club was restarted by Les Davey and Fred Pascoe, who relied on the Kingswood connection. The best player of the era was Gordon Allen, who propped for Bristol in the 1950s. Bob Hesford from Fleetwood joined the club in the 1980s before progressing to Bristol and winning eight England caps. He later returned to Barton Hill as coach. More recently, Ian Pattern began with Barton and moved to Bristol.

Currently Barts are in Western Counties West.

(Thanks to John Rigby)

BATH

"It is said that supporters of Bristol and Gloucester have nothing in common. This is not true. They actually agree on a mutual antipathy to Bath."

Alan Williams

THE ANCIENT CITY of Bath is as famous for its rugby in the 21st Century as it is for its fabulous Roman ruins. The rugby club is one of the oldest clubs in the game, as it was formed in 1865 as 'Bath Zouaves', who took their name from the Zouaves, legendary African warriors. Amongst the founder members was Frank d'Aguilar, an army officer who later played for England.

Herbert Fuller of Bath set a record of six appearances for Cambridge in the Varsity Match. Students were only meant to spend three years at university, even in the 1880s. Fuller overstayed his welcome, enjoyed his rugby, but obliged the university authorities to introduce a three-year limit on players competing in Varsity matches.

Frank Scone was Bath's second international in 1890. Scone was one of many young players who began with local junior clubs and gravitated to the city club. There were rumours that Bath didn't fully embrace the amateur ethos, which was confirmed by their gift of a full set of furniture, worth £50 (a handsome sum in those days), to Scone when he retired in 1899. It was little wonder that the Northern Union clubs repeatedly wrote to the RFU pointing out the "strange remuneration" system that existed at some RFU clubs.

Another source of criticism against Bath was an annual invitation match where the city club played against a junior clubs XV from the city's other clubs. The junior clubs complained that the match was little more than blatant poaching. Not that Bath had much to offer aspiring players because the coffers were empty by 1900. The cause of the financial problems was renting a pitch at the Recreation Ground in the heart of the city, which had proved a disaster because flooding meant matches were continually postponed. Previously the club had played on Lambridge Marshes and Kensington Meadows. Salvation came with the formation of the Bath and District Combination, with the aim of improving the standard of local rugby. The Combination was to provide Bath with a steady stream of talent.

Frederick Belsen was a member of the 1899 British Isles team to Australia. He never returned to Bath, preferring to stay 'down under'. Four years later, R.J. Rogers was selected for the British Isles on the strength of sound performances for Bath and Somerset. Harry Shewring had been an international at Bristol until he retired; he caused some surprise when he came out of retirement and joined arch rivals Bath. In the same era, Tom

White from Bridgwater was capped by England whilst with Bath. He defected to Oldham NU, for whom he played 224 matches before World War One. During the War, he played for the British Army against the New Zealanders at rugby union.

In 1907 winger Vincent Coates joined Bath. Coates (1889-1934) had only one season of international rugby, but scored a record six tries for England. He served in World War One with the Royal Medical Corps, was mentioned in despatches and won the Military Cross on the Somme battlefield in 1916.

The years between the wars began badly for Bath as they lacked experienced players. They even fell out with the county in August 1922 and disaffiliated from the Somerset RU after a dispute. The Honorary Secretary said, "If a player wants to be a member of the SRU, he can join as an individual."

Their most notable player of the era was Arnold Ridley (1896-1984), who didn't win any great honours on the rugby field as a slimly-built winger for Bath, but made a name for himself on the stage. After a distinguished military career, he wrote a play called 'The Ghost Train', which became one of the most successful plays of the 20th Century. Despite this success, Ridley carried on as a journeyman stage actor until television closed the repertory theatres. In the 1960s Ridley took a small part in a new TV series and hit the jackpot for a second time. He played the part of Private Godfrey in 'Dad's Army' for 15 years and became an integral part of one of the greatest comedy series of all time. Ridley was Bath's match secretary and President for some years.

In the 1930s, Bath produced four internationals in Gordon Gregory, Donald Crichton-Miller, Henry Rew and Ron Gerrard. Rew was small by international standards and died tragically whilst serving in the western desert. He was taking the surrender of an Italian unit when an Italian soldier broke ranks and shot him. Gerrard was born in Hong Kong but attended Taunton School, where he excelled at rugby, athletics and cricket. In 1929, he was selected by Somerset to play cricket as a 16-year-old schoolboy. On the rugby field, he could play anywhere in the backs. Freddie Friend of Torquay Athletic recalls making his debut against Bath with the great Ron Gerrard at centre: "Gerrard wasn't particularly big, but he was stocky and very skilful with tremendous elusiveness when you tried to tackle him."

Gerrard made his debut for Somerset against Gloucestershire at Kingsholm and was comprehensively flattened the first time he went near the ball. He got up and played on as if nothing had happened. Eventually, he appeared 42 times for Somerset from 1930 to 1939 and also played 14 times for England. He enjoyed great success, but was eventually dropped by England because he had put on weight and lost his famous speed. The arrival of the 1936 All Blacks found a slimmer Gerrard, who earned an England recall for the Obolensky match. England won, in no small part due to Gerrard's bravery in tackling. Gerrard stepped down from England duty at the end of that season, although he carried on his association with Bath.

Gerrard was decorated for his bravery during the Battle of El Alamein in 1942, but was killed by a landmine shortly after the battle. After his death, he was commemorated by a scholarship at Taunton school and his widow was the first vice-president of Bath.

After World War Two, Bath became a focal point for South West rugby as the arrival of motorways led to increasing mobility. Players from Devon and Cornwall could travel 'up country' and play for the club. Indeed, in 1952 Bath were criticised for recruiting players from the region, including Bristol-based players.

Their most famous recruit was John Kendall-Carpenter, who began with Redruth. Kendall-Carpenter was perhaps the last of the old style forwards who could play anywhere in the pack. He was a schoolmaster by profession, which showed at times. During the 1950s a Bath winger, Ray Farnham, broke clear of the Gloucester defence when a Gloucester fan leapt the barrier and made a perfect tackle to prevent a try. The referee was nonplussed and could only award a scrum. John Kendal-Carpenter, as Bath's captain, was livid. He walked off the pitch and into the grandstand, grabbed the microphone from the announcer and gave the crowd a schoolmasterly dressing down.

Alec Lewis was a Bath and England forward, despite having suffered a serious foot injury during World War Two. He recovered to play soccer for Swindon Town and rugby for England. Other famous Bath players of the era were Laurie Rimmer, Ian Beer and Geoff Frankcom.

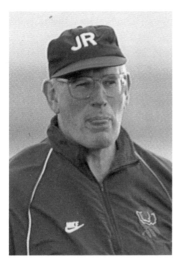

Jack Rowell

It was the 1970s when Bath became a force outside their normal powerbase of the South West. They were previously seen as behind the best nationally because they tried too hard to encourage running rugby. This all changed with the arrival of Jack Rowell from the north east. Rowell had been part of the Gosforth success story. Tall and wiry, Jack was a long way from the traditional view of what English rugby should be. The amateur ethos of 'play the game and ignore the scoreboard' wasn't Jack's way at all. Outside of rugby, he was a successful manager and used the same principles at the Rec. He preached organisation and discipline in the same way that he applied it to the workplace.

Bath recognised that the National Knockout Cup was England's foremost (actually only) national competition in the days before leagues arrived. They won the Cup five times in the 1980s. They attracted huge gates and, more importantly, they became the club that the best English players wanted to join. It was a team of stars: Andy Robinson, Roger Spurrell, Gareth Chilcott, Simon Halliday, David Sole, David Egerton, Nigel Redman, John Horton, Phil De Glanville, Stuart Barnes, Tony Swift, Jon Callard, John Hall, and Jonathan Webb were amongst the best players in the Northern Hemisphere. Rowell also had the best coaching talent on the sidelines in Tom Hudson, Dave Robson and Brian Ashton. Later Jack, Brian Ashton and Andy Robinson would be England's Head Coaches.

Bath were perfectly placed in 1987 when league rugby arrived and were Division One Champions on four occasions in the first six seasons. Rowell departed after 15 years to take over as England coach, but Bath found another saviour in successful businessman Andrew Brownsword, who established Bath as a professional entity. He pumped millions into his club, but other clubs could equal their budget and the good times ebbed away.

Bath's lowest point came after the lifting of the ban on Rugby League players playing union. They played Wigan, the Rugby League giants, in two matches. The rugby league lads won comprehensively.

Bath seemed to be sliding out of the limelight when, in 1998, they won the European Cup, which had become the apex of club rugby in the Northern Hemisphere. They beat the French side Brive 19-18 thanks to the boot of veteran Jon Callard, but it was a flash in the pan and the club plunged to the foot of the Premier League. There was consternation when a merger was floated of Bath and their ancient rivals Bristol. It did not come to pass.

They bounced back in the 2000s with a new crop of stars, such as Steve Borthwick, Mike Catt, Mike Tindall, Iain Balshaw and Kevin Maggs, who were all top-class internationals. Later they recruited more England internationals in Dave Attwood, David Wilson and Lee Mears. Catt proved amazingly durable as he kept his place for Bath and England for a decade. In 2006 he was the Premiership Player of the Year and was also the oldest player to play in the top division.

Mike Catt

In 2003, Bath had a brush with the relegation zone, but they survived to reach the Premiership play-off the following season.

The club were desperate to upgrade the Rec, but the complicated nature of their tenancy on city land meant years of wrangling which never seemed to move the matter forward.

In 2009, Brownsword sold the club to Bruce Craig which sparked an era of change as Ian McGeechan was brought in to help long-serving coach Steve Meehan. Bath brought in a series of overseas players, notably Butch James (South Africa) and Shantayne Hape (New Zealand). In recent time Bath have usually been contenders for the premiership play-offs.

BERRY HILL

"Not the easiest place to visit."
Visiting captain

THE FOREST OF Dean is famous for its mines and rugby. As long ago as 1893 there were 14 rugby clubs in the Forest. Most of the lads from Berry Hill played for nearby Coleford until Berry Hill RUFC was formed in 1893. Coleford lost players, but Bream RUFC felt more aggrieved as Berry Hill's first fixture was away to Monmouth. The opposition were persuaded by Berry Hill to drop Bream because Bream were 'excessively robust' and to give Berry Hill the fixture. Bream were not amused.

The early days of Berry Hill were difficult when an economic depression gripped the mining industry in the 1900s. The club relied heavily on miners for its players and hard times meant that the club and its members struggled. Things were so bad that Cinderford, the top local club, played Berry Hill in a 'benefit match' to raise money for their neighbours.

The mid-1920s saw Berry Hill throwing off their problems and emerging as the best junior side in the Forest by winning their local league, the Forest of Dean Combination, on two occasions. Sadly, the miners' strike of 1926 devastated the area. The only good thing to emerge was that the strikers used their ample spare time to lay out a new rugby pitch at Berry Hill on the Red Triangle Recreation Ground. It was, however, another two years before the pitch was opened with a game against mighty Gloucester. The Cherry and Whites won 21-10.

Berry produced several top-class players around this time, notably K. Salmon, who was a Wales trialist in 1930, and Milsom Short, who appeared for Gloucester and the county before 'going north' to join Hull and Oldham rugby league clubs. It was another 30 years before Berry contributed further to English honours when one of their ex-players, Mike Short, was selected for an England trial whilst with the Metropolitan Police.

The 1950s saw the club's most famous player in his prime. Denis Potter was a modest rugby player, but proved one of the finest playwrights of the 20th century, writing TV plays such as 'Pennies from Heaven' and 'The Singing Detective'. Despite moving to London, Potter kept a lifelong interest in his local club.

Berry Hill were a serious player in local junior rugby, but it was the reinstatement of the Gloucestershire County Cup in 1970 that catapulted them to national prominence. The top South West clubs, such as Bristol and Gloucester, had dominated the original County Cup back in the 1900s, but declined to get involved when the competition was revived. Berry Hill were happy to fill the void. They were County Cup champions in 1983-84, beating Lydney, 1984-85, beating Coney Hill, 1986-87, overcoming Gordon League, and 1988-89, beating Drybrook. They were also runners-up on five occasions.

Victory in the County Cup brought automatic entry to the new National Knockout Cup and the precious chance to meet some of the game's thoroughbreds. In 1984, Berry fought their way through the early rounds to a meeting with Bath, where they were defeated by 24-3. Three years later, the cup run culminated in a losing Fourth Round tie with Harlequins. The following year Berry lost to London Irish at the same stage. In 1989, they beat mighty London Scottish 15-12 in the cup, which helped them win the title of Junior Club of the Year. Berry Hill can also lay claim to having knocked London Welsh out of the National Cup in consecutive years.

It is an accepted fact that Berry Hill has traditionally been a feeder club for Gloucester. In 1984 the England team included four ex-Berry Hill men: Malcolm Preedy, Mike Teague, Steve Mills and John Fidler.

They left behind their junior club days when they won the South West One title in 1993 and were promoted to National League Four, to become the only village side to play at the highest level. At this time, the club had a famous coach in Phil Blakeway, the England and Lions prop forward. Less famous was Julian Horrobin, who set the world record for the fastest ever try. On 22nd November 1990 Horrobin touched down after seven seconds for the club against Cheltenham North.

Berry Hill remain a formidable cup side. They have reached the semi-finals of both the Senior Vase and Intermediate Cup in recent seasons. Their league status has usually revolved around South West One.

BISHOPSTON

BISHOPSTON IS A suburb of North Bristol based around the parishes of Horfield, Stapleton and St Paul's. Originally the area attracted wealthy business people who wanted to escape the smog of the city centre. It took its name from a dispute over land rights between the Vicar of Horfield and the Bishop of Gloucester and Bristol. Rank won out and the Bishop got the land rents and the name. The decision led to a rapid growth in building in the parish.

Bishopston RFC joined the local Bristol Combination. The Club were, however, no major institution as selection meetings were held in the open air, under a gas lamp in Tyne Path off Gloucester Road. Selection meetings were brief as Bishopston only fielded one team on a cow pasture near Horfield Church.

They continued in this casual manner until 1898, when they formally became a registered member of the RFU. In the 1920s they moved in with Cotham Park RFC, who were amongst their oldest opponents. Eventually they persuaded Bristol North School to loan them a pitch and dressing rooms. The school provided everything except hot water for the post-match scrub. The 1930s saw the club playing on Hutton Farm at Hilton, but that ground was lost during the 1939-45 war.

Amongst many players from the club who gained representative honours in the pre-war years was Wally Bryant, who played for Gloucestershire and was an England trialist.

The club was reformed in 1947 and until 1966 played on the Annexe pitch next to the Bristol RFC ground. They enjoyed great success in that period and fielded up to six senior XVs and juniors. The club then moved to a council ground at Bonnington Walk, Lockleaze, where they erected their own clubhouse based on an old RAF hut. Today they play on an annex to the Bristol Combination's ground at Lockleaze.

Bishopston were the best junior side in Bristol in 1966-67. The kingpin of their team was a character known as 'Wallop' Smith, who was rumoured to be the toughest winger in Bristol. Less dangerous was another winger, Graham Fish, who played wearing glasses. He alleged opponents would steal his glasses during mauls, which ruined his afternoon.

The club's original feeder school was Bishopston Secondary, which closed in the 1970s. The break affected the club's performances. Currently they field three senior teams and a wide range of mini and junior sides.

David Sorrell joined the Club from QE Hospital School in 1969 and played at outside-half for the Club when only 16. He went on to play for Bristol, Gloucestershire, England Under 23s and England B.

Other Bishopston players who have won representative honours were Ian Freestone, who played for Zambia v Uganda in 1971, and Trevor Hawkes, who emigrated to Canada and played for Ontario v Japan in 1960.

The club reached Gloucester One in 2005.

BRIDGWATER & ALBION

'The Bricktowners'

BRIDGWATER & ALBION RFC is the product of a merger of two old clubs: Bridgwater RFC and Bridgwater Albion RFC.

Peter 'Bob' Dibble

Bridgwater Albion RFC were known as the 'Bricktowners'. There are records of them operating in December 1875 and playing an away game at Taunton College School. Three years later they played Taunton RFC under primitive floodlights. In 1898 Bridgwater Albion played Swindon and won 62-11, running in 13 tries. The club's golden era was in the years before World War One, when they fielded two internationals in Bob Dibble and Harold Archer. Peter 'Bob' Dibble was a huge flanker with legendary energy who won 18 England caps between 1905 and 1910. Dibble also went on the 1908 British Isles tour along with his Bridgwater team-mate Dr Harold Archer, a product of Blundells who was capped whilst with Guy's Hospital.

Their rivals, Bridgwater RFC, also produced two England internationals in Vincent Coates and Tom Woods. Coates began at Bridgwater RFC, where his father was a doctor in the town. He subsequently moved to Bath, where he was capped by England. Tom Woods played for England in 1908 before switching to the Northern Union.

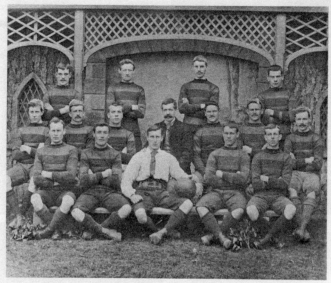

BRIDGWATER ALBION FOOTBALL CLUB, FIRST XV

SEASON 1894-95

S. Boyce   J. Palmer   W. Croker   T. Smith
H. Smith W. Phillips (hon. secretary) C. Sealey H. Williams (treasurer) R. Kingston W. Kingston J. Nicholln
T. Mayo   J. Dibble   G. Bond (captain)   E. Baker   T. Winslade

After World War One, the two clubs merged to form the Bridgwater & Albion RFC. The following year the club hosted the Somerset v All Blacks match, which went to the visitors. B&A did rather better in 1926, defeating Les Primaveres RFC of Paris. The following year Bridgwater provided seven players for Somerset, including Arthur Spriggs, who later won 75 caps.

In the late 1920s, the Swayne brothers represented the club. Jack Swayne, the tallest, was an outstanding forward who later joined Harlequins and came close to an England cap. Dennis Swayne won an England cap despite the burden of medical studies. Another brother, J.W.R. Swayne, was described as a "tough spoiling back row man". He was capped for England whilst playing for Richmond. The same situation arose with another Bridgwater lad, Jim Barrington, who won two England caps after moving to London.

During World War Two, the club formed a casual team called the Bridgwater Barbarians, who operated throughout the emergency.

The club reformed in 1946 and two years later scored an 8-0 victory over mighty Bath. The success of this era brought interest from the English selectors. In 1946 Gordon Barnett was an England reserve and in the 1950s Herbert Bastable was one of the top prop forwards in English rugby, and he also became an England reserve.

In 1951, the club unveiled a 600 seater stand, inaugurated by a match against an international XV. John Kendal-Carpenter, the England captain, did the official opening. Subsequently they installed new floodlights that made the club a popular mid-week venue for county trial matches.

The club may not have produced internationals for a period, but several players went close, notably Dave Hodge, who made his first XV debut at 15 and went onto receive an England trial, whilst winger John Lewis had a trial for Wales.

In the early 1970s, B&A fielded 'crash ball centre' Charles Kent, who was then a local student. He subsequently won five England caps whilst with Rosslyn Park.

In recent seasons Bridgwater & Albion have been in National Three South.

BRISTOL

"Bristol is the place where you could get away from the city in no time at all – you are in the county, the Downs or the port."

Cary Grant

PROBABLY NO CITY in England can claim to be as rugby-mad as Bristol. The district remains proud of its famous city club, but it also has 20 other clubs.

Bristol RFC is comparatively youthful, being formed in 1888, compared to Clifton RFC, which was formed in 1869. A Bedminster RFC existed briefly in the 1870s and played Clifton and Gloucester. Its best known player was W.G. Grace, who appeared for them in the 20-a-side days. Bedminster died out before Bristol was formed.

Clifton was an exclusive club in the 19th Century which relied on players from Clifton College, whereas Bristol RFC was rooted in the smaller clubs in the city. They had names such as Redland Park, Westbury Park, Bedminster, Rockleaze, Carlton, the Arabs, the Harlequins, the Hornets, Oakfield, Vauxhall Rangers, the Swifts and the Rangers and most operated on the Downs, on the north side of the city,. Playing on the Downs was hard work; the players had to carry their own posts to the pitch, erect them and dismantle them after the match. Failure to remove the posts brought a fine from the authorities.

In April 1888, Carlton RFC and Redland Park RFC met at the Montpelier Hotel and merged to form 'Bristol RFC'. The new club was augmented by the players from Westbury Park, which had just folded. There was so much rugby in the city that other clubs took umbrage that Carlton and Redland Park had adopted such a grand name. Certainly it was several decades before Bristol RFC could claim to be the premier club in the city.

Bristol's first captain was A. Gee, who often led a depleted band, particularly to away matches. But soon good players were being attracted to the side, notably 'Fatty' Davies and Tommy Thompson, and even the legendary Arthur Gould did a shift at Bristol in 1897. Thompson succeeded Gee to the captaincy and led Bristol to a rise in their fortunes, a rise that was temporarily halted by the emergence in the city of two professional soccer clubs in Bristol City and Bristol Rovers.

The rugby club's fortunes were boosted in 1908 by the formation of 'the Bristol & District Combination', which tried to promote rugby in the district. The Combination survives to this day.

If Bristol's relations within the city were good, relationships with the RFU were often strained. The club proposed to the RFU AGM that they should be allowed to organise leagues in the area. Rowland Hill, the RFU Secretary, led the opposition with the battle-cry that, "We all know the evils that must spring from introducing leagues". The RFU overwhelmingly rejected Bristol's proposal, but was quite happy to select the city's best players for the national team.

In 1900 Wallace Jarman (1872-1950) became the club's first international. He had come to the selectors' notice after touring Australia with the 1899 British Isles team. Jarman was followed into the England team by W.R. Johnson (1910-1914), which was curious as he was an Irishman, Harry Shewring played for England against the 1905 All Blacks, but his international career was ruined by a dislocated shoulder. Shewring was a member of the 1910 British Isles tour to South Africa and played 30 times at centre for Somerset. The roll-call continued with W.V. Butcher (1903-1905), Norman Moore (1904), J. Lloyd-Mathias (1905-1906), F.S. Scott (1907), P.J. Down (1909) and M.E. Neale (1912), whilst C.S. Arthur won four Welsh caps.

Jack Corsi was never selected for England but was regarded as the best three-quarter in the city. In 1914 he joined Rochdale Hornets NU and scored 120 tries for them in three years.

Bristol had too much box-office appeal to stay on the Downs and looked for a proper stadium where gate money could be raised. The club had been quick to identify that spectators wanted top-class rugby and across the Severn Estuary were some of the best rugby clubs in the world in Newport and

Bristol Downs by Paul Chapman

Meet . . .

Mr. L. J. CORBETT

The Man Who . . .

used to sell the "dummy," and now sells chocolates. Advertising manager of J. S. Fry and Sons, Limited. One of the most brilliant rugby three-quarters Bristol and England have produced. The first Bristol player to captain England. Played as "No. 13" in the international XV. Did more than any other man to revive the "selling of the dummy." On occasions did it so well that he almost deceived himself, and certainly deceived the referee and touch judges. Has 16 English caps. A straight runner and a fine sportsman. Recently became a Rotarian.

WAYFARER

Mr. L. J. Corbett

Meet . . .

Mr. SAM TUCKER

The Man Who . . .

has been Bristol's ambassador in the realms of rugby football. Capped for England more than 20 times. Once he was left out, but they sent for him at the last moment, and Sam flew there by aeroplane. Learned his football at St. Nicholas with St. Leonard's School. Entered big football in 1920. A stevedore. Oranges have been named after him. Once travelled to France with another man's passport to play for England. Got away with it. Now teaches Bristol Rugby Club colts how to play. England's finest hooker.

WAYFARER

Mr. Sam Tucker

Cardiff. Newport were, at the time, the 'Invincibles' and could field an entire team of internationals; Cardiff weren't far behind. Visits by Newport and Cardiff to Bristol guaranteed a gate of over 10,000 spectators, vastly more than visits from London clubs.

The 1920s were Bristol's first golden era, with some of the greatest names in English rugby history appearing for the club: Len Corbett, Reg Quick, plus a dozen other internationals.

Corbett was a willowy centre who won 16 caps for England. He was regarded as the coolest, most unflappable player of his generation. He was legendary for his ice-cool nerve, incredible dummy pass and infectious confidence. He was born in Bristol in 1897 to a rugby family and attended Sefton Park School. He played for Bristol Saracens and Cotham Park before serving in World War One. He was occasionally dropped by England, but finished his international career as its captain. He had a curious relationship with the crowd. He once remarked: "What a city needs is a good soccer club to take the rubbish out of the rugby ground."

Quick was famous in Bristol, but unknown elsewhere. He played 35 times for Somerset, skippering them for six years from 1921 to 1927. He was captain of Somerset the only time they won the County Championship, unfortunately missing the final with injury. He had international trials but was kept out of the England side by A.M. Smallwood, the Cambridge University winger.

Bev Chantrill was a controversial figure at Bristol because the home crowd felt he was a 'big game player' who was usually unavailable for run-of-the-mill fixtures. Chantrill, who began with Clifton, toured South Africa with the 1921 British Isles team. He took a job in London and in 1922 departed for the capital. Some other players also got away. In 1921, Jim Lehy, a brilliant centre, defected to the Northern Union for £600 – a fortune at the time.

Sam Tucker was a Bristol legend. Born into a family of stevedores who worked on Bristol Docks, he was physically the biggest Bristol player at 13 ½ stone. He was educated at St. Nicholas School and began with their Old Boys' club. Tucker joined the Army as a 17-year-old and saw service on the Western Front in World War One. Despite never being picked by Bristol Boys, he graduated to the senior club and earned a reputation as a hard man in a great era. He won 27 England caps; although he nearly missed a France v England match when he couldn't find his passport. He overcame the problem by borrowing a friend's passport and duping the authorities.

In 1930 Sam thought his days as England's hooker were over. The time was 12.30 midday on the Saturday that England were playing Wales at Cardiff and he was in a Bristol restaurant having lunch when a breathless messenger arrived from his office. "You're to play for England this afternoon … Rew is hurt… they've just phoned," the messenger blurted out. The train for Cardiff had left Bristol ten minutes earlier, which left just one option – to fly to Cardiff! That was bold pioneering for those days, but England needed Sam and he was not one to hesitate, although he had never been in an airplane before. Grabbing his bowler hat and rugby bag, he made a bee-line for Filton aerodrome pleading for a plane. "There's no aerodrome at Cardiff," the authorities told him. "Your only hope is to land in an open field." Sam and the pilot bounced into the air in a bi-plane with an open cock-pit. An hour before the kick-off and the duo flew over a packed Cardiff Arms Park and found an open space and landed the plane. Sam dashed into the road and hailed a passing lorry. "A quid if you get me to the ground before the match," he bribed the driver, and with five minutes to spare J.S. Tucker burst into the England dressing-room. He had been given up for lost and the selected reserve, Norman Matthews, was changed ready to play. This hectic afternoon had a story-book ending, for Sam played the game of his life and England won comfortably. He went on to play another five times for his country, but poor Matthews never won an England cap.

After the balmy days of Corbett and Tucker, Bristol felt ill-used by the RFU as no Bristol player won three consecutive caps for 30 years.

At home, Bristol's major event of the inter-war years was in September 1931 when the 'Memorial Ground' was opened to commemorate the club's dead in World War One. The ground was gifted by Sir Francis Cowlin, a local businessman. Previously the club had played at the County Cricket Ground at Ashley Down.

Bristol struggled, like all clubs, during World War Two, but still managed to produce G. Hollis, W.T. Reynolds and F.G. Hill, who all played in Victory Internationals for England.

Good times returned in the post-war years. Without league fixtures, Bristol continued its policy of finding the best opposition, particularly in mid-week. For mid-week matches, they hired Bristol City's ground at Ashton Gate, which could command crowds of 20,000 on Wednesday nights.

This was a strange era for an overtly 'amateur game' as Bristol, Newport and Cardiff played each other twice a season, usually on a Wednesday night, in front of huge crowds. The question was asked at the time: where did all the gate money go? The public paid their shilling (5p) willingly as they wanted to see the Welsh giants rather than what a contemporary described as "a bunch of medical students", a reference to the strong London hospital sides, who had playing strength but few spectators. Curiously, it was the soccer authorities who clamped down on the mid-week matches as they felt the fixtures were affecting gates for the round ball game.

Bristol regained their power and in season 1956-57 they were Britain's top club. That year they had victories over Cardiff, Newport and Leicester and scored 113 tries. Two years later they were again unofficial British champions with 34 victories and 729 points. They were captained by John Blake, an inspirational leader who was unlucky to never be picked by England.

His successor in the Bristol No. 10 jersey was Richard Sharp from Blundell's School. Sharp was called up for his England debut at the last minute. He met and trained with Dickie Jeeps, the regular scrum-half, on the eve of the match and then made a brilliant debut. Sharp eventually won 14 caps and toured with the 1962 British Lions. His partner at Bristol was Peter Ford, who was picked for his England debut at 31 years of age.

As ever, though, it was the Bristol pack which was especially renowned. Great forwards included Bev Dovey, Barry Nelmes and John Pullin. Dovey was a biology teacher who began his rugby at Lydney before playing for Cambridge University and England. In 1967, he led the South of England against the All Blacks. Barry Nelmes arrived at the Memorial Ground as a teenager and had clocked up 50 Bristol appearances before his 18th birthday. He suffered many injuries, but reappeared in England colours in the 1970s whilst playing for Cardiff – one of a handful of Welsh-based Englishmen to be capped by Twickenham.

Perhaps the greatest Bristolian is John Pullin, a rugged West-Countryman who farmed at Aust in the shadow of the Severn Bridge. Pullin won 42 England caps and played seven times for the Lions. He also had a remarkable record as England captain, leading England to their shock 18-9 victory over the Springboks in South Africa and, the following September, England's victory over the All Blacks. He was also one of the few England players to tour with the victorious Lions in 1971. Sadly, Pullin's international career coincided with one of England's lowest ebbs in the Home International Championship.

Other Bristol players were luckier. Alan Morley, a small but flying winger, grabbed a precious try in the 1975 Calcutta Cup match, which gave England a precious win. He was the greatest English try-scorer of his era, touching down 473 times in senior rugby between 1968 and 1980, including 378 for Bristol – a record for a senior club.

At club level, Peter Colston, the Bristol coach, produced enormous improvement in Bristol's fortunes, which led to his appointment as England coach. In true English amateur tradition, he coached the team but wasn't invited to participate in selection.

The 1980s saw Bristol again ranked with the best and Alastair Hignell, Richard Harding and Bob Hesford were England regulars. They helped Bristol finally win the National Knockout in 1983. Three years later the club made the wrong kind of headlines when the RFU reprimanded them after the referee walked off during the Newport match following persistent fighting.

1988 saw the club riding high, as befitted their centenary year, which was celebrated with 31 victories in 39 matches.

The last decade of the 20th Century saw the club below the standard of the previous era. They had excellent players in Ralph Knibbs, Derek Eves, Paul Hull and Simon Hogg, but the star names were heading east – 30 miles east to Bath RFC, which was the rising star. Stuart Barnes, the Bristol fly-half, left for Bath, where he became a legend.

Bristol did have some remarkable internationals. None more remarkable than Dave Hilton, who won 41 Scotland caps before it emerged that he wasn't eligible to play for them. The irony of the scandal was that the International Rugby Board was based in Bristol only a few miles from the Memorial Ground.

The onset of the professional era required a successful rugby club to be at the apex of the financial world. Before professionalism, Bristol had lavished relatively large sums on modernising the Memorial Ground, including a huge new grandstand. The stand was viewed, by some folk, as a white elephant, not least because it was alleged that spectators in the back of the stand couldn't see the full pitch. Financial problems forced the club to invite Bristol Rovers soccer team to ground-share. Unfortunately the rugby club's problems continued and the ground was sold to the soccer team, the rugby team becoming tenants in the stadium they once owned.

In 1998 Malcolm Pearce, a local businessman, tried to turn the tide. Pearce did everything humanly possible to make Bristol a force in the Premiership. He persuaded Mitsubishi to sponsor the club, who changed their name to 'the Bristol Shoguns' after one of the sponsor's vehicles.

Season 2000-01 saw the Shoguns enjoy an excellent season, but the following season was a disaster. The fans were shocked when a move to Oxford was discussed, and then the unthinkable emerged: a merger with arch-rivals Bath. Rescue from this nightmare scenario came, ironically, from Richard Hill, the legendary Bath and England scrum-half. He steadied the ship by signing a team of veterans who prevented the anticipated relegation from the Premiership.

In 2007, Bristol (no longer the Shoguns) finished third in the Premiership and qualified for the Heineken European Cup. Sadly, the good times didn't last and the club was relegated in 2009. Part of Bristol's problems was the inability to retain the services of top-class internationals, such as Martin Corry, Simon Shaw, Josh Lewsey and Kyran Bracken, who went on to do sterling service with other clubs.

As an economy measure, in 2010 coach Liam Middleton divided his time between Cheltenham and Bristol. Recent seasons have seen Bristol valiantly trying to win promotion back to the Premiership. In 2015, they missed out by one point on aggregate in the play-off with Worcester Warriors.

BRISTOL HARLEQUINS

A 'BRISTOL HARLEQUINS XV' played in the 1870s on the city's Downs. However, the first official Bristol Harlequins side was formed in 1885. Five years later, the club rented a pitch at Eastville, which was taken over by Bristol Rovers Football Club. It was a body-blow to Quins, who temporarily closed down. Maybe it wasn't such a body-blow, as a contemporary account describes the Eastville ground as "a mud heap with an old tin hut and no running water".

Harlequins briefly reappeared in 1898, playing at Stapleton Road before disappearing again.

The next reincarnation emerged from Wick Road School in the city. The school switched from soccer to rugby in 1926, but abandoned the experiment in 1929. The rugby fans connected to the school were so upset that they formed Old Wickonians RFC. The club operated from Walsh Farm, Knowle until World War Two. Old Wickonians reformed in 1946, but decided to adopt the ancient name of 'Bristol Harlequins RFC'. Things were so tight that, lacking a set of shirts, Quins bought a spare set from (the now defunct) George's Brewery RFC, which rather dictated what colours the club could choose.

The best players produced by Quins have been Colin Davis, who is one of the greatest point-scorers in the Bristol Combination, and Val Sidoli, one of Bristol's top players of the inter-war years.

Currently Quins play in Western Counties North.

BRISTOL SARACENS

BRISTOL SARACENS RFC is the third oldest rugby club in the city. They were formed in 1896 by disillusioned members of the city's YMCA rugby club. Their first captain was Syd Brookman, who went on to play for Bristol RFC. The Saracens first well-known player was Billy Wicks, who joined in 1898 and served as player and official for 50 years.

During the early years the Saracens ground was at Golden Hill, Bishopston, with changing rooms at the Wellington Hotel, Horfield and the headquarters at the Old England Hotel, Montpelier.

The club moved to Monks Park and changed at the Anchor Hotel on Gloucester Road. Travelling from the ground could only be done on the top deck of a tram car – irrespective of the weather – because people objected to sitting alongside rugby players covered in mud and blood. Later the club obtained the use of a changing hut about half a mile from the Monks Park pitch, which they shared with five other teams (one of which was Broad Plain), the hut having just about enough room to stand up in.

In 1919 Saracens were playing at Radnor Road when Bristol RFC joined them. Bristol shared the Radnor Ground with the Saracens until 1921, when Bristol purchased the Memorial Ground. At the time, Saracens were a very strong side indeed. If Bristol were unexpectedly short of a player, they would often ask Saracens for one.

One player who figured for both clubs was Len Kennedy, a scrum-half from Pontypridd who joined Saracens and was associated with them for 30 years. A forgotten Saracen of the era was 'Gaffer' Jones, who was regarded as the hardest man in Bristol rugby. Another Saracens stalwart was Ted Bakewell, whose association lasted 50 years. Two other notable Saracens of the inter-war years were J.C. Jenkins, who went on to play for Wales, and C. Kingston, who moved to Bristol and won an England trial.

In 1936, Saracens moved to the Blaise Castle, Henbury. 20 years later they moved to a new ground, which they named the Ted Bakewell Memorial Ground and had the best clubhouse in the city. This proved a blessing by drawing new talent from Henbury Estate.

The most famous product of Saracens was John Pullin, the Lions, England and Bristol hooker.

Saracens were placed in Gloucester One at the onset of league rugby and have progressed to the Western Counties division. The club is heavily dependent on its junior teams for new blood, with Andy Blackmore, the Bristol stalwart, being junior coordinator. The team recently included Feao Vunipola, who had won 40 caps for Tonga.

(Thanks to Chris Harding).

BROAD PLAIN

BROAD PLAIN RFC was formed in 1909 as an offshoot of Broad Plain Lads' Club from St Phillips. Games were first held on the Downs outside the city centre. In 1931 a move was made to Beverley Road, Horfield. Four years later the club moved to the Rugby Sports Field, Filton. In 1952 they moved to Combination Ground, Lockleaze. Another change was when blue, maroon and gold hoops were adopted and the club has remained in these colours ever since.

Over the years, many members have been honoured by wearing the colours of Bristol RFC, and of the Combination team, notably Fatty Handford and Bill Claridge, but pride of place must go to Fred Hill, so far the club's only international. Fred played for Bristol for many years between the wars and was capped by England. More recently, both Bob Slocombe and Adrian Godbeer have played over 800 games for the club, and others are not too far behind.

In 2006 Broad Plain achieved their ultimate goal and moved into a new clubhouse in Bedminster. They now run a thriving mini and junior section and field teams at age groups from Under-7 up to colts. The First XV plays in Gloucester 2 and was the city's Junior Team of the Year in 2014.

CAINSCROSS

CAINSCROSS RFC HAS a distinguished history, despite having spent its life in the shadow of Stroud RFC, who were once a first-class club. Cainscross, on the outskirts of Stroud, was founded in 1894 and drew its players from the outlying villages. Even in this small area, Cainscross had a local rival in Ebley United, who gave them their first match (and defeat by 13-3) in October 1894. Ebley were connected with St. Matthew's Church in Cainscross. The two clubs merged in 1896 as Cainscross St. Matthews (later the club became Cainscross & Ebley RFC, then Cainscross RFC).

The merged club enjoyed some measure of success playing other junior clubs and the second teams of the local senior clubs. By 1898, the new club was running three teams, but had won a reputation for being "ragged and dangerous" on account of their lack of sartorial elegance and playing habits.

Unfortunately, Cainscross were hard hit when the loss of their pitch led to a mad exodus of players to Stroud. This sequence of events was to be repeated again and again down the years. Not surprisingly, the relationship between Stroud and Cainscross was often tempestuous. The final straw was when the senior club organised 'The Stroud Cup' for the area's junior clubs, which inevitably brought talented players to the attention of Stroud. This arrangement was common in rugby but seen as a device to solicit players from smaller clubs to their bigger neighbours.

1900 saw Cainscross as Stroud Cup champions, beating Rodborough 11-17. In September 1905 Stroud offered £5 to Cainscross to release a player to them, but, after a heated debate, Stroud dropped the offer to £2. Cainscross retaliated by banning any of their players from joining their neighbours.

Cainscross looked to recruit young players by more orthodox methods. This consisted of inviting lads from the local villages

to a 'game of rugby' and post-match tea party at the White Horse Inn. The game consisted of 50 lads indulging in a version of rugby.

Rugby was slow to restart in the area after the Great War due to hard times in Gloucestershire, and it was 1930 before the club got going again under the leadership of Jack Milton. A local team must have been in existence as a 'Cainscross XV' as they won the 1929 Mid-Gloucestershire Cup. The reformed club repeated this feat five times in the 1930s.

After World War Two, Cainscross achieved 20 victories from 36 matches in 1952–53 and a year later moved into a pavilion on Victory Park. In their Diamond Jubilee season of 1953-54, they celebrated by playing a County XV.

John 'J.V.' Smith is the most famous son of Cainscross. He won four England caps whilst with Cambridge University and Rosslyn Park. In 1956, the famous sports writer Frank Keating joined the club after a spell with Gloucester and Stroud. Keating was Sportswriter of the Year in 1978.

1960 saw an influx of players from another local side that closed: Hoffman RFC. It proved a false dawn as the club soon suffered its own drastic shortage of players.

The club currently play in Gloucester 3.

CHELTENHAM

"Visiting Cheltenham to play rugby in the 1920s meant you encountered people who were most definitely not elderly, shy or retiring – quite the opposite."
C.S. Dingley, 1964

THE GAME OF rugby and the city of Cheltenham go back to the earliest days of the sport. A plaque on the wall of Cheltenham College commemorates that in 1844 the three Acton brothers joined the college from School House at Rugby. Rugby matches between Rugby School and Cheltenham College date back to 1850 and two protégés of Dr. Arnold, Henry Highton and T.W. Jex-Blake, were principals of Cheltenham College. Later a Cheltenham College old boy, A. Woodley, spread the game to the New World when he helped found New York RFC in the USA.

Closer to home, there are records of Cheltenham College playing the 'Town Boys' in 1874. It was, however, another 15 years before Cheltenham RFC was formed. Club rugby had already been around for a while because Cheltenham Whitecross played Gloucester in 1872.

In 1875, two Cheltenham College players represented England, W.E. Collins and E.S. Penott, whilst playing for the London-based Old Cheltonians. Five years later Stuart Neame of Old Cheltonians was capped by England. Old Cheltonians declined in the 1880s, which led to the emergence of Cheltenham RFC.

In February 1885, the College played an exhibition match against Mr. C. Crane's Midland Counties team. College won one goal to two tries.

The following year, a Cheltenham Town RFC was formed at the Cambridge Hotel on North Street the under chairmanship of W.A. Woof of Cheltenham College. The new club was formed by the merger of two existing sides, Red Cross and Charlton Kings RFC. Town RFC had a brief existence and played at Cemetery Road.

The birth of Cheltenham FC owed its origins to the magnificent Maoris of 1888, who captured the popular imagination of sports fans across Britain. Two Cheltenham youngsters, John Hailing and Arthur Perrin, distributed leaflets calling a meeting at the Sydney Arms to discuss forming a new club.

The club's first recorded match was in October 1890, when Cheltenham RFC played Dean Close School on the school grounds. A year later, Cheltenham met Bristol for the first time, with Bristol winning 23-0. They didn't fare any better against Gloucester, who out-scored the newcomers by nine to one.

Season 1894-95 saw a change of jerseys from black and red squares to red and black stripes. At the end of that season, Cheltenham played Leicester for the first time and were described as "one of the leading sides in the West".

Cheltenham were treating the game seriously, as the club records state: "... the players must get fitter. The time for smoking and drinking is not in the rugby season." The club even hired a trainer. Sadly, the season ended on a low note when an outbreak of smallpox occurred in the town. This was a temporary setback as Cheltenham were undefeated the following season.

Notable players of the era included Fred Fry, who set a record of 33 tries for the season, and Geoffrey Unwin, who was capped for England against Scotland in 1898. Seven years later, Cheltenham had the services of three internationals: Unwin, Fred Jacob and the Scotland captain Bedell-Sivright, who guested for the encounter with the 1905 All Blacks. Jacob (1873-1945) won eight England caps with Blackheath and Richmond before teaching at Cheltenham College and playing for the town club.

The All Blacks came to town in 1905 for a match and 8,000 spectators packed the Athletic Ground. Cheltenham lost 18-0 to the tourists, which was a respectable score. Buoyed by the reflected glory, the club helped form the Gloucestershire Senior League, which unfortunately came when they themselves were in decline and they finished bottom in 1909.

The first home-bred Cheltenham international was Leslie Hayward (1886-1938), who won an England cap at centre in 1910. Sadly, Hayward was blamed for England's failure to overcome Ireland in a scoreless draw despite having played most of the match with concussion. He had to be helped from the field and spent the night in hospital. He subsequently emigrated to France.

During the years that followed, an influx of players from either side of the Welsh border helped make Cheltenham into a top side, but their recruitment policy was under scrutiny in 1908 by the RFU after Cinderford complained about illegal poaching of their players. How much truth there was in the accusation we will never know, but 14 years later Cinderford complained to the RFU again. Cheltenham's recruitment policy was so dubious that when Aberavon visited Cheltenham in 1929, the Wizards found nine ex-Aberavon players in the Cheltenham ranks.

The Northern Union also posed a threat. In 1908, the NU persuaded the town council, who owned the Recreation Ground,

to lease the stadium for a professional rugby international, England v Australia. The rugby union club objected, but their landlords allowed the match to go ahead, not least because they pocketed 10% of the gate money from the 4,000 strong crowd. The game was described as "very rough". Fortunately, the NU experiment was short-lived and professional rugby league never reappeared in the town.

Cheltenham's golden era came between the wars, beginning in 1922 with victory over mighty Bristol, which upset the Bristol selectors who accused their players of being unfit and unprepared. The decade saw Cheltenham ranking amongst the finest clubs in England and able to play regular fixtures against the best sides in Britain.

1929-30 was the club's finest season, with 30 wins and two draws in 35 matches, including 24 consecutive home wins. Many of the club's players were Welsh, the best known of which was E. Gwyn Davies who won three Wales caps before 'going north'. His son, Emlyn Hughes, was a captain of the England soccer team and Liverpool FC.

The 1930s saw continuing success, but World War Two halted the club in its tracks. They picked up the reins in 1945 and achieved the double over mighty Cardiff. The England selectors took notice and prop Tom Price won six caps in the post-war years.

Fixtures against the biggest clubs continued into the early 1960s, but decline was inevitable with so many successful clubs in the vicinity. Cheltenham were losing their first-class status and inevitably the precious gate money that was the lifeblood of a top side.

By 1971, Cheltenham had dropped out of the top 32 English club sides. Good players continued to emerge, notably John Hall (North East Counties), Bob Redwood (Gloucestershire), David Protherough (England reserve) and John Fidler (four England caps), but the best players tended to migrate to Gloucester.

In 1981, they left the Rec, which had been their home since the 19th century, for Pittville Stadium.

In recent seasons, Tom Johnson began his rugby at Cheltenham but moved to Coventry and Exeter, where he was capped by England.

At the present time, Cheltenham look to the future with mini and junior rugby, plus by establishing links with the local junior clubs. Today they play at Newlands Park in Southam.

CINDERFORD

CINDERFORD RFC'S FIRST match came on the 27th October 1886, at home to Monmouth. At the time the town had half a dozen coal-mines. The backbone of the rugby club's playing staff were miners, who were vulnerable to low pay and economic depressions. Forest of Dean miners had a terrible life; a six-day week of hard toil for less than £2 a week with no sick pay.

The only positive of being a mining town was that the rugby team were able to travel to away matches on the coal trains. This was needed because the roads in the Forest of Dean were so poor that travelling by horse-drawn wagon was virtually impossible.

The present Cinderford RFC was originally called 'Cinderford White Rose' (the last two words were dropped in 1955). The town also had a number of other clubs with names such as 'Red Rose' and 'Saracens'.

Cinderford's colours were royal blue with an orange hoop, but this changed in 1900 to red, black and amber; colours that survive to this day.

Cinderford were a major force in the mid-1890s, losing only to Gloucester in 1894-95 and being unbeaten the following year. Their best player was Arthur Hall, who moved to Gloucester and Bristol. 1904 was a memorable year for the club when teams such as Llanelli, Neath, Pontypool, Gloucester, Cheltenham and Bristol were all beaten at home.

Because the rugby club's playing staff were miners, it was not surprising that many took seriously offers from rugby league scouts with hundreds of pounds in cash to offer. The principal defection was 'Mad' Arthur Smith, who joined Oldham NU and went on to become a NU international. Smith began his career at Yorkley in the Forest of Dean. The nickname was due to his forceful and enthusiastic style of play. When he returned from the First World War, Smith resumed playing rugby union, despite having a German bullet lodged in his body, which he carried for the rest of his days.

Despite the drain of talent, Cinderford won the 1906-07 Gloucestershire County Cup and the 1908-09 County League Championship, despite competition from Gloucester, Clifton, Bristol and Cheltenham. But all was not well. The rise of soccer in the Forest was making life increasingly difficult for rugby clubs. By November 1912, Cinderford RFC were close to bankruptcy and barely able to field one XV. The rising deficit at the bank meant the club could no longer afford the 4d (1.5 pence) a season to insure the players against serious injury. The club, however, kept going when individuals paid, from their own pockets, for the team to travel to existing fixtures. The 1912-13 season was a sad time, with only seven wins in 29 matches.

The years following World War One saw the pattern of 'feast and famine' continue. On the pitch Cinderford remained a force, losing just six of 35 games in 1922-23 and beating Northampton at Franklyn Gardens in 1926, but the whole area, and the rugby club, were enduring hard times.

The club struggled. Miners were their lifeblood, but the mines were on short time. Miners only worked two or three days a week for 38p a day (underground) or 25p a day (on the surface). By September 1925 Cinderford were broke. Help came with a match between a Len Corbett XV and Bristol RFC to help save them. The following year, they were without a ground because the rent of the Rec was beyond their means. They had lost £170 in 1925-26. A number of their players left to play for the local colliery side. Other players, such as Jack Read, who was considered a potential England international, defected to the NU where he played 483 matches for Oldham.

In 1928 Cinderford had its first international in Alfred Denzel 'Bumps' Carpenter, who was selected for England v South Africa after moving to Gloucester. Playing for England proved an unfortunate experience as Bumps was unaware that the post-match required a dinner jacket – something he didn't own. He attended the dinner wearing his only suit and a scarf.

Bumps was born in Mitcheldean in 1900. He played rugby continuously from the age of 15 to 43, excluding two years in the RAF. He worked at Lightmoor Colliery and started his rugby career with Cinderford before playing for Gloucester from 1928 to 1940, during which time he made 336 appearances. It is known he often walked the 14 miles from home to Kingsholm and back to play for the Cherry and Whites. He played for Gloucestershire in five County Championship finals, winning four of them. He was selected twice for the Rest v England, and proudly recalled, "we beat 'em once". He was selected as a reserve for England more than 20 times (the last time at the age of 38), but his appearance against South Africa in 1932 proved to be his only cap. He started the game at prop but finished it as hooker. He was the first player from the Forest to play for England. Bumps was well respected; a hard man with huge hands, famous for his fitness, stamina and strength and who liked a fight. After retiring from senior rugby, he returned to his roots in the Forest, supporting local clubs. He had the pleasure of packing down at Cinderford with two of his sons, George and Denzel. He died in 1974.

Cinderford RFC closed down during the Second World War when the club's ground became an American Army base. However, a team called Cinderford White Rose kept rugby alive in the town. White Rose continued until 1955, when after winning the Forest of Dean Combination Cup, they changed their name to Cinderford RFC. The change was celebrated when Tom Voyce brought a County XV to play them.

A boost to local rugby was East Dean Grammar School's decision to play rugby from 1953. Around this time, the club bought the Recreation Ground at Dockham Road. They had used the White Hart public house as headquarters, which was run by two dedicated fans in Mary and Bob Beavis, who later became the club sponsors. Born in 1928, Mary Beavis was a true stalwart of Cinderford Rugby Football Club and well-known to legions of players and supporters across the county. Her association with the club began shortly after World War Two, when a group of young men met at the White Hart with the aim of restarting rugby in Cinderford. She took on the role of secretary for the newly re-formed Cinderford club and became the only female honorary secretary in the country, a role she continued to perform for 50 years with the help of her husband. The ground is now known as the Beavis Memorial Ground.

Cinderford have been realistic in recent times and have established a link to mighty neighbours Gloucester. The Cherry and Whites have benefitted with a string of talent flowing from Cinderford, including Ben Morgan, Freddie Burns and Henry Trinder.

In 1998-99, and again in 2000-01, Cinderford lost only one game in each season, and in 2003-04 they reached the quarter-final of the Intermediate cup. They are currently riding high in National One.

(Thanks to Richard Morgan)

CLEVE

CLEVE RFC OF Bristol was founded in 1922 as 'Cleve RFC. Downend' at Park Road, Staple Hill. Subsequently, they moved to pitches on Vassells Park, Fishponds. In 1933 a pavilion was erected at Fishponds and five years later they moved to their present home at Downend (the pavilion being transported along with the teams). In 1947 an extra ground was bought to provide three pitches.

Cleve have a long association with the city club going back to Don Burland, the 1930s England forward, who ran a local public house and was Cleve's president. Don won eight England caps in the early 1930s. He was a burly centre who took a great deal of stopping in full flight.

Other Cleve players have reached the highest level. John Thorne won three caps as hooker for England whilst with Bristol in 1961. In 1966-67 Thorne returned to Cleve after his Bristol days, as did England international Barry Nelmes, who played for Cardiff, and Mike Ellery, Bristol's record try-scorer, who scored 45 tries in a season following his return from the city club. Frank Guard graduated from Cleve to Bristol and was one of the most prolific goal-kickers of the 1970s.

In 1997 Cleve moved to a new clubhouse and ground at 'The Hayfields'. They reached the quarter-finals of the 2004 Powergen Cup and the following year they were South West 2 champions.

The club runs three senior sides on Saturdays and all mini and junior levels, from under 7s to colts on Sundays. In 2015 they were honoured with their first ever county match when Gloucester played Kent at their Mangotsfield Ground.

CLEVEDON

CLEVEDON WAS A lovely seaside town on the north coast of Somerset. Today it is a busy and dynamic Bristol suburb, which owes much to the M5 motorway that runs on the north side of the area. But a century ago, it was a sleepy little port.

Clevedon RFC was founded in 1921. For some years, they played their games behind Hales factory, which was famous for its Swiss Rolls. They were one of Bristol's top sides of the post-war years and the club had a record season in 1957-58 with 24 wins.

Season 1960-61 saw success as Clevedon lost only one game, one of the best records in British rugby. In the side was Welsh international Graham Powell, who joined the club from Ebbw Vale RFC when his work took him across the Severn. Clevedon's finest son is hooker John Evans, who played 600 games beginning in 1975.

Since the reintroduction of the Somerset Cup, Clevedon were winners in three successive years. More recently, Nathan Catt began at Clevedon and moved to Bath, where he played for England U20s. Hooker Hugh Bennett attended Clevedon School before joining the local rugby club. He studied sports science at Swansea University and played for Swansea. RFC before winning his first Wales cap in 2003 and representing them in that year's World Cup.

In the early 2000s Clevedon recorded successive promotions to reach South West One. The promotion run saw them lose three games out of 44. Currently Clevedon are in Somerset 2 North and play on Coleridge Vale Fields.

CLIFTON COLLEGE

"There is a breathless hush in the Close tonight. Play up. Play up and play the game."
Sir Henry Newbolt

CLIFTON COLLEGE OPENED in 1862 for the sons of the city's leading citizens. In actual fact, Bristol Grammar School was over 300 years older but was regarded as not sufficiently elitist for some prosperous Bristolians, hence the opening of Clifton College modelled on Arnold's Rugby School. John Percival, a young master from Rugby School, was the first headmaster.

Percival blended the best features of Arnold's Rugby School traditions with a liberalism that distinguished Clifton from other public schools. The school quickly established a first-class reputation and numbers rose rapidly to 600 by 1879. Rugby Football was the preferred winter sport and there are records of rugby matches lasting 12 days in the 1870s; referees weren't used but play was interrupted to return to the cloisters when dusk fell, only to resume the following afternoon.

The first Cliftonian international was James Bush (1850-1924), who played for England against Scotland in March 1875. The first Welsh rugby captain was J.A. Bevan, who was associated with the college as a schoolmaster. Bevan was blamed for the Welsh defeat and ignored for future selection. Perhaps the most influential Cliftonian was Henry Grylls, who pioneered rugby in Cornwall.

The college has long established links with the Army. Field Marshall Sir Douglas Haig was an old boy. The college's officer corps supplied hundreds of young men to the forces in World War One. The Cliftonian losses on the Western Front were catastrophic. To commemorate the fallen, the school erected a Memorial Arch and pupils are obliged to take their hands out of their pockets while walking through it.

During World War Two, the college was used as the American Headquarters and there US General Omar Bradley planned the D Day Invasion from its hushed cloisters.

The college remains at the heart of Clifton today, but the playing fields have moved to the outskirts of Bristol.

CLIFTON

"Clifton is the kind of place where you can buy incense candles at any time of the day or night – but struggle to find anywhere selling milk."
Tony Marriott

CLIFTON IS ONE of the best addresses in Bristol. It occupies the high ground overlooking the Severn Docks. The college remains, but the rugby team moved out many years ago.

The original Clifton RFC was formed in 1869 by former pupils of Clifton College, which made it the first rugby club in the West County. It had a fine fixture list, including Blackheath, but soon went out of existence due to a difficulty in raising full teams (the school not having many old boys in those days).

Some of the original players revived the club in September 1872. Matches were to be played at Clifton College with "no kicking or tripping allowed" and the school colours of lavender and black were adopted – which have never been altered, although the width of the hoops has changed.

The first match played by the revived Clifton was a win against Sydney College, Bath; indeed, most of the earliest fixtures were against Bath sides. The first full season of 1873-74 saw ten matches played, including a win over Gloucester. The following season, they provided six of the West County's representative side. During the first five seasons Clifton were unbeaten at home and lost only five away games. Season 1875-76 had only one defeat in 23 matches, the victories including a win over a South Wales representative side at Cardiff. The replay was cancelled because the Welshmen could not raise 20 men. 1879-80 stands as the most successful in Clifton's history. They were undefeated and their line was not crossed all season.

They saw themselves as the embodiment of amateur rugby. There was pandemonium at an early AGM when it was revealed that a player's train fare from Cheltenham had been paid by the club.

The first international was James Bush (1850-1924), who played for England against Scotland in March 1875. Bush went on to win five rugby caps and an England cricket cap before touring Australia as a cricketer with his best friend W.G. Grace.

Other early internationals associated with Clifton were William Mobberley (1851-1914), who won an England cap whilst with Ravenscourt Park in 1872 but taught at Clifton College from 1874 until 1913. He played cricket for Oxford University and Gloucestershire. W.H. Birch was the first South African to make his mark in British rugby. He was educated in Bath, where he attracted the attention of Clifton FC, who were then the pre-eminent South West club. A huge forward, Birch was captain of Gloucestershire and the South West rugby sides. Canon Richard Budworth, who won two England caps, taught at Clifton and Durham School. He was headmaster of Durham for 25 years when it produced many fine players. Hiatt Baker is best remembered as the founder of a college at Bristol University. Arthur Budd founded the London Society of Referees and, in 1879, A.K. Butterworth, a member of the Clifton club and captain of the Marlborough Nomads, submitted to the English Rugby Union Committee a new code of laws. Another wonderful character of the era was J.D. 'Punchie' Miller, the second captain. A small man, he played for 30 years.

Initially Clifton were hugely successful, but their fortunes took a dip in the 1890s when poor facilities deterred players and spectators. Matters improved when a ground was acquired at North View in 1899. Four years later, they defeated their oldest opponents, Gloucester – Clifton's first win over their rivals since the old 20-a-side days.

Traditionally Clifton fielded more players and teams than any other club in the South West. They normally began the season by playing Bristol RFC and usually lost as the new club grew in strength.

They resumed rugby after World War One with a victory over the College First XV. Gradually life returned to normal and the club celebrated its Golden Jubilee in 1922 at the Grand Hotel, Bristol with six of the original players present.

In the 1926-27 season Clifton moved to the Eastfield Road ground, which was then shared with Westbury Cricket Club. The first match was against Bristol, led by Len Corbett.

Clifton's best known international of the early 1930s was the Reverend Peter Brook, one of the last rugby-playing clergymen to play for England. In 1931 Brook was badly injured in Paris playing for England against France. Carl Aarvold, the England captain, went over to Brook and said: "You can't die there, it's French soil. Get up!" Brook was lifted to his feet and resumed the game, although he was barely conscious. He recovered to enjoy a long association with the college and the club.

Off the field, Clifton made news in 1932 when they flew a team over to Cardiff to play Glamorgan Wanderers.

After World War Two history repeated itself as the club resumed with a game against the college. However, the link was fading, which was not a serious issue as Clifton had never been a closed club.

The 1950s were a golden era for the club, with a string of internationals wearing Clifton colours: Bob McEwan (Scotland), Peter Young (England), Vic Leadbetter (England), John Currie (England), Steve Richards (England), Roger Hosen (England), Colin McFadyean (England) and Bob Lloyd (England). But perhaps the club's finest servant was Donald Brian, who played for the First XV from 1946 to 1966, clocking up 700 appearances.

The Eastville Road ground was compulsory purchased in 1971, but fortunately Grant Watson, an ex-captain, had an option on a piece of land at Cribbs Causeway (the old Roman Road to Botany Bay) on the north side of the city. Clifton moved there in 1976.

In 1977, they recruited Jack Rowell as coach. He later moved to Bath and became one of the greatest names in rugby.

The arrival of league rugby posed problems for Clifton as their form wasn't good at the time. Placed in South West Two, they produced some fine players, such as Simon Hogg and Chris Bate, but most moved to bigger clubs. It took several seasons for them to assert themselves and eventually they reached National Three and came within minutes of promotion to National Two, but victory for Otley at Fylde robbed them of promotion. In 1990 Alan Morley, the Bristol legend, joined as club coach and led Clifton to an unbeaten season in 1993-94.

In 2012 the club reached National 2 South.

COTHAM PARK

COTHAM PARK RFC was formed in 1901 by an amalgamation of two existing clubs, Bristol East RFC and Redland Park RFC. The club had a range of homes: the Downs, the County Cricket Ground, a pitch on Toronto Road, then moving to Horfield, Southmead and Filton before moving to Failand. In the 1920s Park shared a ground with Bishopston.

Cotham were the great losers when Bristol Grammar School and St Brendan's GS ceased to supply school leavers to the club as the two schools had formed old boys sides of their own.

The best known Cotham player was Wally Reynolds, who moved to Bristol and played for England in a wartime international. Later the club produced three top-class players for Bristol: Derek Griffiths, John Hellings and Mike Fry, who played over 400 games beteen them at the Memorial Ground.

The club's golden jubilee in 1951 was celebrated with a match against Bishopston at the Memorial Ground. In 1959 Park moved to Elm Park, Filton using council pitches. A dispute over running a bar eventually led to them buying a ground at Failand in 1983, with a clubhouse added in1990.

The club appearance record is held by Nick Shopland, who played more than 870 times as a No. 8 over 31 years. Sadly, he died whilst still playing for the club.

Currently Cotham Park plays in Gloucester 2.

DINGS CRUSADERS

IN THE LATE 19th Century there were many rugby clubs in the city of Bristol, notably Dings RFC and Crusaders RFC, who merged to form 'Dings Crusaders'.

Dings RFC took its name from an area of great deprivation behind Temple Meads station, where poverty, crime and disorder were rife and several riots occurred. Despite this drawback, Dings could attract huge crowds of up to 6,000 for local derbies.

The 'Crusaders' took their name from 'the Shaftesbury Crusade', formed by Lord Shaftesbury, a social and industrial reformer in late 19th-century England. The crusade was intended to keep local youth out of trouble. Shaftesbury also provided soup kitchens for the starving. The Crusaders rugby team was also part of the Boys Club Movement in the late 19th Century.

Crusaders' first match was played against Elton St. Michael's in 1898. They made rapid progress and were winners of the Second Division of the Bristol Combination in 1901-02, whilst their rivals Dings were First Division champions.

Both clubs had a common problem: there were no local rugby pitches in the city and matches were played on the Clifton Downs, which involved a three mile uphill trek to Blackboy Hill. The Hill was reached via the colourfully named Whiteladies Road. With so much in common, the two clubs merged to form Dings Crusaders.

Amongst the earliest members was 'Sunny Jim' Peters, who was to become the first black British international. Born in Manchester in 1879 to a West Indian father and English mother, Jim's father worked in a circus and met his end in a lion's cage. This accident forced his mother to hire Jim out to a circus troupe. Things went wrong when he broke his arm and was sacked by the troupe. Aged only 11, Jim was sent to an orphanage in London where he watched Blackheath play rugby. Mother and son were eventually reunited and moved to Bristol. Jim was persuaded to play for Dings simply because they were short of players. He was brilliant and was soon signed by Bristol RFC, for whom he made 35 appearances between 1900 and 1902. In common with many other good players of the era, he moved to Plymouth, where he found a job in the Royal Naval Dockyard, enabling him to play for Plymouth Albion RFC and Devon.

With Jim at fly-half, Devon won two county titles, which led to England selecting him against Scotland. He was dropped for the next England match against the Springboks, but was soon restored and eventually won five England caps. He retained his association with Plymouth Albion, who granted him a testimonial in 1909, although it was forbidden under RFU laws. Albion were, however, a law unto themselves. In the twilight of his playing days, Jim joined Plymouth Northern NU team before 'going north' by signing for Barrow and St. Helens. Neither club saw the best of the little fly-half and he eventually drifted back to Plymouth, where he died in 1954.

'Sunny Jim' Peters was one of dozens of Dings players who gravitated to the Bristol club during the next century. The best known Dings player to follow this path was Arthur Payne, who won two England caps between the wars. Arthur served Bristol for a decade before returning to the Crusaders, where he captained the club and then was coach in the 1960s.

Facilities at Dings improved when in 1948 they moved to a new pitch on the new Lockleaze Estate. The new ground was owned by the Shaftesbury Trust, whose trustees were adamant that a licensed bar was not allowed on the premises and players were expected to attend church regularly. It was 1976 before the rugby club was allowed to run a bar selling alcohol.

Dings players continued to bolster the city club as Colin Kimmins, Graham Trote, Floyd Waters, Trevor Dealy and John Blake became amongst the best players of the era. Kimmins was one of those rare breed of British players who played against the British Lions. Colin was serving in the army in 1962 when the Lions visited East Africa. An East African XV was raised and Colin played.

Dings were Bristol's leading junior club in season 1963-64, and a focal point for their local community.

The arrival of league rugby in 1987 proved a disaster for Dings. The club had heard a rumour that the RFU were planning a Bristol league for clubs in the city. They deferred involvement until the Bristol league was up-and-running, and so missed the boat and were placed in Gloucestershire One. It was 1990 before matters changed when the senior players demanded a more professional approach from the committee. Rapid strides were then made, with the club winning the Bristol Combination Cup and celebrating their Centenary season with victory in the Western Counties League.

Dings continued to produce great players. Dave Hilton, a loose-head prop, arrived at Dings as a junior and progressed to Bath and England Under 20s before suddenly becoming a bone-fide Scotsman and subsequently a Lion. Dave had a long and illustrious Scotland career before it became apparent that he was never eligible. He kept his affiliation to Dings and returned as coach.

Other modern greats who emerged from Dings include Huw Duggan, who began at Dings before joining Bristol and playing in the 1983 National Knockout Cup final, Paul Lloyd, who was one of the best players to ever play for Dings and Bristol, and

Kevin Maggs, who began his rugby at Imperial RFC but lived near the Dings ground. In 1994 he involuntarily joined Dings when they 'kidnapped' him and took him on their Easter tour of Blackpool. He later played for Bristol and Ireland.

The most recent international from Dings is massive lock Dave Attwood, who played at Lockleaze as a teenager before joining Gloucester and being capped by England. He made his senior England debut as a replacement for Tom Palmer in the game against New Zealand on the 7th November 2010, but only established himself in 2014.

Dings rose through the leagues to reach National Two South, but have suffered a constant drain of talent to clubs across the National leagues.

(Thanks to Steve & Chris Lloyd)

DRYBROOK

DRYBROOK IS A small town in the Forest of Dean, where rugby has been played since 1880, when a side called the Good Templars existed. Subsequently there were at least three other teams in the village: the Leopards, Plump Hill RFC and Drybrook RFC. The last named was founded in 1893 and merged with Plump Hill in 1894, the same year they joined the Gloucestershire RFC.

In the early years Drybrook played on a ground in the centre of the village and used several local inns as their headquarters. The original Drybrook RFC disappeared before the end of the 19th Century.

Drybrook was reformed after World War Two. The club purchased its present ground at the Mannings for £600, but by the late 1950s the club was on the brink of closing through lack of numbers. The senior team was disbanded, but a colts team was started and proved an instant success. Eventually a First XV was restarted and when the Senior XV was reintroduced in 1962, the club went from strength to strength.

A clubhouse was built at the Mannings in 1967 and new changing rooms added in 1976. The number of teams being run reached its peak in 1989 when five senior teams were regularly fielded, along with a Saturday Colts XV.

Drybrook have enjoyed many successes over the years, having won the Forest of Dean Combination Cup on 14 occasions. Since the County Cup was restarted in 1970, Drybrook's best performance was to finish as runners-up in 1989, and they have also reached the semi-finals on five occasions. They reached the Second round of the RFU Pilkington Cup in 1989.

Drybrook currently operate in the Gloucestershire Premier League having gained two promotions since league rugby began in 1987. Restructuring has meant that the club lost its status in the Western Counties League in 1999.

They are particularly proud of their mini/junior set up, which is now the largest in the area. With such a large number of young players at the club, officials are confident that the future is bright indeed.

Five players have represented the full Gloucestershire XV. Pat Simmons was the most prominent. He was an England reserve whilst playing at Rosslyn Park. Peter Meek gained an

England schools cap at Under 16 level whilst a pupil at Dene Magna School in 1990. Drybrook's record point-scorer is Chris Treherne, who amassed 5,423 points for the club in 637 games, including 403 tries, between 1979 and 2000.

Season 2012-2013 was a great year for Drybrook, losing only three of 27 games and becoming Gloucester Premier champions. Under coach Frazer McArdle, the club suffered two cup final defeats in a fortnight. They reached the RFU Senior Vase final, but lost 19-10 to Selby, and then lost 9-6 to Cinderford United in the Forest of Dean Combination Senior Cup final.

(Thanks to A.P. Mason)

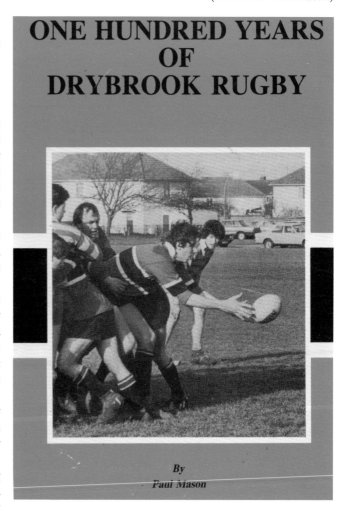

ONE HUNDRED YEARS OF DRYBROOK RUGBY

By Paul Mason

FOREST OF DEAN COMBINATION

"The Forest of Dean has gone downhill since they opened roads in the area."
Anon, 1910

THE FOREST OF Dean Combination is composed of Drybrook, Berry Hill, Cinderford, Coleford, Lydney and Bream. They lie within the ancient boundary of the Royal Forest and owe their roots to the mines of yesteryear. The last pit closed in 1965 but rugby is still a way of life.

Lydney and Cinderford are the best known clubs as they play in the National leagues. Berry Hill were highly successful from

1970 to 1990 before the economics of being a small-town club (pop 2000) proved too much. Drybrook are a small club who are an integral part of the town's life, rather in the tradition of Welsh clubs. Bream are the smallest club in the Forest. Yorkley RFC disbanded in 1983 on the eve of their Centenary.

The Forest has produced only a handful of internationals. Paul Mason, the historian, attributes the lack of caps to an exodus of good players to the Northern Union around 1900. Being mining folk, it wasn't difficult for rugby players to settle in the north, especially with £2 a week paid for playing rugby, more than a miner could earn in the Gloucestershire coalfield for 50 hours underground.

Before World War One, the Forest enjoyed a position of strength in Gloucestershire rugby with three forwards in the county team. However, the 1920s was a terrible decade for the area. A succession of miners strikes brought hard times, especially the 1926 Coal Crisis, which reduced many Forest folk to poverty.

Perhaps the greatest character to emerge from the Forest of Dean was A. 'Bumps' Carpenter, who played for Cinderford RFC and worked at Lightmoor Colliery in the town.

GLOUCESTER

"The RFU view Kingsholm as a piece of scrubland west of Reading."

Mike Burton

GLOUCESTER RFC WERE traditionally famous for tough, uncompromising rugby where the ball is kept in front of their forwards – a style of rugby peculiar to the South West. It was said low scoring was the norm in the South West because avoiding defeat against rivals was the primary aim. Perhaps it has always been so as, in 1880, the local newspaper reported: "The standard of play locally is not as rough as it has been in previous years."

Gloucester RFC is the centre of the county's rugby and traditionally its players come from local junior clubs. The club was formed on September 15th 1873, and the opening match was against the College School. The first captain was Frank Hartley, who came to the city from London and was the prime mover in starting rugby in Gloucester. Initially matches were played at the Spa (the home of the Gloucester Cricket Club).

In 1878 a match was arranged against Rockleaze from Bristol, which was to be played under what should have been four electric lights, but two of the lights failed. The crowd saw little and a riot was only narrowly averted.

Gloucester played in Cherry and White hoops from its earliest days, the choice of colours being dictated by the only available jerseys, which were borrowed from neighbours Painswick RFC.

The move to Kingsholm in 1891 coincided with Gloucester's rise in prominence, notably when they stunned Wales with victories over Cardiff and Swansea. In 1900 they were regarded as the only English team who could visit South Wales and hold their own. On both sides of the border, between 1896 and 1902, they only lost 22 of 201 games.

ONE OF THE EARLIEST TEAMS (ABOUT 1876-77)

J. W. Bayley, J. Bennett, W. A. Boughton, P. B. Cooke, ——, H. J. Berry,
F. Billett, H. J. Boughton.
J. F. Brown (Capt.), W. Snushall, F. Tandy, L. Bubb,
G. J. Dewey, W. Brown, J. F. Grimes.

Gloucester drew their players from local clubs, but it wasn't all peace and light, as in March 1894 Gloucester were hauled up before the RFU for poaching a Stroud player called Sherwell. The hearing also addressed concerns of professionalism about a player called J. Hanman. The RFU found Gloucester guilty of covert professionalism, closed the club for 20 days and levied costs of £150 on the club – a huge sum for the time.

The first great players to emerge were brothers Frank and Percy Stout. Frank was a soccer player who switched to rugby at 17 and made his England debut within two years. Frank won 14 England caps and captained the 1899 British Isles team when the Rev. Matthew Mullineux, the official leader, was dropped. Percy was a great player for club and county, but was lost to the game in 1898 when he moved to Egypt.

W.J. Jackson was considered as talented as the Stouts. He was capped by England ahead of Frank Stout but 'went north' to Halifax. Around this time, two other Gloucester players, Smith and Dovey, were poached by Wigan NUFC.

An England home international match outside Twickenham is unheard of now, but in 1900 Kingsholm staged the England v Wales game, the only Home international game ever held on the ground. Far from being a success, it cost the Gloucester club £750! The club had to spend huge sums on extra stands and other amenities, a capacity crowd being anticipated. The biggest problem was that an estimated 5,000 of the 20,000 crowd sneaked into Kingsholm without paying. The next international visit was an even worse experience as the first All Blacks slaughtered Gloucester 44-0 in 1905. Gloucester were fortunate to acquire a great leader in Arthur Hudson, who led the club to a new level as player and administrator. Hudson won eight England caps, but was so badly injured in 1920, he was forced to retire and took over as club secretary. Also capped by England at the time were Dai Gent, Harry Berry, Billie Johns and Alfie Woods.

Gent was a diminutive scrum-half who later became one of the first rugby writers and commentators. He was the only reporter on the 1950 Lions tour. The tour lasted eight months, but Gent got homesick after three months and went home. The last two test matches went unreported in the UK press.

Woods was a talented but controversial character. He won three England caps whilst with Gloucester, then moved to rivals Cheltenham, which coincided with his appointment as a public house landlord. A year later he moved to Oldham NUFC, with whom he won a championship medal and represented Great Britain on the successful 1914 tour of Australia, where he was accompanied by another ex-Gloucester player in Billy Hall, also playing at Oldham.

Gloucester's first internationals: Harry Berry, Dai Gent, Arthur Hudson and Frank Stout.

Old Blues in 1926, and in the following season, wing three-quarter Sid Brown died as a result of a kidney injury sustained in a game with Aberavon. The rugby community came together and helped the families. Bayliss' family received £1,000 to help his dependents.

Gloucester were consistently one of Britain's top sides in the years between the wars. Cardiff, Newport and Swansea were rivals, but popular visitors as they guaranteed a full house at Kingsholm. In England, Bristol were Gloucester's only serious competition. In 1933-34 Gloucester were viewed as the best club side in England, with 29 wins in 38 matches. The club had six full England players and four more trialists in the 1930s and produced two great rugby players in 'Bumps' Carpenter and Harold Boughton. who were team-mates for club and country until World War Two.

Tom Voyce

Gloucester produced many great characters between the wars, none greater than Arthur Tom Voyce. Voyce played fly-half for England Schools before switching to flanker. He became an army officer and was wounded in World War One, losing an eye. In the 1920s he played 27 times for England. He was a 'tough nut' who was not intimidated. He was a loud, uncompromising forward who was nicknamed 'the King of Gloucester'. He began his rugby career with Gordon League before moving to Kingsholm. At international level, his best years coincided with England's golden era under W.W. Wakefield. The crowd loved Dave Davies and the flying backs, but they were supplied with ammunition by Wakefield, Voyce, Blakiston and company. Voyce was at the heart of the England v New Zealand match in 1925 which was assessed as one of the most unpleasant physical battles in rugby history. He was involved in the brawl that saw Cyril Brownlie of New Zealand become the first international sent off in rugby history. The Welsh crowds hated Voyce, who neither gave nor asked for quarter in the forward battles. He was targeted by the opposition but only once left the field in an international; that was during the 1926 Wales v England match – another regarded as excessively ill-disciplined. He toured with the 1924 British Isles team and was the top try-scorer. He retired from playing for Gloucester in 1927, but served the club for the rest of his life, including as coach from 1929.

In such a climate, it is not surprising that Gloucester suffered several on-field fatalities in the era. Stan Bayliss, a fine forward and clubman, suffered a fatal spine injury when playing against

Bumps was a legend (see Cinderford), but Harold Boughton is forgotten today. His exploits are amazing: schoolboy international at 12 years of age, club debut at 16, county debut at 17 and the best goal-kicker in British rugby. In 1935 Boughton was called up by England as an emergency full-back. He had never played in an England trial but played against Wales, who gave him a 'physical going over'. Between his club debut in 1925 and his last match, Boughton scored over 1500 points – a record for a first-class club. He was much admired 'up north' and one RL club offered him £500 to join them, but he declined. Harold was versatile on and off the rugby field. He was a bus driver by profession and would drive the team bus to away matches, play full-back, take a full part in the after-match drinking and then drive the bus home. Harold and Bumps were captain and vice-captain for season 1939-40 as the wartime authorities allowed Gloucester to carry on playing, although their only opposition was army sides.

Apart from Tom Voyce, selection of Gloucester players by the British Isles team was rare, although the little-known John Gordon A'Bear was selected for the 1936 BI tour to Argentina.

One person surely worthy of mention is the Rev. Bill Phillips, who made 56 appearances for Gloucester between 1934 and 1936 whilst teaching at Cheltenham College. A winger, Bill would play for the Cherry and Whites and then have to get back to the college for evening prayers. During World War Two he served as an army captain, including parachuting into Arnhem. He landed on a panzer tank, the hatch opened and a German said, "For you Tommy, the war really is over." Bill ended up in a prisoner-of-war camp, was released in 1945 and renewed his life-long association with Gloucester.

Since the war Gloucester have had a succession of 'crowd-pullers'; for instance, the mercurial Willie Jones, who was also a Glamorgan county cricketer. His prolific drop-goal feats are said to have been the reason for the eventual reduction in value of the dropped goal from four points to three!

In 1951 Bill Hook was called up by England as a goal-kicker. The broadsheets were skeptical about his selection, but after he kicked a conversion to give England a 5-3 win over Scotland, the Times said, "Hook was the kind of full back we've been hoping for".

John Gwilliam is a contender for the greatest forward in Gloucester (and Welsh) history. Gwilliam was educated at Pontypridd GS, Monmouth School, Cambridge and Sandhurst. After being demobbed, he joined Newport and led Wales to their first Grand Slam since 1908. A schoolmaster, he then moved to Bromsgrove School in 1952 and joined Gloucester for three seasons. At Kingsholm he was regarded as the finest line-out jumper in Britain. He left the club in 1956 and moved to Dulwich College and was later headmaster of Birkenhead School.

The post-war years saw Gloucester produce many great players, including England's full-back, Don Rutherford, evergreen forward Peter Ford, who played 506 times for the club scoring 156 tries, scrum-half Mickey Booth, Dick Smith, a speedy open-side wing-forward, and Bob Cleaves, who scored 239 tries, beating Arthur Hudson's 60-year-old record.

The 1970s saw Gloucester field a great full-back in Peter Butler, who set point-scoring records for his club and county for over a decade but was badly treated by England. Despite being probably the most prolific point-scorer in English rugby at the time he only won two England caps.

Peter Butler

Gloucestershire were regular county champions, with Butler's boot as the principal weapon, and they won the National Knockout Cup in 1972, 1978 and 1982. The club won the SW Merit Table in 1983-84 and continued to produce internationals, none better than Mike Teague, a huge flanker.

At the outset of professionalism, the club was bought by a genuine fan in Tom Walkinshaw. He hired French legend Phillipe Saint-Andre as coach, who brought in 16 of his fellow countrymen. Initially the move worked, as Gloucester won the end-of-season Premiership play-offs and the club reached the semi-finals of the Heineken Cup. Saint-Andre was replaced by Nigel Melville, who won the National Knockout Cup. The vicissitudes of Premiership rugby were demonstrated between 2006 and 2008 when Gloucester were Premiership champions, but lost the title in the play-offs. Dean Ryan arrived as coach in 2010 and afterwards commented that "he signed too many players". The following year Brain Redpath took over and won the new LV Cup.

The stars of the era included Mike Tindall and Phil Vickery, who played in England's Rugby World Cup victory. Tindall had eight years with Bath before joining Gloucester in 2005. He won 75 England caps at centre, but is best known for marrying the Queen's grand-daughter, Zara Phillips. He played for Gloucester for a decade making 181 appearances for the club. Vickery played 145 games for Gloucester from 1995 to 2006 and won 73 England and five Lions caps, but his career was blighted by injury. Currently Gloucester are enjoying better times with the emergence of young England stars such as Billy Twelvetrees, Jonny May and Ben Morgan.

The surprising aspect of Gloucester rugby is despite their reputation for keeping it tough and uncompromising, they are one of the most hospitable clubs to visitors. Also, no club treasures its heritage more keenly than Kingsholm, where pictures of Hudson, Stout, Voyce et al line the corridors.

GLOUCESTER OLD BOYS

GLOUCESTER OB WERE formed at a meeting in the city's Northgate Mansions on 12th March 1904. The aim was to recruit old boys from the main schools: King's, Sir Thomas Rich's, Crypt Grammar and College School to form a new rugby club. It is thought that the club's original colours of blue shirts and white shorts are a link to Sir Thomas Rich's School. The club switched to navy, claret and gold hoops in 1923, adopting Navy for Rich's, Claret for Crypts and Gold from Kings.

At the time, most of Gloucester's schools were soccer-playing and George Romans, the Gloucester captain, felt that there was scope for more rugby in the city. Sid Lane was elected as the first captain of GOB, a post he held until 1909.

The first headquarters of the new club was the Nelson Arms in Llanthony Priory, with the use of a pitch at Hempstead. A transfer of headquarters to the Talbot Hotel in Southgate wasn't a great idea as it involved a two-kilometre walk to the pitch. In 1908 the club moved to a pitch on Denmark Road.

Their first match was against Gloucester 'A' (now the United), which ended in a heavy defeat. But things improved and in season 1905-06 they produced figures of P27 W15 D5 L7. The nature of rugby at this time can be gleaned from Gloucester OB Seconds being unable to find a rugby fixture and taking on Gloucester City Hockey Club, at hockey, and winning! The First XV were unbeaten the following season with figures of P25 W23 D2 F386 A52.

Unfortunately, the demands from the city club for Gloucester OB to loan them players drained their strength and results declined.

The first top-class player to emerge from the OBs was Dai Gent, who won five England caps between 1905 and 1910 and was one of the first rugby writers. Gent achieved his international honours after moving to Kingsholm. This became a well-trodden path as GOB talent joined the city club; a process that irritated many a GOB official down the years.

After World War One, Tommy Voyce played briefly for them before going on to honours with Gloucester and England. Many other OBs went on to better things, notably Arthur Field (Richmond & London Scottish), Stanley Cook (Cambridge University & England reserve) and John Gadd, who played for England.

Gloucester Old Boys were County Cup champions from 1994 to 1996 and North Gloucestershire Combination cup winners on several occasions. Today the OBs operate from the eastern side of the city, near the Oxford Road. They were in South West One for a decade before slipping into Gloucester 1.

GORDON LEAGUE

GORDON LEAGUE WERE for a long time the only kind of league that the RFU would accept. The Gordon League was a Boy Scout-style organisation established in 1886 in memory of General Charles Gordon, the hero of Khartoum. Gordon was an odd sort of hero because he was a mercenary who plied his trade all over the world before choosing to die a martyr's death in Ethiopia. His death sparked a political crisis in Britain that led to the British Government invading the Sudan.

Gordon League boys clubs were formed across Britain in memory of the fallen hero. The Gloucester Gordon League was launched on 5th December 1885. Eventually people began to question the whole Khartoum escapade and government enthusiasm for the Gordon Youth Movement waned and they withdrew their financial backing. Many of the clubs were forced to disband, but the Gloucester branch survived thanks to Miss Agnes Waddy and Ernest Browning. Part of their Gloucester movement was Gordon League RFC, who played its first match in the September of 1885, beating Barton Rangers by one try and one minor to one minor. Ernest Browning scored the winning try and went on to serve the club as a player and an official for a total of 59 years.

Gordon League have produced some great players for the Kingsholm club. David Hollands was born in Gloucester and learned his rugby at Gordon League. He played for Gloucester from 1906 until 1910. At this point, he became one of many fine players to secure employment at Devonport and join Devon Albion. He was rapidly picked for England before 'going north' He joined Oldham RLFC and went on the 1914 Great Britain RL tour to Australia. During World War One, he played for the Devonport Services RUFC.

Sid Smart began at Gordon League and was a Gloucester back row player from 1910 to 1926. He played for England from 1912 to 1914, including winning a Grand Slam. A Gloucester legend, Sid died at Kingsholm during a match.

Another old boy of Gordon league was Tom Voyce, who won 27 England caps from 1920 to 1926 and was perhaps the greatest English forward of the 1920s.

The best-known modern player associated with Gordon League is Peter Ford, who won four England caps in 1964. Ford attended Gloucester Central Modern School before joining the club. He was soon spotted by Gloucester, for whom he appeared over 500 times and was selected 37 times by the county. Later, John Bayliss played for Gloucester and England U21s.

Gordon League made a remarkable impact on the Gloucestershire Cup when it was revived in 1970. They reached the final three times in the next decade and were twice champions, in 1974-75 and 1975-76.

Since leagues arrived, the club were 2003-04 Western Counties North Champions. They currently play in the Gloucester Premier league.

HARTPURY COLLEGE

WHEN LEAGUE RUGBY arrived in England in 1987, Hartpury College was a small agricultural college on the northern outskirts of Gloucester. Yet within 25 years the college side has developed into a National League club and an outstanding centre for the development of talented rugby players.

The college was founded in 1947 by Gloucestershire County Council as The Gloucestershire Farm Institute. It remained relatively unchanged until 1990, when Malcolm Wharton, the new principal, initiated a rapid expansion programme, starting with the provision of a larger variety of further education courses, which saw the number of students rise from 60 to 3,200. The college has a link to the University of the West of England (UWE). Since then the First XV has had a remarkable record of success.

The Hartpury College Rugby Academy was formed in September 2000 in partnership with Gloucester Rugby, consisting of a University side that competed in the British Universities league system and local junior leagues. They rose in consecutive seasons through the Gloucestershire divisions to gain national prominence in 2007 when, in a single season, they won the RFU Junior Vase, the British Universities Championship and the Gloucestershire Premier Division, scoring 1,100 points in the process.

The following years were equally exciting, with an 83-5 victory in the Senior Vase together with becoming champions of the Western Counties and South West leagues.

In 2010, they were promoted to National 3 and won the new RFU National Champions Cup (for level 6 clubs). They reached National One in 2014 despite established players graduating from the college. By 2012 a third of Gloucester's First XV were ex-Hartpury players.

Many of the best young players in the Home Countries have emerged from the college, which has produced 100 internationals in ten years for 11 different countries. The best known have been Alex Cuthbert (Wales), Jonny May and Henry Trinder (England), Matthew Evans (Canada) and Dan Touhy (Ireland).

The college also has the UK's most successful college women's rugby programme, with more than 15 England U20 internationals and two full England internationals.

LYDNEY

'The Tinplates'

THE SMALL GLOUCESTERSHIRE town of Lydney sees itself as the 'gateway to the Forest of Dean' as it lies just outside the border of the Forest. The townsfolk prefer to call themselves 'Severnsiders' and are proud of being one of the best sides in the county, and being able to field a team in National Two from a population of only 8,960.

Tin plate and coal mining were the principal employment in Lydney when the rugby club was formed in 1887 as 'Lydney and Aylburton FC' and using Stockholm Park as a ground. The club was at the time overshadowed by neighbours Coleford RFC, who were the strongest side in the Forest.

The club's first President, Charles Bathurst, must hold the record for the longest tenure in any rugby office as he was club president for 71 years. A local landowner, Bathurst is better known as the 1st Viscount Bledisloe, who became Governor-General of New Zealand. He presented the Bledisloe Cup, which is competed for annually by Australia and New Zealand's rugby teams. Bledisloe can also be remembered for one quote, when he described the New Zealanders as "Nature's gentlefolk", which seems an odd description of some All Black forwards.

The original Lydney club disbanded in 1895 but reformed several years later. Around this time, they moved to Regentsholme, from where they still operate. Regentsholme is picturesquely set with two small stands next to the River Severn.

They were county champions in 1910 and could claim a top-class fixture list. But success was fleeting; an economic decline hit the whole area and Lydney RFC went bust in 1912.

They reappeared in 1919 wearing black and white shirts, which replaced the original colours of a blue jersey with a white sash. Traditionally Lydney played a great number of fixtures in South Wales because of their close proximity to the principality.

The inter-war years saw hard times for Lydney and the whole Forest, which culminated in the Great Depression. Charles Bathurst helped the unemployed in Lydney by giving them land for allotments.

After World War Two, Lydney recovered and had a great season in 1953-54, with six players having county trials. Despite one great season, local rugby was suffering, with only one school, Lydney Grammar School, playing rugby. Subsequently, the school hired Ted Parfitt as rugby master and he was to dominate Lydney rugby throughout the second half of the 20th century.

E.J. 'Ted' Parfitt had played for Llandovery and Newport before crossing the border. He was quickly selected for Gloucestershire, where, as scrum-half, he partnered Willie Jones, the legendary Gloucester fly-half. Under Parfitt, Lydney GS produced 43 schoolboy internationals and four full internationals: Bev Dovey, Trevor White, Peter Kingston and Chris Williams. Dovey, a

biology teacher, was one of the most travelled players of the era, representing Oxford University, Lydney, Rosslyn Park and Bristol, and playing for England. Parfitt produced other players who began with Lydney but who went on to play for top-class sides, notably John Morris (Newport), John Hampton (Rosslyn Park and England reserve), Tom Jones (Devon), Ricky Braybrooke (Army), Paul Price (England Counties), Paul Howell (Bristol), Julian Davies (Bristol) and Gordon Sargent (Gloucester). Peter Kingston started at Lydney before moving to Moseley and Gloucester. He made his England debut in 1975 and was recalled in 1979. Later he taught at Pate's GS for 30 years. The England Women's international Georgia Stevens also played for Lydney.

In 1982 the trend was for Lydney players to move to Gloucester, the Kingsholm club picking up Peter Butler, Brian Vine, Gordon Sargeant and Paul Howells. Perhaps the best player in the club's history was John Morris, who was captain for 11 seasons.

Today the tin plate mines are long gone and have been replaced by smaller industries, but rugby flourishes. In 2003 Lydney reached National Two.

(Thanks to Cyril Bailey)

MINEHEAD BARBARIANS

"Come to Minehead for health, beauty and mental delight."
1960s advertisement

MINEHEAD IS A lovely seaside town on the North Somerset coast. The first known rugby match involving Minehead was against Kellands in 1883. Little is known of the original side.

It was 1923 before rugby re-appeared, with school rugby being played at Minehead Grammar School. Two years later, Minehead and Alcombe RFC was formed by local schoolmasters, who used Alcome Village Hall as changing rooms and used a pitch on Marshfield Road. M & A only survived for a decade, which forced the surviving players to join Taunton.

In 1939, a new side called 'the Barbarians' was formed in the town. The new club opted for the new name to avoid outstanding debts left by their predecessors. Sadly, the outbreak of World War Two bought events to a halt until September 1946.

The restart saw the Parks used as the home ground and the Lido swimming pool as changing rooms. During the war, the Lido had showers installed in the event of a gas attack. Unfortunately, this excellent facility was a mile away from the pitch, which created serious problems. The season began with an 11-3 defeat by King's College, Taunton, but the terrible winter of 1946-47 thwarted all attempts to play a full season.

Things improved, and in the mid-1950s the club gained a lease on the Parks and, in 1958, opened a new clubhouse with a match against Clifton RFC.

Minehead established a useful link with the RAF station at Watchet, which provided new players. This nexus led to Peter Robbins, the Coventry, England and Lions flanker, making occasional appearances for Minehead. Sadly RAF Watchet was closed in the 1960s and Minehead struggled to fill the void.

The 1970s saw Minehead lose their tenancy on the pitch, but they still owned the land containing the clubhouse, which allowed them to barter a deal to stay at the Parks and purchase land at Elliscombe.

They won the Somerset 1 League in season 2004-05 with 19 wins out of 20 games, and the Somerset Premier League the following season with 16 wins from 22 games. Since then Barbarians have consolidated their position in Western Counties West.

OLD BRISTOLIANS

BRISTOL GRAMMAR SCHOOL dates back to the reign of King Henry VIII. The club has kept it links to the old school and 30% of its current First XV are Old Bristolians. OB play at the Old Bristolian Memorial Ground at Failand.

The most famous sportsman who appeared for OB was Tom Graveney, a legendary Gloucester and England batsman of the 1950s, who played full-back for the OB in 1949. Other internationals who began with OB were Rob McEwan (Scotland), John Leieu (Wales), John Currie, Redwood and Colin McFadyean attended Bristol GS and Loughborough University, also played for Cleve RFC and Moseley.

In 1968-69 OBs were the best side in the Bristol Combination.

Currently OB play in Western Counties West after a rapid rise from Gloucester 2. The rise has also included two wins in the Bristol Combination Vase. In 2010 they were voted the city's Rugby Club of the Year.

OLD COLSTONIANS

THE NAME OF Colston is ever-present in Bristol. Edward Colston was a wealthy merchant who became the city's benefactor and established Colston's School in the centre of Bristol. The school opened in 1710 with the aim of providing free education, food and accommodation for 100 poor boys. As the school expanded, fee-paying pupils were introduced, but the school remained true to Edward Colston's vision, and there were still Foundationers receiving a free education until the late 1950s.

The rugby section of the Old Colstonians Sports Club has produced a number of boys with outstanding rugby talent. Henry Shrewring played for England ten times between 1905 and 1907, William Johnson played 16 times for England from 1910 and Tom Brown, the Old Colstonians and Bristol full-back, was also capped for England at rugby. More surprisingly, R.C. Williams was capped for Argentina at rugby in matches against both the English touring side and Chile in 1937. More recently Alan Morley was capped by England seven times between 1972 and 1975 and Austin Sheppard was capped by England twice in the early 1980s. The most recent OC international was Olly Barkley, who emerged from the Colston School XV who won the Daily Mail (Schools) Cup in 2000. After joining Bath, Olly made his England debut in 2001 as a 19-year-old and became a regular in 2004. He later joined Gloucester before moving to France.

The Old Colstonians Sports Club is currently based at the Society-owned ground at New Road, Stoke Gifford on the outskirts of Bristol.

In 2004 OC fielded a teenager who was visiting the school from New Zealand. Ben Smith turned out for the club and looked a fine prospect. He returned to New Zealand and was picked for Otago, the Highlanders and then the All Blacks. Since then he has won 43 caps. From OC to being one of the best players in the world in eight years is a rapid rise for Ben Smith.

OLD CRYPTIANS

CRYPT SCHOOL, GLOUCESTER was founded in 1593 by John and Joan Cooke and used the monks of Llanthony Priory to teach the pupils.

The school adopted rugby union in 1922, but had already established a reputation as a school that produced great rugby players, notably Frank and Percy Stout, who did sterling service for mighty Gloucester. Percy won five England caps in 1898-99. His brother Frank had won his first England cap in 1897, but is best remembered for his feats for the British Lions. He captained the British Isles to three test wins against Australia in 1899 and, four years later, toured South Africa.

The Old Cryptians club itself was formed in Southgate on the 8th October 1925 by eight volunteers under Leslie Haine. From the outset, OCRFC welcomed outsiders because the club couldn't muster 15 Old Cryptians. The club records show the club's principles were stated to be: "A rugby football club, for OBs of Crypt School and others who may be considered desirable, should be formed." Fortunately the club took the name of 'Greyfriars RFC'. A pitch was found at the school playing fields at Llanthony and the YMCA was used as headquarters. Legend has it that the first ever fixture was away to Chepstow, although the result is not known. The first captain was Ron Quinsee.

In 1928 the club went against the usual pattern and dropped the 'open to all-comers' clause and restricted membership to Old Cryptians.

Two years later, OC acquired John A'Bear and Graham Parker. A'Bear moved to Gloucester and captained club and county before joining a small but unfortunate band who played for the British Isles but was never selected for his home county. A'Bear toured Argentina with the 1936 Lions.

Graham Parker was a great figure in Gloucestershire rugby in the late 1930s, playing for OC, Stroud, Gloucester, Cambridge University and England. A large stocky man, Parker was one of the best goal-kickers of the era, as well as being one of the best cricket batsmen in the South West. Parker played in several wartime internationals.

OC captain from 1932 to 1937 was Willie Jones, who later became a legend at Kingsholm. His captaincy included season 1933-34 when OC lost only one match from 22 fixtures.

Gordon Hudson joined Gloucester from Cryptians during the war and played for England in the wartime internationals, scoring four tries against Scotland in 1944. Coincidentally, Arthur Hudson, his father, scored four tries for England against France in 1906.

The 1950s were a golden era at Old Cryptians, with 25 wins in 1955-56 and, two years later, 33 victories from 37. Success was double-edged as the cream of OC talent migrated to Kingsholm, notably Roy Long, Roy Timms, Eric Stephens and Bob Hannaford.

The Hannaford family had a long association with OC and in 1971 Charlie Hannaford scored a try on his England debut against Wales at Cardiff. Charlie was on the fringe of England selection for several seasons but always seemed to miss the final nod.

The same fate befell Peter Butler, a prodigious goal-kicker for Gloucester and the county. He made his England debut on the violent Australian tour which saw his Gloucester colleague Mike Burton become the first England international to be sent off. Butler never had a regular selection for England, although he was generally regarded as the best goal-kicking full-back in the counties.

Perhaps the greatest OC was Cyril Ravenhill, who scored 237 tries in 773 appearances for OC between 1955 and 1997.

The arrival of league rugby saw OCs in Gloucester Div 2 and win a promotion in 1991-92. Currently OC are in Gloucester 1.

OLD PATESIANS

"Followers of the Old Patesians will be provided with the best football, played in the right spirit ... The Old Patesians play the game for the game's sake and the pleasure derived is shared by players and spectators alike."
Gloucester Echo, 1925

OLD PATESIANS RFC are the old boys of Cheltenham Grammar School – also known as Richard Pate's GS. Rugby was played at the school from 1906, but it was another seven years before the old boys rugby club was formed. From the outset OP played on school pitches, and it took 60 years before the club found a permanent home.

OPs were a good side between the wars. The club's biggest match each year was against Cheltenham College, which was reported in the Times newspaper. In 1926 the Times enthused that "The Old Patesians play the game for the game's sake and the pleasure derived by the players and spectators."

The 1950s saw OPs struggling, but they produced an international in George Hastings, who moved to Cheltenham, Gloucester and England.

1975 saw the opening of the ground at Everest Road and an end to the 'nomadic' nature of the club's previous years.

The formation of league rugby saw Old Pats placed in the Gloucestershire leagues. They achieved successive league championships between 1992 and 1994, winning Gloucester 1 and then the Western Counties league. Four years later they won South West Two (South). All this success was eclipsed in 2001-02 when the First XV won South West One on points difference and the Intermediate Cup at Twickenham by a single point against Blaydon.

OLD REDS
(Old Redcliffians)

"Playing top class sides wasn't particularly physical. We had played a club called Old Reds a few seasons before. That taught us a lesson."
London captain, 1987

OLD REDCLIFFIANS RFC was formed by old boys of Redcliffe School in 1918. They began by playing at Redcatch Lane, Knowle, but moved to Redcliffe Athletic Ground, Knowle in 1932. Two years later the club wanted to started a Junior XV and took the complete Redcliffe School First XV as a unit.

There first top-class player was Reg Quick, who was one of the best Bristol players of the inter-war years. A huge figure in the area, Reg was an England trialist but was overlooked in favour of 'up country' players. Other top-class Bristol players to emerge from the club in the era were Frank and Barry Stinchcombe and Alf Lillicrap.

The post-war years were one of the best periods in the club's history. The Firsts went 18 months without defeat and were one of the best sides in the Bristol Combination. In 1958, Old Reds won the Bristol Combination Seven-a-Side Tournament for the first time in its history, and went on to win more cups and

Old Patesians: Intermediate Cup winners and South West One champions 2001-02.

tournaments, regularly having players picked for representative games. At one time they had five players in the Bristol Combination XV, plus players with Bath and Bristol.

In 1966-67 Old Reds vacated Daventry Road, moving to Stockwood Lane, where a new clubhouse was completed for the 50th anniversary season. The Golden Jubilee saw an Old Reds XV play a Bristol XV match, which Old Reds won 20-12.

In 1983, Old Reds qualified for the National Knockout Cup by being runners-up to Bath in the Somerset Cup. Bath became regular visitors to Old Reds matches and persuaded Gareth Chilcott and Richard Lee to move to the Rec. Chilcott became an English rugby legend with his cheeky smile. He played 373 times for Bath and 14 times for England and later became an author and TV personality. Richard Lee played for England B.

In 2010 Old Reds won the Intermediate Cup, beating Northern 42-10, and the following year reached National 3 (South). At scrum-half was Graeme Beveridge, who was physically the smallest Scotland international of modern times. He won six Scotland caps despite being only 5ft 6ins. He joined Reds from Glasgow Warriors – a rare example of a top-class player returning to junior rugby.

OLD WESTONIANS

OLD WESTONIANS RFC was formed in 1928-29 by ex-scholars of the County School, Weston Super Mare. The club played its home games on the school playing fields. Most of their fixtures were with Bristol Combination sides. The highlight of the season was an Easter Monday trip on a steamer across the Severn Estuary to play Old Cantonians in Cardiff.

The playing colours of the Old Westonians were red and yellow. OW closed during World War Two, reformed for a decade before disbanding in 1957.

OLDFIELD OLD BOYS
(Somerset)

OLDFIELD OBs WERE formed in 1950 from the former pupils of Oldfield Boys School on Wells Road in Bath. In 1971 the school merged with the City of Bath Boys' School as Beechen Cliff School.

Oldfield have provided Bath RFC with some fine players. In the 1950s, John Rees began with the club and became captain of the city club. In the 1970s, Oldfield produced two top-class England players in John Hall and Chris Perry. Later they produced Olly Barkley and Freddie Burns.

In 2005, Oldfield were Somerset Premier Champions, coached by Andy Boyce. The club currently play in the Southern Counties and Somerset Premiership.

PAINSWICK

'Queen of the Cotswolds'

PAINSWICK IS THE oldest village rugby side in England. They have a direct lineage of playing rugby back to 1872. The village was originally famous for the production and weaving of red cloth used in army uniforms, until World War One rendered bright clothing obsolete. The greatest Painswick rugby legend concerns red cloth. In the 1870s the club's original colours of red (what else) and white were washed but emerged as cherry and white. The kit was borrowed by Gloucester RFC, who have worn cherry and white ever since.

At this time, the club had a direct link to the oldest roots of rugby as Dr Francis Arnold, the grandson of Thomas Arnold of Rugby School, was the resident GP in Painswick until his death in 1927. He attended St Barts but didn't play rugby.

Currently Painswick play in Gloucester 2 but were in Gloucester Premier in 2004.

ROYAL AGRICULTURAL COLLEGE

THE RAC WERE a serious force in South West rugby for a brief period and also gave Australasian rugby a great gift.

The college itself was formed in 1845 as Fairford Farmers Club as part of the agricultural revolution that swept Britain. Until the mid-19th Century, fluctuating agricultural production and prices was a constant problem, which led to a desire for better education of young farmers.

The original agricultural college was established to reach 'Oxbridge standards' in farming. The Earl of Bathurst donated 430 acres at Cirencester as a home for the school. The 'Royal' prefix was self appointed and only ratified at a later date.

The first students arrived in September 1845 and were an odd bunch. A contemporary account says they were "rough, wild, half-educated" students "who were only sent to Cirencester because nothing else could be found for them". There was no state funding for RAC and students had to find sponsors to pay the fees.

Rugby was played at RAC from the 1860s and for 20 years the college had a first-class fixture list, including Gloucester and Cardiff. But college sides, like RAC, soon fell behind the best club sides and the old adage of 'Men versus Boys' was demonstrated in October 1886 when Cardiff, with seven internationals, hammered RAC by two tries and eight goals to the students' single try. The college reluctantly acknowledged the growing differential and concentrated on local fixtures.

The 1890s saw a great rugby administrator studying at RAC when Viscount Bledisloe completed his studies. He is best remembered as Governor-General of New Zealand from 1930 to 1935 when he donated the Bledisloe Cup.

The best modern player was Robin Cowling, who attended RAC in the 1960s. He subsequently played for Gloucester, Leicester and England.

ST. BRENDAN'S OLD BOYS

ST. BRENDAN OBs WERE formed in 1929 by Douglas Pratten, who was a famous player for Bristol and Gloucester. St. Brendan's College was one of a dozen schools run on public school lines by the Christian Brothers, a tough bunch of Irish educationists who were keen on rugby. Until 1958, Old Brendan's played on the school playing fields. The greatest influence on the club's players in the early days was Elwyn Price, who taught at the college and is regarded as one of the best coaches in the South West.

Down the years, St. Brendan's have produced 50 players for Bristol. The first great player produced by St. Brendan's was John Blake, who became a legendary player, coach and captain of the city club. Since then St. Brendan's have produced a string of top-class players: Mike Rafter, Bill Locke, Nigel Pomphrey, Peter Polledri, Michael Heal, Jim Davidson, John White, Alan Sharp, Peter Colston and Mark Regan. Although most of its best players played for England, Davidson played for Ireland.

Mike Rafter

Mike Rafter was perhaps the best of the group. He was an outstanding flanker for Bristol – as befits the great nephew of Sam Tucker. Rafter won 17 England caps despite being dismissed by one newspaper with the comment "small forwards should have disappeared with steam trains". Today he is club president.

The club originally played at Brislington near Keynsham, but moved to Combe Dingle in Westbury-on-Trim.

Year 2000 found St Brendan's in a parlous state, with only 86 players at all age levels despite a great reputation for junior rugby. Since then the club has clawed itself back from the brink. Today it runs three senior teams, plus minis, colts and juniors. The playing numbers now are 450. The First XV have recently been promoted to the Gloucester Premier division.

(Thanks to Chris Groves)

STROUD

STROUD IS A wool town but had half a dozen coal-mines in the area until the mid-20th Century. Rugby has been played in the hilly Cotswold town since 1871, but it took another two years to establish a side. In 1873 the Rev. John Sibree formed a school at Upper Grange where he included rugby football in the curriculum. Two of Sibree's pupils, Mark Cartwright and Marcus Cartwright, graduated to Clifton College and in October 1873 played in Gloucestershire's first county match.

Amongst the founders were brothers H.A. and H.M. Hamilton. H.A. helped organise the first Varsity match, whilst H.M. was capped by Scotland in 1874. Another founder member was Alec Playne, who was remarkable for being an accomplished player despite being both deaf and dumb.

The new Stroud RFC initially played at Stratford Court, which was owned by J.W.Hellewell, the club president. Sadly, the club lost the ground following the death of a player in 1877. They then moved to Stratford Road, Farmhill.

Stroud were undefeated for two seasons from 1876 to 1878. In October 1878 they took a leading role in forming the Gloucestershire Rugby Union. Prominent players of the era were W.J. Butcher, who was Stroud's captain for nine seasons, and Sydney Howard Smith (1872-1947), who was a great all-round sportsman. He was best known as a tennis player: he was Welsh champion for a decade from 1897 and a beaten Men's finalist and twice Men's Doubles champion at Wimbledon.

Charles Hooper played for Stroud after leaving Clifton College. He moved to London and was capped for England in 1894.

In 1891, Stroud RFC opened its own clubhouse and opened two sides of the ground to spectators, charging 6d (2p) and 3d (1p) for admission. The ground hosted Gloucester RFC in 1896 – with tragic results. The visitors brought 1500 spectators to Stroud at a time when smallpox was rampant in the city. Town officials were hesitant to stop the match, which went ahead. Unfortunately smallpox arrived in the town with the visiting spectators, causing an epidemic which led to many deaths.

Initially Stroud RFC were a fine side in the early 1900s, but the club declined in the years leading up to World War One. The problems continued in the 1920s and worsened with the formation of a new club, the Nomads, who attracted many good players from Stroud RFC.

Better times arose when in 1932 they bought a ground at Fromehall Park, just off the Bath Road, which remains their home to this day. Any visitor to Fromehall soon notices that it is on a flat surface – one of the few level sites amongst Stroud's steep inclines. Fromehall's flatness is a legacy of a massive earth-moving programme in the early 1930s.

In season 1935-36 they won 26 of 35 matches, and three years later lost only three of 29. The best Stroud player of the era was Grahame Parker. Parker was a Rugby Blue and won two England caps as full-back. He also played 70 cricket matches for Gloucestershire, being restricted by teaching duties at Blundell's School in Devon, where he was a housemaster for 15 years.

Stroud has owed a great debt to Marling School, which has produced dozens of good players. The two best known Marling products were A.J. Herbert and J.V. Smith, who both won England caps. Smith had a long association with Stroud and Twickenham, where he was RFU President.

Stroud fielded two other internationals at the time: winger Charles Woodruff, who eventually moved to Harlequins where he was capped by England, and Gareth Payne, who joined Stroud from Pontypridd after winning a Wales cap.

One of Stroud's former juniors has achieved great things in France. In 2015 Nick Aberdanon was voted European Player of Year for his services to Clermont in the European Cup. He began in Stroud minis before playing 207 matches for Bath.

TAUNTON

TAUNTON RUGBY ORIGINALLY relied for its players on the area's three independent schools: King's College, Queens College and, principally, Taunton School. The last named was founded in 1847 as 'The West of England Dissenters Proprietary College', but changed its name to the 'Independent College'. The school was changed when Dr. C.D. Whittaker was appointed headmaster. Whittaker believed in games as an essential part of the curriculum and hired professional sportsmen to teach them. It was James G. Loveday, a master at Taunton School, with H. Newland who formed Taunton RFC in the mid-1870s. The club's inaugural match was against Weston-Super-Mare on the 19th January 1876, which Taunton won by a goal and three tries to nil.

The club had poor facilities and were notorious for the worst set of goalposts in the area. The poor facilities led to the club's temporary demise in the 1880s, but several smaller clubs existed in the town, which inevitably led to calls for the reform of the town side, which finally happened in 1888.

Within a few months, six Taunton players were selected for the Somerset side who played and lost 8-0 to the touring Maoris at Wellington. The first international associated with the club was J.A. McDonald, who had played for Ireland from 1875 to 1884. He joined Taunton in 1889.

Initially Taunton were able to attract top-class opposition, but the club was in dire straits by the end of the century. This occurred despite the presence of Taunton's second international, Reg Forrest, who won six England caps from 1899. He met an untimely death in 1903 after contracting typhoid from the evening meal in the England party's hotel in Dublin. Forrest lingered for two months in hospital before dying. Bert Gunningham was perhaps luckier to not get past an England trial in 1900.

Taunton recovered and were Somerset Cup winners in 1902 before closing down completely in 1904. A year later, Taunton RFC had bounced back and hosted the Somerset v All Blacks match in front of 9,000 spectators. The tourists won 23-0. A year later, the town hosted the Somerset v Springboks match – the home side included three Taunton players.

The town club was, by now, facing opposition from Taunton Albion RFC, who supplied Gerald Kyrke to the 1908 Lions who visited Australasia. Albion disappeared in 1914 and were officially recorded as having merged with Taunton in 1919.

Rugby was flourishing in the town in 1920 as Queen's College, one of the original sources of players, set a world record by beating Huish GS by 171-0 when a try was worth three points.

The greatest Taunton player of the era was 'Rocker' Twose, a great character who won an England trial before switching to rugby league with great success. Bob Dibble, an England international, also played for Taunton, although his best years had been with Bridgwater.

The early 1930s produced several club records. Also, eleven First XV players won county honours and Gordon Gregory progressed to Bristol, from where he was picked for England.

In 1935 Taunton left their long-time home at Eastleigh Road Athletic Ground for Prior Park, which hosted an England trial. The purchase of Priory Park did, however, leave a long-standing

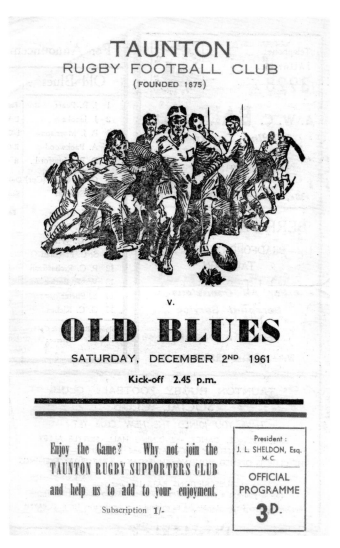

debt that was financed, in part, by leasing the perimeter for greyhound racing.

In 1944 they produced a wartime international in Fred Goddard, who was a tough flanker with a knack for goal-kicking. Goddard was selected for England v Scotland at Leicester whilst serving in the army.

In 1952, Taunton played an unusual match against an 'Old Whitgiftian XV', who were one of the best sides in England. The fixture was secured by Taunton promising their illustrious visitors the princely sum of '40 pints of Beer', worth £1 in those days. Taunton won 26-9, which suggests Whitgiftians weren't in prime condition.

Financial pressure on Taunton arose in 1959 when the clubhouse was destroyed by fire. A replacement opened in 1961, which coincided with the club winning the South West Merit Table and achieving a record 32 wins.

The arrival of league rugby came at a time when the club had lost many of their best players, For a while they 'yo-yoed' between levels 5 and 6.

In 2005 Dave Sims, ex-Gloucester, Exeter and England, was appointed player-coach after 13 seasons at Gloucester. Two years later, Taunton achieved a 100% season and were promoted to National 3 (SW). In 2011 the National 2 (South) club were renamed as Taunton Titans and were being coached by Tony Yapp.

TEWKESBURY

TEWKESBURY IS AN old town at the confluence of the Severn and Avon. The first Tewkesbury RFC dates from 1881 and was formed at the Swan Hotel by Rev. Thurston Rivington. Their first game was against Evesham on the 5th November 1881, which Tewksbury won one try to nil.

The 1906 team were a tough bunch. On one occasion they astonished Gloucester Old Boys by having their post-match bath in the River Severn and then swimming across to the Plough Hotel, where they got changed. By the way, Gloucester won 55-0.

The present club was formed in 1955 as 'Tewkesbury Monks', after their founder, Father Bacon, a monk who ran a youth fellowship. The Rev. Bacon decided rugby was a useful pastime for the boys and organised a side. He was unable to organise any goalposts, but improvised with four scaffolding poles. The side got changed at the town's slipper baths (which was where poor folks got a hot bath in the days before modern plumbing). The 'after match dip' consisted of six inches of lukewarm water in a tin bath. Matches were played on fields on Ashburton Road, which were regularly flooded by the Severn. The club subsequently moved to a neighbouring hillside where the sheep had to be moved before a game.

Tewkesbury's finest player was undoubtedly Phil Blakeway, the great Lions and England prop, who was originally a colt with Cheltenham. Blakeway was on good terms with several Tewkesbury players and played the occasional match for them as a youth in 1970, but was a regular at training. Around the same time, the club leased the Ye Olde Black Bear public house as a headquarters.

Phil Blakeway in action for Gloucester.

In 1985 they went public forming 'TRUFC Ltd.', which enabled them to develop the ground and facilities.

Tragedy hit the club in 2008 when father and son Bram and Chris Lane were killed trying to clear flooding on the pitch. Tewkesbury have planted saplings to their memory.

WALCOT OLD BOYS

WALCOT OB EMERGED in 1895 from a previous Bath side called 'Victoria RFC' that had played on Royal Victoria Park since 1882. Victoria RFC had become Walcot Victoria as they tried to be more closely associated with the Bath parishes of Walcot and St. Stephens.

Many of Victoria's officials were clergymen. The Church of England was a great supporter of rugby to steer young men away from the 'Demon Drink'; ironically, another great source of players was public houses.

Walcot's first known match was against Mr. Ascott's XV at Claverton. The match was drawn. The link with Walcot Church and its vicar, the Rev. James Lunt, was beneficial as the Reverend allowed the players to get changed in the vicarage. Also, the club could recruit players from the local church school. The club's original colours were a Victoria Cross insignia in light blue on the left breast of a black jersey.

After a bright start, the club was reported to be 'going under' and its best players moving to other clubs. Subsequently, Walcot OB reformed when they got the use of a pitch at Batheaston.

Walcot OB were formidable competitors on the Sevens scene, where they were first winners of the Colmer Cup in 1929 and the first winners of the Bath Combination Sevens and the Mid-Somerset Sevens.

The best known Walcot players inevitably gravitated to the city club. Arnold Ridley, the actor and playwright, was a Walcot regular in the 1920s. In the 1960s, Robbie Lye had six years at the junior club before moving to Bath, for whom he played 457 times and was First XV captain. In 1971, Peter Parfitt, the England cricketer, moved from Walcot to Bath and played rugby for Somerset.

Since the arrival of leagues, Walcot OB have been one of the best sides in South West. They currently play in Southern Counties South.

WELLINGTON

'The Serge Town'

THE TOWN OF Wellington (population 14,549) lies on the Devon/Somerset border. It owed its importance to wool and the mills of the Fox family. Mill owner Harry Fox formed the rugby club in 1874. Four years after the formation, his family provided floodlights for the club, which made them amongst the earliest pioneers of night rugby.

In the final quarter of the 19th Century, Wellington rapidly rose to prominence, with the Fox family still eminent. Frank Fox had joint membership with the famous Marlborough Nomads. He won two England caps in 1890 at half-back, but his greatest claim to fame was 'playing' in the 1888 England side against Scotland which never took to the field due to an administrative dispute. Brother Harry never achieved his real potential at rugby as he was killed in a mountaineering accident in 1888. The Fox family erected a grandstand to Harry's memory at the rugby club.

The greatest name associated with Wellington is Sammy Woods, a 6ft tall and 14 stone sporting prodigy. Samuel Moses James Woods (1867-1931) was born in Australia and was perhaps the archetypal (and first) great Australian sportsman. Forthright, physically huge and brilliantly talented, he came to England in 1883 to study at Cambridge University. He liked what he saw and never went home, spending his last 40 years in Somerset and developing a West Country accent.

Sammy Woods

Woods was outstanding with bat and ball for Cambridge, taking 36 wickets in the Varsity cricket matches. It was assumed that he would follow the yellow brick road to London and play for Blackheath at rugby and Surrey at cricket, but he astounded polite society by moving to Somerset, where he played cricket for his adopted county for 20 years and played rugby with Wellington and Wiveliscombe.

Sammy was a lovable rogue who was blessed with a remarkable self-belief that transcended normal acceptable behaviour. He used whiskey as a muscle rub and on one occasion tried to treat a team-mate's dislocated shoulder by simply forcing it back into place. On another occasion he stopped a team-mate's bleeding wound by filling it with chewing tobacco, fresh from his mouth and holding it in place with a piece of cloth. Woods loved walking across the Somerset hills and prepared for such marathons by storing alcohol at strategic points on his intended route. After his sporting days were over, he joined the British Army and fought in World War One. In later life, he gave his profession as 'sports writer', which hid the fact that he devoted his life to sport thanks to a considerable personal fortune.

If Woods was an 'offcomer' to Wellington, that accusation could not be made against the club's other great player, Herbert 'the Octopus' Gamlin, who ranks amongst the finest full-backs in rugby history. Gamlin earned his nickname for his incredible capacity to collar any player who tried to evade his grasp. He won 15 England caps between 1899 and 1904, mainly after he left Somerset for Blackheath. Famous for having extraordinarily long arms, he stood 6ft tall and weighed 14 stone. He specialised in crash-tackling, which was demoralising for his opponents. He is credited with winning the 1902 Calcutta Cup match when England were being over-run by Scotland. The Somerset full-back proved an insurmountable obstacle for the Scots. Gamlin went to a soccer school, but was press-ganged into playing for Wellington Second XV and played at full-back because he did not know the laws of rugby. He made his First XV debut for Wellington at 16 and represented Somerset at cricket and rugby a year later.

Wellington had a great team at the time and produced several other internationals in Percy Ebdon (two England caps in 1897) and A.E. Thomson (three Scotland caps in 1921).

In March 1926 Wellington celebrated their golden jubilee with a friendly match between Devon and Somerset, but the golden days of Wellington wool and rugby were in decline between the wars. The mills disappeared and were replaced by bedding and aerosol factories.

The rugby club retained an excellent fixture list in the 1970s and produced some talented players, notably prop Richard Lee, who moved to Bath and won an England 'B' cap.

Wellington rested in Devon & Cornwall One in 2005, but in five great years rose to Western Counties (West) and also won the Somerset Vase.

WELLS

THE DELIGHTFUL CITY of Wells is dominated by the cathedral and the Bishop's Palace. The rugby club owes its origins to the religious community for, it is thought, that the original rugby club was formed by students at the local theological college.

The club was founded on the 12th October 1876 by a meeting at the Star Hotel. The first game was a big win over Yeovil under Capt. E.M. Hippersley. The good times didn't last as only a month later they suffered a heavy defeat at mighty Bath. A.G. Russ was the club's first 'Hon Sec' and also their first county player.

The mysterious origins of the original Wells RFC are compounded by the fact that four years earlier Harold Freeman played for England and scored the first drop goal in the 1872 match against Scotland. Freeman gave his clubs as 'Marlborough Nomads and Wells FC'. This is the first reference to a club in the town. Freeman was the first of many Oxford University men to find their way to Somerset to study at the Theological College. The next notable player from Wells was J.J. Wilmot, who captained Somerset in 1876 against Devon, an encounter of such ferocity that one player was killed and several seriously injured.

In 1880, Wells pulled off a shock when they defeated Clifton – then the best side in the region. The burning flame of early Wells rugby soon faded and the club ceased playing around 1880.

A Wells RFC reappeared between the wars and were a decent provincial side. This side closed its doors in 1939 and never reformed after the emergency.

A club called Mendip RUFC was formed after World War Two but couldn't find a permanent home. The name of Mendip RUFC was to signify their nomadic existence along the north coast of Somerset. Mendip played on nine separate grounds in a decade. Despite this serious handicap, Wells fielded its only modern international in Alec Lewis, who won ten England caps between 1952 and 1954. Lewis actually began his last international season playing for Wells. This was an interesting time for the club, with Lewis, Bishop Noel Jones and drinks millionaire Keith Showering all travelling to matches in a Rolls Royce.

Alec Lewis later recalled: "They were happy days. Keith would drive me to away matches in his car. He used to pack a hamper of champagne into the boot. We had some good times."

Lewis left the area in 1957 – a sad moment – as Mendip declined. The Knapp Hill ground was sold and the club continued its nomadic existence. They moved to East Harrington, then to the County Showground, then Burcott Road, before moving to Charter Way. The club renamed themselves as 'Wells RFC' in 1965 and opened a new clubhouse in 1985 with a game against a Bristol XV.

Since the arrival of leagues, Wells were 1991-92 Somerset 2 Champions. The club struggled in the early 2000s and had difficulty in putting out a team. Things improved and the club's finest hour came in 2012 when they won the Senior Vase, beating Wath-upon-Dearne 31-22.

Wells had Peter Kennedy as Director of Rugby, who had previously coached Exeter Chiefs and England Women.

WESTON HORNETS

AN EARLY HORNETS side operated in Weston-Super-Mare in the 1880s, but died out long before the present club emerged in 1962. The new Hornets emerged when group of members from Weston-Super-Mare RFC formed a breakaway club. The inaugural meeting was held at the London Hotel in the town. The first game saw a young side, led by Peter Dimery, against St. Mary's of Bristol, resulting in a defeat by 15-0. That season the club played 30 fixtures, with the players changing at Worle School and walking to Hutton Moor. The Golden Lion public house was used as clubhouse.

In 1988 they opened their first clubhouse and later bought their Hutton Moor Ground. In 1995 they won the Somerset Cup. They climbed to South West 2, and in 2005 they reached the Third Round of the National Knockout Cup, losing to London Scottish. Two years later, the First XV won both the Somerset Cup and the Bristol Combination Cup, and in 2013 they won Western Counties North. In 2010, the Hornets Colts were runners-up in the National Colts Cup final to Bedford Blues.

WESTON-SUPER-MARE

"My question is why did the Germans waste bombs on Weston."
John Cleese

JOHN CLEESE MAY have some disparaging remarks about his home town, but Weston-Super-Mare is, to the outsider, an attractive place with more amenities than most English towns. From the rugby standpoint, it certainly has much to offer, with two good sides: Weston-Super-Mare and Weston Hornets, whose grounds are separated by half a mile of dual carriageway.

Weston's first game was in 1875 against Fulland's of Taunton at 'Frank Poole's ground'; the field was later swallowed up by the building of the railway station. The match, played in miserable muddy conditions, ended in a draw. The club did well in its first season with six wins in ten matches – two of the defeats coming at the hands of mighty Clifton, who were one of the best sides in the country at the time.

Weston subsequently moved to Clarence Park, then Clevedon Road, before moving to Sunnyside Road in 1880, which the club bought in the 1930s.

The 1880s were a golden era for Weston (or Weston Rangers as they sometimes called themselves). They produced two internationals in E.L. Strong of England (1882-84) and William Henry Thomas of Wales (1885-91). Little is known of the two internationals, but we know far more about the Smith Brothers (Sydney, Fred and Harry), who all played for Weston and Somerset. Sydney Smith was an outstanding three-quarter who played for the South in an England trial; subsequently injury prevented him getting full honours.

The club certainly had an enthusiast in local medical practitioner Dr. Wilmott, who was known to visit a patient or two on his way to playing in a match. He appeared before the patients dressed for the game in shorts and stockings showing below his coat.

Weston ranked ahead of clubs like Bath in the 1880s. In 1881 they experimented with 'floodlights' for their plum fixture at home to Clifton. 4,000 spectators attended the match at a time when the town's population was only 8,000. Two seasons later, they were undefeated over the whole season, including drawing with Cardiff.

The club had an unusual piece of Oxbridge history in 1901, when two members, the Odgers Brothers played on opposite sides in the Varsity Match.

WSM were Somerset Cup champions twice in the years leading up to the First World War, when the club was famous for its big aggressive forwards, many of whom came from Wales. The policy of recruiting in Wales continued between the wars. Many of Weston's officials were senior staff at the Town Hall and could 'hire and fire' the council employees. In fact, this recruitment policy grew to a level where the club was often in hot water for bending the laws governing 'amateur status'.

Harold Brown, a club stalwart, was a foreman for the town council and openly recruited his staff from South Wales, who were usually top-class rugby players. On one occasion, his policy was criticised by a councillor. Brown replied: "For labouring, you want to find the fittest type of man you can get - and you can't find a fitter man than a good rugby player."

Other critics weren't so easily fobbed off. In January 1929 the Welsh Rugby Union and RFU were astounded to learn Weston-Super-Mare council was advertising for top-class rugby players at the Aberavon Labour Exchange. Amazingly, an RFU enquiry decided that the rugby club were "in no way to blame" for a council policy of recruiting players on their behalf. An acerbic note in Clifton's history records that they had two Welsh fixtures: Glamorgan Wanderers and Weston Welsh.

The club thrived during industrial depression between the two world wars. Conditions in Wales were dire, and the government gave special grants to local authorities to start capital works projects to provide more employment and import labour from depressed areas. Weston Council were extremely generous to their town rugby club, and in April 1924 helped provide an excellent ground. The grandstand was described as "holding 1000 spectators and is the most commodious in the whole West Country".

The club was a popular venue for representative matches and visiting international sides. In 1924, it was home to the Somerset v All Blacks match (played in front of 10,000 spectators) and, two years later, Somerset v Maoris. Later, the 1927 Waratahs and 1931 Springboks trained at Weston on their arrival in the UK. A lesser international came in 1928 when the club hosted a Wales v Rest of Britain baseball game.

The 1930s were a golden era, with the First XV containing a dozen Welshmen, including international Ron Price, who played in Weston's unbeaten 1937-38 team, who scored 875 points whilst conceding only 156. Over the four seasons before World War Two, the club lost only 13 out of 135 fixtures.

At this time, Coventry agreed to give a fixture to the club, thinking it would be an easy afternoon's rugby. Unfortunately for Coventry, Weston had assembled a brilliant team, who won 13-6 at Coundon Road, which elicited the Weston paper to carry the headline, "Coventry beaten by village team", a remark made by one of the home crowd.

It is perhaps unfair to single Weston-Super-Mare for criticism because other local clubs, notably Torquay Athletic and Somerset Police, also had numerous Welshmen. Few of the Weston Welsh returned home after retiring from rugby, although some importations used Weston as a halfway house en route to playing in the Northern Union. NU scouts took great interest in comings and goings at Drove Road in the hope of out-bidding WSM for a talented Welshman.

When the club reformed in 1946, the number of Welshmen had declined and been replaced by ex-Bristol players. In 1951 Reg Quick of Bristol brought an international XV to celebrate the club's 75th anniversary. The council continued to help by rebuilding the grandstand, which had been destroyed by wartime bombing. However, the council annexed part of the rugby ground to build a new railway station.

At least Weston-Super-Mare was producing its own players. In the 1950s Jim Collard won an England trial and Ben Tuthiett set a record for Somerset appearances. The club could also look to the local RAF base at Locking for a steady flow of servicemen, including an Irish international.

Easter tours to Weston were part of rugby club life in the Fifties. They often coincided with the annual Hockey Festival, which could also prove a handful for the local police. Both sets of visitors could behave badly and loved collecting souvenirs such as signposts, notices and other civic property. The town retaliated by placing roadblocks to stop and search coaches carrying rugby and hockey players in an attempt to retrieve the ratepayers' property.

The RAF Locking connection continued, and in 1968 produced a remarkable arrival at WSM. Billy Steele came to Locking with an awesome reputation, although he had yet to play for his native Scotland – or even have a trial. Mighty Bristol moved quickly to get his services and asked him repeatedly to come for trials. Unfortunately Steele missed all three appointments due to injury and Bristol lost interest. Weston saw their opportunity and Steele played four games before Rosslyn Park persuaded him to travel to the capital. Steele was spotted by the Scotland selectors and made his international debut without a trial. In 1974, he became a member of the Invincible Lions who were undefeated in South Africa.

Two other internationals also briefly played for Weston-Super-Mare: Gerry Redmond (1970) and Peter Larter (1967-71). Both played for WSM before being capped by England. A decade later, Nigel Redman came through Weston-Super-Mare's ranks after being educated at Priory School in the town. Redman joined Bath and won 20 England caps.

The 1970s were notable for the two Hazzard brothers, who were the backbone of the Weston-Super-Mare team. Doug later emigrated and played for North Queensland.

Weston reached National 3 South in 2013. Their ladies team are in National 1.

WINSCOMBE

WINSCOMBE RFC WAS formed in 1962 by a group of enthusiasts led by Welshmen Taffy Watham and Dai Davies. An inaugural meeting was held on the 5th September at the Woodborough Hotel. A pitch was found at Homefield, where they played for five years.

On 10th November 1962, the first match saw a 26-12 victory over a Clifton XV under the captaincy of R. Humphries. It proved a false dawn as the club won only two of its first 11 games that year. The following season saw 18 wins in 37 games and the club grew rapidly, winning 25 of 42 games in 1966-67. Sadly, decline followed and results in the 1970s made grim reading.

In 1968 the club moved to Winscombe War Memorial Ground. They shared the clubhouse with Winscombe cricket, hockey and football clubs. In 2000 the club bought land for two additional pitches, and in 2007 these were named the Blomfield Pitches, in memory of the club's late treasurer, George Blomfield, who had campaigned tirelessly to raise money for the purchase. Further development of the club's facilities continues, with the latest stage being the floodlighting of the main Longfield pitch.

The club were Somerset 2 champions in 2003 and have twice been champions of Somerset 1, in 2004 and 2007.

WIVELISCOMBE

'The women less valley'

WIVELISCOMBE IS A delightful village (pop 2,893) on the hilly road from Taunton to the North Coast of Somerset. Wiveliscombe means the 'women less valley'. The name originated during the Black Death, when all the women in the valley died of the plague. The shortage of women is given as the reason for the large number of breweries that grew up in the vicinity. Wiveliscombe has a great rugby history. The tap root of the rugby club was the ten Hancock brothers, seven of whom played for Somerset.

Wiveliscombe was a thriving little town in the mid-19th Century thanks to Hancock's Brewery and Hancock's Bank. It could also boast a market and then the Taunton & Barnstaple Railway rolled into town. Frederick Rooke was an engineer on the railway and it was Rooke who formed the rugby club on the 22nd August 1872 at the Lion Hotel. The first match played by the club was against the Independent School (later to become Taunton School).

The Hancock brothers soon came onboard, including Frank Hancock, who joined the club in 1878 and was rapidly made captain. During his captaincy, Wiveliscombe RFC never lost at home. In 1883 the family opened a brewery in Cardiff and Frank moved across the Severn channel. Whilst in the Welsh capital, he became captain of Cardiff and led them to 26 wins in 27 matches in 1885-86. The single defeat was to Moseley, who felt they had overcome Hancock's secret weapon: four threequarters behind a half-back.

All rugby teams had played the same tactics since the days of the earliest 15-a-side club rugby: a dozen men in the pack and a couple of little men in the backs. Hancock worked out that if your pack could play with nine or ten men and still win the ball, you could play with a half-back and four threequarters, who could score tries. He held goal-kicking and drop-kicking in contempt. Woe betide any team-mate who put boot to ball when Hancock was about. The great man himself didn't practice what he preached as he once kicked a drop goal to save losing to Wellington. Despite his English ancestry, he was capped by Wales and later became a director of Lloyds Bank before returning to Wiveliscombe and helping to run the rugby club.

Froude Hancock was the other brother to win international honours, but for England. A massive man of 6ft 4ins, Froude was nicknamed 'Baby'. He lived in Wiveliscombe but played his best rugby in London with Blackheath, Richmond and Harlequins. He played for England in 1886 and was one of the few non-varsity men picked for Percy Carpmael's first Barbarian team.

Wiveliscombe grandstand

The brothers weren't too welcome at home, where father viewed their rugby obsession with mixed feelings. On occasions the brothers would arrive home on the last train to find 'pater' had not sent a pony and trap to meet them. This meant an eight-mile walk home for Frank and Froude.

Wiveliscombe also produced several other internationals. Even Sammy Woods played for the club whilst working at the Brewery. Two other prominent names associated with the club are Bob Dibble, who played for Taunton and England but turned out for Wiveliscombe whilst he ran a public house in the town, and Mary Hancock. Nobody had longer service to the club than Mary, who replaced Frank Hancock as president and held the post until 1957 when she died aged 94.

Despite these great names, Wiveliscombe RFC declined from World War One onwards. The little town also declined as the brewery and market closed and the government closed the railway. High unemployment meant young rugby players had to leave the town in search of work. The result was a steady drain of talent.

The Recreation Ground is today dominated by an elderly red stone grandstand. It was erected during World War Two by the US Army, who were billeted, en-masse, in the town. The Americans also offered to flatten the slope on the rugby ground (or slopes, as there are several), but some misguided idiot refused the offer and has sentenced innumerable rugby players to a bizarre topography where bounces of the ball are a lottery.

The rugby club were reluctant to join the leagues in the 1980s, but rose rapidly when they did from Somerset 3 to Western Counties, where the travelling costs proved crippling to a small club.

(Thanks to Gary Sharland and Terry May)

CHAPTER NINETEEN

EASTERN COUNTIES

THE EASTERN COUNTIES RFU emerged from several county unions at the end of the 19th Century.

The Suffolk County Football Union was formed in 1884, and there are records of matches between Essex and Suffolk during the middle of that decade. Suffolk approached Kent in 1889 to arrange a Saturday fixture, but were offered a mid-week match against an 'A' team. Suffolk accepted the match at the Rectory Field, Blackheath, but lost by three tries and three minors to nil.

The Essex County Union was formed at Chelmsford in December 1885. The Essex side drew nine players from Saracens and four came from Beckton; the other two players hailed from Wanstead Viceroy. A Norfolk Vacation Club was formed in 1887 and was sufficiently strong to play Suffolk, Essex, St Bart's Hospital and Northamptonshire.

The Norfolk RU originated from a side called Norfolk County Club, who were formed in October 1889. The Vacation Club disbanded in 1892. The fourth county, Cambridgeshire, were only admitted to the Eastern Counties Union (ECU) in 1928.

H.R. Ladell of Norfolk is credited with being the actual founder of the EC Union. He was appointed as the first honorary secretary at the inaugural meeting at Great Eastern Hotel, Liverpool Street, London. The meeting was ostensibly a meeting of the Essex County Union, but it was decided to form an Eastern Counties Cup competition, as well as an Eastern Counties Union, from Essex, Suffolk and Norfolk.

Eastern Counties were included in the Metropolitan group of the County Championships for season 1891-92. Their first County Championship match was against Surrey at the Essex County Cricket Club ground at Leyton on 14th October 1891; Surrey won by 30 to two (a try was only worth two points at the time). The first Eastern Counties XV were: A.P. Snell (Essex and Jesus, Cambridge), Picton Phillips (Suffolk and United Services), L.R.I. Frere (Norfolk and Trinity, Cambridge), G.L. Hanwell (Norfolk and St Thomas's Hospital), H.M. Taberer (Essex and Keble, Oxford), W. Shadbolt (Essex and Viceroy), N.L. Garrett (Essex and Harlequins) (captain); H.P. Mills (Norfolk and Keble, Oxford), J.C. Wilson (Norfolk and Harlequins), C.E. Wilson (Suffolk and RMC Sandhurst), W. Joscelyn (Essex and OMTs), H.A.P. Sawyer (Suffolk and Wickham Park), H.O. Ransome (Suffolk and Trinity, Cambridge), A. Rust (Norfolk), and G. Sparks (Essex and Upper Clapton). EC played and lost four fixtures that season. Their first success was a defeat of Hampshire at Clapton on 21st December 1892 by one goal (five points) to nil.

There has always been more to rugby than playing the game and the early 1890s were notorious for shamateurism. In March 1891 a match was advertised to be played at Dartford between 'A Kent team' and South Essex for the benefit of a member of the Dartford club, but the match constituted a breach of the professionalism laws. Several notable players were scheduled to play. The issue was referred to the RFU.

World War One destroyed rugby in East Anglia, and by 1920-21 there were only two teams in the counties of Norfolk and Suffolk; one at Gresham School, Holt, and another at the Royal Naval Establishment at Shotley. Eventually the region recovered, and throughout the remainder of the century became serious contenders for the County Championship.

Eastern Counties finally made the County final in 1948, but lost to Lancashire in Cambridge.

BANCROFT

BANCROFT IS THE modern name of Old Bancroftians, who were the products of Bancroft's School, Woodford Green, Essex. The school was founded in 1727 with a bequest from the City Company of Drapers.

Old Bancroftians were a soccer side based in Walthamstow from 1894 until 1927, when the club also formed a rugby side. OBs played both codes until 1929, when soccer was phased out.

The rugby club flourished during the 1930s and found a new ground at Kenilworth Gardens, Loughton, including a pavilion with primitive facilities. A notable captain between the wars was Charles Newman, who won the Victoria Cross at St. Nazaire during World War Two. By 1932 the club were fielding four XVs and won the Four Counties Sevens in 1934-35 and 1935-36.

The early 1950s were a great era for OBs, with only 20 defeats in 167 matches over six seasons. The highlight was the 1956-57 season that saw OBs unbeaten. Their best player was an England trialist in R.J. Kent, a scrum-half who later played for Wasps from 1956 to 1961. Kent's return from Wasps in 1961 sparked another golden era, with 19 wins in 22 matches the following season. Around this time D. Main, a Welsh international, played for the club.

OBs were one of the area's leading sides throughout the 1960s, but a decision was made to go open in 1972 and the name of Bancroft RFC was adopted, although the club kept its ties to the old school.

In 1968, Bancroft vacated Loughton and moved to Buckhurst Way, In recent times, the club was rumoured to have been offered the chance to sell the Buckhurst ground to Tottenham Hotspur FC.

Bancroft have a link to international rugby; they toured Denmark in 1970 and played the national side, losing 6-0.

The club entered the league structure in EC5 and achieved four successive promotions, which proved a springboard to reaching the London leagues.

BISHOP'S STORTFORD

BISHOP'S STORTFORD RFC was formed in 1920 and initially played on Dunmow Road before moving to the Town Fields at the Causeway. They relocated to Silver Leys in 1928.

In 1951 it was suggested that the club change its name to 'East Herts RFC'. The idea was well received but never materialised because, at the time, Bishops had only £3 in the bank and a great deal of paperwork was needed to move the money.

The famous local Bishop's Stortford College and the local rugby club were closely associated with the Collett family, many of whose sons – and, latterly, daughters – attended the college. Sir Kingsley Collett was a school governor in the 1960s, and Sir Charles Collett was Lord Mayor of London in the 1930s. Collett House, one of the day boys' boarding houses, was named after the family.

For many years the George Hotel acted as the rugby club's headquarters, with the old stables used as changing rooms. In 1963 the club purchased three old Nissan huts for £50 as changing rooms. Eight years later a new clubhouse was built for £10,000. This was replaced in 1985 by a second building, which was opened with a match against an international XV, attracting 7,000 spectators.

Bishop's Stortford adjusted quickly to the establishment of league rugby in 1987, winning promotion into London Two North in the first season. After 15 years in that league – always in the top half of the table and with very many near misses – they achieved promotion to London One.

The club's finest son is Ben Clarke, who played for Bishop's in the late 1980s before moving to Saracens and becoming an integral part of the England Grand Slam teams of the next decade. He won 40 England caps and toured with the 1993 Lions.

Currently Bishop's Stortford play in National 2 (South), having risen from London North 2 in a dozen years.

BRENTWOOD

THE ESSEX TOWN of Brentwood is primarily associated with the Ford Motor Company, who are the major employer. 200 years ago, it had transport links to the East India Company, with the town housing the company's elephant training school!

The local rugby club was formed on 1st July 1935 at the White Hart Hotel in High Street. The White Hart was to remain the club's headquarters for a quarter of a century. Brentwood's first pitch was at Symes Field in Sawyers Hall Lane, a mile's walk from the White Hart. Initially the field was covered in hay, which had to be cut and stored before matches could begin. Brentwood played there until 1937, when they moved to council pitches on the King George's Playing Fields on Ingrave Road. At the time, local rugby players were a scarce commodity in

Brentwood, but the numbers were augmented by army recruits from Warley Barracks (which was later taken over by Ford).

The club reformed in 1953 after World War Two. The resurrected club struggled at first, but they had an influx of Welsh schoolmasters who were working locally. One of these newcomers was Tony Broom, who became Brentwood's first international when he was capped for the Bahamas in the 1970s.

In 1959 the club moved their changing facilities to Brentwood Hockey, Tennis and Cricket Club on Shenfield Road, where they remained until 1966.

Brentwood were one of the first Essex clubs to establish minis and juniors. Amongst their earliest youngsters was Eric Peters, who learnt the basics with Brentwood's junior section. Peters eventually joined Leicester and was capped for Scotland whilst playing there. Other Brentford players to move on to great things included Chris Wilkins (Wasps and Blackheath), John Tierney (Blackheath) and Peter Harries (Saracens and London Welsh).

The club's most famous old boy is TV actor Ross Kemp, best known as 'Grant Mitchell' in BBC TV's Eastenders. Kemp made regular first team appearances until his work commitments intervened.

Brentwood entered the league structure at London 3 NE level. They were promoted to London 2 North at the end of 1993-94 season. In 2009 they were promoted to London North 1. They were regular Essex Cup contenders, but had to wait until 2015 to become champions.

OLD BRENTWOODS

OLD BRENTWOODS RFC was founded in 1967 by ex-pupils of Brentwood School at the Angel public house in Kelvedon Hatch. In 1970 they found a regular home on Burland Road, Brentwood, which was so difficult to find that the opposition kept getting lost on the way.

OBs won Essex 2 in 1992 and in 2010 they were Essex 1 Champions.

BURY ST EDMUNDS

BURY ST EDMUNDS RFC were formed as 'Bury & West Suffolk RFC' in March 1925. They played four games in their first season, the first being against RAF Felixstowe. The club eventually changed the name to Bury St Edmunds RFC and operated from a ground at Eldo House.

Bury reformed after World War Two in 1947, using a pitch at Perry's Barn whilst the players got changed at the Priors Inn. The club were fortunate when Alan Stephenson, their chairman, bought a pitch at Beeton's Footpath for £400. A decade later they sold the ground, which enabled them to move to a council pitch at Southgate Green and to build a clubhouse.

The outstanding players for Bury over the years have been Henry Lacy-Scott, who played for Woodford, Cambridge and ECs before World War Two, Derek Searle, who played for Warwickshire, and John Farrow, who won Eastern Counties honours in the 1970s.

The club suffered a huge blow in 1974 when it lost 18 members in the Ermenonville aircraft crash that killed hundreds of rugby fans returning from the England v France match in Paris.

Bury were promoted to London North East 4 in 2001. Two years later they won the Suffolk Cup. In 2015 Bury reached National 3. Their colts were National Plate champions in 2007.

CAMBRIDGE

VARSITY RUGBY IN Cambridge dates back to 1839, but it took another 84 years before a city club emerged. Founded in 1923, Cambridge RUFC led a nomadic existence in their early days, although the university helped out by loaning pitches at Caius and Fitzwilliam Colleges. This was regal living compared to one early Cambridge pitch, where dog kennels were used as changing rooms.

It could be argued that some of Cambridge's opposition were so badly behaved that they did not deserve better treatment. Between the wars, a side called Western Wanderers from Middlesex played Cambridge, but their transport broke down on the way home. They had a drink in a nearby pub, but relations between the Wanderers and the pub landlord were so bad that several days later three of the rugby players returned and chopped down the pub sign.

The relationship between 'town and gown' was a better one, as Cambridge RUFC acquired some great players from the Varsity, albeit on a temporary basis. Clem Thomas (26 Welsh caps) and Geoff Windsor-Lewis (two Welsh caps and the Barbarians secretary) made occasional appearances for the city, but it was Dickie Jeeps, the ex-England captain, who changed the history of the club.

Jeeps played for Cambridge for a season after leaving Bedford Modern School. He moved to Northampton in 1949 and was selected for England in 1956, although he had already been picked for the Lions before making his England debut. He eventually won 13 Lions caps and 24 England caps.

Jeeps forged a memorable half-back partnership with Welshman Cliff Morgan during the Lions' 1955 tour to South Africa (which ended in a 2-2 draw). He was back in a Lions shirt for their 1959 tour to Australia and New Zealand (playing in five of the six test matches) and again in 1962, when he appeared in all four tests during the Lions' 3-0 series defeat.

In 1962 he rejoined Cambridge City as player-coach. He attempted to galvanise local interest by trying (unsuccessfully) to emulate Northampton's successful system of feeder clubs. The aim was that the local junior clubs would feed their best players to the city club. The young players would benefit from playing top-class rugby, before hopefully returning to their original clubs.

The Jeeps era was not exactly trouble-free. On one occasion Jeeps took the entire Cambridge side off the field in a match against St. Neots. The local disciplinary committee examined the incident and, finding no precedent, decided to ignore the matter by citing the fact that the referee was not a member of any society.

Jeeps boosted his local talent with top-class outsiders, such as Tony Bevan and the legendary Andy Hancock, who scored

one of the greatest tries in rugby history. Hancock was the England full-back against Scotland in the 1965 Calcutta Cup match. Scotland led with a minute to go when Hancock took the ball in his own 22 and bamboozled the entire Scots team with a stunning 95-yard break that brought a try that gave England a precious draw. He didn't enjoy lasting approval with the England selectors as he was dropped at that end of the season and was never recalled.

Hancock played club rugby for four other clubs (Sidcup, Northampton, Chelmsford and Stafford) and three county sides (London, Eastern Counties and Staffordshire). His sojourn at Cambridge included playing in Cambridge's first ever win over the university in October 1962. The defeated university side included three internationals on the day.

In 2002 Cambridge were London One strugglers, but steadily improved to reach National Two and eventually National One in 2010. Their best known product is Andy Goode, who played for Cambridge after being released by Ipswich Town Football Club. He left Cambridge for Leicester and has enjoyed a 17-year career in the Premiership besides playing for England.

Andy Hancock

Andy Goode

CANTABRIGIAN

CANTABRIGIAN RUFC WAS formed in the 1920s as the Old Boys of Cambridge County High School. The club remained exclusively a closed club until the 1970s, when the school changed to a co-ed sixth-form college. The old school link has gradually died away and the club re-named itself and settled for life in the Eastern Counties leagues.

Cantabrigian can be proud of producing a top-class player in John Jackson Page, known as 'Jacko' Page. Jacko, who was born in Brighton and went to Cambridge University, where he won a rugby blue. He became an England international scrum-half in 1971, but was one of many good players discarded in his prime. He established himself as a master of improvisation with Northampton whilst being ignored by his country. Finally, Page was recalled by England for the 1975 international against Scotland, which England won narrowly. Page was outstanding, but was once again dumped by the selectors.

The club have often topped Eastern Counties One and were 2013 Senior Vase semi-finalists.

Cantabrigian RUFC

CHELMSFORD

IT IS KNOWN rugby was played in Chelmsford in the late 19th century because five players from the original Chelmsford RFC are listed as having represented Eastern Counties in 1895. The sport, however, appears to have died out in the mid-Essex area before World War One.

Rugby in the town was resurrected in December 1920 by a meeting at the Saracens Head Hotel, presided over by Col. Barrington Wells, who was one of the leading RFU figures in East Anglia. A number of the attendees were established players who had already represented the EC and between the wars 16 Chelmsford players represented the region.

In their early days Chelmsford had a string of pitches. The first pitch was at Baddow Road, followed by moves to Wood St, Bruce Grove and eventually to Writtle. After World War Two, fixtures were played at Kings Head Meadows, followed by a move to Parsonage Green (1946), Melbourne Park (1948) and to Coronation Park (1961).

The club has featured many characters, including Jim Smith, who was honorary secretary for 37 years from 1929 to 1966. The club also produced internationals. Flanker Tony Bucknall won 10 England caps between 1969 and 1971 after moving to Richmond. Mike Bulpitt won an England cap as a winger in 1970. He also played for Blackheath and Osterley. Andy Hancock played for Chelmsford in the later stages of an illustrious career.

Currently Chelmsford play in London Two (SE). Their winger, Seb Hill, set a club record when he scored eight tries in 80 minutes as Lowestoft & Yarmouth were beaten 123-0.

COLCHESTER

THE OLD GAME of 'camp ball' was played in Colchester until the 19th century. Camp ball used a pitch of approximately 100 yards in length with small goals at either end. The aim was to carry the ball between the goals. Rugby emerged when camp ball died out. The earliest known football side in Colchester was the 8th Depot Battalion, who in 1866 played both Eton and Rugby rules. The army side were later to rank as one of the best rugby teams in the army.

Colchester is a military town, and for many years there were strong links between the army and the local rugby club. The club also had a steady supply of youngsters from Colchester Royal Grammar School.

The present rugby club was founded in 1928 at the Red Lion on the High Street, with Dr. Alfred Fell (1878-1950) in the chair. Dr. Fell, who had been capped by Scotland in 1901 and who was club president for 20 years, was part of a great three-quarter line. He was born in New Zealand before moving to Scotland, where he studied medicine. He performed well on his debut, but was soon discarded. His many admirers suspected that his Kiwi roots were the principal reason for his rejection, rather than his performances. The local newspaper wrote:

Dr. Alfred Fell

'They do not like thee, Dr. Fell
The reason why is hard to tell.'

Also present at the founding meeting was H.F. Pertwee, the first club captain from 1928-35, and the Rev. T.H. Hollingdale, who appeared for Colchester and had won six Welsh caps whilst with Swansea.

The club has been based at Mill Road since 1978, but they previously played at Lexden Showground (1927), the grammar school (1946), Gasbecks Farm (1948) and Mile End before arriving at their present home.

The greatest name associated with the club is Major General Douglas Kendrew, who won 30 England caps between the wars.

Other Army figures who appeared for Colchester included Ernest Unwin (37 England caps), J.R. Worton (England), Henry Withers (five Welsh caps), Geoff Rees-Jones (five Welsh caps) and John Steeds, one of the great names of 1950s rugby. Steeds played for Colchester whilst he was the England hooker.

Ernest Unwin was a fine all-round sportsman. He played rugby for England and for the 1935 and 1938 Lions. He also played cricket for the army and Essex. He played three times against the 1935 All Blacks – for the army, the combined services and for London. He played for the 1935 unofficial Lions to Argentina before being capped by England. He proved a prolific try-scorer when he was eventually picked for England.

Today the club's links to the army and the grammar school have virtually dried up. The 1990s saw Colchester relegated in three successive seasons before recovering with back-to-back promotions. The club currently play in London One.

HARLOW

HARLOW RFC WAS founded in December 1955 at the Essex Skipper pub in the new town. Many of the founders were Welshmen who had moved to Essex in pursuit of work. In the absence of a pitch, all the eight matches in the first season were away from home.

The first clubhouse was at Parndon Mill, which was a converted pig-sty. Post-match hospitality was in the Dusty Miller pub, which was conveniently across the county line in Hertfordshire, where the pubs opened half an hour earlier!

Harlow won five and lost three of the eight matches in their first season. The first match was played on 28th January 1956 and was an 8-3 victory over Brentwood Seconds. A new bar and club was opened at Ram Gorse in September 1959 with a match against an Essex XV.

Success has come rapidly, with the club climbing from Eastern Counties 3 in 1987 to London Two in 1993. The won the 1994-95 Eastern Counties Cup.

Over the years many fine players have played for Harlow, notably Clive Shell, who won a Welsh cap in 1973. The Aberavon scrum-half was unlucky to be understudy to the great Gareth Edwards. Other good players who represented Harlow include Don Harrigan of Saracens, Haden Davies of Wasps and John Davies of London Welsh.

2015 saw Harlow playing in London 3. They began league rugby in EC1 but rose to London 1 in six years. In 1999 they reached the finals of the Middlesex Sevens.

HERTFORD

HERTFORD WAS THE religious centre of England in Saxon times. It received its charter in 1451 and Hertford Castle was a popular residence of royalty, being only 21 miles from London.

Hereford had many of the problems of Dr Arnold's Rugby School because the East India Company had a college in the town where the students were notorious for rioting.

Hertford RFC was formed in 1932 as 'Old Hertfordians' by a group of former pupils of the town's grammar school. The early club was nomadic, with a variety of pitches being used, beginning at the grammar school playing fields and followed by pitches on Hartham Common (1895), by the sewage works at Rye House (1935) and Ware House, Hoddesdon.

After World War Two, the club played on the Recreation Ground, Station Road, Broxbourne, where the main problem was a potty old lady who collected firewood in an old pram and persisted in using an ancient right of way across the rugby pitch. Referees had to be both vigilant and tolerant.

After a brief (and wet) spell beside the River Lea, the club moved to a permanent home at Hoe Lane. In 1972 the club went open. In 1985 Hertford hosted one of the world's first Golden Oldies, with teams from all over the world.

Hertford rose rapidly after 2001, when they won London 2. Only one defeat in two years saw them win the Intermediate Cup. They reached National 3 in 2010 and were promoted to National 2 South.

HOLT

IN THE EARLY part of the 20th Century, a side called Holt Grammarians had existed in North Norfolk. When they ceased playing, it left a void for rugby enthusiasts in the area.

Holt RFC was formed in 1961. The inaugural meeting was on 30th November at the Feathers Hotel. The first match was played against West Norfolk at Eccles Field on 2nd December 1961. Holt won 3-0. They played at Holt Centre until 1967, until they purchased a ground at Bridge Road, High Kelling. The new pitch was opened with a friendly against an Eastern Counties XV. Changing facilities were provided by the Railway Inn.

Holt have fielded several top-class players: Bob Steven (1962 Scotland cap), John Huins (Welsh trialist) and Neil Poortvliet, who was the most capped Norfolk county player. Their juniors produced Nick and Tom Youngs, who moved to North Walsham and Leicester before playing for England and the Lions.

In 1976 Holt won the Norfolk Cup. At the outset of league rugby, Holt were placed in EC3. They were promoted to EC2 in 1990 and reached EC1 in 1994. In 1997 they reached London 3 (NE) and in 2012 were London 3 champions.

ILFORD WANDERERS

ILFORD WANDERERS WAS formed in 1896 by Frank Potter-Irwin, who was a leading player and referee. Potter-Irwin was also the doyen of EC rugby in the late 19th Century.

In an effort to engender interest in the Ilford district, a county match was organised between Eastern Counties and Middlesex. The match turned into a farce as EC fielded a scratch team. Actually, the EC side was open to anyone from Ilford and Leystonstone who fancied a game. The Middlesex RU weren't amused and warned that the EC might have to play against Middlesex seconds unless things improved.

The best players associated with Ilford are Derek Wyatt and Damian Cronin. Wyatt also played for Ipswich and Bedford and in 1976 he won an England cap before beginning a career as a writer and politician. Cronin is the son of a club president. A huge lock, he won 45 caps for Scotland, including being part of the 1990 Grand Slam-winning side. He also went on the 1993 Lions tour to New Zealand. In the 1988 Scotland v England, Cronin played against Jeff Probyn, the England prop. A decade earlier, the two had been teammates in Ilford colts.

In 1980 the club moved to Barkingside. Wanderers were in the Eastern Counties league in the 1990s, but have recently been in the Essex leagues.

IPSWICH

"The worst thing that ever happened in his rugby career was the claret at Ipswich club dinners.'"

Mark Bailey

IPSWICH RFC WAS formed in 1870, making it the oldest club in East Anglia. But rugby had been played in the town the previous year. The Suffolk town was a flourishing port at the time and a hotbed of rugby as it had at least seven sides:, including the town club, Ipswich Arabs, Ipswich Rovers, Ipswich United, Orwell and St. Helens.

Ipswich RFC suffered from the strength of local opposition in 1881-82, and only won four games all season. They had recovered by the following decade, when they were one of four local sides to take the Eastern Counties Cup – the others being Orwell Works, St. Helens and Ipswich United. Ipswich themselves won the title in successive years.

Orwell Works took its name from an engineering company on the banks of the River Orwell. Despite early success, the works team disappeared in the early 20th century, a fate that also befell Ipswich United, St. Helens and numerous other small local clubs.

Ipswich RFC themselves went into abeyance in 1904 and only reappeared in 1920. The re-birth was orchestrated by Sir Charles Sherrington and the famous player Commander S.F. Coopper. Four years later, the club was strengthened when Ipswich School switched from soccer to rugby, followed by Northgate Grammar School (which was later called Ipswich Secondary School).

The first international to emerge from Ipswich RFC was Geoff Rees-Jones, who moved on to Oxford University and London Welsh before winning five Wales caps in the mid-1930s.

World War Two saw a number of internationals play for Ipswich whilst stationed locally in the services. They included Tommy Harris (England), Peter Candler (England), Derek Teden (England), Maurice Daly (Ireland), Vivian Jenkins (Wales) and Richard Uren (Ireland).

After the war the club left Maidenhall Farm for Humber Doucy Lane. They were Eastern Counties champions three times in the 1970s and provided a number of good players for the region's team, including Peter Langley (England trialist) and Jim Sanders (47 appearances).

Remarkably, Ipswich produced three international wingers. Derek Wyatt went to Bedford via Ipswich and scored a record 145 tries for Bedford. On three occasions Wyatt scored five tries in a match, on five occasions he scored four tries, and in a record 17 matches he ran in three. He made his England debut against Scotland at Murrayfield in 1976. Mark Bailey also progressed to Bedford, Wasps and England via Cambridge University. He won seven England caps in the late 1980s. The third winger was Martin Offiah, who moved to Rosslyn Park before switching to rugby league and was capped by Great Britain. He scored 500 tries in his dual-code career.

Martin Offiah

In recent seasons Ipswich have been near the top of the London leagues.

(Thanks to Stewart Jarrold)

LOWESTOFT AND YARMOUTH

"There is no body of people more inconsiderate than public school boys."

Lowestoft councillor on the prospect of the annual rugby festival in 1954.

THE TWIN PORTS of Lowestoft and Yarmouth owe their importance to their close proximity to Europe, which gives the club the title of the most easterly club in England. The port was famous for exporting cloth in the Middle Ages. However, fishing had become the primary industry by the late 19th century.

Rugby was first played in the district in 1879 by Lowestoft RFC, who became the backbone of the Essex side in the next decade even though the town was not in Essex – Suffolk didn't have a side at the time. Yarmouth, by contrast, were strong supporters of the new Eastern Counties side.

Both Lowestoft and Yarmouth had spells in oblivion. Lowestoft was reformed briefly in 1902, but only established roots in 1921. One of their first fixtures that season was against a Yarmouth XV. This was, however, primitive sport: in 1926 Old Dunstonians from Kent played Lowestoft and were disconcerted to find the match was to be played on a soccer pitch. The home team converted the soccer posts to rugby posts by the simple expedient of tying broom handles to the crossbar.

The merger of Lowestoft and Yarmouth in 1933 galvanised the club into pre-eminence in East Anglia. Many Lowestoft and Yarmouth players have represented the Eastern Counties, with Mike Hepton considered the best. Hepton, a giant lock, was a county regular in the 1950s.

An occasional Lowestoft and Yarmouth player in the 1950s was Dr. Lewis Cannell, who won 19 England caps whilst with St. Mary's Hospital. Rex Richards also played for Lowestoft and Yarmouth after winning several caps for Wales.

The club restarted in 1952 after World War Two. Many London sides used Lowestoft and Yarmouth for their end of season tour, which eventually led to the formation of the Easter Festival. Up to 24 separate clubs would arrive in the town each

Easter and many of the top sides – notably London Irish – headed for the Suffolk coast. L&Y suffered a set-back in 1954 when the annual festival was threatened with a ban by the local council due to fears of 'horseplay'.

The club bought their own ground at Gunton Park, Curton, which was opened on the 5th September 1964 with a match against an EC select. The twin towns won the Norfolk Cup in 1974 and the EC Cup in 1995.

The changing nature of local employment has seen the area suffer. Off-shore oil rigs and tourism have replaced fishing, which has made it difficult to find new players. Lowestoft and Yarmouth have, however, settled into the middle ranks of English rugby.

NORTH WALSHAM

"Redruth against North Walsham is the sort of encounter which makes a set of Roman games look like a vicarage tea party."
Newspaper report, 1997

NORTH WALSHAM (POPULATION 12,463) is a farming community some 20 miles from Great Yarmouth. It has two claims to fame: it can claim to be the smallest town to field a National League team and it was the home of Lord Nelson, the naval hero.

The rugby club was formed in 1962 by John Mansfield, Ken Marshall and George Howard. Mansfield was a police sergeant who felt that directing the aggression of the local youth to the rugby field would reduce problems in the town. Marshall was headmaster of Paston Grammar School and Howard was a P.E. teacher at North Walsham School. The club were able to use school fields at the outset and got changed in a nearby warehouse. Later they acquired a field at Scottow and got changed in the nearby Horseshoes public house.

The club attribute their rapid rise to the size and aggression of their forwards, who epitomised the agricultural life. They qualified for the 1985 National Knockout Cup as East Anglian and Essex Cup winners and gave a good account of themselves before losing to mighty Saracens. Five years later their exploits saw the club become Rugby World's Junior Club of the Year. Five years later they reached round three of the National Cup.

The club has had some outstanding coaches, notably John Currie and John McKay. Currie later became head of Northampton Saints Academy whilst McKay became backs coach of the Australian National side.

In 2000 North Walsham provided the backbone of the Eastern Counties side, contributing six players. That year they reached National 3 South, which had the sizeable drawback of having to travel right along the South coast, including Cornwall. They were relegated to London 1, but bounced back and were unbeaten for a year.

The best players to appear for North Walsham were Tom and Ben Youngs, who were England and Lions players. The brothers began as juniors at Holt RUFC before moving to North Walsham and on to the Premiership. Also, Callum Green began with the club before joining Newcastle Gosforth.

(Thanks to David Horne)

Ben and Tom Youngs both went on to England and Lions success after playing for both Holt and North Walsham.

NORWICH

1881 IS SOMETIMES given as the date of formation of Norwich RFC, but other sources put the date as three years later. The club had several changes of name: Norwich & Norfolk, Norwich Wanderers and Norwich Vacation Club. The Vacation Club was an occasional side composed of students home from university or college.

The original club had an intermittent but successful existence. They were defeated ECs Cup finalists from 1897 to 1899 and cup winners two years later. They must have hit hard times as they were reported to have re-formed in 1903.

Two years later Ernest Roberts (1878-1933) appeared for Norwich. Roberts won six England caps between 1900 and 1908 whilst associated with the Royal Navy College and Devon.

No records exist of the club playing from 1906 until 1920. Indeed, rugby in East Anglia was nearly defunct when R.J. Read of Norwich arranged a match in November 1920 against the Norfolk Regiment led by Captain J. Orton. Four years later the club were playing 42 matches a season, including Thursday fixtures. Between the wars, home fixtures were played at Careys Meadow. The club occupied Fifer Lane from 1955 to 1982, when they moved to Beeston Hyme.

The 1930s saw an outstanding player in J.S. Redmayne, who was capped by EC. After World War Two, the club were honoured with the England trial match in 1955, and a decade later they enjoyed an outstanding season with 32 wins in 40 matches.

They qualified for the National Knockout Cup in the early 1980s and were one of the best clubs in East Anglia, but their fortunes have faded in recent seasons.

OLD STORTFORDIANS

BISHOP'S STORTFORD COLLEGE was opened in 1867 as a non-conformist centre of public school education. The school produced a number of fine rugby players, but was better known for producing cricketers.

There are records of an Old Stortfordians rugby club playing, and losing heavily, to Rosslyn Park 'A' in 1920. Playing flanker that day was Herbert L. Price, who proved one of the best players of the era. Price was educated at Bishop Stortford College, but moved to Blackheath and later Leicester. He won an England trial in 1921. The following year he won his first England cap against Ireland. On one occasion, Price scored a try against Wales without a Welshman touching the ball. He is credited with having played international rugby and international hockey on consecutive Saturdays His international career ended in 1925 when he suffered a broken leg playing for Old Stortfordians, which upset Leicester and England. He is also remarkable for having won a triple blue in water polo, hockey and rugby for Oxford University. Price recovered from the broken leg and finished his playing career with Harlequins in 1932 and later returned to Bishop's Stortford College as headmaster.

The Collett Family had a long association with OSs. Full-back S.B. Collett and flanker R.J. Collett were two of the club's best players between the wars.

By 1925 Old Stortfordians RFC had grown in strength sufficiently to play St. Mary's Hospital, one of England's top sides. The 1930s saw OSs reach middle-ranking status and they were playing an annual fixture against Bishop's Stortford RFC.

OSs disbanded in 1973. A part-time team was reinstated in 1986 for a couple of seasons, but it failed to sustain and was disbanded shortly afterwards.

(Thanks to Maggie Garrett and Stuart Findlay)

RAVENS
(Port of London Authority)

RAVENS CAN BE traced back to October 1875, when the club was formed by staff from the East and West India Dock Co. The name refers to the legendary birds in the nearby Tower of London. In 1882-83 Ravens were recorded as playing Upper Clapton at Hackney, when the opposition were amongst the best in town.

The club reformed when Port of London Authority came into being in 1909 and had to be restarted again in 1925 following World War One.

Currently Ravens play in the Essex Leagues.

SOUTHEND

LITTLE IS KNOWN about the early days of the original Southend RFC beyond the fact that they were formed in 1870 by Captain Charles Theobald at Milton Hall. The original club were a part of Eastern Counties rugby for three decades, but had occasional lapses. They finally folded around 1900.

The club was reformed in 1919 by a group including George Warden, the first secretary. Another founder member was Arthur Chappell, who had organisational expertise as he had run the Bristol Combination.

Within two seasons Southend provided eight players to the Eastern Counties side. The club acquired a ground at Priory Park and organised a popular club knockout competition called the Priory Cup. In the late 1920s they organised a charity cup competition for the Dowsett Cup that raised money for local hospitals in the days before the NHS.

Southend were a good side in the inter-war years, especially in 1923-24, when they won 20 of 25 matches. In the years after World War Two, however, they were a shadow of their former selves, with only one player winning county honours in the 1950s.

Two Southend players did bring credit to the club in the 1960s. Prop Roy Dunn moved to Bristol and played for Somerset, whilst goal-kicker Ken Light played for Southend for 50 years, scoring over 5,000 points. He even turned out in his 70s!

They did, however, produce a champion in the early 1960s, when they hosted the World Beer Drinking Festival. An unknown hero demolished three pints in 13 seconds, so Southend achieved a gold medal in something.

The rugby club were gold medal material in 1981 when victory in the Essex Cup brought qualification for the National Knockout Cup and an appearance on BBC's Rugby Special. In front of the cameras, they lost narrowly to mighty Gloucester.

Eventually they became Essex's premier club, with six players representing Essex and four for ECs. During their spectacular rise Southend were coached by Andy Otto, an ex-Lancashire player.

Sadly, decline followed swiftly as league rugby and professionalism saw Southend's best players enticed to the big money clubs of London. Decline was only arrested in the late 1990s by four successive promotions. Southend eventually reached National 2 before falling back to National 3 South.

SOUTHEND INVICTA

IN 1984 A curious rugby rival to Southend RFC emerged in Southend Invicta, who played rugby league at the local soccer club. Invicta had a good pedigree, being born out of the ashes of the Fulham rugby league club that enjoyed some success in the 1970s. Invicta originally played in Maidstone, Kent, but failed to establish themselves there. Southend United FC offered a home, but after attendances of 86 for Blackpool Borough and 85 for Huddersfield, the league club went into liquidation.

SUDBURY

"Players are asked to remember that Sudbury and Sunbury a
re two distinct places."
Old Whitgiftian notice to players

THE SLEEPY SUFFOLK market town of Sudbury on the River Stour appears in Dickens' Pickwick Papers under the pseudonym of Eatanswill.

The early 1990s saw a new star rise in the east when Sudbury FC reached National 3. This was heady stuff for the team from Suffolk, who were born in 1925 as Sudbury and Halstead RFC. The new club had a county player in Carlton Whitlock amongst their first members.

The following decades saw Sudbury established as a good East Anglian side. They were regular winners of the Suffolk Cup and runners-up in the 1982 EC Cup.

May 1985 was a black month as a disastrous fire destroyed the clubhouse. A new clubhouse was opened within nine months. They literally rose from the ashes by hiring a Kiwi coach, John Phillips, who helped launch the club on a rapid rise to the National leagues. Two of their players – Steve Titcombe and Steve Dyble – were amongst Britain's top scorers in the era.

Sadly, the days in the National Leagues were short-lived, as the costs of travelling all over England for away matches and the cost of players' expenses saw a dramatic downturn in Sudbury's fortunes. An unusual money-saving aspect of the club's decline was that Sudbury retained the services of John Phillips whilst allowing him to simultaneously coach Rotherham – 150 miles away!

WANSTEAD

'The Herons'

WANSTEAD BEGAN LIFE as Leytonstone RFC in 1892 and were a force in Eastern Counties rugby at the time. They faced serious opposition in the borough from local rivals Viceroy RFC, who reached the Eastern Counties Cup final on six occasions, but only won the title once. Viceroy disappeared soon afterwards and were replaced as local cup champions by Leytonstone, who won a hat-trick of EC Cups between 1906 and 1909.

Leytonstone moved to the adjacent borough of Wanstead around 1924 and changed their name to reflect the move. The club's best player was flanker Richard Davey, who won a single England cap in 1931 against Wales. Davey was a much-travelled clubman who began and ended his career in the West Country. Other top class-players to represent Wanstead included Mike Cutter and Dick Turpin, who both captained the Eastern Counties.

The club were forced to move house again in 1972 when their home ground on the Green Man roundabout was commandeered by the Ministry of Transport for motorway development. Wanstead found a temporary home with the Old Blues FC at Hainhault in the next borough before moving to a ground on Roding Lane North.

Wanstead were 2009 Essex 1 Champions and currently play in London 3.

WOODFORD

WOODFORD FOLLOWED A side in the borough called 'Forest FC', who were a private side of Old Harrovians rugby players who changed to association football as 'The Wanderers' and became one of the great soccer sides of the 19th century.

Legend has it that Woodford RFC was conceived in a railway carriage between Liverpool Street Station and the North East London suburbs. The inaugural meeting took place on the 4th August 1924, with Frank Ellison – an ex-Clifton player – appointed honorary secretary. Woodford adopted the traditional Clifton colours of lavender, white and black. The founder members were a distinguished bunch, as they included G. Seward (an England trialist) and Douglas Kendrew, who later won ten England caps. The club also appointed Col. Harold Colley as coach; he had played for Liverpool before World War One alongside Poulton-Palmer.

Woodford's first match was at home to a Old Haileybunans' junior XV and resulted in a 47-0 victory. In their first season Woodford won 12 of 15 fixtures and rapidly became one of the best sides in London. In 1932 they won away to Wasps, taking an unbeaten home record that had stood for five years.

Woodford's original pitch had been next to Woodford Wells Cricket Club in Monkham's Lane, but in 1928 they unveiled a new ground at Higham's with a fixture between two invitation XVs led by Wavell Wakefield and David McMyn, the respective captains of England and Scotland. 'Wakers' team arrived without a hooker and asked the home club to provide one.

Douglas Kendrew – an 18-year-old from Uppingham School – was offered, and thus began a great international career.

Kendrew had his greatest days with Leicester Tigers, but Woodford's second international, Peter Hepburn, remained loyal to the Essex club throughout a long and distinguished career. Hepburn was remarkable because the Scottish selectors rarely, if ever, looked outside Scotland for players – even London Scottish rarely got a look-in.

Hepburn learnt his rugby from Colonel Colley at St. Aubyn's School before winning eight Scotland caps. His two brothers, Guy and Pat, were both top-class players, although Guy lost part of his foot during the war.

After World War Two, Woodford were challenging the finest in the capital, but they never recovered their pre-war glory. The club retained its links to schools such as Uppingham, but went open in the 1970s after previously being restricted to public school and university players.

They won two Essex Cups and the Eastern Counties Cup and were Rugby World's Team of the Year. They have played in London One in recent seasons and their juniors are amongst the strongest in the region. The club's programme was edited for 50 years by Harold Colley, son of the first coach.

(Thanks to the late Harold Colley)

CHAPTER TWENTY – ODDS 'N' SODS

ANTI-ASSASSINS

THE ANTI-ASSASSINS are a prominent northern invitation team who provide opposition for commemorative and charity games, as well as touring all over the world. Three old boys of Sedbergh School, Stewart Faulds and G.S. & S.A. Kenyon, founded the Anti-Assassins club in 1950. Its original function was to play an annual game at Sedbergh against 'the Assassins', a side composed of boys and masters of the famous Rugby-playing Yorkshire school. This series ended in 1956, but today the Anti-Assassins are one of the leading 'nomadic' sides in the country. It has an invited membership of over 250 and raises sides – usually containing some international and county players – for annual games with schools such as Ampleforth, Giggleswick, Mount St. Mary's, Rossall, Sedbergh and Stonyhurst, as well as the Vale of Lune club.

The driving force behind the AAs in recent times has been Peter Hughes MBE, BEM, an international referee from Burnley. Peter has many claims to fame, including a song written about him by Max Boyce, the Welsh folk singer, blaming him for Neath getting beaten. A decade later, he was one of the 57 'Old Farts' who were castigated by Will Carling, the English captain.

The AAs have always had strong links with Bury RFC and in 2003 they merged with the Wooden Spoon charity.

ARMY

"I am convinced that the Rugby Footballer makes the finest soldier in the world…"
Colonel Davidson, 1916

THE BRITISH ARMY is, of its nature, an exclusive world: it has its own rugby union, its own laws and its own great history. The army played a huge part in laying the roots for rugby across the world and army sides can claim to have played the first ever rugby matches in India (1873), Japan (1927), Afghanistan (1878) and Pakistan (1956). Army rugby players usually found a game somewhere, notably in 1931, when the Middlesex Regiment somehow conjured up an away fixture against a 'Khartoum XV'.

The British Army of the 21st century bears little resemblance to the service that ruled the world in Victorian times. The officers and the other ranks were two separate entities in 1854, when Britain entered the Crimean War. The 'other ranks' were largely uneducated, working-class men, whilst the officer corps were almost exclusively upper-class 'toffs'. An upper-class family could purchase a commission for their sons, preferably in the Guards or the Cavalry. Officers of these two exclusive

The army team of 1878.

regiments formed the two sides for the army's first ever match, played on the 27th March 1855 at Balaclava on the Crimean Peninsula.

Four years later, two battalions from the Grenadiers played rugby on the hallowed turf of Lord's Cricket Ground in London. In 1863 a representative from the War Office attended the formation meeting of the Football Association.

The Royal Military Academy, Woolwich became the army's principal rugby headquarters in London. RMA Woolwich was an integral part of the London rugby scene in the mid-1860s. Royal Military College, Sandhurst was Woolwich's arch-rival, but, curiously, the two colleges didn't meet on the rugby field until 1876.

Woolwich and Sandhurst offered ex-public schoolboys a military education before they got sent as young officers to police the Empire. The most remarkable Empire rugby club was the Calcutta Club, based on the 3rd Battalion of the Buffs, who had arrived in India in 1873. The Calcutta Club had a free bar, which was very popular. Members raided the free bar to such an extent that the club imposed charges, which unsurprisingly led to an immediate decline in membership. Rugby was played in India from October to February, but the excessive hardness of the turf spoilt the game. The club was temporarily disbanded, but it was suggested that the Calcutta Club's name be perpetuated by presenting the RFU with a cup to be competed for annually by England and Scotland. The offer was accepted, and the Calcutta Cup was first contested in 1879. Ever since then the trophy has been the reward for victory in the England v Scotland match.

Service rugby had spread throughout the world, but it made an impression at home

The Calcutta Cup

too. Two officers from the Royal Engineers, C.W. Sherrard and C.A. Crompton, played for England in the first ever international. Both men were also members of Blackheath, which has a long association with the armed forces.

In 1878 there were sufficient rugby players in the services for an Army v Navy match to be played at Kennington Oval. The Army lost by a goal and a try to a goal. The fixture led to renewal matches on an irregular basis for the remainder of the 19th century.

The Army Rugby Union itself wasn't formed until 1906. It was the brainchild of three Blackheath stalwarts: Lt. J.C.E. Partridge (Welsh Regiment), Lt. W.S.D. Craven (Royal Field Regiment) and Lt. Clive Liddell (Leicester Regiment). A casual post-match chat led to the idea of a services rugby union. On the 12th November 1906 a meeting was held to inaugurate the organisation. 'Birdie' Partridge had played for Newport, Blackheath, Transvaal and South Africa (one cap, 1903) and helped found Old Alleynians in October 1897. The first committee was composed of representatives from the Cavalry, Royal Artillery, Royal Engineers, Queens, the infantry and the Royal Army Medical Corps. The following year an inter-services tournament took place between the Army and Navy.

Lt. J.C.E. 'Birdie' Partridge'

Four years later the Army XV expanded its boundaries by playing a Kent XV heavily drawn from Blackheath. Although the national army team was totally comprised of officers, the Army RU co-ordinated regimental rugby.

Army rugby played an important part in revitalising the game in Scotland, where in the early 1900s it was struggling. After the Boer War George Usher, who was in charge of army recruiting in Scotland, rekindled interest in the game.

The outbreak of war in 1914 saw huge numbers of troops being mobilized, and the ensuing slaughter on the Western Front brought a cataclysmic change to British society. The traditional officer class drawn from the public schools were amongst the worst to suffer, as one in five ex-public schoolboys were killed as they went 'over the top' with a revolver and whistle to face German machine guns. A young officer, straight from public school, had a life expectancy of three weeks in some parts of the Western Front.

Back in Britain, Rugby was still played by the Army during World War One. Bizarrely, at least one rugby match was played behind the front line; on Boxing Day 1917, the Duke of Cornwall Light Infantry played the Machine Gun Corps at Beaumetz with 150 a side. The officers on horseback acted as referees.

When peace came, the existence of a large standing army benefitted rugby. Many of the best-known players of the era were in the army. In 1923 the Army team could field an all-international back-line drawn from F. Gilbert, J.A. Middleton,

R.M. Scobie, Harold Day, Quentin King, P. Baker-Jones, R.K. Millar and John Worton. Worton in particular did so well for the army, he was selected for England as a scrum-half. His international career was ended when he was posted to China – an occupational hazard for a soldier.

The 1930s were notable for Ireland contributing some great names and characters to army rugby. Victor Pike, Jamie Clinch and H. Mayne were rough customers. Mayne played for the 1938 Lions and helped found the Special Air Service. He had a reputation for incredible courage and for driving his superiors mad at his approach to soldiering. The Irish hooker Victor Pike was from Tipperary and served as an army chaplain. He was one of three brothers capped by Ireland; indeed, Victor scored the winning try in the 1931 Irish win over Scotland. Later he represented Hampshire in two championship wins (1933 and 1936). During World War Two, Pike was chaplain-general to the Eighth Army in North Africa. He left the army in 1960 to become Bishop of Sherbourne.

At local level, army teams were at the best in provincial rugby. The Berkshire County Cup was dominated by the Royal Military College of Science and REME, Arborfield, whilst RMA Woolwich and RMC Sandhurst had first-class fixture lists in the 1920s.

Mobilisation for World War Two brought a curious problem when rugby players in club matches sometimes found themselves on the same rugby field as conscientious objectors. This caused enormous ill-feeling.

The Second World War brought an influx of rugby league players, as it had in World War One. League players were banned from playing union, so it needed a special dispensation to allow professional players to play amateur rugby in the services. The Royal Signals, based at Catterick Camp, was the best side in the army in the 1950s and fielded a sprinkling of rugby league players. The greatest player to appear for them was Billy Boston, a human cannonball, who was also one of rugby league's all-time greats. Another great rugby league player was Eric Ashton, who joined as an unknown Warrington rugby league player. He gained a big reputation in the army and was welcomed back to Warrington with open arms when he was demobbed.

The profile of services rugby diminished substantially in the late 20th century. The defence budget was reduced as the budget of leading rugby clubs escalated, which undermined the status of the inter-services championship. The army could still offer a bursary to young men going to university, and it boasted several internationals, such as Tim Rodber, Rob Wainwright and Matt Stewart. However, the advent of professional rugby offered an alternative avenue for young men who might once have opted for an army career.

The army did benefit from Fijians joining the British Army under a long-standing recruitment programme in the South Sea Islands. In 2014 Semesa Rokoduguni (pictured right) became the first serving

soldier called up for England for 40 years when he was selected against the All Blacks. Although born on the Pacific islands, Semesa qualified for England on grounds of residency.

BARBARIANS

THE BARBARIANS ARE guaranteed a place in sporting history for many reasons, but especially for one magical minute in January 1973, when their scratch team took on the touring New Zealanders. The All Blacks bore down on the Barbarians try line when a fumble gave the Baa-baas the chance to counter-attack. The ball passed through a dozen Barbarian hands before Gareth Edwards scored at the other end of the field. It was perhaps the finest try in rugby history and certainly the most replayed on television.

It epitomised the reckless style of rugby adopted by a team with no money, no regular players, no home and roots that lie deep in a by-gone era. The name is an misnomer, for they are the most civilised of people, and the nickname is thought to come from 'Baw', the ancient Scottish word for football. Legend has it that the Scots played the game in the Middle Ages with the decapitated heads of their enemies.

Percy Carpmael

In 1888 Punch magazine published a cartoon, 'Barbarians at Play', a depiction of Midland Yahoos v North Country Savages playing each other at rugby. Punch sub-titled the cartoon: "The importation of sheer ruffianism into the football field". The cartoon may have been in the minds of a scratch team raised by William Percy Carpmael (1853-1936) to tour the North of England in 1890. The original team was variously known as the Southern Nomads and 'a Blackheath XV'.

Carpmael was a pillar of Blackheath RFC and the RFU. An arch critic of professionalism, in 1895 he submitted a motion to the RFU that anyone who provided information about illegal payments by rugby clubs should be paid £20. The motion was rejected.

The first Barbarians wore a badge of the skull and crossbones taken from School House at Rugby School. In 1890 the team had an Easter tour to Burton, Moseley, Wakefield and Huddersfield. After the match at Huddersfield the high-spirited party returned to their hotel in Bradford, where an 'Oyster Supper' gave birth to the idea of more regular fixtures by a Barbarian FC. All the original party of 21 were Oxbridge men steeped in a Corinthian spirit. On the 1st October 1890, the club held its first Annual General Meeting; it was also the last because the Baa-baas did not think another necessary.

Gareth Edwards in Barbarian colours, scorer of the most famous try in Baa baa, and, arguably, rugby history in 1973.

The following year the party of friends lost to Dublin University, Huddersfield, Swinton and Gloucester, but won against Cardiff. Thus began the tradition of the Easter Tour of South Wales, with matches against Penarth, Cardiff, Swansea and Neath.

Huge crowds queued to watch the Barbarian matches in Wales, which became a massive tradition. The laid-back approach to playing also applied off the field. Before World War One the Baa-baas had a reputation as a rough bunch that drank far too much. Rough or otherwise, Carpmael's originals were eventually replaced by talented rugby players, who were 'gentlemen of all classes' from every part of the British Isles.

The club's reputation on the field was enhanced, during World War One when they organised a series of six 'recruiter' internationals designed to encourage spectators to join the forces.

Edgar Mobbs was a legendary rugby player who was killed in World War One. He was a friend of the Baa-baas, and an annual fixture with the East Midlands was played in his memory from 1921 onwards. It wasn't the first regular fixture, as the Barbarians have played Leicester since 1909.

Between the wars, the Barbarians continued the Easter Tour of South Wales. It was not uncommon for crowds over 30,000 to attend matches. Despite a punishing schedule, the Baa-baas were undefeated on the Welsh tour from 1931 to 1935.

Each Easter, the party were based at the Esplanade Hotel in the sleepy little holiday resort of Penarth near Cardiff. The Barbarians' rules stated that players could drink as much as they liked, but anyone involved the next day had to be in bed by 11pm. One legend is that two Barbarian players once managed to smuggle a cow into their bedroom on the first floor of the Esplanade.

Administering the players has fallen to a small number of officers over the years: Carpmael, L. deLisa, H. Haigh-Smith, Glyn Hughes and Geoff Windsor-Davies.

After World War Two, a tradition developed of touring teams from the Southern Hemisphere playing a farewell match against the Barbarians, which culminated in both sides joining arms and singing 'Auld Lang Syne'. The fixture began in January 1948, when the Wallabies' British tour needed to raise extra money. The Barbarians played the Australians, but lost 9-6. The Barbarians rang the curtain down on every major tour for a generation.

Ironically, the Barbarians' 1973 win over New Zealand marked the end of an age of innocence. Previously the Barbarian selectors would call up 14 established internationals and one uncapped player (an enduring tradition). They would meet on the Thursday before an international match and then try to organise a team. The All Blacks were hurt by the 1973 defeat and by a 14-14 draw in the 1974 rematch. They have made sure they won any subsequent renewals.

The Barbarian brand remained important, but the arrival of leagues meant top clubs were increasingly reluctant to release players for Barbarian matches in case of injury. Even the Easter tour was abandoned.

The Barbarians have fought back by scouring the world for top-class players, but the game has moved on. No longer can a team of talented players guarantee to compete with organised national or top-class club sides. The Barbarians remain a huge attraction and, win or lose, the Baa-baas will remain an important part of rugby into the 21st Century and beyond.

The Esplanade in Penarth, the hotel in which the Baa baas would stay on their Easter tours.

CAMBRIDGE UNIVERSITY

'God damn bloody Oxford'

traditional pre-Varsity match toast

CAMBRIDGE CAME INTO prominence in the 14th century, when seven colleges were opened in the city. The first colleges were founded to cater for non-monastic scholars. The monarch and church employed the scholars as the first civil servants.

Henry VIII forbad the teaching of canon law at Oxbridge and promoted civil law. By the 18th century, every lawyer had to be a Doctor of Law from Oxford or Cambridge. In the 19th century, undergraduates were expected to rise for prayers, spend the day in study and dress for formal dinner.

Sport to the undergraduates was restricted to riding, shooting or fishing, but recreational tastes changed in the 19th century and Oxford v Cambridge sporting matches took place from 1829 when the Boat Race began.

Cambridge University RFC is much more than a famous rugby club; it is actually the body responsible for the rugby activities of all the 28 college clubs within the university. The original CURFC was formed only weeks before the first Varsity match on the 10th February 1872.

Rugby had, however, been played at the university in 1839, when a student called Albert Pell tried to form a club at the university. Spectators of early games on Parker's Piece thought the players slightly deranged. One report told of "a number of Rugby men, mostly freshmen, playing a new game", in which they "made a circle round a ball and butted each other".

Pell's problem was that the players only knew the rules of football they had learnt at their own school (which wasn't necessarily Rugby). In 1848 serious efforts were being made to establish a set of rules acceptable to everyone, which included allowing players to run with the ball and hacking.

The first Varsity Match was played at the Parks in Oxford, with the spoils going to the Dark Blues. The second Varsity match was played at Parker's Piece. Subsequent matches were played in London.

Cambridge played their first matches in pink, but changed to blue and whites in 1876, the same year that matches were reduced from 20-a-side to 15. The change drew the comment from one commentator that: "Oxford and Cambridge are going to the dogs".

The first major Oxbridge character to emerge was Edward Temple-Gurdon, who was Cambridge captain in 1875 and 1876 before being an England regular for a decade. During that era he was only once on a losing side. His brother, Charles Gurdon, who also attended Cambridge, played for England from 1880 to 1886. Another Cambridge international was Charles Wilson, who played for the Light Blues from 1877 to 1880. He won four Rugby Blues, playing in the Varsity match from 1877 to 1880.

Herbert Fuller eclipsed all his contemporaries by playing for Cambridge in six Varsity matches, which elicited the suggestion that he was a professional student. After he finally graduated, a limit was put on the number of times a player could play in Varsity matches.

Cambridge held their own against Oxford University until the 1880s, when their rivals began to dominate. A young Cambridge student, Charles Marriott (1861-1936), proved the catalyst that rescued the series. Marriott learnt from the defeats and galvanised the Light Blues into a side good enough to win five of seven Varsity matches. He later became one of the leading figures of the England team and was RFU Secretary for 17 years.

By 1896 CURFC had become so established that, together with the Cambridge University Association Football Club, they purchased land at Grange Road for the development of a pitch with spectator and changing facilities. Not that changing rooms were over-used. Baths and showers were rare in the days before World War One. Students at Cambridge University were not provided with bathing facilities in their rooms because a term only lasted eight weeks and it was felt students did not need to bathe in term time.

David Bedell-Sivright

Besides Marriott, Cambridge have been fortunate to have been led by some great captains. Andrew Don-Wauchope (1861-1948) won 12 Scotland caps, scoring six international tries. He was followed by another Scots legend in David Bedell-Sivright (1880-1915), who won 22 caps and was captain of the 1904 British Isles team to Australia and New Zealand. Bedell-Sivright was a master of the dribble and was described as "one of the roughest players of his day", which wasn't surprising as he was a Scotland heavyweight boxing champion. Bedell-Sivright was killed at Gallipoli 1915.

The Light Blues next great captain was J.E. 'Jenny' Greenwood, who somehow remained a student from 1910 to 1919. He managed to play in five Varsity matches, despite rules designed to prevent superannuated students lingering in the cloisters purely for rugby purposes. Entry to university in the early 1900s is a mystery to modern minds. Greenwood failed to win a scholarship to King's College, but was excused the entrance examination because he was a fine rugby player. He admitted the standard of admission criteria was "of a very low standard" compared to modern requirements. Greenwood was blunt about Cambridge in 1910 stating: "I really did not do a stroke of work in my first year."

Greenwood was typical of Varsity rugby players, as he was from a wealthy background. Students had to be well-heeled as the cost of being an Oxbridge student in 1900 was approximately £250 a year, which covered fees and lodging. This was twice the annual wage of the average man. University was, therefore, strictly for the wealthy.

The educational standards before the First World War can be gleaned from correspondence between the Hawks club at Cambridge University and the Athenaeum club. It was said nothing was written down because only one undergraduate in either club could read and write. Jenny Greenwood did well from his Cambridge days; he received a third-class degree in law and was immediately offered a job as a director of Boots the Chemists.

After Greenwood graduated, Cambridge had another 'great' in Wavell Wakefield from Sedburgh School. Wakefield is credited with turning Cambridge into the best pack in the country. He reorganised Cambridge university rugby in the early 1920s with an inter-college league, intense preparation for the Varsity match and numbered jerseys in the big matches.

The Varsity match of 1920

His achievements eventually earned him 31 England caps, a huge number in the days before England had foreign tours. Wakefield later became an MP and was raised to the peerage.

Wakefield was helped by Ronald Cove-Smith, who later became captain of Cambridge, England and the British Isles. He won 28 England caps and became a distinguished doctor.

The late 1920s saw Cambridge produce two great scrum-halves in Arthur Young and Wilf Sobey. Young was a particular thorn in Oxford's side. He is almost forgotten by the modern generation, but the tiny player won 18 England caps between 1924 and 1929. Sobey achieved a fraction of Young's greatness, but became a famous public figure, partially due to his rugby partnership with Roger Spong for Old Millhillians and England.

The Cambridge sides of Young and Sobey were aided by an influx of brilliant Welshmen to the Light Blues' colours. In 1927 the Light Blues fielded five Welshmen in the three-quarters for the Varsity match. Windsor-Lewis, Morgan, Rowe Harding, Roberts and Harry Bowcott, who were all to become internationals. Cambridge University were unbeaten in all matches in season 1925-26, scoring 99 points and conceding only 32.

Despite the accusations that some rugby players were sub-standard scholars, one genuine Cambridge student made a huge impression on and off the field. Carl Aarvold, a leggy winger from Durham School, arrived at Cambridge in 1925 with no reputation as a rugby player. He played for the Freshers' XV and was immediately selected for the First XV, becoming one of their greatest ever players. Aarvold's achievements include four wins in consecutive Varsity matches, and a personal tally of three tries. He played on the 1930 Lions tour and won 16 England caps. He later became a barrister and judge.

Many critics maintain that the 1934 Light Blues side was the greatest ever. It contained Cliff Jones, Wilf Wooller, Ken Fyfe, Graeme Parker and Arthur Rees, who all became top-class players. They thrashed Oxford 29-4, scoring six tries.

After World War Two Cambridge had the benefit of the arrival of Mickey Steele-Bodger, who organised a trial match for the Light Blues before the Varsity match, which became a regular fixture. Steele-Bodger won nine England caps and was a national selector.

In the 1950s Cambridge relied on Welsh talent, whereas Oxford relied on Rhodes Scholars. Away from the Varsity XV, 11 colleges had rugby teams who played each other. The cream of the college sides were promoted to the Varsity XV.

The mettle of Cambridge back play in the post-war years is demonstrated by every Cambridge stand-off between 1948 and 1970 winning international honours, except for Pat Briggs, who only made a trial. Perhaps the greatest was Mike Gibson of Ireland, who won a world record 69 caps and made 12 Lions test appearances. Gibson went on five Lions tours and in 1968 he was the first international replacement.

He was not so lucky at Cambridge; he arrived when the Light Blues were in decline. Gibson played in three Varsity matches without scenting victory, but still won a fine reputation. A 'will o' the wisp' three-quarter, he could play anywhere in the backs with equal genius. Many rate Gibson as the finest three-quarter in the history of the game. A teetotal Ulsterman, he had an international career that spanned 15 years.

Gibson was followed by two internationals in Roger Shackleton of England and Iain Robertson of Scotland (who later became the BBCs rugby correspondent). Other top players who represented the Light Blues in the Varsity match include Eddie Butler, John Robbie, Alun Lewis, Marcus Rose and Rob Andrew.

In 1988 Mike Hall of Wales upset the Welsh selectors when he opted to play for Cambridge rather than the national team.

Hugh Lloyd-Davies was the first Blue to switch to rugby league – well, almost. He signed for Barrow RLFC, but is reported to have had second thoughts as he failed to appear at his new club.

Today the Varsity match is not the passport to a lucrative job outside rugby or international honours that it once was, but the pulling power of the two university sides still fills Twickenham each December.

GUERNSEY

THE FIRST REFERENCE to rugby on the island of Guernsey is a match between an Island XV and the Middlesex Regiment at Fort Field. Guernsey played Jersey the following January, but lost heavily. The match became a regular fixture, but it took six years before Guernsey overcame their rivals. Known as the 'Rangers', the original Guernsey side disappeared in the late 1890s.

Welsh and Irish exiles reformed a Guernsey club in the 1930s. They played mainly against army sides. After the war the club was revived by Col. Kenneth Wright (four Scotland caps) and Geoffrey de la Condamine.

Guernsey have risen staedily since 2004. They were champions of Hampshire 1 in 2004, London 2 SW in 2011 and reached National 3 in 2012.

GUY'S HOSPITAL

"Social Historians in the far future will bitterly blame the English for teaching the world a score of ways to waste time."
Karel Capek, 1922

GUY'S HOSPITAL WAS founded in the early 18th century by a successful entrepreneur called Thomas Guy, who had made a fortune speculating on the South Seas Bubble, an 18th century financial scandal. Guy resolved to provide a 'free' hospital for the poor, who presumably included the majority of the speculators in the Bubble.

The rugby club were reputed to be founded in 1843, which makes Guy's the oldest club in the world. The claim is based on the recollections of Dr. Allport, a leading RFU figure in the 19th Century.

Little is known of the early teams, except that their sport was largely in-house because they had no opposition until the 1860s, when other clubs emerged.

When the RFU was formed in 1871, Guy's were regarded as the third best side in London behind Richmond and Blackheath. Matches between Guy's, Richmond and Blackheath were seen as the highlights of the London rugby season.

Guy's played on Blackheath Common for many years. They played – and defeated – Blackheath when 'the club' officially opened their ground at Richardson's Field in October 1877, and were the first guests when Blackheath opened the Rectory Field six years later.

Guys left Blackheath Common in 1872 for a mud heap at Nunshead. A decade later they moved to Raynes Park, where they changed in a cowshed. Raynes Park was a long way from the hospital, so in 1891 the Guy's Hospital Sports Association bought a multi-sport facility at Honor Oak Park.

The Hospital Challenge Cup dates from 1874 and Guy's were the inaugural champions. They dominated the competition for many years, winning 23 of the first 60 finals.

The club's first player picked as an international was unfortunate. Arthur Fagan (1862-1930) was selected at full-back for the 1888 England team that did not play because of a wrangle with the other Home countries. Fagan was never selected again. More fortunate was Willie Mitchell (1865-1905), an unorthodox full-back who won seven England caps in the early 1890s. Mitchell was a founder member of the Barbarians and played in 19 matches on the 1891 British Lions tour of South Africa. He was renowned for turning up for international matches without any kit. For someone who could never find his rugby boots, it was surprising that he went off to find gold in the Yukon. He never did find gold, dying shortly after departing.

Records state that Guy's were a mediocre side in the 1890s, but besides Mitchell, the club could also field H.W. Dudgeon, a flying forward who won seven England caps, and F.O. Stoker, who was capped five times for Ireland as a forward.

The 20th Century brought a golden era for Guy's, with their backs amongst the best. Pivotal to their success was Teddy Morgan (1880-1949), who ranks amongst the greatest Welsh three-quarters. Morgan is recorded as being "small, compact and agile as a monkey. He had a wonderful kick and would tackle anything". He played 16 times for Wales, but is best remembered for scoring the winning try at Cardiff on the 16th December 1905 that ended the first All Blacks' winning run. Although he was the smallest man on the field, he was a tough customer; in one Hospital Cup encounter he was warned by the referee about rough play.

Later it was Guy's' forwards who earned a great reputation. The 1905 Guy's pack contained three England players in A. Archer, G.R. Hind and Arnold Alcock, a postgraduate student who was England's oddest international. Alcock was a decent club player, but he won international selection by a clerical error. The selectors chose 'Slocock' of Liverpool, but the notice of the selection was sent to 'Alcock' of Guy's. He joined the England team at Crystal Palace and took the field against the 1906 Springboks. England managed a draw, which was a good result against the South Africans. Alcock was never again picked for his country, but became a regular at Gloucester (where he worked as a GP) and was club president. Slocock soon regained his place and won 14 caps before dying in World War One.

Guy's had a remarkable association with the British Isles team. The original British teams were heavily dependent upon good players who could spare six months to tour the other side of the world, so medical students were a popular selection. Guy's men who answered the call were A. Ayre-Smith (Australia 1899), E.M. Harrison (South Africa 1903), Teddy Morgan, A.B. O'Brien, P. McEvedy and S. Mackay (Australia & New Zealand 1904), J.P. Tuan, P. McEvedy, H. Archer and G.R. Hind (1908 New Zealand & South Africa). Later R. Cover-Smith captained the 1924 Lions despite playing for a hospital side.

Guy's representation with the British Isles is all the more remarkable because the majority of their contingent were never capped by their country. It is understood that McEvedy and O'Brien were never capped because they were New Zealanders who were studying in London.

This distinction became blurred in later years as the Home countries, it was said, absorbed the colonial students into their national teams with ease. In the early days, hundreds of colonial students came to London teaching hospitals, where cynics suggested their rugby prowess was as important as their studies. This gave rise to an urban myth that ability on the rugby field brought special treatment at exam time, although this was never proved.

The 1920 Hospital Cup-winning team from Guy's was based on South African undergraduates. It consisted of three Englishmen, one Welshman and eleven South Africans. Guy's could also draw on students from the Dental College Medical Schools. Not surprisingly, Guy's were the best side in London in the 1920s.

The 'mature' students from South Africa became so numerous that instructions on the field were shouted in Afrikaans to baffle the opposition. Harlequins overcame this problem by recruiting a South African, who was only selected for the First XV when they played Guy's. An indifferent player, the foreign Harlequin was employed primarily to translate Guy's line-out calls.

Certainly, the Home countries showed special treatment to Guy's colonial brigade in granting national qualification. In 1921 England picked J.A. Krige, a South African, which caused

such a rumpus over eligibility that they avoided taking the risk again.

A huge furore developed over a tough Australian flanker called Doug Keller, who had played for his home nation on the 1947 British tour. He returned to Britain as a medical student at Guy's and claimed Scots ancestry. This was approved by the SRU and he was picked as Scotland's captain. This selection appeared to violate the IRB laws on playing for more than one country, but Keller eventually won a dozen Scotland caps. He later moved to Sheffield after qualifying.

The 1950s were the heyday of Guy's and of hospital rugby in general. The Hospital Cup final was a madcap carnival, with the rugby a distraction in the mayhem. Central to finals featuring Guy's was a battered old milk churn. The milk churn was 'borrowed' by a Guy's team member en-route to a Hospitals Cup match. The club won the Hospitals Cup that year and looked upon the churn as a good luck charm. Since then, the churn is updated with Guy's Hospitals Cup victories.

HOSPITALS CUP

"The Hospitals Cup was once described as 'a disorganised wrestling match between two rabbles having more exuberance than knowledge with players writhing about in mud and caring little for the whereabouts of the ball.'"

Rupert Cherry

VII HOSPITAL CUP FINAL RAG AT RICHMOND

THE HOSPITALS CUP is the oldest competition in rugby. W.E. Collins, the England full-back, represented St. George's Hospital on the United Hospital Committee and suggested to the committee that they hold an annual cup competition. Collins was rebuffed twice, but eventually his suggestion was accepted. The staff and students of St George's had a collection and raised £88 to buy a trophy.

The United Hospitals Committee were very innovative. They ended the law that one drop-goal was more valuable than any number of tries. They ruled in the 1870s that three touchdowns are equal to one try (at goal) and three tries equal a goal (nine points). The side who accumulated most points were victors. They were also the first organisation to introduce touch judges after a massive row between St. George's Hospital and Blackheath. A.W. Pearson of Blackheath gathered the ball in his 25 and ran up the touchline. The medics stopped because they thought Pearson was in touch, but he touched down and turned to find the Medics demanding he be penalised. The row rumbled on, and eventually it was decided to introduce umpires or touch judges.

The Hospitals Cup featured 11 sides and ten games and lasted from mid-January until mid-March. A unique feature of the competition was the unruly behaviour of the crowd, which featured the throwing of flour and red dye on anyone who turned up. Eventually, unruly behaviour was restrained by the deans of the teaching schools.

A curious throwback to street football comes in the tradition of 'rag days' in February, where students do crazy antics for charity. The fun and frolics emulated the old tradition of Shrove Tuesday Football.

In the 1950s, St. Thomas's Hospital discovered an easy way to gain admission to Twickenham on match days. They sent an unauthorised ambulance there, which was always admitted without problems. Inside were a dozen students without tickets, who quietly joined the throng.

ISLE OF MAN

"The average Britisher is an athlete, the English nation an athletic one, and its subjects, both men and women, more universally and generally imbued with the athletic spirit than those of any other race on earth."

Caspar Whitney, 1900

RUGBY HAD BEEN played on the Isle of Man at King William's College since 1861. The college can claim to have been largely responsible for maintaining the island game for over a century.

One College player who learnt his rugby on the Isle of Man was instrumental in creating international rugby. A.H. Robertson of the West of Scotland club was a signatory of the Scots' challenge to England that led to the first rugby international at Raeburn Place, Edinburgh in 1871. Robertson, of course, played in that first international.

King William's has produced seven internationals, two Blues and 50 county players. The best known are C.E. Orr, who played for Scotland 16 times between 1887 and 1892, and E.G. Forrest of Wanderers, who won 13 caps for Ireland between 1889 and 1897.

Away from the college, rugby clubs began to appear on the island from 1873, when Douglas RFC emerged, led by Mr A.W. Moore, who went on to play for Cambridge in the 1874 Varsity match. The best side on the island was Mona, who were formed in 1883 and could boast 200 members and fixtures against Sale and Hull. Their domination was soon overtaken by Douglas. The other sides on the island in the 1890s were King

William's School, Castle Town, Wanderers, Laxey, Foxdale, Ramsey Albert, Peel and Stanley.

The island supplied two players to the 1888 British Isles tour to Australia and New Zealand: Arthur Paul and Arthur Penketh. Penketh and Paul travelled with the team, which took six weeks to reach Australia. Paul was a top-class cricketer for Lancashire, Nottinghamshire and England. After the tour, he moved to the mainland and had a distinguished career with Swinton. Penketh of Douglas, meanwhile, was

Arthur Penketh

never picked for his country. Whilst many of the team were top-class players, the 1888 team were selected largely on their capability to rub along together. Despite the odd selection policy, Penketh and company played 35 matches, won 27, drew six and lost only two. Penketh returned to the Isle of Man after his moment in history and lived to a ripe old age, totally ignored by the sport. He returned to the island to find the Manx RFU had been formed and an annual North v South match was played, based on an imaginary line drawn from Peel to the Douglas town boundary.

Robert Thompson (1869-1952) attended King William's before going to Cambridge. He played on the 1891 British Isles tour to South Africa.

There was a time when there were a dozen sides playing regularly on the island, but gradually they all disappeared. By 1950, Canon E.H. Stebbing wrote in his book 'The Isle of Man': "Rugby football, formerly a very popular game, had almost completely died out."

The Vagabonds in action in 2004.

It was therefore ironic that 1950 should see the revival of the Douglas club, which played a big part in assisting other clubs to come into being. One called the 'Vagabonds' was composed of former pupils of Douglas High School. The other, the 'Ronaldsway Aircraft Club' was mainly composed of employees at the aviation works in the south of the island.

J. Timson, who founded Vagabonds, later played for Davenport. In the 1990s Douglas and Vagabonds joined the mainland leagues, and despite having to fly to every away match, they enjoyed some success.

The Isle of Man has a representative team, with the current squad comprised of players from Vagabonds, Douglas, Ramsey and Western Vikings. Matches are played in Jersey and Dublin. The Jersey match is an annual event, with both sides competing for the Sir Michael Wilkes Cup.

(Thanks to Chris Till and Bob Doughty)

JERSEY

JERSEY RFC ARE the strongest rugby side in the Channel Islands, and certainly the club with the longest history. Rugby was played on Jersey in the 1860s, principally by the local schools. The first recorded club game was in 1870, when St. James Collegiate School XV played 'the Indistinguishable' (the local fire brigade). The school won easily. Three years later a Victoria College team defeated 'Mr Symonds XV'.

Over the next few years various casual sides took the field, usually bearing the name of the organiser (a peculiarity that was never apparent on the mainland). By 1876 the game was established enough to see an Island XV take on the Royal Artillery, and later the islanders played against a St. James Collegiate School and Victoria College Combined XV.

The following season an established round of matches was in place, but playing resources and opposition were scarce. This was at a time when the local newspaper actually recorded the name of every single visitor to the island!

The Wanderers (actually the Jersey XV) were the best side on the island, but they had to rely on school sides for opposition. Eventually a Jersey v United Schools fixture was organised.

Rugby on the islands suffered a body blow with the arrival of soccer in 1890. The only rugby fixture to survive the change was the annual Jersey v Guernsey match for the Siam Cup, which was initially played for by Victoria College and Elizabeth College to encourage rugby on the islands. The Siam Cup was donated by five Channel Islanders working in Thailand in the 1900s. Legend has it that the King of Siam supported the project out of friendship for one of the donors. For such a splendid trophy it had a chequered history. When the colleges on Jersey lost interest in rugby, the trophy was competed for by local army units. When the army sides fell by the wayside, Jersey v Guernsey filled the void. Sporting interest waned so much that the Siam Cup was played for by two darts teams. Eventually it was returned to rugby.

Club rugby reappeared in 1934, when Jersey RFC was formed in Beresford's Café. Things went well initially; Jersey RFC had a kit and a ground, and the annual Jersey v Guernsey competition was revived. The club even affiliated with the Hampshire RU in 1937-38. The new club aroused much animosity by opting to play in black shirts (mimicking the Fascists), a joke that was soon to have echoes.

On 1st June 1940, rugby was forgotten as the German Army occupied the islands. It was seven years before it reappeared.

Jersey in action in 2011.

Appropriately, the Siam Cup became the focus of attention, but first a Jersey-Guernsey XV played Rosslyn Park, Saracens and Portsmouth. In the subsequent season, a Channel Islands XV toured the mainland, but not before Jersey took the Siam Cup, beating their rivals 8-6.

After 70 years the game finally took seed on Jersey in the 1950s, boosted by the popularity of touring teams venturing across the Channel. Unfortunately, Jersey RFC were forced to play on a pitch at Beaumont, which was unplayable in winter due to flooding.

Despite the islands being affiliated to the Hampshire RU, it was 1966 before an island player was first capped by the county when Brian Screen of Jersey played for Hants against Kent.

In 1987 Jersey applied to join the English leagues, but this was only permitted if the club paid all expenses (including the opposition's). Initially this was unacceptable, until a sponsor provided £10,000. Jersey did well to survive in the London Leagues, despite the cost and inconvenience of a dozen matches a season on the mainland.

By 2013 Jersey had reached the Championship after five promotions in eight years. The Jersey government helped the club financially in the hope of promoting tourism. The club has a commitment to develop local talent and in the last decade has produced Fraser Waters and Matt Banahan, who both played for England after moving to the Premiership.

NEWPORT

The 'terror of the tourists'

NEWPORT IS A port clinging to the banks of the River Usk on the coastal plain of South Wales. The town has a long history of steel production, but the steel plants have nearly all gone. The Rodney Parade ground survives, but as the home of the Gwent Dragons, a hybrid merger of Pontypool and the legendary Newport, who once called the 'terror of the tourists'.

During the club's history, Newport have beaten South Africa (twice), Australia, New Zealand and Tonga, with their win against the 1963 All Blacks as the only defeat of that mighty touring side

Newport are a unique rugby club, not least because its ancient origins give the club dual membership of the RFU and the

Welsh Rugby Union, an appropriate fact given that the town and county of Monmouthshire have been part of both England and Wales during a turbulent history.

Newport RFC was founded in 1874 by Tom Phillips, a West Midlands brewer, who bought the local brewery. The club's secretary, Richard Mullock, was a driving force in establishing the Welsh Rugby Union on 12th March 1881, but his club had already joined the London-based RFU and so Newport kept their unique dual status in Anglo-Welsh rugby.

Mullock helped form Newport Athletic Club in 1874. Initially Newport were an association side, but they couldn't get fixtures, so they arranged a rugby match on the 19th December 1875 against the Glamorgan Rugby Club. Newport arrived two men short. Despite this modest start, they were unbeaten from 1875 to 1879.

Mullock was an energetic promoter of rugby and invited Blackheath to play their first ever fixture in Wales against Newport on 20 November 1879. The hefty defeat of his club by the 'Heathens' convinced Mullock that rugby in Wales would only improve by forming a Welsh version of the RFU. Mullock even persuaded the RFU to let a Welsh XV play England at Blackheath on 19th February 1881.

Newport's first great player was Tommy Graham, who hailed from Newcastle-Upon-Tyne but became an adopted Welshman. He won 12 Wales caps and was the first Welsh national coach. At club level, Graham led Newport during their invincible season of 1891-92, with figures of P33 W29 D4 L0 F535 A25. He was club captain for four years, during which time they lost only 15 matches.

Graham's achievements were rapidly eclipsed by the sport's first great player, Arthur Gould, who won an incredible 27 caps from Wales between 1885 and 1897, at a time when three internationals a year were the maximum number of caps available. He was one of six Gould brothers who were born in and played for Newport; three of whom (Arthur, George and Robert) were capped by Wales.

Gould may have been a great player, but he was the centre of a storm that engulfed the Home countries. He was the best known rugby player of his day, but it was a bad time to stick one's head above the rugby parapet. Across the border in England, the Great Schism had brought a proud game to its knees as the RFU fought against shamateurism. Gould hadn't plied his trade in the north of England, but he had played all over southern England before returning to Newport. On his international retirement, he was presented with a £500 testimonial by the Welsh Rugby Union, which was an utter violation of the laws of amateurism. The other countries were enraged, but powerless to stop the money reaching Gould.

Gould is one of over 100 Newport players who were internationals, and nearly 30 Newport men have played for the British Lions. In April 1921, Newport fielded 15 internationals for a match against Bristol. They lost only one game that season, and the following season, they were invincible under captain Jack Wetter. Perhaps the best player in the invincible team was Reg Edwards, who won 11 England caps despite being a Welsh trialist. A team-mate was equally confused about his origins: A.C. Holland caused a diplomatic incident as he had two England trials despite being Welsh by birth and residency.

The 1924 Newport v All Blacks match was one of the greatest in Newport's history, although the Welsh side lost 8-5. Curiously, the Newport crowd were disgusted when Jones of Newport committed a terrible foul on a New Zealander. The crowd howled for Jones to be sent off.

Following World War Two, Newport produced some great players, such as Ken Jones, Bryn Meredith, Malcolm Thomas, David Watkins and Brian Price. Jones was the world's most capped wing, with 47 caps for Wales and the Lions. A 'will o' the wisp' sprinter, he always looked under-nourished, but he was an electric talent. Meredith was a rugged hooker who occupied the Welsh No. 2 jersey from 1954 to 1962, winning 34 caps. Thomas won 27 Wales caps in the 1950s and Price won 32 a decade later. Watkins was the Arthur Gould of the 1960s. A rugby playing genius, he won 21 Wales caps and played for the 1966 Lions before emulating Gould by departing rugby union in controversial circumstances. He was the archetypal Welsh fly-half: small, gifted and mercurial. He switched to rugby league and proved a precious talent for Salford RLFC in their glory days.

Newport have become known as the 'terror of the tourists' because a string of victories over touring teams, notably the 1912 Springboks, the 1957 Australians and the 1963 All Blacks.

Recent times have seen decline as the power in Welsh rugby went west to Cardiff, Swansea and Llanelli. Currently, Newport Gwent Dragons play in the Pro 12 League.

OXFORD UNIVERISTY

"When the team gets a bit stale, a few pints down the pub does more good than training."
G.A. Wilson, 1950 Oxford Captain

OXFORD UNIVERSITY RFC was formed in November 1869. Just over two years later they met Cambridge in the first Varsity Match. The first Oxford side wearing the famous dark blue jerseys contained 16 Old Rugbiens and four players from Marlborough College. Four years later, they could not raise a full team and borrowed Duncan Pease from Cambridge, which makes Pease the only man to have played for both Varsity rivals. The Dark Blues recovered and were the backbone of the England team in the early days. The 1877 Oxford team had three internationals: H. Flower, C. Phillips and F.H. Lee.

1880 saw the first great Oxford innovators in Alan Rotherham, an elusive half-back, and Harry Vassall (1860-1926), who changed the game from a mass scrummage to something like the game we know today. One of the best players of his day, he won five England caps after scoring three tries on his debut. During the Vassall era, Oxford lost only once (to Edinburgh University) in three years and they totally dominated the Varsity Match throughout the 1880s. Vassall introduced trial matches as a way of assessing players, and was one of the first player to develop tactics. In later life, he became a schoolmaster at Repton.

Oxford's next great hero came in 1904 when Adrian Stoop captained the Dark Blues. Stoop learnt his sport at Rugby School, where Harlequins spotted him. The diminutive fly-half

brought a new dimension to back play for Oxford, Quins and finally England. His greatest achievement was lifting back play to a hitherto unknown levels. His lasting legacy to Varsity rugby was scoring one of the best tries in Varsity history when he threaded his way through the entire Cambridge team to score in the 1905 match.

Stoop was one of six internationals at Oxford in the 1900s, when they lost only one Varsity match between 1906 and 1911. The Dark Blues could even overlook Ronnie Poulton-Palmer – an established England player – as a freshman because he was considered too unorthodox to fit in with their line-up. In his day, Poulton-Palmer was considered to be selfish with the ball and hard to play alongside, but Oxford didn't make the same mistake twice, and the following year he scored five tries as Oxford won the Varsity match by 35-3. Poulton-Palmer had been an outstanding athlete during his days at Rugby School, where he played alongside the poet Rupert Brooke. Despite coming from a conventional public school background and having a private income of £20,000p.a. (equivalent to £500,000 in 2009), he championed rugby for all, regardless of class. He was an outspoken critic of the RFU for investigating semi-professionalism in Devon in 1913, which he saw as a class-

based activity. Perhaps Ronnie had in mind the fact that his Varsity team found themselves censured by the RFU that year for paying their players large expenses during a French tour. The allegation was dismissed after the organiser said he couldn't lay his hands on the accounts.

Oxford's reputation for wonderful back play reached its zenith in the 1920s with the all-Scottish back line of Phil MacPherson, George Aitken, Arthur Wallace and Ian Smith. The quartet collected 77 caps in the 1920s, often in the same Scotland team. In the season 1923-24, the Dark Blues suffered only two defeats and won 22 matches. Smith, who was known as the Flying Scotsman, ranks amongst the finest three-quarters in the game's history. Oxford were initially slow to select him, but he scored two tries in the 1923 Varsity match. Wallace and Aitken were part of a new breed called 'Rhodes Scholars', mature students from the Empire. The scholarships were considered rather unsporting in some quarters. They arose from the bequest of Cecil Rhodes, the buccaneering African empire-builder who made a fortune from diamonds and who gave his name to Rhodesia, now known as Zimbabwe. Rhodes had attended Oriel College, Oxford in his youth and wanted graduates from the colonies and the USA to sample life at

Oxford. Many Rhodes scholars came to the old country for a postgraduate course as it looked good on their curriculum vitae, but many simply came for the rugby.

Oxford had a big advantage in having Rhodes Scholars available. They were usually good rugby players and older than undergraduates. One, Alan Valentine, was unique in many ways. He was capped by his native USA at rugby despite the fact that they knew nothing about him. He was picked for the USA team to play in the 1924 Olympics because he already played rugby, unlike many of his US team-mates. Against all the odds, the USA won the Olympic Gold Medal.

Later, America produced the most unusual Oxford Blue of all time. Peter Dawkins played in the Varsity match after a handful of rugby games, although he had previously played top-class American football.

In 1949 Oxford fielded five South Africans who were Rhodes Scholars.

Besides the scholarships, another help to Oxford came from Major Stanley, who had organised rugby in the Army Signals Corps during World War One. Curiously, the original Major Stanley XV was composed largely of 'Northern Unionist', players allowed to play rugby union by an amnesty during World War One. The Major never played rugby at any level, but rose to become an England selector. He first proposed the Dark Blues trial match in 1894, but it wasn't until 1919 when his XV finally took to the field. Oxford benefited enormously from playing an annual trial match before the Varsity match.

Major Stanley

During the 1930s Oxford also benefited from encouraging overseas players. The victorious 1931 team had four overseas players: F.L. Hovde (USA), P.C. Minns (NZ), S.G. Ozler (SA), who was the brother of the legendary Springbok captain Bennie, and N.K. Lamport (Australia). Hovde created a sensation by throwing the ball in from touch with a one-handed flick, all-American style.

Oxford won again in 1932, and in 1933 they were led to victory by 'Tuppy' Owen-Smith, who was brilliant at full-back. It was said, off the field, that he didn't look remotely athletic, but was a top-class rugby player and cricketer nevertheless.

The Dark Blues, like Cambridge, were granted matches against all the major touring teams. In 1957 they defeated Australia 12-6 with a team that included Malcolm Philipps, John Currie and Peter Robbins – all future England greats.

'Tuppy' Owen-Smith

Twelve years later, Oxford achieved one the greatest results in the sport's history when they drew 6-6 with the 1969 Springboks. The match was switched from Iffley Road to Twickenham after anti-apartheid demonstrators threatened to disrupt proceedings. The fixture gave rise to a great urban legend. Following the match, the legend goes that the RFU accidentally gave Oxford's share of the gate to the players. Rumours circulating at the time suggest the team had had a whale of a time before the university search parties were able to locate them.

Oxford rugby had bad runs in the early 1970s and early 1980s, but bounced back with the 1988 side, which is thought to be best in history, with five overseas internationals: David Kirk (New Zealand), Brian Smith, Ian Williams, Troy Coker, Rob Egerton (Australia). Four of that team were Rugby World Cup winners.

Other great players of the era included Simon Halliday, who would become a member of England's 1991 World Cup final team, Hugo McNeil, who won many caps for Ireland, and Victor Ubogo (England) and Bill Calcraft.

After a lean spell, the millennium saw a revival in Oxford's fortunes. They recorded a hat-trick of wins for only the second time in their history. In 2007 Joe Roff appeared for Oxford after he had won 86 Australian caps and been a Rugby World Cup winner in 1999. Two years later, Anton Oliver, the ex-All Black captain, played for the team.

RAF

IN 1917 THE Royal Flying Corps played the first rugby match with air force connections when a RFC side played in Egypt. Back in England, a RFC side led by W.W. Wakefield was formed in 1917 at Cranwell and played in an informal league against the Army and the service teams from New Zealand, South Africa, Canada and Australia. Their first match against the New Zealand army resulted in a huge defeat. Wakefield became sole organiser and selector of the RAF team, albeit on a full-time basis. He also organised divisional sides and an RAF Cup.

The Royal Air Force was formed in 1918 from two existing units: the Royal Naval Air Service and the Royal Flying Corps. The RAF rugby team emerged the following year with fixtures that began with a 10-0 defeat at the hands of the Royal Naval Depot in Devonport. The first RAF trial was played at Rectory Field, Blackheath, comprising the North against the Midlands. The Midlands team included Lieut. Wrentmore, who was a member of the 1912 Springboks.

The backs in the earliest RAF team was composed of flight lieutenants, whereas the front five were 'leading aircraftsmen'. It was a star-studded RAF side, with internationals such as Gerald Cole, George Thom, Robert Simpson and Archie Symington. The side also included the incomparable W.W. Wakefield, whose father had been one of the first civilian air pioneers back in 1902.

The RAF RU club was formerly inaugurated in 1920. Wakefield, who was to become famous as England's three times Grand Slam captain, recognised that the RAF team could never compete with the army and navy unless they played the best teams in the land, so he endeavoured to take on the best. They initially suffered some terrible defeats, but in 1922 they produced a huge shock by beating an Oxford University team. Wakefield led the RAF to the 1922-23 Inter-Services title before resigning his RAF commission and beginning a remarkable career in civilian life.

The role of sole selector passed to Wing Commander Alfred Warrington-Morris, who had won three England caps in 1909 whilst in the Royal Navy. He joined the Royal Air Force in 1917 and became the rugby club treasurer from 1924 until 1962. He was legendary for his meanness; on one occasion the RAF secretary was unable to carry two big bags of soiled rugby kit from a match. He got a taxi and sent 'W-M' the bill for 15p. W-M returned the bill with a cheque for one penny – the bus fare!

In 1922 the RAF beat the Army 26-3, with Cyril Lowe, the England winger, scoring four of the RAF's five tries. Wakefield and Lowe were replaced by a steady stream of internationals. Brothers Victor and George Beamish, both Irish internationals, were the backbone of RAF rugby between the wars. George also captained the Leicester-East Midlands team to victory over Bennie Osler's 1931-32 Springboks. A third brother, Charles, won 12 Ireland caps and captained the RAF for three years. Victor also played a significant part in World War Two. In 1940 he flew 110 Sorties for the RAF and spotted the German warships 'Scharnhorst' and 'Gneisenau' to spark one of the 20th century's greatest naval battles. He was killed in action in 1942.

The RAF was decidedly elitist between the wars. One of the finest players was a young Douglas Bader. In 1930 he played for Harlequins and the RAF. He was tipped for an England trial after playing for Combined Services, but tragedy struck when he lost his legs in an air crash and he never played rugby again. He fought back to become a legendary fighter pilot in World War Two and the subject of a famous film and book called 'Reach for the Sky'.

Another of the RAF's great men was Group Captain R.H.G. Weighill. He was the first fighter pilot to cross the coast of France on 'D' Day – just before dawn – and stayed there in his Mustang directing the fire of the cruiser 'Black Prince' until his fuel situation became critical. He went home for more fuel and was back on patrol again later in the morning. The greatest moment in his life was when, after watching the fleet of small craft heading for the beaches, he radioed back to base: "invasion has begun!" Weighill's rugby started at Wirral Grammar School and then Birkenhead Park. He went on to captain the RAF, Cheshire and England.

Surprisingly, the Inter-Services Tournament was continued during World War Two. Despite the conflict, the RAF often managed to field a star-studded team. The wartime team included many of the best players in the era, such as 'Beef' Dancer, Ray Longland, Joe Mycock, Bert Toft, Weighill and Bleddyn Williams.

The backbone of the post-war RAF teams were the PTI (Physical Training Instructors), who were a way for the service to keep its top rugby players fit and busy. The RAF side was originally selected from hundreds of players because every RAF unit had the power to recommend candidates for trials for the service XV. Every candidate was sent to a series of trial matches, but, not surprisingly, the results could be shambolic. Later a more settled side was selected and they played friendlies against top-class clubs.

In 1948 a strange ban was lifted. Until that year only officers were allowed to wear the RAF rugby club blazer.

The RAF won the Inter-Services Championship in 1947 and repeated the feat on four more occasions over the next 15 years. They fielded 37 internationals in that period, including Don Rutherford, Bob Stirling, Bob Weighill, Peter Yarranton, Phil Judd and Peter Robbins. Weighill and Stirling were both England captains. The service was also fortunate in having the assistance of some superb rugby league players. The 1961 side fielded Alex Murphy, perhaps the finest rugby league scrum-half of all time.

The 1960s saw the decline of RAF rugby due to the ending of national service in 1961, which decreased the number of players available. The RAF looked to its new regular recruits to fill the gap and produced some fine individuals in Ken Wilson, Peter Larter and Billy Steele. Steele played a part in rugby history, as he was the source of the Scots anthem, 'Flower of Scotland'. Steele heard the song back in Scotland, where it had been written in the 1960s, and sang it on the Lions tour, and it was adopted by the Scottish contingent. Within a decade it had become the unofficial national anthem of Scotland. In 1973 Steele was the first non-officer to captain the RAF.

Services rugby still has its lighter side. During the 1970s one of Britain's top-class referees was Air Commodore Larry Lamb, who once arrived late at Coventry. He rushed into the clubhouse in full RAF dress uniform and was met by the Coventry captain, who said: "Sorry, ref, the fancy dress ball was last week."

Despite the decreasing numbers, the RAF still produced outstanding players, notably two England players: lock John Orwin and winger Rory Underwood. Underwood scored 49 tries for England in 84 appearances and toured twice with the Lions in 1989 and 1993. He played 32 times for the RAF, scoring 25 tries.

Two other notable RAF players of the era were Paul Hull and Steve Worrall. Although Worrall did not win a full England cap, he captained the Combined Services to a narrow defeat by the 1993 All Blacks. Hull, who won four England caps, was one of the most versatile three-quarters of the 1990s.

REFEREES

"Unhonoured and unsung"
J. M. Kilburn, 1920

RUGBY FOOTBALL, AS originally played at Rugby School, had no referee or umpires. Disputes were settled by the two captains, who tried to calmly resolve points of contention. Players who broke the rules were fined 'half a crown' (12p) or made to stand on the touchline.

In the 1870s the two captains' decision-making was replaced by two umpires, who stood on the touchlines. Each side appointed an umpire, who had to wear a hat to differentiate him from the players. In 1885 the referee with a whistle was introduced on to the pitch, with the two umpires remaining on the touchlines. The umpires had to wave a flag to attract the referee's attention, but the referee could overrule the touchline judges.

Disputes during matches could be tortuous to resolve. In 1886 the Bristol authorities took issue with a player who struck another player during a match. The authorities were unsure if this was within the laws of the game and penned a letter to Mr. George Rowland Hill, the RFU Secretary, to get his advice. It took four weeks for the Bristol officials to receive Mr. Hill's opinion, which was that the players' behaviour was "not illegal – just objectionable". This elongated process was not unusual as the game developed

1889 was a momentous year for referees. The RFU granted the referee full authority over a game and the London Society of Referees was formed. The LSR was run by Arthur Trollope for a quarter of a century. One of its first acts was to pass a motion that out-of-pocket expenses be paid in exchange for referees controlling matches. Initially out-of-pocket expenses were limited to 37p (7/6). The limit was abolished in 1896, but reinstated three years later when it transpired some referees were earning a living wage by officiating and weren't members of existing referees societies.

Referees found a true friend in the English county unions, whose job it was to see RFU laws were applied. As early as 1890 players were ordered to appear before the county committee for abusing a referee, and the clubs were held to be accountable for the behaviour of their players. Control was applied by fining, cautioning or suspending clubs or players who were found guilty.

Referee's themselves had to reach acceptable standards, and referee examinations on their knowledge of the laws was introduced in 1896.

Neutral umpires had been introduced for internationals from 1882, but usually international referees were selected from the ranks of famous players. The best known English referee of the era was the said Mr. Rowland Hill, who handled the 1889 England v Maoris game. Hill awarded three disputed tries to England, to the disgust of the visitors. Three Maoris walked off the field, provoking a diplomatic incident. Eventually, the tourists apologised (they always had to worry about the gate money being withheld) and the matter was dropped. The accusation that 'the referee's a homer' was to resonate down the years.

Mr. Hill wasn't the only referee to suffer abuse. In 1891 the LSR minutes reported that there was a need "to prevent spectators abusing or molesting referees, whether during or after the matches". In 1913, 'Bim' Baxter, the legendary Cheshire official, officiated in the France v Scotland game. After the final whistle, Bim was roughed up by the French crowd, who weren't overly impressed by his refereeing. It was said Bim, who never lacked self-confidence or spoke French, thought the French were congratulating him on his performance.

Referees had a low profile at this time, except for a handful of famous names such as Hill and Jack Dallas of Scotland. Dallas was the last referee to handle a big match in a formal suit, collar and tie when he was in charge of the 1910 Varsity match. He did,

Conscientious Referee. "WELL, PERHAPS YOU'RE RIGHT, AND I REALLY OUGHT TO HAVE NEW GLASSES."

however, wear nailed shoes to prevent slipping. The 1905 New Zealanders rang the death knell for formal dress because they played with such speed that the old style mass scrummaging became a thing of the past. Referees had to run about for the first time and ended up covered in mud. The formal wear was replaced by rugby boots, shorts and a blazer.

The Great Schism affected referees as officials tended to follow their home club on whichever side they chose: RFU or NU. If the club joined the NU, then their referees followed. The big Northern Union clubs, with their massive playing resources, took many of the best referees with them. NU referees could earn £2 or £3 a match – a sum that represented a week's wages to a working man.

It took nearly a century before rugby union referees could make a living wage from handling games. In the interim, they had to make do with out-of-pocket expenses. Some referees even refused their expenses. One Yorkshire official refused his expenses after a match and suggested the two clubs use the money "to buy a copy of the laws of the game and show it to the players".

At club level, there was moaning and groaning about the 'neutral referees' they were allocated by the county unions. Clubs developed 'preferred lists' of referees who they felt suited them. Tom Crumbie of Leicester was legendary for 'buttering-up' referees.

Below top-class level, referees for club matches were either appointed by the local referees' society or provided by the home club. In 1920 there were 20 official referees in Devon, but the local referees society received only four requests a week for neutral officials. All other matches were handled by local officials.

From 1930 affiliated referees were supposed to send in reports to the county union and clubs were supposed to comment on visiting officials. It was a vexed process. One referee described his visit to one club with the words, "Never Again!", whilst one club said of a referee, "He is fit to referee anywhere – but not here again!"

Every player has a wealth of anecdotes concerning referees. The memories are usually based on narrow defeats decided by controversial decisions. To blame a referee for one mistake is churlish – after all, 80 minutes of rugby, at any level, is strewn with errors by both teams. No doubt the winners in any tight contest don't dispute their victory, whereas the losers may feel aggrieved.

The policy of employing ex-players as international referees continued between the wars. In Britain it was generally accepted that to take unfair advantage on a rugby field was ungentlemanly, but overseas teams were less noble. The 1924 USA team, who came over for the Paris Olympics, described English referees as "crooks". But, to be fair, the Americans themselves had only the scantest knowledge of the laws.

The 1924-25 All Blacks tour brought out, for the first time, the disparity between British referees and the interpretation applied in New Zealand. When the ball was fed to a scrum, the British referees expected scrum-halves to retreat behind the ball in the scrum, whereas the New Zealand scrum-halves stayed at the mouth of the tunnel. This led to much ill-feeling when scrum-halves from abroad were penalised for obstruction, which caused problems. The 1925 sending-off of New Zealand's Cyril Brownlie (the first international to be sent off) caused massive ill-feeling, directed principally towards Alf Freethy, the referee. Freethy had warned both sets of forwards for violence three times in the first ten minutes when Brownlie kicked a prostate England forward. He sent him off, but received little support for his actions, the perception being that the sending-off had brought unwanted disgrace on the game.

Throughout the 1930s referees occasionally made headlines for their eccentric ways. The 1931 Swansea v Bristol match saw the Welsh referee send off the Bristol touch judge for the crime of coaching the Bristol players at half-time.

It was said that until World War Two few referees who handled club matches took much interest in fitness and were content to stand in the middle of the pitch and wait for periodic contact with the teams. Gradual improvements occurred after the war as referees became better trained and fitter. Cyril Gadney and Dr. Peter Cooper organised seminars for referees at Bisham Abbey, and Alan Bean wrote a book on the art of refereeing. Gradually the cream of referees were drawn from top-class players who had been forced to give up playing prematurely due to injury.

In 1957 the London Referees Society was asked by journalists to help them understand decisions by giving hand signals. Arthur Rees, the society's chairman, dismissed the idea out of hand, replying: "Perhaps at the same time, I could stick a yard brush up my backside and sweep the pitch."

The 1970s saw a shift in the status of referees in world rugby. The international authorities recognised that, in both hemispheres, appointing home officials for matches against touring teams was bringing problems of interpretation. On one occasion the home crowd had chased the referee from the field to express their delight at his officiating. British referees in particular were much sought after by the other RFU countries for their impartiality.

In recent times, life has become complicated for referees with a raft of law changes, including the introduction of the sin bin for 'technical offences'. But laws made in Parliament have encroached onto rugby's laws too, and officials have to cope with government directives on health and safety.

Some maverick referees do still appear. In 2007 a male referee was suspended and fined £100 for dropping his shorts during a women's rugby match.

ROYAL NAVY

"I want to produce Englishmen who are useful at a hunt ball – but invaluable in a shipwreck."

J.F. Roxburgh, headmaster of Stowe school

THE ROYAL NAVY provided 67 internationals for the Home countries in the first century of international rugby. The earliest naval rugby players were exclusively ex-public schoolboys studying at RN Dartmouth and Greenwich. They were sufficient in numbers for an Inter-Service game against the Army in 1870. The following year the Navy took part in some of the first rugby to be played abroad when HMS Galatea played the Calcutta FC in India. The earliest rugby in New Zealand is attributed to two Royal Navy warships.

The first Navy player to win international honours was Lieut. Spencer Login (1851-1909) from RNC Dartmouth, who played for England against Ireland in 1875. The next Navy players to win international honours were Engineer Cadet J.F. Shaw and Engineer Cadet C.G. Taylor, for Wales in 1884, and Surgeon-Lieut. J. Chambers, for Ireland in the 1880s.

The Royal Navy RU was formed in 1906 by a group including Spencer Login and George Levick of St. Barts. In 1907 they organised an annual match against the Army, followed by a match with the RAF from 1920. The Navy were so strong they lost only two of the first 12 Army matches and only three of the first 20 matches with the RAF.

The first inter-services matches were billed as the 'Officers of the Navy' v the 'Officers of the Army'. Other ranks weren't considered, but in 1908 Petty Officer R. Gilbert was capped for England as a player from Devonport Albion. Devonport had a first-class fixture list and produced two other England internationals in E.W. Roberts and S.F. Coopper. Devonport Albion RFC were happy to field both servicemen and civilians. They raised the profile of rugby for the other ranks and for the county side of Devon. Until the outbreak of World War One, Albion had claims to be the best side in England.

Hardly any of the Royal Navy's early internationals were from 'below decks'. This is surprising because some of the 'other ranks' were stokers, the fittest men in the Navy. A substantial portion of every warship's crew were stokers who manned the boilers of coal-fired warships. Pre-World War One, warships were floating coal barges with coal stowed anywhere and everywhere. The stokers had to shovel coal from one corner of the ship to the nearest available point in the boilers. The lot of the stokers improved in 1912 when the great naval reformer, Admiral Fisher, persuaded the Navy to switch from coal-fired warships to oil-burners. Gradually the navy's need for thousands of stokers disappeared and the manpower of the Royal Navy was reduced.

W.J.A. Davies

Briefly, in 1919, there was a degree of emancipation as the Navy picked other ranks for the naval team before reverting back to officers only.

The greatest names in Navy rugby were Cyril Kershaw and W.J.A. Davies. Kershaw served as a midshipman in World War One before switching to submarines. After the war he joined the Physical Training School at Portsmouth and fenced for Great Britain in two Olympics before he joined Dave Davies to carve out one of the greatest half-back partnerships in rugby history. Davies was the ultimate fly-half; he had superb hands, devastating speed and a dazzling body swerve. He won 22 England caps, and after making his England debut on a losing side in 1914, he never again tasted defeat in an England jersey.

When Davies and Kershaw ran down the curtain on their illustrious careers, the baton passed to other great players. Harry Stephenson was perhaps the best three-quarter who ever played for the Navy. He won 14 Ireland caps. Upfront, Bill Luddington (1894-1941) was one of the most durable and rugged members of England's great Slam team of the early 1920s team. Subsequently, the Navy produced two more tough forwards in Barney Evans and Charles Webb. The latter won 12

England caps before emigrating to New Zealand and playing for Auckland.

In 1922 an unofficial merit table of 40 London clubs was set up. Royal Naval College (Greenwich) were champions with 87% and Old Blues were second with 85%, but the merit tables were hopelessly flawed because everybody's fixture list was different.

World War Two brought an end to naval rugby and the global nature of the conflict saw ships and men sent across the world. In December 1945, the Royal Navy reformed to play the 2nd New Zealand Expeditionary Force – the Kiwis won 6-5.

Peacetime saw further decline as the Empire and the Royal Navy shrank in size. National Service provided manpower, but its abolition saw the navy fall to 30,000 staff.

Today an annual Navy Sevens begins the rugby year, followed by the Inter-Command Championship, which comprises the Fleet, Royal Marines, Portsmouth, Plymouth, Air Service and Scotland. The Inter-Command Competition provides an opportunity for newcomers to make the Academy squad. The Academy squad is finally merged with the existing First XV as a prelude to picking the navy side for the Inter-Services Tournament and the annual Navy v Army match at Twickenham (which can attract 44,000 spectators).

The old missionary spirit of the navy lives on. In 2004 a navy ship toured the Far East and played rugby matches against sides from Vietnam, China and Korea, a trip that echoed the achievements of HMS Galatea back in the 1870s.

ST HELIERS

ST. HELIERS RFC was founded in 1892 with a match against Victoria College. St. Heliers like to be known as 'the town club', whereas Jersey are the 'island club'.

ST. MARY'S HOSPITAL

ST. MARY'S HOSPITAL RFC was officially formed in October 1865, 15 years after the hospital and 11 years after the medical school had opened. The club had played sporadic matches before its official formation.

St. Mary's quickly established a top-class fixture list that included the other London hospitals, Bedford, Saracens and Wasps. But interest soon declined, and the rugby enthusiasts had to leave their ground near Swiss Cottage for a pitch at Wormwood Scrubs and later Castle Hill.

Good times returned when the number of medical students at St. Mary's was increased in the late 19th century, which enabled the hospital to field a team strong enough to win the Hospitals Cup for the first time in 1900, beating London Hospital.

An integral part of the rugby club's early organisation was Dr. Charles Wilson, later Lord Moran, who became famous as Winston Churchill's doctor. Wilson determined to improve the quality and quantity of the rugby side by hand-picking students entering St. Mary's using criteria not entirely based on intellectual ability. Wilson's medicine worked on the rugby field as the influx of new blood raised the standard of St. Mary's rugby.

1934 saw the arrival at St. Mary's of Owen-Smith, a Rhodes Scholar who was one of the greatest all-rounders in sporting history. Harold Geoffrey Owen 'Tuppy' Owen-Smith (1909-1990) played cricket for South Africa, won Blues at Oxford in rugby, cricket and boxing, before joining St. Mary's. Whilst at St. Mary's, he won 14 England rugby caps. On one occasion his request for a Saturday off from medical studies was refused until it was explained to his boss that he was needed by England.

With players of Tuppy's quality, St Mary's won a second Hospitals Cup in 1931, and then recorded 14 wins in 27 subsequent finals.

In 1936 the club moved to Teddington, thanks to the generosity of newspaper magnate Lord Beaverbrook, who was a friend of Charles Wilson. Owen-Smith returned to South Africa in 1937, but St. Mary's received the services of Tom Kemp from Denstone College, who was later to emulate Owen-Smith by captaining England. Kemp was associated with St Mary's from 1947 until 1975.

St. Mary's was a good side in the late 1940s because the hospital sides were able to keep playing rugby during the war. Most other sides suspended play from 1939 to 1945.

1941 saw St. Mary's fielding one of the greatest midfield trios in rugby history: N.O. Bennett, Nim Hall and Keith Scott. With such a brilliant team, St. Mary's won a hat-trick of Middlesex Sevens titles.

In 1944 Arthur Dickson Wright (father of Clarissa Dickson Wright, the famous TV cook) took over as club president. Clarissa Dickson Wright was four-years-old when she started watching St Mary's with her father, a renowned surgeon.

St. Mary's were so strong in 1945 they were able to boast a first-class fixture list for the first time in their history, and they could field five sides every Saturday. But success was fleeting, and the demands of trying to live up to the golden years proved too strong for subsequent teams.

Lewis Cannell emerged from St. Mary's in the early 1950s as an England player of international stature, and Ivor Beatson was an England reserve. Cannell was an England regular from 1949 to 1955, and under his leadership at St. Mary's they were good enough to win away at Bristol.

The 1960s saw St. Mary's suffer the same problems as all clubs with a narrow recruiting base, as their playing strength couldn't match the resources of the city clubs. Ironically, the era saw a St. Mary's player emerge of the highest calibre: J.P.R. Williams of London Welsh, Bridgend, Wales and the British Lions. Williams was dashing, brave and incredibly talented and was the greatest full-back of his era. He was an integral part of the great 1970s Welsh sides, alongside Gareth Edwards and Barry John. After qualifying, 'J.P.R.' returned to St. Mary's as a registrar and played for St. Mary's B team. Their other best-known player of the era was Trevor Wintle, who won five England caps between 1966 and 1969.

English rugby was changing as the top clubs formed leagues, disguised as merit tables, and the students' team had no place at the table. St. Mary's fixture list changed to clubs who could be described as 'decent middle-ranking'. Talented players still studied at St. Mary's and played in the Hospitals Cup matches, but they chose to play their Saturday rugby elsewhere.

The 1980s saw St. Mary's Hospital RFC cease to be a separate entity when the teaching hospital became part of Imperial College of Science, Technology and Medicine.

CHAPTER TWENTY-ONE
WOMEN'S RUGBY

"I love winners when they cry – losers when they try."
Tom T. Hall

WOMEN'S RUGBY IS a popular sport in the 21st century, but it had a slow journey to popularity. Women have always played a part in rugby; besides nurturing the players of the future, they have also worked hard to run the clubhouse, provide teas for players and raise funds. Their presence in the clubhouse was welcomed as part of Saturdays as they served piping hot food to weary players. But at 7.30pm, the players would sing 'Goodnight Ladies', which signalled that the female of the species was to vacate the premises whilst the men were left to their own devices (i.e. singing bawdy rugby songs).

The slow progress to equality isn't surprising as women's sports in general were virtually unknown when football emerged at Rugby School. Races for unmarried women were known in the 18th Century and married women in Midlothian played street football annually on Shrove Tuesday. At the other end of the spectrum, women fought with bare-knuckles at travelling fairs around the same era.

But in polite society, the Victorian ethos of sport was considered to be alien to women. For women to show their legs was considered appalling – the Victorians covered table legs in case it gave men the wrong idea.

The 1880s, however, saw women expanding their sporting horizons into golf, tennis and other areas. There were even reports of a soccer match between an England Women's XI and a Canadian Army team.

The first records of women playing rugby date from 1885. A school rugby team in Portora in Ireland couldn't field a full XV, so the headmaster drafted in his three sons and his daughter to make up the three-quarters. Miss E.F. Valentine took part in the practices and intra-school games, and some records suggest in their external games as well.

World War One was the major turning point for women in British life. The Suffragette movement was at its height and women were filling the vacancies left when British men went off to war. Women's soccer became a popular spectator sport because the men's game was in abeyance for the duration of the war. A rugby match between Newport and Cardiff Ladies is recorded on 15th December 1917 for war charities. The Cardiff Ladies were employees of Hancock's Brewery (founded by the famous Wiveliscombe rugby-playing family) and a Newport side composed of female employees of the Lysaght Works. Newport won 6-0. The previous year there were reports of women playing rugby in Australia.

If women's rugby failed to establish itself in the 1920s, women's soccer kept its appeal. The participants were a long way from the polite society; the new sportswomen were from poor backgrounds, often mill workers and nurses, who made good footballers because they were used to heavy work.

Women's football boomed between the wars. Many towns had a team. Dick Kerr's Ladies of Preston were the best. They raised £50,000 for charity in 1921 alone and toured the USA and Canada. The FA fiercely opposed ladies' football, but the rugby authorities came to their rescue. When the FA forbade soccer clubs to allow women's teams to use their grounds, rugby provided pitches. Women's internationals were held at Cardiff Arms Park, Newport's Rodney Parade and Odsal Stadium in Bradford.

Women's rugby reappeared in the early 1930s, when a Womens All Blacks team visited England. Little is known of the tourists beyond a single photograph taken in Gloucester. Some people weren't overly-impressed; indeed, one newspaper commented: "A game of football is no more taxing to a woman than doing a day's washing and cleaning."

In Britain women often worked at rugby clubs behind the scenes quietly by making post-match teas or fundraising. But at some big clubs, such as Moseley, women weren't allowed to socialise in the clubhouse at all until 1959.

OUR PHOTOGRAPH of an impressive, even formidable, group of ladies is shown as the result of a letter hon. sec. John Nelson received from a Mr David Dwyer, of Bootham, York, a fourth year student of PE at the University College of Ripon and York St John who is researching the History of Women's Rugby Union for his honours dissertation. He had found reference to women's rugby being played at the Arms Park between Cardiff and Newport in 1913.
John Nelson believes he must be referring to a match on December 15, 1917, played for war charities and at which the above picture was taken and is kept in the club museum. The contestants, reported Danny Davies in his book *Cardiff Rugby Club* "were Cardiff ladies who were mainly employees of Hancocks Ltd, the noted Cardiff brewers, and Newport ladies who were employees of the Lysaght works in the town."
The teams changed in the Grand Hotel in Westgate Street, under the patronage of "Ma" Rosser and the Cardiff captain was Miss E. Kirton, well known as an employee at the Grand.
Oh, yes: Newport won 6-0.

England v Wales in 1988.

In some rugby clubs, an annual match was organised, 'Women v Men'. These were fun matches where the men were expected to show chivalry by having one hand tied behind their backs and allowing the women to win.

From an organised point of view, Loughborough Colleges pioneered the female game in Britain in the 1970s. Their former students later formed Wasps Ladies; whilst ladies sides existed in both Maestag and Newport in Wales, as well as a team called 'Mofia Maidens'.

In England a group led by Carol Isherwood, Deborah Griffin and Sheila Welsh of the Sports Council formed the Women's RFU. They called a series of meetings throughout 1983 that created the RFUW to organise the women's game, a league and a national cup competition. The first non-university clubs appeared the following year when Finchley Ladies was formed by former students of UCL and Leeds University who lived in the capital.

Finchley's pre-eminence was short-lived as the venerable Richmond FC was accused of persuading the Finchley team to move 'lock, stock and barrel' to the Athletic Ground in 1984. This move came after Richmond FC were impressed with the enterprise shown in the first RFUW international, which was played at the Athletic Ground that year.

Two years earlier, the first women's international match had been played in Europe, when France beat the Netherlands 4-0. Also that year, women's rugby was one of the sports included in the Gay Games in San Francisco.

The English women's game grew rapidly after a league and cup system was introduced in 1985. Echoing events a century earlier, the best clubs were based in London, which put enormous pressure on provincial clubs to fund away matches to the capital. A major obstacle for women's rugby was that they relied on club facilities that were used by men on Saturdays, so women had to play on Sundays, which impacted on girls who had to be ready for work on Monday mornings.

In 1985 England played France, but lost 14-8; the honour of being England's first captain when to Carol Isherwood. Six years later, England reached the final of the Women's Rugby World Cup, before losing 19-6 to the USA. England took revenge in the 1994 final. Today the Women's World Cup is a worldwide event and the pinnacle of players' ambitions.

England's pursuit of a second world title proved more elusive than the 1994 win. It began in 2001 when David Shaw of the RFU recognised the importance of academy squads. The creation of the girls' academy was augmented with the recruitment of Gary Street as coach. Gary was previously coach of Aston Old Edwardians and University of Birmingham Women.

This was no luxury jaunt as Gary had to give up a good job and the 15 girls had to accept life as unpaid players. The squad studied at Oldfield Academy and lodged with local families from the school from the age of 16 to 18. From the academy squad, eight received full international honours and five were in the World Cup-inning squad of 2014.

Gary took over as National Women's Coach in 2007 when Geoff Richards returned to Australia. The results have been spectacular, with six Home Nations titles, five Grand Slams and two European titles. But there were lows, not least a last gasp defeat to New Zealand in the final of 2010 Women's Rugby World Cup at the Stoop.

Perhaps this is illustrated best by Gary himself, who said: "The hangover of defeat was terrible. It took months for the whole squad to throw off the agony of going so close – and getting beaten by a more experienced team. It was, however, a massive driver to get it right next time. We went into a four-year plan to be more professional – even if the team weren't being paid. It paid off with us winning the 2014 World Cup at the 20,000-capacity Stade Jean Bouin in Paris. There were ticket touts outside the ground for the first time in the history of women's rugby."

A few months later, the team became the first women's team in a generation to win the BBC Sports Personality Team of the Year award. Also, the whole squad were awarded the freedom of the Borough of Rugby, as the men had been in 2003.

(Thanks to Carol Isherwood, Gill Burns and Gary Street)

2014 WORLD WOMEN'S CUP FINAL

Match Details:

ENGLAND 21 CANADA 9

England: D Waterman (C Allan 46-51); K Merchant (Allan 69), E Scarratt, R Burford (C Large 77), K Wilson; K Mclean (capt), N Hunt (L Toya Mason 77); R Clark, V Fleetwood (E Croker 58), S Hemming (L Keates 53), T Taylor, J McGilchrist (R Essex 53), M Packer (A Matthews 64), M Alphonsi, S Hunter.

Tries: Waterman, Scarratt; Con: Scarratt; Pens: Scarratt 3

Canada: J Zussman (J Sugawara 75); M Harvey, M Marchak, A Burk, J Dovanne (B Waters 59); E Belchos, E Alarie; M-P Pinault-Reid (M J Kirby 72), K Donaldson (L Russell 45), H Leith (O De Merchant 69), L Blackwood, M Samson (K Mack 40), J Murphy, K Paquin, K Russell (capt).

Pens: Harvey 3

World Cup winners at 10 Downing Street.

CLUB INDEX